BAGHDAD

'A richly researched chronicle of a city that was once the learned capital of the world, but whose dizzying apex gave way to a long and miserably bloody decline ... Baghdad's history is not a happy one, but it is fabulous and ghastly and fascinating' Wendell Steavenson, *Prospect*

'This account of Baghdad reaches another level as the story gets closer to our own time ... intense and fascinating. The description of the assassination of the Iraqi monarchy in 1958 is convincing, and vivid, as are details of the reign of terror that Saddam inflicted on his country ... Arriving at the end of this long story of sublime beauty and unimaginable horror, of generosity and greed, of grandeur and pettiness, peace and blood, the events of the past couple of decades since Saddam's invasion of Kuwait seem all the more comprehensible' Anthony Sattin, *Observer*

'The history of Baghdad more than any other city mirrors the ebb and flow that has marked Arab history and civilisation. Justin Marozzi's book is a brilliant, evocative and erudite retelling of the history of this most intriguing of cities ... He knows whereof he speaks, having trudged the streets and visited the monuments and landmarks even where they have been reduced to rubble ... a work of love, and a homage to a place that has somehow survived the depredations of its conquerors, the fractiousness of its population and the duplicity of its rulers' Ali A Allawi, *Spectator*

'A lively, accessible romp through 1,400 years of Baghdad's history ... Marozzi has a journalist's eye for a good anecdote' Eleanor Robson, *History Today*

'An impassioned plea on behalf of whatever vestiges of humanity and culture still exist in the beleaguered and strife-torn Iraqi capital ... impressive testimony to the enduring strength of British travel writing' Michael Burleigh, *Evening Standard*, Books of the Year

ABOUT THE AUTHOR

Justin Marozzi is a Councillor of the Royal Geographic Society and a Senior Research Fellow at Buckingham University. He has broadcast for BBC Radio Four, and regularly contributes to a wide range of publications, including the *Financial Times*, for which he has worked in Iraq, Afghanistan and Darfur. His previous books include the bestselling *Tamerlane: Sword of Islam*, a *Sunday Telegraph* Book of the Year (2004), and *The Man Who Invented History: Travels with Herodotus*.

JUSTIN MAROZZI

Baghdad

City of Peace, City of Blood

PENGUIN BOOKS

PENGUIN BOOKS

UK | USA | Canada | Ireland | Australia
India | New Zealand | South Africa

Penguin Books is part of the Penguin Random House group of companies
whose addresses can be found at global.penguinrandomhouse.com.

First published by Allen Lane 2014
Published in Penguin Books 2015
001

Set in 8.98/12.38 pt Sabon LT Std
Typeset by Jouve (UK), Milton Keynes
Printed in Great Britain by Clays Ltd, St Ives plc

A CIP catalogue record for this book is available from the British Library

ISBN: 978-0-141-04710-2

www.greenpenguin.co.uk

To my dear friend Manaf al Damluji

The story of the City of Peace is largely the story of continuous war; where there is not war, there is pestilence, famine and civil disturbance.

Richard Coke, *Baghdad: The City of Peace*, 1927

Contents

CONTENTS

x

List of Illustrations

33. Baghdad a few hours after the coup, 14 July 1958. (Photograph: PA Photos)

34. Abdul Karim Qasim holding a cabinet meeting, 1958. (Photograph: copyright © Burt Glinn/Magnum Photos)

35. The bodies of Jews hanged in Liberation Square, 27 January 1969. (Photograph: Bettmann/Corbis)

36. Saddam Hussein, 1982. (Photograph: Rex Features)

37. Iraqi soldiers carrying a victim during the Iran–Iraq War, Baghdad, 1981. (Photograph: PA Photos)

38. US soldiers enter the parade grounds during the battle for downtown Baghdad, April 2003. (Photograph: copyright © Christopher Anderson/Magnum Photos)

39. A US marine watches as a statue of Iraq's President Saddam Hussein falls in central Baghdad, 9 April 2003. (Photograph: copyright © Goran Tomasevic/Reuters/Corbis)

40. Canon Andrew White. (Photograph: Dawood Andrews)

41. Emad Levy, 2003. (Photograph: Laurent van der Stockt/Gamma-Rapho/Getty Images)

42. Donny George at the Iraq Museum, Baghdad, 2003 (Photograph: © Steve McCurry/Magnum Photos)

43. Removal of a 1970s statue of al-Mansur, hit by a bomb explosion, Baghdad, October 2005. (Photograph: Reuters/Corbis)

44. Baghdadis relaxing in Al Zawra's park, 2008. (Photograph: © Jerome Sessini/Magnum)

45. Booksellers on Mutanabbi Street, 2013. (Photograph: Justin Marozzi)

46. Aerial view of the shrine of Imam Musa al Kadhim, 2012. (Photograph: Reuters/Corbis)

47. People gather at the shrine of Abu Hanifa to mark the birthday of the Prophet Mohammed, 2009. (Photograph: Reuters/Corbis)

Every effort has been made to contact all copyright holders. The publishers will be happy to make good in future editions any errors or omissions brought to their attention.

List of Maps

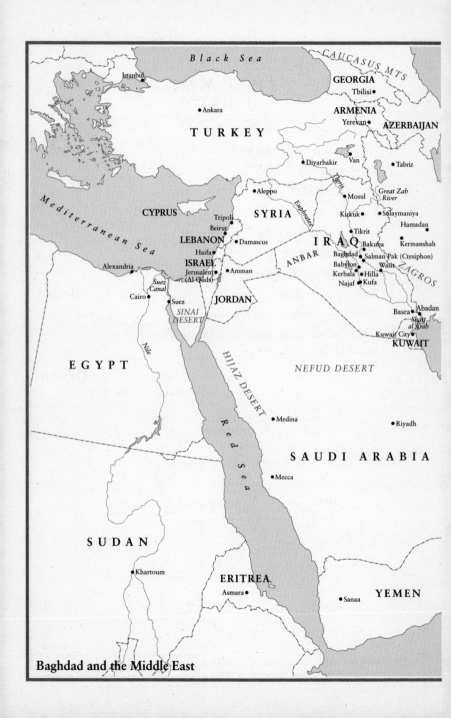

Baghdad and the Middle East

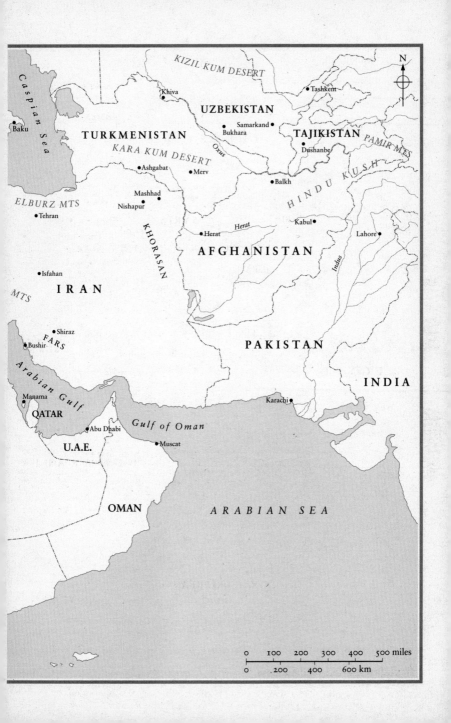

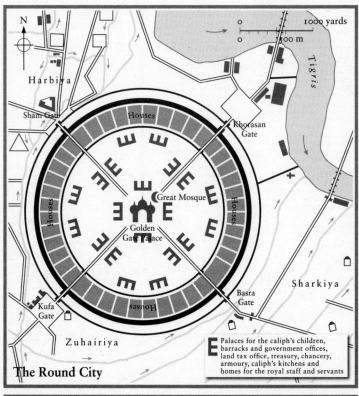

The Round City

N

Harbiya

Sham Gate

Houses

Khorasan
Gate

Houses

Great Mosque

Golden
Gate Palace

Houses

Sharkiya

Houses

Kufa
Gate

Basra
Gate

Zuhairiya

1000 yards

100 m

Tigris

E Palaces for the caliph's children,
barracks and government offices,
land tax office, treasury, chancery,
armoury, caliph's kitchens and
homes for the royal staff and servants

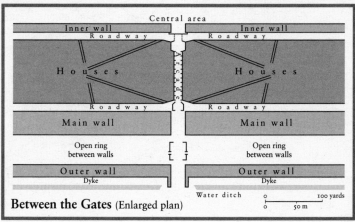

Between the Gates (Enlarged plan)

Central area

Inner wall | Inner wall

Roadway | Roadway

Houses | Houses

Arcade

Roadway | Roadway

Main wall | Main wall

Open ring
between walls | Open ring
between walls

Outer wall | Outer wall

Dyke | Dyke

Water ditch

100 yards

50 m

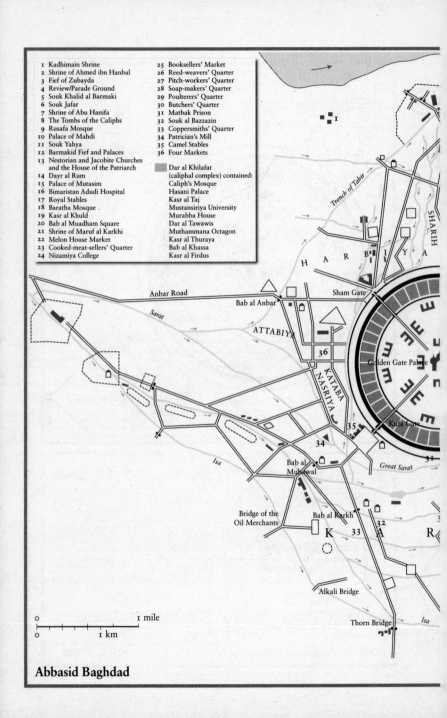

Abbasid Baghdad

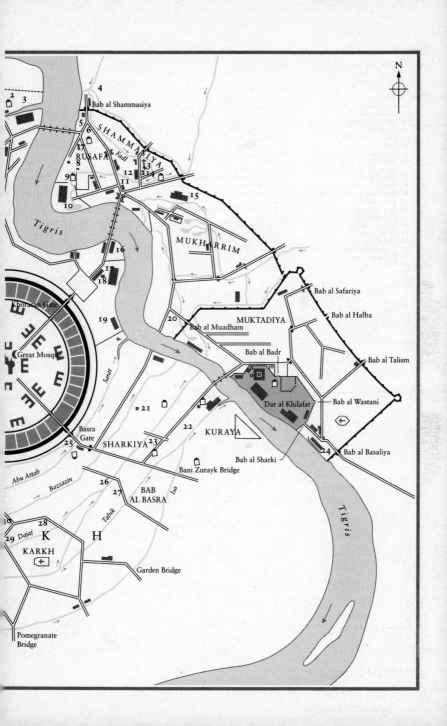

N

Bab al Shammasiya

SHAMMASIYA

RUSAFA

Tigris

MUKHARRIM

Bab al Safariya

Bab al Halba

MUKTADIYA

Khorasan Gate

Bab al Muadham

Bab al Talism

Great Mosque

Bab al Badr

Bab al Wastani

Dar al Khilafat

Basra Gate

Bab al Basaliya

SHARKIYA

KURAYA

Bani Zurayk Bridge

Bab al Sharki

Abu Attab

Bazzazin

BAB
AL BASRA

Isa

Tabik

Dajaj

K   H

KARKH

Garden Bridge

Tigris

Pomegranate
Bridge

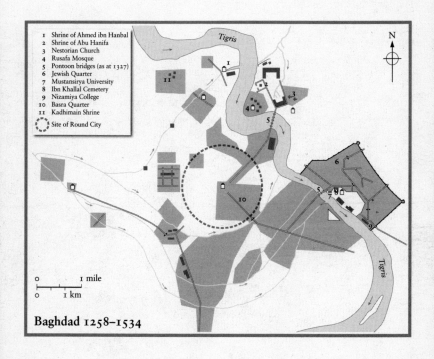

1   Shrine of Ahmed ibn Hanbal
2   Shrine of Abu Hanifa
3   Nestorian Church
4   Rusafa Mosque
5   Pontoon bridges (as at 1327)
6   Jewish Quarter
7   Mustansirya University
8   Ibn Khallal Cemetery
9   Nizamiya College
10 Basra Quarter
11 Kadhimain Shrine

Site of Round City

N

Tigris

Tigris

0   1 mile
0   1 km

Baghdad 1258–1534

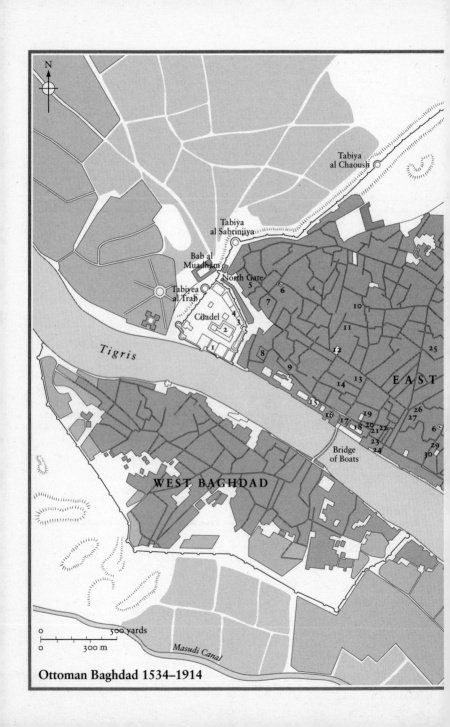

N

Tabiya
al Chaousli

Tabiya
al Sabrinjiya

Bab al
Muadham

North Gate
5

Tabiyea
al Trab

Citadel
4
3
2
1

6

7

8

9

10

11

12

13

14

15

16
17
18
19
20
21
22
23
24

25

26
27

28
29
30

Tigris

EAST

Bridge
of Boats

WEST BAGHDAD

0   500 yards
0   300 m

Masudi Canal

Ottoman Baghdad 1534–1914

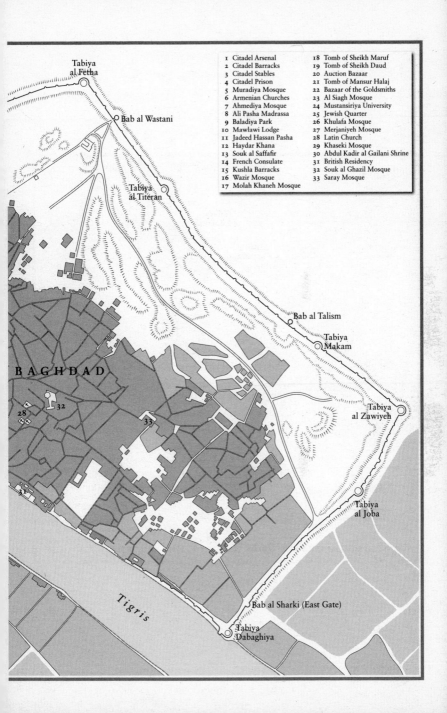

Tabiya
al Fetha

Bab al Wastani

Tabiya
al Titeran

1 Citadel Arsenal	18 Tomb of Sheikh Maruf
2 Citadel Barracks	19 Tomb of Sheikh Daud
3 Citadel Stables	20 Auction Bazaar
4 Citadel Prison	21 Tomb of Mansur Halaj
5 Muradiya Mosque	22 Bazaar of the Goldsmiths
6 Armenian Churches	23 Al Siagh Mosque
7 Ahmediya Mosque	24 Mustansiriya University
8 Ali Pasha Madrassa	25 Jewish Quarter
9 Baladiya Park	26 Khulafa Mosque
10 Mawlawi Lodge	27 Merjaniyeh Mosque
11 Jadeed Hassan Pasha	28 Latin Church
12 Haydar Khana	29 Khaseki Mosque
13 Souk al Saffair	30 Abdul Kadir al Gailani Shrine
14 French Consulate	31 British Residency
15 Kushla Barracks	32 Souk al Ghazil Mosque
16 Wazir Mosque	33 Saray Mosque
17 Molah Khaneh Mosque	

Bab al Talism

Tabiya
Makam

BAGHDAD

Tabiya
al Zawiyeh

28

32

33

31

Tabiya
al Joba

Tigris

Bab al Sharki (East Gate)

Tabiya
Dabaghiya

Baghdad during the First World War

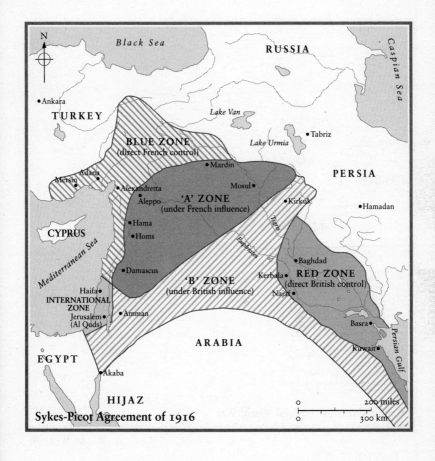

Sykes-Picot Agreement of 1916

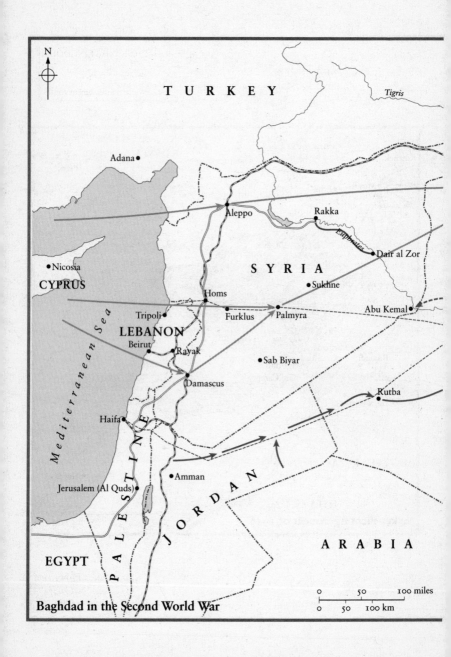

Baghdad in the Second World War

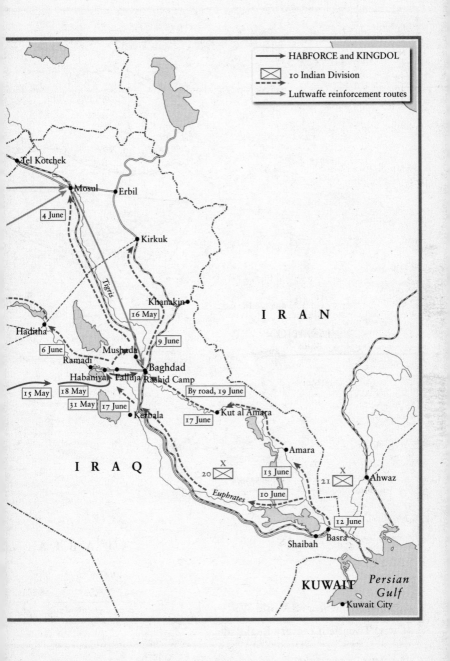

Legend:
- HABFORCE and KINGDOL
- 10 Indian Division
- Luftwaffe reinforcement routes

Tel Kotchek

Mosul · Erbil

4 June

Kirkuk

Khanakin

I R A N

16 May

Tigris

9 June

Haditha

6 June

Ramadi · Mushada

Baghdad

Habaniya · Falluja · Rashid Camp

15 May

18 May

By road, 19 June

31 May

17 June · Kerbala

17 June · Kut al Amara

Amara

20 X

13 June

21 X · Ahwaz

Euphrates

10 June

12 June

Shaibah · Basra

I R A Q

KUWAIT

Persian Gulf

Kuwait City

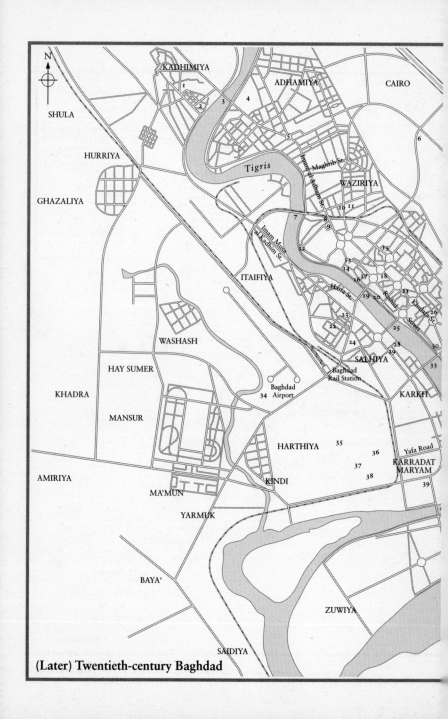

N

SHULA

KADHIMIYA

ADHAMIYA

CAIRO

1
2
3
4

HURRIYA

Tigris

5

Maghrib St.

WAZIRIYA

6

GHAZALIYA

Imam A'dham St.

10 11

8
9

7

Imam Musa
al-Kadhim St.

12

15

ITAIFIYA

13
14

16
17
18

21

WASHASH

Haifa St.

19
20

Rashid St.

Rikabat St.

26

23

22

24

25

28
29

30

SALHIYA

33

HAY SUMER

KHADRA

Baghdad
Rail Station

KARKH

MANSUR

Baghdad
Airport

34

HARTHIYA

35

36

Yafa Road

37

KARRADAT
MARYAM

AMIRIYA

KINDI

38

39

MA'MUN

YARMUK

BAYA'

ZUWIYA

SAIDIYA

(Later) Twentieth-century Baghdad

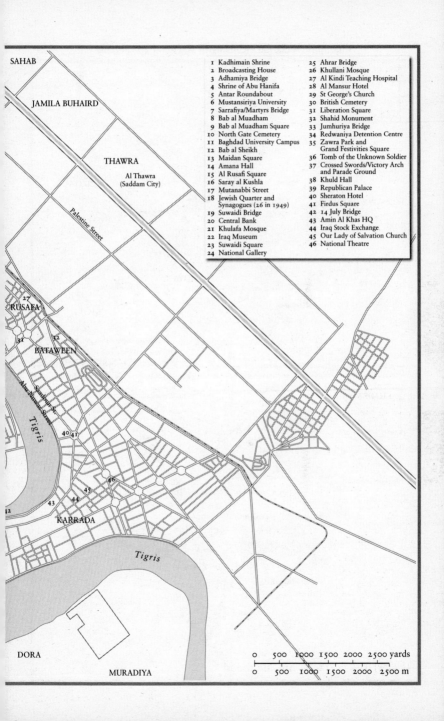

SAHAB

JAMILA BUHAIRD

THAWRA

Al Thawra
(Saddam City)

Palestine Street

RUSAFA
27

31   32
BATAWEEN

Abu Nuwas St.

Tigris

40 41

46

45
43   44
KARRADA

42

Tigris

DORA

MURADIYA

1   Kadhimain Shrine
2   Broadcasting House
3   Adhamiya Bridge
4   Shrine of Abu Hanifa
5   Antar Roundabout
6   Mustansiriya University
7   Sarrafiya/Martyrs Bridge
8   Bab al Muadham
9   Bab al Muadham Square
10 North Gate Cemetery
11 Baghdad University Campus
12 Bab al Sheikh
13 Maidan Square
14 Amana Hall
15 Al Rusafi Square
16 Saray al Kushla
17 Mutanabbi Street
18 Jewish Quarter and
    Synagogues (26 in 1949)
19 Suwaidi Bridge
20 Central Bank
21 Khulafa Mosque
22 Iraq Museum
23 Suwaidi Square
24 National Gallery

25 Ahrar Bridge
26 Khullani Mosque
27 Al Kindi Teaching Hospital
28 Al Mansur Hotel
29 St George's Church
30 British Cemetery
31 Liberation Square
32 Shahid Monument
33 Jumhuriya Bridge
34 Redwaniya Detention Centre
35 Zawra Park and
    Grand Festivities Square
36 Tomb of the Unknown Soldier
37 Crossed Swords/Victory Arch
    and Parade Ground
38 Khuld Hall
39 Republican Palace
40 Sheraton Hotel
41 Firdus Square
42 14 July Bridge
43 Amin Al Khas HQ
44 Iraq Stock Exchange
45 Our Lady of Salvation Church
46 National Theatre

0   500 1000 1500 2000 2500 yards

0   500 1000 1500 2000 2500 m

Shia/Sunni sectarian cleansing of Baghdad 2003–2009

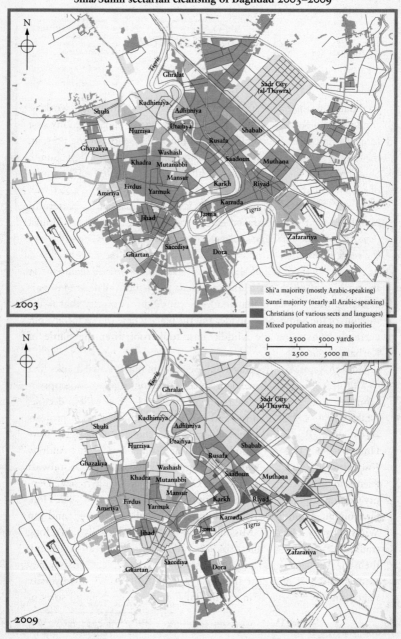

N

Ghralat

Sadr City
(al-Thawra)

Kadhimiya

Adhimiya

Shula

Hurriya

Utaifiya

Shabab

Ghazaliya

Rusafa

Washash

Khadra

Mutanabbi

Saadoun

Muthana

Mansur

Firdus

Amiriya

Yarmuk

Karkh

Riyad

Karrada

Tigris

Jamia

Jihad

Zafarariya

Ghartan

Sacediya

Dora

Shi'a majority (mostly Arabic-speaking)
Sunni majority (nearly all Arabic-speaking)
Christians (of various sects and languages)
Mixed population areas; no majorities

0   2500   5000 yards
0   2500   5000 m

2003

N

Ghralat

Sadr City
(al-Thawra)

Kadhimiya

Adhimiya

Shula

Hurriya

Utaifiya

Shabab

Ghazaliya

Rusafa

Washash

Khadra

Mutanabbi

Saadoun

Muthana

Mansur

Firdus

Amiriya

Yarmuk

Karkh

Riyad

Karrada

Tigris

Jamia

Jihad

Zafarariya

Ghartan

Sacediya

Dora

2009

Acknowledgements

Baghdad is not the easiest place in the world in which to live, work or conduct historical research. For much of the past decade, from my first footsteps in the Iraqi capital in the summer of 2004 until the present, the City of Peace has been a slaughterhouse, an inferno of killing. Sunni, Shia, Jews, Christians, foreigners – all have been targeted in the waves of violence that flooded across Iraq in the aftermath of the 2003 war. This, as I show in this book, is only the latest iteration of a pattern of bloodshed that can be traced across the centuries, sometimes almost indistinct and beneath the surface, frequently all too vivid, right back to the reign of the Sunni Abbasid caliph Mansur, who founded the city in 762 and left a crypt full of Shia corpses – men, women and children – at the time of his death. Strife and instability on a grand scale are inseparable from the history of Baghdad, the capital of a country that is the fulcrum of the Sunni–Shia divide, and the place where the sectarian split currently convulsing the Middle East took root after the Battle of Kerbala in 680.

With that note of long-standing insecurity in mind, I owe thanks first of all to Lieutenant Colonel Tim Spicer OBE for giving me the opportunity to live and work in Baghdad for much of the past decade, establishing a foundation to fund small health and education projects across Iraq. Brigadier James Ellery CBE, the late Brigadier Tony Hunter-Choat, Colonel the Hon. Alastair Campbell, Colonel Andrew Joscelyne, Catriona Laing and many other colleagues were also stalwart friends in difficult times. Lieutenant General Sir John Kiszely, MC, Deputy Commanding General Multinational Force Iraq (2004–5), The Hon. Sir Dominic Asquith, British Ambassador in Baghdad 2006–7, and Jon Wilks, Deputy Head of Mission 2009–10, maintained Britain's long tradition of sending its finest soldiers and Arabists to Baghdad. I thank them for their friendship and for the support of the British Embassy. My former colleague and dear friend Dr Thair Ali of Baghdad University risked his life repeatedly in the line of duty by facilitating all sorts of research in the city. He went far beyond it to help me visit some of Baghdad's most important historical sites at a time when even simple expeditions could be a matter of life and death. I am deeply grateful to him. Thank you above all to my many unnamed colleagues who kept me out of harm's way during my time in Iraq. Too many of them lost their lives over the past decade.

Iraq is not just a violent corner of the Middle East: it is also the cradle of civilization. From Sumerian times in the sixth millennium BC through the Babylonian, Assyrian, Achaemenid, Seleucid, Parthian, Roman and Sassanid periods, successive civilizations have flourished in Mesopotamia, the fertile, irrigated land between the Tigris and Euphrates rivers. For most of the five centuries of Abbasid rule in Baghdad from 762 to 1258, the city represented the pinnacle of intellectual, artistic, scientific and technological achievement on earth, attracting scholars and immigrants from across the world, from Central Asia to the shores of the Atlantic. Iraqis are rightly proud of this legacy. I have been lucky to meet so many civilized and generous men and women who have helped with this book in different and important ways. Some provided critical insights into the history, culture, religion and politics of Iraq, others shared childhood memories of Baghdad in more peaceful times. Many returned from opposition in exile to help rebuild Iraq after the fall of Saddam Hussein. A number of them became friends.

For numerous interviews and conversations my thanks to former Prime Minister Ayad Allawi, former Deputy Prime Minister Barham Salih, Samir Sumaidaie, Iraq's Ambassador to Washington 2006–11, Mowaffak al Rubaie, National Security Advisor 2004–9, who will be better remembered by history as the man who hanged Saddam, Defence Minister Saadoun al Dulaimi, Fareed Yasseen, Iraq's Ambassador to France, Saad Yusef, an advisor to Prime Minister Nouri al Maliki, Dr Abdul Aziz Hamid, former chairman of the State Board of Antiquities, General Nabil Said, Professor Eyad Shamseldeen, Sarmad Allawi and Hadi Allawi. I have benefited from conversations with the controversial Iraqi politician Ahmed Chalabi, who is less well known as an enthusiastic historian of Iraq, and his daughter Tamara Chalabi, author of the spirited memoir *Late for Tea at the Deer Palace: The Lost Dreams of My Iraqi Family*. Tamara Daghestani provided wistful memories of happier times in Baghdad. Her extensive photographic archive on Facebook is a powerful antidote for those who fear the worst for Iraq.

Fatima Fleifel was a delightful and long-suffering teacher who helped me to brush up my Arabic.

In the academic world I am especially grateful to the Abbasid historians Professor Hugh Kennedy, Professor of Arabic at the School of Oriental and African Studies (SOAS), and Dr Amira Bennison, senior lecturer in Middle Eastern and Islamic Studies at Cambridge University, who have provided guidance in person and through their works listed in the Bibliography. Thanks also to the renowned historians of Iraq Professor Charles Tripp at SOAS and Dr Toby Dodge at the London School of Economics, Khaled Al Rouayheb, Associate Professor of Islamic Intellectual History at Harvard University's Department of Near Eastern Languages and Civilizations, Professor Amélie Kuhrt FBA of University College London, and Dr Lamia al Gailani and Joan Porter MacIver, both of the British School of Archaeology in Iraq. For shedding much-needed light on the sometimes murky Ottoman period in Baghdad, my thanks to Professor Norman Stone of Bilkent University in Ankara, Dr Rhoads Murphey at the Centre for Byzantine, Ottoman and Modern Greek Studies at the University of Birmingham, the writers and Ottoman historians Dr Ebubekir Ceylan, Caroline Finkel and Jason Goodwin and Sibel Yildiz. I am extremely grateful to Ali Erken for his assistance in the Ottoman archives in Istanbul. The historian and orientalist Dr Robert Irwin, Middle East editor of the *Times Literary Supplement*, very kindly read my text at a late stage and saved me from a number of errors. Any which remain are, of course, entirely my own. My thanks to His Grace the Duke of Wellington for allowing me access to his private war journal and for a fascinating interview about his experiences in Iraq in 1940. Zaab Sethna and Bartle Bull have been regular companions and astute guides to events and people in Baghdad since I first travelled there. Inspiration, encouragement and knowledge poured from the writers and journalists Con Coughlin, Jon Lee Anderson and Harry Mount, Kwasi Kwarteng MP, Rory Stewart MP, Sarah Hildersley of the British Embassy in Amman, Colonel Robert Bateman, a military historian in the US Army, Peter Francis of the Commonwealth War Graves Commission, the publisher Barnaby Rogerson and the Dutch journalist Aernout van Lynden, who witnessed the first few minutes of the Iraq–Iran War from a Baghdad hotel balcony at dawn on 23 September 1980. The Gertrude Bell Archive at the University of

Newcastle and the photographic archives of the Royal Geographical Society and National Geographic were mines of useful information. A good deal of research in London was made possible by the staff of the much-loved Rare Books and Music room of the British Library.

Baghdad's Jews, who numbered around 40,000 – one-third of the city's population – as recently as 1904, had dwindled to just seven when I first arrived in the city exactly 100 years later. Today that figure is smaller still, and one of the world's oldest Jewish communities, which long predates Iraq's Muslims, is virtually extinguished. Among the Jewish community I consulted outside Iraq, I would like to thank Cordia Ezekiel, who helped her father Max Sawdayee publish *All Waiting to Be Hanged*, his chilling memoir of life in Baathist Baghdad in the 1960s. Like many Jewish families living in the Iraq of President Ahmed Hassan al Bakr and Vice-President Saddam Hussein, their options were execution or escape. The Sawdayee family fled Iraq in 1970. Sandra and Edward Graham, Edward Dallal, Dr Eliyah Shahrabani and George Abda were all generous with their time and thoughts. Karen Fredman pointed me in the right direction in the world of Iraqi Jews in London and gave further help to the writing of this book by regularly walking our exuberant dog at short notice.

During the turmoil of recent years Baghdad's ancient Christian community has also been decimated by violence and driven into exile. The late Dr Donny George, formerly director of the National Museum in Baghdad, gave me a private tour of one of the world's greatest collections of antiquities, which was then closed to the public. The Aegis Foundation made a donation to help restore the building that houses the museum's archives. George and his family were later threatened with death and hounded out of Iraq. He was appointed a Visiting Professor at Stony Brook University in the US in 2006, where he died five years later at the age of sixty. Georges Sada, former Air Vice Marshal in the Iraqi Air Force and author of *Saddam's Secrets: How an Iraqi General Defied and Survived Saddam Hussein*, was an irrepressible companion, together with Canon Andrew White, the charismatic 'Vicar of Baghdad', who has seen so many of his flock cut down in recent years and whose uplifting work on inter-faith reconciliation in Iraq is fraught with danger.

Sincere thanks as ever to my splendid agent, Georgina Capel, a veritable factory of ideas who encouraged this history from the start. The formidable team at Penguin deserve a special tribute: Phillip Birch was the first to commission this book, Stuart Proffitt, Donna Poppy and David Watson were extraordinarily rigorous and sensitive editors, and Cecilia Mackay was tireless in tracking down the most elusive pictures to illustrate this volume so handsomely. Thanks also to Richard Duguid, Isabelle de Cat, Penelope Vogler, Shan Vahidy, Donald Futers and Kathleen McCulloch.

My darling Julia deserves far more than thanks for putting up with her husband living in Baghdad for extended periods, including over a year at the height of the post-war violence, with many more subsequent visits during the following years when the Iraqi capital was anything but the City of Peace. Telephone conversations regularly had to be abandoned as the International Zone siren announced incoming mortars or rockets, a stomach-hollowing prelude to multiple explosions. I thank her and our daughter Clemmie for their love, patience and encouragement.

Finally, this book would not have been possible without the constant support of Manaf al Damluji, a Baghdadi gentleman, diplomat and scholar whose family has suffered, like so many others, from the appalling violence that has afflicted Baghdad in recent years. Manaf has been an erudite and indefatigable guide to so many of the Arabic sources consulted here and a fount of wisdom in all things pertaining to the city he loves. In 2012, after eight years living in Amman as refugees, he and his wife were granted asylum in the US, where they now live together. It is to him that *Baghdad: City of Peace, City of Blood* is dedicated.

A Note on Spelling

Is it to be Mohammed, Muhammad or Mahomet? Should it be the Koran, Quran or Qur'an? Transliterating Arabic is fraught with danger, and can be a pedant's paradise. There are various systems for 'precise' Arabic transliteration, but they are generally very complicated and have little to recommend them aesthetically. My aim has been to make things as simple and comprehensible as possible for the general reader. I do not wish to throw diacritical marks all over the text like confetti, a dot beneath an 's' and an 'h' here, a line above an 'i' or an 'a' there, apostrophes and hyphens crowding in like unwelcome visitors. Asked to choose between *Tārīkh al-'Irāq bayna Iḥtilālayn* (Abbas al Azzawi's *History of Iraq Between Two Occupations*) and *Tarikh al Iraq bayn al Ihtilayn*, I choose the latter without hesitation.

For the most part I have not transliterated the guttural Arabic letter qaf or ق as 'q', preferring 'k' on the grounds that this will be more familiar to readers of English. The caliph some call Qaim therefore becomes Kaim; a *qadi*, or judge, becomes *kadi* and so on. But where usage is extremely familiar to readers, as with Iraq and Al Qaeda, I have retained the 'q' transliteration, so already I am guilty of inconsistency. Likewise with Baghdad itself (Bagdat to some seventeenth-century Englishmen, Bagdad well into the twentieth century for others), I have kept the standard 'gh' transliteration of the letter ghayn or غ. I have chosen to ignore altogether the problematic letter 'ayn or ع – virtually unpronounceable for those who do not know Arabic, and which tends to be variously rendered 'a', 'aa' or even '3' – because what does an apostrophe, or for that matter '3', really mean to the reader who does not know Arabic or the complexities of Arabic pronunciation? Arabic experts will surely know what is meant, and others will hardly notice its absence. So the caliph Ma'mun becomes simply Mamun and 'Iraq becomes Iraq. I prefer not to hyphenate the definite article, so I have Al Mansur and

Al Amin rather than Al-Mansur and Al-Amin at the first mention, Mansur and Amin thereafter.

There are, I know, a number of other departures here from the most rigorous modern scholarly practice. Responding to a plea for clarity from the much put-upon editor of *Seven Pillars of Wisdom* T. E. Lawrence replied tartly: 'There are some "scientific systems" of transliteration, helpful to people who know enough Arabic not to need helping, but a wash-out for the world. I spell my names anyhow, to show what rot the systems are.' I would not dream of suggesting these systems are rot, but less brazenly I have followed his example. And, to answer the question with which I began, the Prophet is Mohammed and the holy book revealed to him by Allah is the Koran.

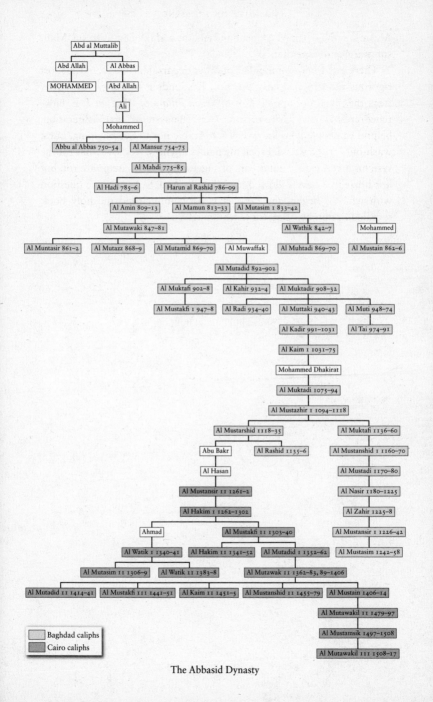

The Abbasid Dynasty

Preface

The old man strokes his beard and shakes his head. He is a bookseller on Mutanabbi Street in the dusty heart of old Baghdad, yards away from the River Tigris. 'The Iranians are controlling us again,' he says, swatting flies from his piles of books. 'We got rid of the Turks and the British, we got rid of the dictator Saddam, we got rid of the Americans, and now it's the Iranians. They're the ones running Iraq,* making trouble for us and causing divisions between Sunni and Shia. By God, some things never change.'

The old man's hostility towards Iraq's neighbour reflects the historical antagonism between largely Sunni Arabs and Shia Iranians. Conspiracies originating in Tehran are a common currency in this city of seven million. Yet what he does not say during his toothy harangue against the old enemy is that, had it not been for some concerted Iranian meddling and intriguing in Iraq 1,300 years ago, Baghdad, glory of the Islamic Empire, once the cultural lodestar of the world and centre of the greatest civilization on earth, not to mention the bookseller's home for eight decades, might never have existed.

*

The revolution had been smouldering since around 719, when plotters in the holy Muslim town of Kufa on the banks of the Euphrates in what is now southern Iraq – today's Iraq was divided into the eastern provinces of Jazira, Jibal, Azerbaijan, Armenia and Iraq – lit the first spark

* The word Iraq is thought to trace its earliest origins to the Sumerian city of Uruk, dating back to around 4000 BC, via the Aramaic Erech and possibly Persian Eragh ('The name al-Iraq, for all its Arabic appearance, is derived from Middle Persian eragh "lowlands",' states *The Cambridge History of Iran*). Lower Mesopotamia, as the Ancient Greeks referred to the Land between the Rivers, has been called Iraq – from the Arabic for vein or root – since ancient times. During the medieval period the terms Iraq Arabi (Arabian Iraq) and Iraq Ajemi (Iranian Iraq) denoted Lower Mesopotamia and central and western Iran respectively. In 1921 the three Ottoman vilayets, or provinces, of Baghdad, Basra and Mosul were united to form the modern state of Iraq.

by sending a clandestine mission to Humayma, an unremarkable little village south of the Dead Sea in Jordan. Here, among the orchards and olive groves of a small country estate, a messenger disguised as a perfume-seller fanned the tiny flames of opposition to the Umayyad Dynasty, rulers of the Islamic Empire from their capital of Damascus, whispering rebellion into the ears of a distant descendant of the Prophet Mohammed's family.

In time, further secret missions were dispatched from Kufa to Khorasan, then the easternmost corner of the Islamic world, a wide-skied region that today stretches across eastern Iran into Afghanistan, Uzbekistan and Turkmenistan. Khorasan, the western half of which was once the ancient region of Parthia, seat first of the Parthian Empire (247 BC–AD 24) then a province of the Persian, was a vast world of steppe studded with the rich and storied oasis cities of Samarkand, Bukhara, Nishapur, Herat, Balkh and Merv, its high-walled capital. Here too were the snow-covered mountain passes, and the waters of the Oxus and Herat Rivers, crashing down from the Pamirs and the Hindu Kush (known to later Arab geographers as the Stony Girdles of the Earth) to water the Kizil Kum (Red Sand) and Kara Kum (Black Sand) deserts. Captured by Alexander the Great in antiquity, Khorasan fell in 650 to the Arab armies from the Arabian peninsula blazing a trail of Islamic conquest. Over the next decades it became a melting-pot, with the Arab conquerors settling alongside the newly converted Turkish nomads, Iranian princes, dirt-poor peasants, prosperous Soghdian merchants and the masters of the Silk Road caravan trade. All were ruled by the Umayyad caliphs from distant Damascus.

After the Prophet Mohammed's death in 632, a succession of four caliphs – Abu Bakr, Omar, Othman and Ali – led the emerging Islamic world until 661, when Muawia, brother-in-law of the Prophet and governor of Syria, seized power and established the hereditary Umayyad Dynasty, which traced its origins to Mecca. Through its expansion of Islamic dominions from its capital of Damascus, it came to rule one of the greatest empires the world had ever seen, extending from North Africa and the Iberian peninsula in the west to Central Asia and the borders of China and India in the east in a relentless procession of military conquests. But over time, opposition to the increasingly autocratic Umayyads grew within Khorasan, encouraged by reports of their astonishingly luxurious lifestyle and neglect of the faith brought by the secret missions from Kufa; here increasing dissent led to a number of armed revolts that were quickly crushed by Syrian troops. The rebels were backing a man described with calculated vagueness as a member of the Prophet Mohammed's family. Oaths of allegiance were sworn to Al Rida min al Mohammed (An Acceptable Member of the House of the Prophet). This ruse, which was central to 'the earliest and most subtle propagandist movement in political Islam', was devised to widen the appeal of the rebellion to the Shiat Ali – or the Shia, to use the common abbreviation – the followers of Ali, cousin and son-in-law of Mohammed and the fourth caliph, murdered in 661.[1]

The Shia considered Ali the first caliph and his uncrowned descendants Mohammed's rightful successors; while orthodox Muslims, or the Sunni, the Ahl al Sunnah wal Jamaah (The People of the Traditions of the Prophet and the Consensus of the Community), instead regarded Ali as the fourth caliph, and last of the Rashidun, or the 'Rightly Guided Caliphs'. This difference was the very root of the Sunni–Shia schism. The Shia, both in Kufa and Khorasan, regarded themselves as the proper inheritors of Mohammed's political and spiritual power. In other words they were, in their own minds at least, those who would most likely benefit from the overthrow of the Umayyads.

The Shia, who were particularly numerous in the Umayyad province of Iraq, regarded the Damascus-based dynasty as Sunni usurpers of a caliphate that should have been ruled by the descendants of Ali. But, in fact, the loyalty of the travelling revolutionaries, though they did not declare it publicly at this time, was to the Abbasids, descendants of the Prophet's uncle Abbas. Although the Abbasid blood ties with the Prophet were flimsy by comparison with those of the House of Ali, their powers of organization had no equal.

In low voices the agents from Iraq promised an Islamic revival, a new dawn in which Arabs and non-Arabs would be equal and united as fellow Muslims, not divided according to the Umayyad tendency to favour the Arab tribes over all other races, irrespective of whether they had converted to the true faith. The message fell on fertile soil. The divisions between the southern Arabian Kalb tribes and the northern Arabian Kays tribes, rivalries that were bedevilling successions and causing bloodshed across the Islamic world, were already consuming the Umayyad Dynasty from within.

The Abbasid movement spread its message of revolution along the

trade and pilgrimage routes to Khorasan through a discreet network of
supporters who adopted roles that allowed them to travel without
attracting undue suspicion: most were merchants and traders, or claimed
to be so, riding along the old caravan routes. They were perfume-sellers
and pedlars, artisans, saddle-makers, apothecaries and arrow-makers.
Between them, the seventy or so Abbasid missionaries known today
represented twenty-five tribes, the entire spectrum of the Arab tribes
settled in Khorasan.

Over the following decades, hatred of the Umayyads and their perceived unjust rule grew, in Khorasan and in Iraq. By the 740s the dynasty
that had proudly built the Umayyad Mosque of Damascus and the
Dome of the Rock in Jerusalem and had led Islam's wars against infidel
Byzantium was facing full-scale rebellion in the east. In 744 three caliphs
came and went, and a fourth, Marwan II, was appointed amid the
chaos. His partiality for the Kays tribes further alienated the Kalb tribes
of Khorasan, driving greater numbers of them into the arms of the
Abbasid plotters, to the alarm of Nasr, the Umayyad governor of Khorasan. 'I see coals glowing amongst the embers, they want but little to
burst into blaze,' he wrote to Marwan, warning of impending disaster.
'Fire springs from the rubbing of sticks, and warfare from the wagging
of tongues.'[2] On 15 June 747 the hitherto covert Abbasid insurgents
revealed their true colours when they unfurled their black banners for
the first time on the outskirts of Merv. Thousands flocked to take up
arms.

The moral leader of this coalition of Shia, Khorasanian and Abbasid
forces was Abu al Abbas, great-great-grandson of Abbas, the Prophet's
uncle. His military chief was Abu Muslim, a shadowy figure of unknown
origin who won fame on the battlefield in a stirring series of victories
over the Umayyads; and infamy off it, having reputedly killed 60,000
people in cold blood.[3] Abu Muslim established himself first as the
essential linchpin between Kufa and Khorasan, then as the Abbasid
movement's pre-eminent military leader, and early in 748 he made himself master of Merv and sent his armies west.

A year later a coup was engineered in Kufa, allowing the Abbasid
revolutionaries to enter the city and take control. Even at this stage
there was still no sign of the Abbasid family members, who had been
ordered into hiding by Abu Salama, the temporizing head of the Kufa
conspirators. Eventually, just as rumours were swirling that a member

of the House of Ali was about to be appointed caliph, local people directed the same soldiers to the Abbasid safe house, where Abu al Abbas was found. In the autumn of 749, although the Umayyads had yet to be finally defeated, he was declared caliph, the Amir al Muminin, or Commander of the Faithful.

In January 750 the Umayyad army of Marwan II met Abbasid forces on the banks of the Great Zab River, a tributary of the Tigris in northern Iraq. With an army of 300,000, the Umayyads were said by the tenth-century Byzantine monk and chronicler Theophanes the Confessor to have outnumbered the Abbasids massively. Borrowing a battle tactic they had observed Umayyad forces use, the Abbasids formed a spear wall, crouching down on one knee with lances pointed directly at their enemy. Marwan's cavalry charged confidently, but the wall held and countless cavalrymen were impaled on Abbasid lances. Of those who were left, many deserted and more took flight. 'One man was seen pursuing a thousand, and two making ten thousand run,' wrote Theophanes.[4] Marwan had the pontoon bridge across the river cut adrift to prevent his soldiers fleeing the battlefield, a decision that condemned huge numbers of them to death by drowning in the waters of the Zab. The rout was soon complete.

Marwan fled across Iraq, then into Syria, finally into Egypt. Damascus fell in April 750, and the fugitive Umayyad caliph was finally hunted down to the Egyptian town of Busir in August. His head was sent back to Abu al Abbas, whose caliphal epithet or throne title was Al Saffa, Shedder of Blood. According to the ninth-century historian Mohammed ibn Jarir al Tabari, the fall of the Umayyad Dynasty was announced on the steps of the mosque in Kufa. The words were those of Daud, the brother of Abu al Abbas:

> Praise be to God, with gratitude, gratitude and yet more gratitude! Praise to him who has caused our enemies to perish and brought to us our inheritance from Mohammed our Prophet, God's blessing and peace be upon him! O ye people, now are the dark nights of the world put to flight, its covering lifted, now light breaks in the earth and the heavens, and the sun rises from the springs of day while the moon ascends from its appointed place ... God has let you behold what you were awaiting and looking forward to. He has made manifest among you a caliph of the clan of Hashim, brightening thereby your faces and making you to prevail over

the army of Syria, and transferring the sovereignty and the glory of Islam
to you.[5]

In another version of a speech whose authenticity is difficult to establish, the fever-racked caliph struggles through his opening address after
receiving the oath of allegiance and concludes with the warning, 'Hold
yourselves ready, for I am the pitiless blood-shedder and the destroying
avenger.'[6]

The once-mighty Umayyad caliphate, which had pushed the frontiers
of the Muslim Empire to the shores of the Atlantic in the west and the
mountains of Afghanistan in the east, had been completely extinguished,
and the Islamic world had a new leader.

Saffa lived up to his name admirably. He devoted most of his brief
caliphate to hunting down and butchering the surviving male members of
the Umayyad family with a dedication that was never less than obsessive.
Only one managed to escape the slaughter and sloped off west to found
the Umayyad amirate of Cordoba in the Iberian peninsula, a tiny sliver of
the Muslim world. Al Makrizi, the fifteenth-century Egyptian historian,
provides some grim detail of this vengeful campaign. Saffa ordered
Umayyad tombs to be dug up and destroyed; exhumed corpses were
'scourged with whips and then crucified'; skulls were used as target practice until smashed into pieces before the remaining Umayyad family body
parts were gathered together and burnt to ashes.[7]

In 754, within four years of his triumph and still in his early thirties,
the Shedder of Blood succumbed to smallpox. On his death, his brother
Abu Jafar, who took the throne title of Al Mansur (The Victorious), was
proclaimed caliph. The brevity of Saffa's intensely violent reign belied
his exceptionally long and glorious legacy, which lasted more than
500 years. The world-changing Abbasid Dynasty, whose extraordinary
achievements are celebrated in the tatty volumes of Mutanabbi Street's
grumpy bookseller, had been born.

I

The Caliph and His Capital: Mansur and the Foundation of Baghdad (750–75)

Baghdad, in the heart of Islam, is the city of well-being; in it are the talents of which men speak, and elegance and courtesy. Its winds are balmy and its science penetrating. In it are to be found the best of everything and all that is beautiful. From it comes everything worthy of consideration, and every elegance is drawn towards it. All hearts belong to it, all wars are against it and every hand is raised to defend it. It is too renowned to need description, more glorious than we could possibly portray it, and is indeed beyond praise.[1]

Mukaddasi, *The Best Divisions for Knowledge of the Regions* (tenth century)

The caliph needed a capital – a new city to become the permanent home of the Abbasid Empire and the headquarters of the Dar al Islam, the Muslim world, a dominion of more than five million square miles stretching from Morocco and the Iberian peninsula to Central Asia.

Until 762, rather like the original Arab tribes that had surged out of Arabia during the great conquests of the seventh century, the Abbasids had shifted from base to base like desert nomads. In the short time since they had displaced the Umayyads as leaders of the Islamic world in 750, they had already made use of four capitals. After a brief and unsatisfactory residence at Kasr ibn Hubayra on the Euphrates, halfway between Kufa and Baghdad, Mansur's predecessor Saffa had built himself a *hashimiya*, or palace headquarters, next to the old Persian town of Anbar on the eastern side of the Euphrates, in what is today western Iraq. The local population there had not taken kindly to the name *hashimiya*, a reference to the Abbasid family's ancestors, and defiantly had continued to refer to the place by its old name, Ibn Hubayra, taken from Yazid ibn Umar ibn Hubayra, the last Umayyad governor of Iraq. Saffa promptly moved to a new site opposite the castle.

Mansur the Victorious had built Madinat al Mansur, the City of Mansur, at Madinat ibn Hubayra, close – too close, in fact – to the rebellious and extremist Shia stronghold of Kufa. A bloody riot within his palace in 758, triggered by Persian fanatics who insisted on worshipping him as their god and then rose up against him when he dismissed them as heretics, must have gone a long way towards persuading him that the quest to find a more suitable base must continue.

To the west, the powerful residual loyalty of Damascus to the displaced Umayyad Dynasty made it out of the question as a potential capital. It was, besides, too far from Persia, which provided the bulwark of Abbasid military power, and too close to the Greek frontier, as the Byzantine incursions that had challenged Umayyad power during its final years had repeatedly demonstrated. After the heyday of Arab expansion in the seventh and eighth centuries, largely although not exclusively in the west, future Islamic conquests were more likely in the east, as was the assimilation of lands already won beyond the Oxus River, so it was in more central Mesopotamia, the Land between the Rivers, that the second Abbasid caliph directed his search. To preserve its independence, the new capital needed to be sufficiently removed from both Basra and Kufa, the two Arab cities that had been founded in Mesopotamia as garrisons for troops during the first century of the Arab conquests.

Mansur was not a man to delegate such an important task to his officials. He led the reconnaissance for his new capital himself, sailing up and down the Tigris from Jarjarya to Mosul, scouting for the most suitable site with his characteristic attention to detail. In itself there was nothing very original in such a search: settlement along this river, which together with the Euphrates once watered ancient Mesopotamia, had taken place from the earliest times. Mesopotamia was able to sustain empires thanks only to its prodigious fertility, remarked on wonderingly in the fifth century BC by the Greek historian Herodotus, who also noted the network of irrigation canals on which it depended.* This extensive and highly sophisticated system of water channels required regular maintenance.

In fact, though Mansur founded the city, settlement at Baghdad long pre-dated the Abbasid caliph. There are a number of hints and suggestions that a community existed here in ancient times, as one would expect of such a favourable location on the Tigris amid productive land. The mighty Assyrian king Tiglath-Pileser I, an Old Testament, slash-and-burn conqueror mentioned in the Book of Kings and the Book of Chronicles (he styled himself 'powerful king, king of hosts, who has no rival, king of the four quarters (of the world)'), certainly campaigned in this area sometime around 1100 BC, and his son is reported to have captured a place called Baghdad, then of little consequence.[2] A name very similar to Baghdad also appears in the geographical catalogues of the legendary Assyrian king Sardanapalus around the seventh century BC. In 1848 the distinguished orientalist Sir Henry Rawlinson, the then British political agent in Ottoman Arabia and later president of the Royal Geographical Society, discovered Babylonian bricks lining the western bank of the Tigris at Baghdad: these bore the royal stamp of another Old Testament anti-hero, Nebuchadnezzar, the Jew-slaying, temple-smashing, gold-loving despot of the sixth century BC. It is not clear, however, whether these had been moved to Baghdad after the Babylonian king's reign, perhaps even by Mansur.

Twenty miles to the south of the future site of Baghdad (and close enough to appeal as a source of building materials for Mansur's new city) lay the evocative ruins of Ctesiphon, the once magnificent imperial capital of the Parthian and later Sassanid Empires, an important city since the first century BC, whose ancient Persian kings had large royal parks and gardens a short sail to the north in the area that became Baghdad. Ctesiphon was built across the river from more ancient Seleucia, founded in the late fourth century BC, which had been one of the great cities of the world in Hellenistic and Roman times. The Arabs

* 'As a grain-bearing country Assyria is the richest in the world. No attempt is made there to grow figs, grapes, or olives or any other fruit trees, but so great is the fertility of the grain fields that they normally produce crops of two-hundredfold, and in an exceptional year as much as three-hundredfold. The blades of wheat and barley are at least three inches wide.' *Histories*, 1.193

referred to the conurbation of Seleucia–Ctesiphon as Al Madain (The Cities). The almost unbroken string of towns and villages along the Tigris gave rise, many centuries later, to the Baghdadi expression that 'A cock could hop from house to house, all the way to Basra.'[3]

A millennium after Nebuchadnezzar, there were communities of Nestorian monks living here, who appear in a number of the foundation legends of Baghdad.* During the seventh century, under the late Sassanid Empire, it was a thriving Iranian settlement with a monthly market, entering the annals of Arab history ingloriously in 634 when an army of the first caliph, Abu Bakr, swooped on Souk Baghdad (Baghdad Market), as it was then known, plundered every piece of gold and silver they could find before galloping off into the desert and leaving the devastated community to sink back into obscurity, until Mansur's epoch-making arrival in 762. It was the first recorded instance of the violence, bloodshed and slaughter that would become tragically dominant features of the city's life in the centuries to follow.

In choosing the Tigris over the Euphrates, Mansur proved himself a shrewd student of geography. First, the Euphrates was the westernmost limit of this spectacularly fertile land. Unlike the Tigris, which was surrounded by productive, irrigated land, the barren sands of Arabia swept right up to its western edge. It was the waters of the Euphrates, through a network of canals, some of which dated to Sumerian times from around 4000 BC, that irrigated the agricultural land between the two great rivers, leaving the waters of the Tigris to be used for the country to its east, along the length of modern Iraq from the Arabian desert and the gates of the Persian Gulf in the south to the snowy peaks of Kurdistan in the north. There was a further disadvantage to the Euphrates that would have impressed itself firmly on the Abbasid caliph's mind: like the Tigris, its course has changed over the centuries, and at this time it disgorged into the murky shallows known as the Great Swamp a little north of Babylon; subsequently, it was impossible to navigate as far as the Persian Gulf (though today the confluence of the two rivers at Kurna,

---

* The Nestorian Church, named after the fifth-century Patriarch of Constantinople, is also known as the Church of the East, the Syriac strand of Eastern Christianity. Christian communities in Mesopotamia, which dated to the first century, were established on a more formal footing when the Council of Seleucia-Ctesiphon in 410 granted official recognition to the Church of the East under its own bishop, known as the patriarch or catholicos (from the Greek, meaning general primate).

north-west of Basra, forms the Shatt al Arab, which empties into the Gulf). Though the Tigris also discharged its waters into the same swamp, it was nevertheless navigable to the southern coast via a series of channels. The benefits to commerce and communications were self-evident.

The ninth-century Arab geographer and historian Yakubi, who compiled *The Book of Countries*, emphasized Baghdad's links to the outside world in suitably portentous comments attributed to Mansur:

> Assuredly, this island [of land between the rivers], bounded on the east by the Tigris and on the west by the Euphrates, will prove to be the crossroads of the universe. Ships on the Tigris, coming from Wasit, Basra, Obolla, Ahwaz, Fars, Oman, Yamama, Bahrain and neighbouring countries, will land and drop anchor there. It is there that merchandise will arrive by way of the Tigris from Mosul, Azerbaijan and Armenia; that too will be the destination of products transported by ship on the Euphrates from Rakka, Syria, the borderlands of Asia Minor, Egypt and the Maghreb. This city will also be on the route of the peoples of Jebel, Isfahan and the provinces of Khorasan. By God I will build this capital and live in it all my life. It will be the residence of my descendants. It will certainly be the most prosperous city in the world.[4]

Mukaddasi, the tenth-century Arab geographer and author of the charmingly titled *The Best Divisions for Knowledge of the Regions*, provided another retrospective endorsement of the site, reporting a wholehearted recommendation offered by one of the district notables to Mansur:

> We consider it advisable that you settle [here] . . . Thus you will be surrounded by palms and be close to water. If, then, one of the districts should suffer from drought, or its cultivation be delayed, another would relieve the situation. Moreover, you are on the banks of al Sarat [a famous canal dating back to Persian times, part of the system of waterways linking the two great rivers], so that supplies can come to you by the vessels plying the Euphrates; the caravans from Egypt and Syria will come across the desert, goods of all different kinds from China will reach you by sea, and from the Byzantines and al Mosul by the Tigris. Again, you are in a place between rivers so that the enemy cannot reach you except by ship, or by bridge, by way of the Tigris or the Euphrates.[5]

The Nestorian monks are supposed to have confirmed to Mansur that the area also enjoyed a favourable climate. Unlike much of the region, its summers were both comparatively cool (something difficult to imagine today, as the mercury inches towards a head-roasting 50 degrees in August) and dry, sparing the district the fatal ravages of fever and mosquito-borne malaria that were so common in Basra and along the Euphrates. Nights were pleasant. The Baghdadi tradition of families taking to the roof to sleep beneath the stars during the hot summer months, which continues to this day, is as old as the city itself.

*

The name Baghdad is probably Persian in origin. Yakut, the thirteenth-century Syrian author of the *Geographical Dictionary* and perhaps the greatest geographer of the Middle Ages, speculated that it derived from *bagh*, meaning garden, and *dad*, the name of the man who owned the garden. Alternatively, *Bagh* might have been the name of an idol, and *dad* a gift, so that the name referred to 'The Gift of the Idol Bagh'. Writing in 1900, the orientalist Guy Le Strange, author of a painstaking study of Abbasid Baghdad, laid the matter to rest. 'The true etymology ... of the name would appear to be from the two ancient Persian words *Bagh*, "God", and *Dadh*, meaning "founded" or "foundation" – whence Baghdad would have signified the city "Founded by God".'[6]

Not surprisingly, Mansur had his own, very personal idea of what the city should be called: Madinat al Mansur, as its predecessor near Kufa had been. Yet, though the city Mansur founded would indeed be the home of his descendants and, for several centuries at least, 'the most prosperous city in the world', the grandiloquent title he gave it conspicuously failed to take hold. The city, or rather the people who flocked to settle there in one of the most astonishing and rapid urbanizations ever seen, preferred the name Madinat al Salam, the City of Peace, or Dar as Salam, House of Peace, a reference to the description of paradise in the Koran: 'God invites you to the House of Peace. He guides whom He will to a straight path. Those that do good works shall have a good reward, and more besides. Neither blackness nor misery shall overcast their faces. They are the heirs of Paradise, wherein they shall abide forever.'[7]

The foundation of Baghdad, like that of many great cities, is enshrined in legend. There is one story related by the prolific historian Mohammed ibn Jarir al Tabari, ninth-century author of the monumental *History of the Prophets and Kings* (whose English translation runs into a dizzying thirty-eight volumes, or around 10,000 pages). In it, a Christian

Mansur is a whirlwind of summary executions. '"Cut off his head!" cried [Mansur], and he was taken and decapitated,' reads a typical line. '[Mansur] gave the order and his head was cut off,' goes another. When it came to killing sworn enemies or his most unswervingly loyal supporters, like the general Abu Muslim, who had helped bring the Abbasids to power, there was nothing remotely sentimental or squeamish about Mansur. The caliph's executions were so numerous, in fact, that there are times when the historian wonders how he found the time to attend to other affairs of state.

Tabari gives us the grisliest example of Mansur's darker side in a memorably sinister anecdote related by the caliph's perfumer, Jamra. She told how, before he left on what would prove to be his last pilgrimage to Mecca, Mansur gave the keys of his storerooms to his daughter-in-law Rita, the wife of his son and heir, Al Mahdi, who was in Iran at the time, with specific instructions to leave the rooms strictly alone unless she was absolutely sure he was dead. Later, once news of the caliph's subsequent death had been confirmed in 775, Mahdi and Rita hurried down to the storeroom, expecting this obscure corner of the palace to be heaving with hidden treasures. Instead they were confronted with the sickening sight of a vast chamber filled with corpses, ranging from those of young children to old men. All were members of the Family of Ali, chilling evidence of the policy Mansur had pursued against the Shia descendants of Ali and his wife Fatima, daughter of the Prophet Mohammed. There was a tag in the ear of every corpse, detailing the name and genealogy of the victim: ruthless violence and meticulous organization combined.

Mansur's methodical persecution of the Alids was an early indication of the destructive tensions between Sunni and Shia in Baghdad and beyond. During the next thirteen centuries this sectarian division would periodically boil over into violence and see the blood flow in Baghdad's streets.

Mansur's meanness was legendary. He was nicknamed Abul Dawanik, the Father of Pennies, a reference to his relentless scrimping and saving. Masudi recorded some telling anecdotes about Mansur in his wonderful book *The Meadows of Gold and Mines of Gems*, an engaging history of the world from Adam and Eve to the Abbasid caliphate. 'Mansur's prudence, the rectitude of his judgement and the excellence of his policies are beyond all description,' he acknowledged. 'He did not avoid the most extravagant generosity when there was something to be had in exchange, but he would refuse the smallest favour if granting it entailed loss.'[12]

At the time of his death, Masudi wrote, Mansur left 14 million dinars and 600 million dirhams in the treasury (a single gold dinar was worth around 20 silver dirhams and each dirham weighed around 3 grams). Nevertheless, 'This great fortune did not prevent him from being miserly, nor did it prevent him from going into details which even a commoner ignores. Thus, he contracted with his cook that the latter should keep the heads, feet and skins in exchange for providing the firewood and seasonings.'[13] Such a hands-on and niggardly approach to accounting had its advantages, not least for his son and immediate successor, Mahdi.

*

In 762 Mansur had the plans of what would be his Round City traced out on the ground in lines of cinders. The perfect circle was a tribute to the geometric teachings of Euclid, whom he had studied and admired. After he had walked through these two-dimensional plans and given his approval, balls of cotton soaked in naphtha (liquid petroleum) were placed along the outlines and then set alight to mark more permanently the position of the double outer walls. Thousands of architects and engineers, legal experts, surveyors and carpenters, blacksmiths, diggers and ordinary labourers were recruited from across the Abbasid Empire. It was the greatest construction project in the Islamic world by far: Yakubi numbered the workers at 100,000, a likely exaggeration but an indication nevertheless of its vast scale. Tabari recorded that each master-builder was paid one carat of silver daily, 1/24th of a dirham, and a day-labourer two to three grains of silver. When an entire lamb cost a quarter of a dirham and a whole dirham bought 30 kilograms of dates or eight litres of oil, such pay was highly attractive.[14]

The royal astrologers Nawbakht, a former Zoroastrian, and Mashallah, a Jewish convert to Islam, declared 30 July 762 the most auspicious date for building work to begin.[15] It was Mansur who, after offering a prayer to Allah, laid the ceremonial first brick. 'Now, with the blessings of God, build on!' he ordered the assembled workers.[16] Like Tamerlane, the Turkic conqueror who descended on the city like a firestorm six centuries later and spent decades adorning his own beloved capital of Samarkand with architectural glories, Mansur revelled in personal supervision and direct control of the building process. Under his command this swelling army of workers surveyed, measured and excavated the foundations, made the sun-baked and kiln-fired bricks that, in the absence of local stone quarries, were the main building material, and raised the fortress-like city walls brick by back-breaking brick. A deep moat ringed the outer wall perimeter, inside which a main wall and a third, inner wall provided additional layers of defence.

The design was startlingly innovative. 'They say that no other round city is known in all the regions of the world,' wrote Al Khatib al Baghdadi, the eleventh-century scholar, whose *History of Baghdad* is a mine of information on the construction of the city.[17]* Four equidistant gates pierced the outer walls, and from each a straight road led to the centre of the city. The Kufa Gate to the south-west and the Basra Gate to the south-east both opened on to the Sarat Canal, a key part of the network of waterways that drained the waters of the Euphrates into the Tigris and made this site so attractive. The Sham (Syrian) Gate to the north-west pointed to the main road to Anbar and on across the desert wastes to Syria. To the north-east the Khorasan Gate lay close to the Tigris, leading to the bridge-of-boats across it.† For the great majority of the city's

---

* Khatib believed the world was divided into seven climes. All but one were inherently imperfect, inhabited variously by Byzantines, Turks, Syrians, Slavs, Chinese and Negroes. At the centre of this unsatisfactory arrangement was the serene land of Iraq, 'the navel of the universe', and at its heart was Baghdad, headquarters of the empire, home of the ruling dynasty and lodestar of the Dar al Islam.

† Keeping up with the changing names of Baghdad's gates over the centuries is an exercise in itself. Sometimes the same gate was known by different names. The Kufa Gate, for example, was also known as the Anbar Gate, both Kufa and Anbar being townships south-west of Baghdad. As the Round City declined and other parts of Baghdad expanded, new gates sprang up on both banks of the city. They came and went during the long cycle of conflict and destruction, sometimes reusing old names (the Khorasan Gate of eastern Baghdad), at other times inventing new titles. Bab al Sultan, named to honour the Ottoman Sultan Murad IV, who liberated Baghdad from the Persians in 1638, was also known as Bab al Muadham (The Glorified Gate), which in turn gave its name to a district of eastern Baghdad that continues today. Bab al Halba (Arena Gate, after the polo field it once overlooked), also in eastern Baghdad, was later known as Bab al Wastani (Middle Gate), sole survivor of the city's medieval gates today. Gates were also renamed. Thus the Bab al Khassa (Private Gate) in the caliphal-palace complex on the east bank was renamed Badr Gate after a favourite slave-turned-minister of the caliph Al Mutadid. The Kulwatha Gate, named after a hamlet in eastern Baghdad, was also known as Bab al Basaliya (Onions Gate), on account of the farms that surrounded it. Today, although it should be known as Southern Gate, it is Bab al Sharki (Eastern Gate), due to the Baghdadis' colloquial habit of thinking of everything from the south – including the famously hot and dusty southern wind – as eastern.

life, a fluctuating number of these bridges, consisting of skiffs roped together and fastened to each bank, were one of the most picturesque signatures of Baghdad; no more permanent structure would be seen until the British arrived in the twentieth century and laid an iron bridge across the Tigris.

Mansur requisitioned iron gates from the nearby town of Wasit, said by Tabari originally to have been made by demons for King Solomon, with additional gates being supplied by Kufa and Damascus. Such was their size and weight that it took a company of men to open and close them. The gateways they protected were equally imposing. 'A horseman with his banner, or a spearman with his lance, could enter the same freely and without lowering the banner or couching the lance,' Yakubi noted.[18]

A gatehouse rose above each of the four outer gates. Those above the entrances in the higher, main wall offered the most commanding views over the city and the many miles of lush palm groves and emerald fields that fringed the waters of the Tigris. We know from Masudi that the large audience chamber at the top of the gatehouse above the Khorasan Gate was a particular favourite of Mansur as an afternoon retreat from the stultifying heat.

The massive brick walls, rising up from the banks of the Tigris, would have been the defining feature of Mansur's Round City. Their circumference was four miles. Khatib recorded a comment by the architect Raba that each course consisted of 162,000 bricks for the first third of the wall's height, 150,000 for the second third and 140,000 for the final section, bonded together with bundles of reeds. Some of these bricks were reportedly 18 inches square and weighed 200 pounds. In one of the various estimations of size and height recorded by medieval historians, the outer wall stood at 60 feet, crowned with battlements and flanked by bastions; but even this was 30 feet lower than its inner counterpart, the main wall, which measured a prodigious 105 feet across at its foundations.[19]

According to Tabari, Mansur asked his famous vizier Khalid ibn Barmak, who came from an aristocratic Persian background, whether he should demolish the ancient ruins of Ctesiphon to provide building materials for his new city. No, Khalid replied, it was a lasting monument to the Arabs' triumph over the pre-Islamic Sassanid Dynasty. Mansur ignored the advice and demolition began. It soon proved much more difficult and expensive than he had imagined. He summoned Khalid and sought his advice a second time. Now that the caliph had started, the vizier replied, he had better 'destroy it to its foundations, for if you do not, it will be said that you were unable to tear it down'.[20] With the capriciousness that was the hallmark of caliphal power, Mansur ignored Khalid's suggestion and, as a result, the ruins of the famous arched palace of Ctesiphon witnessed a fierce battle between British and Turkish forces in November 1915 and still stand to this day, the sole surviving monument of the city.

With Mansur breathing down their necks, supervisors took weights and measures seriously. As an example of the precision with which this urban experiment was undertaken, Tabari tells the story of a man who years later demolished a wall next to Bab al Muhawal, an all-Sunni neighbourhood in the south-western suburbs. He found a brick with its weight of 117 ratls (approximately 115 pounds) clearly marked on it in red ochre. 'We weighed it, and found that it was of the weight that was written upon it,' the evidently impressed man remarked.[21]

Having declined the position of *kadi*, or judge, Imam Abu Hanifa, distinguished founder of the Hanafi school of Islamic law, the largest of the four principal Sunni schools, was appointed one of the four chief overseers of the city's construction, with particular responsibility for brick-making and recruiting labourers.* He pioneered a time-saving way of measuring bricks by the stack with a graduated cane, a great improvement on existing practice. In time, he came to oppose Mansur's rule and duly paid the price. He was thrown into prison and probably tortured, dying in custody in 767, a year after the Round City had been finished.

The four straight roads that ran towards the centre of the city from the outer gates were lined with vaulted arcades containing the merchants' shops and bazaars. Smaller streets ran off these four main arteries, giving access to a series of squares and such houses as there were for the population; the limited space between the main wall and the inner wall answered to Mansur's desire to maintain the heart of the city as a royal preserve. Continuing towards the centre of Baghdad, the roads led to the inner wall and another set of gates, which guarded

* Named after their founders, the four schools of Sunni Islamic *fikh*, based on the Koran, the *hadith* and the interpretations of the clergy are Hanbali, Hanafi, Shafi and Maliki.

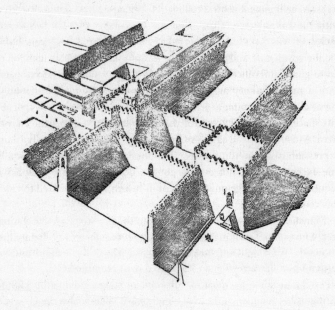

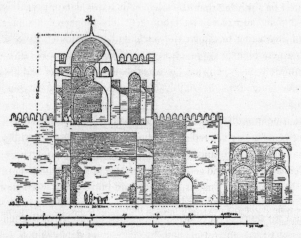

Reconstruction of Baghdad's gates and city walls by the German archaeologist Ernst Herzfeld, who from 1907 excavated widely in Syria and Iraq with Friedrich Sarre, director of the Islamic Museum in Berlin.

access to an immense central enclosure – perhaps 6,500 feet in diameter – with the royal precinct at its heart. An outer circle of this central enclosure was reserved for the palaces of the caliph's children, homes for the royal staff and servants, the caliph's kitchens, barracks for the horse-guard and offices for the treasury, armoury and chancery, together with a public bakery and, to help support the huge expenses of the imperial Abbasid state, a department for land tax. The very centre of this space was empty except for the two finest buildings in the city: the Great Mosque and the caliph's Golden Gate Palace, a classically Islamic expression of the union between temporal and spiritual authority. No one except Mansur, not even a gout-ridden uncle of the caliph who requested the privilege on grounds of ill-health, was permitted to ride in this central precinct.[22]*

Mansur's palace was a remarkable building of some 360,000 square feet whose most striking feature was the 120-foot-high green dome above the main audience chamber, visible for miles around and surmounted by the figure of a horseman with a lance in his hand. Khatib claimed that the figure swivelled like a weathervane, thrusting his lance in the direction from which the caliph's enemies would next appear. Yakut, the high-minded Syrian geographer, declared this 'a cheat and a manifest lie', arguing that 'the religion of Islam is not glorified by such fables'.[23]

Mansur's great mosque survived in various incarnations. It was the first mosque built in Baghdad and, at a prodigious 90,000 square feet, paid dutiful respect to Allah while emphatically conveying the message that the Abbasids were his most powerful and illustrious servants on earth.† Constructed of sun-baked bricks set in clay, with a roof resting on wooden columns, it was reconstructed by Mansur's grandson Harun, who erected a sturdier replacement made from kiln-baked bricks set in mortar. Further restorations and extensions kept it in good shape: when the Persian traveller and geographer Ibn Rusta visited Baghdad in around 903, he admired a 'fine structure of kiln-burnt bricks well mortared,

---

* One sympathizes with this elderly uncle of the caliph. Unmoved by his protestations of decrepit limbs, Mansur said he could be carried into the central precinct on a litter, a mode of transport generally reserved for women. 'I will be embarrassed by the people,' Isa said. 'Is there anyone left you could be embarrassed by?' the caliph replied caustically.

† For all its grandeur, the mosque suffered a striking architectural blunder, which resulted in the *mihrab* niche directing the prayers of the faithful south-west instead of the correct south-south-west to Mecca.

which is covered by a roof of teak wood supported on columns of the same, the whole being ornamented with lapis lazuli'.[24] Almost incredibly, the mosque seems to have survived the devastation wrought by the Mongol warlord Hulagu, grandson of Genghis Khan, in 1258, for it is not mentioned in the list of mosques and shrines he ordered to be rebuilt; in 1327 the high-spirited Moroccan traveller Ibn Battuta, passing through Baghdad at the outset of what would prove a 75,000-mile, twenty-nine-year odyssey, refers to it as still standing. Mansur's mosque, as reconstructed by Harun, thus occupied the heart of Baghdad for more than 500 years. The date of its final demise is unknown. It may have been destroyed by Tamerlane, the self-styled Sword Arm of Islam and Warrior of the Faith, who conquered the city in 1393 and returned to sack it completely and without mercy in 1401, the darkest date for the City of Peace. The names of Tamerlane and Hulagu live in infamy in Baghdad to this day.

The constant threat of rebellion during much of Mansur's twenty-one-year reign dictated that security and law and order were the highest priorities. Each of the four main gates of the Round City had a detachment of 1,000 soldiers. Outside the enclosure of government buildings in the outer circle of the city proper, in the quadrant of houses between the Kufa and Basra Gates, Mansur built the Matbak Prison with 'well-built walls and solid foundations' to keep those who opposed him firmly inside.[25] Such measures were not a failsafe: in 919 a mob broke out and went on the rampage before being recaptured and shut back behind the city's iron gates. Ruling Baghdad has, more often than not, required an iron fist.

Prison, mobs and rebellions are a reminder that for all the Abbasid extravagance and ostentation, the magnificence of the court, the grandeur of royal architecture and the cultural and scientific sophistication which quickly made Baghdad the capital of the world, as we shall see in the following chapters, life for the masses tended to be anything but glamorous. More often than not it was a grim fight for survival, warding off disease, famine and violence on an epic scale. Describing his visit to the city, Ibn Battuta recalled a verse that his father had 'recited to me many a time':

> Baghdad for men of wealth has an ever-open door
> But short and narrow shrift is all she gives the poor.[26]

While princes and poets enjoyed lavish banquets in palaces with wine served in crystal goblets and golden plates piled high with chicken, meat and exotic delicacies, the artisans, traders, retailers, servants, soldiers, singers, dancers, charlatans, cut-throats, beggars and prostitutes – in a word the masses – made do with sparse dinners of onions, beans and radishes, perhaps a vegetable or two and a crust of bread, in a tiny, stinking, one-roomed mud hovel. The abundance of fish and fruit went some way to satisfying the stomachs of the poor, but life in Baghdad for the lower orders was – as it remains today – a fierce struggle in roasting temperatures. The vast, violent, seething slums of Sadr City in north-east Baghdad have their origins in the earliest days of Mansur's capital.

*

What was the final bill for Mansur's gargantuan public building works, this mighty display of capital expenditure? The chronicles do not agree. The generally scrupulous Khatib noted two reports, the first of which said simply that the final expenditure was 18 million silver dirhams; the second claimed that the cost of the city, its mosque, the caliph's palace, the gates and its markets amounted to precisely 4,000,833 dirhams. 'I therefore observe a large discrepancy between the two accounts, and God knows better,' he wisely concluded.[27] But even if the larger of these figures is true, the deep coffers of the notoriously mean Mansur were hardly strained, as we can tell from the huge legacy he left on his death, only nine years after the Round City's completion.

And whatever his wealth, woe betide the man whom Mansur suspected of skimming off funds or merely failing to account for the very last dirham. An official called Khalid ibn al Salt, placed in charge of the expenditure for one-quarter of the city, ruefully reflected on this after it was completed. 'When I was finished with building that quarter, I took all the expenditures to him, and he totalled them with his own hand. Fifteen dirhams remained outstanding, so he detained me because of that some days in the prison of Sharkiya until I paid him.'[28]

On another occasion the cost-conscious caliph summoned an official called Musayab to bring him the chief foreman of the builders. The nervous man was asked how much money he charged for every thousand bricks, but he remained silent. The caliph then ordered him to build a vault in one of the assembly rooms, which took a little over a day, during which Mansur carefully recorded the exact number of bricks and the quantity of plaster used. Summoned to pay the terrified builder once the job was done, Musayab gave him five dirhams, which Mansur immediately declared excessive, and he took back one. The foremen and architects were then ordered to submit all their accounts to Mansur, who checked them 'item by item' against the account for the vault. 'Musayab had to part with more than 600,000 dirhams of the money he had in hand, for [Mansur] held him to it and wrung it out of him so that he did not leave the palace until he had handed it over to him.'[29]

Fiefs throughout the city were given to members of the Abbasid family, to Persian nobles, Arab generals, chiefs of police, judges, chief clerks and court favourites, who proudly saw their names bestowed on lanes and streets and, in the case of the most illustrious, such as the jurist Abu Hanifa, entire neighbourhoods. Yakubi recorded how Mansur granted his most valued clients and commanders lands inside the Round City. Soldiers were given fields around the City, and family members, including his son Mahdi, were allotted land on the outskirts.[30]

By 766 Mansur's Round City was complete. The general verdict was that it was a triumph. The ninth-century essayist Jahiz, a polymath and polemicist who wrote with real style on an astonishing range of subjects (natural history, evolution, Islamic psychology, theology and literary criticism, pigeon-racing, slave-girls, beauty, love), was unstinting in his praise. 'I have seen the great cities, including those noted for their durable construction,' he wrote. 'I have seen such cities in the districts of Syria, in Byzantine territory, and in other provinces, but I have never seen a city of greater height, more perfect circularity, more endowed with superior merits or possessing more spacious gates or more perfect defences than Al Zawra, that is to say the city of Abu Jafar al Mansur.' What he particularly admired was the roundness of the city. 'It is as though it is poured into a mould and cast.'[31]

When a patriarch of Byzantium visited as an ambassador shortly after its completion, Mansur had his vizier Rabi show him around. 'What do you think of my city?' the puffed-up caliph asked his infidel visitor when the tour was finished. 'I thought its construction fine, except that I saw your enemies with you in your residence,' the patriarch replied bluntly.[32] He was referring to the bazaars, home to a transient population of merchants and traders within the city walls. Mansur gave a cool reply in return – but once the patriarch had left, he gave orders that the bazaars were to be moved out of the city and rebuilt in the suburb of Karkh to the south. In time, Karkh, which had been founded by the fourth-century Sassanian King Shapur II, outstripped the population of the rest of

Baghdad and became the commercial hub of the most prosperous city on earth, a position it enjoyed for several centuries. To this day Baghdadis still refer to the west bank of Baghdad as Karkh.

*

The move to Karkh was the first significant departure from Mansur's Round City, a recognition that Baghdad needed to expand beyond its circular walls. As originally laid out, the main markets of Karkh lined the Kufa road south from the city. Streets, markets and quarters in the new district came to be organized by profession or merchandise (a tradition that holds true in much of the Arab world today). The quarters of coppersmiths and poulterers, reed-weavers, soap-makers and cooked-meat sellers all congregated at wharves and unloading points on the banks of the Dajaj (Fowls) Canal, a branch of the Karkhaya Canal, itself a waterway off the Isa Canal, which looped protectively south of the Round City, beyond the Sarat, Abu Attab, Bazzazin (clothes-merchants) and Tabik Canals, and marked the southern limits of Karkh.

The Isa, dug originally in Sassanian times, was regularly praised by medieval writers for never silting up; nor did it ever fail in its water supply. It brought the waters of the Euphrates east to the Tigris and thus supplied Baghdad with the produce of the west. Goods such as Egyptian corn and Damascene silks, borne across the desert by weary caravans, were loaded on to boats and barges at the river port of Rakka on the Euphrates and thence sailed along, via the Isa Canal, to the edge of Baghdad, where they were unloaded amid the hubbub of shouting merchants and swearing boatmen in the lower harbour of Karkh, opposite the southernmost bridge-of-boats. Sweaty canal-diggers and pitch-workers sat alongside the Melon House wholesale fruit market on the Tabik, another branch of the Isa, with oil merchants on the Isa itself. Spaced at regular intervals along this canal were its various, quaintly named crossing-points: Alkali Bridge, named after the detergent used for washing laundry, sold in a market nearby, Pomegranate Bridge, Thorn Bridge and Garden Bridge. Most ornate was the marble Bani Zurayk Bridge, named after a wealthy family of architects of Persian origin.

In northern Karkh, between the Sarat Canal and the outer walls of the Round City, in the quadrant between the Kufa and Basra Gates, well-fed and heavily perfumed Khorasani merchants traded in fine bazzazin fabrics or clothes stuffs. South of this was the Bazzazin Canal, flowing alongside the Fowls Canal, which served the poulterers' quarter. West from here, a world away from these tactile and olfactory delights, was the slave-market, swarming with Nubians and Ethiopians, Takurians from Sudan, Somalis, Tatars, Berbers, Khirgiz, Bantus, Senegalese, Chadians, Franks and Maraghians from Azerbaijan. White eunuchs, castrated in Egypt, were the most highly prized of all and commanded exorbitant prices as domestic servants and harem masters. Catering to other needs were the groups of beautifully dressed and sumptuously scented women huddled together in dread, rounded up from the length and breadth of Arabia and the Abbasid Empire and beyond, with pale-skinned Greek women particularly valued. If the free population of Baghdad was remarkable for its multicultural variety, its bonded men and women were no less cosmopolitan. The girls and young women were selected for their looks and figure, the quality of their singing voice, the breadth of their musical repertoire and their ability to cook delicious dishes for their master and his household. Jahiz described the male ideal of feminine beauty in the ninth century:

Most people who know about women, most experts on the subject, agree in preferring the *majdula*, that is to say the type of woman intermediate between fat and thin. Her figure must be elegant and shapely, her shoulders symmetrical and her back straight; her bones must be well covered, and she must be neither too plump nor too skinny. The word *majdula* conveys the notion of tautness, of firm flesh without superfluous fat. A graceful walk is the most beautiful thing about a woman, and she cannot walk gracefully if she is portly, fat and overburdened with flesh. Indeed, a *majdula* is more often slim, and her slenderness is her best-known feature; this is considered preferable both to the fat corpulent woman and to the thin skinny woman ... A *majdula* is described in prose by the words: the upper part of her body is a stem and the lower part a sand-dune.[33]

West again from the slave-market were the camel stables, a different kind of olfactory experience. To the east, in the outer limits of Karkh, for reasons of hygiene and security, lay the quarter of the butchers; we are told by Khatib: 'they are shedders of blood and always have sharp iron in their hands'.[34]

Slaves, horses and camels, silks, cotton and wool, carpets and hangings, books and paper, copper, gold and silver, jewellery, precious stones, carpentry and hardware, meat, fish and poultry, bread, puddings, fruit and vegetables, herbs and spices – everything was available and everything had its own place. Writing in the ninth century at the time of Karkh's prime, Yakubi gazed approvingly on a scene that managed to combine order with commercial bustle: 'Here every merchant, and each merchandise, had an appointed street: and there were rows of shops, and of booths, and of courts, in each of those streets; but men of one business were not mixed up with those of another, nor one merchandise with merchandise of another sort. Goods of a kind were only sold with their kind, and men of one trade were not to be found except with their fellows of the same craft.'[35]

*

So far, the fledgling city of Baghdad had occupied land only on the west bank of the Tigris. In 768, two years after the Round City's completion, Mansur began to build on the east bank at a kink in the river to the north-east. His purpose in developing this marshy land was quite simple. Rusafa (The Causeway, but also translated as Compactly Built), as it was known, would be the barracks for his army. Tabari explains the decision to settle East Baghdad as a policy of divide-and-rule across the Tigris. An old man called Kutham ibn Abbas, highly regarded by Mansur, reportedly told the caliph: 'Cross over the river with your son and settle him there in a castle. Send part of your army with him there, so that it becomes a separate area from this one. If the people of this side are corrupted, you can use the people of the other side against them, and vice versa.'[36]

Mansur's second building spree was also born of dynastic considerations – the need to establish Mahdi, his son and heir, as a powerful figure in his own right. Before long a new city sprang up across the Tigris, with a mosque and royal palace at its heart, as on the west bank. The two cities were linked by a bridge-of-boats fixed across the Tigris north-east of the Khorasan Gate, beyond an immense review ground. Mahdi provided the royal patronage for a fresh wave of settlement in East Baghdad, granting a series of fiefs to his chief officers. The impetus to expand here was championed equally by the fabulously wealthy Barmakid clan, masters of conspicuous consumption and ostentatious palace-building, who poured in millions of dinars to satisfy an apparently boundless appetite for luxury. (Harun would do the same in the closing years of the eighth century and the beginning of the ninth.) Just as West Baghdad is still known as Karkh, so East Baghdad, thirteen centuries after Mahdi's extravagant arrival, is still popularly Rusafa.

Within a dozen years, buoyed by extraordinary levels of immigration, the population of Baghdad exploded, setting the stage for an extended property boom. Tabari reported how waves of settlers, in addition to the tens of thousands already involved in the construction of the city, flooded in from Khorasan, Yemen, the deserts of the Hijaz, Wasit, Kufa and across the Muslim world. The Middle East had never witnessed anything like it. Baghdad became one of the most multicultural places on earth, a melting pot of races, tribes and languages, united – with a few exceptions – under the banner of Islam.

In no time at all Rusafa had spawned the neighbouring districts of Shammasiya to the north (from the Arabic word *shammas*, or deacon, to describe a quarter housing monasteries and churches) and Mukharrim to the south-east (named after Al Mukharrim ibn Yazeed ibn Shuraih, an Arab military leader who had owned these lands prior to the foundation of Baghdad). Rusafa and Shammasiya were the glitziest districts on the east bank, perhaps in all Baghdad, replete with caliphal and Barmakid palaces, beautiful gardens, broad gates, royal stables, teeming markets, handsome bridges, public baths, shrines and cemeteries sprinkled amongst the necklaces of canals that brought water to every quarter. Mosques multiplied, and a throng of minarets raised the believers' eyes to the heavens. To accommodate the increased levels of cross-river traffic, two more pontoon bridges were added, one upstream of the Round City, the other downstream at the southern end of Mukharrim, providing a direct link to Karkh. Nestorian and Jacobite churches jostled for space among the many mosques. The Nestorians had much for which to thank the Abbasids. With the defeat of the Umayyads in 750 and the subsequent move east to Baghdad, the Syriac Church found itself in a preferred position within the ranks of Christian factions. The Abbasids confirmed this pre-eminence by granting the Nestorian patriarch official jurisdiction over all Christians in the caliphate, which extended from Egypt to Central Asia.[37] As far as the caliphs were concerned, the famed skill of Christian physicians generally, which is touched on in Chapter 3, was a substantial point in their favour. From the time of Mansur, the Bakhtishu family, a distinguished line of Syriac

Christians trained originally in the Persian university of Gundeshapur, provided the Abbasid court with physicians for more than 250 years.

Nobles, judges, court officials and rich merchants vied with each other to build the most fabulous mansions. In a city obsessed with status, Karkh became one of the most sought-after neighbourhoods – as it remains today in the six square miles that make up the government quarter, briefly known as the Green Zone after 2003 – its ascendancy challenged only by Rusafa and Shammasiya on the opposite bank of the Tigris. Marble fountains played in the aristocrats' courtyards and tree-lined gardens; their palaces were adorned with jewel-studded carpets, columns inlaid with ivory and gold, and Koranic verses traced elegantly in gold across the walls.

Just as Rusafa had spread to make new neighbourhoods, so West Baghdad also expanded at dizzying speed. East of the Round City, in the space between the Basra Gate and the Tigris, lay the quarter of Sharkiya, literally the Eastern Quarter, on the site of an ancient settlement famed for its black grapes. In Abbasid times the district was renowned more for the pleasures of the mind, home to both booksellers and papersellers, whose myriad volumes provided the intellectual ballast for the extraordinary cultural, literary, scientific and philosophical renaissance presided over by the Abbasids during the next several centuries. The Souk al Warrakin alone contained more than a hundred booksellers' shops.

Sharkiya also benefited from royal attention. Outside the Khorasan Gate, in the kink in the river below Rusafa, south of the royal stables and exercise grounds, Mansur built his second great palace, the Kasr al Khuld, or Palace of Eternity, with magnificent gardens, an allusion to the Garden of Eternity promised to believers as their lasting reward in the Koran (Sura 25:15). Set on higher ground that was supposedly free from mosquitoes, this became Mansur's favourite palace, conveniently close to the bridge-of-boats connecting West Baghdad to his son's royal enclave in Rusafa. Khatib tells us 'it commanded a remarkable view and revealed superior planning and magnificent architectural construction'.[38] During the civil war between Al Amin and Al Mamun in 811–13, the Kasr al Khuld, together with the neighbouring Palace of Zubayda ('Little Butterball', named after the wife of Harun and mother of Amin), was severely damaged by missiles from siege engines. It lingered on as an unoccupied ruin until 979, when Adud al Dawla, the Buyid ruler of

Baghdad, knocked it down and appropriated the site to build his cele-brated Bimaristan hospital.

To the north of the Round City, beyond the Syriah Gate, was the Har-biya, a quarter named after a certain Harb, whose origins were in the ancient Central Asian city of Balkh and who was appointed chief of the Baghdad police by Mansur. Renowned for its broad streets and thriving markets, this was one of the most popular districts for those Turks and Persians – from Balkh and Bukhara, Kabul, Khiva and Merv – who had arrived in Baghdad on the coat-tails of the Abbasids and been rewarded with fiefs. It lay across the Tigris opposite Shammasiya and stretched west as far as the Anbar road, its northern limits defined by the Trench of Tahir, the northern branch of the Sarat Canal, which was crossed by a series of masonry bridges and gates. One of these, the Iron Gate, served as the gibbet on which the bloody head of the caliph Amin was displayed to the city after his forces had capitulated to his brother's army.

The earlier Christian community had also left its architectural mark in this quarter of the city. Further north, a little beyond Harbiya and the fief of Zubayda, stood the monumental Durta Monastery, a landmark large enough to be considered worthy as the caliph Al Mustakfi's resi-dence in the tenth century. Close by was another Christian place of worship, the Monastery of the Cupolas.

Moving anticlockwise from the Harbiya, we next find the Attabiya, where the world-famous Attabi striped silks and cottons were produced in a dazzling range of colours. The district was named after the Attabiyin, descendants of the honourable Attab, great-grandson of Umayya, ances-tor of the deposed Umayyad Dynasty, who settled in this district of Baghdad during the Abbasid era. Later the name passed into Europe in various guises – *tabis* in French, *tabi* in Italian and Spanish, *attabi* in medieval Latin and *tabby* in English.* As late as 1184, when the Andalu-sian traveller Ibn Jubayr passed through Baghdad, the Attabiya was one of the most prosperous districts in the city. Commercial life continued

---

* Guy Le Strange notes Queen Elizabeth wearing 'a dress of silver and white taby' when meeting the Venetian envoy Scaramelli in 1603 and Samuel Pepys donning his much prized 'false-taby waiste-coate with gold lace' on 13 October 1661. By the time Samuel Johnson published his *Dictionary of the English Language* in 1755, *taby* had become *tabby* and referred both to 'a kind of waved silk' and a cat with brindled markings. 'It is certainly curi-ous,' Le Strange wrote, 'that the common epithet applied to a cat in modern English should be derived from the name of a man who was a Companion of the Prophet Mohammed and governor of Mecca in the seventh century AD.'

immediately to its south with the emporium of the Four Markets, a network of crowded streets, noisy lanes and warehouses heaving with merchandise.

South again, past the sprawling Kataba and Nasriya quarters and a little west of the Kufa Gate of the Round City, at the junction of the Little and Great Sarat Canals, stood a popular Baghdad landmark known as the Patrician's Mill, which housed a hundred millstones and was said to produce an enormous annual rent of 100 million dirhams (in 1900 Le Strange estimated this at £4 million, a scarcely credible £405 million in today's money). If we are to believe the various versions of the story offered by Yakubi, Yakut and Khatib, it seems that a Greek envoy called Tarath had come to Baghdad in 775 to convey the congratulations of the Byzantine emperor on the accession of Mansur's son Mahdi to the caliphate. The ambassador, who had a decent knowledge of engineering, was so pleased with the hospitality he received that he offered to build a mill that would generate annual profits equivalent to the cost of its construction, half a million dirhams, from the millers' rents. The new caliph gave over this sum for the building work, and once the mill had been completed, the envoy's forecast proved entirely accurate. This naturally delighted Mahdi, who, in a very public display of royal generosity, ordered that all the profits be given to the Greek, even after he had left Baghdad – an annual gift, we are told, that continued until his death in 780. Greek or otherwise, the mill marked the southern point of Abbasiya Island, which was named after Mansur's brother, to whom it had been granted in fief. It was a large tract of land circumscribed by the two Sarat Canals, famed for the fertility of its soil, planted with corn and laid out with splendid gardens and perfumed groves, a favourite place for those who liked to promenade in the cooler evenings.

*

This, then, was the City of Peace in the late eighth century, at the dawn of the Abbasid Empire's greatest achievements. It was, in Yakubi's words, 'the crossroads of the universe', a capital unequalled either in the East or West, a city that attracted superlatives as easily as the cool waters of the Tigris flowed through it.

Mansur died in 775 during his *haj* to Mecca, and the throne passed, just as he had planned, to his chosen heir Mahdi. It was, by the standards of the future, blood-soaked successions of the Abbasid caliphate, a model of order and decorum. Mansur died, as he had lived, well. Though his name has been largely eclipsed by that of his grandson Harun al Rashid, Mansur was probably the most visionary and talented of the thirty-seven Abbasid caliphs who ruled from Baghdad. The greatest tribute to his reign was the story of what followed it. Mansur bequeathed a dynasty that would endure for five centuries in the capital he had built, and a treasury that would sustain it. The stage was set for one of the most extraordinary periods in the history of civilization.

2

Harun al Rashid and
A Thousand and One Nights in
Baghdad (775–809)

History and legend unite in placing the most brilliant period of Baghdad during the caliphate of Harun al Rashid (786–809). Though less than half a century old, Baghdad had by that time grown from nothingness to a world centre of prodigious wealth and international significance, standing alone as the rival of Byzantium. Its splendour kept pace with the prosperity of the empire of which it was the capital. It was then that Baghdad became 'a city without peer throughout the whole world'.

P. K. Hitti, *History of the Arabs* (1937)

There debouched in my office the other day an innocent called, if I remember rightly, Frewen, a Major, recently added to I. Branch. He stated that he had been entrusted with the task of compiling a Gazetteer of Mesopotamia and as he had only been 3 months in the country he had come to me for information. Thereupon he produced and read out a series of questions which no one in this universe could have answered. They were either pure tosh or they were things that you can't know. What, said he, was Baghdad like in the time of Harun al Rashid? I don't know – nobody does. People have spent lifetimes of research in trying to form a vague picture of it but they haven't arrived at any real conclusion.

Gertrude Bell, letter to her father from
Baghdad, 3 January 1921

Squinting in the winter sun, a middle-aged man with glasses and a white beard is standing outside a hole-in-the-wall bookshop on Al Rashid Street, poring over a biography of Saddam Hussein. A brown suit that has seen better days, a blue wool cap and a slightly shambolic appearance suggest he is an intellectual. He flicks through the pages of the book, apparently in disbelief, then closes it and turns to his companion, a man of similarly professorial mien. 'Can you believe it, Abdullah?' he says, sucking his teeth and shaking his head. 'We had to see this bastard's bloody face every day for more than thirty years and, now that he's dead and we're in the middle of all this chaos, we still have to see him on the cover of every book and newspaper. Oh my God, the rope is still being dragged. May Allah preserve us!'

Rashid Street is one of the great landmarks of Baghdad. It runs from Bab al Muadham (Sultan's Gate) in the north of the city to Bab al Sharki (East Gate) in the south; it is on the eastern bank of the Tigris, 1,150 feet from the river at its westernmost point. Built in haste by the Ottoman governor and military commander Khalil Pasha to commemorate his defeat of British forces at Kut al Amara in 1916 – described by the historian James Morris as 'the most abject capitulation in Britain's military history' – at 52 feet wide it was intended to facilitate the movement of troops and carriages directly through Baghdad, and to avoid their having to take the much longer route around the city.

It was completed within two months, with the simple if brutal expedient of stretching two parallel ropes straight along the desired line and then demolishing everything that lay in between proving a remarkable, albeit controversial, success. The expression 'the rope is still being dragged', to describe something that continues relentlessly, is used by Baghdadis of a certain generation to this day, as the irate bookworm on Rashid Street bears witness. This being Baghdad, however, whenever the ropes arrived at the roof of a house belonging to a wealthy or influential man, the engineers and foremen were persuaded to bend their line accordingly and the house of a less fortunate neighbour was flattened instead: by the time Rashid Street was inaugurated on 23 July 1916, it was less straight than originally planned. The bends and kinks in its route, smoothed with the passage of subsequent decades, can still be seen today.

The once gracious colonnaded street in which Baghdadi intellectuals bemoan the ubiquity of Saddam Hussein was conceived to provide shade from the searing heat of a Baghdad summer and represented nothing less than a revolution in urban design for the city. Apart from Shari al Nahr (River Street) – a narrow road that ran along the eastern bank of the Tigris linking the city's river port at Masbagha District to the nearby grain warehouses, or *khans* – this was the first major road in modern Baghdad.

Go back to the map of the city drawn by Commander F. Jones and W. Collingwood of the Indian Navy in 1853–4, and Baghdad is a tangled web of crooked streets, alleys and cul-de-sacs (see illustration 20). Of high streets or main roads there is no sign. Unlike Damascus, its neighbour and predecessor as capital of the Islamic Empire, Baghdad has no 'Street Called Straight'. In an essay on Baghdad for the *Encyclopaedia Britannica* of 1902, Major-General Sir Henry Rawlinson, the former British political agent in Ottoman Arabia, made the following observations:

> The town has been built without the slightest regard to regularity. The streets are even more intricate and winding than those in most other Eastern towns; and, with the exception of the bazaars and some open squares, the interior is little else than a labyrinth of alleys and passages. The streets are unpaved, and in many places so narrow that two horsemen can scarcely pass each other; and, as it is seldom that the houses have windows facing the great public thoroughfares, and the doors are small and mean, they present on both sides the gloomy appearance of dead walls.

Such urban design, though baffling to outsiders, served two distinct purposes. Baghdad's gruelling summers, which lasted almost half of the year, required that houses be built close to each other, separated only by the narrowest of alleys. Houses were thereby spared the scorching winds and sun, while pedestrians, and the occasional donkey, were able to come and go along the cool shaded passageways. From a defensive perspective, the labyrinthine network of alleys and tiny streets was superb protection against outsiders unfamiliar with the terrain.

Although Rashid Street began its life as a commemoration of the Ottoman victory over the British, and was officially known as Khalil Pasha Street (Baghdadis preferred the more prosaic Al Jada al Umomiya, or Main Street), such celebrations were short-lived. On 11 March 1917, less than eight months after the street was formally opened, victorious British troops, having driven out the Ottomans, marched through Bab al Muadham, walking over the site of the ancient Sultan's Gate, which in Abbasid times had formed part of the defensive wall encircling eastern Baghdad.

The stories of Baghdad's monuments all too often reflect the bloody history of the city to which they belong. On the right-hand side of Bab al Muadham Square, heading south, stood the *kala*, or citadel, housing the army barracks and training ground. Later, once the Iraqi Army was established in 1921, it became the site of the new Ministry of Defence. Today the imposing gate of the Defence Ministry is remembered as the place where in 1945 Colonel Salahadin al Sabbagh, leader of the failed 1941 coup against the monarchy, was hanged. Revenge came soon enough. During the coup of 14 July 1958, which toppled the Iraqi government and put an end to the monarchy once and for all, the corpse of Crown Prince Abdullah – who had personally sanctioned the colonel's execution and had now been killed alongside his twenty-three-year-old nephew King Faisal II and the rest of the royal family – was dragged through Rashid Street, hacked into pieces and hanged opposite the gate.

The Defence Ministry compound extended to Maidan Square, at the northern end of Rashid Street, where an infinitely bloodier massacre had taken place six centuries earlier. In 1401, the Turkic warlord Tamerlane, Conqueror of the World, stormed the city and ordered every soldier in his army to bring him a Baghdadi head – or two. And they did: 90,000 severed heads were piled into 120 towers – Tamerlane's terrifying battlefield signature. In time the place was called Kala Chiya, Turkish for the Place of Heads. The area's dubious reputation lingered on into the 1920s and 1930s, when it was home to the public brothel, a facility carefully monitored by the British authorities, who, with their mania for order and decency, introduced medical check-ups, issued licences and surrounded the building with a wall accessible through a single gate that was clearly marked 'Public Brothel'. Baghdadis grew to identify regular visitors and street-prowlers along Rashid Street, together with the prostitutes, who were shrouded in black *abayas* and identified by the blue socks the government required them to wear. When flood waters threatened Baghdad one spring night in the 1930s and as many hands as possible were needed to help fortify the sand barrage, the head of police in the neighbouring district of Saray (Seraglio) ordered his officers to seize every man in the brothel and press him on to the rescue team. The next morning there were noticeably fewer government officials than usual reporting for work. The brothel was demolished in 1957.

A decade later, one of the most well-known and popular figures on Rashid Street was the coachman Sheykhan, who of an early evening used to drive a famous prostitute along Rashid Street from Maidan Square to Bab al Sharki, searching for clients. Ordinary people liked him for his ability to blow legendarily loud and long raspberries,* and they would cheer him and his passenger with reciprocal raspberries as he passed down the street.

Evening pleasures here were by no means confined to the illicit. In the golden era of film during the 1930s and 1940s, there were more than twenty cinemas along Rashid Street. There were indoor cinemas for winter and open-air cinemas for the long summer months in a pre-air-conditioning age. An evening in front of the big screen was the major entertainment for Baghdadi families before television arrived in the mid 1950s. Film-lovers could choose from half a dozen cinemas on Rashid Street and neighbouring Saadoun Street: Roxy, Rex, Watani, Aladdin and Sindbad. For those prepared to push the boat out, Khayyam was the most luxurious cinema in the Middle East.

Rashid Street has always been famous for its tea-houses and coffee-houses, patronized by artists and intellectuals. Stroll past Al Zahawi, a threadbare café named after the early twentieth-century Iraqi poet Jamil Sidki al Zahawi, newspaper editor, philosopher and social reformer who championed women's rights, and you will hear the tables clacking and men shouting triumphantly as they slam down their backgammon pieces. In the corner there may be a game or two of chess going on, or a harassed-looking student studying a text. A century ago these tea- and coffee-houses were adorned with huge brass samovars and expensive Persian carpets draped over long wooden benches to help keep customers warm in winter. Some hosted traditional Iraqi *makam* singers;† others drew in customers by paying a *kasakhoon* or *hakawati*

---

* Blowing raspberries is a Baghdadi tradition that dates back to Abbasid times and contin-ues to this day. It is used to mock someone or something.

† *Makam* is one of the most influential genres of classical Arabic music that is thought to date back to Abbasid times. In Iraqi *makam* a singer or reciter is typically accompanied by a four-piece ensemble, the Chalghi Baghdadi, consisting of a hammered dulcimer, a spike fiddle and two types of small drums, sometimes also a tambourine. The essence of *makam* is the semi-improvised musical recitation of poetry within a formal and elaborate structure. A *makam* institute exists in Baghdad to this day.

(storyteller), perched on a high chair complete with wooden sword, to read ancient tales of Arab heroes such as Antar bin Shadad and Abuzaid al Hillali, or racy stories from *The Arabian Nights*. Like its celebrated narrator Sheherazade, who spins out her daily storytelling over 1,001 nights to prevent the serial wife-killing King Shahryar from murdering her, they would eke out their stories, stopping always just before the climax to ensure the customers returned the following evening, when they would plunge into yet another adventure. During the holy fasting month of Ramadan, when Rashid Street's tea-houses and coffee-houses stayed open long after midnight, a popular game was *Muhaybis*, or Ringlet, in which two teams vied with each other to discover a ring discreetly hidden in the hand of one of the players. The losing team would buy the winners a giant platter of local sweets.

If Rashid Street catered for the pleasures of the night, it also offered more spiritual possibilities. The trio of Muradiya, Ahmediya and Haydar Khana mosques, built during Ottoman rule in the sixteenth, eighteenth and nineteenth centuries respectively, lent architectural charm to a street that was vibrantly commercial. Above and behind a beige portal, Haydar Khana Mosque still provides a flash of iridescent blue halfway along Rashid Street, its broad dome picked out in turquoise, navy-blue and yellow, visible from a distance glinting in the sunlight. The historic Mirjan Mosque and its eponymous *khan*, or caravanserai, dated back to 1358, a century after Baghdad's catastrophic sacking by the Mongols. Though the mosque became a casualty of an initiative by the mayor of Baghdad, Arshad al Omari, to straighten Rashid Street during the 1930s (the rope being dragged once again), the magnificent Khan Mirjan – a cavernous building measuring 104 feet by 147 feet with spectacular arched vaults – survived intact. Photographs show the galleried warehouse being used to store grain well into the twentieth century. In its most recent incarnation it houses one of the city's grandest restaurants.

Continuing past Haydar Khana Mosque heading south-east on Rashid Street, a narrow street announced by a slim portal peels off to the right towards the Tigris. Mutanabbi Street, named after the legendary tenth-century poet, is a book-lovers' paradise, with more than 650 feet of shops and stalls selling little else. On Friday mornings Baghdadi intellectuals make a beeline for it. The entrance to the street, blocked by a crowd of amiably pushing and shoving men desperate for their weekly literary fix, is impossible to miss. The place is a maelstrom of activity, with booksellers spreading thousands of new and second-hand titles across the ground on sheets of cardboard or wooden pallets. Browsing bookworms bury their noses inside rare editions and tatty hardbacks, gaudy Korans, English dictionaries and primers, Iraqi histories, magazines – anyone for *Cigar Aficionado* or *Bowhunting*, left behind by American soldiers? – memoirs in Arabic and English, potboilers, perhaps the odd bodice-ripper, serious academic titles – all tastes are catered for. Visitors are greeted warmly here. In a city so often disfigured by appalling violence and bloodshed, the Baghdadis' courtesy and good manners are the stuff of legend and a source of pride.

The traditional Arab saying 'Cairo writes, Beirut prints and Baghdad reads' pays tribute to the city's voracious literary appetite, while disguising the fact that these days Baghdadis do all three. Writing in exile, critically acclaimed Baghdadi authors such as the award-winning Fouad al Tikerly, Mahmoud Saeed and Sinan Antoon have all shone a disturbing light on Saddam Hussein's Iraq, and they will be read for generations to come. The city kept its literary love affair going even in the dark days of the 1990s, when the crippling UN sanctions failed to thwart the most ardent bibliophiles. The latest books from around the world, beyond the reach of the vast majority of Baghdadis, were photocopied and sold at great discounts.

By noon on Fridays, most of the shoppers have drifted off home or settled down to tea or coffee at the Shahbandar Coffee-House, where writers, artists and intellectuals have long whiled away afternoons puffing on *shisha* pipes, chatting about politics over backgammon and sipping endless *istikans*,* small glasses of tea.

At noon on 5 March 2007, just this sort of peaceful scene was shattered when a suicide car bomb ripped through Mutanabbi Street, killing at least thirty and wounding more than sixty-five people. Amongst the dead were three sons of Shahbandar's owner. In time he restored the coffee-house to its former glory, a tribute to the resilience of Baghdadis, demonstrated with such tragic regularity over the centuries. Historical photos of Baghdad once again adorn its walls: pictures of the 1921 coronation of King Faisal I, meaningfully flanked by British military and officialdom, which took place not more than 300 feet away; sepia shots

---

* The word *istikan* is said to have come from the nineteenth-century British observing Indians drinking tea from small containers: East Tea Can became, in Iraq, *istikan*.

of the Tigris in more gracious, pre-skyscraper, days; street scenes and crowded markets; portraits of King Faisal II and Gertrude Bell, the doughty explorer, writer, official and kingmaker who played such a prominent role in the twentieth-century history of Iraq. The place was rechristened the Martyrs' Café after the blast, but will always be the Shahbandar for its older denizens. The rebuilt street was reopened by the prime minister in December 2008, a move welcomed across the city. 'For any intellectual, any educated man, Mutanabbi Street is considered part of his education,' said bookseller Salam Mohammed Abud.[1]

Business was from its very outset the lifeblood of Rashid Street. It was only natural that the first proper street in Baghdad should house its grandest shops and become – as well as offer – the height of fashion. Within a few years of the road's construction, Baghdadi women were soon introduced to extravagant new couture, with glamorous dresses, outfits and accessories imported from Paris and London. Men treated themselves to expensive suits and clothes ('strictly British and made of the finest woven wool', a veteran Baghdadi recalls approvingly), together with silk ties and Colognes. From the 1920s the department store Orosdi-Back vied with Hasso Brothers to provide customers with the latest household wares and electric appliances. An immaculately uniformed doorman would swing open the bright, brass-handled glass doors, and the customer would be greeted with a dash of French perfume to whet the shopping appetite. A treasure trove of elegant and exotic goods, from Bally shoes, cashmere jumpers and fine bone china to silver cutlery, silk eiderdowns and children's clothes made by the chic French label Petit Bateau, from the 1940s to the 1970s it was, as one shopper fondly remembered, 'the Harrods of its day'.[2]

Just before Bab al Sharki was a boutique called Vogue, selling the latest in French fashion, right next to three small outlets run by Baghdadi Armenians: an old-fashioned barber's shop, a coffee vendor and a pastrami shop. 'I used to love going down to see the Vogue boutique and look at the quaint and gleaming three shops next to it, with their proprietors busily serving their clients, while the smell of the freshly ground coffee and the spicy pastrami filled the air, interspersed with the staccato clicking of the barber's scissors,' says Manaf, a Baghdadi in his sixties. 'I once had a haircut there just to soak up the atmosphere. It was absolutely charming.'

Food and fashion aside, from the 1940s Rashid Street was also the place to buy the latest imported cars. Agencies such as the Lawee House, owned by the prominent Iraqi–Jewish family, sold Chevrolet and Buicks, while the Obaida House offered Mercedes. Another wealthy merchant, Hafidh al Kadi, the agent representing Ford, Lincoln and Mercury, was so well known that the square on Rashid Street from which he sold these exotic cars – originally named after King Faisal II – was commonly called by his name. Awestruck boys and ever-hopeful men would stare longingly at the rows of sports cars and saloons glowing within glass-fronted showrooms here and there along the street. Such a major purchase would likely require help from the bank, a number of which maintained offices halfway down Rashid Street. One British bank director who worked on Ameen Square – now known as Al Rusafi Square, after a famous poet of the early twentieth century – kept a vintage Rolls-Royce that old Baghdadis remember fondly to this day. The banks remain in this section of the street.

Beyond the banks, past Agd al Nasara (Christians' Alley), which housed the various abbeys, churches and houses of prominent Christians in the nineteenth and early twentieth centuries, came the studios of the city's two most famous photographers, Arshak and Aboash. Arshak was, as his logo proudly proclaimed, the 'Royal Photographer to the Iraqi Royal Family by special appointment'. Wealthy Baghdadis knew they had arrived at the studios when they saw, attached to the building, a bright display advertising a local cooking oil – the first instance of neon in Baghdad – and a set of traffic lights, the first in Baghdad, installed in 1956. 'It took a little time, and some encouragement from policemen, for drivers to get used to using them,' an elderly Baghdadi reports of the 1950s.

As Rashid Street drew to an end at Bab al Sharki, there was a final building of note. One of the grand houses overlooking the Tigris was home to Field Marshal Colmar Freiherr von der Goltz, German commander in the Mesopotamian Campaign, who died of typhus here on 19 April 1916, ten days before the British surrender at Kut. In one of those curious quirks of history, Lieutenant General Sir Stanley Maude, Goltz's British counterpart, died of cholera in the same house on 18 November 1917. Gertrude Bell subsequently lived here until her death in 1926. Baghdad could be a deadly place.

A place of high style and great riches, where business rubbed shoulders with religion and the pleasures of the flesh mingled with more innocent entertainment and fantastical storytelling, a part of Baghdad in which the most desirable luxuries of the world were available for a price, where poets were prized and literature cherished, kings were crowned, royal patronage disbursed and grand imperial strategies devised. Who, in all of Baghdad's long and rich history, could be more fitting to bear the street's name than the caliph Harun al Rashid?

*

In one important sense the reigns of his two immediate predecessors – Al Mahdi (775–85) and Al Hadi (785–6) prepared the ground for Harun's most extraordinary achievements. After the death of the notoriously austere Mansur, his son and successor, Mahdi, as generous as his father had been mean, showed a much greater interest in literary life and had a particular love for poetry and singing. The two were frequently combined during intimate evening salons with his favourite courtiers, lubricated with liberal quantities of wine. Ibn Khallikan, the thirteenth-century biographer of the Abbasid era's leading figures, tells a story about the famous poet Abu al Atahiya, who, at one of Mahdi's grand public audiences, began to recite what appeared to be an inappropriately risqué verse about a mistress. Two other poets, Ashja al Sulami and Bashar ibn Burd, could scarcely believe their ears on this solemn occasion, having expected their colleague to trot out the customary panegyric extolling the caliph's many virtues. Just as they feared the caliph's wrath would fall upon the bumptious poet – improprieties could be a matter of life or death – Abu al Atahiya's poem deftly switched into an allegory hailing Mahdi as the only man in the world suitable for the office of caliph. That day, as Ashja recalled, Abu al Atahiya was 'the only man who left the audience with a reward'.[3]

Mahdi's son and heir, the short-lived caliph Hadi (unkindly nicknamed Musa Shut Your Mouth on account of his disfiguring harelip), showed considerable respect for learning during his one-year reign from 785 to 786. Masudi describes him as 'hard-hearted, vicious, unapproachable, but nevertheless learned, with a passion for literature. He was strong, brave, energetic, liberal and generous.'[4] Hadi presented the historian Isa ibn Daab with a cushion as a sign that he was welcome to sit with him in the evenings, the only one of his courtiers to be shown such favour. Isa was said to be one of the best-read and most learned men of his age, with an unrivalled command of 'the history and battles of the

Arabs'. In *The Meadows of Gold*, his history of the caliphs, Masudi tells a touching anecdote of the friendship between Hadi and his favourite. On one occasion, the caliph told him, 'Isa, when you are late during the day, or when in the evening you do not appear, I seem to look for none but you.'[5]

In another Masudi story we see Hadi offering a prize for the best verse about the celebrated sword Samsama, which had once belonged to the Arab warrior-poet Amr ibn Madikarib. The poet Ibn Yamin of Basra won and took the basketful of dinars, only to share its contents with his fellow poets and keep the sword. Later, Hadi bought the sword back from him for the magnificent sum of 50,000 dinars.

Born in or around 766, Harun al Rashid (The Rightly Guided) reigned for twenty-three years (786–809). Looking at the five centuries of Abbasid rule from the City of Peace between 762 and 1258, this was no more than a fleeting moment in a grand pageant. The Abbasid Dynasty extended across the reigns of thirty-seven caliphs, a number of whom ruled for much longer periods, yet Harun's fame easily eclipsed them all. His reign represented the pinnacle of Islamic strength and splendour. In the feeble West, his contemporary Charlemagne, king of the Franks, was the most powerful leader, but of an uncivilized, only recently united people. Harun by contrast could consider himself the unchallenged monarch of a mighty empire.

It has been said that in some ways Harun resembled Henry VIII. Both had a certain talent for leadership, and were charismatic and unscrupulous men brilliant at effecting the downfall of those who stood in their way. Yet, where Henry VIII was the ruler of a small kingdom and the equal of his fellow monarchs in Europe, Harun was the master of his age and a supremely confident player on the world stage, feared and revered in equal measure.

For Baghdad, Harun's caliphate was the apogee of glory. 'So great were the splendours and riches of his reign, such was its prosperity, that this period has been called "the honeymoon",' Masudi wrote in *The Meadows of Gold*. In one of those classic stories intended to show a monarch's predestined glory, he describes the court physician interpreting one of the caliph Mahdi's troubling dreams about Harun and his older brother, Hadi. The latter, the doctor is supposed to have said, would have but a short reign. By contrast, the most auspicious future awaited Harun. 'His days will be the best of days and his age the best of ages,' he predicted.[6]

In fact, the heyday of Baghdad lasted from its foundation by Mansur in 762 until 833, with the death of Harun's son Mamun. It was a time when Abbasid power was at its zenith. Throughout those seven decades, Amin was the only caliph who died in Baghdad, testament to the outward-looking nature – and sheer size – of the empire. Caliphs were buried where they died, be it along the pilgrim road across the burning deserts of Arabia (Mansur), in the historical city of Tarsus, onetime capital of the Roman province of Cilicia in what is today southern Turkey (Mamun) or ancient Tus in the Persian province of Khorasan (Harun). The twin demands of *jihad* and *haj*, holy obligations for any Commander of the Faithful, ensured that there was no dilly-dallying in the seat of empire.

Harun, immortalized as the carousing, street-prowling caliph in *A Thousand and One Nights*, continued his family's emerging tradition of cultural patronage and took it to new, superlative heights. Among those he gathered around him were the religious lawyers Malik ibn Anas and Al Shafi, the historians Wakidi and Ibn Kutayba, the poets Abu al Atahiya and Abu Nuwas (whom we shall meet shortly), the musician Abu Ishak al Mosuli, the grammarian Ali ibn Hamza (tutor to Harun's sons), and the fractious humanists Asmai and Abu Obayda. Closest to him of all was the astonishingly rich Barmakid clan, prodigal patrons of the arts and sciences in their own right.

Harun was nicknamed Commander of the Unfaithful, a reversal of the caliph's traditional moniker Amir al Muminin, or Commander of the Faithful, because of his wide-ranging weekly religious and philosophical discussions, but, since he was said to be the only caliph apart from Uthman who was a *hafiz* – meaning he could recite the entire Koran by heart – the nickname was surely unfair. Before he ascended to the throne, Harun had started a club for scientific discussion and maintained his interest in medicine as caliph.

He also championed a burgeoning translation movement, which saw some of the great works of classical Greek, Hindu and Persian scholarship translated into Arabic, revised and in many cases improved, and circulated throughout the Islamic Empire and beyond. Abbasid envoys returned from missions to Byzantium armed with important works by Plato, Aristotle, Euclid, Hippocrates, Galen and others. In addition to the monumental literary collections of royal and official institutions in Baghdad, wealthy private patrons also built up vast libraries that could run into tens of thousands of volumes, providing additional encouragement to the translators. Knowledge was thus transmitted from West to East, ensuring that it survived to pass back, centuries later, into Western civilization, an enormous intellectual service to which we still owe much to this day. The first Arabic translation of Euclid was dedicated to Harun.

In *The Decline and Fall of the Roman Empire*, Gibbon paid tribute to Harun's greatness in his inimitable style, describing him as:

> the most powerful and vigorous monarch of his race, illustrious in the West, as the ally of Charlemagne, and familiar to the most childish readers, as the perpetual hero of the Arabian tales. His title to the name of Al Rashid (The Just) is sullied by the extirpation of the generous, perhaps the innocent, Barmecides; yet he could listen to the complaint of a poor widow who had been pillaged by his troops, and who dared, in a passage of the Koran, to threaten the inattentive despot with the judgement of God and posterity. His court was adorned with luxury and science; but, in a reign of three-and-twenty years, Harun repeatedly visited his provinces from Khorasan to Egypt; nine times he performed the pilgrimage of Mecca; eight times he invaded the territories of the Romans; and as often as they declined the payment of the tribute, they were taught to feel that a month of depredation was more costly than a year of submission.

Harun's career was astonishing: a relentless whirlwind of bloodshed and conquest, pilgrimage and procreation, science and scholarship, palatial building in Baghdad and expenditure on an imperial, never-to-be-repeated scale. Just as Tamerlane adorned his capital of Samarkand with the fruits of his conquests, so Harun lavished money on the greater glory of the City of Peace. Harun's wild extravagances are well known and widely documented. Yet this was no spendthrift ruler without a care for the future of Baghdad and its empire. On his death in 809, according to Tabari, he left the treasury with 900 million dirhams.

By today's standards he was a quick study. When still only eleven, he made his first *haj* to Mecca and Medina, an arduous round trip of well over 2,000 miles and two months across the Nefud and Hijaz deserts in the company of his father Mahdi, from whom he learnt the political advantages of an almost reckless generosity. In 780, at the hoary age of fourteen, he was appointed to lead an expedition against infidel Byzantium and thereby added *jihad* to his burgeoning credentials. As caliph,

Harun displayed a shrewd grasp of symbol and public relations, commissioning a special *kalansuwa*, a tall conical hat in silk, that bore the inscription 'Ghazi wa Haji', Warrior of Islam and Pilgrim.

For Baghdad there was at least one significant consequence of Harun's teenage campaign against the Greeks. When the garrison at the castle of Samalu on the Armenian frontier surrendered to Harun, after a siege of thirty-eight days, it did so on the condition that the caliph spare the Christians' lives and allow them to remain together. Harun brought them back to his capital, where they formed a small Christian community in eastern Baghdad, centred around a church known as Dayr al Rum, the Monastery of the Greeks. It became an important centre for the Christian community, active right up to the arrival of Hulagu's Mongol hordes in 1258. By 1300, like so much of Baghdad, the monastery was in ruins.

By the time of Mahdi's death in 785, the young Harun, scarcely out of his teens, had already experienced the burdens of running an empire, or at least part of it, as viceroy of the west, from the western Iraqi province of Anbar to distant Tunisia, where the Abbasid writ just about extended. His prodigious early achievements were in no small part thanks to the offices of the faithful Yahya, son of Mansur's vizier Khalid ibn Barmak, who was rewarded with fabulous sums of money and other gifts. When Mahdi's son and heir, Harun's brother Hadi, died suddenly after a one-year reign (there were whisperings of skulduggery, including the suggestion that his mother, whom he had publicly snubbed, had ordered a slave-girl to suffocate him while he slept), Harun found himself caliph. He would have been around twenty-one.

Harun had mixed feelings about Baghdad. We hear from Tabari that he referred to it irritably as the *bukhar*, or steam room, hardly surprising given its often savage climate. There were attempts to find an alternative site for a summer capital by the Tigris at Bazabda, where a Roman fortress had once stood in the district of Bakirda, and a royal palace was duly built there, immortalized in the following snatch of doggerel:

> Bakirda and Bazabda for summer or spring
> At Bakirda and Bazabda the sweet, cool fountains sing.
> And Baghdad, what is Baghdad? Its dust
> Is shit, and its heat is appalling.[7]

Yet the same Tabari also attributes the following speech to Harun in 805, when he was en route to yet another campaign against the Byzantines:

> By God, I am passing through a city, and no city more secure or with greater ease of life than it has ever been constructed in East or West. For it is indeed my home, the home of my forefathers and the Abbasids' centre of power whilst ever they endure and keep close control of it. None of my forefathers has ever experienced there any evil or ill-fortune from it, and none of them has ever been injured or wronged there. What an excellent seat of power it is![8]

Mansur's Round City was almost exclusively a west-bank city. Under Mahdi, Rusafa began to emerge as a serious and magnificent rival on the eastern bank of the Tigris, a town of glittering royal palaces clustered around the caliph's palace and mosque on land given as fiefs to a new generation of courtiers. By the beginning of Harun's reign the eastern quarters of Rusafa, Shammasiya and Mukharrim together were almost equal to Mansur's city and suburbs across the river. Harun and the loyal Barmakid family, headed by the aged Yahya as the caliph's vizier, gave further impetus to this irresistible rise of the east bank. The Barmakids moved into fashionable Rusafa, indulging their compulsive palace-building ambitions with a breathtaking chutzpah that, ominously for the vizier and his family, from time to time would raise the caliph's eyebrow. Jafar, Yahya's son and Harun's dear friend and later vizier, spent the fabulous sum of 20 million dirhams building a single palace in the district, and a further 20 million dirhams furnishing it to his extravagant tastes. Wisely he was persuaded to present the palace as a gift to Harun's son Mamun, and in time it became his official residence and the centrepiece of the Dar al Khilafat, the caliphal complex that was home to future Commanders of the Faithful. (In later years it came to be known as the Hasani Palace, after Mamun gave it to his wife Buran as a wedding gift and named it after his father-in-law and vizier, Hassan ibn Sahl, in the Baghdadi tradition of naming places after their owners which continues to this day.) Its grounds are thought to have contained the great Mosque of the Caliphs, whose ruined minaret was still visible well into the twentieth century. In return for their royal service the Barmakids were granted generous fiefs on the east bank stretching right across Shammasiya, marked by names such as Souk

Jafar, Jafar Market, Nahr Fadl, Fadl Canal, Souk Yahya, Souk Khalid al Barmaki and so on.

Harun's reign included a number of architectural highlights, the chief among them the rebuilding of Mansur's by now dilapidated Great Mosque in the Round City, the enlargement of Mansur's Khuld Palace and the creation of Jafar's palace on the east bank. It was Jafar's long vizierate, headquartered in this magnificent building, that initiated the slow but steady drift of government buildings to the east bank, which remained politically and commercially pre-eminent throughout the Middle Ages and into the twentieth century.

Of more lasting architectural importance and value to Baghdad was another monument, on the other side of the Tigris, that can be traced back to Harun's reign, albeit a project conceived in bloodshed, without his support and to commemorate the life of a man he is said to have poisoned. In 799 Imam Musa al Kadhim ('he who can control his anger') – seventh of the twelve Shia imams and direct descendant of Hussain, who was martyred at Kerbala in 680 – died in confinement under Harun. He was buried at Makaber Kuraish, the graveyard of Kuraish (the principal tribe of the Prophet Mohammed and his descendants) in north-western Baghdad, originally laid out by Mansur. Three decades later the imam's grandson Mohammed al Jawad, another likely victim of poisoning, this time under the caliphate of Al Mutasim, was buried in the same place, giving rise to the name Kadhimain, literally the Two Kadhims. The mosque complex became a holy shrine to the Shia, an increasingly important spiritual focus for the heterodox in Baghdad, so much so that in time it grew into an entire district itself, Kadhimiya, enclosed within a loop of the Tigris in north-western Baghdad. The magnificent shrine at its heart is one of the city's great sights to this day. Baghdad has Harun's religious persecution to thank for it.

*

Harun refused to be unduly burdened by the cares of high office. Tabari describes how, when appointing the formidably experienced Yahya as his vizier, he invested in him full executive authority, giving him carte blanche to conduct all government affairs as he saw fit. When he was not directing campaigns against the infidel or leading pilgrims on *haj* to Mecca (as he did in 787, 790, 791, 794, 796, 798, 802 and 804), the caliph was thus free to concentrate on some of the more enjoyable fruits of office.

Night after night, Harun and his court, joined by scholars, poets, diplomats, generals, musicians, judges, sportsmen and the latest favourites, assembled in the palaces to feast and lay waste to the royal cellars, indulging in the ruby-red wine of Shiraz, bewitched by the graceful young women of the harem who were selected as much for their musical talents as for their beauty. As the poet Muslim ibn Walid wrote in characteristically risqué verse, 'What is this life but loving, and surrender to the / drunkenness of wine and pretty eyes?'[9]

We hear of royal banquets with platters of gold and silver set with precious stones, heaving with the finest delicacies, 'egg-apples and stuffed marrows, filled vine-leaves seasoned with lemon, cakes of bruised wheat and minced meat, sliced fillet of mutton cooked in tomatoed rice, a stew of little onions ... ten roast fowls and a roast sheep, and two great dishes, one of *kunafa** and the other of a pastry made with sweet cheese and honey; fruits of every kind: melons, cucumbers, limes and fresh dates'.[10]

Pondering the lithe bodies swaying gracefully before them, Harun's guests tucked into porcelain bowls of *halva* perfumed with orange juice, and sprinkled with cinnamon and ground nuts. Then there were crushed raisins infused with essence of rose, lozenge-shaped, sugar-coated *baklava*, wrinkled figs, bulging grapes, bananas and grapefruit and, hidden amongst vases of roses, jasmine and tulips, mountains of almond cakes covered in syrup that dripped down chins and produced sticky smiles.

Cup-servers brought the men golden jugs and basins filled with scented water in which to wash their hands, rinsing them in ewers encrusted with rubies and diamonds before giving them scent of aloes in small golden pots. Wine was served in goblets of gold, silver or crystal. Eunuchs refreshed the guests with musk and rosewater from jewelled gold sprinklers. While the drinking bouts raged until dawn, the girls sang and strummed the lute, entertaining their drunken audience with the playful scarf dance and the languorous dance of the sabres.

For a time, it was fashionable for well-born men to have affairs with eunuchs. These unusual tastes found royal favour at the highest levels of the state. Amin, Harun's son by Zubayda, the illustrious granddaughter of the caliph Mansur, developed an obsession with eunuchs. Tabari wrote that 'He wished to see no women' and had nicknames for white

---

* *Kunafa* is a type of traditional cheese pastry soaked in sweet syrup.

eunuchs (grasshoppers) and black ones (ravens). A mortified Zubayda resorted to dressing up the most beautiful concubines in close-fitting boy's clothes, cropping their hair short and sending them to him to divert him from this sinful practice. Her ruse worked. Amin was, the chronicles reported, completely captivated.

From its foundation Baghdad was a distinctly patriarchal place, as it remains today. Women have traditionally been confined to the private sphere and generally occupy a minor role in the sources. Yet alongside all the Abbasid caliphs and poets, the mathematicians and musicians, there were of course notable women. Daughter of Mansur's son and heir Jafar, tutored in religion, poetry and literature, Zubayda was one of the most remarkable of her time, famed for her extraordinarily opulent tastes on the one hand, on the other for her overlapping charitable and religious interests and an imaginative act of philanthropy that survives in part to this day. Wealthy from birth, she became immensely rich after marrying her cousin Harun and used much of her fortune as a major philanthropist in her own right. Her court, according to the Abbasid biographer Ibn Khallikan, sounded like a beehive, so great were the number of her maids reciting the Koran day and night. As the caliph's chief wife, Zubayda naturally had the finest jewels and costumes of any woman. Abbasid extravagance knew no bounds: it was said that during the most important court ceremonies she was so laden with gold and precious stones that two servants were required simply to help her stand upright. Her most lasting achievement, however, which gave succour to millions of pilgrims during the following centuries, was the creation of Darb Zubayda, Zubayda's Way, a safe 900-mile route across the desert from Kufa, south of Baghdad, to the holiest city of Mecca. Having observed the hardships suffered during this arduous journey during her own pilgrimages, above all the lack of drinking water, Zubayda spear-headed a vast engineering project to make it more bearable. Wells were bored and reservoirs dug along the route, together with cisterns and state-of-the-art dams with filtering tanks to overcome the problems of sediment. The route was geologically complex and presented formid-able challenges. It had to be cut through mountains, so enormous rocks and boulders had to be cleared and stone paving was required in places. Numerous way stations were built to provide rest for pilgrims and their animals. There were reportedly fifty-four major resting stations along the way, built approximately every sixteen miles (a day's march), with smaller resting places in between. Zubayda took a direct interest in the construction work, and the engineers were ordered to spare no expense. In Mecca itself, she built the first canal to supply spring water to pilgrims at the shrine, who were otherwise entirely dependent on the Zamzam well. To this day the mountain source is known as Ain Zubayda, Zubayda's Well. The final bill was said to run into millions of dinars, paid for from her own pocket.[11]

Dananis, one of the most famous women of Harun's harem, provoked the ageing Zubayda to heights of jealousy after the high-spirited caliph showered the singing slave-girl with extravagant presents, including a necklace worth 30,000 dirhams, ostensibly in recognition of her artistic talents. Ever the survivor, the wily Zubayda subsequently apologized to her husband after listening to the girl sing, and excused her earlier fury by presenting him with ten more exceptionally beautiful slave-girls (who duly produced more royal offspring). Most renowned of the Abbasid queens, Zubayda relentlessly defended the rights of Amin, the only caliph born of royal blood on both sides, to the caliphate over that of his elder brother Mamun. After their struggle for supremacy, which will be described in Chapter 3, she ended her days in prayer and solitude and died in 831.

The harem – and recruitment to it – was an industry all of its own, keeping Harun endlessly occupied with around 200 of the fairest young women, in addition to his four wives. This seems positively ascetic in comparison with the harem of 4,000 that Al Mutawakil (847–61) maintained in the mid ninth century, each one of which he was said to have slept with. Some of their names are still known to us: Diya (Splendour), Sihr (Charm), Dhat al Khal (Beauty Spot) and Hailana (after Helen, probably a Greek). Denied a public role in the life of the caliphate, strong characters from the harem, such as Arib, nicknamed the nightingale of the court for the sweetness of her voice and the thousands of songs and poems she composed, became the stuff of legend. Bought originally by Harun's son Amin, she later joined the harem of Mamun but did not scruple to cuckold him in his own palace, sneaking in her own lover for late-night trysts in an exceptionally dangerous defiance of local custom. Arib was said to have her hair massaged with rich pomades of amber and musk, later sold for a handsome price by her servants.

Much of what we know about Arib comes from the tenth-century historian Abu al Faraj al Isfahani, an avid collector of poems and songs. As an old woman she was visited by two young men who dared to ask her whether she still desired sex. 'Ah, my sons, the lust is present but the limbs are helpless,' she is supposed to have replied. She died in Samarra in her nineties, having enthralled a succession of caliphs.[12]

The harem was no place for a shrinking violet. The poets tell of recurring feuds between women fiercely competing with each other for the caliph's favours and attention and with the royal wives to produce the caliph's son and heir. In one of the more violent encounters Beauty Spot cut off the tip of another girl's nose. In retaliation, her rival tore off the decorative mole that had given Beauty Spot her name.

Catfights were nothing compared with other dangers of harem life. Many women would doubtless have found their elegant captivity utterly stultifying. Perhaps because of this, some experimented with lesbian affairs. If they were discovered, punishment was swift and brutal. Tabari relates the following chilling story in the words of Ali ibn Yaktin, a courtier of Harun's brother Hadi:

One night, I was with Musa, in the company of a group of his companions, when suddenly there came to him a eunuch who whispered something in his ear secretly. Thereupon, the Caliph sprang up with alacrity, saying, 'Don't leave,' and went off. He was away for a considerable time, but then came back, breathing heavily. He hurled himself down on his couch, still breathing heavily for a while until he became calm again. He had with him a eunuch carrying a dish covered over with a napkin. The eunuch stood before him and came forward trembling. We were amazed at all this. Then the Caliph sat up and said to the eunuch, 'Set down what you are carrying,' so he put down the dish. He said to the eunuch, 'Take off the napkin,' so he did this, and behold, the dish held the heads of two slave-girls, with more beautiful faces and hair, by God, than I had ever seen before; there were jewels on their heads, arranged in the hair, and a sweet perfume was diffused from them. We found this a horrific sight. The Caliph said, 'Do you know what these two were up to?' We replied in the negative. He said, 'We received information that they were in love with each other, and had got together for an immoral purpose. So I set this eunuch to watch over them and to report to me what they were doing. In due course, he came to me and informed me that they had got together, so I went along and found them under a single coverlet committing an immoral act. I thereupon killed them.' After saying this he told the slave to take the two heads away ... The Caliph then resumed his former conversation as if he had done nothing unusual in the meantime.[13]

Underwritten by the caliph and his courtiers, men with the deepest pockets – and largest egos – in Baghdad, the market in attractive women could occasionally be frantic. Hugh Kennedy likens it to football transfers, with the most desirable players being traded up, gaining value with each transaction, until they reached extraordinarily exorbitant sums.[14] Thus Harun's father Mahdi bought a girl called Maknuna, 'who took pride in her slender hips and high chest', for 100,000 silver dirhams. Basbas (Caress), evidently in greater demand, cost an eye-watering 17,000 gold dinars. Nor was this a market that necessarily deferred to the whims of the caliph. Inan, a beauty from eastern Arabia who caught Harun's eye and for a time stole his heart, was highly educated and flirtatious, and she was said to be able to hold her own in poetic repartee with the legendary Abu Nuwas. But her master, a man called Natifi, steadfastly refused to sell her, even to the caliph, demanding 100,000 gold dinars and rejecting any attempts to negotiate. Later, when the man died and Inan was put up for sale in the public slave-market at Karkh Gate, Harun tried his luck again. He dispatched his chief eunuch Masrur to the market with instructions to bid up to 200,000 dirhams. Astonishingly, Harun was outbid, even when Masrur gave his presumptuous rival a thrashing and reminded him he was competing with the caliph. Inan exchanged hands for 250,000 dirhams and was whisked off to Khorasan by the unknown man. It was the last Harun ever saw of her.

No less an authority than Tabari wrote how, during the most scorching days of summer, when Harun would take an afternoon siesta in his pavilion, a silver urn was brought in to the caliph in which the royal perfume merchant had blended a fragrant mixture of scent, saffron, aromatic substances and rosewater. Seven tunics of fine Rashidi linen in a feminine cut were then dipped into the mixture, a prelude to the delights to come. Every day, seven girls were brought in to the caliph's chamber, where they observed a meticulously devised protocol. First they removed their clothes and were dressed in the exquisitely scented linen shifts. Then they took their place on pierced seats above piles of burning incense, until their clothes were dry and their bodies were perfumed to the caliph's taste. Only once this elaborate process was complete could lovemaking begin.

*

In the wonderful world of *The Arabian Nights*, a masterpiece of Indian, Persian and Arab storytelling that dates back in its earliest form to the eighth and ninth centuries, Harun's libido is no less extravagant. In the 387th Night, for example, we discover the Abbasid caliph enjoying himself first with two girls, then with three. In 'Harun al Rashid and the Two Slave-Girls', his companions are concubines from Medina and Kufa. The Arabian is massaging his legs, the Iraqi his arms. Understandably all this attention gives Harun an erection, which the girls compete to control. The Kufan girl says to the Medinan, 'I see that you are trying to monopolize our capital and keep it to yourself. Give me my share.' To which the Medinan replies with a remark from the Prophet, 'If someone brings uncultivated ground to life, it belongs to him and his descendants.' Quick as a flash, the Kufan shoves her rival to one side, 'takes Harun's member in both hands' and, not to be outdone on questions of Islamic theology, shoots back with the Prophet's observation, 'Game belongs to the hunter and not to the beater.'[15] As in real-life Abbasid Baghdad, the most desirable slave-girls were prized not only for their looks and musical talents, but equally for their wit and repartee.

In the next story, Harun has evidently decided that, when it comes to taking pleasure with slave-girls, three is more fun than two. This time, they come from Mecca, Medina and Iraq. 'The Medinan stretched out her hand and stimulated his member, giving him an erection, but the Meccan jumped across and pulled it towards her.' The Medinan complains that this is unfair, citing the Prophet's remark about bringing uncultivated ground to life again. Unmoved, the Meccan says this is not so, that the game belongs to the hunter. The Iraqi girl then pushes both rivals aside and confidently declares: 'Until you settle your dispute, this belongs to me.'[16]

Harun deserves his place in posterity in his own right, yet his incomparable fame amongst the Abbasid caliphs, as Gibbon acknowledged, is in large part down to the fantastical world of *The Arabian Nights*. Readers will also know this much-loved book as *A Thousand and One Nights*, a reference to the time during which the indefatigable narrator Sheherazade tells her nightly stories to King Shahryar, a lusty and murderous monarch whose habit of bedding and beheading virgin brides she is determined to break (when the odds are decidedly against her, Shahryar having deflowered and killed a new girl every day for three years). The couple are celebrated in the sculptor Mohammed Ghani Hikmat's eye-catching 1972 bronzes on Abu Nuwas Street on the eastern bank of the Tigris. Shahryar reclines languidly on his pedestal while a slender Sheherazade spins her life-saving stories in front of him.

To say Harun enjoys a starring role in *The Arabian Nights* would be an understatement. He headlines in a dozen stories and sashays boldly through many more, roaming at large as the nocturnal, insomniac caliph, prowling the streets of Baghdad with his loyal companions Jafar the Barmakid vizier and Masrur his executioner, checking on his city and his people, always ready for an adventure, often ending up in a scrape. Harun is one of the charismatic heroes of this freewheeling epic with his imperial capital of Baghdad as his glamorous co-star.

Night after night, as in 'Harun al Rashid and the Fishermen's Chest', the restless caliph wants to explore the streets of his capital. 'One night the caliph Harun al Rashid summoned his vizier Jafar and said: "I want to go down into the city to ask the common people about the governors who have charge of them, so as to depose any of whom they complain and promote those to whom they are grateful." "To hear is to obey," replied Jafar.'[17] The vizier, who is often on the brink of being executed by the irascible caliph, may not suffer from the same bouts of insomnia that afflict Harun but has no choice but to keep him company.

Although this is no trustworthy historical document, *The Arabian Nights* nevertheless provides a compelling picture of life in medieval Baghdad, with its fabulously wealthy merchants, crowded markets teeming with produce, narrow streets and alleys containing houses with projecting balconies and high *mashrabiya* windows that allow the person inside to look out without being seen, its magnificent mosques, luxurious *hammams* and cavernous caravanserais – like the Khan Mirjan – where weary traders and travellers could rest, store their goods and enjoy the delights provided by their hospitable host. As Antoine Galland, the French orientalist and translator of *The Arabian Nights*, wrote of the stories in the early eighteenth century, 'They should also please by what they reveal of the manners and customs of Orientals, of their religious ceremonies, both pagan and Mohammedan; and these subjects are better brought out than in the authors who have written about them or in travellers' narratives.'[18]

The Arabian Nights is a treasure trove of storytelling that has it all: sex and love; intrigue and adventure, danger and death; lavish banquets and debauched revelry; an exotic cast of the utterly weird and the wonderful, from one-eyed hunchbacks and terrifying *jinns* to handsome princes and sublimely beautiful girls with flashing eyes. Haughty viziers share the pages with unscrupulous thieves and confidence tricksters, seductive concubines, derelict fishermen, beggars high on hashish and gorgeously attired courtiers drunk on wine. The stories take swipes at corrupt policemen and lascivious judges, lesbian witches and nymphomaniac man-killers. This is a highly urban world of merchants and money-changers, tailors and barbers, poets and dervishes, singers, schoolmasters and sailors, with none more famous than Sinbad, an *Arabian Nights* celebrity alongside Ali Baba and the Forty Thieves, Aladdin and Harun himself. Rather like Abbasid Baghdad, there is a capriciousness about life in this fictionalized world, such that a man appearing before the mighty caliph is never sure whether he is about to be rewarded with a bulging purse of gold dinars or forced to kneel on the executioner's leather mat to have his head lopped off with a sharp sword.

The epic dreamscape of *The Arabian Nights* has inspired generations of writers, artists, poets and film-makers, whose imagined re-creations of the enchanted world of Baghdad have seeped into Western culture across the centuries. In *Recollections of the Arabian Nights*, originally published in 1830, a youthful Tennyson evokes a dreamily sensuous tableau of the city, slipping along the moonlit Tigris in a playful breeze, 'By Bagdat's shrines of fretted gold, / High-walled gardens green and old,' past scented bowers and lemon groves, sailing by shrines of gold beneath an indigo, star-studded sky. He is taken through an exotic garden,

> Full of the city's stilly sound,
> And deep myrrh-thickets blowing round
> The stately cedar, tamarisks,
> Thick rosaries of scented thorn,
> Tall orient shrubs, and obelisks . . .

'With dazed vision' he reaches the caliph's pavilion, a glittering imperial chamber, with flights of marble stairs and gilt balustrades behind carved

An illustration from an eighteenth-century French edition of *A Thousand and One Nights*. Baghdad and the caliph Harun al Rashid feature prominently in a number of high-spirited tales in this famous collection of Arab, Persian and Indian stories that date back to the eighth and ninth centuries.

cedar doors. Windows reflect the light of a million tapers set in twisted silver. Perhaps inevitably, the poet spies a beautiful Persian girl,

> Serene with argent-lidded eyes
> Amorous, and lashes like to rays
> Of darkness, and a brow of pearl
> Tressed with redolent ebony,
> In many a dark delicious curl,
> Flowing beneath her rose-hued zone;
> The sweetest lady of the time ...

Finally, he comes upon a vast throne set on six columns of pure silver, draped with lavish gold brocade, and there at last is the great Abbasid caliph,

> Sole star of all that place and time,
> I saw him – in his golden prime,
> The good Haroun Alraschid.

Almost a century later, in 1923, the year he won the Nobel Prize for Literature, Yeats wrote *The Gift of Harun Al-Rashid*, a trance-like, Coleridgian poem inspired once again by *The Arabian Nights*, a jasmine-scented world with visions of Harun on diplomatic missions to Persia and at war with the Byzantines, the poet haunted by the beauty of 'a slender bride':

> And now my utmost mystery is out.
> A woman's beauty is a storm-tossed banner;
> Under it wisdom stands, and I alone –
> Of all Arabia's lovers I alone –
> Nor dazzled by the embroidery, nor lost
> In the confusion of its night-dark folds,
> Can hear the armed man speak.

Gertrude Bell may have believed that no one could possibly know what Baghdad was like in the time of Harun al Rashid, as she harrumphed in a letter to her father in 1921, but *The Arabian Nights*, in addition to the many other chronicles of the Abbasid era, suggests no shortage of colourful possibilities.[19] In the story of 'The Porter and the Three Ladies', for example, we get a tantalizing glimpse of a shopping expedition in the well-stocked markets of Harun's Baghdad. A veiled woman with dark eyes enlists the services of a susceptible, unmarried porter.[20] After collecting a jar of wine, she visits a fruiterer's, where she buys 'Syrian apples, Uthmani quinces, Omani peaches, jasmine and water lilies from Syria, autumn cucumbers, lemons, *sultani* oranges, scented myrtle, privet flowers, camomile blossoms, red anemones, violets, pomegranate blooms and eglantine'. After buying meat from the butcher's, she heads to the grocer's for pistachio kernels, Tihama raisins and shelled almonds for a dessert. At the sweetmeat seller's she picks up pastries galore: 'sugar cakes, doughnuts stuffed with musk, "soap" cakes, lemon tarts, Maimuni tarts, "Zainab's combs", sugar fingers and "kadis' snacks"'. With little regard for expense, the foray into the crowded markets of Baghdad continues at the perfume-seller's, where she buys ten varieties of scented water, including some perfumed with water lilies and willow-flowers.

This is no ordinary trip to the market. As is often the case in *The Arabian Nights*, there is a lot more to the story than a housekeeper's quest for fruit and veg. They return to the woman's house, a handsome pillared building whose door is opened by another beautiful girl with eyebrows 'like the crescent moon of the month of Sha'ban', cheeks like red anemones, 'a mouth like the seal of Solomon, coral red lips, teeth like camomile blossoms or pearls on a string, and a gazelle-like neck. Her bosom was like an ornate fountain, with breasts like twin pomegranates; she had an elegant belly and a navel that could contain an ounce of unguent.' A third woman, equally attractive, completes the setting. The house itself is a marvel, with a large courtyard, vaulted chambers, alcoves and fine carvings; it is filled with brocaded curtains, and expensive sofas are set around a large pool on which a lavishly appointed skiff is floating. In the bow of the boat is a couch of gem-studded juniper wood, shrouded in a mosquito net of red satin with pearl buttons bigger than hazelnuts.

Before you can say 'erotic fantasy', a wine-fuelled orgy is under way. One of the girls strips off, plunges into the pool and jumps out on to the porter's lap. 'My master, my darling, what is the name of this?' she asks him, pointing to her vagina. Each time that he volunteers a word – womb, vagina, vulva, cuff, hornet – he receives a sound slap. Eventually she says she calls it 'the mint of the dykes'. The process is repeated with the second girl, and the porter is smartly beaten, until she says that she calls her vagina 'husked sesame'; and then with the third girl, who uses the phrase 'the *khan* of Abu Mansur'. At this point, the porter takes off his clothes, jumps into the pool and then throws himself on to the girls' laps.

> Then he pointed to his penis, and said: 'Ladies, what is the name of this?' before biting and kissing them for every wrong answer. What is its name, then, they ask at last? 'This is the mule that breaks barriers, browses on the mint of the dykes, eats the husked sesame and that passes the night in the *khan* of Abu Mansur.' The girls laughed until they fell over backwards and then they continued with their drinking party, carrying on until nightfall.

If the stories in *The Arabian Nights* are often profoundly fantastical, at other times they merely reflect historical reality. Thus, in 'Harun al Rashid and the Young Bedouin Girl', the caliph, accompanied as ever by Jafar, falls in love with a girl as much, if not more, for her poetic range than for her beauty. Impressed by her ability to improvise verse and fashion it into entrancing songs, he marries her and she becomes a firm favourite.

In the same vein the audacious poet Abu Nuwas pops up from time to time to entertain Harun. The story 'Harun al Rashid and the Lady Zubayda in the Pool' finds the caliph stalking his palace gardens one searingly hot day in Baghdad. He spots his wife cooling off naked in a pool in the pleasure garden he laid out for her, fringed with trees whose dense foliage usually protects the bathers' privacy. Unaware he is watching her, she is standing up, pouring water over herself from a silver jug. 'Modesty led her to put her hand over her private parts, but these were too plump to be entirely concealed,' Sheherazade tells us. Touched by the innocence of the scene and the beauty of his wife, Harun composes a couplet:

> My eyes saw the cause of my ruin
> And separation caused the fire of passion to burn up.

Struck by writer's block, he is unable to finish the verse and so summons Abu Nuwas to do the job for him. What is a tame poet for, after all? After the briefest of pauses, Abu Nuwas, never at a loss for words, extemporizes the verse.

> My eyes saw the cause of my ruin
> And separation caused the fire of passion to burn up,

Through love for a gazelle who captivated me
Beneath the shade of two lote trees.
Water poured over it from silver jugs.
She saw me and then tried to hide it,
But it was too large for her hands.
I wish that I might lie on it one hour or two.[21]

And Harun, delighted with the finished poem, gives Abu Nuwas the hoped-for generous reward. Just as we know this pleasure-seeking poet sailed close to the wind in real life, so in *The Arabian Nights* he continually flirts with disaster. In 'Harun al Rashid and the Three Poets', which finds the caliph fondling a drunken concubine in the palace grounds one night, Abu Nuwas narrowly avoids execution at Harun's hands, saved only – once again – by his wits, when he quotes a verse from the Koran in the nick of time. In 'Abu Nuwas and the Three Boys', the poet is hell-bent on seducing young boys (as he often did in real life). He spies some likely victims:

I passed by two beardless boys and said:
'I love you.' They replied:
'Are you a rich man?'
'Yes,' I said, 'and generous.'
The two boys then said: 'Done.'

Once he has found his willing trio, a long night of singing and drinking begins, the four 'wrapping legs around legs, with no concern for sin or disgrace'.

Perfect pleasure comes only when a man drinks wine
With pretty boys as his companions . . .
We take our wine both neat and mixed,
And slake our lust on whoever falls asleep.

The torrid scene is interrupted by a horrified Harun, whose anger is redoubled at Abu Nuwas' flippant, drunken reaction. He summons the poet to appear before him in his palace the following morning. The executioner Masrur is ordered to strip him of his clothes, tie a donkey's pack saddle on his back, fasten a strap between his thighs, put a halter over his head and lead him around the apartments of Harun's slave-girls to ridicule him before cutting off his head. Coming upon the poet while he is undergoing this indignity, a mystified Jafar asks him what has happened. 'I presented our master the caliph with the best of my poetry and he presented me with the best of his robes,' the poet quips.[22] Harun finds the joke sufficiently amusing to spare him.

The Arabian Nights gives a mesmerizing sense of the sheer ostentation exhibited by the very rich in Abbasid Baghdad. When we learn that Zubayda, famous for her jewel-encrusted slippers, would dine only from plates of precious metal, and that goblets and spoons were of gold or crystal, set on tables plated with gold and silver, Sheherazade's stories suddenly seem less outlandish and exaggerated.

Revelling in bawdy, frequently lavatorial, humour, *The Arabian Nights* certainly reflects at least some of the tastes that prevailed in Abbasid Baghdad, more often than not at the very highest levels of the empire. In the tale of 'Jafar the Barmakid and the Old Bedouin', Harun, Jafar and Abu Nuwas are out one day in the desert, when they come across an old man travelling with his donkey to Baghdad, where he hopes to find medicine to treat his eyes. Harun encourages his vizier to tease the Bedouin, whereupon Jafar prescribes a ludicrous remedy of wind, sunlight, lamplight and moonshine, mixed and applied over twelve months. 'When the old man heard what Jafar said, he stretched himself out over his donkey and gave vent to a disgusting fart. "Take this in return for the medicine you have prescribed," he said. "If I use it and God cures me, I shall give you a slave-girl whose services to you in your lifetime will end your days, and when you are dead and God has hurried away your soul to hellfire, she will smear your face with her excrement."'[23] Harun, who is easily amused in *The Arabian Nights*, falls over laughing and gives the Bedouin 3,000 dirhams for his troubles.

If that exercise in scatological humour sounds a little implausible, consider the real-life story related by Tabari, in which an obsequious courtier presents Harun with a rare blend of perfumes, consisting of musk from the navels of Tibetan musk-oxen, amber from the Sea of Aden, olibanum and other ingredients, created by a master perfumer from Basra. Another courtier, appalled at the pretension, asks for the perfume, boasting, 'May my mother be a whore if I smear any part of my body with it except my anus!' Harun, we are told, is in hysterics. This second courtier throws his tunic over his head, dips his hand into the jar and smears the priceless perfume over his anus, groin and armpits. By now the caliph is 'hardly able to think straight for laughing'. As if this is not enough, the rogue courtier then summons a slave and gives him what's left of the perfume for his wife, who was to follow this instruction from her husband: 'Smear this on your vulva, until I come home and fuck you.' Harun 'laughed till he almost choked to death' and, to add insult to injury, gave the mischievous courtier the scarcely credible sum of 100,000 dinars in reward for the amusement.[24] Tabari makes no further mention of the fawning courtier, who was presumably left seriously out of pocket.

*

On a cold, clear morning in January 803, Baghdad woke to the most astonishing news. In the houses of the great and the good, stunned courtiers could barely believe their ears. In the markets, shocked porters and traders exchanged sotto voce versions of the story that was running like wildfire across the City of Peace. Surely it had to be untrue. The Commander of the Faithful, recently returned from his latest *haj* to Mecca, had executed his dear friend and vizier Jafar the Barmakid, and had put the vizier's aged father, Yahya, and son Fadl, Jafar's brother, under house arrest. Overnight Baghdad had been turned upside down.

The end of the Barmakids' glorious heyday, when it came, was swift and brutal. Tabari tells the story of Harun sending Masrur to Jafar's palace with orders to bring back his head. The bewildered executioner, old friend and boon companion of the vizier returned to the caliph, after the terrified Jafar implored Masrur to make sure Harun was not in his cups and that the instruction was deadly serious. 'Bring me Jafar's head, motherfucker!' the caliph roared.

Three times Masrur queried the order, until eventually Harun could take no more and beat his hapless retainer about the head. 'If you come back to me again and don't bring Jafar's head, then I shall find someone who will first of all bring me your head and secondly Jafar's,' he barked.[25] Masrur was left with no option but to carry out the extraordinary order.

One day, Jafar was the second most powerful man in the Abbasid Empire; the next, his body was hacked into three pieces, each of which was gibbeted for public display on one of the pontoon bridges across the Tigris.

The reason the people of Baghdad could scarcely believe the news – the sight of his head on a gibbet soon dispelled any lingering doubts – was that Jafar, together with Yahya, had been Harun's rock, the cornerstone of a brilliant seventeen-year reign whose hallmark had been peace and prosperity across the Abbasid Empire at the zenith of its power. Yahya had championed Harun's cause when the succession had been in doubt and had been a father figure for the young caliph; Jafar had been Harun's closest friend, adviser and *nadim*, or boon campanion, the veteran of some legendary revels in their respective palaces. Twelve hundred years later, we still do not know why Harun made this decision. It has been suggested that Harun was angry at Jafar's release of a rebel whom Harun had ordered to be kept in custody.

Tabari says Harun had encouraged Jafar to marry his sister Abbasa, so that she – as a married woman – could respectably feast and drink with them of an evening (a royal princess, with no blood tie to Jafar, would never have been permitted to associate with him at the caliph's private drinking parties). According to this story, Jafar was on no account to consummate the marriage, but the laws of physical attraction, inflamed by the pleasures of the grape, took their inevitable course. 'They would then become intoxicated with the wine, and both of them being in the vigour of youth, Jafar would make for her and copulate with her,' Tabari tells us in a story that many find completely implausible.[26] Masudi gives a similar version, introducing the added twist that it was Jafar's mother who, one night when he had returned from a heavy drinking session with Harun, tricked her drunken son into making love to the lovelorn Abbasa, by describing her as a voluptuous, highly educated slave-girl. Only once they'd had sex did Abbasa reveal her true identity, to Jafar's despair. 'You have thrown me away for nothing and brought me to the edge of the abyss,' the horrified vizier said to his mother.[27] Abbasa, Masudi tells us, became pregnant. In time the baby was spirited away to Mecca, but, because of simmering tensions between Harun's chief wife Zubayda and Yahya, the secret came out, and Harun secretly swore revenge.

Colourful and compelling as these stories undoubtedly are, it is far more likely, given what we know of Harun's court, that over the years the caliph had simply grown resentful of the Barmakids' great and unprecedented power, and of their dazzling riches, which were rumoured to rival or even eclipse his own. There were stories of Harun inflicting petty but highly symbolic humiliations on the Barmakids, such as scolding Yahya sharply on one occasion for entering his presence without his permission, despite this being their accepted practice; ordering his pages not to stand up when Yahya came in; and making him ask repeatedly for a glass of water. In the vicious world of court politics, the Barmakids had no shortage of enemies dripping poison into the jealous caliph's ear. We hear of a hunting expedition one day when, turning to survey his vast entourage, a puffed-up Harun asked a courtier, 'Has there ever been so sumptuous a train?' 'Nothing can compare with Jafar's,' came the tactless reply. The popular Baghdad expression 'rich as Jafar', which would certainly have been known to the caliph, must also have grated. In the wake of the steady deterioration in relations between Harun and the Barmakids, it is probable that the tide just simply and very suddenly turned.

After Jafar's pitiless execution, his rotting remains remained on display to the people of Baghdad for two years, until Harun ordered them to be taken down and burnt in 805. The caliph's meticulous accounts show an entry for '10 kirat of naphtha and tow', which related to the cremation of Jafar's body. Yahya died in custody in 805, a broken man of around seventy, followed, three years later, by his son Fadl, Harun's foster brother, whom the caliph had tortured in prison.

Whatever the reason for the fall of the Barmakids, it marked a decisive turning point in the history of Baghdad. At a stroke the torrents of cultural patronage were stemmed, causing, at the very least, a lasting literary loss. The poets, among the greatest beneficiaries of this Barmakid largesse, mourned their passing in apocalyptic verse. They felt the loss most keenly, in their pockets if not also in their hearts. Even in an edited form, Masudi's assorted elegies on the Barmakids run to five pages. The following lines, typical of the reaction in the poets' circle, were composed by Salm al Khasir:

> The stars of generosity are out;
> The hand of benevolence is closed.
> The seas of bounty have ebbed away
> Now that the Barmakids are gone.
> The stars of the sons of Barmak
> Which showed the guide the true path
> Have fallen.[28]

Overnight, the days of plenty were over, said the poet Ashja al Sulami, who had once watched with Bashar ibn Burd as Abu al Atahiya stole the show at one of Mahdi's public audiences:

The Sons of Barmak have departed this world,
But had they continued in power, men
Could not have profited more.
The days of their supremacy were
A perpetual feast for all mankind.[29]

This was an event so momentous that it also found its way into the pages of *The Arabian Nights*, which paid tribute to the Barmakids in the following passage:

the Barmakids were an ornament for the brow of their century, and a crown upon its head. Destiny showered her most favourable gifts upon them, so that Yahya and his sons became bright stars, vast oceans of generosity, impetuous torrents of kindness, beneficent rains. The world lived at their breath, and under their hands the empire reached the pinnacle of its splendour. They were the refuge of the afflicted, the final resort of the comfortless. The poet Abu Nuwas said of them:

Since earth has put you away, O sons of Barmak,
The roads of morning twilight and evening twilight
Are empty. My heart is empty, O sons of Barmak.

They were admirable viziers, wise administrators, they filled the public treasure. They were strong, eloquent, and of good counsel; they surpassed in learning; their generosity equalled the generosity of Hatim Taiy. They were rivers of happiness, they were good winds bringing up the fruitful clouds; it was through them that the name and the glory of Harun al Rashid clanged from the flats of Central Asia to the northern forests, from Morocco and Andalusia to the farthest bounds of China and Tartary.[30]

This 'time of the Barmakids', an expression that has been used for centuries in the Middle East to denote great fortune and abundance, was soon seen as the Abbasid golden age, although in time this was conflated with the reign of Harun. Two generations of Barmakids served Mansur, Mahdi, Hadi and Harun faithfully and to great effect in the most senior positions of state. Perhaps it is not unfair to suggest that, had it not been for *The Arabian Nights*, and the outpouring of Harun-glorifying literature it inspired in subsequent centuries, his star would have shone rather less brightly in the Abbasid firmament after his death.

Tabari certainly took a dim view of Harun's destruction of the

Barmakids. 'Harun's conduct aroused general disapproval,' he wrote. 'The memory of it will live on until the day of judgement, when it will not escape notice that the punishment inflicted on the Barmakids was not an act of political wisdom.'[31]

Much of the remainder of Harun's caliphate was given over to *jihad*, and there were rousing victories against Byzantium in 803 and 806. More troubling was a rebellion in Samarkand led by Rafi ibn Layth, grandson of the last Umayyad governor of the north-eastern province of Khorasan. In the summer of 808 Harun led an army north from Baghdad with his son Mamun, who had been appointed viceroy of the province. By the spring of 809 he had reached the city of Tus, where he fell sick.

The brother of the rebel Rafi was captured and brought before the ailing caliph. Harun summoned a butcher, forbade the man from sharpening his knives and commanded him to dismember the hapless captive – 'the son of a stinking, uncircumcised whore' in Harun's words – boning him like a chicken, limb by limb. 'So the butcher dismembered him until he left him a pile of chopped up limbs,' Tabari recounted, relishing the detail. 'The Caliph said, "Count up the pieces of his body." I counted the pieces, and lo, they came to fourteen.'[32]

It was one of Harun's last acts. On 24 March 809, within a year of his foster brother Fadl the Barmakid's death in custody, Harun died. He was around forty-seven. Many would have expected his reign to have lasted for decades more. Yet, for those who subscribe to the ancient Greek idea that hubris invariably leads to nemesis, there is something grimly inevitable about what happened next.

3

'The Fountainhead of Scholars', Centre of the World (809–92)

Blessed be the site of Baghdad, seat of learning and art–
None can point in the world to a city equal to her,
Her suburbs vie in beauty with the blue vault of heaven;
Her climate in quality equals the life-giving breezes of heaven,
Her stones in their brightness rival gems and rubies,
Her soil in beneficence has the fragrance of the amber- . . .
The banks of the Tigris with their beautifull damsels surpass
(the city of) Khullakh;
The gardens filled with lovely nymphs equal Cashmere,
And thousands of gondolas on the water,
Dance and sparkle like sunbeams in the sky.

Anwari[1]

Basking in caliphal patronage, the City of Peace was fabulously rich from its very foundation. The astronomical sum Mansur left in his treasury at the time of his death in 775 – 14 million dinars and 600 million dirhams, something like 2,640 metric tons of silver – reveal both how quickly his city had prospered and how rapidly the Abbasid Dynasty had consolidated its position at the heart of the Islamic Empire in the wake of the Umayyads' defeat in 750.

Swishing through their ornate palaces in embroidered silks, the royal family sat at the top of the hierarchy, enjoying the trappings of power; yet it was not alone in possessing great wealth. Abbasid courtiers and favourites, famous singers, beautiful slave-girls and wine-quaffing poets all grew rich on the vast pickings available from the caliph's court, where life-changing fortunes could be made in a moment at the ruler's whim (and just as quickly, sometimes fatally, lost).

Beyond the glittering and unpredictable world of imperial largesse, trade also fuelled the rise of Baghdad. The predictions of the district notable who had, according to the geographer Mukaddasi, praised the would-be capital's trade-friendly location on the Tigris to Mansur soon proved to be prescient. Vessels plied the lengths of both the Euphrates and the Tigris, two of the four ancient rivers of Paradise, sand-blown caravans trudged heavily from Egypt and Syria, boats and beasts of burden respectively bringing their wares to the new city whose population was fast learning the delights of conspicuous consumption. Within a few years of its foundation, the city's markets were teeming with merchants selling the products of the world, from silks, gold, jewellery and precious stones to books, spices, exotic fruit, exquisite carpets and long-suffering camels. Within a dozen years a property boom was in full swing, as thousands poured in to speculate and make their fortunes. Mansur's fledgling capital grew into a mighty metropolis and an unrivalled trading emporium, a Rome of the East. Peace brought plenty. With Baghdad at its centre, the province of Iraq yielded four times as much revenue to the treasury as Egypt, the next richest province in the Abbasid Empire. Each year it paid a staggering 160 million dirhams – or about 480 metric tons of silver – to the exchequer.[2]

A series of meticulously administered imperial taxes underpinned this prosperity. The *kharaj* tax was levied on estates, agricultural land and produce. Collection was supervised by the wali or governor of the province, who was then responsible for sending the revenue raised to Baghdad. The *jizya* (capitulation)tax was levied at varying rates on *dhimmis*, protected citizens who were not Muslims and were spared from having to serve in the army in return for regular tax payments. Then there was the *ushr* (tithe) tax levied at 10 per cent on agricultural produce and foreign trade. These revenues were transferred to the Diwan al Kharaj, the taxes treasury, for accounting, and the Bait al Mal, or public treasury. Within the Bait al Mal was the caliph's private treasury and the office responsible for public spending. By far the most arbitrary form of taxation was the routine appropriation of property by caliphs, who diverted the funds raised to both public and personal treasuries.

Baghdad was now supremely well placed to preside over a cultural revolution that was every bit as remarkable as its pre-eminent political and commercial power and, in some respects, even more impressive. Poets and writers, scientists and mathematicians, musicians and physicians, historians, legalists and lexicographers, theologians, philosophers and astronomers, even cookery writers – together they made this a golden age, creating a legacy that far outlived anything bequeathed by those who shone in the city's political and commercial sun. 'Arab Muslims now studied astronomy, alchemy, medicine and mathematics with such success that, during the ninth and tenth centuries, more scientific discoveries had been achieved in the Abbasid Empire than in any previous period of history.'[3] For more than two centuries from the time of Mansur, the city he founded was the cultural zenith of the Islamic world and the intellectual capital of the planet. As Richard Coke wrote in his 1927 study of the city, 'Baghdad was born at an auspicious moment, which predestined the city to become not merely the administrative capital of a mighty Empire, not merely the greatest trading centre of the early Middle Ages, but a focus of world culture and refinement, the goal of every man of talent from Central Asia to the Atlantic.'[4]

The movement of great minds to Baghdad was as extraordinary a phenomenon as the sweep of Arab horsemen from the Arabian desert during the world-changing conquests of the seventh century. Culture required leisure, leisure required wealth, and wealth flowed from patronage and a booming economy. With a swagger born of vast political and economic power, Baghdad evolved into a peerless cultural centre befitting the seat of a dazzling empire.

The outward-looking, intellectually inquisitive attitude of this time – a medieval, Arab version of Greece's golden age in the fifth century BC – was neatly encapsulated in one of the famous *hadith*, sayings, of the Prophet Mohammed: 'Seek knowledge even to China.' This apparently insatiable quest for knowledge was one of the hallmarks of the Abbasid age. At the demise of Umayyad power, Arab knowledge was principally confined to Arabic grammar and poetics; Koranic exegesis; the collection of oral information about the *sunna*, the religious practices and traditions of the Prophet and the fledgling Islamic community; guidelines governing appropriate behaviour for the model Muslim; and a moral, ascetic mysticism. Compared to this narrowly delineated intellectual territory, the Abbasid achievement of generating knowledge of lasting value, across many disciplines from science and law to poetry and mathematics, amounted to an almost boundless new universe.[5]

The distinctive intellectual climate of Iraq was remarked upon by our roving geographer Mukaddasi, who considered it 'the region of men of refinement, the fountainhead of scholars', noting that it had produced 'Abu Hanifa, the jurist of jurisprudents; and Sufyan, the best of the Koranic readers', together with 'Abu Amr, author of a system of Koranic reading'. It was, besides, 'the birthplace of Hamza, and al Kisai: of virtually every jurist, reader and litterateur; of notables, sages, thinkers, ascetics, distinguished people; of charming and quick-witted people', not to mention Abraham himself, 'the Companion of God'.[6] Though he preferred Basra, on account of what he judged to be its greater piety and prosperity in the tenth century, Mukaddasi devoted far more attention to the City of Peace. Said al Andalusi, the eleventh-century Arab historian, credited Mansur with cultivating a new atmosphere of scientific inquiry. There was, he wrote, 'a surge in spirit and an awakening of intelligence'.[7]

Securing the caliph's patronage was the quickest way for a poet or scholar to advance, financially and socially, in Baghdad. The record of the earliest Abbasid caliphs in supporting intellectual endeavour was, with the odd hiccup, exceptional. In fact, it was Mansur himself, never the most generous of patrons, who was guilty of the greatest transgression, when he had Ibn Mukaffa, the father of secular Arabic prose, executed for what were probably political reasons in 756. Thus ended the career of the thirty-six-year-old translator of *Kalila wa Dimna*, a collection of Indian fables that became one of the most loved books in the Arab world, in Ibn Mukaffa's superb translation an international bestseller for almost 2,000 years.

*

By the end of 810, daggers were very literally drawn between the brothers Amin and Mamun. Although he had been at pains to ensure a smooth succession, Harun had bungled it: first, by dividing the empire between Mamun in the west and Amin in Baghdad; then, by specifying Mamun as Amin's heir. The latter already had a son, Musa, whom he was bound to want to succeed him. In an already highly charged environment, where both men had rival courts – and wives – pushing them towards confrontation, it was a virtual guarantee of future discord. A poet quoted by Tabari predicted calamity:

> And he has sown among them recurring warfare
> And has made easy the way for their avoidance of each other
> So woe to the subjects in the near future.[8]

And so it proved. After a hardening of positions, intense manoeuvring by the competing camps and an exchange of increasingly glacial letters ('Son of my father, do not make me come into conflict with you when I willingly grant you obedience,' Mamun wrote in a typical missive), by 811 it was all-out war. A year later Baghdad found itself engulfed by a ruinous, two-year siege that destroyed great swathes of the magnificent city that Mansur and his successors had laboured so hard to build.

Hemmed in by his brother's forces, which encircled Baghdad (two armies under Mamun's commanders, Harthama ibn Ayan and Musayab ibn Zuhayr, guarded access from the north-east and south-east respectively; another under the Khorasani aristocrat Tahir ibn Hussain struck camp close to the Anbar Gate in the western outskirts of the city), Amin found himself master of a diminishing space. He retreated to his great-grandfather Mansur's Palace of Eternity, where he came under constant fire from Mamun's mangonels, trebuchet-like siege engines. The bombardment of stones and missiles grew so intense that Amin was forced to abandon the vast building, having first ordered his servants to torch the audience hall and carpets. It was the end of Mansur's beloved palace, so admired by Khatib for its architectural grandeur and magnificence. Amin retreated to the Round City to make his last stand.

It is important to emphasize that the fratricidal bombardment that now ripped Baghdad apart was two-way. The damage to the city, in other words, was far more extensive than that caused by Mamun's barrage alone. A frantic Amin – Tabari calls him 'distressed and with burning heart' – ordered gold and silver vessels to be melted down and minted into dinars and dirhams to retain his army's loyalty and stem the tide of defections. An instruction was given to bombard the Harbiya quarter, north of the Round City, with naphtha and fire. Innocent civilians were killed in the crossfire in what military commanders today call collateral damage. The poet al Khuraymi, quoted by Tabari, was more expressive:

In every gated street and on every side
there is a siege engine whose moving beam raises its voice.
With projectiles like men's heads taken from pieces
of stone the evil man loads the sling.
It is as if over their heads there were flocks
of dusky sand grouse taking flight in commotion.
The shouts of the men come from beneath them,
while the swinging beams hurl their missiles.
Have you seen the unsheathed swords
that men are brandishing in the markets?
Horses are prancing in its lanes,
carrying Turks with sharpened daggers.
Naphtha and fire are in its roads;
its inhabitants are fleeing because of the smoke.[9]

The poet's 'paradise on earth', an 'abode of happiness' with gleaming palaces, luxuriant gardens and lithe-bodied lute-players, had become 'as empty as the belly of a wild ass', a desolate, fire-scorched hell where widows ran screaming through streets prowled by dogs eating headless corpses. Even the Tigris had lost its beauty. The bodies of drowned men, women and children bobbed in her blood-soaked waters. None was spared the ravages:

I have seen the young men on the field
of battle, their noses defiled in the dust.
Each was a young man who defended those he was
    honour-bound to protect:
kindlers of strife experienced distress in the fray because of him.
The dogs have spent the night by him, mangling him,
their claws stained with blood.
Have you not seen the horses wheeling round
with the men, their hindquarters wounded?
The horses trip over the handsome faces
of the dead, and the skin around their hooves is smeared with blood.
They trample the livers of courageous young men,
and their hooves split their skulls.[10]

The noose steadily tightened around Amin's neck. Tahir cut off all supplies to the city by road and river. Prices soared. The markets were bare. Frustrated at the slow progress, he branded those areas that opposed him Dar al Nakth, the Abode of Promise-Breaking – Tabari particularly mentions the Round City and the markets of Karkh and Khuld to its south-east and east respectively. It was a licence to seize the estates and commercial properties belonging to the Hashimi family, military commanders and senior officials who did not come quickly to declare obedience to Mamun. Amin's regular army was fast losing the will to fight, and the defence of the city increasingly rested on the shoulders of an irregular force of what Tabari and Masudi variously referred to as riffraff, rabble, cutpurses, prisoners, vagrants, street vendors and 'naked ones', the last a reference to their lack of armour. Tahir razed to the ground neighbourhoods south-west of the Round City that resisted the siege. Much of northern Baghdad was laid waste.

Fearing imminent capture, Amin risked everything on a last gambit. He tried to escape by barque, but he was quickly overwhelmed by Tahir's men in skiffs, who threw him into the water. He was seized and held in a bare room with reed mats and cushions with one of his commanders, who later described the blind panic that overcame Amin, reduced to a bedraggled, half-naked wreck in tattered cloth, distraught at the thought of his likely execution. At midnight came the clatter of horses' hooves. A detachment of Persian soldiers rushed in, under orders to put Amin to death. The pitiful caliph tried to resist his executioners, thrusting a cushion at them as they advanced with swords drawn. Masudi quotes his frantic last words: 'We belong to God and to God we return! I am a cousin of the Messenger of God! I am the brother of Mamun!' The assassination party cut his throat, slashed at him 'until his corpse grew cold', and hacked off his head.[11] He was the first Abbasid caliph to die in Baghdad.

*

Mamun's reign from 813 to 833 may have begun in bloodshed but it nevertheless represented a highpoint for scholarly endeavour in the sciences and for the related patronage of the translation movement that no other caliph could match. The creation of the renowned Bait al Hikma, the House of Wisdom, in Baghdad has been traditionally credited to Mamun, though it probably dated to Mansur's era. Although no physical traces of it survive and much of its original activity remains shrouded in mystery, we know that it became the nerve centre of Abbasid

THE FOUNTAINHEAD OF SCHOLARS' (809-92)

intellectual activity, some sort of combination of lavishly endowed royal archive, learned academy, library and translation bureau, with a dedicated staff of scholars, copyists and bookbinders rolling forward the frontiers of knowledge together. By the middle of the ninth century, it was the largest repository of books in the world, according to the Iraqi-British theoretical physicist and author Jim al Khalili, 'the seed from which sprouted all the subsequent achievements of the golden age of Arabic science, from Uzbekistan in the East to Spain in the West'.[12]

The arrival in Baghdad of the new invention of paper from China, which occurred around the time of the city's foundation, allowed translation to flourish, and paved the way for the creation of books, libraries, reading rooms, bookshops and armies of copyists. Roman law, Greek medicine, mathematics and philosophy, Indian mysticism and Persian scholarship – all were harnessed in this rush to understand the world and build on the great works of antiquity. The advancing science of astronomy, vital for such daily functions as determining the times of prayer and the precise direction of Mecca, provided a further spur to cartographers, who in time created a pioneering world map for Mamun. In 828 the caliph commissioned a new astronomical observatory, the first in the Islamic world, to verify the observations made by the second-century astronomer and geographer Ptolemy in his great treatise, the *Almagest*. Some of the greatest scientists of the age were invited to Baghdad during Mamun's caliphate, lured by generous salaries and the prestige of cutting-edge research in the foremost city of the world. The observatory has been called 'the world's first state-funded large-scale science project' and was spectacularly successful, as we shall see.[13] The great and deeply revered Arabic poetry of the Jahiliya, the pre-Islamic age of ignorance, was set down on paper and recorded for history. Every Tuesday, Mamun presided over jurisprudence debates. The Umayyad era had been marked by a cloistered atmosphere of Arab exclusivity, but the intellectual flowering of the Abbasid age was highly cosmopolitan, the court and the elite culture it sponsored open to talented minds from across the empire.

An Arab historian described Mamun in this way:

He looked for knowledge where it was evident, and thanks to the breadth of his conceptions and the power of his intelligence, he drew it from places where it was hidden. He entered into relations with the emperors of Byzantium,

69

gave them rich gifts, and asked them to give him books of philosophy which they had in their possession. These emperors sent him those works of Plato, Aristotle, Hippocrates, Galen, Euclid, and Ptolemy which they had. Mamun then chose the most experienced translators and commissioned them to translate these works to the best of their ability. After the translating was done as perfectly as possible, the caliph urged his subjects to read the translations and encouraged them to study them. Consequently, the scientific movement became stronger under this prince's reign. Scholars held high rank, and the caliph surrounded himself with learned men, legal experts, traditionalists, rationalist theologians, lexicographers, annalists, metricians, and genealogists.[14]

*

Although science and translation dominated Baghdad's cultural landscape from the beginning of the reign of Mamun in 813, it was poetry that prevailed in the earliest years of the Abbasid era. Poets were the celebrities of their day. Unlike the archetypal penniless poet of today, a successful poet in Abbasid Baghdad stood to make great riches once he found a patron, ideally the caliph himself. Hugh Kennedy has likened the poets of this age to rock and roll stars, public figures who were allowed, and to some extent even expected, to behave in ways that would have been unpardonable for less verbally dextrous individuals.[15] Abu Nuwas, perhaps the boldest and most brilliant of Abbasid poets, as we shall see, celebrated illicit sex with a fearlessness that would be met with the hangman's noose in some parts of the Arab world today. More than 1,200 years after this poetic heyday, a stupendous quantity of Abbasid verse still survives, showing just how popular a medium it had become. Much of it is very good, variously tragic, romantic, whimsical, fatalistic, licentious and occasionally hilarious, a tribute to the deep-seated Arab reverence for the richness of the Arabic language.

The repertoire of the Abbasid poet broadly consisted of panegyrics, verses on mournful, unfulfilled, exalted or depraved love, wistful musings on the human condition and the transience of life, and high-spirited praise of the grape.

One of the most popular poets of this time – and by far the most controversial – was Abu Nuwas, 'He of the Dangling Locks', a writer hugely admired by Baghdadis to this day. His name is given to the corniche along the east bank of the Tigris, a gracious, tree-shaded street lined with restaurants serving the Iraqi speciality of *masgouf*, barbecued river fish. A statue of Abu Nuwas stands proudly at the bottom of the booksellers' row, Mutanabbi Street (named after another great Abbasid poet of the tenth century): his right arm is held aloft, as though he is reciting his verse across the water to the city around him. Many consider him the greatest Bacchic poet in the Arabic language. Having left his home in Basra, like so many other precociously talented men of his time, Abu Nuwas moved to Baghdad, arriving around the time of Harun al Rashid's accession in 786. Although he was prodigiously well educated and became a *hafiz* after mastering the Koran at a young age, scandal and blasphemy tended to follow in his wake. As an adolescent he was taken under the wing of an openly gay poet from Kufa called Waliba ibn Hubab, who revelled in homoerotic verse and was evidently thrilled by his conquest of the youthful Abu Nuwas.

According to one anecdote, after the two had eaten and drunk wine together during the evening of their first encounter, Abu Nuwas took off his clothes. Marvelling at his physical beauty, Waliba stepped forward and kissed Abu Nuwas on his behind, prompting the indignant or merely mischievous youth to fart in his face. Waliba roundly cursed him for his vulgarity. Never one to pass up the opportunity for a good line, Abu Nuwas shot back, 'What reward can there be for the man who kisses ass except a fart!'[16]

In one poem Abu Nuwas seems to refer to a deeply dangerous affection for his patron and friend, the caliph Amin:

> I am in love but cannot say with whom; I fear him who fears no one!
> When I think about my love for him, I feel for my head and
>   wonder if it is still attached to my body![17]

In another, he begins by describing the suffering he is experiencing at the hands of his would-be lover:

> O enchanting eyes, you are forever languid,
> Your stare draws out secrets held close in the heart! . . .
> Consider the two of us: you have rent me to pieces, though you
> Are bare of the garment in which Fate has draped me.
> You work to kill me with no hope of vengeance,
> As if to kill me is ritual offering to God.

He plies the object of his desires with wine to aid the conquest:

> So drink the wine, though forbidden,
> For God forgives even grave sins.
> A white wine forging bubbles when mixed – pearls set in gold;
> She was on the Ark in Noah's time –
> Most noble of his shipment whilst the Earth was awash ...

After the drinking bout comes the consummation, followed by a final note of triumphant, even brutal, revenge for the pains suffered. Only in the closing lines do we learn his hapless target is a young man:

> Auspicious stars had risen on this night
> When drunkard assaulted drunkard
> We passed the time kowtowing to the Devil,
> Until the monks sounded the bells at dawn
> And a young adolescent left, dragging delightful robes
> Which I had stained with my iniquitous behaviour,
> Saying, 'O woe!' as tears overcame him,
> 'You have torn away the dignity I had preserved.'
> I replied, 'A lion saw a gazelle and lunged at it;
> Such is the variety of Fate's vicissitudes!'

Abu Nuwas' poetry is especially interesting because of the tension between the desires and transgressions of the wine-drinking, youth-chasing libertine and the pious and contrite reflections of the same man when sober. Among his friends and those with whom he crossed swords were some of the brightest poets and writers of the age: Hussain ibn al Dahak, another Bacchic scribe; Muslim ibn al Walid, who celebrated love and the grape; Abbas ibn al Ahnaf, one of Harun al Rashid's favourites and a master of the courtly-love genre. The incomparable Jahiz, the greatest prose stylist of his generation, was supposedly a pupil of Abu Nuwas, as was the towering jurist Al Shafi, founder of one of the four schools of Sunni jurisprudence.

In this circle of poets and writers that reads like a *Who's Who* of Baghdad's literati, Abu al Atahiya (748–825) was one of the most transcendent voices of the Abbasid era. A man from an extremely modest background in Kufa, at one point in his life he was a penniless pot-seller surviving on his wits. He was part of the great brain drain to Baghdad, where his felicitous flair for language caught the attention of the caliph

Mahdi. Somehow, despite getting into innumerable scrapes, and suffering beatings, exile and imprisonment, he managed to keep his head during the reign of half a dozen caliphs.

During the reign of Mahdi, Abu al Atahiya fell violently in love with a beautiful slave-girl called Utba, who belonged to one of the caliph's wives and who moved him to dash off some fairly impudent, albeit forgettable, verse. The unrequited love became a scandal, and the dishonour brought the girl to tears in front of the caliph. He was summoned before Mahdi, interrogated and then ordered to be roundly beaten. This failed to cool the unruly poet's ardour. Twice he received 50,000 dirhams from the caliph as a token of consolation, which would have convinced most men to drop the chase. Not Abu al Atahiya. Once, to mark the Persian New Year, he presented Mahdi with a jar containing a length of cloth scented with musk, a gift for Nawruz. On the cloth were verses imploring the caliph to give him the woman he so passionately craved. Mahdi was on the point of granting the request when Utba cried, 'Commander of the Faithful, treat me as becomes a woman and a member of your household. Would you give me over to an ugly man who sells jars and scrapes a living selling verses?' Mahdi relented, tempering the refusal with the order to fill the poet's jar with coins. The dejected Abu al Atahiya trudged off to the treasury and got into an argument with the secretaries, demanding they fill the jar with golden dinars, not silver dirhams. Utba happened on the hapless poet–lover in the middle of this exchange, Masudi tells us, and was understandably unimpressed. 'If you really loved Utba,' she said, 'you would not be thinking of the difference between gold and silver!'[18]

Perhaps moved by these misfortunes, the temperamental poet once took the decision to renounce poetry and was promptly thrown into prison as a result. Later, he was called before the caliph and made to watch as a man was beheaded. Mahdi turned to Abu al Atahiya. 'Choose either to make verses or to be sent after him,' he said. 'I shall make verses,' the poet wisely replied.[19]

Later he became a great favourite of Harun, accompanying him on one of his pilgrimages to Mecca and, like all court poets, providing panegyrics to order. Great victories on the battlefield became greater still in verse. Harun's repeated campaigns against infidel Byzantium culminated in the expedition of 806, in which the caliph personally led an army of 135,000 against his enemy and seized and sacked the ancient city of Heraclea on the southern shores of the Black Sea, a victory quickly commemorated by the faithful Abu al Atahiya:

> Did not Heraclea intone her death-song once under attack by the
> king whose designs are Heaven-favoured?
> Harun's threats crash like thunder. His chastisements are terrible and
> quick as lightning.
> His banners, oft visited by victory, float like clouds on the breeze.
> You have triumphed, O Emir of the Faithful; see and taste your
> triumph: here is all the booty; and here the road home.[20]

In later life, Abu al Atahiya had the good sense to move away from romantic verse and panegyric, mining a rich vein of more enduring poetry that lingered on the fleeting nature of life and power. Wine poetry did not always mean high spirits and celebrations of unbridled revelry; beneath the surface lay more bitter tastes:

> Men sit like revellers over their cups and drink
> From this world's hand, the circling wine of death.

Masudi recounts the time one afternoon when a courtier discovered Harun sitting in his palace in tears, a piece of paper in his hands. After regaining his composure, the caliph explained he was not crying because of any worldly affairs and threw the piece of paper to the man. On it were the following lines from Abu al Atahiya, written in a beautiful script.

> Will you be warned by the example of him who has left
> His palaces empty on the morning of his death?
> By him whom death has cut down and who lies
> Abandoned by kinsfolk and friends?
> By him whose thrones stand vacant,
> By him whose daises are empty?
> Where now are the kings and where
> Are the men who passed this way before you?
> O you who have chosen the world and its delights,
> You have always listened to sycophants,
> Take what you can of the pleasures of the world
> For death comes as the end.

'By God,' said Harun, 'it is as if these words were addressed to me alone of all men.'[21]

The triumvirate of great Abbasid poets was completed by Bashar ibn Burd (d. *c.* 784), a mercurial figure whose career illustrated the sort of social and geographical mobility open to the brightest and most ambitious men of letters in the Abbasid Empire. It also highlighted the perils of rising to such heights.

On his grandfather's side, Bashar's family hailed from Afghanistan. He made a point in his verse of contrasting his supposedly noble Persian ancestry and sophistication with the uncivilized, camel-following, lizard-eating Bedouin of the deserts. Much as he may have scorned Arab culture, he himself represented a typically Abbasid fusion of the Arab and the Persian, and was another striking example of how cosmopolitan the new empire had become with Baghdad at its helm.

To look at, Bashar might have appeared an unlikely poet to make it to the top in such a competitive environment. Blind from birth, he was fat, ugly and uncouth, with a face disfigured by smallpox. Much of his poetry turned on his love for the ever elusive beauty Abda:

> Long has grown my night through the love of one who I think
>   will not draw near me.
> Never, so long as the light of the stars appears to your eyes
> Or singing-girl chants an ode in the presence of a tippler,
> Will I have found consolation for Abda, love so overwhelms me.
> If her love were for sale, I would purchase it with many properties,
> And were it in my power, willingly in the vicissitudes of affairs
> Would I ransom her from death with everything I possess.
> My beloved reproached me – and the lover abounds in reproaches –
> Because of a tale that the words of a liar carried to her.
> So I tossed sleeplessly, my locks disarrayed,
> Marvelling at her repelling me – and passion abounds in marvels –
> And I said, with tears covering my breast-bones,
> 'If despair for Abda appears, then my bewailer has already arisen.'
> O Abda, for God's sake, set free from constant torment
> A man who, before you came on the scene, was a monk, or
>   like a monk,
> Keeping vigil all the night, considering the consequences.
> Then passion for a ripe wench deflected him from worship,
> A girl the love of whom preoccupied him from the reckoning
>   of the Reckoner,

A lover, whose heart will never repent of yearning for her,
Suffering in his heart as if of the bite of scorpions.
Even so the lover advances the mention of the beloved ones.
And I feared lest my kinsmen should carry out my bier
All too hastily, ere I should see you in any kindliness.
So when you hear one of my kinswomen weeping,
Mourning, amid the black-robed women, one slain by ripe wenches,
Then know that it was the love of you that led me to destruction.[22]

Bashar's ultimate destruction seems to have come not at the hands of his mistress Abda, however, but, as was so often the case with favourites in Baghdad, as the result of prosaic court intrigue and score-settling. We know that at times he let his eloquence get the better of him, and that he was prone to put into verse thoughts that it would have been wiser to keep in his head. Thus he was sufficiently bold and foolish to criticize the caliph Mahdi himself in verses suggesting the Commander of the Faithful and leader of the Muslim world had become a pleasure-seeking wastrel:

Wake up, Umayyads! Your sleep has gone on too long!
Your caliphate has been ruined, O people! Search
For the caliph of God among the tambourines and lutes![23]

He also stood accused by his enemies of heresy, a crime punishable by death. In the end, though, if we believe the historian Tabari's account, it was neither the caliph nor Bashar's religious enemies who were his undoing. In fact, the whole sorry episode looks like a carefully planned execution. Tabari relates how Bashar insulted the brother of Mahdi's minister Yakub ibn Daud. Spoiling for revenge, the furious minister had a word in the caliph's ear and whipped out some verses purportedly by Bashar, accusing Mahdi of having sex with his aunts, calling for his overthrow and demanding that Mahdi's son Musa be 'shoved back up Khaizuran's cunt', a reference to the caliph's beautiful wife.[24] The poet was summoned to explain himself immediately. Yakub, perhaps fearing that his plot would be revealed and Bashar would talk himself out of trouble with a well-turned couplet, took matters into his own hands and had him quietly murdered in the marshes south of Baghdad.

Poets knew who paid their bills; hence the plethora of panegyric. These often overwrought paeans were not confined to praise of the caliph. The great and the good in Baghdad society were also keen to be celebrated in verse. The dramatic fall of the prodigiously rich Barmakid clan at the hands of Harun in 803 occasioned a huge outpouring of apocalyptic poetry, as we have seen.

*

Poetry may have dominated early Abbasid culture in Baghdad, but music was not far behind. The two were as often as not united by distinguished poet-singers, none more so than Ibrahim al Mosuli, his son Ishak and the prince Ibrahim ibn al Mahdi, son of the third Abbasid caliph Mahdi and a short-lived caliph himself (817–19). Writing in the fourteenth century, half a millennium after this cultural heyday, the magisterial historian Ibn Khaldun wistfully recalled, 'The beautiful concerts given at Baghdad have left memories that still last.'[25] There was no doubt that the courts of Mahdi, Harun, Amin and, to a lesser extent, Mamun were 'the high point of ancient Arab musical culture'.[26]

Music at the court of the Abbasid caliphs catered to the most refined tastes as well as to the most crude. There was a pronounced ambivalence to the art form, born of the religious establishment's condemnation of the moral depravity with which it was so often associated. The caliph Mahdi, though a musical devotee, forbade his youthful sons Hadi and Harun to spend time with singers, an order subsequently followed more in the breach than in the observance.

For clues as to why this was so, we can turn to the great Jahiz, who provides a window into the alluring world of music in Baghdad. He left us a compelling portrait of the singing slave-girl, whose seductive talents went far beyond the musical. 'The singing slave-girl is unlikely to be true and loyal in love, for both by temperament and training she is disposed to set traps and spread nets to catch lovers in their toils,' he warns his readers.[27] Such a girl flirts with her admirer, looks longingly at him, drinks with him 'with gusto', feigns grief at his departure, writes him romantic verses, gives him a lock of hair, presents him with a belt and some sweets at Nawruz, or a ring and some apples at Mihrajan. Sometimes this is genuine, but, Jahiz continues, 'for most of the time she is not straightforward, but employs treachery and wiles to suck her victim dry and then abandons him.' The singing slave-girl routinely plays rival lovers off against each other. 'Had the devil no other fatal wiles, no other badge, and no other seductive charms, singing slave-girls would assuredly meet his purpose.'

Jahiz goes on to explain why these singers were so highly valued:

> [What] makes singing slave-girls fetch such extraordinary prices is simply the desire they arouse ... three senses are involved, not to mention the heart, which makes the fourth: sight, in the contemplation of a beautiful and appetizing slave-girl – for skill and beauty are only rarely found together for the delectation of patrons taking their ease; hearing, as the share of the man who simply enjoys the pleasure of listening to a musical instrument; and touch, in lust and the urge for sexual gratification ... Thus time spent in the company of singing slave-girls entails the most perilous enticement.

Only the finest imaginable line, therefore – and many thousands of dinars – separated the singing slave-girl from the concubine. According to Jahiz, the cleverest girls knew 4,000 songs, each of two to four lines, none of which mentioned God unless inadvertently. 'They are all on such subjects as adultery, procuring, love, youthful dalliance, yearning desire and amorous passion.' From a monarch's point of view, certainly not the stuff of a princely education. Hadi and Harun should have been gaining a knowledge of religion, Arabic language, poetry, philosophy, traditions of justice and good manners – not quaffing wine and enjoying music with these temptresses.

Not all songs, of course, were designed to stir such dangerous passions. The great singer Ibrahim al Mosuli told a tall story of Harun al Rashid bringing together singers in his palace one evening for a special performance in front of the senior members of the court. Having drunk his fill of wine, he ordered a certain air to be sung. The singer Ibn Jami stepped forward and gave his rendition, but Harun was not satisfied. One by one the singers performed, but still Harun was not happy. The singer Miskin of Medina was then invited to try his luck, and astonished Harun with the beauty of his song, so much so that he was ordered to sing it again. Emboldened by the caliph's reaction, Miskin told the caliph how he had once been a slave and tailor with a passion for singing, forced to pay his master a daily tax of two dirhams, after which he was free to pursue his own business. One day he heard a black woman singing a song so entrancing he pleaded with her to teach it to him, which she agreed to do only in return for two dirhams, leaving him unable to pay his tax. 'Son of a whore!' his owner shouted, giving him fifty beatings with the rod and shaving his head and beard, a punishment so severe it made him forget the song. The next day he gave the woman another two dirhams to remind him of it, but then in desperation asked for them back. The woman refused, telling him the four dirhams he had spent would be worth 4,000 dinars from the caliph. To avoid another beating, the trembling slave confessed all to his master and sang him the song, a performance so heart-rending he was spared all tax until his hair had grown back.

'I don't know which I like better, your story or your song,' Harun laughed, 'but I do want to ensure that the black woman's promises are fulfilled.' And so off went Miskin with 4,000 dinars from the caliph.[28]

Like the great poets of the age, the leading singers and musicians were celebrities, some of them spectacularly rich. The life of Ibrahim al Mosuli, as told by Abu al Faraj al Isfahani, author of the monumental *Kitab al Aghani*, or *Book of Songs* (which runs to more than 10,000 pages), offers a classic rags-to-riches story. Ibrahim, who is forever popping up in Masudi, rose from provincial obscurity and a life on the road singing with travelling musicians to make ends meet (one story even has him as a highway robber) to the height of fame and fortune in Baghdad, once his talents had been spotted by passing government officials in the Persian town of Ray and the southern Iraqi city of Basra. Plucked from the regions to adorn Mahdi's court, he and his son Ishak became leading luminaries of Baghdad's cultural scene. Ibrahim directed his musicians with a baton and may have been the first-ever orchestra conductor. Mahdi may not have liked Ibrahim's louche behaviour – the singer was a noted wine-lover, the caliph a dedicated teetotaller – but he had the sense nonetheless to recognize, preserve and reward such uncommon talent, as did his sons and successors, Hadi and Harun, who maintained his patronage.

Ishak estimated that by the time of his death his father had spent 24 million dirhams in the course of his lifetime, in addition to his monthly salary of 10,000 dirhams. Unlike the parsimonious founder of Baghdad, Ibrahim was almost recklessly generous and often entertained great crowds with wine-soaked feasts. No wonder that when he died he was worth just a little over 2,000 dinars. Ishak also prospered. Al Isfahani noted how Princess Ulaya, Harun's half-sister, bought poems from him for 40,000 dirhams to pass off as her own. Like a good member of the Abbasid ruling family, she threatened to have him killed if he ever revealed the truth.

Singers were accompanied by small ensembles consisting of no more than half a dozen musicians, separated from the caliph by a curtain to preserve the dignity and privacy of the monarch. Such politesse was not always scrupulously observed, however, particularly when the caliph and his courtiers were in their cups and the singers were dark-eyed girls swaying seductively in the candlelight. This was a characteristically Abbasid take on the age-old combination of wine, women and song.

Pride of place in such a group was the four-stringed *oud* (from which the English word 'lute' is derived). Then there was the *tunbur*, or mandolin, the stringed instrument, we may recall, that Mansur ordered to be broken over the hapless eunuch's head. Wind came in the form of the charismatic *mizmar*, or reed pipe, like the lute an instrument widely used in Arab music today. If required, percussion came from the *tabl* drum and the *duff* tambourine.

We hear of one occasion when the famous singing-girl Arib sang with the princess Ulaya, the poet-prince Ibrahim ibn al Mahdi and their brother Yakub, who accompanied them on a wind instrument. Arib was much taken by the skill of her royal counterparts. 'I have never heard anything like their singing before and I know I never will again,' she recalled.[29] Today, although many of the lyrics of the songs have survived, together with a good deal of biographical information about the poets and singers, no storehouse of Abbasid music exists, because no system of notation was ever devised.

*

While poetry and song were most prized and tended to receive the greatest accolades during the flowering of Abbasid culture in Baghdad in the eighth, ninth and tenth centuries, in time prose writing emerged also, not least as the most appropriate medium through which to make and record the great strides in the arts and sciences. Both within the translation movement and without, there was an explosive surge in philosophy, history, geography, theology, law, maths, medicine and astronomy. We have already noted how the arrival of paper stimulated a new affection for the written word. It also provided a fillip to the art of calligraphy, in which Baghdad was, once again, a pioneer. Amongst the greatest practitioners were Ibn al Bawab, Ibn Mukla (a vizier who was rewarded for his service to three caliphs by having his right arm

amputated for conspiring against the authorities) and Yakut al Musta-
simi, who created their own schools of calligraphy.

The rise of prose was given an electrifying boost by the prolific polymath Jahiz ('The Goggle-Eyed', *c.* 776–*c.* 868), a prodigiously talented
scholar from a modest background in Basra, who gravitated to Baghdad in the early years of the ninth century under the intellectually
appealing caliphate of Mamun. For Gaston Wiet, the late French scholar
of Islamic civilization, Jahiz was 'probably the greatest master of prose
in all Arab literature', a writer possessed of 'exceptional genius'.[30] His
best-known work among the 231 titles recorded in the latest catalogue
of his works was *Kitab al Hayawan*, the encyclopedic seven-volume
Book of Animals, which drew heavily on the works of Aristotle.[31] Some
of his keenest followers today argue it contained the seeds of what a
millennium later became Darwin's theory of natural selection. The
breadth of his writing was typically Abbasid, ranging from the superiority of black men over whites, pigeon-racing and Islamic theology to
miserliness, the Aristotelian view of fish and whether women should be
permitted to make noises of pleasure during sex. His reaction to some
unkind reviews of one of his books will strike a chord with many writers: 'A group of scholars at once got together to disparage it, impelled
by their devouring energy, even though they knew the book was first-rate
and represented exceptional value. They do this especially when a book is
dedicated to a prince with power to promote or downgrade, to humble
or exalt, to inspire ambition or fear: then they really let themselves go,
like camels in rut.'[32] Highly discursive, anecdotal and revelling in para-
dox, Jahiz was never less than entertaining. Viziers, chief judges and
other members of the Baghdad court competed to pay him substantial
sums in return for dedications in his many works. Had it not been for
his remarkable ugliness and bulging eyes, he might have secured more
extravagant patronage from the caliph Mutawakil, who had considered
making him tutor to one of his sons. As it was, Masudi recorded Jahiz
as saying, 'When the Caliph saw me he found my physical appearance
so repellent that he had me given 10,000 dirhams and sent me away.'[33]

Abbasid Baghdad wasn't all poetry, prose and music. In the ninth
century the city emerged as the intellectual and scientific powerhouse of
the world. We have mentioned the House of Wisdom. Outside its hallowed sanctuary other individuals also made profoundly important

contributions: the Banu Munajim, a courtly family of astronomers and astrologers, opened the Khizanat al Hikma, or Treasury of Wisdom, a library-cum-hostel for scholars. Yahya, one of the family's most brilliant scientists, wrote the first known Muslim-authored astronomical manual.

The trio of Banu Musa brothers, Mohammed, Ahmed and Hassan, pushed forward the boundaries of science in the ninth century, building on the foundations laid by the classical world with their work in geometry, astronomy and engineering. They also were deep-pocketed scientific patrons, commissioning expeditions from Baghdad to Byzantium to bring back new manuscripts for translation and employing teams of translators who received attractive salaries of 500 dinars – something like £15,000 today – a month, equivalent to the pay of senior bureaucrats. Translations became tokens of social advancement in their own right, commissioned by caliphs and ambitious viziers, courtiers, military commanders and Christian administrators.

Amongst the Banu Musa circle was the one-time pagan money-changer Thabit ibn Kura (c. 836–901), who studied with them and became one of the greatest mathematicians of the age, author of at least thirty works on maths and astronomy, and translator of Archimedes, Euclid, Ptolemy, Diophantus and Nichomachus.

Towering over the scientific field within the House of Wisdom was Mohammed ibn Musa al Khwarizmi (d. c. 850), a master of arithmetic and astronomy. Dedicated to Mamun, his groundbreaking work *Al Kitab al Mukhtasar fi Hisab al Jabr wal Mukabala* (*The Compendium on Calculation by Restoring and Balancing*) bequeathed the dread term algebra, scourge of children's schooldays for more than a thousand years, and was also a key conduit for the passage of Arabic numerals into the medieval West. Another of his works, *The Book of Addition and Subtraction According to the Hindu Calculation*, took advantage of the more advanced Indian system of reckoning made available to Baghdad's translators and introduced for the first time the decimal system of nine numerals and a zero, 'the tenth figure in the shape of a circle'.[34] Within a century it led to the discovery of decimal fractions, which were then used to calculate the roots of numbers and calculate the value of pi to sixteen decimal places. Readers who would prefer to forget the horrors of quadratic and linear equations can remember Khwarizmi instead in the word 'algorithm'. The astronomical tables he compiled, known in

Arabic as *zij* after the Persian word *zik* for 'guiding thread', were like-wise landmark scientific achievements, used in the Islamic and later the Christian world for centuries, together with his work on the astrolabe. They are the oldest extant Islamic star tables and enabled users to pin-point the position of the sun, moon and five visible planets, tell the time using stellar or solar observations and predict sightings of a crescent moon – all critical discoveries for the Islamic calendar with its five daily prayers and lunar months.[35]

The biographer Ibn Khallikan described the Banu Musa's painstak-ing experiment undertaken at the behest of Mamun, who wanted to test the accuracy of the ancients' measurement of the world's circumference at 24,000 miles. Off they trooped to the large, level plain of Sinjar, north-west of Baghdad, hammered a peg attached to a line of cord into the ground after measuring the altitude of the Pole Star, and walked due north in a straight line, fastening new pegs and cords as the lines ran out, until they reached the spot where the elevation of the Pole Star had risen by a degree. The distance between the first and last points was 66²/₃ miles. The process was then repeated to the south. Since each of the 360 degrees equated to 66²/₃ miles, the total circumference of the world was therefore 24,000 miles, exactly as the ancients had calcu-lated (the precise figure is actually 24,902 miles). The fastidious Mamun promptly sent them to the plains around Kufa to repeat the experiment. 'They found that the two calculations agreed and Mamun acknow-ledged the truth of what the ancients had written on the subject,' Ibn Khallikan reported.[36]

With scientific results coming in from two astronomical observato-ries, together with confirmation of the earth's circumference and steady progress in both algebra and geometry, the time was ripe for Mamun to commission his famous world map. The Atlantic and Indian oceans became open bodies of water, rather than Ptolemy's landlocked seas. The length of the Mediterranean was refined to 50 degrees of longitude (Ptolemy had estimated it at 63 degrees), much closer to the true figure. *Surat al Ardh* (*Picture of the Earth*), a treatise from the same time, detailed the latitudes and longitudes of more than 500 cities, categoriz-ing towns, mountains, rivers, seas and islands in separate tables, each with precise coordinates in degrees and minutes. Sadly Mamun's world map does not survive, although there have been tantalizing and unveri-fied claims that a fourteenth-century reproduction exists in Istanbul's

Topkapi Museum, but 'the important contribution of al-Mamun's cartographers to the development of the field of mathematical geography cannot be overestimated'.[37]

Drawing on the studies of Philo and Hero on mechanics and pneumatics, Ahmed, the middle brother of the Banu Musa, composed *Kitab al Hiyal, The Book of Ingenious Devices*, an entertaining and mechanically sophisticated guide to making all sorts of machines, including those designed to separate water from wine. It includes what may be 'the earliest example of a programmable machine' in the form of a robotic flute player, which Ahmed called 'The Instrument that Plays by Itself', a complicated creation that uses variations in air and water pressure through conical valve regulators to produce different sounds.[38]

In the field of medicine, the community of Nestorian Christians, together with their Muslim descendants, held sway, with none more illustrious than Hunayn ibn Ishak (808–73), who came originally from the ancient Christian city of Hira in southern Iraq. After working as a translator for the Banu Musa and a stint studying in Byzantium, he returned to Baghdad, where he put together his own stable of translators and earned the highest seal of approval when he was appointed head translator in the House of Wisdom and chief doctor to the caliph Mutawakil. He was precociously talented. At the age of seventeen he translated *On the Natural Faculties*, one of many titles by the second-century Graeco-Roman physician Galen, whose scientific theories dominated European medicine for 1,500 years. Hunayn went on to translate many more Galen works, including *On the Anatomy of Veins and Arteries* and *On the Anatomy of Nerves*. These highly accessible translations of Galen and Hippocrates were amongst his most lasting contributions to medical science, though he was a distinguished scientist and author in his own right, particularly in the field of ophthalmology. His *Ten Treatises on the Eye*, written around 860, includes one of the first ever anatomical drawings of the human eye and is considered 'the first systematic textbook of ophthalmology'.[39]

A well-heeled scholar, Hunayn appears to have followed an enviably sybaritic routine in Baghdad, if Ibn Khallikan's account is anything to go by. A daily ride was followed by a visit to the *hammam*, where he had hot water sloshed over him. After a glass of wine and a biscuit, he lay down to dry off and had a snooze. Then came fumigation with expensive perfumes and a dinner of chicken in gravy, accompanied by a loaf of bread weighing half a kilo, a routine that brought on another agreeable doze. No sooner had he woken up than Hunayn dined on Syrian apples and quinces, apparently washed down with an eye-watering two litres of old wine. Ibn Khallikan makes no mention of time devoted to study.[40]

Another giant in the medical world was Razi (c. 854–c. 935), the great physician and philosopher, practising doctor and author of numerous medical tomes, including studies of smallpox and measles. Known more widely in the West as Rhazes, today he is considered the greatest physician of the medieval world. His careful classification of substances into the four groups of animal, vegetable, mineral and derivatives of the three, outlined in his *Kitab al Asrar* (*Book of Secrets*), represented a departure from the mysteries of pseudo-philosophical alchemy in favour of laboratory experiment and deduction. It thereby prepared the way for the future scientific classification of chemical substances. In *Al Shukuk ala Jalinus* (*Doubts about Galen*), Razi gave short shrift to the Greek theory of the four humours, which subsequently re-entered the medical mainstream through the work of Ibn Sina (Avicenna) in the tenth century. It has been said that, were he alive today, Razi would be 'dumbfounded' to see notions of the four humours persisting within the field of alternative medicine, given his 'passionate condemnation of medical quackery and its dangers'.[41] His understanding of the nature of time as absolute and infinite, requiring neither motion nor matter to exist, was itself ahead of its time and has been likened to Newton's much later theories. When it came to religion and reason and possible contradictions between the two, Razi was radically uncompromising. The following passage represented a succinct summary of his views, only too relevant to the history of Baghdad:

> If the people of religion are asked about proof for the soundness of their religion, they flare up, get angry, and spill the blood of whoever confronts them with this question. They forbid rational speculation, and strive to kill their adversaries. This is why truth became thoroughly silenced and concealed.[42]

From the late tenth century, Baghdad medicine boasted the Bimaristan Adudi, a peerless hospital and medical school built on the ruins of Mansur's Khuld Palace in West Baghdad, famed throughout the world for three centuries and named after the Buyid prince and ruler of the city, Adud ad Dawla. Such was its success that a new quarter quickly sprang up around it.

In the midst of this intellectual ferment in Baghdad, a world in which both arts and sciences flourished spectacularly, the Arabs for the first time explored philosophy. Abu Yusef Yakub al Kindi (c. 800–c. 873), who won distinction as the first 'Philosopher of the Arabs', bestrode the scene in this pioneering field. Kindi, a nobleman of Yemeni origin who was later tutor to the caliph Mutasim's son Ahmed, sought to harness the corpus of Greek knowledge, especially Aristotelian philosophy, to develop Islamic theology. Although he himself could not read Greek, he gathered around him other scholars who could and it was he, more than any other ninth-century scholar in Baghdad, who was responsible for introducing Greek philosophy to the Muslim world. An open-minded thinker, he embraced a rational approach to religion that made him enemies amongst the more cloistered, less intellectually adventurous *hadith* scholars. They were entrenched in their opposition to the pre-eminent role he awarded the intellect in approaching God and deeply suspicious of the Christian company he, like a number of other philosophers, kept for professional and personal reasons. He was the prolific author of 250 works, from his landmark treatise *On First Philosophy* to writings on Archimedes, Ptolemy, Euclid, Hippocratic medicine and, as if that were not eclectic enough, glass manufacture, music and swords. His studies of early Islamic weapons are formidable records in themselves.

There seemed no limit to Kindi's intellectual interests and achievements. He was also a pioneering cryptographer who devised new ways of making and breaking codes and is credited today with establishing what became known as the frequency analysis method, in which variations in the frequency of letters or groups of letters can be analysed to break a particular code. As the Islamic world's first theoretician of music he added a string to the Arab lute, made pioneering advances in musical notation and even attempted to cure a quadriplegic boy through the use of music therapy.[43] In the words of Al Nadim, tenth-century author of the *Fihrist*, or *Catalogue*, a fascinating survey of the literary, scientific and intellectual elite, he was 'the distinguished man of his time and unique during his period because of his knowledge of the ancient sciences.'[44] Today his name is celebrated in Baghdad's Al Kindi Teaching Hospital in Rusafa, north-east of Al Rashid Street.

*

Mamun's reign, a cultural and intellectual highpoint for Baghdad, also marked the end of the most glorious chapter in Abbasid rule. After the halcyon half-century from Mansur's foundation of Baghdad in 762 to the death of Harun in 809, the rupture between Amin and Mamun prefigured a slow decline. The conflict, which shattered the fabric of much of the city and marked the end of western Baghdad as its political and social heart, was the first outbreak of widespread, explosive violence, establishing a pattern of fighting, bloodshed and, in many instances, maniacal cruelty that would recur throughout the history of the City of Peace.

When selecting the site for his new imperial capital, Mansur had been determined to avoid the plague of malaria that was so prevalent in the swampy stretches of southern Iraq. And yet, although he succeeded in this ambition, it was the virus of violence that ultimately proved endemic in Baghdad, far deadlier than any mosquito-borne disease, and carried off untold numbers during the fourteen centuries of the city's life. Dynastic struggles, political assassinations, sectarian strife, torture and execution, all flourished in Abbasid Baghdad, harbingers of the rivers of blood that ran into modern times. All that was missing, at this early stage, were the series of foreign invasions and occupations that would shake – and, during the most apocalyptic visitations, raze – the city to its foundations from the thirteenth century to the present day.

After Mamun succeeding caliphs saw their power steadily ebb away to Turkish military commanders, originally recruited as a loyal personal force of slave-soldiers by his successor and half-brother Mutasim (833–42), son of Harun and the slave-girl Marida. Like the Mamluks of the Ottoman Empire, whom they anticipated, these *ghulams*, as they were known, grew in power until it was they, rather than the caliph, who exercised real authority.

For Baghdad, having basked in imperial splendour since the time of Mansur, the next sixty years from Mamun's death were a humiliating affront. In 835 Mutasim shifted his capital a hundred miles north along the Tigris, building a new city at Samarra, from where he and the next seven caliphs ruled until 892. This dramatic move was partly a reaction to the growing tensions in Baghdad between the local population – especially the elite military class, or *abna* – and the thousands of Turkish *ghulams* that Mutasim had recruited from the steppes of Central Asia and resettled in the city. Baghdadis were resentful of the hordes of Asiatic interlopers, who charged through the streets of the capital on horseback and knocked down anyone, including women and children, in their way; the *ghulams* challenged the established order with sharp-elbowed haste and grabbed lucrative court positions, despite being unable to speak Arabic. Clashes broke out on the streets and in the barracks, and there were a number of murders. And there were additional reasons for local jealousies. The talents of the youthful *ghulams* were by no means limited to the battlefield; they made themselves attractive to the Abbasid courtiers in a variety of ways. 'The same boy could be at once slave, guard, muse and bedfellow to his master.'[45]

Unlike Baghdad, by now a mature city, the new site of Samarra offered unlimited land on which to accommodate the troops. In time, it would prove rather more advantageous to them than to the caliph, as the leader of the Abbasid Empire increasingly became a prisoner in his own palace. With the capital moved to Samarra, Baghdad meanwhile suffered the indignity of being ruled by a series of governors. This dramatic loss of political power and prestige might have been tolerable if it had ushered in a peaceful life for the people of Baghdad, but it did not. In 865, only half a century after the devastating first siege and fratricidal war, the city once more found itself under attack. Following a mutiny in Samarra, the caliph Mustain retreated to Baghdad, leaving behind a court that promptly swore an oath of allegiance to his cousin Mutazz, son of the caliph Mutawakil.

War broke out again. Mohammed ibn Abdalla ibn Tahir, the governor of Baghdad, prohibited river traffic from Baghdad in order to cut off Samarra's food supply from the south. Fortifications began in earnest, and a huge protective wall was raised around both East and West Baghdad, completed on 22 February. Trenches were dug and gates built to shelter the cavalry. The streets were a cacophony of barked orders, armoured soldiers rattling this way and that to shore up defences, panicking families preparing to flee, merchants and booksellers, perfume-makers and coppersmiths, locking up their shops amidst the din of constant hammering from carpenters and engineers constructing catapults and siege engines, giant machines that would be hauled into place on the walls and towers girdling the city.

Shammasiya Gate in north-eastern Baghdad bristled with an arsenal of mangonels, the largest of which was known as Al Ghadban, the Angry One. Baghdadis braced themselves for another deadly and financially calamitous confrontation. The cost of these initial defences was 330,000 dinars, according to Tabari, who provided an almost daily record of the ten-month siege. A long-term cost, for both Baghdad and Iraq, was the terrible damage done to the agricultural infrastructure, following the governor's order to destroy bridges and to flood the canals in the Al Anbar district to prevent a Turkish attack from the north-west. Mesopotamian empires had always been founded on the fertility of the Land between the Rivers and this in turn required a rigorously maintained irrigation network.

Tahir ordered a special draft to defend the city from which few were spared. Tabari recorded an instance of a surprised, possibly incandescent, party of pilgrims from Khorasan, innocently en route to Mecca, press-ganged into the army, together with 'vagabonds' armed with nose-bags filled with rocks and shields made of tar-covered mats. The weapons for the irregular forces were later upgraded to clubs studded with iron nails, which were still a scant match for the professional Turkish army commanded by Mutazz's brother, Abu Ahmed, who positioned his force of up to 12,000 outside the Shammasiya Gate on 10 March. Most of the siege was limited to skirmishes and counter-attacks, with stout defence mounted by both the professionals and irregulars. On 21 March the Baghdadis charged the Turkish camp, looting their belongings and driving many of the attackers into the Tigris, where troops in river boats cut them down. Skiffs piled high with heads unloaded their bloody cargo, which was then hung up on bridges or on top of the walls of Tahir's palace. Tabari says 2,000 of the 4,000-strong Turkish force were killed in this single engagement, a victory rewarded with bracelets for those soldiers who fought valiantly and expensive silk brocade robes for their commanders. 'Anyone reaching the palace of Mohammed with the head of a Turk or Maghribi was given fifty dirhams,' Tabari noted.[46]

Amongst all the interminable attacks and counter-attacks that he reported, Tabari also included some of the more bizarre or tragicomic aspects of the stand-off. At the Shammasiya Gate, for example, a key location that saw the lion's share of the fighting, he wrote about the attacker who threw a grappling hook over the wall and scaled the defences, only to have his head hacked off and catapulted back into the Turkish camp, prompting a hasty and disgusted retreat. Another time, as a North African soldier was scaling the city walls, a Baghdadi defender mistakenly yelled 'Victory to Al Mutazz!' instead of Mustain, an excusable error, one might think, given the frequency with which the caliphate changed hands during the 860s. Alas, the unfortunate man was killed on the spot by his fellow defenders, who considered him an enemy spy. His head was sent to Tahir, who ordered it to be displayed in public above a bridge, notwithstanding the pleas of his mother and brother, who wanted it back. Most outlandish of all was the archer at the Shammasiya Gate faced with a belligerent North African who would routinely approach the gate, bare his backside and fart at the defenders while hurling abuse at them. 'One day,' the Baghdadi recalled, 'I selected an arrow for him, and shot it right through his anus. It came out at his throat as he fell dead.'[47] His body was taken and hung up for public display. Rarely in the annals of conflict has there been such demonstrable need for a rearguard.

For the people of Baghdad, however, there was nothing amusing about the war that raged about them. On 8 September the Turks smashed through the Anbar Gate fortifications on the west bank and poured into the once thriving Harbiya quarter, destroying the shops and workshops of the water-wheel workers and torching everything as they advanced. There was ferocious hand-to-hand fighting in the streets, which once again ran with blood. Another counter-attack saw the Turks withdraw back to their camp, leaving their comrades' decapitated bodies where they lay. Tahir ordered the Anbar Gate to be bricked up to prevent another such incursion. By 24 November, the exhausted population of Baghdad had had enough, and they demonstrated in front of the governor's palace, shouting, 'Hunger! Hunger!' and demanding food in protest at the soaring prices. A month later crowds surged on to the streets again, calling on Tahir either to fight the Turks or sue for peace. Riots broke out, and crowds liberated the women's prison. On 27 December, following the arrival of five boats from Samarra carrying a cargo of flour and other supplies, a rumour swept across the city that Tahir had ousted Mustain as caliph in Baghdad and transferred his allegiance to his adversary Mutazz, the caliph in Samarra. The common people were unimpressed by such brazen opportunism and swarmed through Baghdad, breaking down the gates of his palace, only to be rebuffed by 300 soldiers outside his inner sanctum. Tahir then went through the motions of demonstrating his loyalty to Mustain. In what must have been an extraordinarily dramatic moment, the caliph appeared on the roof of his palace, clad in the Prophet Mohammed's hallowed black cloak and clutching the ceremonial spear of office, assuring the crowds he was under no duress, with Tahir very much in evidence by his side.

Yet the wily governor continued his secret negotiations with Abu Ahmed. By 7 January the talks were official, held in a sumptuous red pavilion pitched outside the city walls. In the Friday prayers on 25 January, Mutazz was announced as the new caliph. Mustain was granted exile in the Hijaz, but he was never allowed to take it. In October, having been ordered to go to Samarra under military escort, he was intercepted by an official known as Said the Gatekeeper and beheaded, together with his old nanny. The gatekeeper was given 50,000 dirhams for the assassination and promoted to chief of security in Basra. Mustain's head was sent to Mutazz. 'Put it there,' the caliph commanded, refusing to interrupt his game of chess.[48] After the game ended, he looked at the head to make sure it was indeed Mustain and ordered it to be buried. Mustain was not the first caliph – or indeed ex-caliph – to be murdered, and he would certainly not be the last.

4

The Later Abbasids: Farewell to *The Meadows of Gold* (892–1258)

Was Baghdad not the loveliest of cities,
A spectacle that held the eye spellbound?
Yes, she was all that. But now her beauty
Is worn away. The north wind of fate
Has made her a desert.
Her people have suffered as have so many before.
She has become an object of pity to nomad and settler.
O Baghdad, city of kings, goal of all desires,
Centre of all the learning of Islam,
Paradise on earth, you who sought wealth and gave
Birth to hope in every merchant's breast,
Tell us, where are they whom once we met
Among pleasure's flowery roads?
Where are the kings, shining amidst their trains
Like brilliant stars?
Where are the kadis, resolving by reason's light
The conundrums of the Law?
Where are the preachers and poets with their wisdom,
Speaking harmonious words?
Where are your gardens rich in charm, the palaces
Along the river banks, the flourishing land?
Where are the royal pavilions I once knew,
Glittering with jewels?

The poet Ali ibn Abi Talib, quoted in Masudi,
The Meadows of Gold

In 892, in an effort to escape what had become the nightmare of Samarra, where the Turkish amirs routinely crowned, dethroned and dispatched caliphs, Mutadid (892–902) returned the caliphate to Baghdad, its home for the remaining 350 years of Abbasid power.* Mutadid, the nephew of Mutazz, was a compulsive palace-builder, launching a prolific reconstruction effort after the damage wrought by the second siege. He chose to live in Jafar's Dar al Khilafat palace complex on the east bank, enlarging it monumentally and laying out new gardens over areas compulsorily purchased and cleared. A second palace, the Kasr al Firdus, or palace of Paradise, sprang up, complete with a park for wild animals (of which more later) and artificial lake. His third palace, a couple of miles to the east on the Musa Canal, was the Kasr al Thuraya, Palace of the Pleiades, which Masudi tells us was connected by an underground passage, two miles long, to the Hasani Palace, originally built by Jafar, in the heart of the caliphal complex, allowing the women of the imperial household to come and go between the palaces with complete discretion, free from the gaze of prying eyes. Mutadid's final palace, or at least its foundations, was the Kasr al Taj, the Palace of the Crown, which in time became the chief official residence – a gilded cage – of the Abbasid caliphs.

Although power was steadily ebbing away from the Abbasid caliphs, as they declined from masters of the civilized world to puppet-rulers maintained in luxurious seclusion within the caliphal complex under virtual palace arrest, their political decline did not entail a parallel architectural decay in Baghdad. On the contrary, as the tenth century unfolded, the caliphs' diminishing sway saw them become masters of little more than their palaces and gardens, enabling royal energies to be redirected exclusively to their beautification. The city remained a sight to behold.

This is evidenced, above all, in travellers' accounts of their visits to Baghdad, one of the earliest and most remarkable of which comes from John Radinos the Patrician and Michael Toxaras, ambassadors dispatched by Zoe, empress of Byzantium, to discuss peace terms with the caliph Al Muktadir in 917, after years of conflict between the rival

---

* The Samarra-based caliphs met their end in varying levels of discomfort. The methods of execution included decapitation (Al Mustain); being bled to death with a poisoned lancet (Al Muntasir); dying of thirst while locked up in a small room without food or water (Al Mutazz); testicular crushing (Al Muhtadi).

empires. The story of their diplomatic mission is told by Khatib al Bagh-dadi, the eleventh-century historian of the city.

Muktadir (908–32), hemmed in by domestic rebellions of his foreign guards, harried by Byzantines and outlying provinces breaking away from the caliphal sway, from Mosul in the north to the Karmathians surging up from Arabia in the south to invade Kufa and Basra, was determined to stage a show of strength and glory before his peace-seeking Greek guests. All the way from the Shammasiya Gate in the north-east of the city to the Dar al Khilafat complex of palaces on the east bank, mounted troops drawn up in two lines sat astride sumptuously capari-soned chargers on saddles of gold and silver, behind lines of parade horses. Behind the troops, as one moved towards the caliph's palace, came the rows of pages of the privy chamber and palace servants, ele-gantly uniformed with swords and ornamental girdles. And five types of beautifully ornamented Tigris boats – the *shadha*, *tayara*, *zabzab*, *zal-lala* and *sumayriya* – as well as assorted skiffs, barques, barges and wherries, were drawn up in formation on the river.*

It was July, and rolling waves of heat shimmered beneath a cerulean sky. The markets and streets, roads, rooftops and balconies of eastern Baghdad heaved with people desperate for a glimpse of the mysterious infidels from foreign lands and the reception afforded them, with shops and rooms overlooking the route rented out at great cost. Would the ambassadors be respectfully greeted and handsomely entertained, before leaving with purses stuffed with gold and silver? Or would they be forced to kneel on a leather mat before the caliph, stretch out their necks and await the blade of the royal executioner? International diplo-macy was a life of unpredictable extremes.

* Since the time of the Sumerians 4,000 years earlier, the Tigris had known a series of trad-itional boats, some of whose designs had barely changed over the millennia. Most popular in Baghdad were the round, bowl-like *guffas*, characterful vessels made of plaited reeds, waterproofed with bitumen inside and out, steered by ladle-like oars, bobbing from one bank to the other in endless motion. Viewed en masse, each weighed down by as many as half a dozen sheep, a dozen Baghdadis, a couple of donkeys and a family's worldly goods wrapped in myriad bundles, or stacked high with bristling sheaves of reeds, they were a striking sight, likened by one writer to 'a thousand huge inverted tar bubbles'. Then there were the *kalaks*, rafts set on a platform of inflated goatskins – the sort of craft considered by Herodotus to be 'the most marvellous thing in the country' bar Babylon (*Histories*, 1.194). Last but not least were the long narrow *bellum* punts, slender, high-hulled *mahayla* cargo-boats with sloping masts, long *shahtur* barges and a picturesque procession of smaller sailboats of various shapes and sizes.

Ushered into the palace of the chamberlain Nasr al Kushuri, the Greek ambassadors were overcome by the magnificence of the setting and the size of his retinue, 'seized by awe and fear', mistakenly thinking this must be the caliph. On they went to the palace of the vizier, Ibn al Furat, a place of even greater splendour, which once again they thought could belong only to the caliph. The vizier sat in an audience room between the Tigris and the palace gardens, hung with brocade curtains and lined with fine carpets, surrounded by servants armed with maces and swords. After a tour of this palace, the ambassadors, by now transfixed, their dread mounting by the moment, were shown into the caliph's presence. Muktadir sat on his throne, flanked by his children. It was, says Khatib, 'a sight that struck them with fear'. The diplomats were promptly dismissed.

In another version of the story, preserved by the eleventh-century court historian Hillal al Sabi, the Byzantine envoys were detained in Tikrit for two months before being allowed to proceed to Baghdad, where they spent a further two months awaiting an audience with the caliph, while he embellished his palace and arranged his furniture to his liking. When the order to appear before him was at last given, 160,000 cavalry and infantry lined the route to the caliph's palaces. After a brief audience, the envoys were given a tour of the palace, staffed by eunuchs, chamberlains and Negro pages. There were 7,000 eunuchs (4,000 white, 3,000 black, Khatib recorded), 700 chamberlains and a further 4,000 black pages. The finest textiles, gathered from across the empire, showed the sophistication and opulence of the Abbasid court:

> The number of curtains which hung in the palaces of the Caliph al Muktadir totalled 38,000. These consisted of brocade curtains embroidered with gold, and magnificently adorned with representations of goblets, elephants, horses and camels, lions and birds. The curtains included large drapes of single and variegated colours from Basinna, Armenia, Wasit and Bahnasa, as well as embroidered drapes from Dabiq ... There were 22,000 rugs and carpets from Jahram, Darabjird and Dawrak. They were placed in the corridors and courtyards where the generals and the Ambassadors of the Byzantine Emperor passed.[1]

This total of 22,000 carpets did not include the choicest rugs from Tabaristan and Dabik, hung in the alcoves and audience halls because they were too valuable to walk upon.

Next on their itinerary was Khan al Khayl, Khan of the Cavalry, a peristyle court adorned with marble columns. On the right side stood 500 horses with saddles of gold and silver, on the left another 500 with brocade saddle-cloths and long head-covers, each animal attended by a smartly turned-out groom. Walking down a series of halls, they passed into the caliph Mutadid's astonishing Park of the Wild Beasts, where animals approached them, sniffed the visitors and ate from their hands. In a court nearby they were introduced to the spectacle of four elephants covered in peacock-silk brocade. Mounted on each beast were eight men from Sind, together with fire-throwers, the sight of which 'caused much terror to the Greeks'. Further zoological surprises awaited the startled envoys, who were already struggling with the heat. First, they were led into a court containing a hundred lions, fifty to the right, fifty to the left, every animal 'collared and muzzled with chains of iron' and handled by a keeper.

There was no indication that this compulsory tour of Baghdad was drawing to a close, and the envoys shot each other discreet, quizzical looks. Next, they were taken to New Kiosk Palace, a pavilion set in manicured gardens. At its centre was a dazzling pool of water in tin, 'more lustrous than polished silver', measuring 30 cubits by 20. Four boats floated serenely upon it, resplendent with gilt seats adorned with brocade and gold work of Dabik. Surrounding the lake were rolling gardens containing 400 palm trees, each 5 cubits high, their trunks encased in carved teak wood encircled with rings of gilt copper, their branches bearing dates in almost every season. Beyond the garden were groves of lemons, oranges and many other fruits.

However impressive the textiles, however splendid the gardens and exotic the wild beasts, the Greeks were more taken by another object. They were led to the Palace of the Tree, named after a tree made of solid silver and gold, weighing an extraordinary 500,000 dirhams, or more than 1.5 tons. 'The tree had eighteen branches, each containing numerous twigs on which were perched gold and silver birds, of many species. The branches, most of which were made of silver, though some were of gold, swayed at given times, rustling their many-coloured leaves, the way the wind rustles the leaves of trees, and each of the mechanical birds would whistle and sing.' The diplomats were more astonished by this precious marvel than by anything else they had seen.

The giddy palace-hopping continued with a visit to yet another royal

1. Detail from an Abbasid Koran by the great calligrapher and illuminator Ibn al Bawab, Baghdad, *c*. 1000. During its Abbasid heyday Baghdad became the unrivalled centre of Arabic calligraphy. Ibn al Bawab, one of the most illustrious Arab calligraphers, perfected a number of elegant cursive scripts. His school of calligraphy lasted until Baghdad was sacked by the Mongols in 1258.

2. 'Sit at dinner tables as long as you can and converse to your hearts' desire, for these are the boon times of your lives,' wrote the tenth-century cookery writer Ibn Sayyar al Warrak. A ninth-century Abbasid blue and white dish with fish design and leafy spray.

3. A tenth-century astrolabe, made in Baghdad by Ahmad ibn Khalaf, epitomising the sophistication and beauty of Abbasid science. Among its many uses was determining the precise direction of Mecca, towards which the faithful would direct their prayers. In the Abbasid Empire during the ninth and tenth centuries more discoveries were made in astronomy, mathematics and medicine than in any previous period of history.

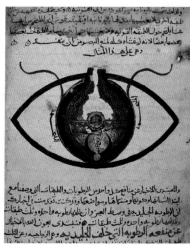

4. The striking tomb of Zumurrud Khatun, wife of the caliph Al Mustadi (reigned 1170–80) and mother of the caliph Al Nasir (reigned 1180–1225). Small holes cut into the dome produce a glowing light inside the vault.

5. An anatomical drawing of the human eye by Hunayn ibn Ishak (808–73), doyen of Abbasid scientists and chief translator in Baghdad's House of Wisdom.

6. The gracious inner courtyard of Mustansiriya University, founded in 1233 by the penultimate Abbasid caliph Al Mustansir (reigned 1226–42), and one of the few remaining Abbasid monuments in Baghdad. Because most Abbasid buildings were constructed from sun-baked and kiln-fired mud bricks rather than stone, any that survive, including this one, have been heavily restored.

7. Soldiers file before the Turkic warlord Tamerlane (1336–1405), presenting him with the severed heads of Baghdadis. According to the chronicles, Tamerlane had his army build 120 towers containing 90,000 skulls after taking Baghdad in 1401. From a sixteenth-century edition of Sharaf al Din Ali Yazdi's *Zafarnama* (Book of Victory).

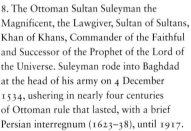

8. The Ottoman Sultan Suleyman the Magnificent, the Lawgiver, Sultan of Sultans, Khan of Khans, Commander of the Faithful and Successor of the Prophet of the Lord of the Universe. Suleyman rode into Baghdad at the head of his army on 4 December 1534, ushering in nearly four centuries of Ottoman rule that lasted, with a brief Persian interregnum (1623–38), until 1917.

9. A genealogy depicting the Prophet Mohammed and the Rashidun, the four 'Rightly Guided Caliphs' (as Sunnis refer to the first four caliphs), produced for Ottoman Turkish patrons in sixteenth-century Baghdad. Mohammed, his face veiled, is surrounded by the Rashidun, beneath his grandfather Abd al Mutalib. To the left is the pre-Islamic Persian king Anushirvan (reigned 531–579).

10. A leaf from a 1224 Arabic translation of the first-century *De Materia Medica* (*The Pharmacy*) of Dioscorides. A wealth of medical, scientific and philosophical texts from the Ancient Greek and Roman worlds were translated into Arabic in Baghdad at the apogee of the Abbasid Empire.

11. The eighth-century caliph Harun al Rashid, one of the central figures in *The Arabian Nights*, with his barber. Persian miniature from a fifteenth-century manuscript of Nizami's *Khamsa* (*Five Poems*). In 1184 the Andalusian traveller Ibn Jubayr was told there were 2,000 public baths in Baghdad. In 1327 the great Moroccan traveller Ibn Battuta remarked approvingly on the city's 'numerous and excellently constructed' baths.

12. The Mongol conqueror Hulagu (1218–65), grandson of Genghis Khan, forces the last Abbasid caliph Al Mustasim to eat gold. This thirteenth-century illustration from Rustichello da Pisa's *Books of the Marvels of the World* is based on Marco Polo's colourful story of Mustasim's execution.

13. Hulagu's scorched-earth sacking of Baghdad in 1258, the most shattering blow the Muslim world had ever suffered, brought five centuries of Abbasid rule to a bloody end. The Tigris was said to flow black from the ink of all the books hurled into the river.

14. A fifteenth-century Persian miniature of the Tigris. Flooding, invariably followed by plague, was a regular and destructive feature of life in Baghdad, killing untold numbers of Baghdadis over the centuries. It was only brought under control with the construction of bunds and other flood defences in the first half of the twentieth century.

residence, in which there were rugs and ornaments beyond counting, bar the 10,000 gold breastplates noted by Khatib. Down they trooped a hallway 300 cubits long, on either side of which hung pieces of armour: leather shields, helmets, bucklers, cuirasses, coats of mail, ornamented quivers and bows. Stationed in rows to the right and left were 2,000 black and white eunuchs.

All in all, the drooping ambassadors were forced to tour twenty-three palaces in the spirit-sapping heat of high summer. But at last, after all these sunlit palaces and gardens, the stunning textiles and wild animals, the priceless metal tree, the parades of cavalry and foot-soldiers with their snorting chargers and extravagant armour, in short, after all the relentless ostentation that Baghdad could muster, the exhausted and suitably awed envoys were taken before the caliph Muktadir for an audience in Kasr al Taj. Three sons sat to his right, two to the left. 'He was wearing a tall *kalansuwa* hat and clothes from Dabik, embroidered with gold. He sat on an ebony throne overlaid with Dabik cloth again embroidered in gold.' To the right of the throne hung nine jewelled necklaces like prayer beads, to the left another seven necklaces of super-sized gems, 'the largest of which eclipsed the daylight with its sparkle'.

The senior Greek envoy, standing before the caliph with arms crossed in humility, said he would kiss the carpet according to custom if the caliph so wished. (When the Iraqi ambassadors made a reciprocal visit to Byzantium, they would only be required to bow before the empress.) The audience lasted an hour. Then Muktadir personally handed his 'long and detailed answer', addressing the question of paying ransoms for captive Muslims in Byzantine hands, to the senior Greek, who kissed it in honour. The ambassadors were then led from Bab al Khassa, the Private Gate, directly to the river, from where they sailed upstream to the palace where they were lodging. On arrival, they were given a gift of fifty purses of money, each containing 5,000 dirhams – this was evidently no occasion for the royal executioner. Their guide Abu Omar was given a robe of honour and a horse. Munis, the eunuch in charge of the caliph's armies, was given 120,000 gold dinars to pay the ransoms and departed, purses clinking, with the Greeks. The diplomatic mission in Baghdad was over.

The Byzantine ambassadors saw Baghdad on the eve of the caliphate's collapse as a political power. While the caliphs remained, physically at least, at the heart of Baghdad life, improving their palaces and designing their gardens, real power was held by the Turkish amirs, who vied with each other to control central Iraq and the revenues it produced, while further afield local chiefs and warlords competed for power, acknowledging distant Abbasid authority with polite letters of deference at best.[2]

Muktadir presided over the caliphate's last gasp as an independent power. The signs of fracturing authority were not difficult to discern. A year after he came to the throne, a Shia Fatimid caliphate was declared in Tunisia; and in 931 the deposed Umayyad Dynasty from Damascus established a rival caliphate in Spain and Portugal. Civil wars and sieges had torn apart much of the landscape, ruining the elaborate irrigation system on which the fertile Land between the Rivers depended to sustain a vast, unified empire. Breached during a military campaign, the mighty Nahrawan Canal, 200 miles long by a quarter of a mile wide, was never properly repaired.[3] By 969 the Fatimids, a Shia dynasty that ruled North Africa from Cairo until the late twelfth century, had taken Egypt.

*

Just as architectural innovation survived political decline, so literary life managed to flourish. Amongst the ranks of prose writers who stamped their mark on the age, the Baghdad-born historian Masudi, as we have seen, left a fascinatingly human, three-dimensional and frequently gossipy portrait of the life of the caliphs, their courts and the cultural revolution; his *Meadows of Gold* is a precious legacy that he bequeathed to future generations. In 'A Conversation with the King of Nubia', Masudi shows the Abbasids debating the qualities of their predecessors: 'At a gathering before Mansur . . . the conversation turned to the Umayyad Caliphs, their conduct, the policies they followed and the reason their power was stripped from them. Mansur said: "Abd al Malik was an arrogant tyrant who did not care what he did. Sulayman's only ambition lay in his belly and balls. Omar ibn Abd al Aziz was like a one-eyed man among the blind. The only great man of the dynasty was Hisham . . . But then their power passed to their effeminate sons, whose only ambition was the satisfaction of their desires and who chased after pleasures forbidden by Almighty God."'[4]

Then there was Ibn Kutayba, the ninth-century philologist, grammarian, historian, literary critic and man of letters; Ibn Durayd (837–933), the charismatic, wine-drinking grammarian, philologist and critic who famously fell off his roof one night and broke his collar-bone, probably after one too many goblets; Suli, the tenth-century memoirist, chess supremo and *nadim* to several caliphs; Yakubi, the ninth-century geographer who left us a riveting picture of the founding of Baghdad.

Abbasid Baghdad was no place for a prude. Poets and writers cele-brated and engaged with the bawdier side of life with a gusto that would make many of their modern counterparts squirm in embarrassment: the titles of the aristocratic author and courtier Ibn al Shah al Tahiri included *Stories about Slave-Boys*, *Adultery and Its Enjoyment* and *Masturbation*.[5] Masudi tells the story of the poet-prince Ibrahim ibn al Mahdi on a boat bound for Mosul one day with his half-brother Harun. The caliph asks him which is the most beautiful of all names. Moham-med, his brother replies, tactfully adding that Harun is the next most pleasing. Harun asks him which name is the most hateful. Ibrahim, his brother replies. Harun is shocked. Apart from Abraham, the name is also shared with the Prophet Mohammed's son. That's why he died young, Ibrahim shoots back, going on to list several famous Ibrahims, all of whom were 'killed, flogged or exiled'. Just then one of the sailors in the royal party shouted out, 'Hey Ibrahim, suck your mother's cunt! Row!'[6] Harun's brother rested his case. The caliph laughed, Masudi tells us, and shook with joy.

Al Tanukhi (*c.* 939–*c.* 994), a retired judge who lived in Baghdad, was the author of the strong-flavoured multi-volume memoir *Kitab Nishwar al Muhadara wa Akbar al Mudhakara* (*The Table Talk of a Mesopotamian Judge*), replete with purportedly true stories of clandes-tine incest, gay and lesbian affairs, enterprising pimps and forgers, wily ministers and ice vendors, ingeniously cruel tortures and executions, extravagant caliphs and concubines, even an instance of cannibalism during a famine in Baghdad. 'Advertising Merchandise', a classic Tanukhi story, typically revels in bawdy humour:

A famous funny Baghdadi man was slowly going down the Tigris in a boat when he passed by a palace overlooking the river with some beauti-ful concubines sitting on its terrace. They started teasing him and he had an immediate erection. He wanted to return their compliment so he pulled up his dress, exposing his rampant staff, and cried like a vendor: 'Fresh asparagus!' One of the girls immediately reciprocated by pulling up her dress, exposing her genitalia, and crying in the same manner: 'Hot oven bread!' All of the nearby fishermen and spectators started blowing raspberries at them.

The following tale, 'A Woman from Hell', is vintage Tanukhi. It makes the Oedipus myth seem positively tame, telling the hideously compelling story of a promiscuous Baghdadi woman with an insatiable sexual appetite who develops an obsession with her handsome son and is determined to act upon it.

The servant told the woman to put the fear of God in her heart and to be content with the other men she was having, but she insisted her wish be fulfilled. When the servant inquired how the young man could be enticed into doing such a thing without creating a scandal, she was told by the woman to go to a scribe in the neighbourhood who composed very eloquent love letters and to ask him to write a letter to her son, brimming with burning emotion, in which she asked him to meet her. She told the servant that the letter should mention the name of their neighbour's pretty daughter. The servant went ahead and delivered the letter to the youth, whose heart was infatuated with the girl. He replied, asking her to meet him and telling her that he didn't have a place where they could meet. The woman instructed the servant to reply to him, saying that she did not have a place to meet either and that she would come to his house. She told the servant to prepare an empty room, fill it with fruits and perfume it. She told the servant to inform him that the neighbour's daughter was a shy young girl who could not bear to be seen in daylight and thus would come at night and stay with him in the darkened room for fear of being seen by any passer-by. Such arrangements were made, and the woman, after seeing her husband off to bed, bathed and perfumed herself, put on her finest clothes and came to the room at night. The youth arrived a little while later and made hot and burning love to her all night until dawn, when he slipped out, and the servant accompanied the woman to her quarters. Sometime later she informed her servant that she had become pregnant by her son and asked for advice, which the servant could not offer. She kept on having sex with her son until she was due to give birth. She then feigned sickness to her husband and asked for his permission to go to her mother's house to be properly nursed. He acquiesced and she went there and stayed with her servant in a separate room, where a midwife came and helped her give birth. She choked her newborn, disposed of its body and returned home a few days later. She wanted to repeat her previous trysts with her son regardless of her servant's protests. Her previous ploy was repeated, and, again, she became pregnant by her son. This time she gave birth to a lovely girl, who was given to the servant to dispose of. The servant could not commit such a crime and gave her to some poor folk who raised her as their own. The mother rewarded them generously on a regular basis, and the young girl was reared in prosperity. Her real mother would see her from time to time whenever she missed her.

The young man got married, to the despair of his jealous mother, and the relation was severed. When the young daughter was nine years old her mother concocted another of her diabolical tricks in which she claimed that she had 'bought' the child as a slave and that she wanted to raise her as her maid. The girl grew up in luxurious surroundings, learned singing and excelled at it. When she reached puberty her mother feared that she might leave the house if she got married to a stranger and thought that the best way to keep her under her wing was to marry her to her son, the girl's father. She contrived another scheme in which the ever-faithful servant convinced the youth's wife that a handsome young soldier who lived next door was madly in love with her and wanted her to answer his love letters. At first she was scoffed at by the young wife, but after persistent efforts the wife relented and answered the forged letters. This was used as material evidence of her marital infidelity and the mother convinced her son to divorce her and he agreed. She also convinced him to marry her young slave-servant and gave him the dowry. He did so and they had children. She is his current wife.[7]

As if this isn't bad enough in itself, the story is being told in front of the abused young man, who astonishingly is hearing it for the first time. Needless to say, he divorces his wife-daughter on the spot. 'He laid his deep curses upon his mother and her pimp of a servant and went away in shame and deep distress,' Tanukhi tells us.

*

Literature, sexually explicit or otherwise, was by no means the only form of entertainment available. Men and women in Baghdad, as everywhere, loved a spectacle. We hear of the occasion when the caliph Mutawakil had five million lightweight dirhams struck in red, yellow and black to mark a festival. He had 700 servants decked out in contrasting colours, and on a windy day they gathered in a domed pavilion with forty doors open to the elements. When the courtiers had encircled him, he ordered them to scatter the multicoloured coins, creating a beautiful, unforgettable scene.

Popular culture catered to this fundamental desire to be entertained in all sorts of ways. Horse-racing, heavily patronized by caliphs and their courts, was wildly popular amongst the upper echelons of Baghdad society. Mansur's son Mahdi built the first *maydan*, a hippodrome, thirty years after the founding of the city. His successors were equally supportive. Amin had one built within Mansur's palace grounds, and his brother Mamun built one specifically for polo within Harun's palace complex. Mutasim had a bottle-shaped racetrack at his Jawsak Palace, while Mutawakil had an ornate, nine-roomed kiosk built from which he would watch the races in comfort. Masudi recorded a happy day for Harun, when his horse came in first, and that of his son Mamun second: a classic father-and-son scoop. In the tenth century the Buyid ruler Muizz al Dawla set up a tree at the racecourse with valuable prizes hanging temptingly from the branches and purses of dirhams clustered around its trunk. The afternoon reverberated to the sound of heavy drums and flutes as Muizz presented the victors with robes of honour. While winners were given these handsome robes, the horse that came in last often suffered the indignity of having a monkey with a whip placed on its back; the lashing of the unfortunate creature was a humiliation for owner, jockey and steed alike.

Then, as now, the horse enjoyed huge status in the Arab world, reflected in an extensive body of Abbasid literature on genealogy, hippology, racing, farriery and the like. The Prophet Mohammed, an accomplished equestrian, considered his enemy's horses part of the rightful booty of battle, and cavalry had been fundamental to the lightning success of the Arab conquests. Although gambling was prohibited by Islam, bets were authorized on horse-racing, archery and foot-racing. Horse-racing may have been too aristocratic a pursuit for the masses, but the common man could content himself with laying wagers on races of dogs, mules, donkeys and, inevitably, camels.

Polo, the king of sports and the sport of kings, was first popularized by Harun, together with archery tournaments, and ball and racket games. He was the first of the Abbasid caliphs to play chess – or at least its precursor, *shatranj*, which reached the Arabs from India via Persia – and backgammon. Once he was forced to strip off his clothes after losing a bet on a game of backgammon with the musician Ibrahim al Mosuli. The popularity of chess, meanwhile, was such that merchants gave slave-girls special training in it to increase their value. We know that Arib, the famous slave-girl of Amin and then Mamun, was prized for her skills at the game, as well as for her legendary beauty and musical talents.

Pigeon-racing was also a hit, and once again the caliphs led the way. Mahdi, Harun, Wathik and Nasir were compulsive pigeon-fanciers and helped to drive up the prices of the most favoured birds to extraordinary heights. 'Pigeons have such a high intrinsic value and such superiority that a single bird may sell for 500 dinars,' Jahiz wrote. 'No other animal can command such a price, neither the goshawk, the peregrine falcon, the saker, the eagle, the pheasant, the cock, the camel, the ass or the mule ... A pair of pigeons is as productive as a landed estate; indeed it will cover the living expenses of a family and bring in enough to allow it to pay off its debts, build fine houses and buy highly profitable shops. At the same time it is a wonderful hobby, a pleasing sight, an education for thinking men and a clue for those given to looking into things.'[8]

The sport was not without its controversies. From time to time the government was moved to order the demolition of rooftop dovecotes to preserve the modesty of women living nearby from peeping Toms, or to put an end to the noise of pigeon-trainers chucking stones at their charges up on the roofs. Enterprising thieves even took to using pigeons as cover for their burglaries, releasing them on to rooftops, then clambering across houses in feigned pursuit.

Animal fighting cut across class divisions and also across the zoological world, from cocks, partridge and quail to the gorier spectacles of dogs, rams, buffaloes and even lions. Some streets in Baghdad, such as the Street of Rams and Lions, paid tribute to this form of entertainment. We hear of the caliph Mutasim organizing a bloody contest between lions and buffaloes that aroused considerable criticism. Tabari tells us how the short-lived reforming caliph Muhtadi (869–70) ordered all the lions in the palaces to be killed and the dogs removed, one reason amongst many for his prompt assassination (he was said to have had his testicles crushed, an excruciating death even by the standards of the

Abbasids). Another time, we are told, Mamun was unable to command the attention of his palace servants, their minds fixed on something much more important than a bossy caliph: a particularly compelling cock-fight.

Wrestling drew great crowds. Some of the more physically adventurous caliphs provided the lead. Amin was a keen wrestler, outdone only by Mutadid, who once fought and killed a lion, albeit by running it through with a sword.

Preachers contended with street hawkers, storytellers and comedians for public attention. Masudi wrote of a famous street storyteller called Ibn Maghazili, who regularly entertained crowds with amusing stories and imitations of Bedouins, gypsies, Turks, eunuchs and Meccans amongst others, peppered with 'all kinds of jokes that would make a mourning mother laugh and amuse a serious man as much as a child'.[9]

The theologian Ibn Akil described the liveliness of Baghdad in the eleventh century. 'The inhabitants appeared to be in a state of continual celebration, not lacking in occasions for the circumcision of an infant boy, or the marrying of a woman. And on Saturdays, there were the assemblies for the modulated recitations of the Quran from the pulpits, fencing and wrestling shows, and boat racing.'[10]

One of the most popular – and gruesome – spectacles of Abbasid Baghdad took place on the three pontoon bridges across the Tigris, which regularly played host to public executions. Rebels were crucified in front of huge crowds, their heads hung on poles to deter other would-be challengers to Abbasid power. We have seen how, in 803, Harun had the body of Jafar cut into three pieces and gibbeted on each of the city's bridges. In 902 Mutadid ordered the body of a rebel known as Wasif the Eunuch to be partially embalmed in resin and hung up, next to its severed head, on one of the bridges, where it remained slowly rotting for more than ten years.*

*

---

* The bridges had their other uses for criminals too. Tanukhi recorded how 'A well-known forger of bonds, letters and official deeds was spotted on a windy day in the middle of Baghdad's main bridge writing on a piece of parchment. When asked what he was doing, he replied that he was forging a letter by a paralysed man whose handwriting was shaky because of his illness. To perfect his forgery he chose the wind-swept bridge in order to give the document a "shaky effect".'

Natural trials and tribulations occasionally added to the city's difficulties. In 940 the dam in the Euphrates at the head of the Isa Canal was breached, causing a great flood that left the worst affected Baghdadis homeless for two years. A year later, Khatib recorded, a powerful storm wreaked havoc on the city and during a night of 'torrential rain, awesome thunder and terrible lightning' Mansur's old palace in the Round City, one of the defining symbols of Abbasid Baghdad with its landmark green dome, was struck by a thunderbolt and destroyed on the spot. "The adjoining mosque was damaged at the same time. Its pulpit, dating back to Harun al Rashid, was rescued and installed in a new mosque.

The year 945 was an ominous landmark for Baghdad. It marked the first time an outsider had occupied the city. Taking advantage of the breakdown of government, Ahmed ibn Buya, the son of a self-made military leader from the mountains of Daylam by the Caspian Sea, seized power from the caliph Mustakfi and took the title of Amir al Umara, Commander-in-Chief. He was also known more evocatively as Muizz al Dawla, the Support of the Empire. Although this represented another humiliation for the depleted Abbasid family, the arrival of a new Shia Buyid Dynasty, which endured for a century, proved something of a boon for Baghdad. First and foremost of his lasting legacies was the construction of a huge dyke, which prevented flooding from streams flowing into the Tigris on the east bank in the Shammasiya lowlands, a defence that was still visible in parts 350 years later. Such a dyke was not entirely altruistic: it enabled Muizz al Dawla to set about building a new complex of palaces on the east bank that stretched across the Shammasiya and Mukharrim quarters, and that came to be known as the Dar as Sultana, or House of the Sultanate. His first palace must have been spectacularly opulent. It was reported to have cost 13 million dirhams, calculated by the historian Guy Le Strange to be worth around £500,000 in 1900, or around £50 million today.[12]

With time and money on their hands, the Abbasid caliphs were allowed by their new masters to indulge their own passion for palace-building, the caliph Al Muti (946–74) adding the Dar al Tawawis, or Peacock Palace, the Murabba Square and the Muthammana Octagon to the caliphal complex. By the closing decades of the tenth century, this palatial enclave of the Abbasids occupied as much land as the entire city of Shiraz.[13]

Muti provided a sobering, if self-pitying, illustration of just how far

Abbasid political power had declined, as evidenced in the following letter he wrote to the Buyid prince Izzud al Dawla, in which money was demanded to finance another *jihad* against the Greeks.

> The Sacred War would be incumbent on me if the world were in my hands, and if I had the management of the money and the troops. As things are, when all I have is a pittance insufficient for my wants, and the world is in your hands and those of the provincial rulers, neither the sacred war nor the pilgrimage nor any other matter requiring the attention of the sovereign is a concern of mine. All you can claim from me is the name which is uttered in the *khutba* [the sermon given during Friday prayers] from your pulpits as a means of pacifying your subjects; and if you want me to renounce that privilege too, I am prepared to do so and leave everything to you.[14]

Among the most celebrated buildings of the Buyid era was the Bimaristan Adudi Hospital, built by Adud al Dawla (ruled *c.* 949–83) in West Baghdad on or around the ruins of Mansur's Palace of Eternity on the banks of the Tigris.[15] The Andalusian geographer, poet and traveller Ibn Jubayr, who arrived in Baghdad in 1184, described the hospital as a prodigious institution, with numerous rooms and wards and all the facilities of a royal residence, where doctors visited the patients every Monday and Thursday to assess them and to prescribe treatments. It was one of the leading hospitals and medical schools in the world, if not the pre-eminent. However effective the water defences, nature could still have its way, as in 1074 and 1159, when the whole hospital was flooded, and again in 1174, when, after forty days of non-stop rain in the Mosul region of northern Iraq, the waters rose so high that boats were able to enter the empty doorways and windows. Although the damage would have been extensive, it was clearly not irreparable, given Ibn Jubayr's admiring account of a decade later. His observation that the hospital was well supplied with water from the Tigris almost looks ironic.

For a snapshot of Baghdad in the mid to late tenth century we must turn to a trio of brilliant minds, the first three Arab geographers of the Middle Ages: Istakhri, writing in 951, Ibn Hawkal, who edited and expanded on Istakhri's work in 978, and Mukaddasi, whose *The Best Divisions for Knowledge of the Regions* was written in 985. Istakhri and Ibn Hawkal reported that in their time most of eastern Baghdad consisted of palaces, those of the Abbasid caliphal complex, as well as the later Buyid additions to the north. Taken together, these two sets of palaces stretched five miles downstream from Shammasiya in what must have been a very arresting sight. In effect, the east bank of the Tigris had become one vast royal enclosure. East Baghdad, as far as the people were concerned, was gradually shifting downstream, reflecting a similar movement on the west bank, where quarters were dissolving into townships and villages. The unitary Abbasid metropolis, vast in scale, imperial in pretension, was evolving into a much more compact and less mighty city. Istakhri counted three great Friday mosques – two in East Baghdad and the mosque in Mansur's Round City in west Baghdad – with Ibn Hawkal adding a fourth at Baratha, West of the Round City. Palaces aside, both Istakhri and Ibn Hawkal emphasized the ruin predominant in many once flourishing quarters, in contrast to Karkh, which remained the richest and best-maintained district, where many of the city's most successful merchants worked. Istakhri estimated the east–west length of the city at five miles.

Full of praise for Mansur's choice of location for his capital city, Mukaddasi nevertheless lamented Baghdad's decline from its apogee of imperial splendour. Only recently it had been 'the most beautiful possession of the Muslims, a most splendid city', yet was 'now falling into ruin and disorder, its splendour departed'. This he attributed to the straightforward loss of political power: 'the authority of the khalifs declined, the city deteriorated, and the population dwindled. The City of Peace is now desolate: the Mosque alone is frequented on Fridays, and otherwise the whole place is deserted. The most populous areas there now are Katiat al Rabi and al Karkh on the western side and on the east Bab al Tak and the neighbourhood of the palace of the Amir.' Mukaddasi was certainly not going to give his readers a rose-tinted portrait of Baghdad. 'I did not find it agreeable, nor anything to admire in it; if I have praised it, it is only in conventional terms,' he sniffed, noting that the city of Fustat in Egypt (which was founded in the seventh century and later absorbed by Cairo) was then what Baghdad had been in its heyday.

Despite his disapproval of what the city had become, Mukaddasi still admired the people's 'wittiness, charm, refinement and correct scholarship', apart from the 'vagabonds', in whom 'depravity was rife'. Sartorially, he was also impressed. 'The people here like to dress well,' he wrote, noticing the 'elegant and varied apparel': clothes made of silk and fine calico, the lofty turbans and the *taylasan*, a pointed black hood or stole thrown over the head and shoulders and worn by men of distinction. Like so many visitors to Baghdad, he was much taken by the beauty of the life-giving Tigris and its river traffic: 'Boats are continually sailed up and down stream, and with considerable skill. At Baghdad the people come and go and cross the river by these vessels: there is constant bustle and stir. Indeed, two-thirds of the charm of Baghdad derives from this river.'

Yet his overwhelming impression was still negative. Proof that every generation thinks the country is going to the dogs, Mukaddasi opined that, 'Day by day the town is going from bad to worse: truly, I fear it will become like Samarra, what with the corruption, the ignorance and immorality, and the outrageous oppression of the ruler.'[16]

The picture drawn of eleventh-century Baghdad by Khatib was more mixed:

There is no city in the world equal to Baghdad in the abundance of its riches, the importance of its business, the number of its scholars and important people, the distinction of its leaders and its common people, the extent of its districts, the width of its boundaries, the great number of its palaces, inhabitants, streets, avenues, alleys, mosques, baths, docks and caravanserais, the purity of its air, the sweetness of its water, the freshness of its dew and its shade, the temperateness of its summer and winter, the healthfulness of its spring and fall, and its great swarming crowds. The buildings and the inhabitants were most numerous during the time of Harun al Rashid, when the city and its surrounding areas were full of cooled rooms, thriving places, fertile pastures, rich watering-places for ships. Then the riots began, an uninterrupted series of misfortunes befell the inhabitants, its flourishing condition came to ruin to such an extent that, before our time and the century preceding ours, it found itself, because of the perturbation and the decadence it was experiencing, in complete opposition to all capitals and in contradiction to all inhabited countries.[17]

To these geographical perspectives of tenth- and eleventh-century Baghdad must be added the very different gastronomical insights of the cookery writer Ibn Sayyar al Warrak because while the most elevated Abbasid minds certainly needed food for thought, they also required something for the stomach. It was no accident that Baghdad – in addition to being Oum al Dunya, or the Mother of the World – acquired the nickname Surrat al Bilad, Navel of the Nations, around this time.

Cookery and cookery writing had started to emerge in the ninth century. The greatest culinary treasure came a century later, in the 940s or 950s, in the form of al Warrak's *The Book of Cookery: Preparing Salubrious Foods and Delectable Dishes, Extracted from Medical Books and Told by Proficient Cooks and the Wise*. Al Warrak's foreign publishers evidently thought this too pithy a title, for the surviving Istanbul manuscript bears the additional subtitle: *The Book of Winning a Lover's Heart and Sparing Him the Need for a Doctor*.

Al Warrak was no trifling amateur. His book is the earliest known and most important culinary record from medieval times anywhere in the world. It contains 615 recipes culled from more than twenty cookbooks by or for caliphs, princes, doctors, and political and literary grandees. More than this, it deals with the best kitchen utensils and ingredients to use, offers a bewildering range of pre-prandial cold snacks, dishes cooked in stoves served with hot bread, porridges and bean dishes, meat stews, braised and fried dishes, and omelettes. There are recipes for outdoor cooking in the *tannur* oven, on the grill and on the spit. Also included are hangover cures, not to mention dishes to improve sexual performance, such as a chickpea drink that 'warms up [the] stomach and kidneys, expels dense excretions and invigorates coitus' and an asparagus dish favoured by Mamun and Ibrahim ibn al Mahdi for the same purpose.[18] Al Warrak even caters for those who suffer from 'wind and flatulence', for whom he recommends a medicinal paste of ginger, Ceylon cinnamon, white cumin, spikenard (related to valerian), honey and dried rose petals.[19]

Al Warrak compiled five recipes for salt alone, including a laxative salt that is also apparently good for gout, facial paralysis, arthritis and spleen-related ailments (rock salt mixed with black pepper, ginger, dried hyssop, asafoetida leaves, celery seeds, Indian leaf, agaricus, scammony resin, garden-cress seeds and safflower seeds). There are rich and refreshing desserts, special recipes for the sick, an array of drinks, both non-alcoholic and the stronger stuff, from sun-fermented raisin wine, date wine and honey wine to rice beer, almond beer and mead.

Food was a cornerstone of Baghdad culture high and low, seen in its most opulent and exotic forms at the caliph's palace banquets; but the city's eateries for the common man were sometimes so popular that the caliph himself would insist on going to them for impromptu downmarket dinners. We know that Mamun went in disguise to a well-known place specializing in *judhaba*, meat roasted in the *tannur*, suspended on a pan of sweet bread-pudding. His courtiers were aghast at such vulgarity and told the caliph that this was food for the masses. 'The commoners drink cold water like we do. Should we abandon it to them?' the caliph replied icily.[20]

The enjoyment of food in a convivial setting was held to be a good thing in and of itself, blessed by no less an authority than the Prophet's grandson Al Hasan bin Ali bin Abi Talib, whose charming injunction was quoted approvingly by Al Warrak in his cookery book: 'Sit at dinner tables as long as you can and converse to your hearts' desire, for these are the boon times of your lives.'[21]

Amongst the most popular recipes were those for Nabatean chicken, named after the indigenous people of Iraq, such as this one, called Nibatiyya, from Ishak al Mosuli:

> Add two plump boned chickens to the pot with onion, sweet and mellow olive oil, soaked and bruised chickpeas and a stick of cassia. Bring to the boil twice, then add a large piece of cheese and salt. Spice with coriander seeds, black pepper, cassia, galangal, spikenard, cloves, nutmeg and ginger, all pounded. Then add noodles with rose water, together with boiled eggs. Simmer until noodles done. Ladle into a bowl. Remove cheese and eggs, cut into pieces and arrange around the boned chicken. You may add a handful of rice and smoked strips of meat. That would be a good thing to do, delicious and scrumptious, God willing.[22]

Ishak al Mosuli was so taken by his recipe he composed an elegy to it:

> Nibatiyya with chicken, as pure as ivory it looks.
> Eating it on a cold winter day is far more beneficial than
>   eating sikbaja.
> Swaying like the waves is the fat swimming on its face,
> Like a luminous full moon shining through its lofty mansion.
> The eggs are stars twinkling from a distance through the dark.
> The egg yolk, sitting in the midst of its white, as beautiful as pure
>   khaluk put in glass.
> The cheese bits showing through are like beaded pearls
>   set on a crown.[23]*

---

* *Sikbaja* was a very popular stew, especially beef soured with vinegar. *Khaluk* was women's perfume, yellow from saffron.

Meat stews were hugely popular. *Sikbaja* was prized at the grandest tables in Baghdad as well as at the most humble. Amin told his uncle Ibrahim ibn al Mahdi that he craved the famous beef *sikbaja* cooked by Ibrahim's slave-girl Bida, made with extra lamb, kid's meat and poultry. 'All he desired was to eat that dish and drink after it until he got intoxicated.'[24] Bida duly obliged, making a landmark *sikbaja* garnished with many types of sausage, sliced sandwiches, thin meat patties, filled pastries, vegetables, herbs and decorations. Amin was so delighted he sent the girl a necklace worth 30,000 dirhams. To his uncle he dispatched three cases of the finest perfumes, three boats, three bags of money and the following verses:

> Here comes Bida with her dish, looking like a garden in spring.
> Approaching thus, the dish looks clad in gowns of light.
> Bursting in colour and aroma, as if from a perfumer 'tis just been
> fetched,
> Emitting scented whiffs and steam, carried by a damsel dazzling
> the eyes with sheen.
> Gorgeous with eyelashes like daring knives of fire in hearts of men.[25]

Cooking was by no means the exclusive preserve of women. Indeed it was an essential accomplishment for the ideal Abbasid man. Expertise in the kitchen was so prized that an aspiring *nadim* had to be able to master at least ten exotic dishes. Masudi tells us that the caliph Mutawakil once smelled an appetizing *sikbaja* stew being cooked by a sailor and asked to try some: it was the most delicious he had ever tasted. There were even Abbasid precursors to the reality television cooking contests of today: cook-offs presided over by as august an authority as the caliph. Mamun and his brother Mutasim were especially fond of such events. Masudi wrote of a competition during Mamun's reign when a random passer-by was hauled off the streets of Baghdad one night and invited into the palace to taste the rival recipes. The man, 'one of the common people', was then given dishes prepared by Mamun, Mutasim, a Greek and the chief *kadi*, Yahya ibn Aktham, without knowing who had cooked which. Fortunately for him, when he tasted the caliph's recipe, he was impressed. 'Well done!' he cried. 'You would think it was all made of musk. The man who produced this must be a very clever cook – clean, imaginative and elegant.' The dishes by Mutasim and the Greek proved equally palatable. When it came to the *kadi*'s offering, however, the common man's judgement was forthright. 'Ugh! By God, whoever cooked this used shit instead of onions!'[26] The *kadi* may not have been amused, but everyone else considered it hilarious. Masudi tells us the man started cracking jokes and so amused Mamun that he was invited back and entered the caliph's service.

Food could also be deployed to advance one's career, as with the grilled chicken on a spit sent by an official to the governor Munis al Muzaffar. It also denoted affection and regard, as when Amin sent a batch of freshly baked biscuits to his uncle Ibrahim. These were no run-of-the-mill treats. Prepared by the famous Nasir al Khabbaz (The Baker), they were made with honey, saffron and almond oil, and luxuriously sprinkled with sesame, pine nuts and almonds. Ibrahim was suitably touched by the gesture and, in the spirit of the times, replied in elegant verse:

> So kind and generous was it of Al Amin to send me a gift of
> *khubz al fatit*, and his affection proved.
> Shaped like perfect discs of equal size, each of which the full
> moon resembles.
> As luscious as honey they taste and like the breeze sweetly perfumed.
> Like silver and gold, white and yellow juxtaposed . . .
> Amin by God protected. May you live a thousand years, forever
> happy. May you not be touched by harm.
> May my thanks to you for the gift, dearest nephew, keep your
> name on the steppes forever alive.[27]

Food then, as today, provided solace for the lazy and unmotivated too. The ninth-century gourmand, gourmet and cookery book author Ibn Dihkana (d. 891) grew so fat that he was unable to get up when the caliph arrived and departed. 'I ate until I got afflicted with chronic diseases. Now I want to eat until I die,' he quipped.[28] Harun's grandson Al Wathik, widely known as Al Akul (The Glutton), was notorious for his weakness for food, particularly aubergines. He regularly polished off forty in a single sitting. Another of Harun's royal relatives, Isa ibn Jafar, grew so fat Harun became worried about him. The doctor diagnosed a simple case of self-indulgence but told the overweight Isa to write his will, because he had an incurable disease. The shock had the desired results, and Isa rapidly lost five notches in his belt.

Fish was always popular, and the poets wrote at length on how to catch and cook them. Ali bin Abbas bin al Rumi, a celebrated ninth-century poet and glutton, composed some lines on a fish party:

> There in your courtyard daughters of the Tigris, in battles
>   doomed forever captives.
> Twisting and turning like sparkling plates of armour, or at times
>   like counterfeit coins.
> White and bright like ingots or better, with fat loaded like small
>   skins of ghee,
> A pleasure to the eyes. Their marrow as luscious as pulling open
>   draw-strings of trousers.[29]

This poet's love of food and undiplomatic verse proved to be his undoing. After he ate a biscuit laced with poison, his days were at an end, the price of mocking the caliph Mutadid's vizier.

A favourite Abbasid recipe was fish in which the head was roasted, the middle poached and the tail fried. None, however, could compete with the most extravagant fish dish ever prepared: fish tongues in aspic, cooked by Harun's brother Ibrahim, the author of an extremely popular cookery book known across much of the Islamic world. Harun, who initially thought the cook had cut the pieces of fish far too finely, asked his brother to explain. When he heard that the dish was in fact made from 150 tongues of carp, the only part of the fish Ibrahim would eat, and at a cost of 1,000 dirhams, he was outraged. He ordered Ibrahim's eunuch to bring him 1,000 dirhams at once in expiation for such 'insane wastefulness' and had the money distributed to the poor. The dish was given to a beggar, and later bought back by the unrepentant Ibrahim for 200 dinars. It passed into Abbasid legend as 'The Fish Dish that Cost 1,000 Dirhams'.[30]

Puddings were an art form in themselves, as they are today in Baghdad, where bakers' shelves buckle under piles of pastries drenched in honey. There was *muhallabiya* (rice pudding); *zalabiya* (fried batter dipped in boiled honey); *katayif* (delicate crêpes filled with ground nuts and sugar, scented with rose water, musk and camphor); *mugharak*, ancestor of the modern *baklawa*; *khushkananaj* (filled pastries pressed into wooden moulds in geometric shapes, especially crescent moons). Coloured sugar and nuts were festooned around the puddings, to make them look like colourful orchards. Layers of white bread were used in some puddings, soaked in water until they expanded, then submerged in sugar and honey. In others, layers of bananas, melons, mulberries and crushed raisins were spaced between the sweetened bread; this was served as a fruit 'casserole'.

There were innumerable recipes for *bazmawarid*, or rolled sandwiches. Ibn Dihkana, a *nadim* to the caliph Al Mutamid and his brother Prince al Mowaffak, had a particular favourite: thick, round bread, cut in half, containing shredded meat from *sikbaja*. One side of bread was covered with finely chopped leaf vegetables and a layer of meat, and then sprinkled with salt, cheese, chopped olives, walnuts, almonds, pistachios and pine nuts. Another layer of chopped vegetables was added and covered with the other half of bread. Once made, the sandwich was pressed under a heavy weight for one hour, cut first into squares, then triangles, and served on a platter. A sandwich fit for a caliph.

The many monasteries in and around Baghdad, where wine was served behind closed doors, provided regular popular entertainment and a whole culinary subcategory was developed to cater for late-night drinking bouts. The eleventh-century writer Shabushti's *Book of Monasteries*, a penetrating survey of early Christianity in Iraq, Syria, Egypt and Arabia, essentially doubled as a *Good Tavern Guide* for Baghdad. 'In how many taverns did I land during the night cloaked in pitch-like blackness!' the irrepressible poet Abu Nuwas recalled. 'The cabaret owner kept on serving me as I kept on drinking with a beautiful white girl close to us.'[31]

Nakl were snacks designed to promote thirst, ward off hunger and delay intoxication; they included modern-day staples such as salted roast nuts and raisins, together with pomegranates, apples, *nabat al sukar*, or rock candy, sugar reeds steeped in rose water, bijoux sausages, filled pastries, grilled swallows and cured meats. Rather more sophisticated than crisps and peanuts.

Al Warrak, a stickler for good manners, wrote at length on the etiquette of dining with friends: he advised on the best way to wash one's hands and to use toothpicks; and believed that a little snooze after dining was a very desirable thing. 'For the accomplished friend or the perceptive boon companion, cleanliness of hands and nails is of utmost importance . . . He should look agreeable; skin radiating with fragrance; face, moustache, and nose, clean, and forehead, immaculate.' Teeth must be clean, beards neatly combed. The turban was particularly important to keep spotless, 'because it meets the eyes of the onlookers more than any other piece of clothing'. The sophisticated Abbasid man 'should perfume himself with incense, musk, perfume and scented powder sprinkled on hair and clothes'.[32]

No one could accuse Al Warrak of leaving any aspect of dining etiquette to chance:

> Soupy grain dishes and stews should be eaten sparingly lest they should drip on his clothes, which might be taken as a sign of gluttony. When eating chicken, he may not disjoint it with his hands lest the fat under the skin or lurking between the joints should spatter on fellow guests in front of him or beside him. A knife is recommended in this case to cut the chicken at the joints. It is uncomely to load the hand with dessert, fill the mouth with hot food, swallow it hurriedly, drink a lot of water, belch audibly, gnaw at the bones, or suck the bone marrow.[33]

Hands had to be washed after the meal but never in sight of the caliph, to whom this was a terrible affront. Al Warrak mentions the case of Al Afshin, the caliph Mutasim's military commander, asking for a hand-basin to be set where the caliph could see it. 'This long-bearded goat is having the basin where I can see him,' barked the caliph. 'Arrest him!'[34] As for 'Manners Observed When Commoners Share Meals with their Superiors and Kings', it was a case of less is more. 'Know that while eating at the table, it is polite to talk as little as possible or not talk at all.' There were good practical reasons for this, 'because talking while eating might cause particles of food to scatter from between the teeth and tongue'. Above all, 'He should avoid informality in his behaviour. He may not sprawl, stretch, yawn, snort, spit, rub his hands, crack his fingers, toy with his ring, or play with his beard and turban.' Among the 'Proprieties Observed When Drinking' was the suggestion to sip, rather than to quaff too freely – and 'When he feels he is getting rather tipsy, he should leave at once while still in control of himself.'[35]

And who could argue with his advice to grab forty winks after eating? 'Taking a nap regularly improves the person's temper and makes the face look radiant with health. It is particularly good for the brain and the heart and is immensely beneficial to knees and joints . . . Additionally, it rejuvenates the heart, pacifies the soul, improves digestion, fertilizes sperm and sustains the body.'[36]

One can only wonder what Al Warrak would have made of the story told to cheer up the caliph Al Radi (934–40) one cold and misty winter night in Baghdad. Radi had offered to give Al Arudi, the tutor to several caliphs and their sons, everything he was wearing and sitting on if he could make him laugh. There followed the story of a man who went to stay at his cousin's house. The host remarked to his slave-girls about his guest's good manners, because the latter had not visited the lavatory for two days. The girls said they would make him go and secretly added a laxative to his drink. The host pretended to be asleep as the purgative took hold. The desperate man asked the girls to direct him to the lavatory. They pretended not to understand and sang him a song. Each time he asked, using a different Arabic word for 'lavatory', they maintained the pretence and launched into a new song. Eventually, his seething stomach could bear no more. He cried out:

> I am dying to shit
> And they torture me with their eternal songs!
> But my patience is at an end and I
> Am going to spatter the faces of these whores!

So saying, he undid his breeches and let fly, says Masudi, covering the mischievous girls from head to toe in excrement. The host pretended to wake up and, having seen his slave-girls in 'this wretched state', accosted his guest.

'Friend, whatever gave you the idea of doing a thing like that?'

'Son of a whore,' replied the other, 'your slaves apparently consider the lavatory as the bridge over hell, for they refused to show me the way there. I could find no better revenge.'

Al Arudi's scatological tale did the trick. Radi collapsed into laughter and gave his tutor rich clothes and carpets worth 1,000 dinars.[37]

*

In 1055, hard on the heels of the riot between rival crowds of Sunni and Shia, which culminated in the sacking of the great Kadhimiya Mosque, and a decade before the Norman invasion of England, the stuttering Buyid Dynasty, riven by internecine conflict between rival princelings, weakened by repeated tribal rebellions encouraged by the Fatimids and threatened by a renascent Byzantium, came to an abrupt end. Tughril Beg, chief of the Seljuk Turks, a Central Asian confederacy of tribes whose accelerating conquests of other warlord dynasties already included eastern Iran, took advantage of the disorder and moved on Baghdad at the invitation of the caliph Kaim. The Buyid leader of Iraq, Al Malik al Rahim, was unable to muster a defence and after only minor skirmishing outside the city Baghdad suddenly found itself under a new foreign authority.[38]

Preoccupied with imperial expansion and campaigns against Byzantium and the Fatimids – the Seljuk Empire at its zenith, in the closing years of the eleventh century, encompassed territory from Central Asia to the Aegean coast – Tughril Beg and his Seljuk sultan successors generally chose not to live in the city during the century in which they held sway. They preferred instead to appoint a governor of Iraq to act on their behalf – an indication of just how little Baghdad meant to the new ruling family. Baghdad was no longer pre-eminent within the Muslim world; yet, for the largely Sunni scholars and court, a Sunni dynasty, as opposed to the Shia Buyids, who had periodically crossed swords with the caliphs on religious matters, was the next best thing to rule by the caliph. It allowed a new institution, the sultanate, to develop, and this came to complement and to support the caliphate, presenting itself as its political and military vanguard.[39] The Seljuk imperial method of assigning cities and regions to sons, brothers and uncles without providing a clear procedure for succession lent itself to instability. It was 'a volatile system of rule, inherently destructive as Seljuk family members forged and broke alliances in a bid for regional supremacy'.[40] Internal divisions within the Seljuk Empire, whose capital shifted between Nishapur, Ray and Isfahan in the eleventh century, and was then divided into western (Hamadan) and eastern (Merv) headquarters for most of the twelfth century, alongside numerous statelets run by *atabeg* princelings, proved auspicious for a significant reassertion of caliphal power, albeit limited to central Iraq.

Cultural life could still thrive amid the turmoil. In 1065, what would become the famous Nizamiya Academy was opened on the river bank south of the caliphal complex, near the modern district of Bab al Sharki. Named after the vizier Nizam al Mulk (d. 1092), one-time ruler of the Seljuk Empire, it numbered many outstanding minds amongst its alumni and scholars: Ghazali (1058–1111), the great theologian, jurist and philosopher, lectured there; Imaduddin and Bahauddin, the biographers of Salahadin, studied there, as did the Persian poet Sadi and Abdullah ibn Tumart, founder of the Almohad Dynasty in Spain. This was also the time of the theologian and Sufi mystic Sheikh Abdul Kadir al Gailani, a twelfth-century Hanbalite preacher whose public sermons were said to be so persuasive that they resulted in the conversion of droves of Jews and Christians to Islam. He came to Baghdad at the age of eighteen and died a famous and hugely revered man. He is considered amongst the great saints of Islam, and his tomb is one of the most visited sanctuaries in Baghdad to this day.[41]

Baghdad was hit by another disastrous flood in 1074. It breached Muizz al Dawla's dyke, damaged the tomb of the illustrious Ibn Hanbal, founder of the Hanbali school of Islamic law, brought tumbling down the underground women's passage linking the caliphal complex to the Palace of the Pleiades and laid waste to much of East Baghdad. One consequence of the destruction was a rush of new building. Baghdadis increasingly started to move out of old Rusafa, much of which already lay in ruins, heading south to form a new quarter, Muktadiya, named after the caliph Al Muktadi (1075–94), clustered around the caliphal complex. In time, assisted by a steady flow of migration from Karkh, this area grew so large that it was recognized as the main part of Baghdad by the caliph Al Mustazhir (1094–1118), who built a wall around it, the ruins of which survived well into the twentieth century.

*

On a stifling August afternoon in 1099 the caliph Mustazhir had a nasty shock. One minute he was relaxing in his *diwan* with his favourites as best he could in the stupor of high summer; the next a dishevelled but obviously very grand visitor burst into the chamber, sweeping past the assembled dignitaries, who looked aghast at this breach of protocol.

The visitor was Abu Saad al Harawi, grand *kadi* of Damascus, whose flushed demeanour was explained by the punishing three-week journey from Syria to Baghdad he had just endured. He had left the Levant in the immediate aftermath of the Franks' seizure of Jerusalem on 15 July, after a forty-day siege, the culmination of the First Crusade. Within two days of its fall, no Muslim had been left alive inside the city walls, and this harrowing news was starting to filter out to the stunned followers of the faith.

The grand *kadi* looked around in disbelief. The caliph's chamber was a picture of indolence and luxury. Exhausted from the road, staggered to see the leader – in name at least – of the Muslim world reclining in sumptuous robes, blissfully unperturbed by the trauma of the Dar al

Islam he was supposed to rule and defend, Harawi forgot where he was, unable to contain his anger. The Lebanese writer Amin Maalouf takes up the story. 'How dare you slumber in the shade of complacent safety, leading lives as frivolous as garden flowers, while your brothers in Syria have no dwelling place save the saddles of camels and the bellies of vultures,' Harawi thundered. 'Blood has been spilled! Beautiful young girls have been shamed, and must now hide their sweet faces in their hands! Shall the valorous Arabs resign themselves to insult, and the valiant Persians accept dishonour?'[42]

Behind him, cowering at this sudden outburst, was a wretched gaggle of refugees. According to the twelfth-century Arab historian Ibn al Athir, 'They recounted in the Diwan a narrative which brought tears to the eye and pained the heart. They demonstrated in the mosque on Friday and cried out for help, weeping and reducing others to tears. A tale was told of the killing of men, the enslavement of women and children and the plundering of property that had fallen upon the Muslims in that revered, august place.'[43]

Mustazhir, still in his early twenties, was not well equipped to respond to the Crusader challenge. A gentle soul, he had a passion for architecture and writing love poetry ('When I stretch out my hand to bid my beloved adieu, the ardour of my passion melts ice'), and a horror of cruelty. His response to the grand *kadi*'s horrifying news was to burst into tears, a reaction that failed to impress his august visitor. 'Never have the Muslims been so humiliated, never have their lands been so savagely devastated,' he chided the caliph.

Powerless to act, Mustazhir expressed his most profound sympathy, both for the refugees and for the loss of Jerusalem to the infidel Franks, and resorted to the politician's classic ruse when confronted by a difficult decision: he ordered an inquiry, to be conducted by seven grandees. 'It is perhaps superfluous to add that nothing was ever heard from that committee of wise men.'[44] The man whose position had once embodied the power, glory and restless energy of Arab civilization had become an impotent puppet.

For Baghdad the twelfth century was an almost unremitting series of riots, conflicts, sieges, fires and floods. Flick through the index of Ibn al Athir's titanic history and the references to violence and natural disaster are dizzying. 'Baghdad, fighting in', 'Urban gangs', 'dissension in' are typical entries, interspersed with the Tigris breaking its banks and infernos roaring through neighbourhoods, consuming everything in their way. Law and order were precarious at best. Between 1099 and 1101, power in the city changed hands eight times in thirty months, with a new master on average every hundred days as the brother princes Barkyaruk and Mohammed, sons of the Seljuk sultan Malik Shah (1072–92), vied for the throne, causing profound disarray across the Middle East.

In 1136 urban gangs in Baghdad and the suburbs rioted again, roaming through the streets and plundering. 'They openly committed murder and violent theft of property and the evil they did was great,' wrote Ibn al Athir. 'The prefect raided Slave-Market Street to seek out the gangs, but the populace of the western quarters rose against him and met him with force. He set fire to the street and a large number of people were burnt to death.' An intermediary sent by the Seljuk sultan Masud was killed, revenge for the suspected assassination in 1135 of the caliph Al Mustarshid, after a reign of seventeen years. The sultan retaliated by giving his men licence to sack Ibn Tahir's harem in West Baghdad, the area where the gangs had been running amok. Sultan Masud put the city under siege for fifty days. Initially unsuccessful, he returned to take the city and depose the short-lived caliph Al Rashid, who was later assassinated. Turbulence and turmoil were the natural order of affairs.

Historians have suggested that the tumultuous nature of Baghdad society, including the relentless procession of riots and rebellions that has afflicted the city for centuries, is partly explained by the fundamental clash of cultures between the urban population and the predatory nomadic tribes that lurked around it. It is worth citing here a present-day Baghdadi perspective, whose thoughts on this cycle of strife and cultural conflict echo those respectively of Ibn Khaldun in the fourteenth century and Dr Ali al Wardi, the historian of Iraq, in the twentieth:

Urbanism was overwhelmed by the forced influence of the nomadic tribes that radically changed the traditional social fabric of the city and injected its crude principles and morals into the Baghdadi society. The tribes retained their boorish customs and never changed them. They had surrounded the city for ages and ogled it with their greedy eyes, craving an opportunity to ransack and burn the modernity of the glorious City of Peace. Over time the ordinary Baghdadi evolved a dual nature: one that represented the sophistication of the city-dweller and another that emulated the nomadic and tribal customs, such as revenge, ransack, destruction of public property and other indescribable practices. The ruling authorities were deeply detested because of their corruption and total disregard for people's needs. The rich bought their heart's desires with bribes to officials while those who could not afford to do so rebelled and mutinied until they were repressed by the rulers. Foreign invasions and occupations, natural disasters, famines and widespread epidemics also played their vicious roles in changing the true Baghdadi character.[45]

The city was under siege once again in 1157, following a complete breakdown in relations between the caliph Al Muktafi, Rashid's successor, and the sultan Mohammed, Masud's successor. Among the witnesses to the two-month siege was a party of pilgrims returning from the *haj* to Mecca, who were, quite understandably, 'much scandalized at the spectacle of the Commander of the Faithful being assaulted in his own capital by the Seljuk Sultan'.[46] The fighting was fierce, with heavy barrages from the siege engines and rival camps brandishing Greek fire, a secret Byzantine weapon that served as a potent flame-thrower.[47] Disease was rife within the city walls, adding to the numerous casualties. Eventually, on hearing the news that his brother was seizing lands in Persia in his absence, Mohammed lifted the siege to attend to more pressing business at home. Muktafi's successful defence of the city marked the end of Seljuk rule in Baghdad and ushered in the brief return of caliphal power.

*

One of the most celebrated accounts of Baghdad dates to this troubled time. On one level it is a brilliantly observed, probably exaggerated, portrait of royal magnificence and constraint, an intimate, occasionally disturbing, study of an extraordinarily reclusive caliph, either Al Mustanshid (1160–70) or his successor Al Mustadi (1170–80). On another level, it offers a powerful, first-hand insight into one of the city's most arresting secrets. To the outside world, Baghdad remained the great Islamic city, the paragon, however reduced, of the Muslim world. Yet, as the Jewish traveller and adventurer Benjamin of Tudela (in Navarre, northern Spain) reported, beneath the Muslim surface was a thriving Jewish population whose prodigious riches provided essential life-support to the caliphate. Benjamin's is the first account we have of Jewish life in Baghdad and is uniquely valuable for that reason alone. He reached the city in the late 1160s or early 1170s (hence the uncertainty about which caliph he is describing), after crisscrossing Europe and the Levant, part of a ten-to-fourteen-year odyssey that took in some of the world's most storied cities, from Genoa, Rome and Constantinople to Samarkand, Cairo and Alexandria, via Jerusalem, Damascus and Antioch.[48]

He reckoned Baghdad to be twenty miles in circumference, surrounded by a verdant land of palms, gardens and plantations. Traders, wise men and philosophers came from far and wide, together with 'magicians expert in all manner of witchcraft'. The caliph's palace encompassed three square miles, including a great walled park with numerous varieties of trees, orchards, wild animals and a well-stocked lake, offering the caliph and his retinue the most lavish hunting. There were fabulous buildings of marble containing columns of silver and gold and carvings made of rare stones. Inside the palace the picture was no less splendid, with 'great riches and towers filled with gold, silken garments and all precious stones'.

Benjamin reported that all of the caliph's brothers and members of his family lived in the palace but were 'fettered in chains of iron, and guards are placed over each of their houses so that they may not rise against the great Caliph'. Such captivity apparently did not prevent them living in 'great splendour'. The princes earned tribute from the towns and villages they owned, allowing a life of royal indolence in which 'they eat and drink and rejoice all the days of their life'.

The caliph's life of palace-bound luxury and seclusion was interrupted only once a year, according to Benjamin, for the Ramadan feast (he does not specify which of the two celebrations it was). Muslims flocked from distant lands across the empire, desperate for a glimpse of the caliph on this exceptional day. 'He rides on a mule and is attired in the royal robes of gold and silver and fine linen; on his head is a turban adorned with precious stones of priceless value, and over the turban is a black shawl as a sign of his modesty, implying that all this glory will be covered by darkness on the day of death. He is accompanied by all the nobles of Islam dressed in fine garments and riding on horses.'

Princes from Arabia and Central Asia, including 'the princes of the land of Tibet', joined the royal procession from the caliphal palace to 'the great mosque of Islam which is by the Basra Gate'. Crowds lined the streets of Baghdad beneath banners of silk and purple cloth, singing, applauding and dancing, saluting him as he passed with the greeting, 'Peace unto thee, our Lord the King and Light of Islam!' In response the caliph kissed his robe, held out its hem and saluted them. He mounted a wooden pulpit in the mosque and delivered a sermon, expounding on their law, after which the mullahs prayed for him and commended his 'greatness and his graciousness'. He blessed his congregation and had a camel slaughtered for them, giving the meat to the princes, who distributed it to the people. After all this commotion, Benjamin tells us, the caliph returned alone to his palace by river, 'and the road which he takes along the river-side is watched all the year through, so that no man shall tread in his footsteps. He does not leave the palace again for a whole year. He is a benevolent man.'

There were two reasons for Benjamin's strikingly positive verdict on the caliph. First was the prosperous condition of the city's Jewish population and, second, its excellent relations with the leader of the Islamic world. The caliph was 'kind unto Israel', the traveller declared, and had many Jewish attendants. He was multilingual, 'well versed in the law of Israel. He reads and writes the holy language [Hebrew].' Benjamin estimated there were about 40,000 Jews, living in 'security, prosperity and honour under the great Caliph', among them great sages and the wise rabbis who headed the ten Talmudic academies, many of them of illustrious lineage. Samuel, the chief rabbi, for instance, could trace his line back to Moses.

The exilarch, the head of the Babylonian Jews in exile, was a man called Daniel, son of Hisdai, styled 'Our Lord the Head of the Captivity of all Israel', who owned 'a book of pedigrees going back as far as David, King of Israel'. Muslims knew him as Saidna ben Daoud, 'invested with authority over all the congregations of Israel at the hands of the Amir al Muminin, the Lord of Islam'. Baghdad's most senior Jew was a powerful figure whose writ extended far beyond the city. It encompassed Mesopotamia, biblical Shinar (Sumer), Iran, Khorasan and Yemen, the lands of the Togarmim (Turks) and Alans (in Georgia and the Caucasus), stretching to the wastes of Siberia and 'the gates of Samarkand, the land of Tibet and the land of India'. Jewish communities across Asia brought him 'offerings and gifts from the ends of the earth'. He owned hospices, gardens and plantations in Babylon and swathes of land inherited from his fathers, none of which could be taken from him by force. He was, said Benjamin, 'very rich, and wise in the Scriptures as well as in the Talmud, and many Israelites dine at his table every day'.

At the time of Benjamin's visit to Baghdad, there were twenty-eight synagogues, situated on either side of the Tigris, of which the principal place of worship was a monument of breathtaking grandeur. 'The great synagogue of the Head of the Captivity has columns of marble of various colours overlaid with silver and gold, and on these columns are sentences of the Psalms in golden letters. And in front of the ark are about ten steps of marble; on the topmost step are the seats of the Head of the Captivity and of the Princes of the House of David.'

Baghdadis may have seen their caliph only once a year, but the city's Jewish leader visited him 'every fifth day' amidst sumptuous ceremony, escorted by Christian and Jewish horsemen, with heralds proclaiming in advance, 'Make way before our Lord, the son of David, as is due unto him.' The Jewish leader was mounted on a horse, dressed in 'robes of silk and embroidery with a large turban on his head, and from the turban is suspended a long white cloth adorned with a chain upon which the cipher of Mohammed is engraved'. After kissing the caliph's hand, he sat on a throne opposite the caliph, 'and all the Mohammedan princes who attend the court of the Caliph rise up before him'.

Benjamin's main preoccupations in Baghdad were observing his fellow Jews and the caliph, but he also provided a valuable insight into the famous Bimaristan Hospital, which he described as 'blocks of houses and hospices for the sick poor who come to be healed.' There were around sixty physicians' stores provided with medicines and any other supplies required by the caliph. 'Every sick man who comes is maintained at the Caliph's expense and is medically treated.' There was also treatment – albeit rather limited by modern standards – for the mentally unwell. The hospital provided care for 'demented people who have become insane in the towns through the great heat in the summer, and they chain each of them in iron chains until their reason becomes restored to them in the winter-time'. While in hospital, these unfortunate patients were provided with food from the caliph's household and, once discharged after monthly inspections to determine their state of mind, given money on their return home. Benjamin was impressed. 'All this the Caliph does out of charity to those that come to the city of Bagdad, whether they be sick or insane. The Caliph is a righteous man, and all his actions are for good.'

Benjamin underscored the essential importance of the Jewish community to the Muslim authorities – which remained true well into the twentieth century – with his observation that at the installation of the exilarch, the Jewish leader gave 'much money' to the caliph, the princes and the ministers. On the day of his investment the exilarch rode in the second of the royal equipages, escorted from the caliph's palace to his own house 'with timbrels and fifes'. Benjamin's remark that 'The Jews of the city are learned men and very rich' held true for another 800 years, until the disasters of the modern age.

*

As a Jewish traveller happening on a vibrant and influential Jewish community in the very heart of the Islamic world, Benjamin was undoubtedly, and rightly, impressed by what he saw. To suggest that Baghdad was free from sectarian strife, however, would be wide of the mark. Although Baghdadis today may frequently attribute the recent outbreaks of hostilities between the Sunni and Shia to the American-led invasion of 2003, as though harmony between the two schools were the pre-existing norm, religious differences have periodically erupted in violence and bloodletting in Baghdad from the city's very birth.

We may recall the ruthless secret war waged by Mansur, the Sunni founder of Baghdad, against the Shia descendants of Ali, and the horror of his son Mahdi in 775 when he discovered a vast crypt full of Alid family corpses, from very young children to harmless old men, every one assassinated on Mansur's orders. In some respects, Mansur's policy prefigured the long pattern of Sunni dominance in Iraq, a frequent consequence of which was the occasionally violent persecution of the Shia majority, a tradition that ran into modern times.

Prior to the Abbasids, Islamic theology had barely existed. While theological questions had arisen during the Umayyad era, these were more concerned with religious and political leadership than with the more intricate questions of doctrine. During the Abbasid era, however, theologians professionalized and proliferated, increasing the scope for *fitna*, or division, within the faith. Religious differences within the Sunni community reared their heads, sometimes fatally, from the time of Mamun, who shocked his court, the religious community and scholars by declaring that henceforth the Mutazilite school of Islam would be the orthodox faith. The Mutazilites believed in the 'createdness' of the Koran, as against the previously orthodox Sunni view that the Koran had existed since time immemorial and been revealed during the time of the Prophet Mohammed. Mamun and Mutasim deliberately patronized

Mutazilite theologians, and strict tests were set for doctrinal purity amongst government officials, an inquisition known as the *mihna*. No less a figure than Ahmed ibn Hanbal, the great Islamic theologian, was called before it and reportedly tortured for refusing to renounce his suddenly heretical views.[49] Tabari recorded the example of a man called Ahmed ibn Nasr, who, in 846, led a failed rebellion in Baghdad against the new orthodoxy. He was brought before the caliph Wathik (841–7), resolutely refusing to accept the createdness of the Koran. He was made to kneel on a leather mat before the caliph himself unsheathed the famous Samsama sword and lopped off his head. During the anarchy prevailing in the early tenth century, the theological balance of power in Baghdad turned full circle, and it was the orthodox Hanbali faction that formed its own inquisition, sentencing leading Shia to be impaled and burnt alive, despite fruitless efforts by the caliph to preserve the peace.[50]

In the riots of 1051, as we have seen, the Sunni took exception to an inscription proposed for a gateway in Karkh, which led to scuffles, the murder of the leading Sunni figure present and, in retaliation for that, the desecration and torching of the magnificent Kadhimiya Mosque, so holy to the Shia. In 1174, shortly after Benjamin of Tudela left Baghdad, there were major religious disturbances in the city, with several serious battles between the Sunni inhabitants of the Basra Gate quarter and the Shia of the Karkh Gate, following the flooding of a mosque. The same two communities were fighting each other again in 1185, with many killed or wounded.

Though most of the sectarian conflicts centred on Sunni and Shia, Jews were by no means immune. In 1177 a group of Muslims from Madain, twenty miles south of Baghdad, came to the city and started to complain about the Jews. Ibn al Athir takes up the story: 'They said, "We have a mosque where we make the call to prayer and perform our prayers and it is next to the synagogue. The Jews have said to us, 'You have caused us nuisance with your frequent call to prayer,' to which the muezzin replied, 'We do not care about that.'" '[51]

A dispute then broke out in which initially the Jews got the upper hand. The Muslims, having been temporarily imprisoned, were later released, only to troop off to the Palace Mosque, where they protested loudly before Friday prayers. Sensing danger, the imam tactfully shortened prayers. Troops came to stop the protests, but the mob was inflamed, angered at the treatment of their fellow Muslims. They broke tiles off buildings and hurled them at the troops, who turned tail and fled.

> The mob then attacked the shops of the apothecaries, because most of them were Jews, and ransacked them. The palace chamberlain tried to stop them but they stoned him, so he fled too. The city was in turmoil. They ruined the synagogue by the residence of al Basasiri and burnt the Torah. The Jews went into hiding. Then the Caliph ordered that the synagogue at al Madain be demolished and converted into a mosque.[52]

Scaffolds were erected in a public square ready for crucifixions of the recalcitrant mob. Refusing to be cowed by this threatening move, the crowd hung dead rats on the crosses. The dispute seems to have petered out after some common thieves were hauled out of their cells, taken to the square and crucified.

The Baghdadi has long been sensitive to any insults, real or perceived, to his religion. The Buyid Dynasty that ruled Baghdad for slightly more than a century until 1055 was, initially at least, ardently Shia. Muizz al Dawla made it obligatory to keep the fast on the tenth day of Muharram, in honour of the great Shia martyr Hussain, triggering a series of disturbances after the Sunni retaliated by introducing a new feast of their own. Muizz al Dawla made precious little effort to calm divisions. Having only narrowly been dissuaded from his intention to depose the caliph altogether, he ordered a denunciation of the Sunni to be posted on mosque doors, causing a new wave of disturbances from an angry mob.

Religion was very much on the mind of another distinguished visitor to Baghdad in the early summer of 1184, less than twenty years after Benjamin of Tudela had passed through. The Andalusian geographer and poet Ibn Jubayr arrived in the city with a caravan of pilgrims, having just witnessed a mob scene south of Baghdad in which many men and animals had died crossing the Euphrates in a stampede.

His first impressions tended towards the gloomy. Although Baghdad was still the Abbasid capital, 'most of its traces have gone, leaving only a famous name. In comparison with its former state, before misfortune struck it and the eyes of adversity turned towards it, it is like an effaced ruin, a remain washed out, or the statue of a ghost. It has no beauty that attracts the eye, or calls him who is restless to depart to neglect his business and to gaze.' Two exceptions to this dismal verdict were acknowledged. First was the Tigris, which ran between the eastern and western parts of the city 'like a mirror shining between two frames, or like a string of pearls between two breasts. The city drinks from it and does not thirst, and looks into a polished mirror that does not tarnish.' Second, the bewitching and well-known 'beauty of its women ... so that if God does not give protection, there are the dangers of love's seductions.'[53]

Reading the account of his fortnight's stay in Baghdad gives the distinct impression that Ibn Jubayr did not go out of his way to enjoy himself. Certainly he regarded Baghdadis with a gimlet eye, casting aspersions on their hospitality, accusing them of parochialism, vainglory, hypocrisy and bad behaviour. This was no overawed visitor from western shores:

> As to its people, you scarce can find among them any who do not affect humility, but who yet are vain and proud. Strangers they despise, and they show scorn and disdain to their inferiors, while the stories and news of other men they belittle. Each conceives, in belief and thought, that the whole world is but trivial in comparison with his land, and over the face of the world they find no noble place of living save their own. It is as if they are persuaded that God has no lands or people save theirs.

Any outsider hoping for a decent welcome from his fellow Muslims would quickly be disabused of such a naive presumption. The foreigner was there to be fleeced:

> The stranger with them is without fellowship, his expenses are doubled, and he will find amongst them none who do not practise hypocrisy with him or make merry with him only for some profit or benefit. It is as if they are forced to this false form of friendship as a condition of gaining peace and agreement in their lives together. The ill-conduct of the people of this town is stronger than the character of its air and water, and detracts from the probity of its traditions and its reports.

Of course, Ibn Jubayr's reactions to Baghdad said as much about him as they did about the city's inhabitants. Judging by how he spent his time, he was one of the more high-minded visitors to the City of Peace. Rather like the Byzantine envoys whizzing around from palace to palace, Ibn Jubayr seems to have dashed from sermon to sermon, marking each sheikh, fakih and imam for his performance. He approved, for example, of the 'quiet and grave discourse' of the sheikh and imam Radi al Din al Kazwini, head of the Shafis, another of the four schools of Islamic jurisprudence, and the leading theologian at the illustrious Nizamiya College. The Andalusian watched the cleric move his congregation to tears. Switching schools, Ibn Jubayr later enjoyed a sermon by the sheikh, fakih and imam Jamal al Din Abul Fadl ibn Ali al Jawziat, head of the conservative Hanbalis, who was so well regarded he lived in a house adjoining the caliph's palaces. He was, said the Andalusian, 'the wonder of all time, and the consolation of the faith', a man of the highest learning, who spoke with 'bewitching eloquence', punctuating his sermon at each paragraph with the rhyming opening verses of the Koran, recited earlier in an affecting display of faith by twenty readers. The penitents shouted out in admiration and fell on him 'like moths on a lamp'. Every man held up his forelock for the holy man to cut. 'Some fainted and he raised them to him in his arms.' By modern standards it might have bordered on the heretical, but for the twelfth-century traveller it was 'an awesome spectacle which filled the soul with repentance and contrition, reminding it of the dreads of the Day of Resurrection'. In fact, for Ibn Jubayr, this one sermon justified the entire expedition to Baghdad. 'Had we ridden over the high seas and strayed through the waterless desert only to attend the sermon of this man, it would have been a gainful bargain and a successful and prosperous journey.' It must have been quite a performance. In yet another sermon, again by Jamal al Din, this time at Bab al Badr in the square of the caliph's palaces, whose belvederes overlooked it so that the caliph and his family could conveniently listen, Ibn Jubayr said the congregation lost all control. 'Eyes poured forth their tears, and souls received their secret longings. Men threw themselves upon him, confessing their sins and showing great penitence. Hearts and minds were enravished, and there was great commotion. The senses lost their understanding and discernment and there was no way to restraint.' As if this were not enough, the preacher also recited 'erotic poems of great passion and of remarkable sensibility', throwing petrol on to the flames of rapture and devotion. Judging by Ibn Jubayr's account, Jamal al Din was the most charismatic and accomplished rabble-rouser of his day.

Travellers provide compelling portraits of Baghdad through the ages, particularly during the city's long decline from Abbasid metropolis to provincial backwater in the Middle Ages, when the sources become much quieter. The visitors bear witness to the rise of new quarters and the eclipse of the old, and observe the destruction of war and the ravages caused by fire, famine and flood. Ibn Jubayr described western Baghdad as 'wholly overcome by ruin', albeit with seventeen quarters, each the size of a separate town, with two to three public baths and a large mosque in eight of them. The four largest quarters were Kuraya, where he lodged close to the Tigris, Karkh, Bab al Basra and Sharih. West Baghdad consisted largely of orchards and walled gardens that supplied fruit to the eastern part of the city, the long-established home of the caliphs and Mansur's great mosque.

Although he never seemed to tire of sermons, Ibn Jubayr was also a dedicated monuments man, who found the time to seek out the tombs and shrines of pious men, above all that of Maruf al Karkhi, the much loved patron saint of Baghdad; the shrine of the Imam Abu Hanifa; and the tomb of Ahmed ibn Hanbal, 'May God hold them all in His favour.'

East Baghdad, rather than its shattered western counterpart, was now the heart of the city, arranged on the grandest scale, with 'magnificent markets' and 'a population that none could count save God Most High'. There were three great mosques, the Caliph's Mosque, the Mosque of the Sultan and Rusafa Mosque, which contained the tombs of the Abbasid caliphs. There were simply too many district mosques to estimate their number. As for seats of learning, there were around thirty colleges in eastern Baghdad, each one of which was said to outdo the finest palace. Nizamiya College was exceptional: 'A great honour and an everlasting glory to the land are these colleges and hospitals.' One sheikh told Ibn Jubayr that those who wished to while away mornings, afternoons or evenings soaping themselves down in public baths could choose from around 2,000, doubtless an exaggeration but nevertheless a sign of their abundance. Most were faced with bitumen, 'so that the beholder might conceive them to be of black, polished marble'. At this time, set in the wall erected around the city by the caliph Mustazhir, there were four gates in eastern Baghdad: Bab al Sultan, Bab al Safariya, Bab al Halba and Bab al Basaliya.

For Ibn Jubayr, like Mukaddasi two centuries before, Baghdad was past her best. Political power had ebbed away, and the once mighty Abbasid caliph was shut away in his palace 'in sumptuous confinement', while others ruled in his stead. A life of luxury and ostentation was the consolatory order of the day. 'The lustre of this reign consists only in pages and negro eunuchs,' he observed drily. 'To be short, the state of this city is greater than can be described. But ah what is she to what she was! Today we may apply to her the saying of the lover: "You are not you, and the houses are not those I knew."'

*

Ibn Jubayr's visit to Baghdad came when the caliph Al Nasir (1180–1225), an unusually vigorous and ambitious leader, was still in his twenties. His long reign was marked by a renewed flourish of caliphal power, which saw Iraq, western Persia and eastern Syria acknowledge Baghdad's sway. Nasir took advantage of the instability brought about by competition between Seljuk sultans, princes and atabegs to build an effective power base and the caliphate regained much of the lustre lost during preceding centuries. His reign also coincided with the final collapse of the Seljuk Empire, when Sultan Tughril III was routed in battle by the Khwarizmid Shah Takash in 1194. Although much of the canal system, foundation of the empire's prosperity, lay neglected, with the once mighty Nahrawan Canal partially silted up, Nasir embarked on a number of public building works in Baghdad, including the demolition of the ruins of the old Buyid palaces in Rusafa, the installation of Salahadin's Crusader cross in the Nubian Gate of the caliphal complex, the rebuilding of the Halba Gate (commemorated with an inscription that remained intact until 1917, when the retreating Turks blew up the gate), a temporary dam on the Tigris and the restoration of the tomb of Sheikh Maruf al Karkhi. For some time the growing power of the Khwarizmid Dynasty in Persia threatened the caliph, Sultan Mohammed going so far as to announce the deposition of Nasir and the Abbasid family, prior to launching an assault on Iraq. Nasir was saved by the intervention of a very different enemy from the east that demanded his full attention. The Mongol wave was about to come crashing down on Muslim lands.

Yet Abbasid culture would not end with a whimper. Intellectual life continued to flourish as late as the reign of Al Mustansir (1226–42), the penultimate Abbasid caliph in Baghdad. In 1233, in an effort to eclipse the Nizamiya College and all other seats of learning in the city, he founded the university that bore his name, the Mustansiriya. One of Baghdad's most enduring and magnificent monuments, a rare jewel of Abbasid architecture that survives to this day at the southern end of

Baghdad's Old Quarter on the east bank behind a sky-grazing portal of exquisite inscriptions and geometric motifs, it is revered in the city as the oldest university in the world.

'Imagine, this is all that remains from the Abbasid time,' says my friend Thair, an academic at Baghdad University, during an impromptu visit one morning. 'Can you believe it? Everything else has been destroyed. But look how beautiful it is and I think you can understand how great the Abbasids were.' He is right. In a city in which violence has been endemic from the very beginning, there is a strange serenity about the place that stems perhaps from an architectural style that marries simplicity with silencing grandeur. It is one of the few survivors of Hulagu's onslaught in 1258. Defiance and nostalgia are set in every stone.

Alongside a blue-tiled dome winking in the morning sun, a minaret casts a stately shadow over proceedings. Once beyond the portal, which tapers up into the blinding sky, we are suddenly swallowed up in sheer, heat-filled space, desolate shrubs and a solitary palm tree for company amid the rows of empty arches that frame the courtyard on two storeys. 'This is peaceful, isn't it? Not like the other Mustansiriya,' Thair says with a sarcastic laugh. 'You only find students killing professors in Baghdad!' He is talking about the modern Mustansiriya University, established in the 1960s in a campus in north-eastern Baghdad, which in 2009 was temporarily closed by the prime minister Nuri al Maliki in an effort to purge a student gang that was accused of murdering, torturing and raping fellow students, and killing university professors and administrators.[54]

In this sun-drenched heart of the Abbasid Mustansiriya's campus were the four colleges representing the four orthodox schools of Sunni Islamic *fikh*, based on the Koran, the *hadith* and the interpretations of the *ulema* clergy: Hanbali, Hanafi, Shafi and Maliki. When they were not nose-deep in the books and manuscripts available in the prodigiously well-stocked library, students and teachers alike were able to take advantage of the latest medical treatments from a new on-site hospital (supplied with equipment from the Adudi Hospital), a *hammam* in which to luxuriate and a bountiful kitchen. The entrance hall was graced by a monumental clock, elaborately powered by water, that announced prayer and study times.

This was also the era of another giant of Arab geography, widely considered the greatest of them all. Yakut's *Geographical Dictionary*, published around 1226, represented 'perhaps the greatest storehouse of geographical facts compiled by any one man during the Middle Ages', a treasure trove of information about Baghdad on the eve of the Abbasid Dynasty's demise.[55] Three decades later, in around 1256, Ibn Khallikan published *The Obituaries of Eminent Men*, better known as his *Biographical Dictionary*, a masterful, highly anecdotal survey of some of the greatest men of his time. Two years later, half a millennium after Mansur founded his imperial capital, it was time to write the obituary of the Abbasid Dynasty itself.

*

The five centuries of Abbasid rule had witnessed a stunning efflorescence of culture. It is no exaggeration to say that Baghdad in the eighth and ninth centuries represented the highpoint of human civilization anywhere on the globe.

'As Baghdad had risen suddenly, a brilliant meteor in the sky, so was her fall long, slow but inevitable; she had drawn all the strings of Islamic life to her, had stamped them with her own individuality, and had set them loose again. The city's work was done.'[56] Richard Coke's summary is too bleak. Intellectual and cultural life did not suddenly expire once Baghdad's military and political heyday had passed.

The age of its monopoly on intellectual brilliance started to draw to a close with the steady decline of the caliphate from the middle of the ninth century. Other cities within the Eastern orbit were forging distinct cultural identities, developing courts and attracting their own constellations of talented and ambitious stars, from the Central Asian strongholds of Samarkand, Balkh and Khiva to the Persian centres of Tabriz, Isfahan and Shiraz. Sultan Mahmud of Ghazni transformed an obscure provincial town into one of the world's great cities within the space of his own lifetime. To the north of Baghdad, sharing the Tigris River, was the developing city of Mosul, while further west was the ancient Syrian citadel of Aleppo. In North Africa, Cairo was emerging, and further west still the seeds of Andalusian culture were taking root.

Masudi traced Baghdad's cultural demise to the mid-ninth-century reign of Mutawakil, traditionally seen as the last great Abbasid caliph. 'Mutawakil abolished free thought, philosophical disputes and the things which had preoccupied men's minds under Mutasim, Wathik and

Mamun,' he wrote. 'He re-established orthodoxy and submission to traditional religious values.'[57] Received opinion, said Masudi, was henceforth the order of the day. A religious hardliner without the intellectual interests of his father, Mutasim, or brother Wathik, both of whom preceded him on the throne, Mutawakil nevertheless had a taste for architectural grandiloquence. The Great Mosque of Samarra, which he commissioned at the start of his reign, was a stunning legacy to world civilization.

In fact, life in Baghdad had become more turbulent well before this. Harun's reign, described by Hugh Kennedy as 'the Edwardian summer of the caliphate', was followed by the ruinous civil war between the brothers Amin and Mamun from 811 to 819 – including the siege of 812 to 813 – that brought the city to its knees. Baghdad's pre-eminence took a further blow when the caliphate moved its capital to Samarra in 835. By the last decade of the ninth century, faced with the growing power of the Tulunids in Egypt, the Samanid Dynasty in Central Asia and rebel authority in Persia, the caliphal dominions were narrowing to Iraq, western Persia and parts of Arabia and its neighbours.

Yet the Abbasid intellectual legacy completely transcended these short-term political vicissitudes. By the middle of the tenth century, the enormous scholarly advances in Baghdad had resulted in an entirely new corpus of knowledge, and when later generations organized this vast body of information into encyclopedias and manuals in both the Arab world and Europe, it was Arabic texts, rather than Greek or Persian manuscripts, that they studied. After the brilliant zenith (another Arabic word) of the eighth and ninth centuries, the city steadily lost political and military power and much of its sparkle, if not its cultural prestige. Yet, by comparison with that long, gentle decline of Abbasid Baghdad, what followed next was nothing less than a catastrophe.

5

'This Pilgrimage of Destruction': The Mongol and Tatar Storm (1258–1401)

You have doubtless learnt from men of high rank and low what punishments the Mongol armies have inflicted on the world and its peoples from the time of Genghis Khan to the present day: the humiliation, thanks to eternal God, of the dynasties of the Khorezmshahs, the Seljuks, the sovereigns of Dailam, the Atabeks and other princes renowned for their grandeur and power. Since the gates of Baghdad were not closed to any of these races, each one of which had established its dominance, how then can entry to this city be forbidden to us, we who possess so many forces and so much power? We have warned you already and we say to you today: rid yourself of feelings of hatred and hostility, don't struggle against our standard, because you will be wasting your time. Therefore, without revisiting the past, let the caliph agree to dismantle the city's defences and fill up the moats, let him hand over the administration to his son and come in person to us in good time. If, however, he refuses to attend, let him send us his Vizier, Suleiman Shah, and the Devatdar [vice-chancellor], so that all can convey our intentions to him, word for word. If he obeys our orders, it will be unworthy of us to demonstrate any hatred towards him and he will remain in possession of his states, his troops and his subjects. But if he refuses to listen to our advice and prefers to follow the path of opposition and war, deploying his forces and naming the battlefield, we are committed and ready to fight him. And once I lead my forces to Baghdad in righteous anger, while you are hiding, from the highest heavens to the depths of earth,

I will bring you crashing down from the summit of the sky,
Like a lion I will throw you down to the lowest depths.
I will not leave a single person alive in your country,
I will turn your city, lands and empire into flames.

If you have the heart to save your head and your ancient family,
listen carefully to my advice. If you refuse to accept it, I will show
you the meaning of the will of God.

Letter from Hulagu Khan to the caliph Al Mustasim,
September 1257
Rashid al Din, *Jami al Tawarikh* (*Compendium of Histories*)

Oh, young man, barely started on your career, who shows such
little desire to live, who, drunk with the happiness and riches
of ten days, believes you are greater than the whole world,
who thinks your orders have the irresistible force of destiny, why
do you ask of me what you have not the slightest chance of
obtaining?

Do you believe with your greatest efforts, the strength of
your armies and your bravery,

You can bring a star tumbling down into your chains?
The prince forgets that from the east to the west all the worship-
pers of Allah, whether kings or beggars, young or old, are slaves
of this court and make up my armies. The moment I give the
order to these defenders of my realm to come together, I will
begin by finishing the business of Iran, after which I will con-
tinue my march to Turan and will put everyone where he belongs.
Certainly the face of the earth will be covered with troubles and
disorder but I am neither eager for vengeance nor hungry for the
consideration of men ... I do not want my subjects to be the
victims of passing armies, above all when I and Hulagu Khan
have but one heart and one language. If, like me, you have sown
the seed of friendship, why do you talk of dismantling defences
and ramparts? Follow the path of wellbeing and return to Kho-
rasan. If, however, you want war,

Do not hesitate and do not have any excuses
If you have decided to fight

I have millions of cavalry and infantry, all ready for war.

Who, when the moment of vengeance arrives, will dissolve the waters of the sea?

Caliph Al Mustasim's reply to Hulagu Khan
Rashid al Din, *Jami al Tawarikh* (*Compendium of Histories*)

As the massed Mongol armies of Hulagu Khan swept westward across the Asian steppe in 1257, Baghdad faced the greatest danger in its history. The braggadocio of the caliph Mustasim's correspondence suggested he had seriously underestimated his adversary. Hulagu, Lord of the Ascendant, later founder of the Ilkhanate state that encompassed Persia, much of the Middle East and Central Asia, was the grandson of Genghis Khan, the Scourge of God and Ruler of the Universe. He was also the brother of Mangu, Great Khan of the Mongol Empire since 1251. To celebrate Mangu's accession, it had been decided to launch two large-scale expeditions. In the words of the Persian historian Rashid al Din (1247–1318), author of the prodigious *Jami al Tawarikh*, a grand literary project to justify Mongol power over Iran), Mangu 'turned his august attention toward the subjugation of the farthest East and West of the world'.[1]

Kublai Khan, brother of Hulagu and Mangu, was to command one expedition against China. Hulagu, 'upon whose forehead he [Mangu] had observed the signs of conquest, sovereignty, royal majesty and fortune', would lead the other, which was aimed against the troublesome, dagger-wielding Assassins (Hashshashin, a radical Shia sect of Nizari Ismailis) in their mountain fortresses of northern Iran, the Ayubid states of Syria, Mamluk Egypt and the caliphate itself. Hulagu's self-appointed mission was also to ride to the rescue of the oppressed Christian communities of the Middle East and Caucasus, which were, as Rashid al Din dutifully assured his readers, 'seeking justice against the Heretics'.[2] Though not generally known for their mercy, the Mongols were tolerant towards Christians. Some Mongol tribes had been converted to Nestorian Christianity over the preceding centuries, and both Hulagu's mother and wife were Christians. Hulagu's later diplomatic approaches to the Christian West were also born of a hard-headed desire to forge an alliance against the Mamluks of Syria.

In recent years the ailing caliphate had already felt the cut of Mongol steel. In 1219 Genghis Khan had led his armies into Central Asia, sacking and storming some of the greatest cities of the world – among them Bukhara, Samarkand, Urganch, Termez, Balkh, Merv, Herat and Nishapur – with terrifying ease. He and his hordes employed terror as a strategic weapon, pouring molten gold down throats, disembowelling the dead and the dying, levelling cities, raping and pillaging freely. By 1221 the Khwarizmid Empire, which ruled Persia and swathes of Central Asia, unable to contend with the waves of Mongol warriors streaming west, collapsed. Mongol raids into northern Iraq followed, with the capture of Mosul, Mardin and Nisibin triggering a series of counter-attacks from the caliphate. Mongol incursions into the heartland of the caliphate became an almost annual fixture until 1238, when Mustansir boldly declared *jihad* and drove the invaders out. By the time Mustasim (1242–58) became caliph, however, the Mongols were beginning to reappear across the eastern horizon with ominous regularity.

History's verdict on the caliph Mustasim has been almost universally damning. For Sir Henry Howorth, author of a four-volume history of the Mongols (1876–1927), Mustasim was in a 'state of mental imbecility' when Hulagu arrived in the Middle East.[3] The Scottish orientalist Sir William Muir, a former president of the Royal Asiatic Society who, in the late nineteenth century, wrote about the rise, decline and fall of the caliphate, was even more brutal. Mustasim, he charged, was 'a weak and miserly creature, in whose improvident hands the caliphate, even in quieter times, would have fared ill'.[4] Modern historians have not been much kinder. John Saunders, a twentieth-century expert on the Mongol conquests, considered him 'weak, vain, incompetent and cowardly'.[5] For the Iraqi historian Professor Farouk Omar Fawzi, Mustasim was a frivolous leader, more concerned with the pleasures of his harem and hunting grounds than with the defence of the realm. He blamed the caliph's notorious miserliness for the disastrous neglect of his army, with soldiers being recruited only at times of external danger and then disbanded to save money, a short-sighted policy that resulted in mass desertions and even defections to the Mongol ranks.[6] In the light of how Mustasim's reign ended, and the epoch-shattering consequences of its demise, such vituperation is hardly surprising.

Although much of the criticism heaped upon Mustasim, the last Abbasid caliph in Baghdad, has a whiff of predictability, it is difficult to dismiss it entirely as made with the benefit of hindsight. From his first encounter with the Mongol khan, which began with the exchange of letters quoted above, while Hulagu was still camped beneath the walls of Hamadan, more than 260 miles to the north-east, Mustasim struck the wrong note, responding with provocative bluster rather than with strategic calculation. This blunder was subsequently compounded by a series of serious political and military errors that culminated in catastrophe. All along there were alternative courses of action open to him.

For instance, Mustasim could have apologized to Hulagu for failing to provide the troops the Mongol had requested for his expedition against the Assassins. He could have dispatched high-level envoys to Hulagu's camp, as requested. Certainly he could have started dismantling his defences, a relatively painless task. However unpalatable it would undoubtedly have been, he could even have offered his nominal submission in return for sparing Baghdad the carnage of a full-scale Mongol assault. While Mustasim's army had been neglected and below-strength for years and the caliphate was no longer the all-conquering power it had once been, the utter ruthlessness and destructive fury of the Mongol armies were well known and feared across Asia. The size of Hulagu's army is not entirely clear. Although two fifteenth-century sources put it variously at 70,000 and 120,000, modern scholars have estimated it at up to 300,000.[7] Whatever its exact strength, there is little doubt that it was a horizon-filling force that struck terror across Asia. As the two sides approached each other, there was therefore a delicate ballet to perform. Far from exhibiting grace and finesse, Mustasim's choreography looks clumsy and naive at best, utterly lumpen and uncontrolled at worst.

To add to the weakness of his position, Mustasim's court was deeply divided, with his Shia vizier Ibn al Alkami allegedly playing a dangerous double game, according to later Sunni writers, quietly encouraging a Mongol assault through back channels to Hulagu, while at the same time reducing the strength and numbers of the Baghdad garrison.[8] In this context, Mustasim's response of immediate defiance, pushing Hulagu to an all-out attack that the caliph was ill-equipped to withstand, appears extremely reckless. Another letter was dispatched to Baghdad as Hulagu prepared for war:

Eternal God has lifted up Genghis Khan and his family in honour. He has given us an empire of the whole world from east to west. Every man who has sincerely submitted to us can be sure of keeping his goods, his wife, his children and his life. He who resists will have nothing. The love of great things, riches, pride, the illusions of fleeting happiness have so completely seduced you that the words of well-intentioned men make no impression upon you, and your ears are closed to the advice and warnings of those who are closest to you. You have completely abandoned the path followed by your father and your ancestors. Now all you can do is prepare for war because I am going to march against Baghdad at the head of an army as numerous as ants and grasshoppers.[9]

The Mongol envoys were mobbed in the streets. Diplomacy, barely under way, had quickly run its course. Hulagu ordered his armies to converge upon, and surround, the City of Peace. General Baiju, conqueror of the Seljuks, was to march south from Rum (Asia Minor) via Mosul to encircle Baghdad's western flank. Hulagu's Christian general Kitbuka led the left wing from Luristan, a province in western Iran that lay among the Zagros Mountains. Mongol contingents from the Golden Horde, which stretched from Eastern Europe to the frozen wastes of Siberia, approached from Kurdistan, while Hulagu himself led the main body of the army from Hulwan in western Iran.

In an effort to pre-empt the attack, an Abbasid force of 20,000 crossed the Tigris to confront the Mongol right wing, attacking it west of the city. The Mongols retired to the Dujail Canal, which linked the Euphrates to the Tigris, encouraging the Abbasid forces to advance farther west after them. It was another miscalculation. Overnight the Mongols broke open the dykes, flooding the country behind the caliph's army and drowning the majority of these troops. On 18 January, Hulagu began investing Baghdad from the east, closing in on the walled city of palaces and law colleges, rambling bazaars, ancient tombs and manicured gardens. In the more florid language of Wassaf, the fourteenth-century Persian court panegyrist and historian of the Ilkhanate, 'the eagle standard of the ilkhan, the bird of good fortune, proudly raised its neck from the head of fury and the fire of the fight burst forth, and the wood on which it fed was the doom of Baghdad.'[10]

On 30 January, the assault began on all sides, and the Mongol siege engines – mangonels, ballistas and battering rams – went to work, high above ground level on mounds constructed by Hulagu's forces from the burnt bricks scattered about beneath the city walls. The population of Baghdad found itself under a terrifying bombardment of rocks, palm trunks and flaming naphtha. 'The city was filled with thunder and lightning by the striking of stones and the flares from the naphtha pots; a dew of arrows rained from the cloud of bows, and the inhabitants were trampled underfoot by the forces of weakness and humiliation.' The city, Wassaf wrote, was 'besieged and terrorized' for fifty days, although most historians put the bombardment at a week. 'The arrows and bolts, the lances and spears, the stones from the slings and catapults of both sides, shot up to heaven at top speed like messengers of the prayer of the just, and briskly fell down like the judgement of fate. The people were killed, both from inside and outside, or were carried away wounded.'[11]

Underlying all Hulagu's military campaigns, like those of his grandfather Genghis before him, was the most meticulous preparation. He now ordered pontoon bridges to be laid across the Tigris both above and below the city, to seal off all escape routes by river. A force of 10,000 Mongols with siege engines were placed upon them, to prevent anyone from fleeing. Fearing imminent disaster, Mustasim's vice-chancellor made a frantic attempt to escape. Immediately the Mongol engines came creaking and pounding to life in a crescendo of destruction, launching volleys of stones, arrows and burning naphtha at him, overturning his three boats and killing everyone in them, except the horrified official, who hurried back into the besieged city. Mongol archers fired arrows into the city from six sides of Baghdad, bearing notes promising to spare the lives of the *kadis*, doctors of law, sheikhs, descendants of Ali, merchants and everyone who had not taken up arms against Hulagu. The pressure on the besieged increased to breaking point.

By 1 February, after the tower flanking one of the gates had been pulverized by the sky-filling bombardment, Mongol forces had captured the entire length of the eastern wall, the key to mastering the city. Panicking, Mustasim sent another deputation to Hulagu in a belated effort to stall for time. True to Mongol practice and traditions, however, Hulagu was now committed to the fight, determined to press home his advantage and disinclined to discuss terms, his initial instruction for Mustasim to submit having been refused. The bombardment continued. Two further delegations were dispatched, the first led by the caliph's second son, Abdul Rahman, the second led by his eldest son and heir, Ahmed, accompanied by the two-timing vizier, both bearing magnificent gifts for the Mongol khan. Mustasim's options were narrowing, and he prepared to surrender.

Rashid al Din tells the story of Suleiman Shah, the commander-in-chief of the caliph's army, who had been victorious over the Mongols in earlier encounters, being seized by the Mongols and taken to Hulagu's camp, together with 700 members of his household. He was bound hand and foot. 'You are an astrologer who understands the portents, good and evil, of the stars. How is it you did not foresee these events and forewarn your master?' Hulagu asked him. 'The Caliph was led by his destiny and would not listen to the advice of his faithful servants,' Suleiman lamented.[12] He and his entire household were put to death in a mass execution. The vice-chancellor and his eldest son were also executed, their heads hung up on display in a gibbet.

On 10 February, after the destruction of the Basra quarter of Baghdad, the Abbasid caliph, accompanied by his three sons, together with 3,000 of the city's most distinguished figures, including sayids (descendants of the Prophet Mohammed), imams, *kadis* and numerous grandees, left the city and entered Hulagu's camp to offer a formal surrender. They were received graciously, the Mongol khan instructing Mustasim to cease all resistance and issue a proclamation in the streets ordering the entire population to lay down their weapons and leave the city so that an inventory could be made. The order was given.

Hulagu now entered Baghdad in triumph, made his way to the caliph's palace and summoned Mustasim. From Baghdad's perspective, the worst appeared to be over. The caliph had surrendered, and it was now only a matter of negotiating terms. Husbands and wives hugged each other hard and dared to hope amid the desperate fear and uncertainty. Yet anyone who knew the Mongol art of warfare would have recognized such hopes as illusory, if not delusional. Having expended his energies and those of his bristling armies on bringing Baghdad to its knees, once Mustasim had declined the initial offer of submission, Hulagu was duty-bound, according to Mongol tradition, to take his revenge; in so doing, he would issue a dreadful warning to any other ruler considering resistance. In the long history of Baghdad, this was the city's darkest hour.

As terrified Baghdadis trooped out of the city and handed themselves in, in groups, to Mongol forces, hoping for the mercy they had been promised, they quickly discovered the awful truth. They were taken to camps and hacked down in cold blood where they stood. Several hundred thousand probably went to their deaths in this way, pleading vainly for mercy in a cacophony of slashing swords. In his history *Al Bidaya wal Nihaya* (*The Beginning and the End*), Ibn Kathir, the fourteenth-century Syrian historian and commentator on the Koran, described how Hulagu's men butchered the scholars, scientists and religious doctors, the cream of Baghdad society. 'The man was summoned from the Abbasid palace of the caliph and he would come out with his children and women. He was taken to the cemetery of Ibn al Khallal [today the Khullani Mosque and square in Khulafa Street] opposite the reviewing stand, where he would be slaughtered like a sheep and they would capture whomever they fancied from among his daughters and servants.'[13]

According to Rashid al Din, the Mongols killed 800,000 in Baghdad, a figure cited by both the thirteenth-century historian Minhaj al Siraj Juzjani and Hamd Allah Mustawfi Kazwini, the fourteenth-century Persian historian and geographer. In the fifteenth century the Egyptian historian Al Makrizi put the death-toll, implausibly, at two million. Although medieval sources are notoriously inaccurate with such figures, there is little doubt that Mongol forces, never squeamish about shedding blood, committed a massacre of twentieth-century proportions. Hulagu himself was more conservative in his estimate of numbers killed. In a letter to Louis IX of France in 1262, he admitted to 200,000.[14]

With the mass executions largely complete – there would be stragglers to cut down within the city walls and over the next few days more would emerge from hiding – Hulagu gave his men licence to rape, kill and plunder. Christians and Jews alone were to be spared. Baghdad was now consigned to flames, as the Mongol khan had promised. Whole neighbourhoods crackled and burnt to the ground in the inferno. The great Abbasid palaces were consumed in the blaze, alongside the mosques and law colleges, the tombs of the caliphs, the markets, libraries, and street after street of homes. Beneath a blank sky, Baghdad, once the most sophisticated civilization in the world, went up in smoke. The destruction of what had been the world's greatest city was unfathomable. According to Rashid al Din, only a few simple houses belonging to oxherds and foreigners survived. Wassaf takes up the story.

> Then they swept through the city like hungry falcons attacking a flight of doves, or like raging wolves attacking sheep, with loose rein and shameless faces, murdering and spreading fear . . . The massacre was so great

that the blood of the slain flowed in a river like the Nile, red as the wood used in dyeing ... With the broom of looting they swept out the treasures from the harems of Baghdad, and with the hammer of fury, they threw down the battlements head first as if disgraced. The palaces whose canopies, on account of their ornamentation, had made the seats of paradise hide in shame and cover their shortcomings, were demolished ... Beds and cushions made of gold and encrusted with jewels were cut to pieces with knives and torn to shreds; those hidden behind the veils of the great harem ... were dragged like the hair of the idols through the streets and alleys; each of them became a plaything in the hands of a Tatar [Mongol] monster; and the brightness of the day became darkened for these mothers of virtues.[15]

Juzjani described some of the carnage in detail. He wrote of a group of Mongol soldiers slitting open and disembowelling a corpse, so that they could fill it with plundered pearls, precious stones and gold. Some deliberately broke their swords at the hilt to stuff their scabbards with looted treasures. Then there was the Mongol soldier who discovered forty suckling babies lying in the streets without their mothers, starving in the open. To put them out of their misery, he killed every one.

Ibn Kathir also included some harrowing scenes reporting how the Mongols 'entered the city and slaughtered all they could of its men, women and children, the elderly, middle aged and the young. Lots of people had to hide in wells, toilets and sewerage ducts and remained hidden there for days. Groups of people congregated in caravanserais and closed their doors. They were forced open by the Tatars who broke them down or burned them and entered. People inside escaped to the roofs, where they were pursued and murdered. Roof gutters ran with their blood to the alleys. May God's will be done.'[16]

We are told the Georgians, who unlike Mustasim had offered troops to Hulagu at Tabriz, took particular relish in putting the Muslims to the sword. This was a time for Christian revenge, divine retribution for five centuries under the Muslim yoke. 'During the time of Baghdad's supremacy, like an insatiable bloodsucker she had swallowed up the whole world,' wrote the Armenian chronicler Kirakos of Ganjak. 'Now she has been punished for all the blood she has spilled and the evil she has wrought, the measure of her iniquity being filled.'[17]

Established in the caliph's palace as Baghdad burnt to ashes and the blood of its people ran through the streets, Hulagu mockingly played the role of guest to Mustasim's host. Rashid al Din recorded the exchange. 'You are the master of this house receiving us as your guests,' the Mongol sneered. 'Now tell us what presents worthy of us you have to offer.' Mustasim presented him with 2,000 robes, 10,000 pieces of gold and precious stones galore. It was not enough to satisfy Hulagu. 'The treasures above ground are one thing,' he chided the caliph. 'Now tell me where are your *hidden* riches.'[18] Mustasim ordered a cistern to be dug up, filled to the brim with pieces of gold, each one weighing 100 mithkals, or around half a kilogram.

The personal dignity of Mustasim, proud ruler of the world's greatest dynasty for almost half a millennium, must have been crushed completely when Hulagu made his next demand. An inventory of the harem revealed the caliph had 700 wives and concubines and 1,000 eunuchs. Mustasim pleaded with the Mongol to spare him a hundred women, 'on whom the sun and moon had never shone', a request that Hulagu granted.[19] The caliph chose a hundred of those related to him by blood, and the rest were shared amongst the khan and his commanders. It was, perhaps, a posthumous tribute to Hulagu's grandfather Genghis Khan, who told his generals, 'Man's greatest good fortune is to chase and defeat his enemy, seize all his possessions, leave his married women weeping and wailing, ride his gelding, use the bodies of his women as night-shirts and supports, gazing upon and kissing their rosy breasts, sucking their lips which are as sweet as the berries of the breasts.'[20] Mustasim's 1,000 eunuchs, less immediately appealing to the warriors of the steppe, were put to the sword.

The indiscriminate killing went on for between a week and forty days, depending on which chronicle is consulted. However long it lasted, all agree that the dead and the dying lay piled in rising mounds in the streets. Baghdad had turned into a putrid ghost town. At last Hulagu called an end to the slaughter, in response to pleading from the Baghdadis and to the advice of his commander Kitbuka, who said that unless it stopped there would be no one left to supply the Mongol army with money or provisions. 'Baghdad remained bereft and empty except for the scum of people,' Ibn Kathir recorded. 'Corpses were massed like hills in the streets; rain had fallen on them so they were starting to decompose and the city stank from the corpses. The air was polluted and thus it led to a rampant plague that spread to Syria, leading to the death of many people due to the infected atmosphere. People had to suffer exorbitant prices, plague and death. May almighty God's mercy befall us.'

By the time a general pardon was proclaimed, those Baghdadis who had managed to survive underground in filthy cells, canals and sewerage ducts returned to ground level looking, in the words of Ibn Kathir, like 'exhumed corpses'. They had avoided the maniacal killing spree, only for the most part to succumb immediately to the severe plague raging across the city.[21]

Even though this was the coldest time of the year, the stench of decomposing corpses soon became unbearable. It was so noxious that, on 20 February, Hulagu left the city to avoid serious infection, returning to camp several miles away, in possession of the mountains of priceless treasure that had been carefully accumulated during the five centuries of Abbasid rule.

The Mongol had one more important question to decide: what to do with Mustasim. Opinion, perhaps inevitably, was divided along sectarian lines within the Muslim community. Some Sunni warned of disaster in the event of putting the caliph to death, predicting a catastrophic earthquake. The Shia astrologer Nasir al Din of Tus disagreed, arguing that no such disasters had occurred at the deaths of John the Baptist, the Prophet Mohammed and his grandson, the Shia martyr Imam Hussain. On 21 February, after considering the advice, Hulagu had Mustasim, his eldest son and five loyal eunuchs executed near the village of Wakf, outside Baghdad. His demise was lamented in verse by the poet Sadi:

> Well it were if from the heavens tears of blood on earth should flow
> For the ruler of the Faithful, Al Mustasim, brought so low.[22]

There are differing versions – some of them fairly lurid and farfetched – of Mustasim's death. There is a famous story of Mustasim starving in front of tables groaning with gold and silver plates and precious stones which can be traced back to three Christian accounts from around 1300: the French chronicler Jean de Joinville, the Armenian nobleman Hayton of Corycus and, most memorably, Marco Polo all cite it.

Marco Polo wrote of an astonished Hulagu, having taken Baghdad by storm, discovering a tower full of riches, 'the greatest accumulation of treasure in one spot that was ever known'. Summoning the caliph, he asked Mustasim why he had not used the gold to pay his soldiers to defend Baghdad against the Mongol invasion. The caliph remained silent. 'Now, then, Caliph, since I see what love you have for your treasure, I will give it to you to eat!' Hulagu taunted Mustasim, locking him up in the 'Treasure Tower' and ordering that no food or drink be given him. 'So the Caliph lingered in the tower four days, and then died like a dog.'[23] The extravagant story of death by gold, popularized by Longfellow's poem *Kambalu* ('I said to the Kalif: "Thou art old, / Thou hast no need of so much gold . . ."'), was not corroborated by any contemporary Muslim writers.[24]*

According to less exuberant accounts, Mustasim was rolled up in a carpet and trampled to death by horses, in accordance with the Mongol *yasa*, or customary law, that prohibited the spilling of royal blood. Perhaps the best clue to Mustasim's final hours comes from the Egyptian historian Ibn al Furat, who may well have met in person those Baghdadis whose fathers and grandfathers had fled in 1258 from the city to Cairo, where Mustansir II, first in a line of Abbasid puppet caliphs, was installed in 1261. His account includes the taunting over Mustasim's gold but ends – more convincingly – with the classic Mongol execution reserved for royalty, designed so as not to shed blood:

> Then Hulagu gave command and the Caliph was left to starve, until his case was that of very great hunger, so that he called asking that something might be given him to eat. And the accursed Hulagu sent for a dish with gold in, a dish with silver in and a dish with gems in, and ordered these to be set before the Caliph al Mustasim, saying to him, 'Eat these.' But the Caliph answered, 'These are not fit to eat.' Then Hulagu said, 'Since you knew these were not fit to eat, why did you make a store of them? With some of these you might have sent gifts to propitiate us and with others you could have raised an army to serve you and defend yourself against us.' And Hulagu commanded them to take forth the Caliph and his son to a place outside the camp, and they were here bound and put into two great sacks, being afterwards trampled underfoot till they both died – the mercy of Allah be upon them.[25]

Of Mustasim's three sons, two were killed and only Mubarak was spared, at the request of Hulagu's wife Oljai Khatun; he was sent east

---

* It was not mentioned by Juzjani, writing in around 1260, or any of the following: Abul Faraj (1286); Rashid al Din (1300); Fakhri (1300); Hamd Allah Mustawfi Kazwini (1330); Ibn Khaldun (1380); Suyuti (1500).

and married off to a Mongol woman. A daughter was also spared, sent as a gift to Hulagu's brother, Great Khan Mangu. Before she got there, according to Rashid al Din, the party stopped at Samarkand, where she asked permission to visit the tomb of Kusam, son of Abbas, to pray. 'O God, if this Kusam, son of Abbas, my ancestor, hath honour in Thy presence, take this Thy servant to Thyself and deliver her out of the hands of these strange men,' the distraught woman sobbed, at which point she collapsed on the tomb and died.[26] In one of history's most brutal volte-faces, the Mongols visited on the Abbasid family the Abbasids' destruction of the Umayyad Dynasty five centuries earlier.

Having destroyed Baghdad, stolen its treasures, slaughtered its inhabitants, seized and raped its women and exterminated the Abbasid line, Hulagu finally left on 8 March. In the light of this wholesale destruction, there is something almost ironic in his order to reopen the bazaars. Nevertheless, a force of 3,000 Mongol cavalry was dispatched to clear the bodies from the streets, restore order and rebuild houses. Mustasim's infamous vizier Ibn al Alkami was reappointed to the position, lending weight to the charge of treachery levelled against him. For years to come, Muslim schoolbooks bore the inscription 'Let him be cursed of God who curses not Ibn al Alkami.'[27]

In marks of favour to the Christian community (the protection of which had been amongst the ostensible reasons for the military campaign), one of the caliph's palaces was assigned to the Nestorian patriarch, and a large plot of land inside the caliph's sanctuary was handed over for the construction of a church. Given its hugely symbolic position in the heart of the hitherto quintessentially Islamic royal city, this was a shattering humiliation. Rebuilt and restored innumerable times over the centuries, the church still stands in Khulafa Street in downtown Baghdad, presiding over the interminable traffic jams so cursed by Baghdadis. To this day its increasingly beleaguered congregation still worships in the time-honoured tradition that would have been familiar to its predecessors in the earliest days of the city:

Your Majesty, O Lord, a thousand thousand heavenly beings worship, and myriad myriad of angels, hosts of spiritual beings, ministers of fire and spirit with cherubim and holy seraphim, glorify your name, crying out and glorifying, 'Holy, Holy, Holy, God almighty, heaven and earth are full of his glories' . . .

The city's pillaged treasures were gathered together: part was sent in tribute to Mangu in Karakorum, the rest taken to be stored in a specially constructed treasury on Kaboudi Island in Lake Urmia, north-western Iran, where Hulagu was buried on his death in 1265.

The Dar al Islam had suffered a number of checks and setbacks in previous centuries. Umayyad power in Spain had collapsed in 1031, and North Africa had been ravaged from coast to coast by the Arab nomads of the Banu Hillal, a confederation of Bedouin tribes originally from the Arabian peninsula, in the same century. The Seljuk Turks had stormed into Persia and the eastern caliphate, while, most recently of all, Frankish Crusaders had invaded the Levant, seized the holy places and annexed part of Syria and Palestine. But Hulagu's invasion of 1258 was on an altogether different scale. It reduced Baghdad 'from the peerless seat of Islamic dominion to a shabby outpost of the Ilkhan Empire'.[28] It was, by far, the most shattering blow the Muslim world had ever received and imperilled the very future of Islam.

*

For one Baghdadi, at least, the fall of the City of Peace was less a cataclysm than a godsend. The story of Ahmed ibn Amran illustrates the astonishing career possibilities afforded by ruthless treachery. A former slave, Ibn Amran had a lowly, if eccentric, position, employed by the governor of Bakuba, north-east of Baghdad, to massage the soles of his master's feet and lull him to sleep during the long, hot summer afternoons. One day, Rashid al Din reported, during a particularly soporific spell, he dropped off on the job. Forced to explain himself on pain of a good beating, he said he had had an extraordinary dream in which he had been appointed governor of Baghdad, a revelation that resulted in a sound thrashing for his impertinence. Later, as Hulagu's Mongol army advanced on Baghdad, Ibn Amran discovered it was running out of provisions. He shot an arrow with a message attached into the Mongol camp, saying he had important information and requesting an interview with an officer. He duly conducted the Mongols to some hidden granaries, which contained enough supplies for a fortnight. After the sacking of Baghdad, Hulagu rewarded Ibn Amran handsomely, appointing him vizier with command of all the districts east of the city. He was tickled pink.[29]

Under the Mongol administrative reforms, the region was split into two provinces: Iraq Arabi, or Iraq of the Arabs, consisting of Lower

Mesopotamia, with Baghdad as its capital; and Iraq Ajemi, or Iranian Iraq, the mountainous region to the east, headquartered at Isfahan. The territory was placed under the command of the eldest son of Abuka, Hulagu's son and heir. This was humiliating proof, if any more were needed, that Baghdad's influence had been diluted to the point that it did not even command the province of Iraq, let alone an empire. The governorship of the city went to a distinguished Persian official, Ala al Din Ata Malik Juvayni, who had never tickled toes for a living, and hailed from a family that had produced a number of the most senior ministers in the Mongol Empire. Apart from his excellence in administration, which allowed Baghdad to begin the tortured process of rebuilding, Juvayni had a literary flair, which brought him lasting fame as the author of *Tarikh i Jahangusha* (*History of the World Conqueror*), a thirteenth-century account of Genghis Khan's Mongol Empire.

Juvayni was no scholarly dilettante, but a politician of serious mettle. He proved sufficiently steely to survive a number of intrigues against him, including one that saw him accused of amassing an illicit private fortune. For this alleged offence he was given a prohibitive fine, forced to wear a humiliating Chinese wooden collar and, when he proved unable to pay the total fine, imprisoned, tortured and paraded naked through the streets of Baghdad. Redemption – and reinstatement – came in 1282, when he was released by the new ilkhan, Sultan Ahmed Khan (Hulagu's son Tagudar, who had very publicly converted to Islam and changed his name). The governor's most troublesome critic, an inveterate plotter, was then torn to pieces by a vengeful mob in Baghdad (his head remained in Baghdad, while other pieces of his body were sent to different corners of the empire: his tongue to Tabriz, feet to Shiraz and hands to Isfahan).[30] Juvayni died a year later.

Baghdadis had lost their Abbasid Dynasty, but the new Muslim convert was determined to show they had not lost their religion. This message was at the heart of his coronation address to the city:

In the name of the most Merciful God. There is no god but God, and Mohammed is His Prophet. We who are seated on the throne of sovereignty are Muslims. Make it known to the inhabitants of Baghdad. Let them patronize the *madrassas* (colleges), the *wakfs* (religious foundations), and their other religious duties as they were accustomed to do in the time of the Abbasid Caliphs, and let everyone who has claims upon the various charities attached to the mosques and colleges be reinstated. Do not transgress the laws of Islam, O people of Baghdad. We know that the Prophet (may God grant him peace and pity) has said: 'This faith of Islam shall not cease to be triumphant till the day of resurrection.' We know that this prophecy is true, that it emanated from a true prophet, that there is only one God, unique and eternal. Rejoice, all of you, and make this known throughout the province.[31]

Religious tensions and differences resurfaced intermittently in Baghdad during this time. Many Muslims felt ill-disposed towards the Christian community, which had shown where its true loyalties lay on Hulagu's arrival at Baghdad and had scandalized many orthodox Baghdadis by building a church, as we have just seen, in the caliphal complex of palaces, traditionally the heart of Islamic authority. In 1268 the Nestorian patriarch, flexing his muscles, refused Juvayni's order to release a Christian man who had converted to Islam and was under threat of execution. Not for the first time, the mob demonstrated it was the real power in Baghdad: rushing in terror through the streets, with a crowd baying for blood at his heels, the patriarch narrowly escaped with his life, only to be exiled from Baghdad by Juvayni. In 1271 another rush of anti-Christian feeling prompted the government to imprison all the city's clergy, who were suspected of plotting against the governor. With the arrival of Sultan Ahmed as ilkhan, the court became distinctly less friendly to Christians, and many Nestorians converted to the ruler's new faith. In time, sensing the period of Christian influence in high places was drawing to a close in Baghdad, the Nestorian patriarch left the city and withdrew his official seat to the relative safety of the northern highlands at Erbil, in what is now Iraqi Kurdistan.

Baghdad's long-standing spirit of conflict ensured that religious sensibilities were not confined to its own citizens, be they Christian, Muslim or Jew. Sultan Ahmed's religious conversion had upset many within the Mongol nobility. Within two years of his accession he was faced with a revolt led by his nephew Arghun, Hulagu's grandson, who ransacked the treasury in Baghdad and extorted money for his rebellion from the terrified citizens of Baghdad. In 1284 Ahmed was captured by his own officers and put to death by having his back broken. Baghdadis were never less than inventive in devising unusual methods of torture and execution.

One of the most remarkable governors of Baghdad was Saad al Dawla, a Jewish physician raised to the highest office in a quintessentially Muslim state, eventually being promoted to grand vizier. His elevation, the great patronage it conferred and the energy with which he exercised it, especially among relatives, was met with predictable tirades against him and his co-religionists. While the Mongols resented his monopoly of power over tax revenues, Muslims were outraged by a Jew having authority over them. As one Baghdad poet complained:

> The Jews of this our time a rank attain
> To which the heavens might aspire in vain.
> Theirs is dominion, wealth to them does cling,
> To them belong both councillor and king.
> O people, hear my words of counsel true
> Turn Jew, for Heaven itself has turned a Jew![32]

Saad's royal protection disappeared with the death of Ilkhan Arghun in 1291, an event that triggered his immediate assassination and a wider campaign against Baghdad's Jews. A frenzied mob attacked the Jewish quarter, and many were killed on both sides. Baghdad's Jews came under renewed suspicion during the reign of Ilkhan Oljaitu (1304–16), when they began to convert to Islam in large numbers. Unconvinced of their sincerity, the vizier Rashid al Din ordered all new converts to eat a dish of camel's meat seethed in milk, a particularly vindictive decree, since this represented a double transgression against Jewish dietary law. Jews were also forbidden from visiting the shrine of the prophet Ezekiel at Kifl in south-eastern Iraq, one of the most important Jewish sites in the country. These punishments, however troubling, were as nothing compared to those that awaited Baghdad's Jews in the coming centuries.

*

In 1327, seven decades after the conquering hordes of Hulagu had laid waste to Baghdad, a rather sunnier visitor arrived in Baghdad. Author of the charmingly named volume *A Precious Gift to Those Who Contemplate the Wonders of Cities and the Marvels of Travelling*, he was two years into what would turn out to be an odyssey of 75,000 miles and twenty-nine years. The indefatigable and irrepressible Moroccan was the undisputed 'Traveller of Islam', whose long journeys saw him dining with sultans, khans and emperors, escaping from pirates, marrying wives at the drop of a hat, siring children on multiple continents, crossing deserts, dodging the Black Death and finding unexpected employment as judge and courtier. He hopped on to camels, mules and horses, boarded junks, dhows and rafts, clambered on to ox-wagons and, whenever necessary, travelled by foot, with an unmistakable spring in his step. His name was Ibn Battuta.

His route to Baghdad had taken him to the famous Iraqi cities of Kufa, which was beset by 'violence' and 'desolation'; Hillah, where the 'factional strife' was uninterrupted; and Kerbala, where 'fighting continues interminably' between two factions.[33] In other words, he was admirably prepared for the City of Peace.

Every traveller to Baghdad had his (very rarely 'her' until the twentieth century) own interests, some more peculiar than others. For Ibn Battuta it was baths – they were to the high-spirited Moroccan what sermons were to the Andalusian traveller Ibn Jubayr in 1184. A spa-lover before his time, he was hugely impressed by the bath-houses' state-of-the-art facilities and particularly taken by their generosity when it came to pampering their customers with fluffy towels:

> The baths at Baghdad are numerous and excellently constructed, most of them being painted with pitch, which has the appearance of black marble. This pitch is brought from a spring between Kufa and Basra, from which it flows continually. It gathers at the sides of the spring like clay and is shovelled up and brought to Baghdad. Each establishment has a large number of private bathrooms, every one of which has also a wash-basin in the corner, with two taps supplying hot and cold water. Every bather is given three towels, one to wear round his waist when he goes in, another to wear round his waist when he comes out, and the third to dry himself with. In no town other than Baghdad have I seen all this elaborate arrangement . . .[34]

Ibn Battuta reported two fixed pontoon bridges across the Tigris: they carried a continuous traffic of men and women from one bank to the other, night and day, an activity that gave 'unending pleasure' to the people of Baghdad.[35] His comments on the city tend to echo those of Ibn Jubayr, which may perhaps be a bit of old-fashioned plagiarism. West Baghdad was 'for the most part in ruins', reduced to thirteen quarters and many orchards and gardens. The hospital mentioned by Ibn Jubayr was now 'a vast ruined edifice, of which only vestiges remain'.

Yet, however devastating Hulagu's ransacking of Baghdad had been, the city's east bank had evidently managed to recover in the intervening decades, for Ibn Battuta described a place of many bazaars and colleges. The Moroccan man of letters was thrilled to visit 'the wonderful Nizamiya College, the splendour of which is commemorated in a number of proverbial phrases'.[36] His favourite seat of learning, however, was Mustansiriya University, one of Baghdad's finest ancient monuments, a stone's throw from the Tigris. 'All four schools [of Islam] are included in it, each school having a separate *iwan* with its own mosque and lecture room. The teacher takes his place under a small wooden canopy, on a chair covered with rugs; he sits in a grave and quiet attitude, wearing robes of black and his turban, and with two assistants on his right and left, who repeat everything that he dictates.'[37]

Flighty and frivolous one moment, earnest and erudite the next, the Moroccan shared his Andalusian predecessor's interest in tombs, mentioning that of Abu Hanifa near the Rusafa Mosque; the tomb of Ahmed ibn Hanbal, 'held in great veneration by the inhabitants, most of whom follow his school'; and the shrines of several Sufi saints, which he mistakenly ascribed to the east bank.

Ibn Battuta was no prude. An incorrigible gossip, he couldn't resist including the following scandalous story about Sultan Abu Said (1316–35), also known as Bahadur the Brave, then ruler of Baghdad. Abu Said had been married to an extremely beautiful woman called Baghdad Khatun, who held complete sway over him and enjoyed high position for most of their married life. In later years, however, he married another woman, called Dilshad, 'whom he loved with a violent passion, and neglected Baghdad Khatun. She became jealous in consequence, and administered poison to him in a kerchief, with which she wiped him after conjugal relations. So he died and his line became extinct.' Local amirs seized the provinces and vowed revenge on the woman. Her assailant 'came to her while she was in the bath-house and beat her to death with his club. Her body lay there for some days, with only her pudenda covered with a piece of sacking.'[38]

*

If Ibn Battuta bore sad witness to the physical ruin into which much of Baghdad had fallen, he missed the extreme political disarray and steady disintegration of the Mongol Ilkhanate that followed the end of the reign of Abu Said, the last great Mongol ilkhan, whose childless death in 1335 triggered civil war. In the eight years following his death, a total of six puppet ilkhans – including Sati Beg (1338–9), the short-lived first female ruler – came and went in a confusing flurry of plotting and bloodletting, as rival provinces of Iran pressed their claim to the throne.*

The city that had until only recently been the centre of the civilized world, treasure-house of the Dar al Islam and a formidable military power was becoming a more or less defenceless possession fought over by a succession of chancers. Its vertiginous decline was such that, by 1339, the City of Peace was merely the winter capital of the rump Jalayirid state, a Mongol territory encompassing northern and eastern Iraq and western Iran, carved out of the collapsing Mongol Ilkhanate by an ambitious vassal. The summer capital of this fledgling state was the ancient city of Tabriz in north-western Iran.

While these political problems were reducing Baghdad to a pitiful state, natural disasters also continued to stalk the city, creating further misery for its beleaguered population. In 1356 the waters of the Tigris swept through the defences in a terrible flood that washed away several districts. The same thing happened, more extremely, in 1374, when it was said that 40,000 Baghdadis died in the flooding. By this time the Ilkhanate was in freefall, with local wars in Persia, Azerbaijan and Iraq, together with repeated uprisings and assassinations in Baghdad opening the way for the opportunistic Sultan Ahmed Jalayir, one-time ruler of Sultaniya and Tabriz, to invade Iraq in 1383 and seize power in Baghdad.

As tumultuous and damaging as all this factional fighting was for Baghdad, it was as nothing compared with what would shortly follow.

*

On the morning of 23 July 1401, the inhabitants of Baghdad woke to another searingly hot summer day. The Tigris glittered as it slid slowly through the city on its journey south. Much of the city's skyline – dun roof terraces, the green thrust of palm trees, iridescent, blue-tiled mosque domes – was blurred in the shimmering haze. Only the minarets

---

* The five ilkhans were puppets to the short-lived Jalayirid and Chobanid dynasties, which emerged from the wreckage of the Ilkhanate.

poked through the rolling waves of light, standing silently like warning exclamation marks. Yet the silence was not one of peace, but of imminent calamity. Looking out at a vast enemy army encamped around their city, a horizon-filling host of savage-looking soldiers, sappers and cavalry divisions, smoking campfires and ermine-lined imperial tents, 'the astonished inhabitants no longer looked upon their city as the house of peace, but as the palace of hell and discord'.[39]

They were right to be alarmed. The noose around Baghdad was tightening with every day that passed. For the previous six weeks, Baghdad had been under siege, encircled the length of its six-mile circumference, according to the fifteenth-century Persian court historian Sharaf al Din Ali Yazdi, by a host of Tatar forces bent on rapine, plunder and slaughter. The Tatars were a Turkic people of Mongol origin, descendants of Genghis Khan's hordes, who had converted to Islam after their settlement in Central Asia. These countless thousands of warriors were loyal to the fearsome Temur, self-proclaimed Sword Arm of the Faith, Lord of the Fortunate Conjunction, Emperor of the Age and Conqueror of the World. Better known in the West as Tamerlane, he had surged out of the Asian steppe in 1370, at the outset of an extraordinary career of conquest in which he had fallen on the great cities of Asia one by one like a firestorm. Like Hulagu's forces almost 150 years earlier, the eastern invaders had built a bridge-of-boats over the Tigris and stationed archers downriver to prevent the inhabitants escaping. Upriver, two royal princes guarded the approaches to the city. All escape routes had been cut off.

Earlier in the year, having plundered Sivas and Aleppo, Tamerlane had turned on Damascus, sacking it in a frenzy of killing. The great Umayyad Mosque, symbol of the ruling dynasty that had been swept aside by the Abbasids, centrepiece of the city Baghdad had displaced as capital of the Islamic Empire, was torched. It was, said Ibn Arabshah, the fifteenth-century Syrian author of a poisonous biography of Tamerlane, nothing short of a 'pilgrimage of destruction'.[40]* Now the Unconquered

---

* Arabshah had good reason to despise Tamerlane. At the tender age of eight or nine, he was captured by Tamerlane's forces during the sacking of Damascus in 1401 and carried off to Samarkand as a prisoner with his mother and brothers. Although he subsequently enjoyed an illustrious career, serving as confidential secretary to the Ottoman sultan Mohammed I, he never forgave Tamerlane for the terrible scenes of rape and pillage he had seen the Tatar hordes commit. Hence chapter headings such as 'This Bastard Begins to Lay Waste Azerbaijan and the Kingdoms of Irak' and 'How that Proud Tyrant was Broken & Borne to the House of Destruction, Where He Had His Constant Seat in the Lowest Pit of Hell'.

Lord of the Seven Climes had his eyes on a greater historical prize and 'descended to Baghdad with troops countless like ants, moths and locusts'.[41] Its people feared the worst, for all knew what happened when Tamerlane took a city that had previously slipped out of his grasp.

Even as the besieged tried not to confront their worst fears, they could hear a sickening, grating noise: Tamerlane's sappers were resolutely undermining the city walls, yard by subterranean yard. Panic-stricken, the defenders struggled to repair the mined walls as they began to collapse about them.

Yet perhaps there was still hope. Rumours were circulating that Tamerlane's princes and amirs had been pleading with the emperor to order an all-out assault, a request he had refused, the apologist Yazdi later explained (somewhat implausibly), on the grounds that the inhabitants would soon come to their senses, realize their mistake and beg forgiveness from the emperor. Tamerlane, according to this account, did not want to see the fine city of Baghdad 'entirely ruined'.[42]

Baghdadis shivered at the memory of the last time Tamerlane had arrived outside the city walls. Yazdi recorded how, on 10 October 1393, the Tatar descended with his innumerable hordes, an army that stretched for more than five miles north and south of the city. What particularly stunned Baghdadis was the sight of this great host swimming across the river with all their armour and equipment, a feat that made the citizens 'bite their fingers in wonder'.[43] Wisely, they opened the city gates to Tamerlane, whose army then plundered 'whole treasures' left by its terrified ruler Sultan Ahmed – who had fled ignominiously at his approach, first to Hilla, thence to Egypt, abandoning both his army and family in the process. Yazdi likened the Tatar troops to 'armies of pismires [ants] or grasshoppers, they covered the fields, pillaging on all sides'.[44] Although the Sword of Islam fell on the necks of hundreds of thousands more Muslims than either Jews or Christians during his bloody career of conquest, Tamerlane nevertheless always took pains to appear a devout Muslim ruler. Thus it was that he ordered all the wine discovered in Baghdad – *haram*, or forbidden by Islam, although covert drinking had been a feature of the city's life from Abbasid times – to be poured into the Tigris. He also took all Baghdad's scholars and learned men, in addition to Sultan Ahmed's wives and children, into captivity as intellectual ornaments for his beloved imperial capital Samarkand, Pearl of the East. These prisoners included 'the masters of the renowned

Baghdad school of book illumination, who had enjoyed the protection of Sultan Ahmed'.[45] Those who remained were forced to pay a punitive tribute for their lives.

This time, surely, would be far worse. In the eight years since Tamerlane had brought his army to Baghdad, Sultan Ahmed and his vassal-cum-ally Kara Yusef, leader of the Black Sheep Turkmen tribes, had flouted his authority repeatedly, and Ahmed had retaken Baghdad. It was an affront that could not go unpunished. Fearing the retribution that he would undoubtedly inflict, Sultan Ahmed briefly considered a defence of the city and brought Turkmen troops from Kara Yusef for the purpose, only to panic and take flight again when Tamerlane's approach had been confirmed. The two men escaped to Aleppo and sought refuge at the Ottoman court in Anatolia. At this moment of great danger, Baghdad was leaderless.

By noon, the summer inferno was too intense for the defenders to remain standing on guard on the shadowless city walls. The 'violence of the heat', Yazdi reported, was such that 'birds fell down dead' in mid-flight, and armoured soldiers 'melted like wax'.[46] Boiling in their armour, the sweating soldiers propped up their helmets on sticks behind the ramparts in a clumsy attempt to convince the Tatars they were still on guard, abandoned their positions and droopily returned home.

It was the cue for Tamerlane, far too cunning to be taken in by such a simple ruse, to order a general assault. The Tatar trumpets sounded, kettle drums shook the air in a barrage of noise, and the army stormed the city. Those Baghdadis who had been cowering behind the walls and now peered gingerly over them to see what was happening were met with a terrifying vision. Countless scaling ladders were being lifted up and slammed against the lofty walls. A seemingly unstoppable torrent of soldiers surged up them, as massed ranks of archers behind them loosed volley after volley into the city. Within moments one of the emperor's most trusted commanders, Sheikh Nur al Din, had mounted Tamerlane's dreaded horsetail standard, crowned with a half-moon, on the city walls. 'Faraj [governor of the city] and the inhabitants of Bagdad were struck with fear,' Yazdi wrote, 'so that they fought not so much out of bravery as from despair.'[47]

There was no way out for the besieged. Many Baghdadis, fearing the whole city would be massacred, frantically threw themselves into the Tigris with their families, only to be cut down by the archers wait-ing below. Others took to small boats and chanced their luck on the river, but were quickly felled by the vicious volleys of arrows. Faraj and his daughter tried to escape in a boat, but it was shot at and cap-sized. In an echo of the unsuccessful escape attempt made by the caliph Mustasim's vice-chancellor under fire from Hulagu's forces in 1258, they both drowned in the Tigris. Tamerlane's boatmen retrieved Faraj's soaking corpse and dumped it unceremoniously on to the river bank.

For the second time in his career, Baghdad belonged to Tamerlane. Those Baghdadis who already knew the Conqueror of the World's fear-some reputation for butchery must have been completely transfixed by the news, for there was an inevitability about what would follow the city's fall. Through three decades of calculated savagery, terror had been used to strike fear into his enemies' hearts, to rid newly conquered ter-ritories of opponents and to minimize the risks of future rebellion. It encouraged prompt surrender, since defiance would meet only with the swiftest and most terrible retribution. No matter how magnificent or illustrious a recalcitrant city had once been, it would be reduced to a smoking ruin, decapitated corpses piled high in the streets, their severed heads built into great towers and set alight as flaming beacons, totems of his wrath, to mark another conquest.

The retaking of Baghdad had vexed Tamerlane and cost him many men. Mercy – except for the religious leaders and scholars who threw themselves at his feet, begging pardon and quarter, and were given robes of honour and escorted to safety – was out of the question. 'He turned towards the city the reins of anger and destroyed whatever his hand obtained, by flood and fire and overshadowed them with dense clouds of affliction, after he had attacked like thunder and lightning,' wrote Ibn Arabshah.[48]

In practice this meant one of his most vengeful orders. Each of his soldiers, Arabshah reported, must fetch him two Baghdad heads.

> They brought them singly and in crowds and made the river Tigris flow
> with the torrent of their blood throwing their corpses on to the plains,
> and collected their heads and built towers of them; but they slew violently
> of the people of Baghdad about ninety thousand. Some, when they could

not have Baghdadis, cut the heads of Syrians who were with them and other prisoners; others, when heads of men were wanting, cut off the heads of ladies of the marriage-bed.[49]

The slaughter was so rampant, and Tamerlane's orders so feared, that some were reduced to killing their companions to bring the emperor the requisite number of heads. Even Yazdi, Tamerlane's most stalwart apologist, admitted that the conqueror 'spared neither old men of fourscore, nor children of eight years of age. No quarter was given either to rich or poor; and the number of dead was so great that no one could count 'em up.'[50]

The physical destruction of Baghdad came next, and again it was complete. In Yazdi's account, 'Temur gave orders that there should not remain one single house in the city unrazed.'[51] Mosques, colleges and hospitals alone were to be spared, according to Yazdi, doubtless with an eye on Tamerlane's posthumous reputation, though after events in Damascus, including the devastation of the Umayyad Mosque, whether they actually were seems highly improbable. Tamerlane's traditional practice was to visit wholesale destruction on recalcitrant cities. Markets, caravanserais, hermitages, monasteries, palaces and Ibn Battuta's beloved bath-houses went up in smoke. Arabshah confirmed how the Tatar 'laid waste the city', sacking it and plundering its 'hidden wealth'. He 'overturned the whole city from top to bottom', leaving in his wake a scene of total desolation.[52]

This was the time of the annual *haj* to Mecca, the holiest time in the calendar for Muslims. Having put 90,000 – mostly Muslims – to the sword, the Sword Arm of Islam now went serenely on a pilgrimage to the tomb of Imam Abu Hanifa in eastern Baghdad, a graceful shrine topped with a white cupola, 'to implore the intercession of this saint', without a touch of irony.[53] When Hulagu sacked Baghdad, as Baghdadis still recall with a wince today, the Tigris was said to flow black from the ink of all the books hurled into the river. After Tamerlane fell upon the city, the chroniclers had it flowing red with blood.

While Tamerlane said his prayers at the shrine, his soldiers were putting the finishing touches to the 120 towers of skulls they had erected around the flattened city.[54] Vultures circled above the ruins of Baghdad, dropping out of the sky to pluck eyes from their sockets. Owls and crows made their nests in the remnants of royal palaces. The air was putrid with the stench of corpses decomposing fast in the midsummer heat.

Tamerlane's 'pilgrimage of destruction' was nearing its end. Baghdad, like Antioch and Acre, Baalbek and Beirut, Hama and Homs, Damascus and Aleppo, before it, lay in ruins. The 'city of peace', wrote Arabshah, had become 'the house of surrender'.[55]

6

Black Sheep, White Sheep (1401–1534)

*The long age of poverty, confusion and neglect that followed the
Mongol inroad has repelled the historians alike of Hammurabi
and of Cyrus, of Seleucus and Khasrau and Harun. Darkness of
varying depth falls over Iraq history from the hour when the light
of the Khalifate was extinguished until the present century.*

Stephen Hemsley Longrigg, *Four Centuries of
Modern Iraq* (1925)

Baghdad shivers beneath a crushing cobalt sky. It is a piercing winter's
morning. For those acclimatized to the customary inferno, when the
head-crushing heat scrambles minds and ignites arguments that flare up
instantly and just as quickly subside, the cold is a sharp shock. Baghdadis wear heavy coats and mournful expressions. Staccato bursts of
gunfire rifle across the city. Sirens wail in the distance. American Black
Hawk helicopters surge across the skyline, gunners levelling their weapons towards unknown targets. 'This is an interesting day for sightseeing,'
my friend Thair jokes as we set off in a convoy of armoured vehicles to
Kadhimiya, home to the greatest Shia sanctuary in Baghdad and one of
the four Atiyat Aliyat, or Shia shrine cities of Iraq.* The city is not at
peace.

Conflict is an unhappily appropriate backdrop for a visit to the
Kadhimain shrine. Over the centuries it has often been the flashpoint in
riots between Sunni and Shia. One of the worst encounters came in
1051, when a group of Sunni took exception to a proposed inscription
for a gateway in the district of Karkh, south of Mansur's Round City.
The suggested legend, in praise of the caliph Ali, was held to be

---

* The four Atiyat Aliyat (sublime thresholds) are Kadhimiya, Najaf, Kerbala and Samarra.

blasphemous in the eyes of the orthodox. Words were exchanged, a fight followed, and the leading Sunni figure was killed. At his funeral the next day the quarrel was renewed, escalating into a full-blown riot that spread to Kadhimiya. The crowd of Sunni agitators plundered the shrine, seized the gold and silver fittings, ripped down the brocade curtains, removed the numerous jewels and set the complex on fire. According to the Arab historian Ibn al Athir (1160–1233), author of the magisterial *The Complete History*, the great teak domes above the shrines of the two holy men were consumed by the flames, which then spread to the tombs of Jafar, son of the caliph Mansur, two Buyid princes, Harun al Rashid's royal consort Zubayda and their son and later caliph Amin.

Leaving the Green Zone through Assassins' Gate, a kitsch sandstone arch whose name gives pause for thought, the convoy arrows north-west down Haifa Street, parallel to the Tigris. The river likened by the twelfth-century geographer Ibn Jubayr to a shining mirror and a string of pearls is a curmudgeonly grey sludge today. Here and there among the concrete tower blocks we rush past are handsome, broad-fronted villas with bow windows, Ionic columns, elaborate balconies and painted pediments and panels, a free-spirited exercise in classicism tinged with the East. Most are marked by gunfire from the fighting that raged here recently. The security guards, former British Army soldiers, alternate between dark mutterings about the danger of the route ('Best place in Baghdad to run into a vee-bid, we should have taken 14 July Street')* and enthusiastic discussions about women and weapons. American forces have nicknamed Haifa Street 'Grenade Alley' and 'Purple Heart Boulevard' after numerous attacks from insurgents.

On a map of Baghdad the Tigris traces a facial profile through the city. Kadhimiya resembles a boil above the large nose formed by the districts of Karkh and Karadat Maryam to the south, bound to the north, south and east by the river. Our route to it takes us across ground on which Mansur's Round City once stood. It was Mansur who designated this land north of his walled city Makaber Kuraish, the graveyard of Kuraish, the principal tribe of the Prophet Mohammed and his descendants. He used it as the cemetery for members of the Abbasid dynasty and their cousins, the Alawites. His eldest son, Jafar, was first to be buried here in

---

* VBIED is the acronym for Vehicle-Borne Improvised Explosive Device.

767, but it was the burial here of Imam Musa al Kadhim here in 799, followed by his grandson Mohammed al Jawad in 834, that proved the more lasting influence. Today Kadhimiya is a district of gilded domes and minarets (there are fifty-two mosques), narrow alleys, covered markets such as Souk al Musakaf, Astrabardi and Fadhwa, booksellers, pilgrim guesthouses, crowded gold markets, the Jama Agd Assada and Al Jawadin libraries, and restaurants offering the local specialities of date juice and *bakila bi dahn*, broad beans in oil. It is a place for pious pilgrims, peckish shoppers and bookish intellectuals alike.

We branch off north-east on to Imam Musa al Kadhim Street. Several minutes later, a pair of golden domes thrust into a cluttered skyline and we have arrived. It is still early in the day, but the wide, pedestrianized street of shops and hotels is already busy. 'Most of these people are pilgrims,' Thair says. 'Iraqis and Iranians. They come to visit and pray at the two graves inside that are kept in gold structures beneath the domes, ornamented by hand and decorated with verses from the holy Koran. On Fridays and Saturdays they say there are half a million visitors here.' Young couples patrol the lines of gold shops like generals inspecting a parade, pausing here and there to pick up a piece of jewellery and talk to a shopkeeper. 'This is their traditional visit to Kadhimiya. They're about to be married so they come here to buy the wedding rings and the bride's set of jewellery that is part of her trousseau. Kadhimiya is very famous for its goldsmiths in Asharif Arredi, Bab al Kibla and Bab al Murad, who make their jewellery and everything else by hand. They're highly skilled and the same family can produce generations of goldsmiths.' Thair sighs. He is unmarried. 'You know, it's expensive for the man. According to custom he must pay for all the jewellery. That can be thousands of dollars.'

We walk and talk, and the shrine rears up before us behind a blue-tiled arched portal. It is wrapped in a walled enclosure adorned with rolling Kufic script of verses from the Koran, its gates clad with intricately worked tiles that are a riot of blue, yellow, green and white. These tiles pay tribute to an artistic heritage that dates back to Abbasid times, when the city was the world centre for glazed ceramics. The vastness of the site – the walls measure almost 135 metres by 200 metres – seems purposefully designed to humble the visitor into a sense of religious awe. There is no question of going in. Originally built at some point during the time of Harun al Rashid, expanded in around 947 by the

Buyid ruler Muizz al Dawla, who had two wooden domes and a surrounding wall built, in its current form it dates back to the sixteenth century, when the Persian Shah Ismail I took Baghdad in 1508 and embarked on a comprehensive renovation. Fully restored after decades of neglect during Saddam Hussein's regime, today it is one of the city's most magnificent sights. Its twin domes, swathed in golden tiles that flash like beacons in the sunlight, are visible from afar, flanked by a cordon of four slender, golden-tipped minarets.

It is not difficult to imagine the uplifting effect it must have had – and continues to have – on tired pilgrims at the end of their gruelling journey to Baghdad. 'They'd have been struggling across the desert for such a long time then suddenly they see this amazing colour in contrast to all the brown brick buildings around it, these great domes rising out of the groves of palm trees close to the river,' Thair says. At night, illuminated in swathes of green neon, with white bulbs glowing along the four lines of lights that link the minarets together, the Kadhimain shrine is an arresting vision of the old and the new, the burnished gold of its twin bullet-like domes and minarets blazing like fire across the skyline above the brilliant lights of the gold shops. This is the glittering Shia counterpart to the Sunni shrine of Abu Hanifa, which lies across the Tigris just over a mile to the east. Where Abu Hanifa is understated to the point of drabness, Kadhimain is colourful and showy to the point of ostentation. If the defining sectarian divide within Islam runs through Iraq, nowhere does it feel more acute than in this small stretch of land and water between these two shrines.

In its current glory Kadhimain is also a triumphant symbol of defiance. For all the onslaughts it has suffered, it is one of Baghdad's greatest survivors, enduring the vicissitudes of the city's history through fire, flood and plunder. The list of casualties goes back centuries. After the disaster of 1051, its main dome was destroyed by fire in 1225, then rebuilt. In 1258 Hulagu visited the full fury of his Mongol troops on the sanctuary, plundering and setting fire to it. Having been rebuilt again, by 1300 it was once more a ruin, victim of two serious floods of the Tigris. Seven centuries later, it was targeted, together with other places holy to Iraq's Shia, in a number of attacks linked to the global terror group Al Qaeda and its supporters. The worst loss of life in recent years came on 31 August 2005, when almost 1,000 Shia pilgrims commemorating the death of Imam Musa al Kadhim were killed in a stampede across Aimma (Imams) Bridge triggered by rumours of an imminent terror attack.

The street is filling steadily. Heads turn. The foreign sightseer in body armour is attracting stares. 'Come on, it's time to leave,' says Thair. 'We have been here long enough. It's not safe.'

*

For the century and a half that separated Hulagu's and Tamerlane's annihilating visits to the City of Peace, Baghdad had at least been able to dream of future glory. Although Genghis Khan's grandson had snuffed out the Abbasid caliphate and hurled Baghdad into the abyss, the city had gingerly recovered and hauled itself back to its feet, to the extent that it could perhaps aspire to the greatness of its new rival, Tabriz, summer capital of the Jalayirid state, 350 miles to the north-east across the mountains of Kurdistan. After Tamerlane's second attack in 1401, such dreams were entirely crushed.

The physical ruin inflicted by the Mongol and Tatar conquerors was the first obvious consequence of the storm they unleashed upon the city. The jewels in Baghdad's architectural crown – the splendid caliphal palaces, the grand mosques and the sumptuous royal parks of the Abbasid age – had all been obliterated. Yet houses, mosques and marketplaces could be rebuilt relatively easily. Baghdad's most fundamental problem was how to deal with the legacy of Hulagu's calculated destruction of the elaborate network of waterways, dykes and headworks upon which the city's prosperity had long depended. Since ancient times the wealth, power and success of Mesopotamia had been underpinned by flourishing irrigation systems. The civilizations and empires of the Sumerians, Babylonians, Assyrians and Persians had all been founded upon an exploitation of the fertile Tigris and Euphrates Rivers.[1] After these networks were ripped up, it did not take long for the waterways to silt up and fall into complete disrepair, a situation that the remaining inhabitants of the city stood little immediate chance of changing. The slaughter of Baghdad's population ensured that the repair and then regular maintenance required to resuscitate the infrastructure was simply out of the question.

To the physical destruction inflicted by Hulagu and Tamerlane must be added the far longer-lasting political decline ushered in by their invasions. Here the historian must lay the greater blame, or indeed credit, at the feet of the earlier conqueror. However steeply it had declined over the centuries, the Abbasid caliphate in 1258 still represented the Islamic Empire and, even if honoured more in the breach than in the observance, the unity of the Muslim world, from the shores of North Africa to the roof of the world in Central Asia. Baghdad had owed its greatness to being the headquarters of this continent-spanning empire. On the eve of Hulagu's assault it had still been the flag-bearer of Islamic rule, but overnight the flagpole was uprooted and then smashed to pieces. Baghdad's primacy, the fruit of centuries of labour, conquest and culture, was over.

The second storm wiped out the limited recovery the city had made since the first. When Tamerlane fell on Baghdad, the city was still – in the Syrian writer Ibn Arabshah's words – 'more famous than can be described and the aroma of its excellence and merits more fragrant than can be shown'; but its political significance bore little relation to the importance it had enjoyed until 1258.[2] From an ailing imperial metropolis, the city became simply the winter capital of the state that had emerged from the ruins of Hulagu's Ilkhanate in Iraq and western Persia. Its position as the centre of the Dar al Islam was receding into memory; while Iraq languished, other powers were emerging to the west and the east.

The withering of literary life completed the unhappy trio of desolations suffered by Baghdad in the wake of Hulagu's and Tamerlane's offensives. As the wounded City of Peace left the stage with a weary bow, after a stirring performance that had lasted more than six centuries, the great throng of writers exited the theatre. With the demise of the Abbasid court, there was precious little chance of finding literary fame and fortune in Baghdad. The era of the gold-scattering patron of the arts was gone.

Poets, those itinerant fortune-seekers like Abu Nuwas and Abu al Atahiya, purveyors of literary lustre to the metropolis, were no longer irresistibly drawn to Baghdad. The great geographers – Yakubi, Mukaddasi, latterly Yakut – had been and gone in that sparkle of Abbasid science and discovery, together with those formidable historians of the Abbasid era, Tabari and Masudi. Without an imperial dynasty, whose glory and fortunes they could trumpet in grandiloquent prose, there was no longer any need for court chroniclers and panegyrists.

As a result, Baghdad entered a dark period into which little historical light intruded. In the 1470s Venetian envoys left a smattering of descriptive detail about the court of Uzun Hassan, leader of the White Sheep (Ak Koyunlu) Turkmen tribes. From the late fourteenth century and for most of the fifteenth, the White Sheep vied with the Black Sheep (Kara Koyunlu) Turkmen for control of Baghdad and its territories, across an area that encompassed present-day Armenia, Azerbaijan, eastern Turkey and swathes of Iran and Iraq. Both were unruly confederations of Turkic tribes, pastoral nomads whose origins are obscure. It has been suggested that the names derived from the predominant colours of their flocks.³

These Venetian ambassadors prefigured a new source of information about medieval Baghdad. Literary travellers started to arrive in fits and starts from the 1550s, leaving high-spirited accounts that, in the absence of many other records, have been greedily welcomed by the historians of the city.

*

In the aftermath of Tamerlane's invasion, Baghdad's future soon lay chiefly in the hands of two men. Their lowly status, in comparison with the Abbasid caliphs of old, underlined the humiliating and painful relegation inflicted upon the city. The Jalayirid chief sultan Ahmed and his brother-in-arms Kara Yusef, leader of the Black Sheep Turkmen, were hardly world leaders who bestrode 'the narrow world' like colossi, but ambitious local chieftains.

Learning that the ever-factious Baghdadis had wasted little time in driving out Tamerlane's appointed governor, they returned from Anatolia in 1402 and briefly repossessed the city. In response, Tamerlane, preparing for war with the Ottoman sultan Bayazid, his greatest adversary in the Muslim world, dispatched four cavalry divisions, one led by his grandson Mirza Abu Bakr, to settle the uprising. According to the fifteenth-century Persian chronicler Mirkhwand, Ahmed, who had had little warning, immediately turned tail, as was his wont, and fled across the river, wearing only his shirt.⁴ In a telling demonstration of how little Baghdad now mattered, Tamerlane abruptly withdrew his forces from Iraq to reinforce his campaign in Anatolia, allowing Ahmed, lingering like a bad smell, to return once again. By now Baghdadis knew enough of the Jalayirid leader to feel distinctly jaundiced towards him. 'Ahmed was not altogether popular in the city, partly owing to his tyrannical treatment of the people ... partly to the fact that, when any trouble arose, he seemed to have the knack of saving himself at the expense of the community at large.'⁵ The balance of power in the relationship with Kara Yusef was also changing, the one-time vassal-turned-ally steadily emerging as the stronger partner. A subsequent dispute between the two men saw Ahmed doing what he did best – fleeing from Baghdad – this time, reportedly, on a cow.⁶ A later military mission by Mirza Abu Bakr saw both men captured by the sultan of Egypt's forces and imprisoned in Damascus, where they swore a secret alliance for future endeavours.

After the head-severing horrors he had inflicted the length and breadth of Asia during thirty-five years of constant campaigning, Tamerlane's death in 1405 was met with a continent-wide sigh of relief. Baghdad was refortified with walls that would stand, despite numerous sieges and assaults, until the nineteenth century. Ahmed and Kara Yusef were released from captivity, a move that enabled the former to return, disguised as a dervish, to take up the reins of power in Baghdad, to the likely chagrin of its put-upon citizens; while the latter consolidated his position in Kurdistan. In the spirit of the times, the alliance between Ahmed and Kara Yusef proved short-lived. In 1410, having just prised Tabriz from the hands of his former collaborator, Ahmed was wounded in battle and discovered hiding in a garden. Initially loath to do away with the man he had once served, the Black Sheep leader was eventually prevailed upon to have Ahmed quietly strangled.

Ahmed was not greatly missed by Baghdadis. Janus-like in his extremes, he was at once a high-minded intellectual and a cruel, scheming, opium-addicted hedonist. Away from the battlefield, he was an enthusiastic poet, painter and musician and a generous patron of artists such as Abd al Hay and Junaid Baghdadi, who evolved what came to be known as the Jalayirid style of Persian illustration. *Diwan*, Ahmed's beautifully illustrated volume of poems, would not have disgraced a better-known poet. He might have earned more lasting fame, perhaps, if his efforts to lure the great Persian poet Hafiz to Baghdad had succeeded. All we are left with, however, are a couple of tantalizing lines from the master that suggest he had at least entertained the invitation:

> In Shiraz we did not find our way to our goal;
> Happy that day when Hafiz shall take the road to Baghdad!⁷

In another poem, Hafiz praised Ahmed as 'a King of kingly descent' and the 'Soul of the World', likening him improbably (even by the standards of a panegyric) to Genghis Khan. Again, there was the suggestion that the poet had longed all along to make the City of Peace his home:

> No rose-bud of delight bloomed for me from the earth of Fars:
> O for the Tigris of Baghdad and the spiritual wine![8]

*

As low as Baghdad had fallen, the city's fortunes had further to sink. Hard on the heels of Ahmed's death, the City of Peace, long accustomed to royal rule, suffered the piercing indignity of falling under the command of first one slave, a man called Nakhasis, then another, Abdul Rahman, after a period of renewed disorder and violence. Kara Yusef's army soon put an end to this, inaugurating a Black Sheep Dynasty that would rule Baghdad, however nominally, until 1468. His son Shah Mohammed was appointed governor of the city, a position he held for twenty-three years.

The nominal rule of the Black Sheep, and the White Sheep who later supplanted them, reflects the fact that Baghdad's power had shrivelled to the point where it was little more than an isolated oasis of historical curiosity in a political desert that owed its allegiance to an ever-shifting whirl of tribal confederations. There was a literal element to the desert as well: once fertile fields that had fed the heartland of the empire now stretched into the sand-strewn horizon, offering no more than the scrubbiest grazing to wandering flocks. The always fine distinction between 'the desert and the sown' had blurred. Thus, within the short space of several generations,

> there was little except gigantic ruins to suggest that Iraq had ever been the proudest province of the great Abbasid Empire, or the seat in earlier ages of world-famous cities and active civilizations. The land that had once figured as Paradise in all the holy books of the Semitic religions, [was] now turned into an arid, treeless desert, across which swept every storm with irresistible force, upon which fell alike the pitiless heat of summer and the lingering floods of winter, fed by the errant waters of the great rivers, now for the first time since the great inundation of Noah freed from all direction and control.[9]

The Egyptian historian Al Makrizi (1364–1442) left an exceedingly bleak, pointedly brief portrait of the city in 1437: 'Baghdad is in ruins.

There are neither mosques, a faithful congregation, calls to prayer, nor souks; most of the palm trees are dried out. It cannot be called a town.'[10] When the Venetian merchant and explorer Nicolò de' Conti passed through in 1444, en route to Basra, he barely devoted a paragraph to the city, confusing Babylon with Baghdad, as many medieval writers did, giving the briefest mention to the plethora of ancient ruins and contenting himself with the bland observation that it was eight days' journey thence to Basra and another four to the Persian Gulf.[11]

Around the same time as de' Conti's visit, Baghdad fell to Jahan Shah, perhaps the greatest leader of the Black Sheep line. Initially a vassal of Tamerlane's son Shahrukh, after the latter's death in 1447 he declared independence, styled himself 'sultan' and 'khan' and set about the expansion of his fledgling realm. Under his energetic rule, the Black Sheep dominions expanded to encompass parts of Anatolia, most of Iraq, central Iran, Fars and Kerman, stretching south as far as the strategic Shatt al Arab waterway that divides Iraq from Iran. His rule was not without its problems, however. He was beset by persistent rebellions, including that of a mutinous son, Pir Budak, governor of Baghdad, who revolted against him, precipitating a year-long siege, which ended with the son's surrender and death. The end for Jahan Shah was equally bloody: in 1467 he was killed by the White Sheep chief Uzun Hassan (The Tall), who thereby ended the dynasty of the Black Sheep, his bitter adversaries, notwithstanding a brief, unsuccessful and ultimately fatal attempt by Jahan Shah's son Hassan Ali to reign in his father's place. True to form, the City of Peace did not buckle under to its new masters without a fight. Another siege had to be raised, yet another governor killed, before Baghdad grudgingly acknowledged Hassan's power.

Although Baghdad was of little interest to foreign powers at this time, there being nothing within it to excite imperial greed, the empire of Uzun Hassan was nevertheless assiduously courted by the Venetians, who were preoccupied with the rise of Ottoman power in the Mediterranean at this time. Hassan himself had good reason to oppose the Ottomans, having crossed swords with Sultan Mehmed II's army repeatedly in the early 1470s. Ambrosio Contarini, one of the Venetian envoys who visited the White Sheep court in Tabriz during the winter of 1474/5, left a portrait of Hassan. The king was very fond of his wine, he observed, drinking it with every meal, to the accompaniment of singing and flute-playing from his musicians. About seventy years old, he was tall and thin and generally 'a good liver . . . of a very merry disposition', but, like many drunks, 'when too far gone, was sometimes dangerous'. The decades of devotion to the pleasures of the grape had taken their toll: 'His hand trembled when he drank.'[12]

Distinguished visitors to Baghdad in this era who left a record of their experiences are few and far between. Where once the city had been the goal of every writer, scholar, scientist, poet, musician, lawyer or theologian, not to mention the most beautiful singing-girls and concubines, medieval Baghdad had abruptly dropped off the thinking man's – and singing-woman's – itinerary. Hafiz might have confessed in verse to a longing to travel to the city, but his poetic dream was never realized.

The great Persian poet Jami spent four months in Baghdad in the winter of 1472/3, an extremely disagreeable experience that he later reflected on with a flash of bitterness. He was travelling from Iran on *haj* to Mecca, and while living in the City of Peace had made an excursion to the holy Shia city of Kerbala. A disgruntled servant and his brother used this visit to doctor and highlight some verses Jami had written attacking religious 'dissenters', which became a cue for the Shia population of Baghdad to explode in a paroxysm of rage against the poet. Jami was forced to appear at a public assembly and to defend himself before the governor of Baghdad and his court, the religious authorities from the Hanafi and Shafi schools of jurisprudence, and large numbers of religious fanatics. Revealing his original text, which demonstrated the falsity of the charges against him, he triumphed against his accusers.

There was some consolation in revenge. First, he had his adversary's moustache shaved off in public. A more embarrassing fate awaited the brother of the de-moustached servant, who was made to wear a dunce's hat before being mounted on an ass, backwards, and paraded through the city's streets and bazaars. Such a public payback must have been gratifying to Jami, but the deeply unpleasant and no doubt highly intimidating encounter in Baghdad left an indelible scar. He later marked the occasion in a *ghazal*, or verse:

> O cupbearer, unseal the wine-jar by the brink of the Shatt,
> And wash from my memory the unpleasantness of the Baghdadis.
> Seal my lips with the wine-cup, for not one of the people of this
> land is worth discussion.

Expect not faithfulness or generosity from the unworthy;
Seek not for the virtues of men from the disposition of devils.[13]

The old ghosts of intrigue and regicide that had so haunted Baghdad returned after Uzun Hassan's death in 1478. 'Prince followed prince, intrigue and violence rent the loose and mutinous empire.'[14] Succession crises stalked the kingdom, the low-point of treachery reached when the mother of the White Sheep ruler Yakub Mirza poisoned her son in 1490, a murder that triggered yet another round of plotting, fighting and assassinations.

No longer a political or military force, nor even master of its own destiny, Baghdad was tossed to and fro in a storm of instability. The White Sheep Dynasty was tearing itself apart. Rival descendants of Uzun Hassan were embroiled in civil war. While the White Sheep Empire was drawn into this vortex of bloodletting, to the east a new power was on the rise. It was an auspicious moment for another foreign invasion.

*

The dawn of the sixteenth century saw Persia renascent. In the closing years of the preceding century, a descendant of the famed Sufi ascetic Sheikh Safi, founder of the eponymous Safavid holy order in Ardabil, north-western Persia, was attracting notice, less with his Koran than with his sword. As infant leader of the order, Ismail, grandson of the White Sheep ruler Uzun Hassan, began to rally his followers, and in 1499, at the delicate age of twelve, made his bid for power in Persia, supported by growing numbers of militants and revolutionaries. After defeating Alwand, one of the White Sheep rulers, in a momentous victory that opened the door to Tabriz, he proclaimed himself Shah Ismail in 1501.

Gruesome stories emerged from the taking of Tabriz. Pregnant women were massacred; the bodies of noblemen buried in cemeteries were disinterred and burnt; 300 prostitutes were lined up in public and cut in half; thieves were beheaded, their heads thrown into fires. Ismail was even reported to have had his stepmother beheaded, after discovering she had been married to one of the nobles who had fought at the Battle of Derbent (in Dagestan), where his father had been killed. 'From . . . Nero to the present, I doubt whether so bloody a tyrant has ever existed,' wrote an Italian merchant of the time, who had perhaps not heard of Genghis Khan, Hulagu or Tamerlane.[15]

Within a year, all of western Persia acknowledged Ismail's power, and further provinces fell to the messianic founder of the Safavid Dynasty, one by one.[16] Ismail may have been a holy man, but he was far from backward on the battlefield. After a brutal campaign in northern Persia, he had two captured enemy officers roasted on a spit and served up as kebabs.

For the first time since the Arab armies had stormed through in the surging conquests of the mid seventh century, Persia was a distinct entity once again. After 850 years of rule by Arab caliphs, Turkish sultans and Mongol khans, Persia was at last under Persian rule, with the Shia faith established as the official state religion.[17] In 1508, after defeating Murad, the White Sheep ruler of Iraq, Ismail sent his general Lala Hussain to seize Baghdad, which was taken without a fight. The Iraqi historian Abbas al Azzawi writes of how Hussain was installed as governor of Baghdad and Iraq with the grandiloquent honorific Khalifat al Khulafa, Caliph of Caliphs.[18]

Partly in celebration of Baghdad's capture, partly in pious pilgrim-age, Ismail visited the city within a year of its fall. He made little secret of where his religious loyalties lay, according to the Iraqi historian Abdul Aziz al Duri, levelling the tombs of Sunni saints and executing some of the city's leading Sunni figures, while lavishing money on the Kadhimain shrine and making the pilgrimage to the sacred Shia cities of Samarra, Kerbala and Najaf.[19] Not content with the deliberate destruc-tion of Abu Hanifa's shrine and that of the Hanbali preacher Sheikh Abdul Kadir al Gailani, the new Persian authorities issued the inflam-matory order for Sunni mosques to be converted to Shia mosques. One thousand miles to the north-west, exaggerated stories of Ismail's mas-sacre of Sunni ran through the thronged bazaars of Istanbul.

Yet, for the first time since most Baghdadis could remember, the City of Peace started to live up to its ancient moniker. Baghdad and the holy cities of Iraq supported the pronounced Shia inclinations of their new overlord, while the scattered tribes along the rivers respected his religious prestige. Persian merchants beat a path to Baghdad, adding commercial heft to this atmosphere of religious tranquillity. Twenty years or so passed without a major disturbance.

Such peace and calm, however, were not the natural order in Bagh-dad. Having been fought over for many decades by Black Sheep and White Sheep Turkmen, the city now found itself the focus of rivalry between two far more powerful adversaries: to the west, the Sunni Ottoman Empire of Sultan Selim the Grim (1512–20); to the east, the emerging Shia Safavid Empire of Shah Ismail. Optimists might detect in this some evidence of Baghdad's growing importance, but the status of the warring parties offered little consolation to Baghdad's embattled population.

The disappearance of the White Sheep territories as a buffer state between the two powers gave rise to conflict, heralded by the ritual exchange of bombastic threats. Ismail sent envoys to Selim, bearing gifts of a staff of gold, a handsome saddle and a richly mounted sword. 'Ismail, great Sovereign of the Persians, sends to you Selim these gifts, quite equal to your greatness, as they are worth as much as your kingdom; if you are a brave man, keep them well, because I will come and take them from you, together with your head and kingdom, which you possess against all right, as it is not proper that the offspring of peasants should bear rule over so many provinces.'[20]

Selim, we are told, had to restrain himself from a natural impulse to kill the ambassadors on the spot. After his courtiers had calmed him down, he confined himself to cutting off their noses and ears. He replied: 'Selim, great Sovereign of the Turks, replies to a dog without taking the least notice of his baying, telling him that if he will show himself, he will find that I will do to him what my predecessor Mahomet did to his predecessor Ussun Cassano [Uzun Hassan].'[21]

Religion was the ostensible *casus belli*, with Selim adopting the self-appointed role of defender of the orthodox faith. To demonstrate his credentials before embarking on his campaign, he outlawed the Shia faith within the empire and took the small precaution of butchering up to 40,000 Shia across his dominions. He also had all family members whom he considered to be potential usurpers killed, *pour décourager les autres*. Selim may have been an accomplished poet, but there was little evidence of a poetic sensibility in his astonishing willingness to shed blood. As he once remarked to his grand *mufti*, 'Is it not permitted to put to death two-thirds of the inhabitants of the empire for the greater good of the remaining third?'[22] Although Ismail's physical courage was widely commented upon – a contemporary Italian traveller thought him 'as brave as a game cock, and stronger than any of his lords' – his army was heavily outnumbered and was duly routed by the Ottomans at the Battle of Chaldiran in 1514.[23] Selim's army entered Tabriz in triumph.

The defeat had a profound effect upon Shah Ismail, who never again took to the field, despite a series of territorial losses during the next decade. He went into mourning, donning black clothes and a matching turban, and dyeing his military standard black. In northern Iraq, the Persian khan gave way to an Ottoman pasha. Truculent tribes played off one foreign master against another. And in Baghdad, the governor's grand honorific 'Caliph of Caliphs' offered the thinnest disguise of the loosening Persian hold. In 1528 a man called Dhul Fakar, nephew of the city's governor, demonstrated this weakening grip when he assassinated his uncle on a mountain pass in northern Iraq, before marching south and seizing power in Baghdad. Knowing he stood little chance of holding it without external support, and sensing which way the wind was blowing, the upstart rebel struck coins in the name of the Ottoman sultan, whose name was also read in the *khutba*, or Friday sermon, the traditional recognition of authority. Messages shot off to Istanbul, accompanied by the symbolic keys to the city, pledging allegiance and pleading for support.

Overnight, Baghdad slipped out of the Persian Empire and into the Ottoman. For the next two years it remained in Ottoman hands, until Shah Tahmasp I, son and heir of Ismail, vowed to reclaim it in 1530. When a series of straightforward military assaults proved unsuccessful, he resorted to subterfuge, recruiting Dhul Fakar's brothers to assassinate him in cold blood. Nevertheless, from the time Dhul Fakar seized power, Istanbul considered itself the rightful owner of the keys to Baghdad. Possession of the city was an important part of the Ottomans' effort to legitimize their claims to pre-eminence in the Middle East. Its lustre may have gone but its name, and the memories it evoked, remained a powerful symbol. Shah Tahmasp's audacious retaking of the city, therefore, represented a direct attack on the Ottoman sultan, Selim's descendant Suleyman the Magnificent, and a descent into the abomination of Shia heresy.

The Persian triumph proved but a brief respite. Rumblings of war, increasingly menacing since the mid 1520s, grew louder, as Sultan Suleyman, the Magnificent, the Lawgiver, the Lord of His Age, sought to impose himself across the lands held by the boy-shah Tahmasp. As ever, the pretexts for war were not difficult to devise for those bent on conflict. Incidents along the frontier, where the governor of Bitlis had defected from Ottoman to Persian service, admirably served the purpose, together with conveniently drafted *fatwas* justifying the war and demanding the extermination of Shia. Safavid territory also threatened Ottoman ascendancy over the trade routes linking south-east Asia to eastern Europe. With control of the route through the Red Sea and Egypt assured after the Ottoman defeat of the Egyptian Mamluk Sultanate at the gates of Cairo in 1517, from which time Ottoman rulers proclaimed themselves the rightful successors of the Abbasid caliphs, Istanbul's ambitions turned towards the trading route through Iraq and the Gulf.

Suleyman's 'Campaign of the Two Iraqs' – a reference to the Mongol-era division of the territory into Iraq Arabi (Lower Mesopotamia) and Iraq Ajemi (the mountainous country to the east) – thundered into life, and by 1533 his grand vizier Ibrahim Pasha was marauding in the northern highlands. On 16 July 1534, after Kurdish fortresses along the frontier near Van surrendered, Tabriz fell to Ottoman forces, and Suleyman entered in person to receive and dispense imperial largesse to the dutiful local khans and begs. Rather than face him in battle, the Persians retreated. After an exhausting crossing of the Zagros Mountains, in which many of the 200,000-strong army died, the Ottomans reached the Mesopotamian plains. The way to Baghdad was open.

In the City of Peace, pandemonium reigned: news of the Ottoman advance, liberally mixed with apocalyptic rumours, was causing panic. The governor, Mohammed Khan, was the recipient of letters playing on his Tekke Turkmen ancestry in an effort to induce his defection to the Ottomans. Mohammed was unimpressed by the argument, but equally unconvinced by the rumours that Persian reinforcements were at hand. The sheer force of Ottoman arms satisfied him that resistance was futile. He resolved to abandon Baghdad and flee to Persia. His fellow tribesmen, who were prepared to present the keys to the city to Suleyman, disagreed. When he urged them to leave with him, they mutinied and seized the ancient Mustansiriya University as their base. Mohammed gave his last throw: resorting to deception, he feigned a change of heart and sent his leaders out to welcome Suleyman, before discreetly crossing to the right bank of the Tigris and slipping away with his household and Shia supporters to Persia.

Reports of his escape quickly reached the Ottoman sultan, who dispatched Ibrahim Pasha with an advance guard to occupy Baghdad. The grand vizier entered the city without resistance and closed the gates as a precaution against looting. Everything was ready for Suleyman's grand entrance on 4 December 1534.

History does not record what went through the minds of Baghdadis as they set eyes on this vast army of invaders camped outside their city. Invited to pay their respects at Suleyman's lavish makeshift court, the cream of Baghdad society – the tribal aristocracy, lawyers, scholars, imams and the great merchants – probably saw the wisdom of deference, charm and outright sycophancy, praising the Ottoman's martial valour and Islamic purity, welcoming the new caliph to the most famous city of caliphs, regaling their new masters with tales of Baghdad's past greatness and the certainty of its return to glorious days under the sultan's visionary leadership. Many Shia looked on appalled by these Sunni foreigners, terrified by the persistent rumours swirling through the souks that there was going to be a general massacre of the heterodox, just as Selim had ordered the slaughter of Shia across his empire only twenty years earlier.

Yet Suleyman appeared determined to propitiate his new subjects, Shia and Sunni alike. He made a great show of stately pilgrimages to the Shia shrines at Kadhimiya and the tomb of the great Sufi leader Maruf al Karkhi, patron saint of Baghdad. In the eastern district of Adhamiya, which remains a fiercely Sunni area to this day, he ordered a sumptuous restoration of the tomb of Abu Hanifa, destroyed by the Shia Iranian occupiers. The site had special significance for the Ottomans, who favoured the Hanafi school of Islamic jurisprudence over the Hanbali, Maliki and Shafi schools. The shrine, rebuilt with a soaring dome, with a mosque and hospice added to the complex, became a place of Sunni pilgrimage for centuries to come. Suleyman's miraculous 'rediscovery' of Abu Hanifa's tomb was a deliberate echo of Sultan Mehmed II finding the tomb of the Muslim saint Ayub Ansari at the time of the conquest of Constantinople, and fall of Byzantium, in 1453.[24]

Continuing his religiously inspired building programme, Suleyman built a dome over the tomb of Sheikh Abdul Kadir al Gailani and also completed the restoration of the Kadhimiya shrine, begun in 1519 by Shah Ismail, whose family claimed descent from Imam Musa al Kadhim and who had adorned the complex with a glittering, sunlight-catching covering of faience. Less luminous, more practical works followed in the form of canal maintenance and the construction of a dyke that bore Suleyman's name to protect Kerbala from the inundations of the Euphrates.

Suleyman stayed in and around Baghdad for six months, resting his army after the most gruelling winter campaign over the mountains of Kurdistan and receiving countless surrenders and pledges of allegiance from cities and fortresses far and wide. Suleyman Pasha, former governor of Diyarbakir, in south-eastern Anatolia, was promoted to become the first Ottoman governor of Iraq, with a garrison of a thousand musketeers and a thousand fusiliers under his command.

In an energetic vindication of his moniker, the Lawgiver spent a considerable amount of time organizing a new system of administration for the mass of territory he had acquired. A new *kanunname*, or law code, was proclaimed. Although it resembled the existing Safavid code in many ways, significantly it eased the general tax burden and annulled a number of illegal and abusive practices. Suleyman was determined to demonstrate that Ottoman justice was superior to that imposed by the Safavids.[25]

Although the City of Peace had fallen into foreign hands yet again, it had done so without bloodshed. For Baghdadis who cared about such things, there was perhaps further solace in knowing that those hands belonged to the leader of the Islamic world. Suleyman the Magnificent, Sultan of Sultans, Khan of Khans, Commander of the Faithful and Successor of the Prophet of the Lord of the Universe, was no provincial Black Sheep or White Sheep chieftain.

7

Of Turks and Travellers (1534–1639)

Ashika Bagdad irak deyildir.
To the lover Baghdad is not far distant.
Turkish proverb[1]

As dawn broke over Baghdad on 27 October 1574, revealing the familiar silhouettes of palm trees, city walls, lance-like minarets and sun-bleached domes, a stiff-legged traveller stumbled into the suburbs. He was half-way through an epic, three-year journey to 'the Eastern countries'. Setting off from the town of Augsburg in southern Bavaria, he had sailed from Marseilles to the ancient Syrian port of Tripoli, travelled across the desert from Aleppo in a caravan of camels and asses to the town of Bir on the Euphrates, whence he had taken a river boat as far as Falluja, a short distance from the City of Peace. This was no idle Grand Tour, thrill-seeking adventure or dalliance with the dark arts of espionage; Leonhard Rauwolff was in Baghdad on business.

Rauwolff was a German physician, botanist and would-be trader, dispatched by his brother-in-law to discover and to study new drugs, medicinal plants and other herbs that would be of commercial value to the family business. His first impressions of the city were not entirely complimentary: he likened Baghdad to Basle on the Rhine, 'but nothing near so pleasant, nor so well built' because the streets were 'pretty narrow' and the houses 'miserably built', many reduced to one storey, while others were 'quite in Ruins'. The decrepit, blackened churches were 'so much decayed that you shall hardly find a whole one'.[2]

Long gone was the tone of hushed awe and exalted praise of the Abbasid-era traveller. Magnificence had given way to desolation. West Baghdad, once home to the rich, teeming markets of Karkh, was now more of 'a great Village than a Town'. East Baghdad alone was handsomely fortified with walls and ditches. The only sights worth seeing were the camp of the Turkish pasha – or 'Bashaw' – and the grand bazaar on the Persian side of the Tigris. Rauwolff mentioned the bridge-of-boats, but the river once likened by the Andalusian writer Ibn Jubayr to 'a mirror shining between two frames, or . . . a string of pearls between two breasts' was 'so dark and dull, that it [was] a dismal sight to look upon' and flowed so quickly it made him dizzy.[3]

Summoned to meet the pasha in a 'very ordinary' room in his camp, which was partially redeemed by elegant decorations and delicate tapestries, he found himself questioned closely about the purpose of his visit and the merchandise he was carrying. The pasha ordered him to go away and reflect on his situation, and Rauwolff understood only too clearly that the intention of the interview had been to 'screw a present out of us'. He affected not to grasp any of this, subsequently Presented his passes from the pasha and *kadi* of Aleppo, both of which were in order, and escaped without a penalty, taking care to walk away from the audience backwards, 'for if you turn your Back to any one (although it be a far meaner Person) they take it as a great incivility, rudeness and disparagement'.[4]

If Rauwolff had entertained hopes for the sort of epicurean treats that had delighted Abbasid palates in the days of the celebrity chef and writer Ibn Sayyar al Warrak, he must have been enormously disappointed. Since there were no inns catering to the hungry traveller – or Baghdadi – it was a case of buying food in the market and cooking it yourself. 'Every one boileth for himself what he hath a mind to', al fresco, in front of his lodgings.[5] The accommodation was anything but sumptuous. As there were no beds, tables, stools, chairs or benches in the rooms, his bed was the ground, his cloak doubling up as sheet and mattress. Food was in short supply: the area of cultivated ground in the once fertile 'Land between the Rivers' had shrivelled to the point where Baghdad was no longer self-sufficient and depended on imported provisions, including grain, wine and fruit, chiefly brought down the Tigris from Mosul.

Yet, for all its decline, eight centuries after the caliph Mansur had been advised to found his city at this trade-friendly location on the banks of the Tigris, Baghdad was still a bustling emporium. There was, Rauwolff noted, 'a great Deposition of Merchandises', with goods coming by land and river, particularly from Asia Minor, Syria, Armenia,

Constantinople, Aleppo and Damascus, carried onwards to Persia and the Indies. On 2 December the German watched twenty-five boats arrive with a cargo of 'Spice and other precious Drugs', which had been brought by sea from the Indies via the Gulf port of Hormuz, and thence to Basra, where smaller river craft ferried it north to Baghdad in a journey of up to forty days. Merchants in Basra and Baghdad were able to keep up a 'good correspondence' by carrier pigeon. When laden boats put in at Baghdad, the traders who were taking the spices on to Turkey pitched their tents in open areas outside the city, hiding their cargo as discreetly as possible beneath sacks for security. They were so numerous that from afar they looked like a massed army rather than a multitude of merchants.

Baghdad was not only a centre of the spice trade; it also dealt in other, even more valuable commodities. Amongst the merchants Rauwolff met was a jeweller carrying diamonds, chalcedonies, rubies, topazes and sapphires, expertly concealed from the prying eyes of customs officials, who were tasked by the 'extraordinarily covetous' pasha of Baghdad to confiscate such treasures whenever possible.[6] Coral and Egyptian emerald were also exported to the Indies, together with saffron, chermes-berries, dates, tamarinds, figs, almonds, silks, Turkish handkerchiefs and, above all, fine horses. As a result of all this commerce, Baghdad was a highly cosmopolitan place, with Arabs living alongside Persians, Indians, Turks, Armenians and Kurds. Well represented amongst the biggest merchants, Persians also predominated among the more spiritually inclined foreign visitors, with crowds passing through Baghdad regularly on *haj* to Mecca. One day Rauwolff watched a caravan of 300 such pilgrims arrive with camels and horses. For centuries past, the City of Peace had grown used to these desert-parched travellers arriving before the city walls in straggling caravans.

The German noted the enduring enmity between Turks and Persians, a relationship that, for several centuries, had direct consequences for Baghdad. Although Persians got on with the Christians, he wrote, 'as for the Turks, because great and bloody Wars arise often between them, they hate them very much, and call them Heretics.'[7]

For the time being, at least, the Turks had the upper hand, a superiority Rauwolff felt was amply reflected in their attitude: 'So great an Opinion have the Turks of themselves, that they really believe, there is no other Nation, that can conquer the World so as they.'[8] This sense of innate, effortless superiority would not be unknown amongst Englishmen when their turn came to govern Baghdad almost 350 years later.

*

Rauwolff was an astute observer of Baghdad during the two months he spent in the city. Although credulous at times – his otherwise sober account included tales of three-headed insects and the Persian shah's private collection of unicorns – his admiration of its lively commerce prefigured the growing European interest in trading opportunities with Baghdad and the much later rivalry between Germany and Britain that would find its keenest expression in the second half of the nineteenth century.

Rauwolff's *Curious Travels and Voyages* is also important to the story of Baghdad on a broader level. He is one of the earliest, mostly European, travellers who begin to arrive from the mid sixteenth century, returning with a series of reports that are particularly valuable in light of the declining number of other sources for this era. Most of the first century of Ottoman occupation, dating from Sultan Suleyman's capture of Baghdad in 1534, remains shadowy due to the later destruction of the city records, so much so that the precise succession of the Turkish pashas who held sway here is not known. More generally, there is a steady retreat into provincial obscurity to contend with, a development akin to drawing a veil over the city, leaving a discernible outline but disguising the most vivid, tantalizing details. Given this unfortunate historical lacuna, travellers' tales are particularly useful. Roving medieval monks and merchants, noblemen, writers, adventurers and explorers – all bring back a mass of information on Baghdad, its architecture, its people and their customs, religion and trade, and much more besides. Most of this literature may be European, reflecting Eurocentric tastes and prejudices of the time, but, for all the caveats, we are indebted to these travellers for the sheer wealth of detail they bring to the picture of a city that had shuffled off centre-stage. Rauwolff's *Curious Travels and Voyages* was preceded, for example, by accounts from Venetian merchants such as Cesare Federici, who arrived in 1563, and the aristocratic jeweller Gasparo Balbi, whose journey to Baghdad in 1579 was beset by 'many lions and Arab theeves'.[9]

A good deal of the most basic information about the imperial administration of Baghdad survives. As it entered the expanding Ottoman realm as the principal city of an *ayalet*, or province, of the empire, the city fell under a new administrative hierarchy, at the top of which sat the pasha. His most senior officials were the *kadi* and the *daftardar*, or treasurer. Underpinning this authority was a corps of Janissaries,* imperial troops loyal – in theory, at least – to Istanbul, together with the locally recruited forces who formed the pasha's personal guard. A council of notables acted as a check, albeit partial, on the pasha's powers.

These apparently neat and formal structures disguised the informal but very real limitations on the authority of Baghdad and the pashas of the time. There were, for instance, many Shia who objected to the foreign rule imposed by a distant Sunni power and managed their cooperation accordingly. Beyond the city, in areas such as Najaf, Kerbala and the stretching desert where Baghdad notionally held sway, were the ever-fractious tribes who remained a law unto themselves. Central control petered out a paltry forty miles west of the capital, with a swathe of land running along the Euphrates from Falluja to as far south as Kufa and Najaf falling under tribal authority. At Ana, further north along the same river, the sheikh of the Abu Risha tribes exacted tolls from caravans plying the desert route between Aleppo and Baghdad and was recognized by Istanbul as a power in his own right. Then there was the sultan himself, always a threat to overweening pasha power, however removed from the scene. Closer to hand were the Persians, a constant Shia menace to Sunni Ottoman authority. Revolts, riots and upheavals were regular, sometimes ruinous.

Insularity reigned. 'The city began more and more to resemble an isolated island in a sea of desert waste, inhabited only by lawless and aggressive pirates. Her life, once in close touch with the leading thought of half the world, now began to be thrown in completely on itself; her inhabitants ceased to take much interest in the happenings of even adjacent towns.'[10] Irrespective of its decline, Persians always looked to Baghdad as an important station on the holy road to Mecca, passing the sacred Shia cities of Najaf, home to the shrine of Ali, cousin and son-in-law of the Prophet Mohammed, and Kerbala, where the Prophet's grandson Hussain and his half-brother Abbas lay. It was also home

---

* The Janissaries were elite Ottoman infantry, founded in the fourteenth century. Recruited as youths mostly from Christian communities, they underwent rigorous Islamic education and military training to become the Ottomans' crack fighting force. Janissaries could – and frequently did – rise to the highest positions within the Ottoman Empire.

to a significant number of resident Persian merchants trading with Isfahan and Tabriz. For the Ottomans, Baghdad's value lay in its strategic location, which gave access to the Persian Gulf, the link between India and the Mediterranean. And for the Sunni rulers of much of the Muslim world, possession of the city, notwithstanding the regrettable heresy of the Shia, was the historically legitimizing prize.

*

The first Englishman to reach Baghdad was the London merchant John Newberry in 1581; he sailed again, in 1583, on the *Tiger* to Syria, accompanied by fellow merchants John Eldred and Ralph Fitch, the jeweller William Leedes and the painter James Story in a ground-breaking journey commemorated in a line in Shakespeare's *Macbeth* ('Her husband's to Aleppo gone, master o' the Tiger').[11]

From this moment, trade with Baghdad became an avowed priority for England, initially through the Aleppo offices of the Levant Company – which was established in London in 1581 and which immediately financed the Newberry mission to Baghdad – and later through the East India Company (which had to wait until 1798 for representation there).[12]

Eldred considered Baghdad 'a place of very great traffique, and a very great thorowfare from the East Indies to Aleppo'. He described the ingenious way in which merchants from Mosul brought their goods to the city on *kalaks*, rafts set on a floating platform of inflated goatskins 'blowen up full of wind in manner of bladders' and tied together. On arrival the goods were duly traded, the timber of the raft was sold for firewood and the goatskins deflated, packed on asses or camels for the journey back north by land, ready to be reused on the next commercial expedition downstream. Like a number of travellers to medieval Baghdad, Eldred mistakenly thought he had discovered the ruins of 'the olde tower of Babel', which he judged 'almost as high as the stone worke of Pauls steeple in London'.[13]

European interest in trading opportunities with Baghdad was all very well, but their accounts reveal that they were desperately confused by the baffling weights and measures and multiple currencies operating in Baghdad, all of which they needed to understand in order to do business. Newberry did his manful best to report on the prices of local commodities. In a letter published by the writer and geographer Richard Hakluyt of 20 July 1583 he noted that cloves and maces were 5 'duckats' the 'bateman', a bateman weighing 7 pounds and 5 ounces. Cinnamon was 6 duckats; nutmegs 45 'medins' the bateman, 40 medins being one duckat; ginger was 40 medins, pepper 75 medins and turbetta 50 medins. Neel was 70 duckats the 'churle', a churle being 27.5 'rottils . . . of Aleppo'. Silk, much finer than the Persian variety, was 11.5 duckats the bateman. Newberry's next letter, dated 21 September, testified to the regional clout of the Portuguese and Venetians. It was written from Hormuz Prison, the Englishmen having been denounced as spies to the Portuguese authorities by a Venetian merchant who did not welcome foreign rivals on his patch. 'It may be that . . . they will cut our throtes, or keepe us long in prison,' wrote Newberry, who had a taste for the dramatic. 'Gods will be done.'[14] In fact, they were released after two months, unchanged except for the artist Story, who had unexpectedly become a monk.

In 1583 fellow Englishman William Barret also tried to make sense of the local currencies, in a passage that would surely challenge the most enthusiastic supporter of imperial measurements to reconsider his or her aversion to metric. Like most travellers to Baghdad at this time, he confused modern Baghdad with ancient Babylon, believing the former to have been built on the site of the latter.

> The currant mony of Babylon are Saies, which Say is 5 medines, as in Aleppo, and 40 medines being 8 Saies make a duckat currant, and 47 medines passe in value as the duckat of gold of Venice, and the dollars of the best sort are worth 33 medines. The roials of plate are sold by the 100 drams at prise, according as they be in request: but amongst the marchants they bargaine by the 100 metrals, which are 150 drams of Aleppo, which 150 drams are 135 single roials of plate: but in the mint or castle, they take them by the 100 drams, which is 90 roials of plate, and those of the mint give 5 medines lesse in each 100 drams then they are woorth to be sold among the marchants, and make paiment at the terme of 40 dayes in Sayes.[15]

No doubt his correspondent was thoroughly enlightened.

*

Although the Mongol storm had shattered for ever Baghdad's primacy as imperial metropolis, it did not entirely end the city's importance as a centre of religious study, literature and the arts. The work of the great poet Fuzuli (whose self-appointed, attention-grabbing pen name meant 'Presumptuous' or 'Impertinent'), written in Azerbaijani, Turkish, Persian and Arabic, hints at the cultural richness that could still be found here. Having received patronage from Shah Ismail and the Safavid governors of Baghdad, he deftly switched sides – and sects – on Suleyman the Magnificent's capture of the city in 1534, dedicating a *kaside*, or ode, to the sultan and, in case this was not enough, addressing three additional favour-currying verses to the grand vizier, the chief *kadi* and the pasha of Baghdad respectively. His promised stipend, which was supposed to be extracted from the surpluses of the endowments belonging to the Shia sanctuaries, failed to materialize, however, an experience that no doubt inspired his caustic *Sikayetname*, or *Complaint*, in which he railed against Ottoman bureaucracy and corruption and regretted his failure to be made court poet: 'I greeted them, but they didn't accept it as it was not a bribe.'[16]

After a long hiatus, the illustration of books also resumed in earnest in Baghdad from the middle of the sixteenth century, and towards its close received a significant fillip from religious sponsors. The Ottoman reconstruction of Sunni shrines and theological schools resulted in, among other things, the Mawlawi *tekke*, or lodge, a local branch of the Mawlawi Order, originally founded in the central Anatolian city of Konia by the thirteenth-century Sufi poet and mystic Jalal al Din Rumi.

Numerically small during its early years, by the fifteenth century the Mawlawi Order of dervishes had grown considerably in both size and influence in the Ottoman court in Istanbul and among its aristocracy. This was the order whose dervishes, or Sufi ascetics, practised the Sema, a whirling dance that was one of several rituals, along with singing and chanting, reciting poetry and prayers and playing musical instruments, designed to convey the performer to religious ecstasy. From the fifteenth century, sultans, some of whom were followers of the dervishes, were presented by heads of the order with a sword symbolizing the legitimacy of their reign. A century later Ottoman nobles were building and supporting Mawlawi centres across the empire. Around 1600, the Mawlawi lodge in Baghdad became a centre of artistic excellence, with at least two highly eminent calligraphers working there: Nusayra Dede, who was fêted by the courts of India and Iran; and Abdul Baki al Mawlawi, better known as Kusi, who inscribed a number of dedicatory panels on several important buildings in Baghdad, including that of the lodge itself. At this time Baghdad was also home to two great scribes, Mawlana Hassan Ali and Mawlana Baba.

A recent study has shown that there was a vibrant and highly idiosyncratic 'Baghdad school' of miniature painting in the city for nearly two decades, from around 1590 to 1606. Its most important patrons and clients were the Mawlawi Order, which commissioned illustrated biographies of Mawlana Rumi and the Sufi saints; the pashas of Baghdad, who wanted world histories and genealogies either for themselves or as deferential gifts to the sultan; and well-heeled Shia customers interested in illuminated versions of the tragedy at Kerbala, the battle of 10 October 680, at which Umayyad forces routed an army led by the Prophet's grandson Hussain.[17] Since none of these were royal patrons, the art was spared the stiffness and formality of traditional court style, rejoicing instead in an eclectic approach that drew on the cosmopolitanism of Baghdad, its religious history and its location at the commercial crossroads between Turkey, Europe, Persia and India. The great majority of the surviving illustrated manuscripts are devoted to purely religious subjects: Adam's fall and expulsion from Paradise; Abraham thrown into the fire; the Prophet Mohammed on his *minbar*, or pulpit, in Medina; the iconography of Baghdad's saints; the lives of the Sufi mystics; events from the life of Ali, this last 'unique in the history of Islamic painting', according to Milstein.[18] Very unusually, too, there is a picture of the Prophet's daughter Fatima in a manuscript of Fuzuli's *Hadikat al Suada* (*Garden of the Blessed*) that bursts with colour.

There is a striking realism in these miniatures, which eschews the usual focus on court life and lavishes attention instead on the city, its monuments, its inhabitants and its visitors. Here are Turks and Persians, Indians and Arabs, in different dress, young nobles and dandies in flat turbans, warty beggars with alms-bowls, quiet scenes in private houses, handsome gardens in soothing green, the blazing colours of crowd-filled bazaars. More exotically, there are highwaymen and demons casting sinners into the fire, morbid executions, bloody sieges, desert-weary caravans and high-spirited parties.

*

The Ottomans had good grounds for their view that Iraq was an area of dissent, much of it deliberately stoked by the Safavids, and it comes as little surprise that religious divisions continued to cause tensions in and around Baghdad in this period. Under Shah Tahmasp (1524–76), longest-serving of the Safavid monarchs, the Persians paid stipends to fifty men in the shrines of Najaf and Kerbala, both within the province of Baghdad, to recite verses day and night in praise of the illustrious Shia leader, or the man the Ottomans called the Evil-Doing Shah. This, Istanbul feared, was a dangerous and deliberate policy to rouse discontent against the rule of the Sunni sultan.[19] In a *firman* (royal decree) of 1573, the *beylerbeyi* (governor-general) of Baghdad province was ordered to 'destroy' these fifty men. In 1577, ahead of an anticipated war with the Persians, the same official was commanded to investigate heresy in his province and to 'punish seditious persons ... whose removal is necessary', an Ottoman euphemism for execution; he duly found that there was 'no end to the heretics and misbelievers' operating in his province. In 1582 the climate was so poisonous that Sunni intriguers were breaking into the houses of innocent men, leaving a Kizilbash crown on their table as a sign that the person had been identified as a heretic Shia.* People were thrown into prison on no more than the hearsay of their fellow citizens in Baghdad and beyond.

Although the Sunni–Shia divide was the most significant in terms of numbers, religious splits – and the violence they all too frequently engendered – were by no means exclusive to Muslims. In 1552 a schism in the Nestorian Church led to a rebellious faction entering into full communion with Rome and emerging, a year later, as the new Chaldean Church under Shimun VIII, the first Patriarch of Babylon, a position that exists to this day.† The birth of a new church was a bitter pill for the original patriarch, Shimun VII, to swallow. Rather than turn the other cheek with Christian good grace, he conspired to have Shimun VIII arrested by the Ottoman authorities, by whose hands he was tortured and executed, providing the fledgling church with its first martyr. And in 1628 another new Christian element arrived in Baghdad, when Father Juste of Beauvais founded a Capuchin convent in the city; the Capuchins remained until they were replaced by the Carmelites in the early eighteenth century.

On 29 September 1598, one of the most flamboyant foreign visitors

* The Kizilbash (literally Red Head) movement was named after the red headgear worn by supporters of the Safavids. The term was also used derogatively by the Ottomans to describe the Shia sects of Asia Minor.
† The term had hitherto been used only for the Chaldean Church of Cyprus.

arrived in Baghdad. Sir Anthony Sherley was an English knight-adventurer – and rogue – of the old school. In the course of an astonishingly experience-filled life, he was imprisoned by Queen Elizabeth I and King James I, knighted by the French king Henry IV, made prince and ambassador by Shah Abbas I, sent to Morocco by the Holy Roman Emperor Rudolph II and appointed admiral of a fleet by the Spanish king Philip III. Tales of his hobnobbing with the Persian shah, known to Englishmen as the 'Sophy', and of the prodigious fortune that the Englishman had acquired from the association, even found their way into Shakespeare's *Twelfth Night*.* Sherley's mission was twofold: to encourage trade between England and Persia, and to stir up the Persians against the Ottomans.

Having had goods worth 6,000 crowns, including his most precious emerald cups, confiscated by officials on his arrival in Baghdad, Sherley was not in the most diplomatic of moods when he was granted his audience with the light-fingered Hassan Pasha of Baghdad. According to his companion George Manwaring,

> when Sir Anthony came before him, the Bashawe did look for great reverence to be done him, but . . . Sir Anthony came boldly in, and did not so much as once bow himself, but did sit down by him without any entreating. Whereupon the Viceroy, looking very grim upon him, told him he should be sent in chains to Constantinople to the Great Turk, and all his company should have their heads cut off, and set upon the gates of Baghdad.[20]

Sherley was unfazed. He had time briefly to admire the commercial opportunities on offer in Baghdad, which boasted 'excellent goods of all sorts and very cheap', while Manwaring found it 'a place of great traffic with merchants forth of the East Indies, Armenians, Persians, Turks, and Venetians, and many Jews'.[21] But then Sherley caught wind of an order from Istanbul to Hassan Pasha to seize the party of Englishmen and one Frenchman and send them to the sultan. They escaped with a caravan of Persian pilgrims, after the extraordinary generosity of a Florentine merchant called Signor Victorio Speciero, whose courtesy went so far as to reimburse Sherley for his losses.

---

* Act II, Scene 5: Fabian: 'I will not give my part of this sport for a pension of thousands to be paid from the Sophy'; Act III, Scene 4: Sir Toby Belch: 'Why, man, he's a very devil; I have not seen such a firago . . . They say he has been fencer to the Sophy.'

In 1603 another Englishman, John Cartwright, paid tribute to the city's auspicious location on the Tigris, by which 'Bagdat' was 'very aboundantly furnished with all kind of provision, both of Corne, Flesh, Fowle, Fish, and Venison of all sorts; besides great store of Fruit, but especially of Dates, and that very cheape'. Baghdad was three miles in circuit, a city of sun-dried brick and low, flat-roofed houses. It was neither 'so great nor so faire' as Babylon, on the ruins of which he thought it had arisen.[22]

Few new buildings rose to grace Baghdad's skyline in this era. Among the more remarkable were Murad Pasha's Muradiya Mosque, erected in 1570, Hassan Pasha's mosque known as Jami al Wazir and, more interestingly, the famous caravanserai, coffee-house and bazaar built by Cigalazada Yusef Sinan Pasha in the 1590s that also bore his name. This quickly became an extremely popular corner of Baghdad, regularly crowded with craftsmen and merchants. It gave birth to the local proverb 'His house has turned into a Khan Jighan', a corruption of his name. The genitals of prostitutes and women of easy virtue were also likened to Khan Jighan, to reflect the heavy traffic they encountered. Cigalazada earned lasting posterity by reconstructing Jami al Sagha (Goldsmiths' Mosque), which still stands in a neighbourhood close to Mustansiriya (today passers-by will see a venerable coffee-house, dense with smoke from *nargeelas*, or hookahs, occupying its entrance). He also restored the Mawlawi Lodge, again still standing and now known to Baghdadis as Asafiya Mosque, with its slender minaret and rising pair of blue domes that overlook the Tigris.

The Portuguese explorer and adventurer Pedro Teixeira arrived in Baghdad on 4 October 1604, a balmy time of the year that no doubt reinforced his impression that the climate was 'very pure, temperate and healthy'. He was impressed by the single bridge of twenty-eight boats, which was made fast to the city walls on the eastern bank and to houses on the western bank by 'great iron chains'. Every night, during Friday prayers, and at times of high wind and flooding, it was cast apart in mid-stream, half of it lying parallel to each bank.

During his two-month stay in the City of Peace, Teixeira recorded the first description of a new social phenomenon that was, in time, destined to sweep the world: the coffee-house, where men – and only men – would gather to chat. 'They sit in order, and it is brought to them very hot, in porcelain cups holding four or five ounces each. Every man takes his own in his hand, cooling and sipping it. It is black and rather taste-less; and, although some good qualities are ascribed to it, none are proven. Only their custom induces them to meet here for conversation, and use this for entertainment.' Coffee-house owners laid on other attractions to bring in the customers, such as music and, above all, 'pretty boys, richly dressed, who serve the coffee and take the money'.[23] These establishments were popular at night in summer and by day in winter.

There were few other public buildings of note, according to the Por-tuguese. He mentioned the Mustansiriya College, the great Mosque of the Caliph, vaulted markets, a couple of other mosques and, of course, the seat of the pasha's authority, the citadel, standing on the east bank in what is today the Bab al Muadham district. This last, home to the pasha and up to 2,000 of his troops, was more 'spacious than strong' and built of brick walls 1,500 paces in circuit; guns were mounted on its bastions, and the whole enclosure was surrounded by a ditch 8 cubits deep and 12 wide. The land around the citadel, flat and cultivated, was often flooded in winter and had to be crossed by boat. The total force to defend Baghdad was 14,000 cavalry and infantry, consisting of Turks and other nationalities, of which about 5,000 (including 1,500 Janissar-ies) lived in the city, the rest in garrisons and posts.

Although the pasha had 'absolute and supreme command in peace and war', there was a 'protector', appointed by the Ottomans, whose role was to assist strangers and stand up for them and any merchants against the abuse of royal power. During his stay Teixeira saw Ottoman officers imprisoned and the pasha forced to abandon one of his pet projects.

The Portuguese explorer was impressed by the looks, nature and manner of Baghdadis, who spoke Arabic, Persian and Turkish, of which the last was most popular. 'The men, who go mostly on horseback, dress cleanly and richly; as do the women, of whom many are very handsome and most have fine eyes. In the streets they wear always mantles called *chaudeles* [chadors], but not black, and over their faces veils of silk or gauze, black or purple, so that they see all and cannot be seen.' Such feminine modesty was not always sincere, he thought, noting how some women never failed to 'drop their veils on purpose' at times.[24]

He estimated there were between 20,000 and 30,000 houses in Bagh-dad, of which 200 to 300 – or 1 per cent – belonged to the city's Jewish

15. Harun al Rashid receives envoys from Charlemagne in Baghdad, 786. The 1864 painting by the German artist Julius Köckert (1827–1918) is a classic example of European Orientalism, emphasizing the perceived exoticism and sensuousness of the Middle East.

16. A Baghdadi woman wearing a black face veil, from the late eighteenth-century *Zenanname* (*Book of Women*).

17. Baghdadi women playing the popular Middle Eastern game *mankala*, a watercolour from François-Marie Rosset's *Costumes Orientaux*, published in 1790.

18. A nineteenth-century drawing of Baghdad from the Tigris by Lieutenant James Fitzjames of the Royal Navy, a member of Captain Francis Rawdon Chesney's Euphrates Expedition of 1835–37.

19. A portrait by Henry Pickersgill of the British traveller James Silk Buckingham and his wife in Arab costume. When Buckingham reached Baghdad in 1816 he reckoned the British Resident, Claudius Rich, was 'the most powerful man' in the city after the Ottoman pasha.

20. Map of Baghdad drawn up by William Collingwood in 1853–54. The young midshipman was forced to resort to 'all kinds of subterfuges', including scribbling down bearings, measurements and paces on his shirt cuffs and tails, 'to lull [Turkish] suspicion'.

21. A pontoon bridge over the Tigris, 1914. For almost 1,200 years, until the first fixed structure was commissioned by the British in 1932, pontoon bridges and boats were the only means of crossing between the east and west banks of the river.

22. The British Residency in Baghdad, 1917. The prime riverside location and the monumental size of the embassy made a striking architectural statement of Britain's position and influence in Iraq. Britain's Iraq Mandate lasted from 1920 to 1932.

23. Baghdadis paddling across the Tigris in a *guffa*, the traditional round vessel made from plaited reeds and waterproofed with bitumen. Viewed en masse on the river, they were likened by one writer in 1914 to 'a thousand huge inverted tar bubbles'. In the background is a European steamship.

24. British troops of the 4th Hampshire Regiment enter Baghdad through the Bab al Muadham Gate on 11 March 1917, ending four centuries of Turkish rule. 'We shall, I trust, make it a great centre for Arab civilization and prosperity,' wrote Gertrude Bell.

25. The coronation of Iraq's first monarch, King Faisal I, in Baghdad's Saray al Kushla, Palace of the Military Barracks, 23 August 1921. Sir Percy Cox, British High Commissioner, is at extreme left, next to Sir Kinahan Cornwallis, the king's advisor. General Sir Aylmer Haldane, the British Commanding Officer, stands to Faisal's left. Behind the throne is Faisal's ADC, Tawfik al Damluji, and on the far right is Mahmud al Gailani, the Prime Minister's son.

26. King Faisal I sitting next to Sir Sassoon Eskell (centre, with white beard and fez), the Iraqi Jewish statesman and financier in Baghdad, 1920s. In 1909 Eskell was one of six parliamentarians representing Baghdad in Istanbul and a decade later was one of the architects of the Iraqi state. In 1904, Baghdad's Jews numbered around 40,000, a third of the city's population.

27. The Alliance Israélite Universelle set up its first Jewish school in Baghdad in 1865. The Laura Kedourie School for Girls, pictured here, another Alliance project, opened its doors in 1911 and soon established itself as the leading school for Jewish girls in the city, under the direction of its formidable principal Madame Bassan.

28. Gertrude Bell in the British High Commission in Baghdad in 1924, surrounded by British colleagues and Iraqi ministers. Oriental secretary, Arabist, explorer, kingmaker, co-architect of modern Iraq, Bell was a formidable figure. 'I know every Tribal Chief of any importance throughout the whole length and breadth of Iraq.'

29. Iraqi bishops celebrate Iraq joining the League of Nations and the end of the British Mandate at a reception hosted by King Faisal I in the royal palace on 6 October 1932. Christians, like Jews, long predated Muslims in the ancient land of Mesopotamia.

community. Of these, around a dozen families claimed to be descended from the Jews of the first exile, to Babylonia, which dated to around 586 BC. The Jews lived in a separate ward and had their own synagogue; most were 'very poor'. Ten houses belonged to Armenian Christians, while the Nestorians occupied eighty.

Although Teixeira, like some of his predecessors, praised the abundance of good, cheap provisions, how greatly the commercial area of Baghdad had shrunk can be gauged by his observation that there were no more than seven or eight streets of shops and workshops, and the same number of caravanserais to provide lodging for travelling merchants. The most popular industry appeared to be textiles, employing more than 4,000 wool, flax, cotton and silk weavers 'who are never out of work'. Baghdad also had its own mint, where gold, silver and copper coins were struck.

Pashas came and went. In 1607 trouble broke out when Mohammed Tawil, a Janissary captain in the Baghdad garrison, seized power in another reminder of the fragility of the Ottoman grip on power. Istanbul dispatched Nasir Pasha, one-time grand vizier and then governor of Diyarbakir, to subdue the upstart. Marching south with a force of 40,000, Nasir was roundly defeated in 1608 as a result of treachery within his own ranks. After the failure of this expedition, Istanbul was ignominiously reduced to recognizing Mohammed Tawil as pasha. Any hopes the rebel had of profiting from his hard-won power disappeared only days later, when he was fatally stabbed by Mohammed Chalabi, the man who had built a lodge in the city for the Mawlawi whirling dervishes. Instability and turbulence remained the bloody norm. In 1610 alone, Baghdad saw a total of five pashas rise and fall.

The Roman nobleman Pietro della Valle injected a welcome note of romance into the story of Baghdad with his arrival on 20 October 1616. Stocky, and sporting a goatee and an earring, Della Valle was a casualty of love – he had been rejected as a suitor – who had vowed to go on a personal pilgrimage to the East. He could be whimsical and occasionally precious, whining about the loss of his Italian underwear during the journey to Baghdad, 'since Turkish linen is generally not so good'. Never one to downplay the dangers of desert travel, he described how, when he walked off a stone's throw from his tent 'to obey the call of nature' at night, he took his sword and arquebus with him 'with the firm resolve to fight with our breeches down if need be'.[25] Yet, for all his Latin pretentiousness, Della Valle was also erudite and enterprising. Plunging into the Bible, Koran and the ancient Greek historians and geographers Herodotus, Strabo and Diodorus, he refuted the generally held assumption that Baghdad was the Babylon of old and was perhaps the first person correctly to identify the ruins of Babel as the site of ancient Babylon, 55 miles to the south of the Iraqi capital today.

Della Valle found West Baghdad more like 'a large, open suburb, without walls' than a city, evidence of the more precipitate urban decline on this bank of the Tigris. Most of the houses had their lower floor beneath street level 'because of the great heat experienced in the summer'. Families remained in these basement rooms, dark and usually windowless, for hours on end during the hottest part of the day. When they preferred fresh air, Baghdadis sat in their courtyards, or what they called their *diwans*, 'apartments which are open all along one side like great loggias'.[26]

These pleasant architectural reflections in Baghdad were interrupted by a domestic tragedy. One afternoon, while one of his servants, Lorenzo, was humming a tune and preparing salad in the kitchen, a second servant, Tommaso, rushed in and stabbed him twice in the back.

> You can imagine my horror first at the enormity of the crime itself – a man who had long served me faithfully, murdered, for absolutely no reason, almost in my very arms. But further, I was alarmed at the thought of how this affair might end. We were in a country subject to the Turk, and in a town, far away from the court, where we had neither ambassador nor consul; where justice meant nothing and where everyone – especially Christians – might hope to receive the most ruthless treatment.[27]

With his well-practised flair for self-dramatization, Della Valle pondered the possible punishments that lay before him: prison, a heavy fine, torture, forced conversion to Islam or, dare he even think it, death by impaling. Eventually the crisis was resolved with the help of an unconventional Maltese merchant friend. Lorenzo's corpse, its bleeding wounds plugged by cotton swabs, was packed into a corded wooden crate and delivered to the Maltese. That night the merchant took it by boat to the outskirts of the city and discreetly tipped it into the Tigris, the river that has been a dumping-ground for dead bodies from the very foundation of the city to the present day.

Della Valle had already experienced more dramas – many of them self-afflicted – in one journey than most people encounter in a lifetime. Now, just as he was recovering from his domestic murder in Baghdad, at the age of thirty he fell madly in love with a beautiful eighteen-year-old girl called Maani Joerida, an aristocratic Christian of mixed Syrian and Armenian blood. It was an ardent and lightning courtship in which the unstoppable Roman rolled over first her mother's, then her father's objections, squared Turkish officials with the requisite bribes and married his 'Babylonian love'. It was a great love affair, lent added drama by the Roman pen, but it ended in tragedy: after a miscarriage, she died at the age of twenty-three.

*

Della Valle's arrival in Baghdad coincided with a renewed burst of Persian mischief, as a force marched into the province of Baghdad in December 1616 and sacked the large town of Mandeli, north-east of the city. The pasha sent around 8,000 men against them but keenly felt the need not to disrupt the free passage of commercial caravans 'because of Baghdad's dependence on provisions from Persia'.[28] This minor Persian incursion was, however, merely the harbinger of a far deadlier crisis for Baghdad. According to the historian Stephen Hemsley Longrigg, who was not generally given to overstatement, 'in the history of humanity the story deserves a place as a *locus classicus* of treachery'.[29]

By 1619 an officer of the Janissaries called Bakr the Subashi had become the most powerful man in the city, outstripping the weak Yusef Pasha. During Bakr's absence campaigning against Basra in 1621, a plot was devised, under the leadership of Mohammed Kanbar, Bakr's foremost enemy, to do away with this pretender. Word of the intrigue reached Bakr's son and his military deputy, who acted swiftly to take control, seizing key buildings, blockading streets and surrounding the citadel, into which the pasha had retreated. A letter was dispatched to Bakr, who marched on Baghdad immediately. After the pasha had been killed by a stray shot, Kanbar soon surrendered, having received a guarantee of his personal safety – but, like so many such promises, it was casually disregarded. In keeping with the historical genius for cruelty that Baghdad's rulers had exhibited during the past ten centuries, Bakr devised a peculiarly unpleasant execution for Kanbar and his two sons. They were put in chains and lashed to a boat filled with sulphur and bitumen, pushed into the middle of the Tigris and set alight. Bakr watched entranced until his enemies had been burnt to cinders, their blackened corpses finally sinking with a hiss into the waters. Further massacres followed, with the saintly *mufti* of Baghdad, a senior religious scholar, one of the most prominent victims.

Bakr's attempt to have his self-appointment as pasha confirmed by Istanbul was rebuffed. Grand Vizier Mir Hussain sent the Ottomans' own man, Suleyman Pasha, to take up the reins of power in Baghdad, assisted by Hafiz Ahmed Pasha, governor of Diyarbakir. Initially victorious against the force sent to depose him, Bakr was subsequently routed and forced to negotiate. He continued to insist on his pashalik, a position that was completely unacceptable to his opponents.

While these simultaneously elevated and sordid affairs of state were in flow, the ordinary people of Baghdad were suffering abject misery. A famine, brought on by a severe drought, was so extreme that looting broke out as prices soared. In their desperation for food, exacerbated by the arrival of thousands of Arabs – pouring north from the roiling plateaux of Nejd in the Arabian peninsula in a similar fight for survival – Baghdadis were reduced to ghastly depths, and instances of cannibalism were reported.

Opportunism soon crossed the line into outright betrayal. Bakr sent a letter to Shah Abbas, accompanied by the keys to Baghdad, which he offered to the Safavid monarch in return for the governorship of the city. A Persian army was rapidly mobilized under Sufi Kuli Khan, governor of Hamadan, and took to the field, massing along the frontier. Learning of the underhand plot with the Persians, Hafiz Ahmed Pasha reluctantly confirmed Bakr as pasha, the cue for the latter to renege on the commitment he had just made to Shah Abbas. In demonstration of his new-found attachment to the Ottoman cause, Bakr started to hang Persians upside down from the city walls.

In the summer of 1623 Shah Abbas arrived in person at the head of an army to invest Baghdad. Once again conditions in the city deteriorated sharply and then sunk to abominable levels. Baghdadis were reported to have eaten dogs, children and corpses. A steady stream of deserters, climbing over the city walls, joined the Persian camp. Unbeknownst to Bakr, his son Mohammed, who was holding the citadel, had entered into a secret correspondence with the shah, promising to deliver Baghdad over to him in return for the governorship of the city, just as his father had. Mohammed's proposal was accepted.

Late at night, on 28 November 1623, after he had allowed large numbers of Persian troops into the citadel, Mohammed opened the city gates. Persian trumpets sounded across the city, and Abbas was proclaimed lord of Baghdad. In what Herodotus would have recognized as a classic case of hubris meeting with nemesis, Bakr had been undone by an instance of treachery that had outdone even his own. He was dragged before Abbas, where he saw his turncoat son, resplendent in Persian robes of honour in sumptuous silk, sitting next to the shah. Then he was tortured with exquisite slowness and put to death, along with his supporters. Many were burnt alive. After this, a general amnesty was proclaimed to reassure the terrified, half-starved inhabitants of the city.

It proved illusory. Persian soldiers rounded up the richest Baghdadis and tortured them to reveal the whereabouts of their fortunes. Once again the balance of power between Sunni and Shia had been turned on its head, and once again it resulted in bloodshed and destruction. Thousands of Sunni, including the *mufti* of Baghdad – a position that had its attendant dangers – were killed; thousands more were taken back to Persia as prisoners and sold into slavery. In a sad echo of 1508, the shrines of Abu Hanifa and Sheikh Abdul Kadir al Gailani, architectural jewels of Baghdad, were ransacked and almost entirely destroyed. More heartening was the behaviour of the guardian of the shrine in Kerbala: set the task of compiling a list of Baghdad's Shia population, who were to be spared any outrages, he included the names of many Sunni. Shah Abbas left the bloodshed of the city for a celebratory tour of the holy cities, returning in triumph to his capital of Isfahan, and Sufi Kuli Khan took charge of Baghdad.

The fall of Baghdad in 1623 was another exercise in ruination. Drained by the annihilation of its Sunni community, the population plunged abruptly, only partially offset by the incoming Persians, for the most part soldiers, merchants and administrators. Damage lay unrepaired: many siege-shattered houses were left as empty shells; schools became stables. As it shrank, the footprint of the city retreated from much of the land in East Baghdad that was encircled by the old city walls of the twelfth-century caliph Mustazhir, leaving a desolate tract of open ground that remained a wilderness of brackish, brick-strewn pools well into the twentieth century.

Yet the Persian control of Baghdad, though Shah Abbas could not have known it in 1623, was only the briefest interregnum in the four

centuries of Turkish rule from 1534 to 1917. Nor was it a happy inter-
lude, since, for much of the decade and a half it lasted, Baghdadis were
forced to view a host of Ottoman soldiers beyond their walls, doing
their utmost to recapture the city. The loss of the City of Peace rankled
in Istanbul, which was resolved to retake the forlorn prize from Isfahan.
In late 1625 Hafiz Ahmed Pasha, by now promoted by Sultan Murad IV
to grand vizier, while retaining the governorship of Diyarbakir, led the
first Ottoman siege, concentrating his efforts on the southern wall near
the Gate of Shadows. After trenches, emplacements and redoubts were
ready, the siege proper began with a devastating explosion of fifty mines
and a series of assaults. Prices rose (a ratl* of wheat soared to seven
silver dirhams), sinking the population of Baghdad into further wretch-
edness; another famine redoubled the suffering. For more than seven
months Baghdad resisted, its resolve stiffened by the shah's dispatch of
a large relief force, which harried the Ottomans continuously. Three
pitched battles were inconclusive but took a heavy toll on both sides.
Famine and disease were rife within the Ottoman camp, and conditions
started to resemble those within the city walls. The stalemate was punc-
tuated with flurries of negotiation. In one round of talks the Persians
offered to swap Baghdad for control of Najaf, but in vain. Relief for
the city came at last when mutiny broke out in the camp of the hard-
pressed Ottomans. Hafiz Ahmed briefly found himself under siege in the
already wrecked shrine of Abu Hanifa. When discipline broke down
entirely and the Janissaries refused to fight on, the siege was
abandoned.

In 1630, after Hafiz Ahmed had been demoted for his failure, the
Ottomans tried their hand again, sending another grand vizier, Husrev
Pasha, to besiege Baghdad. Arriving in August, he launched his assault
in October, directing his attack against the northern wall. For almost
two months the city was under fire from Ottoman artillery and mines
aimed at toppling the bastions. Husrev Pasha came within an inch of
taking the city, but the sheer massiveness of Baghdad's fortifications,
combined with the severe strain on supplies, not least on ammunition,
frustrated the attack, and in December the Ottoman forces departed,
having again failed to achieve their objective.

* A ratl was a dry measurement for small, usually food, items across the medieval Middle
East. In Baghdad it varied from aproximately 300g to 500g over the centuries.

The virtually constant state of war that engulfed the population of the City of Peace during this time had desperate consequences. During the Persian governorship of Bektash Khan from 1632 to 1638, the population of Baghdad dropped 70 per cent, putting battle casualties to one side. The greatest catastrophe of siege warfare was not so much the deaths caused by pitched battles and bombardment as the twin demons of disease and famine that followed in their wake. Thus, the French Ottomanist Robert Mantran estimated that Baghdad's population fell from a high of 40,000–50,000 in the late sixteenth century to just 15,000 the following century as a result of epidemics rather than the depredations of siege warfare.[30]

*

In 1664 the French traveller Jean de Thévenot, an accomplished linguist well versed in the rigours of Turkish, Arabic and Persian, published the blandly entitled *Relation d'un voyage fait au Levant* in Paris. During four years of long journeys in North Africa and the Middle East, he had notched up the imaginative traveller's usual store of adventures. His travelogue revels in exploits such as climbing Mount St Catharine in the Sinai Desert and disinterring ancient graves in Alexandria, and includes numerous diversions, amongst them discourses on circumcised women, how to make lemon sorbet, Persian astrologers, and a woman who pulled worms out of children's ears.

Thévenot, who had had an eventful journey down the Tigris from Mosul, enlivened by various attacks from naked thieves, jackals and a buttock-eating lion, spent four days in Baghdad in the spirit-wilting heat of August 1664. It was a city one could walk around in two hours. Although it contained 'fair bazaars and lovely bagnios' built by the Persians ('generally all that is goodly in it hath been built by them') and a handsome citadel of white stone, he found the city strikingly 'ill peopled', considering its size. There were a great many empty places in it, without a soul to be seen, he reported, 'and except the bazaars (where there is always a great confluence of people) the rest looks like a desert'. The sieges and battles that had preceded his visit had reduced Baghdad's once fertile environs to a whitish, salt-glazed plateau, 'where grows nothing but wild caper-shrubs, and land-caltrops'.[31]

Thévenot's agreeable account of his travels contained an extremely important document. To give it its full name in the seventeenth-century translation, it was 'A Relation of what past at the Taking of Babylon, otherwise called Bagdat, by Sultan Amurath Emperour of the Turks; Translated from a Letter written from the said City by the Grand Signior's Chief Faulconer to Mustapha Bey, one of the Sangiacks of Egypt, at Caire', written on 29 December 1638 (or '22 of the Moon of Chaban').[32] It is precious because it contains a detailed, eyewitness account of Sultan Murad's siege of Baghdad, which began, after a march of 110 precisely planned stages, on 15 November 1638, 104 years after his predecessor Suleyman struck camp outside the city walls. Apart from twenty guns, which remained with the army, the Ottoman artillery was lashed to the customary *kalak* rafts of inflated goatskins and floated down the Tigris from Mosul to Baghdad.

The sultan's personal camp was pitched on a small bluff by the river, close to the shrine of Abu Hanifa, which he pledged not to enter until victory had made him a worthy pilgrim. In front of the royal pavilion he had a high tower built that offered a wide view of the battlefield and the city, his army placed 'out of danger of the Enemies Guns'. Orders were issued to his viziers, pashas and senior commanders to put their men into battle formation. The sultan and his personal corps faced the battle-worn citadel and the north-western face of the city walls opposite the Muadham Gate; the forces under the agha (commander) of the Janissaries and the *beylerbeyi* of Rumelia, west of the Bosphorus, were drawn up before the north-eastern flank, opposite the broad cylindrical Halba (Racecourse) Gate (later known as Bab al Talism, Talisman Gate, for its unusual inscriptions). Further east, completing the encirclement down to the Gate of Shadows, were forces under an admiral, two senior generals of the Janissaries and the pashas of Anatolia and Siwas. Inside Baghdad, the defence of the city was led by its governor, Bektash Khan.

Although Baghdad's power had dwindled sadly through the centuries, its defences were nonetheless prodigious. The account of the Ottoman officer Ziyaeddin Ibrahim Nuri, who wrote a history of the campaign, gives some idea of the challenge facing the sultan's besieging force.[33] Nuri counted a total of 211 towers, with 52 crenels between each pair, guarding the circumference of the city walls, which he measured at 27,309 paces. Yet, since each of the more than 10,000 crenels should, ideally at least, be defended by five men – consisting of two musketeers, a bowman and two assistants – Baghdad required a small army merely to defend its walls. These walls – 80 feet high, 30 feet wide at moat level, tapering to a still powerful 22 feet at their top – were constructed of shock-absorbent brick reinforced with heavy earthen ramparts. Unlike brittle stone, they were therefore able to withstand heavy bombardment.

After riding around his camp on a royal inspection, Murad ordered his sappers to throw up general defences 'where the Cannon of the Town could annoy us' and also to construct three huge ramparts, 'higher than the Walls of Bagdat', made of earth, timber and faggots. The twenty cannon that were installed on each one immediately started to unleash a ferocious barrage against the city. Fire and black smoke spat out from the booming guns, and the helpless people of Baghdad took to their basements to escape the onslaught.

Murad then called his commanders together for an eve-of-battle address. He spoke to them deploying the classic combination of rousing encouragement and stomach-hollowing threats. First the fear of God: 'You Mufti, Viziers, Beylerbeyis, Bashas, Sangiacks, and all the rest of you, whom God has put under my Obedience, do not think I have come here just to turn back again without taking this city: No, I have come with this great number of soldiers faithful to the law, to conquer or die here, and therefore each and every one of you must make the same resolution.' The stirring call to arms ended with a chilling promise: 'For I am resolved to kill any man who does not do his duty, no matter how great he is, with my own hands.'

Then the appeal to higher motives: there was no greater prize than dying well, he roared, none more lasting than the glory of 'killing an enemy of the Faith', which would bring the reward of eternal paradise. And, finally, just in case anyone had forgotten his original warning, he reminded his commanders that 'if I find that any of you do not go into battle to fight willingly, I'll kill you with my own sword.'[34]

Murad led from the front, taking charge of all aspects of the block-ade, from intelligence to logistics. He had surgeons' tents pitched next to his own and made regular tours to visit the wounded, distributing cash to those most in need. Thévenot cites the sultan's payment to 700 men in a single day as evidence of how 'furious' the fighting was, a figure that may strike the modern reader, familiar with the vastly magnified horrors of twentieth-century conflict, as almost quaint. Morale amongst the besiegers was high. One day, Baghdadis woke to see a vast and indistinct line filing towards the city, partially eclipsed by the sand

and dust stirred up by its passage. It was a caravan of 10,000 camels, bearing provisions from the sheikh of the Abu Risha tribes to be distributed amongst Murad's forces. The siege-starved Baghdadis could only watch as their enemies devoured camel-loads of fresh food. After days of the pounding bombardment, the Ottoman artillery started to make inroads into Baghdad's defences, opening breaches in the north-eastern section of the wall. Baghdadis took heart from the rumours that Shah Safi (a louche and careless monarch addicted to opium) was marching west to relieve the city. He was, but his force of 12,000 was far too weak to tip the balance, and an Ottoman army sent under the pashas of Tripoli and Aleppo to intercept it forced his humiliating withdrawal back to Persia. Baghdad was on its own.

Murad's impatience grew with every hole that appeared in the city walls. His calls for a general assault were met with a plea for caution from his grand vizier, who emphasized that there were lines of trenches and barricades that acted as an inner line of defence. Ramparts were built closer to the city, and the heavy cannon continued their crushing bombardment, smashing down whole sections of wall and blowing up houses, markets, public baths and mosques. Dead bodies once again lay untended in the streets, now reduced to a fetid chaos and squalor.

At last, on Christmas Eve 1638, the fortieth day of the siege, the order was issued for an assault along the battered eastern flank. Trumpets sounded – a hideous noise for the inhabitants of Baghdad, who knew only too well its meaning. Riding in at the front of his men, the grand vizier was killed 'by a Musquet-shot in the Head'.[35] Officers were cut down to his left and right in the tumult of the attack, but the torrent was irresistible. With Ottoman hordes pouring through the breached defences, the besieged Baghdadis faced imminent defeat. The Persian colours and standards were quickly lowered. Overwhelmed, outgunned and shorn of his defences, Bektash Khan took the only sensible course of action remaining to him and surrendered.

Christmas Day 1638 opened with rain coursing down from a lowering, leaden sky; it was so intense, said the chief falconer, that soldiers could not keep their matches alight. Head bowed, Bektash's deputy, the captain of the arms, went to the newly appointed grand vizier 'with a Scarfe about his Neck, and his Sword wreathed in it, which is an Ignominious mark of Submission'. He begged pardon and mercy for himself and his master, which, once granted, was the cue for Bektash Khan to appear in person. The Persian governor of Baghdad was conducted into the sultan's presence by a double line of Ottoman guards. It was a scene of 'great Pomp and Magnificence' – here we must allow for the conventions of court sycophancy – in which Bektash Khan was 'so confounded at the lustre of so great Majesty ... that his Blood was chilled, being able to say nothing but God be praised, God be praised'. He threw himself to the ground, begged for mercy and, after it was bestowed, answered numerous questions, apparently to the sultan's satisfaction. Next, he was presented with a sable-lined vest, a dagger and girdle set with precious stones and a valuable ensign with a plume of heron's feathers. Then he was directed to proclaim the surrender to his army and the people of Baghdad: those who agreed to serve the sultan were welcome to do so; those who didn't would be dismissed without their weapons; and those who resisted would 'be put to the Sword'.[36]

The outbreak of violence that followed is shrouded in the inevitable murk and confusion of war and the passage of centuries; why it happened will never be clearly established. The chief falconer claimed that Ottoman soldiers from the grand vizier's corps had begun to 'plunder the Houses', prompting a furious reaction from six Persian khans, who called on their men to resist. The Turkish chronicle *Gulshan i Khulafa*, however, specifically blamed the ill-conceived resistance of the Persian commander Mir Fattah. Either way, after their extraordinarily long campaign – the march alone to Baghdad had taken 197 days – there would have been a fierce desire to reap what the soldiers considered a just reward: much, if not everything and everyone, especially women, would have been considered fair game. Others yearned for revenge for the loss of their comrades. In spite of the amnesty, 'our men were so hot upon Slaying and Plundering' that they killed everyone they came across – 'God knows what a vast number of Persians died in this Action.'[37]

The rump Persian resistance continued under a body of 15,000 men. When Sultan Murad learnt of this, 'he commanded all the Soldiers of the other Posts to enter the Town, and put all to the Sword.' When the powder magazine at the arsenal caught fire and exploded, killing many Turks, the sultan determined to give no quarter. Ten thousand Persians fought to the death; 5,000 surrendered. These last were put under the guard of a *beylerbeyi* to prevent their massacre. Spotting this great mass of prisoners passing before his pavilion, the grand vizier called his commanders and said, 'Why do we give Quarter to those Dogs who have no Faith, and never keep their word?' In a rush of blood he ordered his men to 'cut them in pieces', deliberately disobeying the sultan's orders and taking full responsibility for the action. Murad sent for him 'in great Rage', asking him the reason for this gross act of disobedience, and the grand vizier explained away the massacre of the heretic Shia so convincingly that the sultan took off his royal vest there and then and gave it to him, 'praising him for what he had done'.[38]

According to the chief falconer's eyewitness account, a total of 31,000 professional soldiers and 20,000 volunteer defenders were put to the sword. The violence spread to the Ottoman camp, swarming with refugees from the city, and many were beheaded where they stood. Desperate men in Baghdad were said to have been so terrified of what the Ottomans might do to their families that they killed their wives and young children themselves. As many as 5,000 valuable horses were hamstrung to prevent their use by the enemy.

Bektash died from poison, either administered by his wife in the Ottoman officer Nuri's account or taken in suicide, according to the *Gulshan i Khulafa*. He was found dead and 'buried like a Dog'.[39]

*

The new ruler of Baghdad summoned the Persian ambassador and gave him instructions for the shah: he was to release those pashas and officials he had imprisoned, return all territories captured by Murad's great-grandfather, Sultan Suleyman the Magnificent, including Tabriz, and to present his tribute and other gifts. 'Otherwise I declare to him, that though he hide himself in the Earth like a Pismire, or flie in the Air like a Bird, he shall not escape my hands. And I will reduce his whole Country to such a state, that there shall not be a House standing ... there shall not a pile of Grass be left within his Kingdom; and that I will afterward Chase him before me, as a Hunter does his Prey.'[40]

Orders were given to rebuild the city and repair its fortifications, customary from those, like Hulagu and Tamerlane, who had just destroyed them. There was also something inevitable about the lavish restoration of the fallen shrine of Abu Hanifa, now adorned with golden lamps, precious stones and the finest silk carpets, in the aftermath of the blood that flowed through the streets of Baghdad. Sultan Murad was by no means the first in Baghdad's turbulent history to combine ostensible piety with killing on an industrial scale, and he was certainly not the last.

Sultan Murad appointed Hassan Pasha Kuchuk 'The Little' as the new governor of Baghdad. On 17 February 1639 the victorious sultan of sultans marched at the head of his army through the Bab al Talism, which immediately afterwards was bricked up, never to be used again. Photos survive of this handsome monument, which dated back to at least the late twelfth century, its brick-filled arch looking oddly incongruous in a city gate. It stood proudly guarding the eastern approach to the city until, in 1917, it was blown up by the retreating Turkish Army, as Ottoman control of Baghdad gave way, after 383 years, to the British.

8

Plagues, Pashas and Mamluks
(1639–1831)

When the [Abbasid] state was drowned in decadence and luxury ... and overthrown by the heathen Tatars ... then it was God's benevolence that He rescued the faith by reviving its dying breath and restoring the unity of the Muslims ... He did this by sending to the Muslims, from among this Turkish nation and its great and numerous tribes, rulers to defend them and utterly loyal helpers, who were brought ... to the House of Islam under the rule of slavery, which hides in itself a divine blessing. By means of slavery they learn glory and blessing and are exposed to divine providence; cured by slavery, they enter the Muslim religion with the firm resolve of true believers and yet with nomadic virtues unsullied by debased nature, unadulterated by the filth of pleasure, undefiled by ways of civilized living, and with their ardour unbroken by the profusion of luxury ... Thus one intake comes after another and generation follows generation, and Islam rejoices in the benefit which it gains through them, and the branches of the kingdom flourish with the freshness of youth.

Ibn Khaldun, *Kitab al Ibar,*
The Book of Precepts (fourteenth century)[1]

After the vicious drama of Sultan Murad's victory, Baghdad quietly slipped into the shadows, as if, having summoned all its energies to contend with the Iranian menace for so many of the past 130 years, it could do nothing more than collapse into a sun-baked torpor. The decline of Safavid Iran helped to ensure peace for the next eight decades, through weariness if not amity. For as long as Iran threatened Ottoman power, distant sultans had taken a keen interest in this troublesome yet illustrious possession. Now that the foreign threat had been extinguished, Baghdad largely faded from imperial view, coming to notice only during the struggles for power that were one of the few consistent features of Baghdad life. Viziers and sultans might regularly fume that Baghdad was not paying its proper dues into the imperial coffers, but, as they could do little about it, this quarrelsome corner of the Ottoman Empire was left more or less to its own turbulent devices.

Shorn of international significance, the city collapsed in on itself. Pashas came and went in quick succession, their short-lived pashalics of little moment. For the rest of the century few men were able genuinely to impose themselves on Baghdad or rise above an atrophied political landscape scarred by petty intrigues and relentless bloodletting. The historian surveying the depleted sources of this unhappy era is tempted to observe that Baghdadis possessed a savage genius for assassinating their leaders, a talent that by this point had been honed for almost a thousand years. A painful succession of poisonings, strangulations, stabbings and beheadings, interspersed with death from disease and the occasional eccentrically bloodless retirement, brought the total of Baghdad's pashas to thirty-seven over a sixty-five-year period (each one thus averaging twenty-one months in office), a record that makes the solitary, cataclysmic regicide of Charles I of England at this time seem positively pacific by comparison.

Pashas rose and fell against a backdrop of regular tribal revolts outside the city, and murderous mutinies and garrison uprisings inside it, With some notable exceptions they struggled to withstand attacks from the increasingly aggressive desert Bedouin. In the countryside the irrigation system fell into further disrepair. Baghdad was a hardship posting, then as now, and most pashas looked at their office as an opportunity to obtain as much plunder as they could, and as quickly as possible, while still surviving to enjoy it. State corruption was endemic, another tradition that has continued to this day.

Largely undistinguished by their achievements in office, many pashas were only remarkable for their colourful nicknames. First amongst them was Hassan Pasha the Little, an Albanian appointed in the wake of the Ottoman sultan's reconquest of Baghdad, only to be deposed within weeks amid criticisms that he lacked the requisite ruthlessness. Soon followed Hussain Pasha the Mad, who earned his moniker by making nocturnal patrols through the city in an echo of Harun al Rashid's celebrated undercover missions by night. One of the most irascible of Baghdad's rulers in the seventeenth century was surely Musa Pasha the Fat, a eunuch so obese he was unable to walk. The disability was said to be responsible for his legendary displays of wrath, during which he would pronounce mass death sentences on suspected supporters of his unfortunate predecessor, Ibrahim Pasha, whose assassination had been ordered by Istanbul. Musa Pasha was deposed in 1649, making way for the unusually mild-mannered Ahmed Pasha the Angel, who served less than a year in office before being promoted to grand vizier. In this later role Ahmed instituted a system of fiscal reforms in which fixed assessments were introduced and taxes farmed out, a well-intentioned policy for which Baghdadis had little reason to thank him, as droves of corrupt but powerful tax-collectors descended on their city, and others across the empire, to squeeze out revenues with impunity.

Of the moniker-less Murtada Pasha, the Turkish chronicle *Gulshan i Khulafa*, one of the principal sources for this period, relates how his door was always open to the poor, so much so that one night a Bedouin stole into the city, surreptitiously made his way into the pasha's private apartments and woke him up to make a complaint. Rather than cutting his head off on the spot for such impertinence, the pasha is reported to have asked the tribesman to bring him his writing desk, on which there and then he composed the order for the wrong to be righted. Famed on the one hand for his severity in maintaining law and order, and on the other for his kindness to the poor, he was also notorious for his support of prostitution and displays of palace pornography, decorating his rooms with 'strange and obscene pictures'.[2]

Then there were Musa Pasha the Little, brave-hearted Mohammed Pasha the White – who faced down a mutiny of his troops by riding out alone to deal with the rebels in a striking show of fearlessness – and Mustafa Pasha the Hunchback, a former agha of the Janissaries with a weakness for cannabis cakes and opium. An unstable heavy drinker, Mustafa was prone to wine-fuelled explosions of rage that sent his panic-stricken servants scurrying from his chambers to avoid the arbitrary executions he was so fond of ordering. Later came Mustafa Cotton, a juvenile reprobate and debaucher; Ibrahim Pasha the Tall, who was consumed by one of the ever-rumbling rebellions in Basra; Ahmed Pasha the Drunkard; and Ahmed Pasha the Merchant, who imprisoned his predecessor for not leaving his accounts in order.

If Baghdadis thought little of their constantly changing, frequently murderous and only occasionally capable leaders, it is fair to say that foreign visitors also thought little of Baghdad itself at this time. We have a perspective of Baghdad in the mid seventeenth century from the august explorer, trading pioneer and diamond dealer Jean-Baptiste Tavernier,* whose trailblazing travels across Europe and Asia later landed him the patronage of the Duke of Orléans. Tavernier arrived in 1652, after a nine-day journey downstream on the Tigris from Mosul. His initial impression of the City of Peace was sniffy:

> In general, the City is ill built, there being nothing of beauty in it but the Bazars, which are all arched, else the Merchants would not be able to endure the heats. They must also be watered three or four times a day, for which office several poor people are hired upon the public charge. The City is Full of Trade, but not so full as it was when in the hands of the King of Persia, for when the Turk took it he killed most of the richest Merchants.

He noted five domed mosques, decorated with 'varnished Tiles of diverse colours'.[3] Despite the depopulation of the bazaars, Baghdad was still 'mighty full of People', attracting merchants and a regular flow of Shia visitors come to pay their devotions to Ali, in addition to the 'continual passage' of *haj* pilgrims bound for Mecca.

Tavernier wrote of the ancient sectarian divide between the Sunni, whom he called 'Observers of the Law', and the Shia, who were 'Rasedis or Hereticks'. A Frenchman who probably missed his glass or two of wine, he noted that 'The Rasedis will not drink with a Christian or Jew and hardly with a Mahometan of another sect. The chiefest of the City are of this sect.' The small Christian community consisted of 'Nestorians, who have a Church, the Armenians and Jacobites, who have none but go to the Capuchins to confess'.

Largely unimpressed by the city's architecture, Tavernier was no more sympathetic to local customs. He found the funeral practices

---

* Tavernier was a voracious traveller, a latter-day French Ibn Battuta. He notched up an astonishing 180,000 miles during six major voyages over forty years. He was famous for discovering the vast, 112-carat Tavernier Blue diamond that he sold to Louis XIV in 1669 for 220,000 livres, the cash equivalent of 147 kilograms of gold. The diamond was subsequently cut down into the French Blue, a peerless treasure within the Crown Jewels, and, later still, the deep blue, 45-carat Hope Diamond, which currently sits in the Smithsonian National Museum of Natural History in Washington, DC.

particularly excessive: 'As to their Funerals, when the Husband dies, the Wife plucks off all her Head-gear, and lets her Hair fall about her Ears, and then besmears her Face with the Soot of a Kettle, and frisks and leaps about ridiculously.' Family, friends and neighbours met at the house of the dead man, where 'the Women yell like mad People, beating on Drums'. As the body was carried to the grave, crowds of poor people preceded it 'singing most dismal Dirges'.

Tavernier estimated Baghdad's population at 14,000, the lowest figure ever recorded in the city's history and an indication of how low it had sunk from the zenith of the Abbasid era. In 1663, more than a decade after Tavernier's visit, the Jesuit priest Manuel Godinho passed through Baghdad en route to Portugal from India, 'in the service of both majesties, both divine and human'. Although he had enjoyed the 'exceedingly palatable' locusts fried in butter during his gruelling journey by land from Basra, he had only narrowly avoided death after running out of water and was reduced to sucking lead balls to assuage his thirst. Godinho paid tribute to the 'amiable and courteous manners' of Baghdadis, while arguing that 'they had lost their ancient reputation for valour and were not trusted by the Turks in any affair of importance'. The Portuguese traveller reckoned Baghdad's population at 16,000, consisting of Turks, Arabs, Kurds and Persians, with around 300 Jewish families.[4] We have seen how fellow Frenchman Jean de Thévenot provided further evidence of demographic decline during his visit in the height and heat of summer in 1664, commenting on how 'ill peopled' the city had become. Beyond the bazaars, he wrote, 'the rest looks like a desert.'[5]

Thévenot also referred to one of the enduring miseries of Ottoman rule for the long-suffering Baghdadis. 'The Soldiers here are very licentious, and commit all imaginable insolencies, their officers not daring scarcely to punish them.' Several weeks before his arrival, he wrote, the pasha had been poisoned to death 'because of his tyrannies', with the agha of the Janissaries strongly suspected of having had a hand in his assassination.

Within five years of Tavernier's visit, after unseasonably heavy rains, Baghdad was hit by a particularly serious flood, when both the Euphrates and Tigris broke their banks, turning the plains west of the citadel into an immense, frothing lake. The waters swept through the streets, knocking down a number of the tallest buildings, flooding the canals and undermining the foundations of the city walls, which left Baghdad perilously vulnerable. Orders were dispatched to Diyarbakir, Kirkuk and Mosul to send troops for the defence of the City of Peace.

In 1689, towards the end of this luckless period, the harvest failed and a severe famine devastated Iraq. The *Gulshan i Khulafa* reports that Baghdad was teeming with Arab and Kurdish tribesmen who had flocked in from the barren countryside to beg for scraps of bread. The streets were full of the dead and the dying. Then came the inevitable post-flood plague, which carried off more than 100,000 in three months. The treasury was bare, the pasha resigned, and the Janissaries were mutinous. Baghdad once again was mired in crisis.

*

After a bewildering procession of inconsequential pashas for most of the seventeenth century, the first half of the eighteenth was dominated by just two men, the beginnings of a new, relatively stable, quasi-hereditary dynasty.

Hassan Pasha was of Georgian origin, raised in Istanbul as the son of one of Sultan Murad's sipahis, or Ottoman cavalry officers. Intelligent and courageous in battle, he was promoted to a series of royal appointments, including the positions of vizier and *wali*, or governor, of the ayalets of Konia, Aleppo, Urfa and Diyarbakir in quick succession. In 1704 he was made governor of Baghdad. Had Istanbul known how he would rule, specifically how he would manage the succession, doubtless it would never have appointed him, because, during the 130 years that followed, Ottoman sultans found themselves completely powerless to appoint Baghdad's pashas. Humiliatingly for Istanbul, from the time of Hassan Pasha, such decisions were taken exclusively in Baghdad, and the Sublime Porte – the Ottoman government – was reduced to the indignity of merely confirming these appointments.* In fact, Hassan Pasha was doing nothing more than emulating the Ottoman practice of importing child-slaves from Circassia, Georgia, Daghestan and the Caucasus, schooling them in special colleges, converting them to Islam and training them to form an elite, pale-skinned cadre of civil servants and military officers – the Janissaries. Istanbul approved the policy at the time, in order to allow Hassan to suppress the ever unruly tribes and

---

* 'Sublime Porte' was the French translation of the Turkish word 'Bâbilâi' (High Gate or Gate of the Eminent), the official name of the gate that gave access to the principal government buildings in Istanbul. Over time it became shorthand for the Ottoman government.

thereby to maintain the notional flow of taxes to the imperial treasury. By doing so, however, he was also building up a force that would serve as the foundation of Mamluk rule in Iraq. A new Office of the Incomers was established and commissioned to buy and train the regular cargo of fresh-faced boys.[6] The Mamluks were Hassan Pasha's equivalent of the Janissaries.

One probably unforeseen consequence of this mass importation of young boys was pederasty, which was forever associated with the Mamluk era (1704–1831). Homosexuality was said to thrive in the dormitories where they slept, supervised by tutors, while depraved Baghdadis reportedly enticed the boys to commit 'unthinkable' acts. The stigma of these youthful indiscretions did not disappear on later promotion. A Mamluk who was known to have indulged in homosexual practices in his past was routinely referred to as 'that broken-eyed fellow', a reference to his supposedly shame-faced inability to look people in the eye, and the expression is still current in Baghdad to this day.[7]

In office, Hassan proved a robust and successful defender of Baghdad's authority. He came to power promising to cut off heads and did not disappoint. 'As brigands, you will be dealt with Islamically as brigands and we will reach you even in the ends of the earth. Your beheading is nothing new to us,' he announced prior to putting down, in short order, challenges from the Bani Lam, Khazail, Shammar, Aniza, Hamid, Saada and Rafi tribes;[8] these tribe-bashing campaigns lasted continuously over a period of eleven years.[9]

In 1708 he sent a large army south to Basra, eventually breaking the hold of the powerful tribal confederation of the Muntafik, who were said to have lost 100,000 of their men. As a reward for this hard-won victory, Istanbul gave him the right to nominate the city's governor, and Basra became a dependency of a progressively more assertive Baghdad.

Under the rule first of Hassan Pasha, and then of his son and successor, Ahmed, Baghdad's territorial tentacles spread with newfound confidence. In the north, its writ was felt in Mosul and Kirkuk and, however partially, in other Kurdish areas such as Amadiya, Sulaymaniya and Koy Sanjak. The province of Baghdad expanded to encompass Mardin and the famous commercial centre of Urfa in south-eastern Turkey, renowned for its trade in cotton, leather and jewellery. And its control of the southern port city of Basra, gateway to the east and rich in revenues from the dates it grew in abundant palm groves, meant that

Baghdad was able to dominate the northern trade routes and influence all commerce between the Gulf and Syria.[10]

The Mamluk-era historian Abdul Rahman al Suwaidi wrote of how, in 1716, Hassan 'lifted the ugly cruelties' by eliminating the punitive *baj*, or gate tax, on sheep and agricultural produce, a corrupt system under which 'Even from the peasant farmers who entered Baghdad to sell eggs, one egg would be taken.'[11] He also cut the *tamgha* tax imposed on all *kalakjiya*, the owners of the inflatable-goatskin rafts, which was collected in the form of firewood. Recalcitrant tribes might have resisted paying taxes with every sinew, but Hassan won lasting respect by using the money to effect good public works, constructing new bridges and canals, founding mosques, making grants of lands and funds to be used for religious purposes, thus earning himself the affectionate nickname Abu Khairat, or Father of Charity. Nor was his piety sectarian: he gave the Carmelites permission to establish a mission in Baghdad in 1721. In 1722, a year before his death, Hassan received a *fatwa* from the Sheikh al Islam, the supreme religious authority within the Ottoman Empire, sanctioning military force against Safavid Iran, a state already teetering on collapse after its invasion by Mahmud Khan, a particularly brutal Afghan prince. Taking advantage of Iran's weakness, Peter the Great of Russia and the Ottoman sultan Ahmed III moved in to carve up the Shia kingdom and enlarge their empires, the honour of taking Hamadan falling to the new governor of Baghdad, Ahmed Pasha, whose father, Hassan, had died at Kermanshah during the campaign.

Ahmed Pasha ruled from 1723 to 1747, with a judicious two-year break from 1734 to 1736 to pacify a jealous grand vizier in Istanbul. Although most of his time was preoccupied dealing with rebellious tribes and a renascent and hostile Iran under the ebullient Nadir Shah, he nevertheless managed to consolidate the gains made by his father, ensuring that Baghdad was only nominally subject to Ottoman authority. Many silk-robed, high-turbaned grandees swishing about the corridors of Topkapi Palace in Istanbul resented Baghdad's autonomy. While sultans did their worst to bring upstarts to heel, a policy that included numerous assassination missions, wily Mamluk pashas did what they could to stay alive.

Lieutenant William Heude, a young British officer in the Madras Military Establishment who passed through Baghdad in 1817, described one of several attempts on Ahmed Pasha's life. The sultan once sent an envoy with a *firman*, or decree, for Ahmed's head. With a formidable network of agents and friends, both in the city and on the main roads, the pasha usually heard of such plots before the messenger reached Baghdad and was able to intercept the *firman* or assassinate its bearer. In this case, however, the envoy had travelled so secretly and quickly that Ahmed Pasha learnt of the plot with only hours to spare. So he rode out of the city with his most senior officers under the pretence of playing *jareed*, 'a warlike game in practice amongst the Turks', in which cavalry officers raced at high speed on their mounts and threw blunted lances at each other.[12] At the gates of Baghdad, Ahmed met the official carrying his *firman*, greeted him with exquisite courtesy and invited him to play. Unable to refuse, the man found himself pitted against the pasha, who armed himself with 'a steel-pointed javelin, hurled it at his insidious but unsuspecting adversary with all his force, and killed him on the spot'. The messenger's papers were opened, sealed up again and sent back to Istanbul with a letter expressing the most profound condolences for the 'unfortunate accident' that had befallen him.[13]

Heude also told the story of how one of Hassan Pasha's slaves, Suleyman, won his freedom by saving Ahmed's life when the pasha's lance broke during a lion-hunting expedition outside Baghdad. Everyone else was too frightened to intervene, Heude reported, because Ahmed always insisted on killing his quarry alone, 'lest he should lose the entire honour of the chase'.[14] Suleyman was repaid immediately with the hand of Ahmed's eldest daughter, Adila, in marriage, a handsome tribute that was a decisive factor in his later promotion and one that carried within it the seeds of a future dynasty.

The stability of the first half of the eighteenth century, which Baghdadis must have considered almost an alien condition for their city, was only relative. It did not preclude a savage siege in 1733, when Nadir Shah, at the outset of a career of conquest so brilliant and bloody that historians have called him the Napoleon of Persia and a second Alexander, invested the city.[15] The invading army defeated Ahmed's forces sent out to defend the city, cut off the grain caravan routes from the south and occupied Karkh, where Nadir Shah celebrated the great Iranian New Year feast of Nawruz in deliberate and ostentatious splendour, distributing 7,000 robes of honour to his officers and showering gold on the fortunate few who had been invited to a sumptuous banquet. From their city's threatened walls, Baghdadis watched in horror as

2,700 towers rose ghoulishly from the desert plain, each within musket shot of the next. Iranian boats enforced the blockade, and a huge camp-city estimated at 300,000 grew up around two large forts upstream of the city. Only a third of this huge population were fighting forces, the rest being traders and artisans, slaves and camp followers. The finery and plenty without the city walls – supplies here were cheap and plentiful – contrasted all too visibly with the increasing misery and hunger within. Without the requisite heavy artillery to breach the defences, Nadir Shah had to rely on starving Baghdad into submission. As the months wore on and spring gave way to the torrid blasts of summer, conditions within the city worsened, as attested to by Joseph Emin, later a prominent figure in the Armenian liberation movement. Aged six, he lost his mother and brother during the siege and years later recalled how 'the Mahometans were reduced to eat the flesh of horses, asses, dogs, cats, and mice'.[16] Visceral images rise from the sources for this time. A beautiful young woman was spotted in an alley tearing at the carcass of a donkey with a sharp knife; when asked what she was doing, she said she had consumed nothing but water for five days. Ali al Wardi writes of starving people eating cotton seed and virgins selling their bodies for a loaf of bread.[17]

In a gesture of mock pity for the city's dry-throated hunger, Nadir Shah sent cartloads of watermelons into Baghdad. Ahmed Pasha returned the gesture with a batch of delicious fresh bread and a bravado note assuring the Iranian that this was their daily diet. He also invited an enemy delegation to an ostentatious banquet, which was said to have shaken Nadir Shah's faith in the efficacy of the siege.

Emin left an amusing story of how, after one of Ahmed Pasha's levees during the siege, the governor gave Mr Dorrel, a British resident of Basra and a close friend, a tour of his fortifications, boasting how Nadir Shah would never be able to take the city. The pasha asked the Englishman what he thought of Baghdad's defences. '"May it please your highness, if an European army besieged it instead of Nadir they would have taken the place in five days time." Which expression made the Basha turn pale, and he said, "Gavoor, if I had not sworn, I would cut off your head."'[18]

The rescue of Baghdad from the clutches of Nadir Shah owed less to the stoutness of its walls or the quality of its bread than to the arrival of Topal Othman Pasha the Lame, a grizzled Greek former grand vizier, crippled during an earlier campaign and prized by the Ottomans as the finest soldier in the empire. After various manoeuvres between the two sides, battle was joined on 19 July. In a symbolic display of strength, Othman eschewed the litter in which he had been carried throughout the campaign and mounted his horse for the first time to rally his troops. 'I saw him riding like a young man, sword in hand, his face radiant and his eyes sparkling,' wrote his doctor Jean Nicodème.[19]

For nine hours the fighting raged, advantage tilting this way and that. In one furious encounter Nadir had his horse shot under him. A replacement mount later threw him, causing instant panic amongst the Iranian forces, who thought their inspirational leader had been cut down. The Ottomans pressed home their advantage, Nadir's once invincible army started to fall back, and he was forced to order a retreat. For the Iranians, it was a catastrophic defeat, which saw their earlier triumphs right across Iraq reversed in a single day. Nadir lost perhaps 30,000 men, many hacked down in headlong retreat, slaughtered by Ahmed Pasha's garrison. But victory for the Ottomans also came at a heavy price, with up to 20,000 lost.

In the city, which had been starved of supplies for seven months, conditions were dire. Although estimates of 100,000 for the number of those who died during the siege look excessive, given that Godinho had reported a population of around 16,000 in 1663, it is clear the losses were staggering.[20] As so often in its history, the Tigris was used as a liquid cemetery. Disease rifled through the city in the wake of the corpses left to putrefy in the dizzying heat of midsummer. The scenes were so dreadful one must question Ahmed's account to Istanbul, in which Baghdadis young and old flocked to their liberator Othman Pasha 'to lick the dust off his feet'.[21]

Twice more Nadir Shah attempted to take Baghdad: first in the autumn of 1733, when the Ottoman hero Othman Pasha the Lame was shot dead in battle; then in 1742, when subsequent uprisings in Iran demanded his swift abandonment of the campaign in Iraq. Peace was signed between the Iranian and Ottoman Empires in 1746, followed the next year by the deaths of the two men who had personified this generation of the ancient conflict between Iran and Iraq. First to die was Nadir Shah, by now lost to illness, savagery and a maniacal inclination to kill many of those closest to him. In a dark imitation of his hero and fellow Asiatic warlord Tamerlane, he had taken to building towers from his victims' skulls. He was assassinated eight weeks before Ahmed Pasha died on campaign.

During Ahmed Pasha's long and unusually successful reign, Baghdad had expanded its sway to encompass an area greater than that of modern Iraq, from the mountains of south-eastern Turkey beyond Syria in the north, to the warm waters of the Persian Gulf in the south. If the glories of the city's Abbasid pre-eminence remained deeply buried in millennial memory, he had nevertheless restored a measure of pride and power to its diminished reputation. Baghdad may no longer have lorded it over vast swathes of North Africa and the Middle East, but it enjoyed considerable autonomy, bordering on independence, within the empire to which it was formally subject, contributing little more than a trickle in revenues to the exchequer in Istanbul. And the steady stream of pale-skinned Mamluks that flowed unchecked from Georgia to Baghdad would form the basis for a new dynasty that wielded power entirely at its own pleasure, not at that of the Ottoman sultan. For the next eighty years successive sultans bridled at this defiance of the imperial writ, but were able to do nothing at all about it.

*

The middle of the eighteenth century found Europe savouring the intellectual riches of the Enlightenment. In France, Diderot's famous *Encyclopédie*, first published in 1751, drew on contributions from the most celebrated *philosophes* of their age, including Voltaire, Rousseau and Montesquieu. The English had Hobbes and Locke, the Scots Hume and Smith. Prussia was a decade into the long, modernizing reign of Frederick the Great, an epoch set to music by Bach, Haydn and Mozart in turn. Enlightenment political ideals of liberty and democracy, as embraced by Jefferson, Franklin and Paine amongst others, underpinned the 1776 revolution that saw Britain's thirteen American colonies become the independent United States of America.

Half a world away in Baghdad, there was rather less intellectual ferment; yet two highly significant developments for the future of the city must be noted. In 1750, after three years of turmoil following Ahmed Pasha's death and the subsequent failures of four sultan-appointed pashas to hold Baghdad in the teeth of local opposition, his father's former Mamluk slave Suleyman took power in Baghdad, initiating a dynasty that would last for almost a century. Of more enduring relevance was the establishment, in 1798, of a British trade agency, initially a branch of the Basra Office of the East India Company and one of the earliest symbols of growing European interest in Iraq.

Suleyman was a larger-than-life character. For Baghdadis, he was Suleyman the Lion; the Bedouins nicknamed him Abu Layla, Father of the Night, either after his nocturnal investigatory prowls around Baghdad in the manner of Harun al Rashid, or possibly because of the timing of his successful expeditions against the desert tribesmen. Fearless and punitive on the battlefield, he was loved by Baghdadis for keeping the menacing tribes at bay. More than half a century after his death, songs were still being sung in his honour in the city.[22]

Dr Edward Ives, a former naval surgeon who passed through Baghdad in 1758, noted that Suleyman contributed no revenues to the Ottoman sultan, making false claims for fictitious repairs to the city's fortifications. As a result of this, the sultan had tried to have him assassinated several times, sending three or four messengers with a secret mandate for his head, but Suleyman's 40,000 Janissaries would not countenance it. Thanks to his effective intelligence network, he had 'always made it a rule to send the heads of those very messengers to Constantinople instead of his own'.[23]

Suleyman continued what Hassan and Ahmed before him had begun, increasing the numbers of imported boy-slaves, establishing a special school for their tutoring and appointing numerous Mamluks to senior positions, to the detriment and intense disappointment of Turkish and Baghdadi families, who saw their power steadily ebbing away.

While his military and political prowess was unquestioned, Suleyman's unusual domestic arrangements were considered less impressive and even lent themselves to *sotto voce* satire by the braver Baghdadis. His wife, Adila Khatun, ran the strictest of domestic regimes and did not allow her husband to have any other wives, lest they produce rival offspring. Perhaps it was this restriction, highly unorthodox for the time, which accounted for his alternative choices. The historian Stephen Hemsley Longrigg reproached Suleyman for 'a private life made disgraceful by the vices of his race', but would not elaborate beyond the starchy observation that Dr Ives had provided 'sufficiently vivid details' in his memoir.[24] Ives was indeed more forthcoming. 'Shocking to relate! We were informed that he kept upwards of twenty boys for his unnatural gratifications,' he wrote.[25]

Since its foundation almost exactly a thousand years earlier, Baghdad had always been a resolutely patriarchal society, and political power was reserved exclusively for men. Women's position was in the home, with their families. Adila Khatun did not see things that way. In popular gossip the Lion became the diminished, hen-pecked husband, as William Heude explained: 'The chief cause of complaint against him, however, was the extreme deference he generally showed to the opinion and wishes of his wife; who, being the proud daughter of a pasha of the first rank, and both proud and ambitious, could scarce forget that notwithstanding his present high dignity, her husband had once been her father's slave.'[26]

As far as men were concerned, women had no business involving themselves in the public sphere, but the arrival of the formidable Adila Khatun thrust conventional wisdom on its head. She threw herself into political life with an energy that scandalized Baghdad on the one hand and terrified it on the other, going so far as to abrogate her husband's decrees and orders according to her wishes. Everyone understood only too clearly the risks involved in opposing her. Blithely disregarding all the prevailing notions of impropriety, she held political salons and received both men and women callers, bestowing the gift of an embroidered silk scarf to identify the wearer as a member of her court. Those Turks and Arabs she thought needed buying off received extravagant pelisses and cloaks.

As high officials discovered, to their cost, Adila Khatun was not a woman to be trifled with. Immensely wealthy as a pasha's daughter, powerful and unscrupulous, she used her position to promote favourites (for a fee) and to eliminate rivals. She was implicated in several political assassinations, including that of Ahmed Agha, the entirely innocent husband of her sister Aisha, whom Adila had wrongly suspected of plotting against Suleyman. She was also deeply involved in the plot against Salim Pasha of Kurdistan, a long-standing irritant who had aligned himself with the Iranians and launched a number of raids deep into Iraq. In 1758 Adila persuaded Suleyman to lure Salim to Baghdad, where he would receive forgiveness for his past misdeeds, confirmation of his office and several other honours. He travelled south and presented himself at the palace, was received with great fanfare and presented with an extravagant silk, fur-lined pelisse. Moments later Suleyman's retainers rushed at him, removed his weapons, put him into shackles and dragged him off to a cell, where he was left for nine days, then strangled to death.

Ives described how Adila defended her place at the very summit of Baghdad society with admirable tenacity. The wife of the *kahya*, the pasha's deputy, had ordered craftsmen to make her a sumptuous *takht-revan*, or litter, which was reserved exclusively for people of 'the first rank'. Shortly after it was finished, and just as she was getting ready for her debut outing in this splendid status symbol,

> she received a message with the Haram's [wife of the pasha] compliments, declaring to be informed what vehicle was now left by which it was possible for the Basha's lady to manifest the superiority of her rank over the Kahier's wife; and intimating that if she was unacquainted with any other method for keeping up the distinction between them (as the Haram herself confessed she wholly was), it would be esteemed obliging in her to lay aside all thoughts of making use of the Takht Revan she had ordered to be built. The compliance of the Kahier's lady was unavoidable, and probably so was her mortification.[27]

The remarkable Adila ushered in a unique and all too brief era in which women, or at least those of the royal household, were able to exercise considerable power over the life of Baghdad. Unwilling to cede such influence after Suleyman's death in 1762, Adila devoted herself to undermining his controversial successor, the Iranian-born Ali Pasha. She spread rumours that he was a fanatical Shia, convinced the Mamluks that he was going to have them killed and whipped up a mutiny supported by her sister and brother-in-law Omar Agha, a senior military officer. Ali Pasha was reduced to the ignominy of fleeing Baghdad dressed as a woman, in which shameful disguise he was apprehended and executed. Omar, Adila's preferred candidate, duly became pasha and ruled Baghdad until 1776.

From the time of Adila until the fall of the Mamluk Dynasty in 1831, royal women effectively occupied the centre-stage of political life in Baghdad, even if actual power was wielded more discreetly in the wings. On the death of a pasha, his wives dominated the struggle over the all-important inheritance that would help a pretender to establish his claim to the pashalik. Thus the rich wife of Omar Pasha, who governed Baghdad from 1764 until his assassination in 1776, was said to be the true force behind his rise to power; while Suleyman the Little, pasha from 1807 to 1810, was able to remain in office only thanks to his wife's prodigious fortune. The short-lived rule of Said Pasha (1813-16) was founded on the financial support provided by his mother.

Daughters were used as a means to extend a pasha's political network: married to the strongest or most loyal Mamluk, they bound him into the family, securing his dependence through capital. These techniques, however, were no guarantee of stability, since more often than not each mother-leader of a Mamluk household would be fighting others on behalf of her own putative pasha. From 1790 to 1831 the most important factions in Baghdad, beyond Suleyman the Great (1780-1802) and his sons' immediate supporters, were led by former Mamluks who had married into Suleyman's family.[28] Rivalry could be fierce, often fatal. These royal women tended to occupy positions that were more stable than those of their husbands, because they were able to remain in the background, accumulating fortunes from their privileged status. And they were spared the summary executions that invariably followed political defeat for the men.

Women were also employed in more traditional roles. A curious character called Mohammed al Ajami (The Iranian) inveigled his way into the inner circle of Abdullah Pasha, Omar's successor from 1776, by forming a musical troupe with his mother and two extremely attractive sisters. Mohammed sang, his mother played the tambourine, and his sisters danced and catered to the pasha's carnal needs. The ambitious Iranian made no secret of his delight in procuring girls for his pasha. 'If it hadn't been for this honourable career, I wouldn't have been where I am today!' he is reported to have boasted, having risen to high office on the backs of his sisters.[29]

*

On 8 January 1766, two years after another Iranian invasion that brought a renewed outbreak of plague in its wake, the German explorer and cartographer Carsten Niebuhr arrived in Baghdad as part of a scientific expedition sponsored by King Frederick V of Denmark. During his extensive travels, which had taken in Egypt, Arabia, Yemen and India, Niebuhr had visited Persepolis and the Behistun Inscription in western Iran, where his careful research had prepared the ground for the decipherment of cuneiform, one of the world's earliest scripts, dating back to fourth-millennium BC Sumer. Within ten days of his arrival in Baghdad, after heavy snows in the north, the Tigris rose alarmingly, smashing the chains of the traditional bridge-of-boats and sweeping the whole structure away in a mighty rush of water. All of the country around Baghdad was flooded, and his hopes for mapping the city in fine detail were dashed.

Niebuhr found much of the area within Baghdad's city walls on the eastern bank of the Tigris 'entirely without buildings and uninhabited'.[30] He counted at least twenty mosques with minarets and a further 250 without. There were many public baths and half a dozen caravanserais for the big merchants. His visit coincided with an especially harsh winter: in early February, he reported ice half a finger's width in depth; twenty people froze to death overnight. Dr Edward Ives, like many British and European visitors at this time, probably had unrealistic expectations of Baghdad, fabled city of the caliphs, and was disappointed by the architecture. 'The public buildings are better than those of Bassora,' he wrote with a touch of pomposity, 'but the best would be esteemed unfit for a private gentleman of a thousand pounds a year in England.' The streets were very narrow, the covered bazaars long, their roofs punctured at intervals to allow in light and ventilation. The pontoon bridge of thirty-nine boats was 'floored with date trees, flags, horse-dung, and slime or mud; it is very badly railed.'[31] Ives, who was something of a naturalist, described the pigeon-crowded mosques and churches of the city with affection. He greatly admired the storks, known as 'Leg-leg' by Baghdadis, which made their nests on minarets and conferred blessings worth 'more than a field full of sheep and camels'. A family living in a house where storks nested was considered very fortunate. As always, religion was not far from the surface, even in the field of ornithology: 'If a Christian should happen to kill one of them, his life would be in danger.'[32]

Whatever the complaints of visiting European gentlemen, it would be a mistake to consider this a period of architectural stagnation in Baghdad. On the contrary, the numerous monumental mosques erected from the sixteenth century to the nineteenth showed Baghdad had not forgotten its distant yet unique heritage as the cornerstone of the Dar al Islam. There was the glittering Muradiya of 1578, which dominated the northern end of Rashid Street; Hassan Pasha's dun-coloured, many-domed

Saray Mosque (1704) at the entrance of the Kushla barracks; the high-walled Ahmediya (1796) overlooking Maidan Square, where Tamerlane committed so many of his atrocities; and the blue-domed Haydar Khana (1826), also on Rashid Street. Hassan Pasha also established the neighbourhood adjoining the Kushla, which to this day is known as Jadeed (New) Hassan Pasha, an evocative district of faded, once handsome Ottoman buildings. The formidable Adila Khatun was a great architectural patron and built several schools and two mosques, one of which can still be seen. Her Khan al Takiya, built as a courthouse, survived until 2010, when it was demolished to make way for a new building.[33] Curiously, given the ancient enmity between them, Baghdad relied heavily on the Iranian model of religious architecture from the late sixteenth century to the early nineteenth, copying structural forms and epigraphic styles and adorning domes and minarets with the quintessentially Iranian, sun-catching blue faience tiles.

A word of warning should also be given about the pervasive sense of decline at this period. As André Raymond has shown, Arab cities grew dramatically during several centuries of Ottoman rule. Defining the city centre as the area around the great mosques, together with the main markets and caravanserais, often walled, he estimated the size of sixteenth-century Damascus at around 9 hectares, Aleppo at 11 and Cairo, second city of the Ottoman Empire, at 58. By 1837 the cities had expanded astonishingly to 313, 367 and 660 hectares respectively. During the same period Baghdad spread out like the Tigris in high flood, growing almost thirty times, from 12 to 340 hectares.[34]

Niebuhr ruefully noted that Baghdad's scholars had long since abandoned the venerable Mustansiriya College on the eastern bank. He found its kitchen was now used as a toll-house and much of the rest of the complex was a caravanserai called Otmedani Khan. Niebuhr's sobering discovery of just how far Baghdad had fallen from the cultural glories of the Abbasid era would have shocked, saddened and perhaps infuriated caliphs such as Harun al Rashid and Mamun, who had expended such energy on sponsoring intellectual and artistic endeavour. Though sciences were once accorded considerable prestige in the city, Niebuhr wrote, today they were valued less than in either Cairo or in Yemen. He met few people who could read or write and failed to find a single shop in Baghdad where he could buy old books: 'If anyone wants to build up a collection of books ... he has to wait until someone dies, when the dead man's books are carried through town, like old clothes, and the town-crier auctions them off.'[35]

Decline did not preclude splendour. Niebuhr admired Omar Pasha's personal guard of 800 cavalry, 'magnificently dressed and mounted on beautiful horses'.[36] He estimated the total number of forces the pasha could theoretically put into the field at 36,000, but in practice he thought the core army was barely more than 10,000 strong. Commenting on Baghdad's limited and poorly organized defences – the half-dozen cannons on each of the citadel's ten bastions had no gun-carriages – he echoed the remarks made thirty-three years earlier by Mr Dorrel, the British friend of Ahmed Pasha, concluding that 'A European enemy could very easily make himself master of the city.'[37] The British would take the same view in 1917. Ives was also struck by the sartorial elegance of what he called 'cap-gentlemen', the aghas whose dress he considered 'very neat'. A senior Mamluk official might wear a green or white turban, made of linen or camel's wool shawl-cloth. Alternative headgear was a stiff cloth bonnet, black and quilted and at least twelve inches high, around which white or green linen cloth was twisted. A long shirt was tucked into linen drawers beneath another pair of loose camel-wool trousers. Sewn to the ankle of these trousers was a pair of thin yellow slippers without heels, worn within another pair, the outer set left by the door when entering a house. The dapper gentleman would wear a close-fitting, calf-length buttoned tunic over the linen shirt, and over this another tunic of similar length, with fine linen lapels, buttons at the wrist and 'an open petticoat-like tail'. The addition of a fine sash, trimmed with gold or silver embroidery, gave the ensemble added panache; and an embroidered handkerchief accompanied a timepiece in a pocket under the lapel. Finally, a third tunic, silk-lined and made of fine cloth or shawl-cloth, was worn loosely over the other layers, either buttoned or open, and usually thrown off at home. The above was considered summer wear, winter dress differing only in the material worn rather than in the number of layers. Ives marvelled at the numerous styles of headwear, the most impressive being three feet high with huge circumferences, covered with fur.[38]

Such gorgeously dressed officials were part of a highly stratified order of Mamluks, which by now dominated public life to such an extent that being an indigenous Baghdadi severely restricted one's career opportunities.

The training of the Mamluks' apparently limitless pool of Caucasian boys consisted of reading, writing, swimming, horse-riding and martial skills. Some were destined for the upper echelons of the pashalik, where they would rub shoulders with the leaders of the great families; others would serve in the pasha's bodyguard, at court or in the civil administration. Once their training was complete, most Mamluks joined the pasha's inner circle, where they could rejoice in positions such as Agha of the Wardrobe, Agha of the Coffee, Agha of the Carpets, Warden of the Private Apartments or Commander of the Georgian Guard, the last consisting of three regiments of 1,000 soldiers each – in theory at least.

Mamluks in the pasha's outer circle were assigned to public-administration duties, and could find themselves working as scribes, tax-collectors or, in some cases, extremely senior government officials.

Given this formal structure of the pashalik, there were few avenues to distinction available for the bright or ambitious Baghdadi. Senior religious and legal figures such as the *kadis*, *muftis* and *nakibs* were recruited from the clerical aristocracy, while the senior financial position of *sarraf bashi*, banker to the pasha, was traditionally occupied by a representative of one of the influential Jewish banking families. The *khaznadar*'s duties might include those of the pasha's private treasurer, the commander of the inner circle of servants or the chief inspector of taxes, and sometimes encompassed all three, while the *daftardar* was the public treasurer in the direct service of Istanbul, later also the army commander. The trio of Ottoman Porte officials, namely the *kadi*, *daftardar* and *agha* of the Janissaries, were senior authorities, but in practice no match for the pasha's entourage, reinforced by Mamluk military might. The pasha's deputy and chief minister was the *kahya*, whose chief function all too frequently was to be the scapegoat for any military or other serious reversal.[39]

Power was represented and exercised in administrative *diwans*, or assemblies, completely dominated by Mamluk officials; and in the less influential consultative *diwans*, which had a broader membership that included leading figures outside the Mamluk class, such as the *nakib* of Baghdad, various *muftis*, the preachers from Sheikh Abdul Kadir al Gailani and Abu Hanifa mosques and former governors living in Baghdad.*

* The *nakib* was the representative and head of Baghdad's gentry, chosen to represent the city's notables in meetings with rulers and foreign visitors. Abdul Rahman al Nakib, a direct

The closing decades of the eighteenth century were the golden era of the Mamluk Dynasty in Baghdad. The Georgian-born Suleyman the Great, the only pasha to enjoy such a moniker in four centuries, ruled as governor of the three provinces of Baghdad, Basra and Shahrizor from 1780 to 1802, during which time the external threat from Iran receded altogether and there was no significant challenge to these territories. Although they faced a growing menace from the fundamentalist Wahabis in the deserts of Arabia, which Suleyman proved unable to eradicate, his personal position was unshakable for twenty-two years.* It was founded on prodigious energy (especially for a man who had become pasha at sixty), notable displays of courage and relentless military campaigning to reinforce Mamluk authority and to curb that of the restless tribes and Janissaries. Pashas' campaigns against the tribes of the marshes, deserts and mountains were 'monotonously frequent' in Iraq.[40] Suleyman made more headway in such expeditions than most. Reining in the tribes reinforced the stability necessary for diplomacy and trade with Europe, which he promoted vigorously. The burgeoning revenues from this commerce permitted the lavish expenditure every pasha required to retain power amongst numerous rivals and factions and funded a court whose magnificence was widely acknowledged.

Where there was trade, the British were never far away. The first Englishman to arrive in Baghdad, it may be remembered, was the London merchant John Newberry in 1581. Two hundred years later, in a striking indication of its growing influence in Iraq, Britain was intimately involved in Suleyman's rise to the pashalik. William Latouche, the British Agent in Baghdad, facilitated Suleyman's appointment, serving as a private intermediary with Istanbul, to which he sent considerable sums of money on the would-be pasha's behalf. The pasha's gratitude was acknowledged in 1782 with orders for arms and ammunitions from Bombay, and regular consignments, sometimes accompanied by European instructors, followed. A year later Suleyman authorized the appointment of an East India Company Agent in Baghdad; and in

descendant of Sheikh Abdul Kadir al Gailani, was the last person to hold the title. He was Iraq's first prime minister before the crowning of King Faisal in 1921.

* Mohammed ibn Abdul Wahab (1703–92) was a firebrand and religious reformer from the Arabian peninsula. He studied in Basra and urged a return to a pure Islam, based on the Koran and the *sunna*, or traditions of the Prophet Mohammed, untainted by modernity. An alliance with the Al Saud family in the mid-eighteenth century formed the basis of the strict version of Islam that continues in Saudi Arabia to this day.

1798 he went a step further and granted the Company permission to establish a permanent British Resident in Baghdad. In the admittedly partial judgement of the East India Company's first Resident in Baghdad, the British diplomat and writer Sir Harford Jones Brydges, who knew him well, 'Suleyman was, perhaps, as fine a specimen of a Turkish Pasha as ever existed.'[41]

After the almost halcyon days of Suleyman the Great in the closing years of the eighteenth century, Baghdad entered the nineteenth beset by troubles. In 1801 plague returned to the city, driving the ailing, octogenarian pasha to the healthier town of Khalis, north of the capital. In the same year a Wahabi force of 6,000–7,000 camel and horse surged north from Arabia and sacked the sacred Shia city of Kerbala, massacring several thousand inhabitants and looting the peerless, gold-filled shrine of Imam Hussain, before riding south on animals piled high with the treasures of Shia Islam. For the now invalid Suleyman, it was a blow from which he never recovered, and on 7 August 1802 he died.

Baghdad returned on his death to its default position of political strife and instability. Once again pashas came and went, the manner of their execution being the most interesting aspect of their time in office. Suleyman's successor, Ali Pasha, was assassinated while at public prayers in 1807. In 1810 Suleyman Pasha the Little, escaping from rival forces, sought sanctuary in the tents of the Shammar Toga tribe; disregarding the time-honoured Arab traditions of hospitality, they lost no time in cutting off his head. There followed Abdullah Pasha the Tobacconist, who struggled to assert his authority before a successful revolt broke out led by Said, a son of Suleyman the Great. Deserted by his supporters, Abdullah and a small group of followers were strangled, buried, disinterred and decapitated in 1813.

Said Pasha was an extravagant, pleasure-seeking youth who lacked the iron personality required to keep a grip on power in Baghdad. Questions were raised about his judgement after he made a series of dubious appointments to senior positions and incurred immense private debts to fund a ruinously lavish court. In the absence of his brother-in-law Daud, frequently away campaigning loyally on the pasha's behalf, his advisers consisted of 'a foolish mother, a worthless friend and a buffoon'.[42] As security started to unravel, from within and without Baghdad, Istanbul began to take a closer interest in a province that for too long had behaved like an independent ally rather than a vassal province. Sultan

Mahmud II withdrew his support for Said and ordered his dismissal, turning to Daud after some imperial wavering. Said's initial success on the battlefield led him to dismiss his forces, whom he could barely afford to pay, a premature and complacent act for which he was soon punished. With Daud scattering coin amongst the all-powerful Georgian Guard, Said's support began to melt away and he was reduced to making a last stand in the citadel. On 20 February 1817, Daud entered Baghdad and was proclaimed pasha. At night the newly appointed agha of the Janissaries approached the gates of the citadel, showed the guards his signet of authority and quietly made his way into the pasha's private apartments. Reassured by the agha's soft words, Said's doting mother unlocked the door. The end came quickly. 'While the mother clung around her devoted son, in distracted agony shrieking and imploring mercy . . . their victim was struck down with a battle-axe and a headless trunk alone remained in his parent's arms.'[43] A pasha's hubris, in this case Said's earlier treachery towards Abdullah, once again, brought about his nemesis.

*

A curious portrait hangs in the coffee room of the Royal Geographical Society in South Kensington. An exuberantly bearded, handsomely dressed man sits next to his wife, wearing a deep red, gold-embroidered tunic worn over green and white linen robes. The beautifully worked hilt of a dagger thrusts out with a martial flourish from beneath a striped sash around his waist. His turban, a luxurious concoction of white linen, rises a good foot above his forehead. His wife, whose little finger he holds affectionately, is a modest counterpoint to this elaborate finery, hen pheasant to his peacock. She wears a robe of faded pink with matching headpiece, her hair tied into several waist-length braids that are neatly tucked behind her back beneath a patterned sash. While the husband gazes admiringly at his wife, she looks at the artist with something approaching melancholy.

At first glance, the bearded man might be a Mamluk pasha. Yet the legend beneath reveals he is James Silk Buckingham with his wife in the Arab costume of Baghdad. Buckingham, a prolific English traveller and writer, arrived in Baghdad in the summer of 1816 and was a guest of Claudius Rich, the then British Resident and an historian of Babylon and Iraqi antiquities. An observant writer, Buckingham paid particular notice to the establishment of the British Resident, which by this time reflected Britain's position as the second power in Iraq after the Ottomans. The Residence, which had originally consisted of several homes, was now 'one of the largest, best and most commodious in the city'.[44] Rich presided over a large multicultural staff consisting of an English surgeon, an Italian secretary, several dragomen (interpreters), a number of Janissaries, grooms and servants ('Turks, Arabs, Georgians, Persians and Hindoos'), a company of sepoys as bodyguard and a diminished troop of European hussars. The British Resident lived and travelled in some style:

> A large and commodious yacht was always kept ready for excursions on the river, under the care of an Indian Serang and crew. The stud of horses was large and choice; and everything belonging to the Residency was calculated to impress ideas of great respect on the minds of the inhabitants . . . The fact is, indeed, that Mr Rich was universally considered to be the most powerful man in Baghdad, next to the Pasha; and some even questioned whether the Pasha himself would not at any time shape his own conduct according to Mr Rich's suggestions and advice, rather than as his own council might wish.

Other aspects of his visit impressed him less. Echoing Niebuhr's unhappy discovery half a century earlier, Buckingham found literature 'at so low an ebb here, that there is no one known collection of good books or manuscripts in the whole city, nor any individual Moolah distinguished above his contemporaries by his proficiency in the learning of his country'. He estimated Baghdad's population rather vaguely at 50,000–100,000, of which Jews numbered more than 10,000. They included the remarkable David Sassoon, who, in 1817, became the treasurer of Baghdad, following in the footsteps of his father, Saleh. Yet, however thriving the Jewish community had become, the markets did not pass muster with Buckingham, possessing 'an air of meanness which I have never before observed in any large Turkish city'.

Disappointed by the literature, disgruntled by the language, Buckingham was a difficult man to impress. Baghdadi Arabic, he wrote, was 'very bad; scarcely anything more harsh in sound or more barbarous in construction and the use of foreign words can be conceived than the dialect of Baghdad'. He did not think much of Baghdadi women either. High-born women were not attractive and had poor complexions, while their lower-class sisters were darker-skinned and occasionally 'so barbarously tattooed as to have the most forbidding appearance'. In his evident admiration of the Georgian and Circassian women, 'decidedly the handsomest by nature and the least disfigured by art', Buckingham shared the tastes and prejudices of the Ottoman sultan, not to mention his many pashas throughout the empire. As Voltaire wrote in 1734,

> The Circassians are poor and their daughters are beautiful, and so they use them as their chief export. They supply beauties to the harems of the Grand Turk, the Sophy of Persia, and those who are rich enough to buy and keep this precious merchandise. With the most honourable intentions they train these girls to fondle and caress men, to perform dances full of lasciviousness and sensuousness, to rekindle by all the most voluptuous artifices the desires of the high and mighty masters for whom they are destined.[45]

Daud's eventual triumph over his erratic master, Said, ushered in the golden sunset of the Mamluk Dynasty. Contemporary accounts of Daud speak of a slightly quixotic figure capable of extremes, recklessly generous and extravagant one moment, irrationally greedy and parsimonious the next. When it came to domestic luxury, there was no restraint. The sparkling splendour of his court was said to rival that of the imperial capital. He was considered cowardly and irresolute as well as capable of extreme bravery, a modernizer who demonstrated a lively interest in reforming the army, developing textile and munitions industries, clearing canals, building bazaars and founding a printing press, yet was equally opposed to the march of progress, especially when it threatened the very survival of the Mamluks. In this post-Enlightenment age of revolution and progress, the dynasty of slaves looked more anachronistic by the day, above all to Istanbul.

Much of Daud's time as pasha was occupied by renewed hostilities with a resurgent Iran. In 1818 the shah's son Mohammed Ali Mirza, prince of the province of Kermanshah, invaded Iraq, following treasonable correspondence from Mahmud Baban of Kurdistan, who joined forces against Daud. The attack on Iraq was officially justified by the perennially poor treatment of Iranian pilgrims visiting the holy Shia sites. But these narrow local enmities mirrored wider differences between shah and sultan. Border disputes were the convenient precursor to all-out conflict, and Daud was instructed by Istanbul to make all necessary preparations. A series of military encounters, from minor skirmishes to larger engagements, was marked by regular reversals, defections, disease, regroupings, negotiations, siege preparations and recriminations against treacherous tribes. The death of Mohammed Ali Mirza hastened the end of the conflict, which was formalized by the Treaty of Erzurum on 28 July 1823. 'Henceforward the Sword of Enmity shall be sheathed, and every circumstance shall be avoided, which may produce coldness or disgust, and may be contrary to friendship and perfect union,' it read.[46] By reaffirming the imprecise border that dated back to Murad IV's conquest of 1639, the treaty failed to eliminate the potential for further conflict. The treaty was confirmed in 1847, after the findings of a mixed boundary commission that for the first time included British and Russian representatives. Final demarcation of this troublesome border, however, had to wait until 1914.

A glimpse into the pomp and circumstance of Daud's court comes in an account by the Indian Army officer Major George Keppel, who stayed in Baghdad in 1824, shortly after hostilities with Iran had ended. Riding on horseback, Keppel was preceded by an officer carrying a silver baton of office, topped with a filigree gilt ball. His own horse was lavishly bridled and caparisoned in rich velvet patterned with gilt and silver studs.

> The Pasha's secretary sent several of his servants to attend us, and we were met at some distance from the palace by a deputation of janissaries. On passing through the gates of the palace, we entered a spacious court, where the Pasha's troops were drawn up ... At the gate of the second court we dismounted; here the principal officers of the Pasha received us, and ushered us into his presence, to which we passed though two lines of janissaries, who, standing with their arms folded, preserved an immovable gravity. The hall of audience was fitted up in the Oriental style, and decorated with numerous small looking-glasses of a triangular form, which had a curious and dazzling effect. In one corner was seated the Pasha, supported by cushions.[47]

Keppel felt the grandeur of his entrance was better suited to an ambassador than to the private traveller he was. Yet there were good reasons for this pro-British show. In 1820 Daud had tangled with the British Resident Claudius Rich, after announcing the arbitrary doubling of customs duties on all British goods, in breach of agreements with

Istanbul. When Rich expressed his intention to pursue the matter in Bombay with the board of the East India Company, the pasha immediately forbade his departure from Baghdad and sent troops to surround the Residency. These soldiers were greeted by a bristling force of sepoys, Arabs and Europeans in defensive positions. In the intense stand-off that followed, Daud blinked first. A compromise was hastily devised in which the pasha's forces were withdrawn and Rich was allowed to leave the following spring.

Further cracks appeared in the pasha's power. In 1826 came a dramatic moment in Istanbul, when the modernizing young Sultan Mahmud II moved decisively against the Janissaries, whom he considered a reactionary and corrupt force standing in the way of his reforms, especially those that involved the adoption of modern military methods of training, gunnery and other innovations. Mutinies and defeats on the battlefield had strengthened Mahmud's determination to push through the reorganizations that up to that point had been vigorously resisted. This time the inevitable mutinies that followed the order for a proportion of the Janissaries to submit to new training were faced down. Cannons rumbled into action against the Janissaries' barracks, which within minutes were reduced to an inferno. Eyewitnesses put the number killed at 6,000, with thousands more hunted down and killed across the empire in what became known as the Auspicious Incident.[48] Mahmud had struck at the heart of traditional military power, the Janissaries were abolished at a stroke, and serious consequences – together with more bloodshed – loomed in Iraq.

In Baghdad, Daud Pasha ordered a meticulously choreographed parade in which eighteen companies of Janissaries were strategically stationed in the centre of the great Ottoman palace of the Saray. While the sultan's decree announcing their abolition and the formation of a new force was bellowed out, the raging thoughts of mutiny that followed the immediate reaction of astonishment were cooled by the rectangle of field guns trained upon them and the rows of Mamluk soldiers ready to cut them down at a moment's notice. After a tense silence, the Janissaries threw down their fur *kalpaks* and replaced them with the headgear of the new Nidham Jadeed Army that had been announced. To the gunners' great relief and no doubt that of Daud, the artillery pounded away in celebratory volleys rather than initiating the mass execution that had been feared. For once Baghdad lived up to its moniker, and the transition from the Janissaries, so violent in Istanbul and throughout Ottoman lands, was entirely peaceful.

In 1830, in the aftermath of the Ottoman–Russian War, which had resulted in Sultan Mahmud's humiliating defeat, imperial eyes turned again to Baghdad. Daud had conspicuously failed to provide any support to his sultan. Mahmud now dispatched the envoy Sadik Effendi to Baghdad, whose mission was to enforce the pasha's retirement and replacement by a non-Mamluk successor. The envoy was greeted with the greatest ceremony and cordiality, a scrupulous observation of diplomatic protocol that he refused to reciprocate, ignoring the military display and official reception that had been prepared at the Saray. Daud responded the next day with a calculated display of rudeness, rising only at the very last moment to greet his visitor. On the third day of the visit, by which time the atmosphere was glacial, Sadik Effendi at last revealed his mission. It was a predictably difficult meeting: voices were raised and accusations hurled. The envoy promised the senior official Suleyman Agha, the pashalik, only for the man to rush back to Daud to confess what had happened. It was time for a final Mamluk solution to an Ottoman problem. A council of war was called and the action required quickly settled. On 19 October 1830 a specially detailed corps of Daud's Mamluks slipped into the envoy's lodgings and removed his retainers before smashing their way into his room and strangling him on the spot. An exquisitely crafted letter of condolence, accompanied by the ritually lavish presents, was rushed to Istanbul, expressing the pasha's most sincere regrets that the esteemed envoy had succumbed to cholera.

There was no question of Mahmud falling for such a weak ploy. The Ottoman sultan declared Daud a renegade and appointed a new pasha, Ali Rida, a junior army officer from outside the Mamluk ranks. Rida began his march south from Aleppo in February 1831 but quickly halted, as it seemed quite possible that nature would achieve the desired end without recourse to arms.

In March 1831 disaster struck. The plague, which had been coursing through Tabriz the previous summer, spreading south to Kirkuk and Sulaymaniya in the northern highlands, reached Baghdad, breaking out initially in the Jewish quarter. The British Resident tried to persuade Daud to introduce a quarantine but was told in response that any prophylaxis was contrary to the laws and spirit of Islam. As a result, no medical precautions were taken.[49] Caravans from plague-infested areas passed in and out of Baghdad unrestricted, freely passing on the disease, which now ran unchecked through the city. After initial inertia, many Baghdadis thought of escape, but the various ways out of the city were fraught with danger. All land routes were in the hands of tribesmen who would happily slit their throats for a few coins, while boats on the Tigris for all but the cream of society were few, full and known to be infested. Christians barricaded themselves in their homes, shunning contact with fellow citizens in a desperate effort to avoid the disease, but still the plague swept through the city. Having seen the authorities refuse to take the necessary precautions, the British Resident and his staff left by boat to Basra.

Piecing together various accounts, the daily death-toll appears to have risen from around 150 on 4 April to 1,100 on 12 April and continued at 1,500–3,000 until 27 April.[50] During this time the English traveller James Wellsted was living in a house that overlooked all the others in his neighbourhood. He watched the numbers of those sleeping on the roofs around him fall off daily. In one house the twenty-five men, women and children who had taken to their roof terrace dropped to just six in three weeks and then disappeared completely.[51]

Things fell apart. The normal life of Baghdad was suspended as the city slipped into a Dantean vision of hell. Bodies piled up in the streets because the living could not keep up with the dead. Food supplies dwindled then disappeared; the water-carriers vanished, along with soldiers, court officials and the last vestiges of government. In the midst of this terror law and order broke down altogether. Bands of ruffians, high on opium and reeling from strong spirits, prowled deserted streets brandishing daggers, sabres and matchlocks, searching for easy prey, of which there was no shortage. Roaming from house to house, they robbed and pillaged with impunity, frequently killing the homeowners and stripping their corpses of any jewels and valuables.

One man racked by fever described how he was lying on a pallet on the first floor of his house, being tended by his devoted wife, when thugs smashed in and rushed upstairs. The homeowner, stretched out next to two plague-ridden corpses from his household, was too sick to move. 'I read their purpose in their looks,' he recalled, 'but I was stricken and could not lift a finger to save her for whose life I would gladly have forfeited my own.'[52] With a gleaming knife in one hand, one of the thieves approached her, ignoring the couple's desperate cries for mercy, and stabbed her repeatedly. The feverish husband watched helplessly as she bled to death beside him, then fell into unconsciousness as the assailants stripped them of their jewellery and fled. Although there were heart-warming instances of camaraderie and self-sacrifice for loved ones, onlookers described a general collapse of morality and decency as the plague did its worst.

Baghdad was sinking fast. Yet the plague was only the first phase of nature's attack on the city. In the first week of April the weather had turned. Heavy clouds massed, thunder and lightning crashed across dark, lowering skies, and more rain than Baghdadis could ever remember poured from the heavens. Streets turned to mud. On 12 April the Tigris started to rise. During the night of 20 April it burst its banks, overrunning the city in a terrifying deluge. Wellsted, who was still taking refuge from the plague on his roof, left an eyewitness account of what happened that night:

> I was sleeping at the top of the house when the flood burst upon us, and was awakened by the roar of the waters rushing past the hall. I remained perfectly quiet, convinced no human exertion could avail me. No outcry accompanied the convulsions; I heard no shriek nor wail; but, as I seated myself on the upper part of the wall, I could perceive several bodies, their white dresses gleaming amidst the turbid waters, silently sweeping by.[53]

The floating corpses were amongst the 15,000 Wellsted reported killed that night. The heavy death-toll included children, plague sufferers and the weak and elderly. Many of the dead were those who had managed to survive the disease after burying less fortunate relatives. In the early hours of 21 April the waters started to subside. By sunrise it was a stream that could be waded through. Wellsted lowered himself gingerly to street level by rope. 'Hardly had my feet touched the ground, when, with a mighty crash, down came the house. A lucky escape!'[54]

Baghdad had not been so fortunate. The plague, with the help of the savage flood, had carried off between half and two-thirds of the city's population.[55] The structural damage to the city was beyond comprehension. Within hours of the first rush of water, hundreds of houses had fallen down, their foundations undermined. A day later 7,000 houses lay in ruins, many of them burying their owners and tenants alive. On 26 April a section of the city walls near the Muadham Gate crashed to the ground and part of the citadel collapsed. The dervish hostel within the revered Sheikh Abdul Kadir al Gailani Mosque, pillaged by the Iranians in 1508, ransacked and largely ruined in 1623, was lost completely to the waters. While ravenous dogs tore at the limbs of corpses submerged in mud, the prize Nejd mares of the pasha's stable clattered through the empty streets.

Daud was almost alone. Where once thousands of immaculately uniformed Mamluks, Janissaries, aghas, court officials, servants and the doe-eyed women of his harem had waited on his every command, his retinue had shrivelled to one old woman who tended him as he lay sick in an empty, flood-ravaged palace. The magnificent, high-spirited banquets he hosted here only recently must have seemed a cruel memory, as he contemplated a bowl of fish scavenged from fishermen.

With the flood waters receding and the worst depredations of the plague past, Daud pinned his hopes on relief; yet his miseries were only compounded by the news that the army of his rival, Ali Riha, had arrived at the city walls, commanded by Kasim Pasha of Mosul. The sultan's decree deposing Daud was read aloud, triggering an almost inevitable uprising within the city, but this soon fizzled out. Demoralized, weakened by disease and abandoned by all but a handful of retainers, Daud fled to the home of a friend, supported in his saddle by an Ethiopian slave. In a city where nothing remained secret for long, the pasha's hiding place was quickly discovered, and he was transferred to house arrest. Kasim Pasha and his entourage rode into the city and were greeted by the meagre ranks of Baghdad's notables and escorted into the Saray. The transition had been swift and bloodless.

Baghdad's genius for producing terrible violence from moments of tranquillity was undimmed, however. Kasim's forces, which included ill-disciplined desert Bedouin, went on the rampage. Rumours spread that those who had served Daud would be done away with, persuading many that Kasim was now the man to remove. On 13 June, carried along on a wave of outraged emotion, a crowd of Mamluks, Baghdadis and tribesmen of the Ughail surrounded the Saray and attacked. Kasim's early surrender was not enough to prevent further tragedy for the city.

The audience-hall of the Saray, one of the greatest monuments of Baghdad, was torched in a blaze that spread fast through the elegantly arcaded building, ripping down gilt apartments and consuming the many riches not already looted. The finest carpets went up in smoke, together with exquisite artwork, Damascene silks and royal furniture. Priceless jewellery, sets of armour, inlaid mirrors, the treasures of a continent – everything was lost. Daud was restored to power with the remnants of an army, but his position appeared weak.

Recognizing that he needed to put an end to the affair in person, Ali Rida marched from Mosul to Baghdad and ordered a blockade. The city that had come through a shattering plague, barely survived one of the worst floods in living memory and was mired in division and recrimination now found itself under siege in the gasping heat of summer. Since the defenders numbered little more than 1,000 under arms, and Ali Rida had two infantry and two cavalry regiments at his disposal, in addition to 12,000 irregulars, the issue appeared clear. For two and a half months, the stand-off continued. Prices rocketed in the bazaars, which struggled to provide the most basic food supplies. Regular desertions and constant intrigue weakened the city's resolve. There were inconclusive skirmishes outside the city walls, and a desultory bombardment was maintained. When Ali Rida received instructions from Istanbul to withdraw, he determined on a diplomatic solution, offering Daud a pardon in return for his surrender. The consequences of refusing this generous offer, it was made clear, would be utter ruination. A final act of treachery during the night of 14 September 1831 ensured the city fell into Ali Rida's hands. He received Daud with the dignity due to a Mamluk pasha, and the two men exchanged cups of coffee in the time-honoured tradition of ritual caffeine.

Strange to record, in the light of the history of Baghdad and the many difficulties he had caused Istanbul, Daud was not executed. The pardon was honoured, and the last Mamluk pasha spent the remainder of his days in the service of an imperial authority he and his slave-pasha ancestors had so artfully resisted. He was appointed wali of Bosnia, then promoted to the high office of president of the Council of State before receiving the governorship of Ankara. In 1845 he became the highly respected guardian of the shrine at Medina. He died in 1851, after an extraordinary life that saw him go from free-born Christian boy to Muslim slave, and then, successively, to grandee, all-powerful pasha, penniless prisoner and fugitive on the brink of execution, before an unexpected pardon allowed him to spend his last twenty years in the highest offices of the Ottoman Empire, enjoying the hard-earned respect of a venerable old man.

It was a fate that would have been envied by his former Mamluk friends and colleagues. On the third day of taking office, Ali Rida called a general *diwan*, a council of notables, in Baghdad, where the imperial decree confirming his appointment as governor of Baghdad, Aleppo, Diyarbakir and Mosul was read; it was the first time a pasha had been granted command over all these provinces. The old title of caliph, abandoned in 1517 and less relevant than ever, was reintroduced. In practice, however, the new pasha held sway only in Iraq. All the Mamluk structures and positions were summarily abolished. In front of him, surrounded by his Albanian troops, stood the orderly lines of proud Mamluks, now officially an anachronism. Ali Rida's retirement to a private room was the cue for his forces to slaughter them where they stood. Those who survived the initial volley of musket shot were cut down by sabres. Others in the city were hunted down and killed.

The dynasty of slave-pashas that had ruled Baghdad for 130 years with so little interference from Istanbul that it had become virtually independent, that had restored power, style and grandeur to a city that had sunk into provincial obscurity, had been completely extinguished.

9

Empires Collide (1831–1917)

Balik baştan kokar.
The fish putrefies from the head downwards.

Turkish proverb

Question: *When it occurs that enemies attack the Islamic world,
when it has been established that they seize and pillage Islamic
countries and capture Muslim persons and when his Majesty the
Padishah of Islam [Ottoman Sultan Mehmed V] thereupon
orders the jihad in the form of a general mobilization, has jihad
then, according to the illustrious Koranic verse: 'Go forth, light
and heavy! Struggle in God's way with your possessions and
yourselves; that is better for you, did you know', become incum-
bent on all Muslims and has it become an individual duty for all
Muslims in all parts of the world, be they young or old, on foot
or mounted, to hasten to partake in the jihad with their goods
and money?*
Answer: *Yes.*

Sultan Mehmed V, declaration of jihad,
Istanbul, 11 November 1914[1]

Less than a century ago, the Abu Hanifa Mosque in the north-eastern
district of Adhamiya was surrounded by groves of palm trees that
tapered off towards the banks of the Tigris. Today it is ringed with
tarmac – wide boulevards and car-jammed roads – but still overlooks
the river towards the end of Imam al Adham Street,* which stretches
from Maidan Square in the south, continues past the mosque and shops

---

* Imam al Adham: the Greatest Imam, i.e. Abu Hanifa.

that were bombed and looted during the 2003 war and crosses the Aimma Bridge to Kadhimiya. The few palms that still penetrate the skyline rise up from a cemetery that was the original raison d'être of Adhamiya, founded in the earliest years of the city as a graveyard for the most notable Baghdadis. Foremost among them was Imam Abu Hanifa, the founder of the Hanafi school of Islamic jurisprudence, largest of the four Sunni sects. After his death in 767, probably at the hands of Mansur, his grave became a place of pilgrimage.

'This is where the caliphs and their families were buried in the middle and late Abbasid era,' says my friend Manaf, who has accompanied me on a visit to Adhamiya, a Sunni heartland of Baghdad that is enclosed on three sides by a loop of the Tigris. 'Khaizuran, Harun al Rashid's mother, was buried nearby so it came to be known as Khaizuran's grave-yard. In one of these streets is the shrine of Um Rabia, daughter-in-law of Mustasim, the last Abbasid caliph who was slayed by the invading Mongol hordes.' For a moment I have tantalizing visions of stumbling across the graves of the greatest Abbasid caliphs, but Manaf quickly dispels them. 'The tombs of the caliphs have disappeared during the floods and devastations that afflicted the district during Baghdad's many dark periods,' he says quietly.

Like the Kadhimain shrine it almost faces across the Tigris, the Abu Hanifa shrine has been destroyed, rebuilt and expanded a number of times over the centuries, a barometer of the city's changing fortunes as Shia (Persian) and Sunni (Ottoman) invaders have come and gone. In 1066, a theological school was established here, which lives on today as a religious institute. The complex was high on the list of places to visit when Ibn Jubayr reached Baghdad in 1184. He wrote of 'a shrine, superbly built, with a white dome rising into the air, containing the tomb of the Imam Abu Hanifa'. In 1327, the Moroccan traveller Ibn Battuta likewise paid his respects here, admiring the mosque for its charity towards the poor. 'Over it there is a great dome, and a hospice at which food is served to all comers. In the city of Baghdad today there is no hospice in which food is supplied except this hospice. Magnified be he who brings destruction and change to all things.'[2] The complex was then expanded by the Ottomans, first by Suleyman the Magnificent in 1534, and later by Murad IV in 1638. By the nineteenth century it was surrounded, in addition to the acres of palm groves, by the four neighbourhoods that form the heart of Adhamiya today: Safina (ship),

Nassa (low ground), Harra (hot ground) and Shuyoukh (tribal leaders). Urban development accelerated rapidly from the early twentieth century, when the population was estimated at 2,000, to in excess of 400,000 a century later.

Today, by comparison with the Kadhimain shrine on the opposite bank of the river, the Abu Hanifa shrine is a monument of Spartan simplicity. The bricks are the colour of the desert, with matching twin domes and a solitary minaret. Even the clock tower, a much later addition, is almost severe in its lack of colour. 'You should see the shrine on the Prophet's birthday,' says Manaf. 'It's the focal point for the Sunni throughout the Islamic world and the birthday celebrations are one of the major events in Adhamiya. Great ropes of light bulbs are strung up between the minaret, the central dome and the clock tower. It's an extraordinary sight.' He points up towards the four-faced clock, visible at the top of the tower beneath the Arabic letters spelling الله (Allah). 'It might not look like much but that is a special clock. It was completely handmade by Abdul Razzak Mahsoub, a brilliant Baghdadi ironsmith with no education but his basic Mesopotamian gift of making and creating the unthinkable. Not a single part was imported. He made the clock piece by piece in his workshop. When it was completed in 1925 it worked with unbelievable perfection, sounding the hours and half hours. It won first prize in the Baghdad Fair in 1932, and Mahsoub presented it as a gift to adorn the entrance of the shrine.'

A US Department of Defense website lists the Abu Hanifa shrine among the major historical and cultural sites of Iraq. 'Most of the important historical landmarks in or near Baghdad are named after past political or religious figures (Sunni or Shia) or are associated with events in the history of the city or the history of Islam that can make these monuments high-value targets,' it says. With sad irony, US forces themselves damaged the shrine when they hit the clock tower with a rocket on 11 April 2003. Red graffiti has been daubed across a section of wall. It reads: 'Be patient, be patient, Baghdad. The army of the Invader will be swept away.' On 23 November 2006, the mosque was damaged again in a mortar barrage during a savage renewal of sectarian strife that once again pitted Sunni against Shia. Just as Kadhimiya has been the epicentre of some of the worst atrocities against Baghdad's Shia in recent years, so Adhamiya has encountered equally mesmerizing levels of violence against its Sunni inhabitants. In 2007, the ferocity and regularity of attacks here was such that desperate US forces announced they were building a three-mile wall around Adhamiya – inevitably dubbed the 'Great Wall of Adhamiya' by soldiers – 'to break the cycle of sectarian violence' and deny access to death squads and militia groups.[3] Yet the blood continued to flow.

Manaf's eyes light up as we pass several traditional Baghdadi houses along the Tigris, where a string of small restaurants spread along a winding road, offering the Baghdad speciality of *masgouf*, grilled river fish. 'They are wonderful traditional houses of yesteryear,' he enthuses. 'Outside, you have a closed balcony with peeping spaces overlooking the alley where the house stands. Inside, rooms run off a courtyard that provides sunlight and fresh air. Stairs lead up to more rooms on the first floor then, best of all, the open roof where sleeping during summer time has always been a unique Baghdadi experience. You have the fresh breeze of the river wafting across the beds laid side by side beneath mosquito nets. When there is a full moon families enjoy their dinner on the roof – it's like an extraordinary Baghdadi moonlight sonata. Drinking water is kept in clay pitchers that keep the water cool naturally. Once the flies start coming in at dawn and the hot sun rises, you can continue snoozing below in the cool lower courtyard which has a tree or two to cast some shade.'

Imam al Adham Street runs through the historical home of Baghdad's predominantly Sunni aristocracy. Alongside Antar roundabout, marked by a statue of an Arabian knight brandishing a scimitar astride his stallion, is the former Royal Olympic Club ('they used to have magnificent clay courts where young men played tennis in immaculate whites'). South of the Abu Hanifa shrine, in a semi-circular slice of land lined with evergreens and palms, is the war-damaged Royal Mausoleum, a secular counterpart to Sunni pre-eminence, designed by the British architects Mason and Dixon in the early 1930s. Beneath its great turquoise dome, flanked by two smaller ones, lie the slim marble tombs of the three kings of Iraq – Faisal I, Ghazi and Faisal II, together with their queens and princesses – under the watchful eye of Ghanem Jamil Ali, an elderly guard who grumbles about the American occupation and the soldiers who smashed King Faisal's marble tomb cover: 'They said they were looking for weapons.' South-east again, past the palm trees of Maghrib Street, the Royal Court stood for half a century until it was pulled down in 1975 and replaced by a glass and aluminium rest-house for army officers. A cultural counterpoint across the road is the former building of the Institute of Art: 'Its theatre, classrooms and gardens saw the most brilliant generation of Iraqi artists, actors and sculptors blossom into creators of beauty just like their Sumerian, Babylonian, Assyrian and Arab predecessors,' Manaf says. To our west is Sarrafiya Bridge, a clunking iron structure built by the British in the late 1940s. 'It used to have a train track that ran alongside the car lanes, and as a boy it was a joy to be with all our friends cheering as the steam train rattled along high above the street, blowing its whistle.'

We continue down Imam al Adham Street, slicing south through Rusafa. Manaf points out an occasional grand villa and mourns the destruction of many more, discussing his preferred architectural style of the 1930s, once seen to splendid effect on Zahawi Street, named after the Iraqi poet. He mentions Taha Street, once home to prime ministers and a medley of ministers, political leaders and military generals, and suddenly we have reached Bab al Muadham – the famous Abbasid gate through which conquerors marched their troops, remembered in name only today after the gate was demolished in 1922 – with Maidan Square, site of Tamerlane's head-severing outrages in 1401, within sight.

'Adhamiya has been the theatre for so many important events over the years and has this powerful spirit about it,' says Manaf. 'It has housed and bred so many of Baghdad's notable people – politicians, doctors, generals, engineers and artists. I just hope it will produce such fine people again.'

*

For Baghdad, the Mamluks were the last gasp of medievalism. The advance of the nineteenth century, bringing new technology and new ideas of progress within a more orderly imperial setting – from trains, steamships and the telegraph to flourishing trade and oil exploration – helped lift it from stagnating backwater to thriving international city. With the Mamluks' departure, the shrivelled city exchanged virtual independence for formal loyalty to the empire, slipping into the keen embrace of what became modern – or at least modernizing – Turkey.

For centuries Baghdad had exerted a powerful centripetal attraction. In its Abbasid heyday, students from the Atlantic coast to Afghanistan had flocked there to pursue their studies alongside some of the world's most distinguished scholars. As often as not during Baghdad's tempestuous history, the foreign visitors appearing outside the city walls had less elevated pursuits in mind. Untold thousands of them had been soldiers from distant as well as neighbouring lands, bent on conquest, and slaughter, rape and pillage.

As medievalism began to give way to modernity, a new species of foreign invader thrust his – it was rarely her – way into Baghdad. Gone were the teeming masses of sword-wielding Mongols, Tatars, Iranians and Turks from the East. In their place came softly spoken civilians from the West. Where the old invaders had issued blood-curdling threats to torch the city and put its people to the sword (which were all too frequently realized), the nineteenth-century gentlemen from England, Germany or France would never have dreamt of something so vulgar and uncivilized.

On the contrary, the handsomely suited and moustachioed European would murmur, he had made the long and arduous journey to Baghdad in the name of bringing the gifts of modern civilization to a city that had once been its very byword. He made modest inquiries about possible trade concessions; spoke confidently about the enormous benefits of travel by steamship and about how the coming telegraph would revolutionize business in Baghdad for ever; and dangled the prospect of iron-clad investments, first in the British-led Euphrates Valley Railway Company and later in the German-led Baghdad Railway Company.

True, the city had declined from a glorious metropolis of two million to an unremarkable provincial town of anything from 20,000 to 50,000, depending on how many had been carried off by the most recent instances of flooding and outbreaks of plague; yet there was a growing sense, both within Baghdad and beyond, that the worst had passed, that the city was on the move. Rapid technological change was afoot and new inventions were multiplying at a disorienting speed. More than a thousand years after the caliph Mansur had chosen the 'crossroads of the universe' as the site for his imperial capital, the advent of steam and the railway were returning Baghdad to the world map. The old desert road to India, revived with trains rather than camels, threatened the traditional sea route linking Europe and Asia via the Cape of Good Hope. Ali Rida Pasha was quick to renew the privileges of the East India Company, a growing influence in Iraq. Baghdad's destiny was beginning to be shaped by Western rather than Eastern influences

After his brutal disposal of Mamluk troops, an entirely traditional act of violence in the history of the City of Peace, the new pasha hunted down their wives and families in order to subject them to torture. Ali al Wardi has chronicled some of the spirit-testing techniques employed. Secured to a *falaka*, a thick wooden bar with a rope tied between its two ends to immobilize the victims' feet, these hapless men and women were then caned until their bare feet were swollen and oozing blood. To encourage confessions of hidden treasures, red-hot iron rods were held agonizingly against bare flesh.[4]

However little this differed from previous regimes, Ali Rida set a new tone for Ottoman government in Iraq. At its most superficial level, the difference was sartorial. The once flowing robes and elaborate turbans of Baghdad's pashas gave way to European dress with a local twist: coats, cravats and collars, set off with a red, blue-tasselled fez, de rigueur for the new class that dominated at court, the effendis. To the ire of many Baghdadis, especially clerics and the older generation, smooth chins likewise displaced the magnificently bushy beards of old. Moustaches – calumny of calumnies! – were regularly trimmed. This sartorial code was given added impetus by the series of liberalizing Tanzimat (reorganization) reforms which started under Sultan Mahmud II in 1839 and continued until 1876. The Tanzimat was a fundamental reordering of the state and its institutions through a series of imperial edicts and decrees. Ottoman subjects were granted rights guaranteeing their security and property. The army was reorganized and professionalized. A new criminal code was introduced, based on the French model, with European-style courts and equality before the law, irrespective of religion. Tax collection was standardized, again according to the French system, and the traditional *jizya* tax on non-Muslims was ended. New paper currency was launched. Factories replaced guilds, ministries of health and education were established, together with universities, teaching schools, a central bank, stock exchange, post office and Academy of Sciences. Slavery was abolished in 1847 and homosexuality was decriminalized in 1858, more than a century before Britain. Much of what the reformers adopted was considered best European practice. By the time such zealous innovations reached distant Baghdad, however, the enthusiasm with which they had been launched in Istanbul all too often had long since disappeared.[5]

The early part of this period differed little in its concerns and tragedies from previous eras. Despite repeated warnings from the British

Resident to quarantine the pilgrims visiting from Iran, plague returned three times between 1831 and 1834, as the pasha's greed for levying taxes on the visitors took precedence over basic questions of health. His policy towards the ever-feuding tribes around Baghdad consisted of divide and rule, first bending towards the Iniza tribe when the Shammar put the city under siege in 1832, then seeking the help of the Shammar to rid the city of its lingering liberators. Obese and indolent, he was a notorious alcoholic and lecher. Continued flooding further added to the city's difficulties, cutting the population again and shattering Baghdad's already depleted stock of buildings. Two-thirds of Rusafa's structures were ruined, and across the river in Karkh the picture was even worse. Daud Pasha's palace at the Saray complex was verging on collapse. Ali Rida later ordered it to be rebuilt as barracks for his soldiers, sorry evidence of the general state of affairs. In time Baghdadis came to know it as the Saray al Kushla, Palace of the Military Barracks, a recognition of the twin uses to which it had been put. It was chosen for King Faisal's coronation in 1921 and still stands today, lending a proud, monumental style to the riverfront.

Within a few years of the devastating plague and flood, the British traveller Baillie Fraser arrived in Baghdad, leaving a surprisingly jaunty description of the city. His first sight of it made a favourable impression on him. 'The walls, in the first place, present a more imposing aspect – constructed as they are of furnace-burned bricks, and strengthened with round towers, pierced for guns, at each angle . . .'[6] The houses, which rose several storeys, were also attractive and well built. Fraser estimated the population at 60,000. However damaged the city may have been, he still counted 200 mosques, six colleges and twenty-four public baths. The fabled Mosque of the Caliphs had dwindled to a solitary minaret, the dilapidated Mustansiriya, the oldest university in the world, was doubling up as a customs office, and of course the pasha's Saray Palace was ruined.

Looking back on the early years of this phase of Turkish rule in Iraq, Stephen Hemsley Longrigg, a senior official in the Iraqi government during the British Administration of the 1920s, perhaps inevitably found little to praise. While admitting that new standards had been set and some improvements made, his overall verdict, typical of a British administrator of his time, was scathing: 'if government be judged by the freedom and happiness of subjects, the new era showed no great advance upon the old; security was as low, justice as rare, exaction as cruel, pol-icy as foolish.' The new official class was 'Literate but not otherwise educated, backward but decorous in social habit, uniform in a travesty of European dress, exact and over-refined in the letter of officialdom, completely remote from a spirit of public service ... contemptuous of tribe and cultivator, persistent speakers of Turkish amongst Arabs and, finally, almost universally corrupt and venal'.[7] The British had a very different understanding of progress.

*

The 1830s saw Baghdad opening to the world, or, rather, being opened up by outsiders, primarily by Englishmen. In 1830, John Barrow, second secretary to the Admiralty, proposed to establish the Geographical Soci-ety of London – from 1859 the Royal Geographical Society (RGS) – with a group of like-minded gentlemen and explorers, including three dukes, nine earls, twenty-four various members of the peerage and gentry and a hearty crowd of naval and army officers.[8]

The RGS spearheaded a golden era of exploration in many corners of the globe, in which surveyors and cartographers frequently led the charge. One such was Captain Francis Rawdon Chesney, who, with the blessing of Ali Rida and a grudging *firman* from Istanbul, led the Euphrates Expedition of 1835-7, co-financed by the British government and the East India Company. Fired up by the prospect of opening a new overland route to India, Chesney took two steamboats to the Euphrates. One, the *Tigris*, foundered in a squall, with the loss of twenty lives. More happily, the *Euphrates* navigated the river of the same name all the way from Birecik in Turkey to Basra, though, given the obvious dif-ficulties of the upper Euphrates, it was considered an unsuitable route for a fast steamer link to India. For his strenuous efforts in Mesopota-mia, Chesney was awarded the RGS's Gold Medal in 1838.

On the more promising Tigris, meanwhile, Chesney's deputy, an Irish thruster by the name of Lieutenant Henry Lynch, was steaming the length of the river in a series of bold journeys from 1837 to 1842, which led to the establishment of the famous and profitable Lynch Company with his brother Thomas, a future consul-general for Persia in London. In a remarkably prescient letter written in the aftermath of an Anglo-Persian crisis in 1839, Henry wrote from Baghdad that 'there could be no difficulty in marching armies along these rivers.'[9] In 1862 the brothers launched the Euphrates and Tigris Steam Navigation Company, which operated a service between Baghdad and Basra, with onward transport to India, until the 1930s. Fearing British dominance on Iraq's water-ways and taken aback by the angry mobs protesting against the British concession, the Turkish government moved to establish a rival company, which in 1867 became known as the Uman-Ottoman Administration. It was to little effect. Abdul Kareem al Allaf, the historian of Baghdad during the nineteenth and twentieth centuries, notes that it was out-stripped from the outset by the much more modern and efficient Lynch operation.[10]

Competition on the Tigris increased over time, hence the licence, recorded in the Ottoman archives on 20 June 1910, granted to two Baghdadi merchants, Abdul Kadir Pasha al Khudairi and Jafar Chalabi, for the operation of two ships and six ferries on the Tigris between Baghdad and Basra. Ottoman sensitivities lingered. Under the terms of the licence, 'Ottoman flag to be hoisted on both ships and ferries' and 'Licence cannot be surrendered to foreigners'.[11] Transport commanders, officers and army personnel were to be carried at half-fare and state bags and mail for free. Net profits were taxed at 10 per cent. Khudairi was a wealthy man from a renowned family. His palace, which still stands at the end of Rashid Street, overlooking the river, was given to the soldier-scholar Field Marshal Colmar Freiherr von der Goltz in 1915. The Chalabi family is similarly well known today.

A charming 1912 photograph by the Armenian photographer Z. G. Donatossian, who ran a famous studio in Baghdad, shows the Turkish governor of Baghdad and a group of his officials, immaculately dressed in dark cloaks and fezes, embarking on a small Turkish steamer to attend the inauguration of the Hindiya Barrage, a flood defence on the Euphra-tes built by Sir William Wilcox, the great expert on irrigation who was advising the government in Baghdad at the dawn of the twentieth cen-tury. There were hopes – often romantically unrealistic – that modern techniques would restore a measure of glory to the regional breadbasket of old. As the Englishwoman M. E. Hume-Griffith grandly declared after eight years living in the Middle East, 'Irrigation in Mesopotamia will change the whole face of the country; vast stretches of desert will be transformed into a garden, ruined villages will be restored, a new kingdom may be born, and Babylon possibly rebuilt.'[12]

The arrival of the British in 1917 spelt other, more aesthetic changes for the Tigris. To the ancient flotilla of *guffas*, *kalaks*, *bellum* punts, raked-mast *mahayla* cargo-boats, *shahtur* barges, barques, scruffy skiffs and wherries was added a dramatic new river craft. Specially provided for General Maude, commander of the Mesopotamian Expeditionary Force, the *glisseur* was the fastest boat in town, a surface-skimming, racket-making, motor-powered contraption capable of a crowd-shocking 35 knots. Staring into the slick surface of the river, Baghdadis and visitors alike must have contrasted the tranquil and timeless boats of the East with the noisy and powerful vessels of the West. For the Tigris, the arrival of steam and motors was nothing less than a riverine revolution. Apart from the dramatic reduction in journey times, the sight and sound of the river changed for ever.

*

While his colleagues were exploring the rivers of Iraq, Commander James Felix Jones of the Indian Navy was compiling an extraordinarily detailed secret map of Baghdad. With British influence in Iraq on the ascendant, the Ottoman authorities were completely hostile to any foreign mapping project, which was understandably viewed as a precursor to further expansion at a time when Britain and Russia were competing energetically over India. Undeterred, Jones discreetly dispatched Midshipman William Collingwood to record his clandestine measurements in the labyrinthine streets of Baghdad from 1853 to 1854. Faced with 'very unpleasant restrictions', the enterprising youth resorted to 'all kinds of subterfuges to lull suspicion' and had 'many narrow escapes' as he sweatily scribbled down his bearings, measurements and paces on his shirt cuffs and tails.[13] The result, first published in Bombay in 1857 and kept hidden from the Ottoman authorities until they requested a copy to assist with municipal reforms in 1912, was the *Ground Plan of the Enceinte of Baghdad the Capital of Irak-Mesopotamia, called also Dar es Selam and Medinet al Kholafa*, the most comprehensive map of the city yet.

It is a beautiful illustration, surmounted by an evocative river-level view of the city from opposite the British Residency, whose flag is flying at a height almost deliberately calculated to annoy the Ottomans. The Residence sits at the northern end of acres of date-palm groves that tuft up into the skyline above the buildings, together with the slender minarets of Molah Khaneh, Al Siagh, Merjaniyeh, Khaseki and Souk al Ghazil mosques, travelling from north to south.

In Jones and Collingwood's Baghdad, Rusafa is like the greater half of a piece of toast sliced vertically, crust on top, sprawling across 591 acres. The broad blue band of the Tigris cuts the slice in two, replete with tiny numerals that are the soundings of the river measured in feet at the lowest season (ranging from 2 feet south of the city walls to 36 feet north of the city). The once mighty citadel is the first monument of note on the north-westernmost corner of Rusafa, its prison, stables, gun sheds, magazine, artillery equipage stores, barracks and tombs fastidiously noted. Immediately south is the Ali Pasha Madrassa, then the harem belonging to the pasha's Saray Palace, together with the Kushla barracks, a swathe of grand riverfront property extending to the hospital and Wazir Mosque just north of the sole pontoon bridge.

South of the British Residency lie the steamers' depot and anchorage point. To its north-east, in the heart of Rusafa, is the holy cluster of the Latin church, two Armenian churches and the Chaldean and Syrian church. The large Jewish quarter begins just west of the ruins that lie within the old city walls, white islands of desolation amidst tracts of brown desert. North and south of Rusafa, nature takes over with large patches of irrigated green fields and, on the river bank itself, acres of date-palm groves and orchards. A series of tiny roads fans into Bab al Wastani, the easternmost gate in the Abbasid city walls. None lead to Bab al Talism further south along the same stretch of wall, bricked up since Sultan Murad IV's victorious exit in 1639. Karkh, or western Baghdad, is a shrunken morsel of 146 acres sandwiched between the Tigris to the east, palms to the south, the crumbling tombs of Zumurrud Khatun,* wife of the caliph Mustadi, sheikhs Maruf, Daud and Mansur al Halaj, and brick kilns to the north, with lush green fields and the Masudi Canal to the west.

Jones's 'Memoir on the Province of Baghdad' gives the reader a wonderful flavour of the workaholic zeal exhibited by one of the British Empire's most conscientious servants. He measured the circuit of eastern Baghdad, including the riverfront, at 10,600 yards, that of the western section 5,800 yards. Painstakingly he listed by name the 91 coffee-houses, 46 bazaars and 39 mosques of Rusafa and the 7 main mosques of Karkh, together with each and every *mahalla*, or quarter, and its

---

* Collingwood and Jones mistakenly mark the tomb of Zumurrud Khatun as that of the more famous Zubayda, wife of Harun al Rashid, a common error. Zubayda was buried at the Kuraish graveyard in what is now the Kadhimiya shrine, next to her son Amin. Both graves have long since disappeared.

caravanserais and baths. An enthusiast to the core, he admired the Talisman Gate 'as fresh as if it were but a recent work'. On the ten round towers of the city walls he recorded a number of handsome, large-calibre cannon. 'Most of them were cast in Baghdad, which cannot now boast of a foundry capable of making a small ordinary cannon,' he wrote. Occasionally there is the confident swipe of a man who did not lack self-confidence. The vernacular tongue, for instance, is 'an impure Arabic, extremely corrupted amongst the Christian population, perhaps the most ignorant of a singularly ignorant community of men, such as is found within the walls of Baghdad.'[14] Merchants tended to speak Turkish and Persian, workers and porters Kurdish, Luri and Chaldean. Hebrew and Armenian were known only to a few. And thirteen languages could be heard over dinner at the British Residency.

There is something about Jones and Collingwood's sheer, relentless thoroughness that makes the modern reader smile. In a survey of the trades and their respective daily wages, Jones recorded the master goldsmith at the top of the pile, with 50 piastres a day, closely followed by the gem-polisher, master sword-maker, silver designer and master tailor, all on 40. A master tentmaker received 30 to 35, his counterparts in shoemaking and tanning 30 and 25 respectively. A silk-cord-maker could count on 20, a mounted musketeer 15, a coffee-house boy 10 and the bazaar watchman a measly 5 a night. He listed the 19 Turkish gold coins in circulation, with their weight and exchange rates, from the lirah or majeedi worth 430 piastres to the ghazi khairi worth 84.

Then there are the medicines and drugs available in Baghdad's bazaars, an exotic list taking in absinthe, nitric acid, asafoetida, bastard saffron, black betelnut, black naphtha, arsenic, camomile flowers and camphor, dill seed and dragon's blood, euphorbium, olibanum and opium, fenugreek, fennel, flea-wort, Arabic gum, hemlock, manna, mercury and myrrh.*

---

* Jones's prodigious report also lists the produce available in the city's markets: mulberries, mutton, mustard, milk, biscuits, butter, beef and bullocks, broccoli, beans, candles, camels, coffee, cream, cheese, fish, flour, fowl, sheep, salt, sugar, suet, pigeons and partridges, peaches, pomegranates, pears and plums, melons, nectarines, apples, apricots, figs, dates, grapes, limes, lemons, quinces, oranges, artichokes, almonds, hazelnuts, pistachios, walnuts, raisins, turnips, tomatoes and truffles, chillies, cucumbers, cabbages, carrots, pumpkins, potatoes, mushrooms, onions, barley, wheat, Indian corn and millet, tobacco, oil, soap, charcoal and firewood. For those of his readers who may have fancied a drink, he helpfully listed brandy, champagne, sherry, beer, country *arrack* and Persian wines, 'only procurable occasionally and the supply always limited'.

There are even some lovingly sketched portraits – based on the earliest known photographs taken in the Middle East – of Sheikh Maruf's domed tomb among a knot of palm trees, the upended tack that is Zumurrud Khatun's (and not Zubayda's) tomb, massive-walled Baghdadi houses with windows projecting on to the river, the shaded courtyard of the British Residency and a twin-masted steamer at rest in its Tigris depot.

*

While smears of white steam from these new machines became a common sight on the river in the second half of the century, innovations by road proved far less compelling. The reason for this lack of progress was straightforward. There was only one street in the whole of Baghdad through which a wheeled vehicle could pass. A proper city road had to wait until the Great War reached the city. Until then, crooked, labyrinthine alleys were the main thoroughfares. As a result, Baghdad's merchants continued to use those age-old beasts of burden: the long-suffering camel, horse and donkey, and their human counterpart, the Kurdish porter. For other travellers, the most popular option was to journey by caravan – mule, donkey, horse or camel. The well bred and well heeled, together with women and elderly men, could recline out of the sun and rain in the questionable comfort of a mule-drawn carriage or camel-drawn *takht-revan* cabin. A teeth-rattling journey from Baghdad to Bakuba, Hilla and Kerbala would take around twelve hours. Horses were the sports cars of their day, conferring considerable prestige on their owners. The same, sadly, could never be said for the unfortunate donkey, forever maligned in the Arab world. The Hasawi donkeys that traced their pedigree to the town of Al Hasa in Saudi Arabia were popular choices, and to this day Baghdadis use the word *hasawi* to describe a perfect idiot.

In 1865 the enterprising Frenchman the Comte Edmond de Perthuis travelled from Damascus to Baghdad, an unnecessarily difficult journey that he thought would be vastly improved if opened up to carriages. The marauding desert tribes en route, he reckoned, could easily be bought off. A number of Baghdad's merchant families agreed and were willing to float his company, but the Turkish governor, Namik Pasha, his nose already out of joint from the success of the Lynch steam operation and the failure of its Turkish counterpart, was quick to shut down the scheme. The aristocratic Frenchman was warned not to get involved with the desert tribes and sent packing. Comfortable, air-conditioned transport between Beirut, Damascus and Baghdad had to wait until 1923, when Norman and Gerald Nairn, two brothers from New Zealand recently demobilized from the British Army, established the Nairn Transport Company and 'The Overland Desert Mail Service' operated by a fleet of sky-blue coaches.[15]

To rivers and roads must be added railways, or at least multiple efforts to establish them. In 1857, the year of the Indian Mutiny, the Euphrates Valley Railway Company was established in London with a view to slashing travelling times to the East – for mail, military and mercantile interests. The company forged an alliance with the European and Indian Junction Telegraph, with which it shared a number of directors. Chesney, by now a general, was appointed consulting engineer and joined on the board by Henry Lynch. Its champions touted Baghdad as a business centre in its own right, pointing out that in recent times it had exported annually 2,000 mule-loads of pearls, silk, cotton, stuffs, shawls, coffee, gall-nuts and indigo to Erzurum in north-eastern Turkey, with more sent to Mosul, Diyarbakir and Urfa. 'Baghdad, from its matchless situation, would, with the slightest fostering care, become a grand centre of English, Arab, Persian and Eastern commerce, and nothing is wanting to distribute it widely and increase it greatly but the advent of steam.'[16] Nothing, that is, apart from the support of investors and the British government. As late as 23 June 1871, Sir George Jenkinson, MP, was calling for a Select Committee to examine the project's merits. By that time, the Suez Canal – 'the highway to India' – had been open almost two years, and interest had declined.

As London, Berlin and Paris looked east and west, they saw Asia and the Americas connected by steam-powered shipping to the great centres of world trade. Yet, there on the periphery of Europe sprawled the vast mass of Asiatic Turkey, virtually removed from these new globalizing connections. The days when Baghdad could be considered a magnificent prize were long gone, but 500 miles to the south-east lay the port of Basra. Link Europe to the Persian Gulf with a steel road and, theoretically at least, you had a faster route to the East than either the long-winded Cape of Good Hope or even – the most ardent railway promoters insisted, with figures to prove it – the Suez Canal.

Thus the genesis of the Baghdad Railway Company, 'the kind of half-mad imperial enterprise *fin de siècle* Europeans excelled in'.[17] The line was to begin at Konia in Turkey, travel south-east to Aleppo and onwards to Mosul, Baghdad and finally Basra. Construction began in 1903, and by 1912 the Baghdad Railway Company employed 16,000 people, from German engineers, Italian carpenters and Greek explosives experts to unskilled Turkish, Kurdish and Arab manual labour.[18] With the sultan's support, Kaiser Wilhelm had tweaked British noses, embarking on a project that threatened London's supremacy in the Persian Gulf, a bulwark for India. By so doing, he also introduced a new German flavour to Baghdad. The British government had only itself to blame. Despite various efforts to resuscitate it, the Euphrates Valley scheme had died an unremarkable death. Its later Tigris equivalent, supported by British business interests, proved no more successful at securing British government backing.

Ultimately it was the German-led company that was to bring the railway to Baghdad from Berlin, though not without huge gaps in the line, endless squabbling between Germany, France, Britain and Turkey, and the fatal interruption of the First World War. For Germany, the line offered a connection to its eastern colonies and the prospect of a foothold in the Persian Gulf. Britain, whose dominance in colonial trade was directly threatened, was determined that the Baghdad Railway should not become an exclusively German enterprise that would, fretted Sir George Clarke, secretary of the Committee of Imperial Defence in 1905, 'undoubtedly inflict grave injury upon our commerce, and must ultimately destroy our political influence in Southern Persia and in the deltas of the Tigris and Euphrates'.[19] Writing in 1918, Morris Jastrow, a former president of the American Oriental Society, summed up the British perspective on the pre-war railroad rivalry: 'It was felt in England that if, as Napoleon is said to have remarked, Antwerp in the hands of a great continental power was a pistol levelled at the English coast, Bagdad and the Persian Gulf in the hands of Germany (or any other strong power) would be a 42-centimetre gun pointed at India.'[20] As war approached, such fears heightened, and the Baghdad Railway became an integral part of the German policy to ignite a *jihad* against the British Empire, to encourage Afghanistan and Persia to attack India as German allies and to seize hold of the Suez Canal.[21]*

The new technology was not confined to transport. Telegraphs and postal services also moved with the times, bringing Baghdad into more rapid communication with the outside world. In 1856 the East India Company approached the Ottoman authorities with a view to introducing a land line between Syria and the Persian Gulf. Once again, Istanbul took a dim view of the meddling British and refused to guarantee the scheme. Instead, a year later, the British and Ottoman governments agreed to erect a telegraph line financed by the Ottomans and built by British engineers. By 1861 Istanbul and Baghdad were connected, and the lines were quite literally buzzing – so much so that many tribesmen, disconcerted by this strange invention, believed they were inhabited by the devil.

Establishing these lines of communication between the hub of empire and its outlying provinces was all very well, but in a province like Baghdad, where violence was endemic, such infrastructure required protection. Thus we see a telegram of 16 April 1861 from the governor of Mosul to the telegraph directorate appointing thirty men from the Shammar tribe to 'guard the telegraph lines and protect them from the Arabs'.[22] Timely postal services took a little longer to get going. The British Residency still relied on a traditional service by camel to Damascus, a journey of eleven days. Letters and packages could take as long as forty-five days to reach London. In 1868 Taki al Din Pasha approved the establishment of British–Indian post offices in both Baghdad and Basra, a service that was superseded within a decade by an empire-wide Ottoman postal system.

Baghdad had been prised back from the upstart Mamluks with great relief by the Ottomans, but, as the nineteenth century wore on, the city steadily became less of an Ottoman possession and more of an international question, its fate to be determined by external powers. Within the city, foreign rivalries were played out on an almost daily basis.

---

* The lasting irony was that, although conceived by the Germans, the Orient Express, as the line was popularly known, came to be associated with very British derring-do. It was immortalized in *From Russia with Love*, one of the better James Bond novels, Graham Greene's *Stamboul Train* and, above all, Agatha Christie's Hercule Poirot favourite, *Murder on the Orient Express*.

During the pashalik of Mohammed Najeeb, who succeeded Ali Rida in 1842, the British and French competed vigorously in everything from trade and political power to pomp and circumstance. With his own retinue of immaculately turned-out sepoys, the grandest steamer on the Tigris and an enviable budget from which to dispense largesse amongst the tribal leaders, the British Resident was generally able to outclass his French counterpart. As a rule, the pasha awarded the British precedence during his audiences. We hear of a classic diplomatic bust-up in 1845, when yet again the British Resident preceded his French colleague in offering his congratulations for the holy festival of Eid. Affronted by what he perceived as a snub too far, the French diplomat sent a junior official in his place, a decision that infuriated the pasha. In 1846 his soldiers attacked the French Consulate and went unpunished for this outrageous breach of protocol. Istanbul weighed in to clip the pasha's wings, and a banquet was hastily arranged at which the French consul was given precedence over the British Resident.[23]

Haughtiness and self-importance were by no means exclusive to the British. We hear from the historian Abbas al Azzawi of one occasion when a Frenchman came across Namuk Pasha (who had ousted Mohammed Najeeb in 1851) and his retinue making their way through the city. Unwisely the Frenchman refused to dismount from his horse to demonstrate suitable respect, as protocol demanded. For this lack of etiquette he was hauled down from his stallion and given a sound beating by the pasha's guards. France was quick to demand compensation for the affront, and Istanbul duly removed Namuk Pasha from his position.[24]

The French were in trouble again in 1868, when the French consul paid a visit to Taki al Deen, one of the many short-lived pashas of this time, to present his compliments on the sultan's birthday. Acutely aware of his own importance, the consul noticed that the *kadi* did not stand up to salute him. He promptly grabbed his beard – a heinous insult in a culture wherein the beard is a mark of honour – and told the judge he was duty bound to stand up. The *kadi* refused and the Frenchman swept out, blaming the behaviour on religious bigotry. The incident almost led to riots, with Baghdadis quick to see it as an insult to the Islamic religion. They called for an attack on the French Consulate and the execution of the consul, but the army prevented bloodshed by encircling the consulate. The pasha summoned Baghdad's grandees, severed all relations with the consul and demanded his withdrawal. Istanbul had him removed and, to soothe French feelings, expelled the *kadi*.[25]

To European rivalries in trade and diplomacy must be added behind-the-scenes scuffles over religion. The scramble for influence within the city could be witnessed in the various efforts to establish new churches. On 24 February 1869 Taki al Deen wrote to the prime minister's office in the Porte, petitioning the authorities to prohibit the establishment of a Protestant school in Baghdad. As there were only thirteen Protestant houses with a combined population of thirty-five, he wrote, a separate school for them was not justified. Besides, the pasha feared, there were hidden motives behind the move to open a new school: 'the State of England shall seize upon such an opportunity to expand its influence in this province . . . and it will open the way for the missionaries to foment sedition. Hence, such establishment does not harmonize with wisdom and politics.'[26] London believed the message bore the imprint of French pressure: France had a strong presence in the Catholic schools that dated back to the eighteenth century and saw itself as their foremost supporter. For Paris, Protestant interfering was unwelcome. Many Baghdadis considered the constant interference by external powers equally unwelcome; yet, as the century wore on, Great Power rivalry within Baghdad, above all that between Britain and Germany, only intensified.

*

One of the few pashas of Baghdad to earn lasting respect took office in 1852. Mohammed Rashid Guzligli the Bespectacled, the first governor in the Ottoman Empire to wear glasses, managed to resuscitate the ailing silk industry, double the city's revenues, combat corruption amongst the tax-collectors, pay long-overdue military salaries, export grain to the Hijaz and keep the warring tribes at bay.[27] Born a Georgian Christian, he had been forced to convert after his abduction by the Turks as a child. There were rumours about his religious convictions and stories of secret Bible readings, sensitive issues in a city in which holiness and fanaticism were never too far apart. Tackling the rumours head on, according to the historian Suaad Hadi al Omari, he built a small mosque at his own expense.[28] He was hard pressed, however, to accommodate Istanbul's constant demand for money to fund its Crimean War commitments. With rumours rife of an Iranian invasion of Iraq during this conflict, London sent two battleships to the Shatt al Arab waterway, which separates the two countries. The invasion never materialized.

There was always a fine line between maintaining order and self-defeating severity when governing Baghdad, as the short-lived Omar Pasha, a Hungarian Muslim convert who had had a good Crimean War, quickly discovered. Appointed in 1858, he was ousted in 1859, having imposed mandatory military service in Baghdad, a policy that succeeded only in uniting the tribes against him. Once the tribesmen had inflicted an ignominious defeat on his army, Istanbul lost little time in removing him.[29]

While some of Baghdad's rulers left barely a mark on the city, others passed into folklore for their deeds, both real and imagined. Haj Ahmed Agha, a powerful henchman in the pasha's circle, was known as a nasty but also whimsical figure. There is a story dating back to the early 1860s in which an old woman whose son was mistreating her went to see him in his office to file a complaint. Moved by her tale, Agha ordered his officials to find her son and make him carry his mother on his back through the streets of Baghdad. Off she went, accompanied by a bailiff, to look for her son. A sudden feeling of remorse and guilt then over-came her, at which point she decided to spare her son the public humiliation and pointed instead to an unknown passer-by. The bailiff read the astonished man Agha's order and told him to carry his mother on his back, encouraging him with some lusty blows from his trun-cheon. Staggering under the weight of the strange old woman, he passed his brother's shop in the market.

'Who is this woman you are carrying, brother?' he asked.

'Why, that's our mother, don't you know?' the poor man replied sarcastically.

'Our mother? She's been dead for the past twenty years!'

'Yes, I know, but go explain it to Haj Ahmed Agha!'

To this day, Baghdadis of a certain age still use the expression 'Go explain it to Haj Ahmed Agha!' when trying to make logical things clear to illogical people.[30]

Of Baghdad's many nineteenth-century pashas, one man stands out above all others. His portrait occupies pride of place in Longrigg's study of Ottoman Iraq and shows an earnest man in spectacles and fez, half his face hidden beneath a full beard and vast moustache, smartly turned out in black coat and white shirt. That he governed for only three years but is still considered a towering figure to this day is testament to the profound changes he brought to a city that in many respects had remained a medieval enclave.

Midhat Pasha was, above all else, a modernizer. He entered Baghdad on 30 April 1869 at the age of forty-six, his credentials as a reformer firmly established during a decade in the Balkans, where the Danubian *vilayet* he governed was considered a model province of the empire.* A man of unquestioned integrity, unusual in a governor to say the least, he quickly introduced severe punishments for officials caught taking bribes, the first pasha of Baghdad to do so.[31]

His short-lived tenure as governor of Baghdad, during a glittering career that subsequently saw him appointed grand vizier, the highest office in the empire, proved a whirlwind of innovation. A printing press and newspaper (*Al Zawra*) appeared for the first time. Military factories provided an economic fillip; before Midhat Pasha, the uniforms of soldiers in Iraq could best be described as shambolic; a modern cloth-weaving factory, the Abbakhana, brought some uniformity to the chaos, while a new almshouse, orphanage and hospital, together with numerous schools, testified to the humanity of his vision.[32]

It was in the neglected field of education that Baghdadis noticed the greatest changes during Midhat Pasha's administration. Thanks in no small part to his civilizing reforms, it has been estimated that literacy in Baghdad rose from around half a per cent in 1850 to 5–10 per cent in 1900.[33] The Madrassat al Sanayi, a vocational training school, was established to teach orphans useful trades such as carpentry, black-smithing, weaving and other handicrafts. Midhat Pasha also set the tone for later nineteenth-century improvements, such as the *idadi*, or second-ary, military schools, including the Idadi Rashdi Military School, from which the most promising students would be earmarked for further education at the Mektebi Harbiya Military Academy in Istanbul. The first batch of Iraqi recruits to pass the course graduated in 1881. In 1917 the Idadi Rashdi was replaced by Al Markaziya Secondary School, an increasingly prestigious institution that continues to educate the best and the brightest Baghdadis today. The school hall still bears the name

---

* Introduced in 1867 as part of the ongoing Tanzimat reforms, the vilayet was the new term for a province of the Ottoman Empire, replacing the previous ayalet over the next two decades. Present-day Iraq consists of – but is smaller than – the three Ottoman vilayets of Baghdad, Mosul and Basra.

of one of its most famous occupants, Miss Gertrude Bell, who worked there when the British Army used the building as its headquarters.

Midhat Pasha's ambitious reforms revolutionized educational opportunities in a city that had once been the centre of world scholarship. A summary by the historian Mohammed Rauf Taha al Shaikhli gives a sense of how far the city had slipped from its more glorious days. By 1890, a census year, Baghdad had a total of 11 state schools educating 1,351 children. These were in addition to the 8 Christian schools (1,440), 21 Jewish schools (550) and 27 Islamic schools preparing their students for positions as imams and preachers. Finally, for the most basic primary education of reading, writing and simple arithmetic, there were around 34 local mullahs who ran classes at their homes or at mosques.[34]

Midhat Pasha's Baghdad could even boast a tramway, albeit a curious, two-tier, horse-drawn contraption, to ease the mass transport of pilgrims to and from the suburb of Kadhimiya. In its time, it was considered state of the art for the Middle East. As the 1920s wore on, however, and rumours of long-mooted electrification failed to materialize, Baghdadis had to make do with the occasional substitution of Fordson tractors for horses.[35]

Midhat Pasha's energy was prodigious. His biographer Sadik Damluji records how, as part of his far-reaching reforms, he successfully imposed mandatory military service in Baghdad, despite the predictable and vigorous opposition.[36] Less successfully, he founded the Tapu Land Registry in a well-intentioned but poorly executed attempt to calm perennial tribal tensions by settling land ownership; the ambitious scheme dissolved into official corruption, tribal apathy and popular distrust.[37]

Architecturally, Midhat Pasha's legacy was mixed. On the one hand, public buildings thrust up into the skyline, older monuments such as the Saray al Kushla were restored, and the silted-up Saklawiya Canal (the renamed Isa Canal of Abbasid days) linking the Tigris to the Euphrates was dredged and reopened. Baghdadis could also thank Midhat Pasha for the city's first public park, the Baladiya (municipal) Park, on the grounds of what is today the Medical City complex overlooking the Tigris in the Bab al Muadham neighbourhood of eastern Baghdad. Before this was opened, families who wanted fresh air, green spaces, flowers and running water had to make the long trek over to the orchards and groves beyond the eastern gate of Bab al Sharki or north of Adhamiya.

And Midhat Pasha had even grander plans, ones that went beyond the City of Peace: the new towns of Nasiriya, to the south-east of Baghdad, and Ramadi, to the west, were born on his watch.

Yet disasters also resulted from Midhat Pasha's modernizing zeal. By far the most tragic was his demolition of Baghdad's venerable city walls, the massive Abbasid defences that had withstood – and succumbed to – so many foreign invasions and attacks over the centuries. The intention had been to replace them with grand, tree-lined boulevards in the European tradition. In the end, the walls were destroyed, but the boulevards never built and the debris remained. Six decades later, Baghdadis were still grumbling at the ruins of these once famous and formidable defences that lay all around them.

Had the pasha's ambitious plans been realized and the city's filthy, overcrowded little streets been replaced, perhaps in the opening years of the twentieth century Baghdad would not have been rife with disease: malaria, sandfly fever, bilharzia, hookworm, dysentery, typhoid, smallpox and cholera foremost amongst them. One of Baghdad's most disfiguring ailments of the nineteenth century was particularly linked to Adhamiya, home to an infamous tannery, which attracted swarms of sandflies. Their bite transmitted the parasites that caused cutaneous leishmaniasis, creating the terrible facial scars popularly known as the 'Baghdad mole', 'Baghdad boil' or the 'Adhamiya Stamp'. Until the 1950s, when the disease was finally eradicated, unfortunate Baghdadis who bore the tell-tale marks were known as 'true Adhamiyis'. That basic public services such as water, sewerage, electricity and street-cleaning were rudimentary at best, non-existent at worst, merely compounded the problem. Little wonder that Baghdad came to be known, in a pointed adaptation of its celebrated Abbasid moniker, as 'the city of 1,001 smells'.[38]

To be fair to Midhat Pasha, unlike so many of his predecessors, he did his best to prevent contagious diseases – in particular the plague – arriving with the corpses of Persians whose families were burying them alongside the holy shrines in Iraq, especially in Kerbala and Najaf. To prevent further outbreaks of disease a decree was issued stating that burials could take place only one year after death.[39] As ever, some enthusiasts took to bending the rules and smuggled in the remains of their loved ones earlier than allowed, having first treated the body with lime and then arsenic to separate the flesh from the bones. After being left in the sun to dry, the skeleton was put into a coffin and the flesh into a separate bag for the journey to Najaf. Ali al Wardi tells the ghastly story – faint-hearted readers look away – of one famished Iranian in a funeral caravan chancing upon a bag of meat. He promptly took it, cooked it and ravenously devoured it, scarcely believing his good luck. The owner of the remains discovered his loss, saw what had happened and flew into a rage. 'You've eaten my father!' he screamed. 'You've eaten my father!'[40]

As far as Istanbul was concerned, the Midhat Pasha reformist experiment was an unqualified success, not least because during his brief rule tax revenues from Iraq reached the unprecedented heights of 1.1 million Ottoman lira. Impressed by this figure, the Porte wanted more, but Midhat had had enough and tendered his resignation in 1872, after governing Baghdad for three memorable years.[41]

*

For one ancient community in Baghdad in particular, the nineteenth century was a time of great change and growing prosperity. Yusef Rizk-Allah Ghanimah, the historian of the Jews of Iraq, tells the extraordinary story of how in 1845 the twenty-seven-year-old Romanian Jewish timber merchant Joseph Israel suddenly quit his business, said goodbye to his doubtless bewildered wife and child and embarked on the fabulously improbable task of finding the ten lost tribes of Israel. Israel, who styled himself 'Benjamin II', in honour of Benjamin of Tudela, who had travelled to Baghdad almost 700 years earlier, arrived in 1847 and discovered a thriving Jewish population. 'In Baghdad there are 3,000 Jewish homes and their knowledge and professions helped them to compete in commerce and the general professions and they flourished in these areas,' he wrote. 'The Jews seized commercial opportunities and among them were great merchants and businessmen who did business with distant countries and uncomfortable nationals and foreigners.'[42]

Baghdad's Jews lived voluntarily in their own quarter on the east bank. Travellers over the centuries were invariably impressed by the profusion of synagogues in the City of Peace. Israel counted eight. By 1949, there were twenty-six.[43]

The British cartographer James Felix Jones thought the city was ahead of its time in its relations between the faiths. 'Nor, perhaps, can

of 1890, the population of Baghdad was 149,941, of which Muslims numbered 134,459 (almost 90 per cent), Jews 13,182 (9 per cent) and Christians a modest 2,300.[49] By 1904, according to an estimate by the French vice-consul in Baghdad, the Jewish population had virtually trebled to 40,000, meaning that Jews represented around a third of the total. In 1910 H. D. Shohet, author of a British consular report, put the number of Jews in Baghdad at 45,000–50,000.[50] Making use of the most recent Turkish figures available, the *Arab Bulletin* of October 1917, intended by the British Army intelligence officer T. E. Lawrence, the future Lawrence of Arabia, to be a 'secret magazine of Middle East politics', reported that Baghdad contained 101,400 Arabs and Turks, 80,000 Jews (or almost 40 per cent of the city's population), 12,000 Christians, 8,000 Kurds and 800 Persians.[51] While one has to be fairly cautious with these figures, based on censuses where officials had to take the male householder's word for granted, the upward trend is still striking. By 1936 the Iraq Directory numbered the 'Israelite community' at around 120,000 nationwide.[52]

Shohet put his finger on the Jewish success in Baghdad: '[Jews] have literally monopolized the local trade and neither Mohammedans nor Christians can compete with them. Even the few leading Mohammedan merchants owe their prosperity to the capable and industrious Jews whom they have for years employed as clerks. The Jewish clerks are practically the managers of their firms.'[53]

The most popular products for Jewish merchants were Manchester piece goods, imported from Britain and exported on to Iran via local offices in Manchester, London, Kermanshah and Hamadan. Since the eighteenth century, and more especially during the second half of the nineteenth, Baghdadi Jews had scattered to the four winds, setting up trading posts across the length and breadth of Asia, maintaining business connections with Baghdad from Bombay and Calcutta, Rangoon, Hong Kong, Shanghai and Japan.

It hardly needs saying that frictions and disputes with the majority Muslim community were common in Baghdad, a city in which lasting harmony between its inhabitants was invariably elusive. According to Muslim law, the Jews were *dhimmi*, a protected minority, exempt from military service and free to practise their faith in return for a poll tax and land tax. As second-class citizens they were also obliged to dress differently from Muslims, distinguishing themselves by their headgear.

Trouble broke out in 1889, after the death of the revered Rabbi Hakham Abdullah Somech. The Muslim guard outside the tomb of the high priest Joshua, on the right bank of the Tigris outside Baghdad, where the burial was to take place, refused the Jewish gravediggers entrance unless he was given a large *bakshish* tip of £50. The gravediggers refused. After an altercation, around 2,000 Jewish mourners forced their way in, and the burial got under way, only for a group of Muslims armed with clubs to wade in and start attacking the Jews. In a memorandum of 29 October 1889, Morris Cohen wrote how they 'began to lay about them furiously on all sides. A scene of wild confusion ensued. The suddenness of the attack so far from town and at night too, induced many of those who were able to leave the courtyard to take flight towards the town in fear of a general massacre. Many persons received severe blows on the head, face and arms, others having fallen down, were trodden on in the general confusion.'[54] The chief rabbi was arrested the next day and sent to prison.

Telegrams of protest buzzed down the line to the sultan and grand vizier in Istanbul, to the Board of Deputies, to the Anglo-Jewish Association and the Sassoon family in London, and to the Alliance Israélite in Paris, signed by seventy distinguished Jews of Baghdad. The governor immediately ordered the arrest of all those who had signed the telegrams. In London, British Jews protested to the British prime minister, Lord Salisbury. Writing on 30 October, Surgeon-Major R. Bowman of the British Residency reported that a total of ten rabbis and sixty other Jews had been arrested during the disturbance. Some had been taken to prison in 'a barbarous manner', tied to the tail of the mule ridden by the arresting police officer.

Cohen's report provides a depressing picture of the difficulties faced by Baghdad's Jews at this time. The Muslim attitude to Jews, he wrote, had become 'decidedly unfriendly', to some extent a Middle Eastern reflection of rising anti-Semitism in Europe, particularly in Germany and France, and Russia, where pogroms were already underway. Petty humiliations were common. 'A respectable merchant whom I know intimately was violently insulted by a Mussulman in a coffee-house full of people, for having removed his fez on a warm afternoon and put it on his knee for a moment.' Worse, during a recent outbreak of cholera, Cohen had observed how at the Bab al Muadham the quarantine was enforced on Jews only by order of the governor, while Muslims and

Christians were allowed to pass freely in and out of the city. Yet nothing was heard of these incidents: 'the Jews are afraid to complain to the authorities; hardly expecting any justice where so much injustice has already been experienced. Counter-accusations are so common here and so easily maintained by the aid of false witnesses that the Jews are ordinarily inclined to suffer their grievances in silence rather than raise still greater ones by complaining.' In his report to Lord Salisbury, Colonel Tweedie, the British consul-general, echoes this view of the mal-treatment of Jews: 'The prescriptive right of doing as he pleases with a Jew is here held to belong, in virtue of his natural and religious super-iority, to every Moslem.'

Commercially and financially strong by the close of the nineteenth century, the Jewish community in Baghdad had long been accustomed to second-class social and political status. On the one hand, Baghdad's Jews enjoyed unrivalled control of the city's domestic and international trade, yet they were also forced to endure all shades of persecution, from petty harassment to outright violence. Then, in 1908, came the bombshell of the Young Turks Revolution, when discontent within the army, piled on to political dissent led by a combustible mix of secular-ists, nationalists and liberals, ignited into military rebellion. Sultan Abdul Hamid II was forced to restore parliament and the short-lived inaugural constitution of 1876 (brainchild of Midhat Pasha, by then the grand vizier of the Ottoman Empire) that he had suspended thirty years ear-lier. The orthodoxies of the Ottoman Empire were turned on their head. Power had leached away from the sultan and now flowed towards the new nexus of authority, the Young Turks' Committee of Union and Pro-gress. The talk in Istanbul was of liberty and reform.

Overnight, Jews became full citizens, as the official *dhimmi* status was abolished. In one of the most extraordinary moments in their long history, Baghdad's Jews – together with their co-religionists across the empire – stood for the very first time on an equal footing with Muslims. In 1909 the Baghdadi Jew Sassoon Eskell was one of six parliamentar-ians representing the city in the new elective assembly in Istanbul, a position that would have been unthinkable at any other point in Bagh-dad's history.[55]

For the Jews of Baghdad these were halcyon days. The promise of greater glory in the twentieth century seemed to unfurl before this uniquely talented community – but it was not to be. Their very visible success in a hot-headed Muslim city bore inherent dangers. As the British ambassador noted in his annual report for 1909, 'The growing wealth and influence of the Jews in Mesopotamia has contributed also to the discontent; they have got all the trade in their hands, and by invading the better quarters of the town and forcing up all the prices they have succeeded in bringing on themselves the hatred of the Moslem population – a sentiment which they heartily reciprocate.'[56]

Yet only thirty-two years after Sassoon Eskell's inspiring political triumph, catastrophe struck, as we shall see in Chapter 10.

*

Spurred on by Jewish energy, Baghdad revelled in business great and small. Apart from high finance, the city bustled with the din of everyday commerce. Although the main industries were not yet industrialized – textile workshops, shoemaking, silver-working, copper-smithing, brick-making and boat-building – a new breed of export-processing factories had started to rise into the Baghdad skyline. By 1889 the entrepreneurial Lynch brothers had two steam presses, which together could pack 30,000 bales of wool a year. Another group, Darby Andrews, operated similar facilities. At the turn of the century the American firm MacAndrews & Forbes & Company built a plant with hydraulic presses where thousands of tons of licorice root were dried, baled and exported – a godsend for lovers of chewing gum, sweets, tobacco and beer the world over.

Pacing the streets from one of the city's 118 warehouses to another, flitting from souk to souk, walking along the banks of the river, Baghdadis breathed in the assorted smells of a re-emerging metropolis, from the exotic perfumes of the spice markets and the sickly stench of the tanneries to the fresh – and putrefying – fish of the Tigris. From houses preparing for wedding-day celebrations issued the enticingly sweet aromas of home-cooked specialities: *shakkar borek*, baked sheets of pastry interlaced with almonds; *mihalabi* rice pudding flavoured with essence of orange blossom; the delightfully chewy *man al simma* (manna from heaven) flavoured with pistachios and cardamom; the classic, sugar-drenched *halawa* with shaved carrots, cardamom and saffron; dainty round *claytcha* cakes stuffed with dates; burma, glazed pistachio nuts wrapped in vermicelli.

Baghdad entered the twentieth century if not in the rudest health, then at least at three times the size it had been ignominiously reduced to by the 1830s. And, although little more than a sleepy corner of the Ottoman Empire, itself the Sick Man of Europe, as Tsar Nicholas I is traditionally said to have called it in 1853, it found itself the object of increasing international attention – and competition. Once again it was at the heart of world affairs, albeit no longer master of its own destiny, as it was in Abbasid times past.

As the century entered its second decade, there was a notable hardening of Turkish attitudes to British interests in Baghdad. For the brave new world of the Young Turks, bristling with secularism, nationalism and reform, such ostentatious British privileges as the Indian sepoy guard and the *Comet*, the British Residency's extravagant military launch bristling with guns, were pure anathema – and anachronism. In 1910 the offices of the Lynch Company, an irritatingly successful reminder of the inefficiency of its Ottoman rival in the steam-transport business on the Tigris, were destroyed. This was a prelude to the subsequent demolition later that autumn of other British properties in Kadhimiya. In the same year, in a highly symbolic indication of the direction in which power was shifting in Baghdad, Germany's first wireless station was established at the Bab al Wastani, a massive thirteenth-century monument on the east bank, sole survivor today of the medieval walls that were demolished by Midhat Pasha.

Great Power rivalry was intensifying by the year in Baghdad. In the aftermath of its defeat in the Russo-Turkish War of 1877–8, Istanbul had given Germany the precious role of reorganizing the Ottoman military. From 1885 to 1895 this mission was led by the German baron Colonel Colmar Freiherr von der Goltz, a name that would become ominously familiar to British soldiers in Mesopotamia during the Great War.[57]

*

Politics was all very well for the political class, but ordinary Baghdadis were much more transfixed by a very different rivalry that unfolded in 1910 and was the talk of the town. Sarah Khatun was a very young, extremely rich and extraordinarily beautiful Armenian-Iraqi woman who had inherited a great fortune and vast estates, including rambling fruit groves, in and around Baghdad. The large family house was on Rashid Street and looked directly on to the Tigris. Rumour – and much of the story has the ring of bazaar gossip about it – had it that her properties were so extensive that it took a train half an hour to pass through them. Since the death of her father, a philanthropist who founded the first girls' school in Baghdad in 1901, she had been under the guardianship of her uncle, who had control of her fortune. On a fateful August evening in 1910, Nazim Pasha, the massively moustachi-oed Ottoman ruler of Baghdad, held a charity ball on a river ship ablaze with lights and coloured with flags. Here, amid the pompous foreign consuls and their buttoned-up wives, he set eyes for the first time on Sarah, partially hidden beneath a veil, and was completely smitten. He was sixty-two, she was seventeen. He laid siege to her, initially posing as a friendly figure who could help liberate her from her uncle's exacting guardianship, later proposing marriage, a proposal she swiftly rejected – she already had a fiancé. Her cousin Daniel tried to kidnap her from her house, getting her on to a boat he had left in front of the house, only to be beaten back by her neighbours' servants, who had got wind of the plan. The pasha responded by arresting her servants, sending her hapless fiancé on military service in Kirkuk and ordering the police to break into her house to seize her. One step ahead, Sarah climbed over her garden wall and sought refuge in the house of her neighbour, Herr Hesse, German consul in Baghdad. Unimpressed by the protection of diplomatic immunity in the teeth of the lecherous pasha's pursuit, the German smuggled Sarah to the nearby house of Daud al Nakib, whose family was descended from the great Sufi imam Sheikh Abdul Kadir al Gailani. From here she was taken to the home of Sayid Abdul Rahman al Gailani, doyen of the city's notables and later the first prime minister of Iraq, who granted her sanctuary. Forced to bide his time, Nazim Pasha put the house and neighbourhood under surveillance, and the police were ordered to arrest her on sight. During her attempt to break through the cordon fully veiled in a horse-drawn carriage, the police tried to apprehend her but were beaten back by crowds from the Bab al Sheikh neighbourhood (named after Sheikh Abdul Kadir al Gailani, whose popular shrine is located there). News of this deepening scandal had reached Istanbul by now – poems and songs mocking Nazim Pasha were doing the rounds through the city – and a Turkish reporter duly arrived in Baghdad. His article, which included an interview with the unfortunate Sarah, caused a sensation and led to vigorous protests from the Iraqi members in the Ottoman parliament in early 1911. Undeterred, Nazim Pasha procured a medical report declaring Sarah was insane in an attempt to have her locked up. By now desperate to escape, Sarah disguised herself as a French nun, made her way to the ancient Mustansiriya University, where Basra-bound ships were moored at that time, and boarded a Lynch Company boat in the protective company of a French nun and a Spanish monk. Tipped off by the ubiquitous spies – keeping secrets in Baghdad had always been a formidable challenge – the pasha's police tried to prevent her departure but were prohibited from boarding by the British captain. Still Nazim Pasha refused to accept Sarah's rejection of his suit and tried to argue that she had been forced to convert to Catholicism by the French nuns and must therefore be rescued from Basra. As the Lynch boat drew in at Basra, where the pasha's strongmen were ready to seize her on the quay, the captain had her transferred to a waiting British steamer, which spirited her away to safety in Bombay via Bushir, where she was briefly looked after by Sir Percy Cox, then British Resident of the Persian Gulf, later Britain's first High Commissioner in Iraq. Nazim Pasha was removed from his position in Baghdad, a move celebrated across the city and in *The Tyrant of Baghdad*, a poem by the popular poet Al Zahawi that praises 'a noble girl of well-known chastity' and mocks the 'offender of Iraq'. As Gertrude Bell wrote to her father in 1911, 'Nazim was more than the town could stand . . . they would rather have the devil to rule in Baghdad'.[58] In 1913, by then chief of staff of the Ottoman Army and minister of war, he was assassinated in Istanbul. Freed at last from his unwanted advances, Sarah moved from Bombay to France, returning to Baghdad after the Great War. There she played a leading role in stopping the forced evacuation of Iraqi-Armenians to death camps in Turkey and devoted much of the rest of her life looking after Armenian refugees. She died in poverty in 1960, having exhausted her fortune through good works and the fraud practised against her by a disreputable lawyer. She is remembered today in Baghdad's Camp Sarah, a tribute to her sale of land on generous terms to house the masses of Armenian refugees.[59]

*

When war was declared, Baghdad braced itself for conflict. In Istanbul the figurehead Sultan Mehmed V ordered a general mobilization. Then, on 11 November 1914, a dramatic ceremony unfolded in the mighty Fatih Sultan Mehmed Mosque, one of the most venerable monuments on the Istanbul skyline. Constructed by, and named after, the sultan's mighty predecessor and namesake, the conqueror (*fatih*) of Constantinople in 1453, the mosque could hardly have been a more apposite venue, standing on the ruins of the Byzantine Church of the Holy Apostles. Here, the sultan and caliph received the Sword of the Prophet from Ürgüplü Hayri Bey, the Sheikh al Islam, and declared global *jihad*. By December, hundreds of English, French and Russians were interned in Damascus.

German-subsidized *jihad* pamphlets, helpfully translated into Arabic, Persian, Urdu and Turkic, were printed off and distributed throughout the Ottoman Empire. On 8 April 1915, Jesse Jackson of the US Consulate in Aleppo sent a typical example to Henry Morgenthau, the American ambassador to the Porte. It read: 'The killing of the infidels who rule over the Islamic lands has become a sacred duty, whether it be secretly or openly, as the great Koran declares in its word: "Take them and kill them whenever you come across them."'[60]

Britain was not slow to respond to this threat to its interests in Mesopotamia and the Persian Gulf. Oil was rapidly becoming a Great Power prize. Germany had been interested in oil here since the 1870s, and in 1901 one of its missions returned with the enticing, perfectly accurate news that the region was a 'Lake of Petroleum'.[61] Three years later, the Ottoman government gave the Anatolian Railway Company, controlled by Deutsche Bank, a concession to explore for oil in Mesopotamia. Over the next decade it was joined by the Anglo-Persian Petroleum Company and Royal Dutch Shell Oil Company, the competing groups combining to form the Turkish Petroleum Company in 1914, only for war to wreck these best-laid plans.[62] From this time the potential of the Ottoman province of Basra – both to protect British energy interests in Persia and to supply oil itself, which was essential for Britain's oil-fuelled Royal Navy – figured centrally in British strategic planning, not least as the Ottomans entered the war with the Germans on the side of the Central Powers.[63]

Landing near Fao on 6 November, the Anglo-Indian Mesopotamia Expeditionary Force under the command of Brigadier-General Walter Delamain quickly seized this southern town and fort. Delamain's orders were to protect the oil refineries, tanks and pipeline at Abadan, and to proceed to Ottoman-held Basra only in the event of hostilities being declared. With news reaching the British of war breaking out, this became an immediate ambition. Delamain's reinforcements, commanded by General Sir Arthur Barrett, struck north to Basra. After enduring fighting in hideous conditions of thick dust, alarming mirages and rivers of mud, they formally took it on the 23rd.

Thus began what one historian has termed 'mission creep on a grand scale'.[64] In a telegram sent immediately after Basra fell to the British, Sir Percy Cox, chief political officer of the Expeditionary Force, called for the offensive to continue. 'I find it difficult to see how we can well avoid taking over Baghdad. We can hardly allow Turkey to retain possession and make difficulties for us at Basra; nor can we allow any other Power to take it.'[65] The advance north began. Kurna, a region of reed beds, hoopoes, kingfishers, grebes and herons, thought to be the site of the Garden of Eden, fell on 14 December. Within a year of landing at Fao, Britain was committed to taking Baghdad.

Plotting and king-making continued apace, much of it within the highly significant McMahon–Hussain Correspondence of July 1915 to January 1916. On 24 October 1915, as Britain worked towards the 1916–18 Arab Revolt within the Ottoman Empire, Sir Henry McMahon, British high commissioner in Egypt, wrote to Sharif Hussain of Mecca, assuring him Britain would 'recognise and support the Arabs in all regions' with some modifications. 'With regard to the vilayets of Baghdad and Basra, the Arabs will recognize that the established position and interests of Great Britain necessitate special administrative arrangements in order to secure these territories from foreign aggression, to promote the welfare of the local populations and to safeguard our mutual economic interests.'[66] Quite what these 'special administrative arrangements' were remained undefined.

In fact, there was considerable confusion over political and military objectives within the tangled knots of British bureaucracy on three continents. First, the military suffered from having a chain of command that was half in India, half in Britain. The India government and India Office both envisaged Basra as falling under permanent British rule, while Baghdad should be ceded by Turkey and made a British protectorate with a local administration. Lord Kitchener, secretary of state for war, had more imperial designs and wanted all of Mesopotamia annexed by the British Empire. Prime Minister Asquith and the Foreign Secretary Sir Edward Grey opposed such an annexation but were not against the push towards Baghdad, which was also being strongly urged by British business interests and individuals such as Lord Inchcape, who had significant investments in the Persian Gulf.

Such statecraft – both lofty and low – was of little immediate concern to Baghdadis as the war wore on. In Baghdad, feelings towards the centralizing power of the Committee of Union and Progress – which had started as a revolutionary umbrella organization including the Young Turks, only to become the empire's sole legal political party after it seized power in a 1913 coup – were decidedly mixed. The climate worsened. In the spring of 1915 the poet and newspaper editor Abdul Hussain al Uzri was rounded up from his house in Kadhimiya on the orders of Nur al Din Bey, commander-in-chief of the Ottoman Imperial Sixth Army headquartered at Baghdad. His crime was to have written and published inflammatory editorials criticizing Ottoman policy and calling for self-determination and independence. He was carted off and imprisoned in Kayseri, ancient Caesaria, in the heart of Anatolia, where he was joined by other Baghdad literati who had fallen foul of the Ottoman regime, including the Jesuit scholar Père Anastase-Marie Karmali.[67]

War was already spreading misery to Baghdad by April 1915. In an eyewitness account, the distinguished explorer and orientalist Alois Musil – a Czech Lawrence of Arabia – noted the terrible damage caused by the war and flooding:

> The streets of the inner town, through which it was hard to move in 1912, gaped emptily, the shops were mostly closed, the coffee houses only half filled ... groups of soldiers appeared occasionally here and there ... In the Christian cemetery east of the high road leading to Persia coffins and half mouldering skeletons were floating. On account of the Cholera which was ravaging the town (three hundred people were dying of it every day) the Christian dead were now being buried on the new embankment of the highroad, so that people walking and riding had not only to pass by but even to make their way among and over the graves ... There was no longer any life in the town, formerly one of the busiest in the Orient.[68]

In October the Turks closed down the Laura Kedourie School, requisitioning it as a military hospital. The Alliance boys' school was also taken.

By mid October, Barrett's replacement, Major-General Charles Townshend, commander of the 6th (Poona) Division, was marching on Baghdad under the orders of General Sir John Nixon, commander of the Indian Expeditionary Force. As an Indian Office memo of 6 October to the Inter-Departmental Committee on the Strategical Situation in Mesopotamia expressed it, an occupation of Baghdad would 'revive British prestige in the Middle East' and put Britain 'in a position to cut German communications to Persia'.[69]

Baghdad, despite its centuries of decline, was still a romantic name to conjure with in the corridors of the British Empire. Whereas for most Ottoman officials earmarked for a posting there, Baghdad was a dread word and a trial of sun-baked remoteness ('a rumour will come back even from Baghdad', went the proverb), many British policymakers by contrast thought of it as an 'irresistible lodestar', at least when gazed at from afar.[70] A rousing victory here would stir British hearts and compensate for the lack of success in Gallipoli and the German invasion of Serbia.

The Turks' winter defeat at Shaiba, an attempt to retake Basra, brought about a reshuffle of their military leadership in Baghdad. Field Marshal von der Goltz swept into Baghdad on 15 December with thirty German officers to be welcomed by carefully orchestrated and obediently cheering crowds of children. Baghdadis soon heard about the German commander's ruthlessness and severity. Some witnessed it first-hand. Working as a teenage messenger for the Turkish command headquartered in the citadel, Hadi Abdul Hussain – the future father of the Iraqi politician Ahmed Chalabi – watched in horror as a teaboy who had inadvertently spilled tea on the general's documents was cruelly flogged. By contrast, and to the confusion of many dog-hating Baghdadis, von der Goltz doted on his curly-tailed Turkish Kangal sheepdogs.[71]

For the British, the road to Baghdad lay through the town of Kut, on the banks of the Tigris 100 miles to the south-east. It was there that Britain, after a failed advance on Baghdad, suffered one of the worst military humiliations in its history of empire. A shattering Turkish siege started in December 1915 and continued for five months, despite efforts by T. E. Lawrence and Aubrey Herbert to bribe the British out of trouble. By the time Townshend offered his unconditional surrender on 29 April, conditions inside the town resembled something out of the apocalypse. Photographs of emaciated, saucer-eyed Indian Army survivors, with ribs pressing through parchment skin, still make harrowing viewing. 'This last part of the siege was a bad time, hungry, sick, overworked,' Major Ernest Walker of the 1st Indian Field Ambulance wrote at the time. 'Biting flies and mosquitoes increased apace. Our dead stank, dead Turks stank. Never can I forget the *cats*, starved of course, eating dead Turks & feeding out of their skeletons. Diarrhoea began & fever, scurvy got worse.'[72]

Townshend had lost 4,500 men before the siege and a further 3,800 during the ordeal. The three failed attempts to break the siege cost 23,000 Allied lives. Yet the surrender did not put an end to the suffering. A dreadful trial still awaited the unwitting prisoners.

*

Baghdadis saw some of the miseries inflicted by the siege at first hand. In mid May, still reeling from a near-fatal attack of cholera that had spared him the first leg of the forced march from Kut, RAF Flight Sergeant P. W. Long chugged into the city as a prisoner on board the beaten-up armoured supply ship *Julnar*. Captured from the British after one of their unsuccessful attempts to break the siege, it had been so badly raked from bow to stern that onlookers thought it resembled a floating sieve.

Like so many travellers before him, Long was entranced by his first sight of Baghdad. 'I shall never forget the beautiful picture that came into sight as we rounded a bend in the river near Karrada, a suburb of the city,' he wrote in a post-war account of his captivity. 'Turquoise-blue domes and slender minarets peeped above the dark green palm fronds and formed the background. The steely-blue sky was mirrored in the waters of the Tigris and in the foreground was an island, reed-covered, and the hunting-ground of a flock of long-legged herons.'[73]

Beneath loudly clacking storks, the upper balconies of riverside houses were crowded with unveiled Christian girls and women shouting 'Bonjour!' and 'Good morning!' to the haggard new arrivals. Things took a turn for the worse once the British and Indian prisoners had crossed the bridge-of-boats into West Baghdad, where they were ordered to march through a crowded 'filthy bazaar' in which 'Bearded Arabs in flowing kaftans and red-fezzed youths gazed at us in amazement and disgust.' The atmosphere darkened. Groups of women 'with tattooed faces and ragged clothes shrieked at us and spat on the ground to signify contempt'. Then,

> one of the tattooed ladies came close to me and spat full into my face.
> Entirely forgetting the fact that I was a captive, I clawed weakly at the

hag's throat. Behind me the nearest soldier brought the butt of his rifle crashing down between my shoulders, and I was knocked sprawling into the filth of the roadway. I rolled on to my back in time to receive the point of his bayonet through my bottom lip as he made a vicious lunge at me ... the blood flowed freely down the front of my chin and on to my ragged shirt, giving me a ghastly appearance. The spectators among the crowd cheered wildly at this little side-show, and the women shrieked, 'Kaffir, kelb ibn kelb!' ('Unbeliever, dog son of a dog!') at me as I staggered back to my place in the ranks.[74]

Reeling through the souk with a burning, head-spinning fever, Long was one of 300 prisoners forced to camp in the open air at Baghdad railway station. One night he was woken by the screams of two sick Englishmen who had been using the trench latrines, only to be attacked by a group of Arabs and left naked and groaning on the ground, covered in vicious knife cuts and heavy bruises. During the nine days in Baghdad, sunstroke, starvation and disease carried off many of the prisoners.

Initially, at least, the British and Indian officer prisoners from Kut were treated much better. On 9 May 1916, Captain Edward Sandes disembarked at the former British Residency, now a Turkish military hospital. Dripping with sweat under heavy packs, the British captains and subalterns were made to march through the city, behind the Indian officers, 'to be exhibited exactly as in a Roman triumph, except that we wore no chains and had our full complement of clothes'.[75] They passed the infantry barracks at the citadel and filed through the North Gate and out on to the desert plain towards the vast Turkish cavalry barracks, surrounded by sheets of water, which was to be their home for the next four days. Within moments the famished officers were surrounded by a noisy mass of Baghdad's hawkers selling oranges, onions, local cigarettes and sweet cakes at extortionate prices. British majors, colonels and generals made a more dignified journey, the most senior among them by carriage, to the Grand Babylon Hotel near the gently bobbing bridge-of-boats.

While the other ranks struggled for their lives, Sandes and colleagues were chartering phaetons to the Imperial Ottoman Bank to change money, thence to the redoubtable American consul Charles Brissel, who gave them 'excellent liqueur brandy, coffee and cigarettes' and advanced three liras in gold per man'.[76] Major Ernest Walker, who reached Bagh-dad on 5 June, was allowed to while away pleasant evenings with his fellow officers in a club overlooking the Tigris and to dine in some splendour. 'The Club was really a hotel or café on the banks of the river with a nice lawn, chairs at little tables, whisky, soda and *ice* ... We stayed to dinner and had a good feed with a quart of red wine & very excellent coffee.'[77]

One day during his enforced stay in Baghdad, Flight Sergeant Long's ragged band of half-dead prisoners received a surprise VIP visitor. Enver Pasha, the Turkish minister of war, had come to inspect them. He reassured the survivors of the nightmare of Kut: 'Your troubles are over now, my dears; *you will be treated as the honoured guests of the Sultan*.'[78]

In fact, General Townshend was one of the few Kut prisoners to be treated as an honoured guest of Sultan Mehmed. After Khalil gave a dinner party in Baghdad in his honour, Townshend travelled north with the coffin of Field Marshal von der Goltz, who had died of typhus shortly before the fall of Kut (there were rumours he had been poisoned by the Turks), and spent the rest of the war in great comfort on a small island near Istanbul.

A very different journey awaited Long and several thousand fellow prisoners: a forced desert march of 500 miles in searing heat of forty degrees, during which they were deprived of proper supplies of food and water and bullied, beaten, burgled and buggered by their guards. Racked by colic, scurvy, dysentery or cholera, frazzled by sunstroke, many simply staggered off the roadside to their death or died where they stood. By the end of the marathon trek to prison camps in Turkey and Syria, 1,306 of the 2,680 British NCOs and privates taken captive at Kut had died and 449 were unaccounted for. Of the 10,486 who served with the Indian Army, 1,290 died and 1,773 remained untraced.[79] It was one of the most brutal and bloody military marches in history.[80]

*

The British public was horrified by the disaster at Kut. Kipling expressed the popular fury at the bumbling incompetence in his poem 'Mesopotamia', published in July 1917:

> They shall not return to us, the resolute, the young,
>   The eager and whole-hearted whom we gave:

But the men who left them thriftily to die in their own dung,
   Shall they come with years and honour to the grave?
                    . . .
Shall we only threaten and be angry for an hour?
   When the storm is ended shall we find
How softly but how swiftly they have sidled back to power
   By the favour and contrivance of their kind?
                    . . .
Their lives cannot repay us – their death could not undo –
   The shame that they have laid upon our race.
But the slothfulness that wasted and the arrogance that slew,
   Shall we leave it unabated in its place?

Yet the débâcle at Kut also hardened British resolve. Major-General Sir Stanley Maude was put in command of all Allied forces in Mesopotamia in late July 1916. In a secret note written in that year, the under-secretary of the India Office wrote of the desire to 'efface the memory of the failure at Kut' – and the appropriate response immediately presented itself. 'The Taking of Baghdad would undoubtedly impress the Middle East' and put Britain on course to dominate in the region.[81] By February 1917 Prime Minister Lloyd George was saying to Sir William Robertson, chief of the Imperial General Staff, that 'you must give us Baghdad if you possibly can'.[82]

As British forces pressed towards Baghdad again, the conditions in the city worsened. Coppersmiths in the Souk al Saffafir metal market went into hiding after watching Turks haul their colleagues away from their shops and conscript them. In several public squares the bodies of army deserters were strung up to rot on poles. Streams of wounded poured into the city daily. The narrow streets were made narrower still by the makeshift open coffins in which corpses lay beneath fetid swarms of flies. The prices of basic supplies such as sugar and wheat rose drastically. Baghdad became a giant refugee camp as destitute women from the villages south of the city flooded in, fleeing from the fighting.

Hampered from effective military resupply and manoeuvring by the tiny streets, in May 1916 the Turkish military governor Khalil Pasha, with the encouragement of the German command, made a decision that would change Baghdad for ever. A 52-foot-wide avenue, running from the South Gate through Maidan Square and alongside Mirjan Mosque to the northern gate of Bab al Muadham, parallel to the Tigris, was cut through Rusafa. Everything in its way, including the supposedly protected Haydar Khana Bazaar, which was *wakf*, or bequeathed property, was levelled. Only the homes of those who could afford serious bribes were spared.

The authorities, keen to mark their success at Kut, opened Khalil Pasha Street – the future Rashid Street – with great fanfare in July. Its route, said the intrepid American newspaperwoman Eleanor Egan, who spent time in Baghdad with General Maude and the British command in 1917,

> required some lack of consideration for the feelings of the inhabitants and the property owners. There was no question of investigating or respecting proprietary rights. The street was simply cut through. And some of the property owners were so cast down by it that to this day they have not troubled to remove from the half-cut-away buildings the evidences of human occupation. They left pictures to dangle forlornly on the walls of rooms, and bits of furniture here and there to become weather-beaten and unsightly. They look horribly exposed and ashamed.[83]

By March 1917, Turkish troops were digging trenches outside Baghdad to defend against the relentless British advance, and officers were requisitioning merchandise from all over the city and sending it by rail to Samarra. On 10 March a sandstorm of unusual ferocity fell upon the city. Khalil Pasha called a council of war in the Khirr Pavilion to confront his unenviable position. On the one hand, he was under stiff pressure from Enver Pasha to make a stand, and his heavy-handed German allies had issued a hardly less urgent recommendation to launch a counter-attack. On the other, his field commanders were highlighting that their defensive forces were too depleted to face a more powerful adversary on the front foot and emphasizing the profound dangers and difficulties of a sudden, unplanned retreat from Baghdad. At 8 p.m., after a final private conference with his chief of staff, Khalil Pasha made his decision. The order was given for a general withdrawal to a line 19 miles north of Baghdad. A telegram was sent to Istanbul in which the pasha announced 'the sorrowful necessity of abandoning Baghdad'.[84]

There was time for a last-minute scorched-earth farewell. Every factory in town was to be destroyed, together with the German wireless station, various British offices and seven new aeroplanes in their crates.

Ammunition was dumped in the Tigris, and the bridge-of-boats burnt. Baghdadis cowered in their cellars as the terrible boom of Turkish salvos shook their houses. Sand streamed through the city in thick gusts, causing panic and confusion. On pain of being shot for desertion, Turkish troops hurried through the city towards the North Gate, providing the cue for Baghdad's mobs to surge on to the streets, gutting the shops and stealing anything they could lay their hands on, from heavy bedsteads and iron railings to merchants' safes and park benches. Amidst the chaos, Khalil Pasha and his entourage boarded a train to Samarra, washing their hands of Baghdad. As the Turks marched out of the City of Peace, there was time for a final act of vandalism. The Bab al Talism, the thirteenth-century jewel of the Abbasid caliphate – which had been bricked up to prevent future conquerors following in the footsteps of Sultan Murad IV, who had taken the city in 1638 – was blown to smithereens.

The manic Turkish artillery and the explosions sent a deep red glare into the sand-filled sky. Shortly before midnight, Maude's 35th Brigade set off up the right bank of the Tigris. At 1.35 a.m. the 39th Brigade reported that it had occupied enemy trenches on the left bank and Baghdad appeared to be in flames. At 2 a.m. the 35th occupied enemy positions and an hour later the order to advance was given. By 6 a.m. a Black Watch patrol under 2nd Lieutenant Houston had taken control of Baghdad railway station, three-quarters of a mile outside the city, and the troops were searching for an appropriate trophy to lift. Amongst the graffiti they encountered were the defiant legends, '100 Tommies = 1 Askari' and the touchingly mistaken 'It is a long way to Baghdad'.

A little after dawn, two squadrons of British cavalry trotted towards the city. Outside the South Gate they met a deputation of Arab and Jewish grandees bearing a petition from the city's merchants and a plea from the admirable American consul for British troops to take Baghdad without delay, since Arabs and Kurds were ransacking it from top to bottom. In the priceless words of the commanding officer of the King's Own, as reported by the war correspondent Edmund Candler, 'By Jove! I believe these fellows are bringing us the keys of the Citadel!' Amongst the unofficial welcoming party were attractive unveiled women, 'whose forwardness was almost embarrassing to men who had seen nothing in the shape of a woman for years beyond black bundles filling their pitchers on the Tigris bank'.[85]

Within the hour, three battalions of the 35th Brigade – the 1/5th Buffs, the 37th Dogras and the 102nd Grenadiers – were making their debut in commandeered *guffas* across the Tigris, and half an hour after that the Union Jack was flying from the venerable citadel as British and Indian troops fired over heads to break up the crowds of looters.

At 8.30 a.m. a British naval flotilla of seven gunboats – including *Firefly* flying the White Ensign over the Turkish – left Bawi, a village four miles north of ancient Ctesiphon, south-east of Baghdad, accompanied by General Maude in the *P. 53*. At 3.30 p.m., on 11 March, Maude disembarked at the British Residency in one of the most discreet entrances any conqueror of Baghdad had ever made.

The British had arrived at what Maude's troops called 'the old Turkey-cock's city of Haroun al Rothschild'.[86]

10

A Very British Monarchy: Three Kings in Baghdad (1917–58)

The English have conquered this country, they have expended their wealth and they have watered the soil with their blood. The blood of Englishmen, of Australians, Canadians, Muslims of India and idolaters has drenched the dust of Iraq. Shall they not enjoy what they have won? Other conquerors have overwhelmed the country. As it fell to them, so it has fallen to the English. They will establish their dominion. Khatun, your nation is great, wealthy and powerful. Where is our power? If I say that I wish for the rule of the English and the English do not consent to govern us, how can I force them? And if I wish for the rule of another, and the English resolve to remain, how can I eject them? I recognise your victory. You are the governors and I am the governed. And when I am asked what is my opinion as to the continuance of British rule, I reply that I am the subject of the victor.

The *nakib* of Baghdad to Gertrude Bell,
February 1919[1]

Our weather is just like us. Hot one day, cold the next. We too flare up until you think the universe will fall to pieces, then subside until you think not a spark is left in us.

Jabra Ibrahim Jabra,
Hunters in a Narrow Street (1960)

Battered by war, consumed by flames, reverberating to the sound of explosions, with an abject population virtually reduced to starvation and many of its buildings completely levelled, the Baghdad that General Maude entered on 11 March 1917 bore no resemblance to the fabled Abbasid city of old. Confronted by squalor, misery and destruction whichever way they turned, the British were quickly disabused of any romantic associations they may have carried on first glimpsing the heart-stopping blue and gold domes, the slender minarets, and the date palms and orange groves reflected in the languid mirror of the Tigris at dawn or dusk.

The official British History of the Great War notes that the outskirts of Baghdad were littered with 'corpses and bones of dead animals'. Marching into the city, the Anglo-Indian forces were confronted with 'miserable-looking and rather dilapidated houses of mud-brown brick and ... narrow filthy streets'. 'There were no sanitary nor scavenging arrangements, noxious smells abounded and hundreds of diseased and half-starved dogs roamed everywhere.'[2]

Having slogged it out in the desert and malarial swamps in spirit-wilting heat and bone-numbing cold alike, having longed for an idealized Baghdad in which to rest and perhaps even to set eyes on a woman for the first time in more than a year, the general feeling amongst British troops, unsurprisingly, was one of 'great disappointment' and 'disenchantment'. As the war correspondent Edmund Chandler, one of the first into Baghdad, noted drily, 'Romance flies before revelation.' In fact, 'there was to be no rest; all the djinns of Baghdad could not raise a single glass of beer'.[3] The offensive against the Turks continued to the north and the west.

To add to the British rank-and-file's disillusion, the retreating Turks had left hidden explosives throughout the city. The proud-walled citadel was sheathed in the black smoke of petrol-fed fires, 'with trains ready laid [with explosives] to the ammunition stores'.[4] Maude's forces struggled throughout the day and following night to extinguish them.

Within the city in which British business had prospered for decades, 'Not a single piece of British property was left standing except the Residency, a rather imposing building on the river-front which reminds one forcefully of the days when Great Britain maintained a special and somewhat stately relationship with the Turkish Empire.' Appropriated as a military hospital, even that was 'dirty and unkempt beyond anybody's power to describe', wrote the horrified – and vigorously pro-British – American correspondent Eleanor Egan.[5] This depressing picture is supported by the British Official History, which reported that the larger buildings that had been commandeered by the Turks as medical facilities were 'indescribably dirty and verminous'. 'Sanitation had to be taken in hand energetically' before the city was ready for occupation, including the provision of hospital beds for 7,000 sick and wounded.[6] The narrow streets clattered to the sound of soldiers on patrol, conducting house-to-house searches for weapons and policing the bazaars, most of which had already been ransacked and now lay gutted and smouldering. Baghdad's mobs had been quick to exploit the few hours of lawlessness between the Turks' departure and Maude's arrival. Jewish merchants reported combined losses of two million francs between 2 a.m. and 9 a.m. on 11 March.

Crowds of Baghdadis – Arabs, Jews, Iranians, Armenians, Chaldeans and the various Christian sects – came out to meet the new conquerors. 'They lined the streets, balconies and roofs, hurrahing and clapping their hands,' Candler reported. 'Groups of schoolchildren danced in front of us, shouting and cheering, and the women of the city turned out in their holiday dresses.'[7] Less than a century later Baghdad would welcome American soldiers with an equally short-lived enthusiasm.

Despite the squalor and destruction, Egan, who had been put under the wing of Maude and his command, found the conquered city utterly absorbing and exotic. Through the crooked streets passed an unending procession of headwear: turbans, tarbushes, topees, straw hats, skull-caps, traditional Arab *agal* headbands, elongated felt tubes worn by the Lur and the Kurd, brimless top hats of the Bakhtiari, the occasional black astrakhan from the north. There were bare-footed Bushir coolies in English frock-coats, Bengalis in wraparound *dhotis*, Madras servants with rings in their ears, scholarly-looking Chinese with straw hats and spectacles. Green-turbaned sayids, descendants of the Prophet, rubbed shoulders with black-gowned Iranians, Parsees and wild-looking Zanzibaris, Swahilis and Abyssinians, Greeks and Jews, Christians of all hues from Chaldaean and Armenian to Sabaean, Nestorian and Jacobite. She admired the 'Persians and Arabs and Oriental Jews at their everlasting drowsing over coffee and hubble-bubbles', hundreds of unveiled women in gorgeously coloured *abayas*, 'Kurd porters staggering under unbelievable burdens', the 'droves of coolie women all but lost to view under loose enormous bundles of twigs and desert grass roots'. Then there were the 'lordly turbaned Moslem elders' in black flowing robes, 'red-fezzed Jews in misfit European clothing' and 'handsome Persians in high white lambswool caps and long silken coats of many colours' that reminded her of Joseph. She was particularly struck by the 'Christians of ancient Chaldean stock', who wore Arab costume but had blue eyes and were 'white skinned as a German'. The only dark note came from the East African slaves, men and women 'black as ebony and with shifty eyes full of inquiry and resentment'.[8]

While his colleagues wrote letters home full of fond longing, dry military wit and the odd reference to Ali Baba and the Forty Thieves and Sinbad the Sailor, Bombardier George Coles of the 38th Brigade lost no time in seeking out the nearest dive. He found one in which 'About 100 Arabs were lounging on wooden settees yawning and drinking tots of mint tea while an Armenian girl was dancing the Salome on a raised platform to the music of a piano and two weird stringed instruments.' The performance climaxed with the girl 'in a frenzy – as naked as she was born . . . the East with the lid off!'[9]

In London, news of the fall of Baghdad was met with sabre-rattling relief. 'The British Flag over Bagdad', proclaimed *The War Illustrated*; 'End to German Dreams of Eastern Empire.' Maude's capture of the city had dealt Germany 'the heaviest blow it has suffered in the war and the Ottoman Empire the most damaging blow inflicted upon it in a quarter of a thousand years'.[10]

On 19 March, Maude issued his famous Proclamation of Baghdad, drafted by the British politician Sir Mark Sykes, founder of the Arab Bureau and co-author of the secret 1916 Sykes–Picot Agreement that, unbeknown to the Arabs, divided the Ottoman Middle East into spheres of British and French influence and control. The proclamation referred explicitly to past Abbasid glories, Mongol depredations and Ottoman iniquities in Baghdad.

Maude began by reassuring Baghdadis that

> our armies do not come into your cities and lands as conquerors or enemies, but as liberators. Since the days of Halaka [Hulagu] your city and your lands have been subject to the tyranny of strangers, your palaces have fallen into ruins, your gardens have sunk in desolation, and your forefathers and yourselves have groaned in bondage. Your sons have been carried off to wars not of your seeking, your wealth has been stripped from you by unjust men and squandered in distant places.

Next came a swipe at the Turks, whose promised reforms had proved a tragic chimera. Great Britain, by contrast, was determined that 'you

THE BRITISH FLAG OVER BAGDAD

End to German Dreams of Eastern Empire

ON March 11th, 1917, Lieut.-General Sir Stanley Maude, in command of the Mesopotamian Expeditionary Force, occupied Bagdad, and so dealt the German Empire the heaviest blow it has suffered in the war and the Ottoman Empire the most damaging blow inflicted upon it in a quarter of a thousand years. For Germany the capture of the city means the end of her dream of dominion in the East, towards which she was reaching slowly along the Berlin-Bosphorus-Bagdad Railway line. For Turkey it means almost certainly the disruption of her Empire in Asia, consolidated among the Moslem peoples when Bagdad surrendered to Murad IV, on Christmas Day, 1638. With her Empire in Europe also tottering to its fall, it means the final elimination of Turkey from the Powers of the world.

Politically, the event is of transcendent importance in the East. It restores British prestige, undoubtedly shaken by the earlier failure to relieve Kut-el-Amara. It frees Persia from the Turkish occupation of some 30,000 square miles of her territory. It secures the frontier of India. It stills Mohammedan unrest throughout the East. It opens up the possibility of a great and far-reaching revival of the Arab race. Strategically, too, it is of great importance. It enables us to co-operate with the Russians advancing from Persia, and, still further compromise the Turks' line of retreat from Bagdad; and, in any case, it seriously threatens the whole efficiency of the Turkish armies to help the Germanic Powers. With every mile of the railway that falls into our possession we shall interfere more seriously with their means of moving reinforcements and supplies northwards, and so increase the weight that they have already become upon Germany, which is their real military base.

Chiefly, however, because of its extraordinary picturesqueness will the capture of Bagdad first impress the imagination of the world. The very name of the city is redolent of romance. It stands in that great plain which is the focal point of immemorial associations, whose history covers at least five thousand years and rings with names that still are magnificent. Bagdad itself was founded in 762 by Al Mansur, first of the Abbasid Caliphs, who thought it desirable to move the capital of the new dynasty from Damascus, where the Ommiades had held their Court. He built it on the site of an infinitely old village, on the west bank of the Tigris, and for five hundred years it remained the seat of the Caliphate until Hulagu, grandson of Genghis Khan, and his Mongol hordes carried and sacked it in 1258. At its zenith Bagdad really was the city of which we dream when we read of Haroun al-Raschid in "The Arabian Nights"; in the heart of a district made fertile by a wonderful system of irrigation canals, with exquisite gardens, fairy palaces, flourishing colleges whence learning spread the whole world over, priceless libraries and works of art, and wealth beyond the dream of avarice.

After the Mongol invasion Bagdad ceased to be the spiritual home of Islam. Its glory had departed. Hulagu had destroyed the whole system of irrigation and Mesopotamia was blasted. Once again Bagdad was sacked—by Tamerlane, in 1410, and after a prolonged and chequered history, Murad IV. besieged it, accepted its capitulation, and, after a most bloody massacre, turned it into the seat of a Turkish Pasha. But its geographical position kept it a chief point on the great highway to the East. As such it attracted the covetous eyes of the German Kaiser. As such it became of vital importance in the Great War; and as such it has passed now into the possession of the British Empire.

Lieut.-Gen. Sir STANLEY MAUDE,
General Officer Commanding the Mesopotamian Expeditionary Force, who captured Bagdad, March 11th.

When Lieutenant-General Sir Stanley Maude's British and Indian troops marched into the city on 11 March 1917, after 383 years of Ottoman control, Baghdad fell to the British Empire.

should prosper even as in the past, when your lands were fertile, when your ancestors gave to the world literature, science, and art, and when Baghdad city was one of the wonders of the world'.

Maude emphasized the 'close bond of interest' between Britain and Baghdad, whose merchants had been trading together in 'mutual profit and friendship' for 200 years. The Germans and the Turks had made Baghdad a centre of power from which to attack Britain and her allies in Persia and Arabia; 'Therefore the British Government cannot remain indifferent as to what takes place in your country now or in the future.'

There was another – ominously vague – reassurance about Baghdad's political destiny. Britain did not wish 'to impose upon you alien institutions' but hoped that 'the aspirations of your philosophers and writers shall be realized', with Baghdad flourishing under institutions in accord with its 'sacred laws' and 'racial ideals'. Maude drew Baghdadis' attention to events in the Arabian Desert, where the Arabs had 'expelled the Turks and Germans who oppressed them and proclaimed the Sharif Hussain as their King, and his Lordship rules in independence and freedom'.*

The proclamation concluded with a rousing crescendo. 'Many noble Arabs have perished in the cause of Arab freedom, at the hands of those alien rulers, the Turks, who oppressed them.' Great Britain was committed to ensure that 'these noble Arabs shall not have suffered in vain. It is the hope and desire of the British people and the nations in alliance with them that the Arab race may rise once more to greatness and renown among the peoples of the earth.'

O people of Baghdad remember that for 26 generations you have suffered under strange tyrants who have ever endeavoured to set one Arab house against another in order that they might profit by your dissensions. This policy is abhorrent to Great Britain and her Allies, for there can be neither peace nor prosperity where there is enmity and misgovernment. Therefore I am commanded to invite you, through your nobles and elders and repre-

---

* Hussain ibn Ali, Sharif and Amir of Mecca from 1908 to 1917, broke with the Otttoman Empire in 1916, when he led the Arab Revolt, supported by the British, and proclaimed himself King of the Hijaz and Sultan of all Arabs a year later. As a Hashemite, descendant of Hashim ibn Abd al Manaf, great-grandfather of the Prophet Mohammed, he enjoyed special status within the Muslim world. In 1924, after the dissolution of the Ottoman caliphate, he proclaimed himself caliph, but was defeated in the same year by Abdul Aziz Al Saud, his chief rival in the Arabian peninsula and later the first king of Saudi Arabia.

sentatives, to participate in the management of your civil affairs in collaboration with the political representatives of Great Britain who accompany the British Army, so that you may be united with your kinsmen in North, East, South, and West in realizing the aspirations of your race.

In Baghdad the proclamation largely fell on deaf ears.[11] In London it occasioned severely raised eyebrows. As the Speaker of the House of Commons observed in a withering aside during a debate on 21 March, 'I am afraid it contained a great deal of Oriental and flowery language not suitable to our Western climate.'[12]

*

For Baghdadis, accustomed to centuries of Turkish rule, 11 March 1917 was a sudden, shocking change of cast. The sartorial switch alone was immediately striking. Overnight topees and ties replaced turbans and fezes. From the all-important perspective of religion, the transformation was equally abrupt. Distant infidels supplanted neighbouring co-religionists, however loathed those co-religionists had become. Culturally, the arrival of the British was nothing less than a revolution. As the ranks of languid pashas and effendis scattered to the winds, they were replaced by the ruddy-faced, straight-backed servants of the British Empire fizzing with zeal. Politically speaking, to judge by Maude's proclamation, arbitrary, capricious rule was going to be replaced by something closer to 'independence and freedom'. The only thing the British appeared to have in common with the Turks, apart from their natural bossiness, was a tendency to sport bristling moustaches.

If the Turks had been indolent, the British seemed possessed of a maniacal energy for 'improving' things, from sanitation, bridge-building and road repairs to irrigation, constitutions and government. As the ten-volume Iraq Administration Reports of 1914–32 spectacularly attest, they were also inveterate compilers of lists. Thus, to take a typical example, in his annual report for 1917, Brigadier-General C. J. Hawker, whom Maude appointed military governor of Baghdad, provided an overview of his department's activities. This document's various categories wonderfully encapsulate British interests and priorities of the time. Under 'Cruelty to Animals', he noted there were 266 cases of cruelty to animals prosecuted. One hundred animals had to be destroyed due to their 'deplorable condition'. Baghdad's canine population, usually unlamented by the city's population, now came in for particular attention – and care. Under 'Dogs', Hawker reported the distressing news that the Military Police had 'shot and buried' 4,917 diseased animals. When it came to 'General Sanitation', 'The emptying of cesspits was taken energetically in hand, and during one week 281 cartloads and 161 donkeyloads of cesspit refuse were removed to the cesspit refuse area.' The 'Disinfecting Depot' was especially busy. In one week it disinfected 6,694 items. 'Grain supplies' in January averaged 60 tons of sales daily. 'Vaccinations' were also going well, with 3,929 Baghdadis inoculated in January alone. Yet, for all this progress, Hawker was bound to add a distinctly British caveat. 'The population of this town is on the whole most amenable to carrying out regulations, but after centuries of misrule they naturally require considerable education before they can assimilate modern ideas concerning sanitation, cruelty to animals, the necessity of giving truthful evidence, and other such matters.'[13]

This was the era of remarkable British officials such as Sir Percy Cox – Supposi Kokkus to Baghdadis – Maude's chief political officer and later the first high commissioner in Iraq. An Old Harrovian protégé of Lord Curzon and a brilliant Arabist, he was at this time in his early fifties. When not immersed in political plotting, he would spend hours amassing a collection of Mesopotamian birds. Some arrived in Baghdad dead; others, including a large eagle, very much alive. For a while it lived on a perch in Cox's house and fed on bats that flew across the Tigris of an evening, were netted in his garden and put on ice overnight by Lady Cox (since the eagle preferred eating bats for breakfast rather than dinner).

Cox, a shrewd soldier-diplomat who had been British Resident in the Persian Gulf in Bushir for a decade before the war, was instrumental in creating the modern state of Iraq, above all by deciding in 1922–3 the borders that divided it from Jordan, Najd (Saudi Arabia) and Kuwait. He was assisted in this monumental task by his no less extraordinary oriental secretary, Gertrude Bell, a formidable woman respectfully remembered – and in some cases revered – by Baghdadis today as 'Miss Bell'. Bell was the first woman to achieve a First in Modern History at Oxford, the first woman to be awarded a prize by the Royal Geographical Society and the first woman officer in British military intelligence. She added to these laurels by making an important first traverse in the Alps, and in 1897, having only recently learnt Farsi, by publishing an anthology of Hafiz's poems in translation. Edward Browne, the leading authority on Persian literature, judged it, with one exception, 'probably the finest and most truly poetical renderings of any Persian poet ever produced in the English language'.[14] Her brother-in-law, Vice-Admiral Sir Herbert Richmond, drew a light-hearted cartoon depicting her as the most powerful woman in the British Empire:

> From Trebizond to Tripolis
> She rolls the Pashas flat
> And tells them what to think of this
> And what to think of that.[15]

Bell, who never married and had no children, considered herself the midwife who helped give birth to the new state of Iraq. Sometimes she saw herself in a rather more elevated role. As she wrote to her mother on 5 December 1918, 'I feel at times rather like the Creator about the middle of the week. He must have wondered what it was going to be like, as I do.'[16]

Then there was Cox's deputy, the God-fearing imperialist Sir Arnold Wilson, later civil commissioner for Mesopotamia, nicknamed 'the Despot of Messpot' for his leading role in suppressing the Iraq Revolt of 1920, the violent gestation that prefigured the formal birth of Iraq a year later.

Dominating this all-British cast was 'The Man of Mesopotamia', as his admirers nicknamed him, General Sir Stanley Maude, regularly seen riding out in Baghdad. A photograph taken in the summer of 1917 shows the immaculately turned-out Old Etonian in spotless army uniform with polished boots, a vast moustache and imperious bearing, every inch the servant of the British Empire. He is surrounded by British and Indian staff, who seem smaller by comparison. A recently raised Union Jack hangs limply amongst the date palms behind them.

These early days of British Baghdad were full of promise – as they would be with the American-led invasion almost ninety years later. 'We shall, I trust, make it a great centre for Arab civilization and prosperity,' an excited Bell wrote to her father on 10 March 1917 as British troops approached the city.[17] In her first letter from Baghdad, written on 20 April, the high-spirited Bell reported that it was all 'wildly interesting'. She had 'lots of thrilling things to do . . . Baghdad is a mass of roses and congratulations! (They are genuinely delighted at being free of the

Turks.)'[18] Maude, a keen horseman, reported similar atmospherics later that summer:

> The people are all delighted to see us, and whenever I ride out in the evening one is met with smiling faces and salutations everywhere. I have only been twice assaulted so far, once by a man and once by a woman, who rushed out from the crowd and insisted on kissing my boots, which I hope they liked. All round outside, too, our troops are received in a most friendly manner, though of course, as you know, the Arab character is a treacherous one.[19]

As always when they were abroad, the British knew just what was needed to make life more bearable in Baghdad. 'The new club is being laid out with polo ground, racing tracks, lawn tennis courts, cricket and football grounds, [and] golf course,' Maude wrote on 6 September. He had just been to a moonlit party of musical chairs and dancing given by the 'Nursing Sisters' in a house on the river.

Yet Maude's personal triumph in Baghdad was extremely short-lived. On 14 November, he took Eleanor Egan to a Jewish school for an evening's entertainment, which ended with a cup of coffee. A couple of days later, he went into the office, feeling unwell, and called for his doctor, who prescribed rest and milk. Renowned throughout the army as a workaholic, at lunchtime he reluctantly returned home, to the same house overlooking the Tigris in which the German Field Marshal von der Goltz had died the previous year. At 6 p.m. Colonel Willcox, consulting physician to the Forces, gave an initial examination and later diagnosed a virulent form of cholera. Maude had had milk in his coffee in a neighbourhood where cholera and the plague were rife; Egan had not. Though insisting that his men be inoculated, Maude had always refused any inoculation himself, claiming a man his age was immune. At 7.45 p.m. 'an acute attack of cholera commenced with great suddenness, and in a few minutes a state of extreme collapse occurred.' At 4.30 p.m., on 18 November, he fell unconscious and died peacefully at 6.25 p.m.

'At the end it was all very beautiful,' wrote Reverend A. C. E. Jarvis, who was with Maude during his last hours.

> His immediate personal staff, the doctors, nurses and orderly stood round the bed. Outside the measured tread of the Ghurka guard. A peaceful calm

filled the room. I began the service of Commendation at five minutes past six, and at twenty-five minutes past six, just as I was uttering the words:

Rest Eternal grant to him, O Lord,

And let Light Everlasting shine upon him

he peacefully entered Paradise. Thus our beloved commander left us, victor, as always, over the last great enemy.[20]

Maude's death, so soon after the game-changing conquest of Baghdad, came as a profound shock to Baghdadis and Britons alike. Speaking in the House of Commons on 4 March 1918, Prime Minister Lloyd George paid tribute to a commander who had 'found British prestige at a very low ebb in a quarter of the globe where prestige counts for much ... the dramatic capture of Baghdad sounded throughout the East. These were amongst the finest feats in military history, and they had a magical effect on the fame and position of Britain throughout the whole of the East.' Maude's triumph in Baghdad had destroyed Germany's 'cherished dream'.[21]

Maude was buried on 19 November in the then bleak, unwalled desert cemetery beyond the North Gate in a crowded funeral attended by the great and the good of Baghdad, together with numerous devoted officers. Bell thought the burial service 'more than usually thin and unconvincing in that wide desert', until the 'indescribably stirring conclusion' of the bugles sounding the Last Post across the city. 'I knew him very little,' she wrote, while acknowledging his gifts as a military commander. 'He was always very polite and agreeable but not interesting.'[22]

Maude's grave is marked by a large, damaged memorial in Baghdad's North Gate War Cemetery just off the busy Safi al Din al Hilli Road in the Waziriya district of Rusafa, a poor part of town opposite a section of the Baghdad University campus and the old Bab al Muadham neighbourhood. In the same cemetery lie the graves of the British and Indian officers and men who perished during the death march from Kut and in the prison camps of Anatolia. Many of their headstones and crosses were damaged or destroyed during the violence that swept over the city like an avenging angel in the aftermath of the American-led invasion in 2003. 'There were many car bombs and mortar attacks in this area – Al Qaeda and other militias,' said Jasim Koli, the disconsolate guardian of the cemetery, during a visit one spring afternoon, pointing to a smashed stone cross tossed into the unmowed grass. Unlike the customary British war cemetery, pristine and scrupulously maintained, it is a ragged place, exhausted by neglect and surrounded by danger. There is a sign announcing a renovation of the site at the entrance but it is dated 1997 and has been shot up by a machine gun.

Of the 6,889 Commonwealth casualties buried here, largely British and Indian, 4,160 are remembered by name:

- 5633 Sepoy Afzal Khan 126th Baluchistan Infantry died 3 October 1918
- 4770 Sergeant G. Anderson 13th Hussars died 5 March 1917
- 2779 Lance Daffadar Amin Chand 10th Duke of Cambridge's Own Lancers died 3 September 1920
- 2056 Private C. J. Aslett 7th Dragoon Guards died 7 October 1916
- JUM/1941 Driver Ashraf Khan Mule Corps died 28 September 1918

There are 2,729 unidentified burials, some sharing a common grave. The nameless dead are commemorated in that stock but deeply moving phrase used by the Commonwealth War Graves Commission:

A Soldier of the Great War – Known unto God

Walking along row after row of these toppled graves that stand like crooked teeth in this sun-cracked field, a death-filled enclave within a city that has known more war than most, is a briefly suffocating experience. This is a place of dignity and crushing sorrow. A memorial plaque reads 'These are they who came out of great tribulation.'[23]

*

From Maude's capture of the city in 1917 to the birth of the new nation of Iraq in 1921, the whirlwind of activity did not let up. There were keen internal rivalries and tensions within the British camp, with early divisions appearing between Cox and Maude over political administration. Further differences existed between T. E. Lawrence's 'Sharifian' camp – which sought to appoint as king a member of Sharif Hussain of Mecca's family, his sons Faisal and Abdullah were leading candidates – and Cox's deputy, Wilson – a committed opponent of Arab independence who favoured the idea of a high commissioner (Cox), without an Arab amir or other head of state, backed by Arab ministers with British advisers. Even on the civil side, differences ran deep. In one 'appalling scene' Wilson raged at Bell for her behind-the-scenes king-making and accused her of undermining official British policy.[24] Bell became a relentless advocate of Faisal, leader of the ongoing Arab Revolt against the Ottomans with his brother Abdullah and their Bedouin guerrilla forces, harrying enemy supply lines by repeatedly blowing up sections of the Hijaz railway and attacking Turkish garrisons, backed by Allied officers including Lawrence.* Although Lawrence later described the campaign as 'a sideshow to a sideshow', the Arab Revolt nevertheless helped tie down 30,000 Ottoman troops in the desert and hastened the defeat of the Turks.[25]

For some Baghdadis, it was not long before the gloss came off the British liberation. Contrary notes sounded across the Middle East and on the other side of the Atlantic. First, in the aftermath of the Bolshevik Revolution of 1917, the secret Sykes–Picot Agreement was exposed, revealing British and French designs in the region – to the intense embarrassment of the British, the glee of the Ottomans and the dismay and anger of the Arabs. 'Administratively absurd and morally lamentable', at a stroke it undermined Maude's proclamation with its apparent support for the 'cause of Arab freedom'.[26] On 8 January 1918, President Woodrow Wilson's Fourteen Points speech to Congress raised the prospect of self-determination. Then, like a bombshell, came the Anglo-French Declaration of 8 November 1918, calling for 'the establishment of indigenous Governments and Administrations in Syria and Mesopotamia'.[27] It was a rallying call to nationalists throughout the region. As a fuming Arnold Wilson recalled, 'it would have been difficult to arouse more sound and fury, not to speak of heart-burnings and intrigue, than have been created in Baghdad' by the declaration and the plebiscite that followed.[28]

The fires of resistance had already been kindled. In 1918 Al Ahd al Iraqi, the Iraqi Covenant, was formed as the Baghdad branch of Jamiat al Ahd, the Covenant Society, an underground group of Arab nationalist officers within the Turkish military, a number of whom had fought with Faisal during the Arab Revolt of 1916. In February 1919, after the British refused to allow an Al Ahd delegation to attend the peace talks in

---

* Abdullah later became the first Amir of Transjordan (1921–46) and then the first King of Jordan (1946–51), founder of the Hashemite monarchy which survives today.

Versailles, a rival resistance group, Haras al Istiklal, the Independence Guard, a majority Shia group, joined the fray in Baghdad under Mohammed al Sadr, son of the distinguished Shia Ayatollah Hassan al Sadr* (the Sadr name would return in the aftermath of the 2003 invasion). Revolution was in the air.

In 1919 Arnold Wilson arranged a rigged plebiscite, consulting tribal leaders – rather than the general population – across Iraq on their views towards 'a single Arab state under British tutelage' and whether it should be placed under an 'Arab emir'.[29] It reported the vast majority in favour of continued British control.

In March 1920 Grand Ayatollah Shirazi issued a *fatwa* prohibiting cooperation with the occupying forces, a policy that ceded political space, influence and ultimately power to the minority Sunni population. Yet resistance to British rule was by no means confined to the Shia. On 23 April a meeting was held in Baghdad behind the studded closed doors of Hamdi Baban, a Kurdish grandee. Present were those leading the movement for independence, including Mohammed al Sadr; Yusef Suwaidi, his Sunni counterpart; Jafar Abu al Timan, a prosperous Shia merchant; Rifat Chadirchi, a Sunni landowner in his seventies; the Sunni Sheikh Said Nakhshbandi and his brother the judge Abdul Wahab al Naib; Fuad al Daftari, formerly a representative of Baghdad in the Ottoman parliament; Sheikh Ahmed al Daud; and Fatah Pasha, a Sunni landowner from Kirkuk.

If growing numbers of Baghdadis were beginning to wonder whether their destinies were being decided not by their own leaders but by the Great Powers, as the Paris Peace Conference of 1919 had strongly indicated, two days later the San Remo Conference of 25 April 1920 – scrambled together to divide up the Ottoman Empire within days of Syria declaring its independence – lit the nationalist fuse. It granted Britain a League of Nations Mandate over Mesopotamia, with responsibility for creating a modern state out of the three former Ottoman vilayets of Baghdad, Basra and Mosul. London no longer seemed so interested in Arab freedom. 'Instead of enjoying Arab rule with a measure of British assistance, the people found themselves subjected to British rule with nominal Arab assistance.'[30] Al Ahd al Iraqi, which in March had declared

---

* An ayatollah, from the Arabic *Ayatu Allah* (Sign of God), is a senior cleric within the Shia hierarchy, an acknowledged master of Islamic law and philosophy.

the independence of Iraq – envisaged as the three Ottoman vilayets of Baghdad, Basra and Mosul, under Amir Abdullah, brother of Faisal and son of Sharif Hussain of Mecca – now issued a proclamation calling on the people to resist. Within weeks, much of today's Iraq was in full rebellion.

From Kerbala came a fiery *fatwa* declaring service in the new British administration unlawful. The Iraqi political scientist Ghassan Atiyah, author of a study of early twentieth-century Iraq, records a British police report noting that 'Bolshevik talk in Baghdad is on the increase.'[31] Soon the mosques of Baghdad, Sunni and Shia alike, thundered to impassioned calls to resist the infidel occupiers. There was a sudden and remarkable unity between these frequently adversarial sects, such that traditional Sunni Maulud services in honour of the Prophet Mohammed's birth were also held in Shia mosques and even combined with the Shia Taziya rituals of condolences on the martyrdom of Hussain. Mass meetings assumed an alarming momentum. Nationalist poetry and patriotic speeches coursed through the city. The arrest of a young government employee for making a speech deemed 'dangerous to public order' was the trigger for unrest and a mass demonstration. The British sent in armoured cars, the mob attacked them and shots were fired over heads. Beneath the shimmering blue dome of Haydar Khana Mosque, fifteen Baghdad notables, styled *mandubin*, or delegates, were elected to negotiate with the administration. Wilson agreed to meet them at the Saray on 2 June, together with an additional twenty-five prominent Baghdadis – including Jews and Christians, communities not represented amongst the original fifteen. The atmosphere was tense, and feelings were running high. Wilson apologized for the delay in establishing civil government but was met with demands for a national Arab government. There were 'shouts of abuse and hisses', which Wilson considered were 'intended as a sort of declaration of war'.[32] Writing to her father on 14 June, Bell spoke of the growing 'passions of the mob' and the nationalists' 'reign of terror'. She thought the answer was Faisal's brother Abdullah. 'Abdullah is a gentleman who likes a copy of the Figaro every morning at breakfast time. I haven't any doubt we should get on with him famously.' 'Bagsful of letters' were going to the tribes daily calling for all-out resistance. Bell doubted whether there would be a revolt, but it was 'touch and go'.[33]

Notwithstanding Bell's doubts, armed rebellion broke out across the

Euphrates within two weeks of her letter and quickly spread, following British arrests of tribal leaders. The size of the British Army was then a little over 60,000, consisting of 53,000 Indian troops and 7,200 British, of whom 26,000 were non-combatants.[34] With such limited forces at his disposal, General Sir Aylmer Haldane, recently appointed General Officer Commanding, could not immediately contain a revolt that within weeks had travelled up the Euphrates, right across Iraq and into the Kurdish north. In August, Najaf and Kerbala declared *jihad*. As the atmosphere became more hostile, Jews and Christians in Baghdad fretted for their future in Iraq. During the inferno of midsummer, rebels were in charge right across Iraq with the exception of the three main cities of Baghdad, Basra and Mosul. Security was concentrated in Baghdad, epicentre of the nationalist camp, where by August the rebels found organized public opposition almost impossible. The British were forced to resort to overwhelming force – including the bombing of the holy city of Kufa, sacred to the Shia as the site where Ali, cousin and son-in-law of Mohammed, was killed in 661 – to suppress the revolt.

Public opinion in Britain was turning against this expensive adventure in the desert. Writing in the *Sunday Times* on 22 August, disillusioned by the post-war realpolitik, T. E. Lawrence warned, 'The people of England have been led in Mesopotamia into a trap from which it will be hard to escape with dignity and honour.' It was an excoriating article that condemned Wilson's 'bloody and inefficient' administration as a 'disgrace to our imperial record', worse than the Turkish system it had replaced. While Istanbul had used 14,000 local conscripts and killed a yearly average of 200 Arabs to keep the peace, Britain kept 90,000 men with aeroplanes, armoured cars, gunboats and armoured trains, and had already 'killed about ten thousand Arabs' that summer. 'How long will we permit millions of pounds, thousands of Imperial troops, and tens of thousands of Arabs to be sacrificed on behalf of a form of colonial administration which can benefit nobody but its administrators?'

Wilson's time at the British helm in Iraq was drawing to a close, hastened by an uprising that cost what many in Britain felt was an unforgivable quantity of blood and treasure: £40 million, three times the subsidy given to the Arab Revolt, and an estimated 6,000 Iraqis and 500 British and Indian soldiers killed.[35] A shattered Wilson described himself in a letter to his mother of September 1920 as 'a radical young man trying unsuccessfully to introduce radical principles into the wholly unfruitful and stony soil of a savage country where people do not argue but shoot'.[36] The British, who did their fair share of shooting, only regained order by the end of October, by which time Cox had returned to replace Wilson and form a provisional Arab government.

Combing through the British archives of this time, there is an occasional air of unreality about the official record. In his annual report for 1920, for instance, Lieutenant Colonel W. B. Lane, inspector-general of civil jails in Mesopotamia, euphemistically wrote on 20 March 1921 of 'an eventful year'. Baghdad Central Jail had housed 1,934 convicts. The disturbances had required the opening – and subsequent enlargement – of a new, barbed-wire, extra-mural jail at Bab al Wastani. On 21 June there was a 'concerted attempt at escape'. The prison warders' buckshot ammunition merely aroused 'contempt'. Rifles and ball ammunition concentrated the prisoners' minds, 'and no trouble occurred.' On 29 July, as Baghdad braced itself for another turbulent procession from Kadhimiya, there was once more an escape attempt. Prisoners rushed two British warders, who fended off the attackers with revolvers, shooting dead two prisoners and wounding six.[37]

One of the most lasting and damaging consequences of the Iraq Revolt was to bring to the surface again the age-old differences between Sunni and Shia. Gertrude Bell's description of the majority population as 'primitive' and 'Shiah obscurantists' was the prevailing British view. The Shia believed they had dealt the death blow to the British military occupation, only to see themselves largely excluded from power.

'To show how fully the Arab populace believed that we were beaten I am told that seven men who were Court Martialled and shot at the Military Prison for attacking a sentry, when entering that Prison, laughed and joked saying that it was no use their being put there because the British would be out of the country in a fortnight,' Lane noted.

As the Iraqis discovered, the British would not be leaving quite so quickly.

*

At exactly 6 a.m., on 23 August 1921 – following months of feverish plotting and interminable bureaucratic infighting in Baghdad, London and Cairo, an abortive stint on the throne in Damascus, another rigged plebiscite and a stage-managed but lukewarm reception on his arrival in Basra – Faisal emerged from his apartments in the great Saray. Clad from head to toe in khaki, he descended the steps flanked by Sir Percy Cox, resplendent in white diplomatic uniform covered in ribbons and stars; General Sir Aylmer Haldane, ramrod straight in military uniform; Faisal's topee-wearing adviser Colonel Kinahan Cornwallis; and a gaggle of brisk-footed ADCs. They entered the vast courtyard and paced along the long path of carpets, past the guard of honour of the 1st Battalion Dorsetshire Regiment, to a three-foot-high dais, watched every step of the way by a crowd of 1,500 grandees, senior officials and tribal leaders who stood up to receive them. With the party were Mahmud al Gailani, the eldest son of the *nakib* of Baghdad (who was too elderly to attend), and Hussain Afnan, secretary of the Council of State. Those Baghdad notables who arrived late at the Saray were, to their great shock and disgust, barred from entering by Arab police officers.

The thirty-six-year-old Faisal took his seat on a hastily improvised throne made from packing-case wood that was said to betray the distinctly unIslamic signs of its origin: Asahi Beer.[38] As the dignitaries settled in their seats, Faisal looked along the front row, spotted Gertrude Bell, caught her eye and received a discreet salute in return. Bell thought Faisal looked 'very dignified but much strung up – it was an agitating moment'. Then Hussain Afnan stood up and read a proclamation written by Cox, announcing that Faisal had been elected king by 96 per cent of the people of Mesopotamia – long live King Faisal I of Iraq!

Out came the new national flag. Extending from its mast, over horizontal stripes of black, white and green, was a red triangle containing two white seven-point stars, a design inspired by the flag held aloft during the Arab Revolt. In the absence of an Iraqi national anthem, the band played 'God Save the King'. As the twenty-one-gun salute thundered across Baghdad, Mahmud al Gailani struggled to make his prayers heard. Faisal then stood to address his people. He thanked Iraqis for electing him as their ruler and expressed his gratitude to the British for their support and sacrifices towards the Arab cause of liberation. He reminded his audience of Iraq's glorious history. Yet the former 'cradle of civilization and prosperity and the centre for science and knowledge' had tragically declined since those heady days. 'Security was lost, anarchy ruled, work became scarce, the waters of the two great rivers were lost in the bottom of the sea, the land that was once lush and fertile became barren.' Only solidarity would allow Iraq to grow great again. Faisal called on all his countrymen, regardless of religion, tribe or sect, to unite.

'For me nobody is distinguished except by knowledge and ability. The nation, as a whole, is my party. I have no other.'[39] Concluding with this rousing call to Iraqi patriotism, Faisal pledged to hold parliamentary elections and establish democratic government with British help. The coronation ceremony came to an end, the crowd dispersed, and Mesopotamia had become Iraq, a new nation with a new king. 'It was an amazing thing to see all Iraq, from north to south gathered together,' Bell wrote. 'It is the first time it has happened, in history.'[40]

The official photos of the coronation leave little doubt about the real power quite literally behind the throne. Faisal, a slight man, is a shrunken figure dwarfed by the high-backed throne and the towering figures of Cox, Cornwallis and Haldane, who stand around him. The preponderance of military hats, topees and ladies' sunhats in the front row likewise make Britain's driving role unmistakable.

For all Britain's overweening influence, this was also a time when the leading figures in Baghdad began to assume a more prominent role in the political life of the city – and of the newly formed Iraq. The pool of rich, powerful families in the capital was not especially large. Putting the biggest merchants and most renowned religious leaders to one side, there were probably only around twenty leading families in the city. As often as not they were mired in feuds, not unlike the families of medieval Italy. Their names – Pachachi, Suwaidi, Chadirchi, Chorbachi, Chalabi, Daghestani, Shawi, Rawi, Daftari and Kubba – recur regularly in the lists of ministers until the military coup of 1958. Some of this first generation of Iraqi politicians were the grandfathers of the generation of politicians that rose to prominence after the American-led invasion of 2003.

Thus the Cabinet formed on 10 September, under the premiership of Abdul Rahman al Gailani, the doddery *nakib* of Baghdad, contained some very familiar faces. The minister of finance, for example, was the prominent Baghdad Jew Sassoon Eskell, who had represented Baghdad in every parliament in Istanbul since 1908, had held ministerial office and was 'probably the man who carried most weight' after the *nakib*, according to British officials. 'His wisdom and integrity are universally appreciated.' The minister of defence was Jafar Pasha al Askari, a former major-general of Faisal, recently returned from a year as governor of Aleppo under the Arab government of Syria and a veteran of the Arab Revolt. In the absence of Hassan Pachachi, who did not want to abandon his lucrative private legal practice, the distinguished lawyer Naji al Suwaidi was appointed minister of justice. The education ministry went to the famous Shia cleric Mohammed Ali al Shahristani. Izzat Pasha Kirkuli, a native of Kirkuk originally of Turkish descent, who had held high military office under the Ottomans and earned 'a great reputation throughout Mesopotamia', was appointed minister of works.[41]

Shia participation in what many Iraqis considered a British puppet government was controversial in Baghdad. When Abdul Hussain Chalabi was appointed education minister in 1922, the year in which the RAF assumed command of British forces in Iraq until the Second World War, Sheikh Mahdi Khalisi, an influential cleric in Kadhimiya, accused him of heresy, banned him from the gold-domed shrine for breaking the *fatwa* and stuck up posters on the walls of the shrine explicitly forbidding him from entering.[42]

For much of the next four decades, Baghdad was home to a protracted struggle for influence between Britain and Iraq. The city was riven by violent, frequently fatal, divisions between the pro-British camp and the rising tide of nationalists, led by new Shia political parties such as Watani (Nationalist), Nahda (Awakening) and Hizb al Hurr (Free Party). Within a year of Faisal's coronation, and to their great shock, Cox and Bell were heckled in the grounds of Kasr al Rihab, the Royal Palace, as they offered their congratulations to the king on the anniversary of his accession to the throne. Led by royal officials, a crowd of 400 nationalists shouted, 'Down with the mandate!'[43]

Opposition to the British Mandate was widespread, and often fierce. Resistance to the Anglo-Iraqi Treaty – intended to put a more palatable gloss on the mandate's fiction of full Iraqi sovereignty – was also vehemently expressed, in print and in more forceful ways. It was eventually signed in 1922, ratified in 1924 and then replaced with a new treaty in 1930, by which time a number of oil discoveries had increased Iraq's importance to Britain.

Oil was rarely out of the picture after this. From 1928, the reconstituted Turkish Petroleum Company, along with the Shell Group, the Anglo-Persian Oil Company, the Compagnie Française des Pétroles and the Near East Development Corporation of the US as its principal shareholders, dominated the field. As Stephen Hemsley Longrigg noted drily, 'The claims put forward by the heirs of the late Sultan Abdul Hamid, a formidable body of Turkish princes and princesses, to the ownership of all the oil of the old Ottoman Empire, and much besides, were not then or later taken seriously in Iraq.'[44]

*

Beyond the ever-boiling world of Iraqi politics was Gertrude Bell, who bequeathed Baghdad – and Iraq – a lasting cultural legacy in the form of the Iraq Museum. Appointed Honorary Director of Antiquities in 1922, a year later she founded what was initially called the Baghdad Archaeological Museum with a view to housing and preserving the country's precious ancient objects, which dated from the earliest human civilizations of Sumer and Akkad to the Assyrian, Babylonian, Mesopotamian and Iraqi eras. Before this, the international archaeological expeditions from Europe and America that were already returning to Iraq were taking their finds to foreign shores. A plaque in the museum, which in 1966 was relocated to its present site in the Salihiya district of western Baghdad, commemorates her achievement in creating this profoundly important institution, which represented a shared history and national lifeblood for the new country.

GERTRUDE BELL

Her memory the Arabs will always hold in reverence and affection.

She created the Museum in 1923

Being then Honorary Director of Antiquities for the Iraq

With wonderful knowledge and devotion

She assembled the most precious objects in it

And through the heat of Summer

Worked on them until the day of her death

On 12th July, 1926

King Faisal and the Government of Iraq

In gratitude for her deeds in this country

Have ordered that the Principal Wing shall bear her name

And with their permission

Her friends have erected this Tablet

Bell's extraordinarily voluminous correspondence from Baghdad provides vivid descriptions of life in the city from 1917 to her death in

1926. The domestic scenes that she evokes are particularly charming. In July 1920 she is hand-feeding fried egg to a baby mongoose, a gift from the son of the mayor of Baghdad. In August 1922 she writes of an evening bathing and picnicking party with the king: 'We roasted great fishes on spits over a fire of palm fronds – the most delicious food in the world – I brought carpets and cushions and hung old Baghdad lanterns in the tamarisk bushes where we kept simple state in the rosy stillness of the sunset. "This is peace!" said the King. "This is happiness!" We lay on our cushions for a couple of hours after dinner . . . I have seldom passed a more enchanting evening.'[45]

There are games of bridge with Faisal, tea parties, church prize-givings, excursions to watch patriotic plays, regular complaints about the pitiless heat, ridings out to meet notables in their mulberry arbours, dinner parties with visiting MPs and secretaries of state, starry palace banquets, grand balls at the Residency, affectionate asides about the king's son and heir, Ghazi, 'a dear little boy with charming manners', disquisitions on the health of her beloved spaniel Peter. In later years, fending off personal unhappiness and the loss of her professional status as king-maker-in-chief, she charts progress at the museum, worries about cataloguing difficulties and makes plans for the Babylonian, Assyrian and Arab rooms. 'I foresee that I shall be very boring about museums for some time to come!'[46]

Bell's unexpected death during the early hours of 12 July 1926 – attributed to poisoning by sleeping pills – caused a sensation and profound sense of loss in Baghdad. Her funeral that evening was attended by Iraq's leaders and the Regent Ali representing King Faisal. Mourners and troops lined the streets. Grief at Bell's death, just short of her fifty-eighth birthday, was not confined to the pro-British camp. *Al Alam al Arabi*, the nationalist newspaper, praised her astonishing commitment and achievements. 'The true sincerity of her patriotism, free from all desire for personal gain, and the zeal for the interests of her country which illuminated the service of this noble and incomparable woman makes her an example to all men of Iraq.'[47]

Her sandstone tomb lies, like that of Maude, in a tatty graveyard full of broken headstones: the British Cemetery in the traffic-choked district of Bab al Sharji. Few visitors make it here these days. In 2005, Tamara Chalabi, the writer and daughter of Ahmed Chalabi, the Iraqi politician, planted a ring of jasmine trees and date palms around the grave 'in recognition of Gertrude Bell's historic contribution to Iraq'. When I visited it some time later, despite the best efforts of the grave keeper Ali Mansur, most had died.

*

While nationalist newspapers bashed the British, berated the Cabinet and railed against the 'slavery' imposed by the treaty – prompting in response a 'Law for the prohibition of harmful propaganda' – development in Baghdad accelerated in the early twentieth century. Traditionally neglected, education started to receive greater focus within the city. Al al Bait University, an initiative of King Faisal, opened its doors in 1923, initially offering a single course in Islamic theology before broadening its curriculum. An American secondary school for boys opened in 1921, one for girls in 1925. A modern fire service was introduced, and street lighting started to illuminate the darkest depths of the city's thoroughfares.

Al Rashid Street grew ever livelier in front of its arcade, as memoirs attest, carrying a noisy and eclectic stream of traffic through the city: barefoot pilgrims, tribal visitors from the Euphrates, grain merchants, Jewish clerks and accountants, British businessmen, irrigation experts, political advisers, tattooed, kohl-eyed girls tottering beneath trays of yoghurt precariously balanced on their heads. From neighbouring Samaual Street came the cries of the mobile food-sellers offering *turshi* (pickled vegetables) and boiled egg with mango pickle sandwiches. By the 1930s, gramophones in cafés were blaring out the latest Egyptian love songs and traditional Iraqi melodies; live entertainment took the form of weekly poems from Mullah Aboud Karkhi and songs from popular singers such as Sultana Yusef, Zakiya George, the falsetto Rashid al Kundarchi, the Jewish cantor Yusef Huresh and, perhaps the most glamorous of all, Salima Pasha, the moon-eyed, rosy-lipped heart-throb of Baghdad.[48]

Western-style hotels, a handful of European shops, numerous commercial agencies and three banks – the Eastern, the Ottoman and the Imperial Bank of Persia – catered for the growing number of foreign visitors to a city on the move. In 1924 the doors of the chic Alwiya Club, where Gertrude Bell would spend long evenings hobnobbing in the last few years of her life, opened for the first time. The club remains a pillar of the city's establishment today.

One of the many travellers who descended on Baghdad around this time was Donald Maxwell, a naval reserve officer who had been an official artist to the Admiralty during the First World War. His memoir *A Dweller in Mesopotamia: Being the Adventures of an Official Artist in the Garden of Eden*, teems with evocative pictures of his travels across Mesopotamia, undertaken for the Imperial War Museum. His experiences of Baghdad were mixed. By night he found the city alluring, if not quite equal to his romantic imagination, fed by the splendour of Harun al Rashid and the overwrought world of *The Arabian Nights*. Moonlit skies revealed *guffas* gliding across the Tigris in the wake of the chugging steamer *Puffing Billy*, silhouettes of slender minarets, narrow streets beneath elaborately latticed projecting windows. By day, however, the sun bludgeoned colour out of this enchanted cityscape to reveal earthier realities. 'We expect so much when we come to the real Baghdad, and we find so little,' Maxwell wrote, 'so little, that is, of the glamour of the East. Few "costly doors flung open wide", but a great deal of dirt. Few dark eyes of ravishingly beautiful women peering coyly through lattice windows, but a great deal of sordid squalor. Few marvellous entertainments where we can behold the wonderful witchery of Persian dancing girls, but a theatre, the principal house of amusement in Baghdad – and lo, a man selling onions to the habitués of the stalls!'[49] There was one unexpected perk. Having failed to see Oscar Asche's musical comedy hit *Chu Chin Chow* in London, Maxwell managed to fight his way through crowds of camels, beggars, British officers and Ford cars – an increasing presence on the streets – to watch Ali Baba, 'the wine-bibbing babbler of Bagdad', being sent up on his home turf. Baghdad was captivated by the show.

Expecting softly swaying palm trees and burnished golden domes, travellers were often disappointed to find their carefully cherished dreams swamped by the ubiquitous Mesopotamian mud. Mud featured highly in Maxwell's account of Baghdad. Even the Tigris was 'café au lait' rather than limpid blue. 'I have often thought since these days of mud in Mesopotamia that a vast fortune might be made by some one who could find a commercial use for a substance, as slippery as oil, as indelible in staining properties as walnut juice, and as adhesive as fish glue.'[50] The extraordinary prevalence of mud, easily forgotten in a modern Baghdad submerged beneath asphalt and cement, was remarked upon by the English traveller and writer Robert Byron in 1937:

It is a mud plain, so flat that a single heron, reposing on one leg beside some rare trickle of water in a ditch, looks as tall as a wireless aerial. From this plain rise villages of mud and cities of mud. The rivers flow with liquid mud. The air is composed of mud refined into a gas. The people are mud-coloured; they wear mud-coloured clothes, and their national hat is nothing more than a formalised mud-pie. Baghdad is the capital one would expect of this divinely favoured land. It lurks in a mud fog; when the temperature drops below 110, the residents complain of the chill and get out their furs. For only one thing is it now justly famous: a kind of boil which takes nine months to heal, and leaves a scar.[51]

The indomitable explorer Freya Stark arrived in Baghdad in 1931. Her love of the East had been kindled at the age of nine when an aunt gave her a copy of *The Arabian Nights* for her birthday. Years later Charles Doughty's *Arabia Deserta* led her to immerse herself in the Middle East. Her portraits of Baghdad for the *Baghdad Times* were collected and published as *Baghdad Sketches* in 1932. There are amusing asides on her smelly slum lodgings, where a miasma surged up from her cistern every night like a 'Babylonian fiend', making her wonder whether a Sumerian ancestor may not have been buried beneath the courtyard. In Baghdad, she reckoned, 'happiness and sanitation are not held to have any particular connection'. The land was so low and flat that there was no question of drainage. 'This is what makes it so depressing for Officers of Health and so amusing for people who like to study microbes.'[52] One of her most enchanting vignettes is the description of a boat ride across the 'lion-coloured' river to a dinner party with the cunning, watery-eyed Old Salih the boatman, a 'rather disreputable-looking old Charon' who kept a trail of thrashing fish threaded alongside the boat. 'Kindness to fish did not enter into Salih's catalogue of merits, but he was great on fasting, which is a lucky virtue to be fond of if one is very poor.'[53] One day, after a generous advance of 10 rupees from Stark, he vanished altogether, never to be seen again.

Stark was entranced by the life of the Tigris, with its myriad craft from all the ages of man, its barefoot, river-bank traffic with women carrying water jars on their shoulders, the low winter mists and 'yellow slabs of sunset shallows' when the water buffaloes came down to drink. Perhaps her favourite time of year was the holy fasting month of Ramadan: after a drowsy day the city would suddenly leap to life and she would leave a gathering of women friends discussing their variously unsatisfactory husbands and wander through crowded streets after midnight. 'It is always strange and like a dream to walk in starlight among the narrow ways: but now in Ramadan it is fantastic. The whole city rustles and moves and whispers in its labyrinthine alleys like a bee-hive swarming in the dark. One cannot distinguish faces; the murmuring figures glide by like flowing water.'[54] Unlike some of her fellow travellers, Stark reserved her fiercest criticism for the British. She was particularly unimpressed by the expatriate women of Baghdad, whom she felt tended towards the rude and ignorant. Stark's travels forced a dreadful conclusion: 'The British appear to be popular wherever they go until they come to settle with their wives.'[55]

For many Baghdadis, British culture was intoxicating (often literally), sometimes mystifying, frequently reviled. Alcohol was widely available and abused. Historically despised, dogs were suddenly doted upon by the pith-helmeted brigade, whose wives seemed not to know their place. Most shockingly of all, there was a lot of flesh on display. As Richard Coke noted in the later 1920s,

the present-day European, with his free and easy manners, his love of strong drink and dogs, his brusque contempt for the little courtesies of life, is the very opposite of what the Arab has been brought up to consider becoming in a gentleman. Even more so does this apply to his consort, the modern European lady, with her loud voice and mannish appearance, her cocktails, her long cigarette-holder, her habit of appearing at public functions in clothes that leave practically nothing to the imagination. The respectable husband or father, far from being impressed with the value of the Western lady's 'freedom', thanks God in his heart that his womenfolk are not as the woman of the unbeliever.[56]

For a time, at least in the most glittering circles of Baghdad society, this spirit caught on – and the shapeless, all-covering *abayas* came off. Among the many wonderful pictures from the family archive of Tamara Daghestani, granddaughter of Field Marshal Mohammed Fadhil Pasha al Daghestani, there is a series taken from a Red Crescent fashion show held in Baghdad's Al Amana hall in the early 1950s. Elegant models in floral-print summer dresses, natty suits and floor-length, décolleté ball gowns sashay boldly down the catwalk, gazed at admiringly by rows of glamorous, unveiled women. Speaking in 2011, Tamara said, 'Some of my younger friends are rather scandalized by it. When they see my beautiful mother in a low-cut dress, they ask me what on earth she is wearing. I tell them, "You've all gone backwards!" The older ones love it. It makes them proud to be Iraqi. What's tragic is that you could never imagine it happening today.'[57]

*

From the very beginnings of Baghdad and the era of its founder, Caliph Mansur, who (as we saw in Chapter 1) liked to keep the bodies of his many victims preserved in a subterranean storeroom with their names and genealogies sewn into their ears, strongmen have been an inescapable part of the city's story. All-powerful Abbasid caliphs, brutal Mongol and Turkic conquerors, Turkmen tribal chiefs, Iranian shahs, Ottoman sultans and pashas, overweening Mamluks, aghas and Janissaries – all made themselves masters of the City of Peace by shedding blood on a grand scale. Whatever their many differences, they were united in one important respect: none suffered from squeamishness.

In the first half of the twentieth century, a new strongman emerged to fit the changing, less bloody, character of the times. His name began to appear with monotonous regularity in the long list of Iraqi Cabinets from the early 1920s to 1958. Appointed defence minister on 20 November 1922, having already served as the first director-general of the Iraqi police force, Nuri al Said (The Happy One) was rarely absent from the Cabinet for the next thirty-six years, generally occupying the positions of foreign minister or defence minister when he was not serving one of eight terms as prime minister. He was first appointed premier in 1930; his last ministry was in 1958. Iraqis knew him by his nickname: The Pasha.

Said unquestionably had the right pedigree to play a leading role in Iraq. Born in 1888, he had been a member of the underground Al Ahd movement in Baghdad and had had a brilliant war in the desert with Faisal and Lawrence as a Baghdadi staff officer, later becoming chief-of-staff to Jafar Pasha al Askari, his brother-in-law. He commanded the Arab troops which took Damascus in 1918 and was rewarded with the position of chief-of-staff to Faisal during the latter's short-lived reign on the Syrian throne in 1920. Lawrence, not a man given to easy or excessive praise of his colleagues, thought Said's 'courage, authority and coolness' made him an ideal leader. 'Most men talked faster under fire, and acted a betraying ease and joviality,' he wrote.

'Nuri grew calmer.'[58] Meeting him for the first time in February 1921, Gertrude Bell was equally impressed. 'The moment I saw him, exceedingly slender and lithe, with a small pointed face and grey eyes that gradually awoke as he talked, I realized that we had before us a strong and supple force with which we must either work or engage in difficult combat – too difficult for victory.'[59]

Said, a pragmatist as much as an opportunist, announced his pro-British inclinations early, signing the Anglo-Iraqi Treaty of 1930, which conferred all responsibility for Iraq's defence and internal security on Baghdad, while granting Britain the right to move troops across Iraq, to supply advisers and materiel to the army, and to maintain two major RAF airbases in Iraq, one at Shaiba near Basra, the other at Habaniya near Baghdad. The treaty, always controversial, set the foundation for relations between Britain and Iraq for the next three decades, and established Said's pro-British credentials, which would ultimately cost him his life. In 1931, backed by a parliament stacked with his allies, Said pushed through an oil agreement that gave the Iraq Petroleum Company an exclusive concession in northern Iraq, together with tax exemptions, in return for annual payments of gold prior to any oil being exported. Although oil had been discovered near Kirkuk in 1927, it was not exported until 1934. Thanks to Said's scheme, oil revenues jumped from virtually nothing in 1930–31 to 20 per cent of all government income just a year later, going some way towards relieving the worst effects of the global depression.[60]

In the early years of King Faisal's reign, security in Baghdad was far from perfect, and for young women in particular life was especially dangerous. By far the greatest proportion of murders in the city – around 100 a week – was the killing of young women by their brothers for carrying on alleged affairs that had, in their eyes, dishonoured the girl and her family. 'The offending part of the woman's body was cut out with a knife.'[61] Unmarried pregnant women could also be taken to a remote place by their male relatives, killed and secretly buried in a practice known as *gasl al arar*, or washing away the shame. Subsequent autopsies revealed that a number of the accused women had been virgins. Women could also be killed for contacting their fiancé before the wedding night. The men who perpetrated these 'honour' killings were frequently praised by the newspapers for their 'noble' actions.[62]

From the arrival of the British in 1917, and especially in 1941–58, we find a 'Baghdad throbbing with a vigour long unknown, a middle class in continuous growth and already intensely articulate, a modern education still meagre in content but extending in bounds, paved roads, railroads and air services gradually spanning more and more of the country, a commerce still hesitant but in a lively mood.'[63]

For the country's elite, these were halcyon days. Faisal set the tone for this happier era, entertaining regularly in his palace, playing bridge in the evening, shooting black partridge in Amara. He took a particular interest in oil companies, the national budget and the Haifa–Baghdad railway. Lunchtimes would often see him motoring a few miles out of town to present a cup at the racecourse, where big crowds of horse-mad sheikhs in traditional robes and headdress shared paddocks with Europeans in suits and panamas, rushing between the Tote and the barrier to back one of their horses or another fancied, desert-bred mare. Arab jockeys milled about in bright jackets and peaked caps, with a few of the more traditionally minded sporting the head-cloth. Faisal watched the races from his special pavilion, often wearing his trademark, widely imitated fore-and-aft cap that Baghdadis called the *faisuliya*.[64]

Although the monarchy was intended to provide Iraq with a certain stability, political life continued with a turbulence that would have been familiar to the Abbasid caliphs of old. Baghdadis watched as governments came and went with bewildering speed. From 1920 to 1958 the average life of a Cabinet was just eight months. And, worryingly for Iraq's future, these early years of the monarchy had, in the eyes of many Shia, entrenched Sunni power through Faisal's patronage of the Sharifian officers with whom he had fought during the Arab Revolt.

In 1932, anxious to avoid further expense administering a turbulent and increasingly nationalist Iraq, the British joined forces with Iraq's rulers to declare the state-building process satisfactorily completed – despite manifest administrative, financial and military shortcomings. The British Mandate officially came to an end, and Iraq joined the League of Nations as an independent state, albeit still closely yoked to Britain.[65] On 20 June 1933, King Faisal travelled to London to mark the closing of an era, visiting Westminster Abbey and riding in state to Buckingham Palace in an open carriage with King George V, escorted by the Life Guards. In newsreel and photographs of the time the two men radiate monarchical splendour in military uniform, white-plumed hats, white gloves, regal moustaches and beards, a spaghetti of gold embroidery and innumerable medals across their chests.

This splendid picture was almost immediately eclipsed by tragedy. On 8 September, less than three months after the royal visit to Britain, the fifty-year-old Faisal died in Switzerland, where he had been receiving treatment for a weak heart. All of Iraq was plunged into mourning. The king's body was flown back for a state burial, and the streets of the capital were thronged with wailing women beating their breasts in a deafening display of mourning. Enormously popular, physically courageous, extraordinarily gallant, patient to the point of serenity and politically brave, Faisal had successfully steered Iraq towards independence – his great goal – had held the new nation together in the face of awesome challenges and put it on the path to modernity, notwithstanding the ethnic and sectarian fractures that always conspired to elicit bloodshed from peace. As the king wrote shortly before his death, in words that would surely have struck a chord with many Iraqi leaders from 1933 to the present: 'In Iraq, there is still – and I say this with a heart full of sorrow – no Iraqi people but unimaginable masses of human beings, devoid of any patriotic idea, imbued with religious traditions and absurdities, connected by no common tie, giving ear to evil, prone to anarchy, and perpetually ready to rise against any government whatever.'[66]

*

Crowned king in 1933, Faisal's only son, Ghazi – a twenty-one-year-old Arab nationalist with markedly different views towards British influence from those of his father – was quickly steeped in political intrigue. He supported the 1936 coup, led by General Bakr Sidki, which saw a civilian government replaced by a military regime, thereby earning Baghdad the dubious distinction of having hosted the first coup within the modern Middle East. On 29 October military planes rumbled over Baghdad, dropping leaflets signed by Sidki, self-proclaimed commander of the National Forces of Reform, demanding the resignation of Prime Minister Yasin al Hashimi. The army began to move on Baghdad, and the city came under bombardment. The government resigned; Said was exiled to Cairo, the prime minister to Istanbul; and Defence Minister Jafar al Askari, hero of the Arab Revolt, was murdered in an assassination that was duplicitous even by the standards of Baghdad. A precedent for military intervention to topple civilian governments had been set in Baghdad, one that would echo long over the Middle East and beyond.

Sidki was, depending on one's view of Iraqi history, uniquely ill-equipped or perfectly suited to take charge. He was the mastermind of the notorious massacre of Assyrians, descendants of the ancient Assyrians of Mesopotamia, when, on 11 August 1933, an Iraqi Army machine-gun company drove into the Assyrian Christian village of Simayl, north-west of Mosul, and methodically shot every man, following disturbances in the region. The number of those killed was 315, including four women and six children.[67] Overall, as many as 3,000 were killed in more than sixty villages during several days, most of them in cold blood. As part of the subsequent cover-up, the massacre was presented as a combination of Assyrian rebellion, British conspiracy to undermine and control the country and the heroic patriotism of the Iraqi Army, whose soldiers were rewarded by victory parades in Mosul and Baghdad, where triumphal arches were erected with melons pierced with daggers representing severed Assyrian heads. According to the Iraqi writer Kanan Makiya, the Simayl massacre was 'the first genuine expression of national independence in a former Arab province of the Ottoman Empire'.[68] Faithful to the long tradition of Iraqi regime change, Sidki was himself murdered in 1937.

The atmosphere in Baghdad in the late 1930s darkened. The Palestine Question, dominated by an intensifying conflict between Jews and Arabs and increased Jewish emigration from Germany, hardened opinions against the Jewish population. The Nazi regime's increasing engagement with Baghdad achieved the same end. Berlin offered long-term credit, invited schoolboys to Youth Rallies in Berlin and spread Nazi propaganda to willing ears within the Iraqi Army. Baghdadis who tuned into the Arabic-language broadcasts of Radio Berlin grew used to the daily greeting from its blue-eyed Iraqi presenter Yunis Bahr, a friend of the Nazi propaganda minister Joseph Goebbels: 'This is Berlin. I greet the Arabs. My brothers, people of Iraq, swell out the earth.'[69] There were definite shades of the Hitler Youth too about the Futuwa, the Iraqi Youth Movement. In 1937 Ghazi established his own palace radio station, Al Zuhour, which he used to air nationalist critiques of British foreign policy; it was also used to make the claim, for the very first time, that Iraq had the right to sovereignty over the oil-rich British protectorate of Kuwait, sowing the seeds for future bloodshed and tragedy. Sympathies for Hitler grew, and in 1938 bombs were thrown in Baghdad's Jewish quarters. In late 1939 Baghdad received a famous, destabilizing visitor when Haj Amin al Hussaini, the grand *mufti* of Jerusalem, leader of the failed 1936–9 Arab nationalist uprising against British colonial rule in Palestine, was granted sanctuary in the city. Over the next two years the man described by the British as an 'arch mischief-maker' became immensely influential within the Iraqi government, a lightning rod for the raging local opposition to a Jewish home in Palestine.[70]

Amid the turmoil in Baghdad, some things remained reassuringly – or perhaps defiantly – the same. The youthful Ghazi maintained a regal court with an extravagant hospitality to match. On 31 March 1937 a banquet was held in the king's honour in the royal palace. Entertaining the party as they consumed their ten-course meal were the royal musicians, who played ten pieces of music, opening proceedings with an overture from one of Suppé's operas, followed by a graceful serenade by Moszkowski and a Mascagni fantasy, together with pieces by Verdi, Strauss and Wagner. The sumptuous royal evening came to an end with a rousing aria from Verdi's *Aida*.

Like many young men, Ghazi liked sports cars. Unlike many men in their twenties, he could afford them and maintained an exotic fleet. Described as 'a brilliant high-speed motor driver' who had raced around Brooklands racetrack in England at the tender age of twelve, he was also a keen pilot and flew his own Percival Gull, a single-engined British racing aircraft.[71] Over the years Baghdadis had grown used to seeing the young king roaring about in sports cars such as the 150-horsepower Auburn Speedster. On 4 April 1939 the young king's taste for speed got the better of him, and Ghazi's reign ended in a thumping crash of metal when he smashed his convertible into an electric-light pole near the palace. He died several hours later from multiple head injuries. Suspicions about the death lingered in Baghdad, which had long provided fertile soil for conspiracy theories. Some of the more outlandish, enthusiastically encouraged by Radio Berlin, suggested that the British secret service had had the monarch murdered. Passions ran high, and tens of thousands attended the king's funeral in Baghdad. At Mosul, the British consul was attacked and killed by an angry mob.

But for the monarchy itself, life continued. The king was dead, long live the king. Ghazi's three-year-old son Faisal II was proclaimed king under the regency of his uncle Prince Abdul Illah. The succession was ensured, but there was little hope of stability. Governments continued to be appointed and just as quickly collapse in an increasingly febrile atmosphere. Although Baghdad was not directly involved, the outbreak of war in September 1939 made itself immediately felt. Prices rose in the markets, families stockpiled provisions, businesses panicked, and there was a run on the banks. A State of Emergency was declared. A cabal of four anti-British colonels, nicknamed 'The Golden Square', started to exercise growing power behind the scenes. Many leading Iraqis believed it was merely a matter of time before the Axis powers defeated Britain, and so secret channels were kept open to Berlin and Rome. Baghdad was bitterly divided between those, like Said, in favour of honouring the Anglo-Iraqi Treaty and the anti-British party of the generals, the press and much of the public

On 31 March 1940, after the latest Said administration had fallen after just six weeks, the nationalist lawyer Rashid Ali al Gailani, whom London considered virulently anti-British, became prime minister. London shuddered, whispered in the regent's ear, and Rashid Ali was prevailed upon to step down on 30 January 1941. Then, on 1 April, the drama intensified with a military coup in which Rashid Ali, backed by the Golden Square and buoyed by German promises of assistance against Britain, seized power and declared a Government of National Defence. Fearing for his life, the regent fled to the American envoy, who spirited him out of Baghdad, wrapped up in a carpet in the back of his American Legation car, to the RAF base at Habaniya; from there he was taken to Basra and then on to Amman. Pro-British politicians were arrested, many others fled, and relations between Britain and the new regime chilled to freezing point. With Germany scoring victories in the Balkans and North Africa, and the prospect looming of a breakthrough into the Middle East, Britain's position in Iraq suddenly looked distinctly precarious.

There followed one of the strangest conflicts of the Second World War. Overriding General Archibald Wavell, Britain's overstretched commanding general in the Middle East, who maintained he did not have enough troops to deploy to Iraq, Churchill ordered the mobilization of a force to safeguard British interests. Troops began arriving at RAF Shaiba near Basra on 17 April.

For the next month Baghdad was gripped by war and rumour. A blackout was imposed; schools and businesses were closed; radio stations broadcast interminable martial songs, military propaganda and threats to deal with the 'internal enemy' once Britain had been defeated. The grand *mufti*, spoiling for a fight, declared *jihad*. Jews, widely despised as British clients, were rounded up by the police, accused of assisting the enemy. A Jewish woman was detained for wearing an *abaya* through which a shiny silver button could be seen, supposedly a signal to the British planes overhead.[72]

On 29 April, 250 British civilians were evacuated from Baghdad and a further 500 took refuge in the British Embassy and the American Legation. Iraqi forces mounted a siege of Habaniya, and soon the skies over Baghdad thundered to the sound of Wellington and Blenheim bombers as the British bombed the attackers and destroyed the Royal Iraqi Air Force from the air. On 6 May a mob armed with cudgels and daggers surged into the Jewish Meir Elias hospital, where enemy agents were rumoured to have been based, shot the pharmacist dead, beat up patients, looted the buildings and set fire to the complex. After capturing Falluja on 19 May, British forces advanced east to Baghdad. The young Lieutenant Arthur Wellesley, the future eighth Duke of Wellington, was assigned to 'Habforce', a composite unit drawn up from elements of the 1st Cavalry Division and other infantry and artillery regiments. Its tortuous route from Palestine to Baghdad included a forced march across the desert with constant harrying by marauding tribesmen, occasional bombing by Messerschmitt Bf 110s and interminable delays brought on by floods and broken bridges and bunds caused by Iraqi demolitions of the Euphrates system. As they closed in on Baghdad, Lieutenant Wellesley and his troop came under heavy fire and were forced to dodge from dune to dune to escape enemy riflemen and Vickers machine guns. 'I felt like an Aunt Sally at a fairground shooting range but at the same time there was a little pang of exhilaration rather like jumping several big fences out hunting.' His first sight of the city, announced by the golden dome of the Kadhimain shrine, was 'tremendously impressive, a magnificent site' beyond acres of palm trees and open desert. Standing on the outskirts of Baghdad, he watched streams of refugees pouring out of the city. 'I heard a voice say, "What a sad, pathetic sight." It was Glubb Pasha, commander of the Arab Legion.'[73] Baghdad surrendered on 31 May. The following day the reinstalled regent, Abdul Illah, who had returned on a British destroyer, held a *majlis*, or assembly, in the Palace of Flowers. Public hangings of the officers behind the coup followed. For the British, the spring of 1941 was a victory; for one of the city's most ancient populations, it was an irrevocable tragedy.

*

On the night of 1 June, just when Baghdad's Jews thought the British success had delivered them from destruction and were celebrating the festival of Shavuot with spiced chicken and a bottle or two of *arak*, a chilling cry could be heard across the streets of the capital: 'Cutal al yehud!' ('Slaughter the Jews!').[74] Fires lit up the skyline, and marauding gangs surged through the streets. The violence had started earlier that afternoon, when demobilized soldiers started to attack Jews on the Khurr Bridge. The men in uniform were enraged to see Jews parading about in their finest clothes, which they mistakenly took to indicate a celebration of the British victory rather than the religious feast. Bodies of Jews, machine-gunned, stabbed or shot where they stood, started to turn up in different parts of the city. An Iraqi friend of Freya Stark reported he was 'wading in blood' in Ghazi Street.[75] At Bab al Sheikh, Jews were pulled off buses and beaten to death in the streets. From the old quarter of Bataween came the sickening screams of women being raped. Guided by the red hands and swastikas daubed across the doors of Jewish homes, the gangs conducted an orgy of slaughter. Babies and children were tortured and put to death with unfathomable cruelty. An elderly man who had refused to give up his savings had his throat slit.[76] In a mixed Jewish and Muslim quarter, a mob set a house alight and paraded through the streets gleefully holding up what one boy thought was a piece of meat: it was the breast of one of his mother's friends.[77] As the killing spread like a storm, Jews barricaded themselves in their cellars behind reinforced doors. Order broke down so completely that army and police officers led looting parties all along Rashid Street. Finally, on 2 June, a 5 p.m. curfew was imposed with security forces ordered to shoot on sight. Around 60–70 were shot dead that afternoon.

The number of Jews killed was estimated at around 200. The number of Muslims killed, consisting of rioters, members of the security forces and those who had tried bravely to defend their Jewish friends and neighbours, was even greater. Baghdad's Jews, who on the eve of this pogrom represented a third of the city's population, called the events of 1 and 2 June *farhud*, an Arabic word for violent dispossession. They had been failed by the Committee for Internal Security, by Iraqi police and army units and by the British forces on the edge of Baghdad, none of whom had lifted a finger to help them. For many it was the death-knell of any lingering hopes that they could ever really belong in the new Iraq. Conceived in Nazi hatred, exported to the heart of Mesopotamia, the Farhud pogrom shattered Jewish dreams and hastened the end of more than two millennia of largely peaceful coexistence. It was a tragedy from which Baghdad has never truly recovered.

The following years were to confirm the tragic wisdom of Jewish fears. In the aftermath of the foundation of the Israeli state in 1948, when Baghdad declared Zionism a capital offence, the city's Jews came under violent attack again. From July 1948 to December 1949, around 800 Jews were expelled from public positions without any compensation or benefits. Jewish businesses were harassed and hit with punitive taxes, Jewish banks had their licences revoked, and police swarmed through Jewish areas, using the discovery of a Zionist underground movement as an excuse to arrest and torture men and women at will.[78] In 1950 Israel passed the Law of Return, promising immediate citizenship to any Jew. 'Jews! Israel is calling you – come out of Babylon!' a Zionist manifesto proclaimed. A year later the Baghdad government allowed Jews to leave Iraq on condition – not disclosed at the time – that they forfeit their Iraqi nationality, together with all property and assets. They were allowed to take no more than $140 out of the country, together with 66 pounds of luggage. Removal of jewellery was explicitly forbidden. Sensing which way the wind was blowing, Iraqi Jews signed up in their tens of thousands. From May 1951 to early 1952 Israel's Operation Ezra and Nehemiah, also known as Operation Ali Baba, airlifted more than 120,000 Jews out of Iraq. By the end of the operation only 2,000 Jews from a population in Iraq of around 150,000 hung on in Baghdad. The prisoners of Nebuchadnezzar, a community which had lived in Iraq for twenty-five centuries, predating Christians and Muslims alike, had been hounded into near-extinction.

Among the few Jews who remained were wealthy families such as that of the young George Abda, whose father was a big landowner and estate agent who rented houses to the chief *kadi* and the Spanish and German ambassadors and was a confidant of government ministers. Born in 1942, Abda recalls innocent afternoons playing with homing pigeons, escaping on swimming expeditions on the Tigris in *dahur* rowing-boats and whiling away hours at Nadi Melhab, the Jewish Club,

practising tennis and volleyball. Every month the six-storey family home, complete with a French bathroom and an animal menagerie consisting of a gazelle, lambs, pigeons, cat, dog and chickens, played host to opulent all-night parties. 'There'd be a hundred people there drinking whisky and *arak* all night, with *makam* musicians and belly-dancers.*
Baghdad was very special in those days, and Jews were all right under the king. In the 1940s and 1950s they were almost running the country.' He sighs, perhaps contemplating his family's subsequent exile from Iraq in 1959. 'The problem is Baghdadis get very angry very quickly.'[79]

*

Divisions deepened within Iraqi society. In Baghdad the monarchy began to appear increasingly isolated, extravagantly removed from the concerns of the common people.

In 1946 the iconic Egyptian singer Oum Kalthoum, undisputed queen of Arab music to this day, arrived in Baghdad to sing at the youthful king's particularly opulent birthday celebrations. The Iraqi Communist Party rose as a potent mouthpiece for those who harboured grievances against a system of government that was a byword for repression and persecution, in which Britain still retained a uniquely privileged position. Extraordinarily, no other country was entitled to maintain an embassy in Baghdad until 1946. Elections were rigged; the power of the Sunni minority was entrenched; the Shia masses were disenfranchised (the first Shia prime minister, Salih Jabr, was appointed in 1948); political parties more often than not were merely vehicles for powerful personal interests; and life in the steaming slums was invariably nasty, consistently brutish and frequently short.

In early January 1948 Iraqis learnt, to their shock and, in many cases, disgust, that Britain and Iraq had been conducting secret negotiations. Signed on 15 January, the Portsmouth Treaty extended British military privileges and political influence for another twenty-five years. Strikes

---

* Drinking alcohol has a long history in Baghdad that dates back to Abbasid days and even earlier, with the ancient Christian communities and their taverns. When Kermit Roosevelt, the soldier son of the American president Theodore Roosevelt, reached the city while serving with British forces in Mesopotamia during the Great War, he spent a good deal of time drinking *arak* and whisky. 'The Koran's injunction against strong drink was not very conscientiously observed by the majority, and even those who did not drink in public rarely abstained in private,' he wrote. See his *War in the Garden of Eden*, p. 136.

were called, and soon the streets of Baghdad, the locus of so much dis-order and killing since the earliest days, were a mass of noise and fury. For Baghdadis, this was the *wathba*, or the leap, a protest movement on a grand scale, attended by members of the Communist, National Demo-cratic, Independence and Liberal parties, together with the urban masses. The police responded by firing indiscriminately into the marchers.

Crowds from Karkh surged past a police unit blocking their passage and swarmed on to the bridge in an effort to join forces with their fel-lows on the Rusafa bank. No sooner had the first of them set foot on the other side of the river than an armoured-car detachment unleashed 'piti-less fire' upon them, killing and wounding several immediately. Turning round in panic, the others tried to reach the opposite bank, but were 'spattered with machine-gun fire from the top of a khan in Suwaidi Square. The bleeding of the crowd was terrible. Bodies lay all over. Some were entangled in the iron of the bridge. Others had dropped into the river below and were carried along by the current.'[80]

*

After the turmoil of the 1940s, Baghdad enjoyed a rare period of stabil-ity and cultural renaissance. Iraqis of a certain age – and class – still go misty-eyed when the 1950s are brought up. 'Ah, those were the golden days for Baghdad,' an Iraqi friend told me once, with a wistful sigh. 'After all the wars and fighting that came before, and comparing it with the ugliness that followed, it was a glorious, elegant time.'

Awash with oil money, the city was coming of age in the twentieth century, attracting some of the world's most celebrated figures from academe and the arts. Moving away from the traditional dependence on British firms, the Iraqi government embarked on a series of major archi-tectural commissions, most of them modernist in spirit: the Italian architect and designer Gio Ponti created a building for the Ministry of Development and the Development Board, a body established in 1950 by Said to lead the country's charge into the modern era with the not incon-siderable assistance of 80 per cent of the country's oil revenues. Alvar Aalto of Finland was invited to design the National Art Gallery, William Dunkel of Zurich the central bank. Responding to the needs of an urban population that rose by 90 per cent to one million in the decade from 1947 to 1957 the government commissioned Constantinos Doxiadis, the Greek architect and town planner, to design extensive housing schemes

30. A Red Crescent fashion show in Baghdad's Al Amana Hall, early 1950s. 'Some of my younger friends are rather scandalized by it,' said Tamara Daghestani, granddaughter of Field Marshal Mohammed Fadhil Pasha al Daghestani, acting governor of Baghdad. Note the absence of hijabs.

31. A twentieth-century (1952) Hollywood take on the caliph and his harem. 'We hardly recognize her with her clothes on,' one reviewer wrote of its co-star Gypsy Rose Lee.

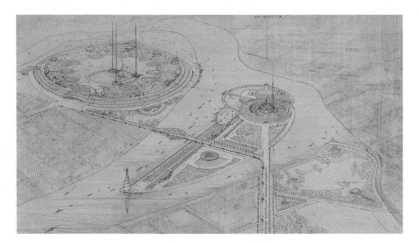

32. The American architect Frank Lloyd Wright's extraordinary design for central Baghdad, 1957. A 100-metre statue of Harun al Rashid rises from a spiral minaret modelled on Samarra's ninth-century Great Mosque on the island he named 'Edena' (centre), southwest of a million-dollar complex containing an opera house, cultural centre and museums. At top left is Baghdad University and at bottom right a botanical garden.

33. Jubilant crowds take to the streets of Baghdad on 14 July 1958, hours after the bloody military coup that overthrew the Iraqi monarchy and ushered in a new era of republican turbulence. The Baghdad mob has been a potent, unstable and often barbaric force in Iraqi politics since the foundation of the city.

34. Major-General Abd al Karim Kassem, leader of the 1958 coup (*bottom right*), chairs a public Cabinet meeting shortly after the revolution. Having survived an assassination attempt involving the young Saddam Hussein in 1959, the nationalist Kassem was executed and replaced by his former revolutionary comrade and pan-Arabist Abdul Salam Aref in 1963.

35. A 'perfect, masterly, cold-blooded, wicked, diabolic' display 'to gratify the Baath Party's lust for power', wrote the Jewish eyewitness Max Sawdayee of the regime's hanging of nine Jews in Liberation Square on 27 January 1969. 'It shakes one to the bones. It shakes even one's faith in humanity.'

36. Saddam Hussein, President of the Republic of Iraq (1979–2003). Saddam was also Chairman of the Council of Ministers, Commander-in-Chief of the Armed Forces, Chairman of the Revolutionary Command Council, General Secretary of the Regional Command of the Arab Baath Socialist Party, Leader-Struggler, Knight of the Arab Nation, Hero of National Liberation, etc.

37. Iraqi soldiers carry a wounded colleague in Baghdad during the Iraq–Iran War, 1981. Though most of the conflict was felt in the south, Baghdad still experienced the terror of rocket attacks and the grinding poverty brought on by the eight-year war. Henry Kissinger famously said of the conflict, 'A pity they both can't lose.'

38. American soldiers of the 3rd Infantry Division enter the Crossed Swords parade grounds during the battle for Baghdad, April 2003. The 'Victory Arch' was formally opened to the public in 1989 by Saddam, the 'Hero of Peace', to commemorate Iraq's 'defeat' of Iran. The dissident Kanan Makiya called it 'Nuremberg and Las Vegas rolled into one.'

39. U.S. Marine Corps Assaultman Kirk Dalrymple watches as a six-metre statue of Saddam Hussein is toppled in Firdus Square, central Baghdad, 9 April 2003. A British journalist described the event as 'the most staged photo-opportunity since Iwo Jima'.

40. 'Christians that remained have been tortured, killed and kidnapped.' Canon Andrew White, the Anglican 'Vicar of Baghdad', ministers to a mixed Chaldean, Assyrian, Orthodox and Armenian Catholic flock that has been savagely reduced by the raging violence of recent years. They speak Aramaic and Syriac, the most ancient of Christian languages.

41. Emad Levy, the last Rabbi in Baghdad, 28 September 2003. Dating back to the Babylonian Captivity in the sixth century BC, the Jewish population of Iraq, one of the oldest and most significant Jewish communities in the world, has been hounded almost into extinction.

42. 'This is one of the greatest catastrophes in the history of Baghdad. It's a crime against the heritage of mankind.' The late Dr Donny George, director of Baghdad's Iraq Museum, originally founded by Gertrude Bell, surveys the wreckage of the Assyrian Gallery in the aftermath of the looting of 8–12 April 2003.

43. Baghdad municipal workers remove the statue of the Abbasid caliph Al Mansur, founder of Baghdad, after it was hit by a bomb in October 2005.

44. Life continues: Baghdadis relax at the zoo in Al Zawra's grand park, one of the city's most popular places to visit at the weekend, 3 May 2008.

45. 'Cairo writes, Beirut prints and Baghdad reads,' runs the Arab saying. On Fridays Baghdad's bookworms head for Mutanabbi Street, named after the great tenth-century poet, with more than 200 metres of bookshops and stalls.

46. The magnificent shrine of Imam Musa al Kadhim, one of Shia Islam's twelve imams, and his grandson, Mohammed al Jawad, in the heart of Kadhimiya, the northwestern district of Baghdad. From its origin in the mid ninth century until the present day, the Kadhimain shrine has often been the flashpoint of riots pitting Sunni against Shia, the traditional sectarian faultline that has long bedeviled Iraq.

47. Baghdadis gather to celebrate the birthday of the Prophet Mohammed at the shrine of Abu Hanifa, founder in the eighth century of the Hanafi school of Islamic law, the largest of the four principal Sunni schools, and a leading figure in the construction of Baghdad. Situated in the northeastern district of Adhamiya across the Tigris, it is the Sunni counterpart to the Kadhimain shrine.

across the city. This was necessitated by the mass migration to Baghdad of peasants from the southern marshes of Iraq. Driven out of their ancestral lands by the salination of the region and the lure of better-paid jobs in the city, they exchanged primitive conditions in the marshes for mud-hut shanty towns in Baghdad. With education rapidly moving centre-stage, Germany's Bauhaus giant Walter Gropius began work on plans for Baghdad University, following his visit to the city in November 1957. The great Swiss modernist Le Corbusier, who visited Baghdad at the same time and gave a lecture on modern architecture to the Society of Iraqi Engineers, was invited to design a new stadium and sports complex, later the Saddam Hussein Gymnasium. The plan was to introduce a new style of urban architecture in Baghdad that paid overt tribute to the ancient cultural traditions of Mesopotamia. In the words of the head of Baghdad University, 'It will return the golden era of Baghdad during the Abbasid reign.'

In March 1956 the British architects and town planners Minoprio and Spencely and P. W. Macfarlane designed a master plan for the city. Flood-control measures were introduced along the Tigris, finally ending the tradition of catastrophic inundations of millennia. For the first time in Baghdad's history, a series of new wide streets cut through the ancient city centre, while Karkh and Rusafa were linked with new bridges. A year after the master plan was conceived, King Faisal II cut the ribbon on several boulevards and bridges, opening them to motor traffic.

Had the decade ended differently, Baghdadis might today be enjoying Frank Lloyd Wright's extraordinary million-dollar opera house, cultural centre and museums on an island in the Tigris, staring at a towering, 300-foot statue of Harun al Rashid atop a spiral minaret modelled on Samarra's ninth-century Great Mosque, decorated with camels and their lance-carrying riders ascending the curving walkway.

After spotting an entirely bare island while flying over the city looking for a suitable site in May 1957, the American architect, one month shy of his ninetieth birthday, was told it was royal property. During a subsequent meeting with Faisal, Wright explained his plans for the island and the young king listened appreciatively. 'Well, he put his hand on this island place on the map and looked at me with an ingratiating smile and he said, "Mr Wright, it is yours," the American recalled. "Now that converted me to monarchy right then."'[81]

Swept up by the historical associations of the city and the homeland of the world's oldest civilizations, Wright romantically dedicated his 'Plan for Greater Baghdad', a series of drawings mostly dated 20 June 1957, to 'Sumeria, Isin, Larsa and Babylon'. The island was christened Edena, in honour of the supposed site of the Garden of Eden, around 120 miles south of Baghdad. Wright planned a bridge from the island that would connect to a King Faisal II Boulevard running north-east to the public buildings near the city's main train station and airport. Running south-west, the same road was oriented towards Mecca. A second bridge would cross from the south-eastern corner of the island to the new university campus Wright envisaged, before Gropius was involved, on the east bank at the bend of the river in the park south of the Karrada district.

There is no question Wright's radically inspiring vision for post-war Baghdad, with its monumental yet graceful designs on a grand, exotic scale, would have changed the face of the city for ever. Yet the 'Plan for Greater Baghdad' remained just that. Ruled out on grounds of cost and sheer extravagance, the grandiose scheme never went beyond the drawing board. One clue to its failure, perhaps, lay in Wright's description of the project as 'worthy of a king'. By the summer following Wright's visit to Baghdad, those words alone ruled it out as completely unacceptable.

Architecture was only one among many creative fields to flourish. The 1950s witnessed a broad cultural efflorescence in Baghdad. Established in the early 1940s by the distinguished Turkish *oud* player and classical composer Sharif Muhiddin Targan, the Institute of Fine Arts produced a new generation of artists. There were painters and sculptors such as Jawad Salim, Faik Hassan, Suad and Layla al Attar, Mohammed Ghani, Khalid al Rahal and Ismail al Turk. Fresh from the Slade School of Fine Art, the British artist Ian Auld and the Cypriot potter Valentinos Charalambous set up a department of ceramics at the institute. Among the musicians and composers were Jamil Bashir, former head of the Baghdad Radio Orchestra, and his brother Munir, Ghanim Haddad and Salim Hussein. Salman Shukur, another virtuoso *oud* player, directed the institute's Oriental Music Department for three decades, while the redoubtable Madame Moeller from Switzerland, together with the pianist Julian Hertz and the violinist Sandu Albu, both from Romania, held sway in its Western Music counterpart.

Then there were the pioneering poets and writers Al Sayab, Al

Malaika, Al Bayati and Abdul Malik Nuri, who became torch-bearers for modern Arabic literature, read and admired across the Arab world. Art exhibitions became increasingly popular. Classical concerts and recitals, of both traditional and Western music, attracted large cosmopolitan audiences of Iraqis and foreigners. From the late 1950s, the Iraqi National Symphony Orchestra became a central part of the city's musical life. Baghdadis could watch many of these events on televisions, which became popular additions to street cafés at this time.

For movie-lovers too, this was a memorable decade. Well-heeled customers tended to gravitate towards the ornately designed and inevitably more expensive cinemas, where they would watch the latest British and American films, sipping fizzy drinks and munching on one of the thirty types of freshly made sandwiches from the Sharif and Haddad restaurant and sandwich stall, one of the best-loved and most famous eateries on Rashid Street. In the mid 1950s the Khayyam Cinema ushered in a new era of even greater luxury for Baghdad's cinema-goers and was generally considered the finest in the Middle East. American-designed, it revelled in louche, velvet-covered walls, huge murals depicting Persian scenes from the poet Omar Khayyam's quatrains, twinkling lights in the ceiling and deep swivelling chairs. Baghdadis who remember it say it was the finest theatre they have ever visited. Those with more modest budgets and perhaps less cosmopolitan tastes would have headed to the cheaper cinemas, which showed Egyptian films in Arabic.

Intellectual life was rooted in a culture that was open to the world. The British historian Arnold Toynbee came to lecture in Baghdad in 1949, where he compared notes on exile with the Palestinian-Iraqi émigré Jabra Ibrahim Jabra, a Cambridge-educated novelist, poet and critic, author of *Hunters in a Narrow Street*, the story of a doomed Christian-Muslim love affair set in 1950s Baghdad. In 1956 the pre-eminent historian of Byzantium and the Crusades, Sir Steven Runciman, flew in to lecture and to attend an arts festival marking the inauguration of the Society of Iraqi Artists.

Amateur dramatics and professional theatre alike thrived. During Runciman's visit, a reception was given in his honour by Suham Shawket, a talented amateur actor-producer who had put together a small salon of like-minded friends to stage Graham Greene's 1953 play *The Living Room* in his elegant reception rooms on the banks of the Tigris. Across town, in another Ottoman-era riverside house, with two storeys and a wide, starlit courtyard, so beloved by British diplomats, George Bernard Shaw's play *Man and Superman* wowed an audience that included Lord Jellicoe, the then assistant secretary-general of the Baghdad Pact. American expatriates in Baghdad formed another group and staged Truman Capote's *The Grass Harp* in the British Council, with a second performance in the Alwiya Club. The audience of Brits, Baghdadis and Americans had to dash home after the performance to change into black tie for an Iraqi Red Crescent Society charity ball at the Amana Hall.[82] Political and diplomatic visitors to Said's grand riverside home recalled elegant, starlit soirées eating *masgouf*, that age-old Baghdadi delicacy of barbecued river fish, in his gardens, and feeding his flocks of ducks, swans and geese from pans piled high with bread. For the social, political and business elite, these were glorious days.

For the many Baghdadis and Iraqis left outside this charmed circle, life was rather less glamorous and considerably more deadly. In 1956 infant mortality in the city's sweaty, reeking slums was estimated at 341 in every 1,000 pregnancies.[83] The densely packed mud hovels, stretching into the horizon beyond the earth bunds piled up high to protect the eastern bank of the city from flooding, were a city apart and a stain on Baghdad's reputation. Conditions were shockingly basic. In the torrid blasts of midsummer, the heat was intolerable. In winter, families shivered on mud floors beneath patched blankets without heating. Although the great epidemics of plague and cholera were largely things of the past, typhoid, tuberculosis, malaria and eye diseases continued to run riot through the overcrowded population.[84] Discontent seethed through the slums with them.

*

While Baghdad society glided serenely from one black tie gala event to another, removed from popular concerns in a sumptuously upholstered, gilded cage, nationalist tensions mounted. In 1955, Said signed the Baghdad Pact, linking Britain, Iraq, Turkey, Iran and Pakistan in a defence alliance that was intended to combat Soviet influence in the Middle East. Instantly violently unpopular at a time when virulently anti-Western Arab nationalism was on the rise, it was condemned across the region, with opposition led by the Egyptian dictator Gamal Abdul Nasser's fiery broadcasts on Voice of the Arabs radio. Syria refused to join. In Jordan the young Anglophile King Hussain wavered, before bowing to public opinion. Whipping up an anti-Western frenzy, Nasser was contending for Arab leadership with Said, the senior Arab statesman of the Middle East, in a twentieth-century resumption of the ancient rivalry between the peoples of the Nile and Euphrates valleys, first witnessed in the competition between Thebes and Babylon. Within a year of the Baghdad Pact, the Suez Crisis changed the Middle East beyond recognition. Humiliated by President Eisenhower, Britain withdrew its forces from Egypt, together with France and Israel. British influence in the region was never the same again, and in Baghdad the loss of British prestige was palpable. The nationalist wave was poised to crash over Iraq.

Said was appointed to his eighth and final premiership on 19 May 1958. Staunchly pro-Western and anti-Communist to the last – when Nasser nationalized the Suez Canal Company in 1956, he advised Anthony Eden to 'hit him now, hit him hard' – he had long been seen by the masses as a British and American stooge. Writing in 1964, Dr Fadhel Jamali, former prime minister and foreign minister, argued that this tireless support of the West put the veteran politician on a collision course with the Iraqi public, a constituency that had never been of great interest to him.

> Wasn't the United States of America the close friend and main supporter of Israel at the expense of Arab rights to their homes? Wasn't Britain the attacker of Egypt as well as the first cause of the Palestine tragedy? Wasn't France the attacker of Egypt as well as the killer of hundreds of thousands of Arabs in North Africa? Free political activity and a free press in Iraq would, in most cases, have turned anti-Western and not anti-Communist. Nuri's job was a thankless one. He fell, in a sense, as a victim of Western policies in the Arab World.[85]

The Pasha's last period in office was also one of his shortest. Less than two months later, Said, hero of the Arab Revolt, one-time comrade of Faisal and Lawrence of Arabia, and steely Iraqi politician bar none, was dead.

*

Baghdad had changed almost beyond recognition between 1921 and 1958. Summarizing some of the most visible developments, Gerald de Gaury, a British Army officer, Arabist and close friend of the Iraqi royal family, noted how paddle steamers, camels, horses and horse cabs had given way to public buses, taxis, private cars, bicycles and a tramway. Once relying on word of mouth and a solitary government newspaper, Baghdad's contact with the outside world was now assisted by fifty Iraqi and regional Arabic newspapers, together with radio stations, television channels and a number of European publications. Where only recently education had generally been extremely limited and restricted to *madrassas*, in which religious lessons were conducted in Arabic, students could now improve their prospects at the secondary, technical and law schools, as well as learning a foreign language, usually English.

Many women had abandoned the strict, age-old conventions surrounding their sex and were 'largely emancipated'. Oriental singing and dancing, including boys impersonating women in theatres, had shifted towards more Europeanized cabaret, and cinemas showed Westerns, thrillers and surprisingly risqué films with no shortage of flesh on display. Alcohol was more freely available, especially at the nightclubs that sprang up in the more affluent neighbourhoods. Glass-fronted shops, crammed with the latest luxuries such as televisions, fridges and washing machines, lined the streets, where the occasional Rolls-Royce Silver Ghost slummed it with oversized Cadillacs, Buicks, Chevrolets, Fords, Oldsmobiles and the doughty Vauxhall Veloxes. Sartorial codes had changed too. The traditional Arab dress of flowing robes and headdress now competed with close-fitting European suits, shirts and ties. Although the popular diet of rice, unleavened bread, kebabs, dates, milk and *arak* liquor remained largely intact, the way of consuming it had evolved. Fewer ate with their fingers and had turned instead to knives, forks and spoons.[86]

However, the 1950s, a decade that had witnessed such a remarkable flowering of Baghdadi life amidst the upper echelons of society, if not for the perennially neglected masses, ended with a vicious jolt.

*

At around 8.15 on the morning of Monday, 14 July 1958, a breathless Iraqi Army officer rushed up to the shuttered house of Sharif Hussain Ali, a relative and close friend of King Faisal. He had lost his hat, his shirt was unbuttoned, and he looked distraught. 'They are dead!' he said in choking gasps. 'They have killed them all – God have mercy on them. Go quickly, while you can!'[87]

Sharif Hussain, whose house lay within several hundred yards of the royal palace, had spoken to the king only an hour and a half earlier. At around 6.15 a.m., bursts of gunfire sounded out near the palace. As the shooting grew heavier, Sharif Hussain called the palace on a private line. The twenty-three-year-old king told him he was besieged. Armed soldiers, brandishing their weapons aggressively, had just entered the palace grounds. From further off came the roar of an angry mob of young men from the *sarifa* squatters' settlement east of the city. Desperately poor and disenfranchised, living in makeshift reed huts without water or electricity, they were eager supporters of the Nasserist message that was bombarding Baghdad's airwaves with calls for a class war and a struggle against Britain and her stooges, the Iraqi king and his regime. 'Al mawt *lil malik!*' ('Death to the king!') came the growing cry beyond the palace walls. '*Al mawt lil Abdul Illah!*' ('Death to the Crown Prince!').[88]

Inside the palace, an ashen-faced Faisal was listening to Baghdad Radio – now renamed Free Iraq Radio – which was already broadcasting, among the martial music and the nationalist songs, the extraordinary news that a revolution led by Major-General Abd al Karim Kassem was under way. At 6.30 a.m. the voice of Colonel Abdul Salam Aref, Kassem's number two, came on air. In 'Proclamation number 1', addressed to the 'Noble People of Iraq', he announced that the Iraqi Army was liberating 'the beloved homeland from the corrupt crew that imperialism installed' and called on his brethren to support 'the wrath that it is pouring on the Rihab Palace and the house of Nuri al Said'. In terms that prefigured the tone of Iraqi governments for the next six decades, he urged his countrymen to report all 'offenders, traitors, and corrupt people so that they could be uprooted'. 'Citizens of Baghdad, the Monarchy is dead! The Republic is here!'[89]

As the net closed around the royal family, Faisal's chauffeur recommended that they make a break for it in the car, leaving by a still-open gate on the road to Diwaniya, south-east of Baghdad, but the king insisted on staying. Neither he nor the crown prince would countenance flight. More troops continued to arrive. Terrifyingly for those within its walls, an infantry anti-tank gun started to shell the palace at around 6.45 a.m., setting off an explosion at the ammunition stores and a fire that began to blaze through the upper hall of the palace, making escape even less likely. At 7.45 the Royal Guard surrendered.

Then, a few moments before 8 a.m., as the shooting subsided, through the smoke and chaos came shouts from a Captain Abdul Sattar Saba al

Abusi, an unknown army officer offering to take the king and his party to safety outside the country in the royal cars. Despite their misgivings about entrusting themselves into the hands of a complete stranger, the royal party reluctantly agreed and followed the officer and sergeant. They numbered around fifteen and included King Faisal, the crown prince, his wife, Hayam, his mother, Queen Nafisa, and his sister, Princess Badiya, the aide de camp Lieutenant Thabit and assorted palace servants and retainers. On the point of leaving, the crown prince's wife, wearing only a nightdress beneath her coat, rushed back inside the palace to put on some more practical clothes. When they were in the middle of the palace courtyard, close to the fountain, the officer suddenly swung around, aimed his submachine gun at the royals and cut them down from behind, triggering wild shooting on all sides. The members of the royal family were killed instantly, except for Faisal, who died of his wounds later, en route to hospital, and Hayam, who had been saved at the last second by turning back to change her clothes. Recalling the assassination years later, Captain al Abusi, who had not been party to the coup planning and joined the rebels only on hearing that morning's radio appeal, said he had been in a 'state of frenzy', as if blinded by a 'black cloud' and had pressed the trigger 'unconsciously'.[90]

Although the rebels' treatment of the crown prince's corpse was undeniably barbaric – hands and feet hacked off, mutilated, dragged naked through the streets, hung up as a spectacle, driven over repeatedly by cars, until nothing was left but a piece of spine and flesh – the violence and cruelty were merely twentieth-century echoes of the long-established patterns of regime change – and explosive mob behaviour – in Baghdad. Exceptional to many readers, they were grimly familiar in the City of Peace.

One more man lay in rebel sights. 'The man has not been born who can assassinate me,' the pistol-toting Said once boasted. Yet for all the bravado, Said was, by the summer of 1958, a deeply unpopular man. 'His countrymen fear, respect, or stand in awe of Nuri,' a journalist wrote in an interview with the prime minister in 1957. 'They do not love him, and though he has been managing their country's affairs since before most of them were born, few Iraqis know him as a human being. He rules them as a dictator, with an indifference to their opinion that verges on contempt.'[91]

Tipped off that murder was in the air, Said fled across the river in a fishing boat in his pyjamas, desperate to find the veteran senator Sheikh

Mohammed al Araibi, the head of the marsh tribes around Amara, who could have been instrumental in devising an escape route from Iraq. The east bank of the river was crawling with armed men, so he returned to the other side and was smuggled into a friend's house in Kadhimiya, hidden in the boot of a car. The radio reported a bounty of 10,000 dinars on his head. The next day he took the dangerous decision to return to central Baghdad, to the Bataween quarter, to search out the sheikh. Fearing that a young man in the house had turned him in, he rushed out into the streets disguised as a woman, with Madame Astarabadi, the wife of a political friend, as his companion. Within moments, Said was recognized by a grocer, who had spotted pyjamas peeping out beneath the *abaya* and called out to the neighbourhood for help, reminding everyone of the precious bounty at stake. Said turned to face his pursuers and fired his pistol at them. He and his companion were both killed in the returning fire. After his body had been formally identified in hospital, it was buried in a cemetery by the North Gate, only for a mob of revolutionaries to disinter it later and haul it through the streets by rope; they then drove cars over it repeatedly, before mutilating it further and finally setting light to the diminished trunk.

Some Baghdadis took the words of Free Iraq Radio – 'Today is a day to kill and be killed. Down with imperialist agents! . . . Death to the traitors and agents of imperialism!' – as a licence to slaughter. Within a few hours of the revolutionary broadcasts, the capital's streets were swarming with nationalists, Communists, pan-Arabists, *sarifa* slum-dwellers, rampaging thugs – a seething Baghdad mob at its most vicious. General Sadik Shara reported how rebels descended on the swish New Baghdad Hotel at around 9.30 a.m., ripped out the telephones, ransacked the office and seized more than twenty foreigners, including three Jordanian ministers, three American businessmen and two Britons. They were then shoved into a military truck. Just outside the Ministry of Defence a mob attacked the vehicle. Ibrahim Hasha, deputy premier of the Arab Union, was killed instantly when a stone hit him on the head. A young Swiss or German was grabbed by the head and pulled out of the truck. Eight men set about beating him with iron rods until he died. Then they cut off his head. The three Americans were also killed. According to General Shara, once the gates to the ministry opened, those still alive on the truck jumped down and made a run for it. 'Anyone who could not reach the gate was killed and dismembered.'[92]

A large crowd broke into the British Embassy compound. The ambassador opened his door only to hear a bullet fizz past his ear. Parts of the embassy were looted and torched. Colonel Graham, the comptroller, was killed. Mobs tore down the statues of Faisal and Maude. Finally sobered by the uncontrollable violence they had fomented, the revolutionaries declared a curfew and martial law.

More than thirty people had been killed in the course of the day. By the standards of many regime changes, the bloodshed had been limited, but the three most important men in the country – the king, the crown prince and the prime minister – were all dead.

Ultimately, the British association with the monarchy proved far more important in Iraqi minds than its noble descent from the Prophet Mohammed. The Hashemite monarchy of Iraq, whose origins lay in the desert war that had brought Ottoman rule in Iraq to an end, had been annihilated, never to return. Exactly 700 years after Hulagu's Mongol soldiers destroyed the 500-year-old Abbasid Dynasty, a small band of Iraqi Army officers destroyed a monarchy in its infancy, six weeks before its thirty-seventh anniversary. Five months after the coup, the American ambassador at that time, Waldemar Gallman, wrote of Said, 'Iraq lost her best leader towards an eventual life of dignity and decency, and her strongest bulwark against recurrent chaos, if not savagery.'[93]

By noon, Major-General Kassem was installed in the defence ministry and Iraq had a new leader. Baghdadis did not know it yet, but the golden years were over.

Coups, Communists and Baathists:
The Mother of All Bloodshed
(1958–)

Our people in truth are builders of dictators.
Hashim Jawad, minister of foreign affairs, 1959–63[1]

Ando kull mufatih bi jaybo.
He has all the keys in his pocket.
Baghdadi saying about Saddam Hussein

Within a few weeks of the 1958 coup, a Special Supreme Military Court, presided over by Colonel Fadil Abbas al Mahdawi, a cousin of Kassem, was trying 106 people accused of 'plotting against national security and corrupting the government machinery'.[2]

The proceedings of the kangaroo court, which was the hottest show in town, made shocking and compulsive daily viewing. Seating was limited in the old parliament building, and tickets were distributed amongst the regime's cronies. The televised hearings, broadcast in the evening after working hours to maximize the audience, were the main attraction in Baghdad's street cafés. Across the capital Baghdadis in their tens of thousands tuned in their radios to listen to the bloodthirsty colonel cursing and taunting the defendants in their small fenced enclosure, encouraging the spectators to join in and haranguing Britain, America and, later, Nasser. Death sentences were as numerous as confetti, pronounced with glee as a cause for celebration. At a party in the Baghdad Railway Club on 31 December 1958, Mahdawi announced that his New Year's gift to Iraq was another twelve executions.[3]

The show trials and the droves of executions and prison sentences they brought continued well into 1959. This was vindictive retribution against the *ancien régime* and entertainment for the masses, as the correspondent for the *Daily Telegraph* made plain on 19 May 1959: 'The mob revel equally in the viciousness of Judge Mahdawi's depraved Punch and Judy show. Baghdad on a trial night is a terrible city, guffawing and gloating from end to end over the poor wretches in the dock.' The atmosphere poisoned the entire city. 'Across the wide Tigris in the darkness the dreadful orchestration of evil can be plainly heard. The brutish laughter of the court-room, picked up on thousands of radio and television sets, is magnified by a whole city full of sadists.'[4]

*

At around 6.30 p.m., on 7 October 1959, Prime Minister Abd al Karim Kassem was being driven south along Rashid Street in his army vehicle, a Chevrolet estate. One civilian car drove ahead, while a military escort followed further behind. As the convoy was making its way slowly through the crowded, traffic-filled central district of Ras al Karya, gunmen burst out from behind the broad pillars lining the street on both sides and started to fire into Kassem's car at short range. Some witnesses reported that a grenade was also thrown. The driver, Corporal Kadhim Aref, was instantly hit, and the car screeched to a halt. In the back of the vehicle Kassem threw himself to the floor. Having ascertained that the prime minister was injured but alive, his ADC, Major Kassem Amin al Janabi, got out of the Chevrolet to return fire but was immediately hit and fell to the ground. In the chaos that followed, police officers and soldiers took charge of the battered car and rushed the prime minister to the Dar as Salam Hospital, where he was admitted shortly after 7 p.m. and taken directly to the operating room.

Visiting Kassem in hospital on 10 October, the American ambassador, John Jernegan, was met with a classic show of Iraqi bravado. Although he looked 'a little weak', the prime minister was 'eager' to discuss the assassination attempt from his hospital bed and recounted how he had been shot by 'twelve to fifteen bullets'. One of his assailants had been about to throw a grenade but had dropped it and fled when Kassem had drawn his pistol and started shooting. Kassem asked the American whether he had seen the bullet-riddled Chevrolet, reduced to a colander on wheels. When Jernegan said that he had seen the car and wondered how anyone could have walked out of it alive, Kassem 'smiled and said he had been sure he would not be killed and had actually laughed as shooting began'.[5]

Kassem was wounded in the right hand, upper-left arm and shoulder. Two men were killed in the bungled assassination attempt: Kassem's driver and one of the assailants. The others fled down two narrow alleys running off Rashid Street, next to the Rafidain Laundry.

One of the members of the six-man Baath Party* assassination squad was a twenty-two-year-old who had just been released from prison due to lack of evidence in the murder of a civil servant. Wounded by crossfire in the attack, he fled first to his hometown of Tikrit and then, in a dangerous and dramatic journey, across the desert to Damascus. He had notched up his first murder at fifteen, his second at twenty, and was embarking on a long career that would be notable, even by Iraqi standards of violence, for persecution, torture, sadism and mass murder. His name was Saddam Hussein.

*

Coups and attempted coups became almost a way of life for Baghdad in the years after 1958, as power on the streets oscillated between Communists, Baathists and the pan-Arabist Free Officers of Iraq. Internal rivalry between the nationalist Kassem, who was supported by the Communists, and his pan-Arabist deputy, Abdul Salam Aref, who was urging Iraq's union with the United Arab Republic of Egypt and Syria, deepened the divisions in the immediate aftermath of the revolution.

In 1956 Baathists scarcely numbered 300. They grew rapidly: in the months after the 1958 coup, they claimed 300 'active members', 1,200 'organized partisans', 2,000 'organized supporters' and 10,000 'unorganized sympathisers'.[6] By 1976 Baath Party membership and organized supporters numbered 500,000, doubling to 1 million in 1980 and reaching 1.5 million in 1984.[7] Baghdadis grew accustomed to the Baathists' rhyming street chant – '*Al Wahdah Bakir, Bakir ma il Asmar Abd al Nasser*' ('Unity Tomorrow, Tomorrow with the Brown Abd al Nasser'), which alluded to Nasser's dark complexion.

Kassem established his pro-poor credentials quickly with a series of

---

* Founded in Syria in 1947, the Baath (Renaissance) Party was a political movement whose ideology was an amalgam of socialism, anti-imperialist nationalism and pan-Arabism, Its mantra was 'Unity, Freedom, Socialism'. Despite its pan-Arabist ambitions, it took power only in Syria and Iraq.

populist measures, including cutting the cost of bread from 6 fils to 4 fils and of the large oval loaf *samoun* from 20 to 8 fils. State-controlled rents were dramatically reduced: of rooms by 20 per cent, houses by 15–20 per cent and shops 10–15 per cent. The working day was limited to eight hours; night shifts were restricted to seven. In 1959–60 Kassem had a whole suburb built for the mud-hut-dwellers of Baghdad, with more than 10,000 houses constructed, together with new roads, markets, schools, medical dispensaries and public baths. He named it Al Thawra (The Revolution), forerunner of the vast, north-eastern district of Sadr City that is home to around 2.5 million (mostly Shia) Baghdadis today.

Twice Aref tried to dislodge his one-time ally, and both times he failed. It was not until his third attempt that he was successful. On Friday, 8 February 1963, he left his home in Adhamiya for early-morning prayers before meeting Colonel Ahmed Hassan al Bakr at the Fourth Tank Regiment headquarters at Abu Ghraib, a town just west of Baghdad. There he got into a tank, returning to Baghdad to seize control of Broadcasting House by the right bank of the Tigris. Three Hawker Hunters and four MiG-17s from Habaniya screamed over the city, terrifying residents for two hours as they directed a relentless rocket attack on Kassem's defence ministry headquarters, the heavily fortified heart of the regime. Shortly after 9 a.m. Baghdad Radio broadcast 'Communiqué No. 1': 'Sons of the valiant people, units of our valiant army, listen to this good news: after our heroes, the eagles of the air force, destroyed the den of the criminal traitor, and after all our military units moved forward proclaiming the revolution ... our brothers, the officers and troops of the defence ministry rose up and killed the criminal traitor.'[8]

Kassem was not dead, but his position was becoming more desperate by the minute. Donning green Al Haras al Kawmi Nationalist Guard armlets for the first time, more than 2,000 Baath Party militia, many armed with submachine guns, poured out of Adhamiya. An assassination detachment drove to the house of Brigadier Jalal al Awkati, commander of the Iraqi Air Force, and shot him dead on his doorstep. By 10 a.m. the Eighth Brigade and Fourth Tank Regiment were deployed, and the city was under siege. Anticipating support for Kassem from the sprawling slums of eastern Baghdad, tanks took up positions on the Bund, the flood-defence embankment commanding the area.

In a frantic effort to defeat the coup, Husain al Radi, the Communists' first secretary, drafted a proclamation, which was pasted on walls, distributed by hand and read aloud to crowds in the streets sometime after 10 a.m. It was a fiery call to action. 'To Arms! Crush the Reactionary Imperialist Conspiracy! . . . Masses of our proud struggling people! To the streets! Sweep our country clean of the traitors!'[9]

Workers, porters and artisans, together with the destitute from the poorest quarters and eastern shanties, surged through the streets towards the ministry, angrily waving sticks. Mustering at Karrada, Agd al Kird and Kadhimiya, Communist demonstrators tried to force their way down Abu Nuwas Street to relieve the Ministry of Defence, but many were mowed down. Since Kassem had refused to arm them – the Communists had committed massacres in Mosul, Kirkuk, Erbil and Basra in 1959, and he feared they would become a source of instability for his regime – 'they had the tragic appearance of sheep rushing forth high-spiritedly to the shambles'.[10] Over on the Karkh side of the river, bakers, fishermen and vegetable-sellers from Kraimat and Shawaka districts rushed Broadcasting House but were driven back with heavy losses.

More radio communiqués followed in rapid succession, calling for the surrender of the leadership and announcing the closure of Baghdad airport and the country's borders. Kassem's hold on the country shrank steadily, until he controlled only the ministry and its garrison of 600. The battle for his headquarters began at 3 p.m. At 5.30 p.m. tanks and armoured cars burst through into the compound, and the remnants of the garrison surrendered. After a vicious room-by-room assault, Kassem called Aref to beg for safe conduct to Turkey but was told to surrender at Shaab Hall at 7 a.m. the following morning. There he was arrested and driven to Broadcasting House, where Aref, Bakr and the Free Officers violently abused him to his face. A hasty court martial was held, and death sentences were pronounced on Kassem and his two generals, the former hanging judge Mahdawi and Taha al Sheikh Ahmed. According to one version, Kassem asked his former comrade whether this execution was to be Aref's recognition of the mercy he had shown Aref after his failed coup attempts. Aref replied that the matter was not in his hands. Kassem gave a gesture of disdain and turned to face the firing squad without a blindfold. At 1.30 p.m. he and his henchmen were lined up against a wall and machine-gunned. Their bodies were buried at night in an unmarked grave.[11]

For a week many Iraqis refused to believe Kassem was dead, and the masses of Al Thawra took on the army and Baathist militia in some of the bloodiest street battles for years. To persuade the people that Kassem had indeed been eliminated, the new regime broadcast a television clip night after night showing a soldier holding up the bullet-ridden, open-mouthed corpse, propped on a chair, spitting in Kassem's face for good measure. The mutilated bodies of Mahdawi and Ahmed lay slumped beside him. In response to the efforts of thirty Communist soldiers to oppose the coup, Aref had twenty-five 'counter-revolutionaries' executed in what was then the largest judicial mass execution held in an Arab country since the war. Bakr was appointed vice-president and prime minister.

Stability was entirely elusive, and Baghdad remained a turbulent city throughout the 1960s. Attempts to effect regime change through violence were proving addictive. In 1964 a planned Baathist coup was foiled by security forces. According to one of the plans, Saddam Hussein and colleagues were to storm the presidential palace, break into a conference room where President Aref and his ministers were meeting and machine-gun the lot of them. Instead, Saddam spent the next two years in prison, where he burnished his growing credentials for revolution and violence. Released in 1966, he was appointed deputy secretary-general of the Baath Party's Regional Command by his cousin Bakr. Then, on 17 July 1968, senior army officers and their Baath Party allies struck. They seized Broadcasting House, the Ministry of Defence and the Republican Guard headquarters and, for the seventh time in the past decade, a military coup was announced. President Abdul Rahman Aref, brother of the previous president, who had died in a helicopter crash, was hustled out of Iraq on a plane; the prime minister and his Cabinet were arrested, and Bakr was declared president. Saddam was appointed his deputy, and, through a tight control of the numerous security and intelligence agencies, he steadily and ruthlessly increased his power over the next decade.

The Baathists were in power in Baghdad. This time, they had no intention of losing it.

*

While crowds of long-haired music lovers in Britain and America rocked to the Rolling Stones, the Beatles and Bob Dylan, Baghdadis had to make do with a very different sort of mass entertainment.

On 27 January 1969 men, women and children woke up to hear the radio announcer urging them to celebrate this 'holy day' of 'joy and happiness' by going down to Liberation Square. There they discovered an extraordinary sight. Nine Jewish corpses were hanging from improvised scaffolds, each one erected 220 feet from the next. This macabre procession of death stretched across the vast square, the largest public space in the city. All of the bodies, whose feet dangled six feet from the floor, bore the traces of severe torture. Some had broken arms and legs; others had had their chests smashed in; some had been set on fire; and others had had their hands cut off. As part of the ritual humiliation they had been dressed in cheap brown linen trousers and shirts and left barefoot.

Crowds of school and university students, workers, soldiers, policemen, Baath Party officials, Palestinians, barefooted villagers from outside Baghdad poured in to relish this punishment of 'Israeli spies'. Many cheered and broke into song and dance. They cursed the dead, spat on them and hurled stones at their twisted bodies. Saleh Omar al Ali, a hoarse-voiced senior Baath Party official, urged the crowds into a frenzy over a microphone:

> You great people of Iraq! The Iraq of today shall no more tolerate any traitor, spy, agent or fifth columnist! You foundling Israel, you imperialist Americans, and you Zionists, hear me! We will discover all your dirty tricks! We will punish your agents! We will hang all your spies, even if there are thousands of them! Great Iraqi people! This is only the beginning! The great and immortal squares of Iraq shall be filled up with corpses of traitors and spies! Just wait![12]

For those who could not make it to Liberation Square that morning, television cameras helpfully relayed gruesome close-ups of the dead men, panning slowly over each victim from head to feet, showing blood dripping from noses and ears, hovering over the sheet of white paper identifying each man and his supposed crime, lingering over the prominent legend JEW.

By 11 a.m., when President Bakr arrived at the square, standing in an open army jeep to bask in the great 'victory' over Israel with his defence minister, Hardan al Tikriti, a Jewish eyewitness, Max Sawdayee, estimated the crowds at 200,000. For the traumatized Sawdayee, and for everyone else who was there that day, it was an unforgettable sight – deliberately so. The innocent men, he thought, looked like 'nine angels of death ... as though to prophesy disasters and catastrophes that will befall this miserable country in the near future'. It was a 'perfect, masterly, cold-blooded, wicked, diabolic' display, a meticulously staged execution of scapegoats 'to gratify the Baath Party's lust for power'. 'It shakes one to the bones,' he wrote in his diary later that day. 'It shakes even one's faith in humanity.'[13]

*

During the earliest years of Baghdad, the caliph Mansur had built himself the Kasr al Khuld, the magnificent Palace of Eternity whose luxuriant gardens evoked the Koran's famous 'Garden of Eternity' that was to be the believers' reward for their faith. In time it became his favourite royal residence, praised for its architectural grandeur and 'superior planning'. It was perhaps appropriate, then, given Mansur's history of bloodletting, that in 1979 the latter-day Khuld Hall should be the stage for one of the most chilling episodes in Baghdad's recent history. It was masterminded by the man who had steadily taken control of all the levers of power in the Iraqi state since 1968, and in its ruthless execution bore all the hallmarks of his own 'superior planning'. It also demonstrated the same complete lack of concern for eliminating his rivals that had characterized Mansur's caliphate 1,200 years earlier.

On 17 July, after considerable encouragement from his vice-president, Bakr announced he was stepping down from the presidency for 'health reasons'. Saddam was made president. Then, on 22 July, having successfully ousted his former patron, protector and relative, Saddam convened an extraordinary conference of around 1,000 senior Baath Party members from across Iraq. None knew what was about to unfold. Since Saddam had the entire proceedings filmed *pour encourager les autres*, it is possible to watch the putsch, to observe the very moment when Baath Party rule succumbed to the will of one man, when an authoritarian regime crossed the line into total dictatorship.[14]

The grainy black-and-white film opens with Saddam sitting coolly on one side of the stage, puffing away on a large Cuban cigar, alongside Taha Yassin Ramadan, the new vice-president and head of the Popular Army, the Baath Party's militia; Izzat al Douri, Saddam's deputy in the party and deputy secretary-general of the Revolutionary Command Council; foreign minister Tarik Aziz; and Saddam's cousin and chief-of-staff

General Adnan Khairalla. To the delegates' surprise Ramadan announces 'a painful and atrocious plot'. You can sense the sudden terror when he adds that all the plotters are in the room. Saddam rises to his feet, sleek in a tailored suit. Supremely calm, he puts his cigar to one side and starts addressing the conference hall without notes.

'We used to be able to sense a conspiracy with our hearts before we even gathered the evidence,' he says. 'Nevertheless we were patient and some of our comrades blamed us for knowing this but doing nothing about it.'

He then invites Muhie Abdul Hussain Mashadi, who only days earlier was secretary-general of the Revolutionary Command Council, to reveal the 'horrible crime'. Again, the sense of unfolding terror is palpable. Haggard from his prison torture – he was threatened with having his wife and daughters raped and murdered in front of him if he did not confess – Mashadi launches into an exposé of the plot against the regime. He says since 1975 he has been part of a Syrian plot to overthrow Saddam and Bakr to promote union with Syria. He gives names, places and dates of meetings. While he speaks, the camera shows Saddam puffing away on his cigar again, looking profoundly bored.

Saddam returns to the podium. After explaining his attempts to understand the conspirators' motives – 'they had nothing to say to defend themselves, they just admitted their guilt' – he ends his speech with a short declaration. 'The people whose names I am going to read out should repeat the party slogan and leave the hall.'

The names of the conspirators are read out; men in wide-lapelled suits stand up and are quickly bundled out of the conference centre by armed Baath Party security personnel. Back on his cigar, Saddam watches as each man declaims the Baathist mantra, 'One Arab Nation with an Eternal Message! Unity, Freedom, Socialism!' One man whose name has been called out dares to question the justice of these proceedings. Saddam cuts him off without raising his voice, reminds his audience of Mashadi's confession and, with real menace in his voice for the first time, says, 'Itla, itla!' – 'Get out, get out!'

Moments later, when the list of traitors has finished, the surviving party members jump to their feet – imagine the relief – and break out into cries of 'Long live Saddam!' and 'God save Saddam from conspirators!' Some are sobbing, prompting Saddam to reach for a tissue and wipe away a tear, still clutching his cigar with the other hand. Ali

Hassan al Majid, later nicknamed Chemical Ali for his role in gassing the Kurds in 1988, gives a few rousing words in support of Saddam, who descends from the stage to mix with his fellow party members, inviting them to join the execution squads that will shortly be assembled.

On 8 August, twenty-two of the fifty-five Baathists convicted of conspiracy against the regime were executed in the Khuld courtyard. The film of these 'democratic executions' shows blindfolded men kneeling in the dust, arms tied behind their backs. A pistol, a personal gift from Saddam to each member of the execution squads, is held against the temple and fired; the victim jerks to the ground, blood darkening the earth around him. Some of the executioners are less effective than others, and once in a while a professional has to finish off the job. Thus Saddam's half-brother Barzan al Tikriti administers the *coup de grâce* to Adnan Hussain al Hamdani, head of the president's office since 1973, appointed deputy prime minister only in July. While he writhes on the ground in his death throes, his wife is enjoying a shopping trip in Paris with Saddam's wife, Sajida Hussein.[15]

The Khuld purge cemented Saddam's total control in Iraq. There were few in Baghdad who did not understand, once news of the plot was broadcast on the day of the executions, that any opposition to Saddam would now be fatal.

*

At dawn on 23 September 1980, the young Dutch journalist Aernout van Lynden was woken by a colleague in Baghdad. He rushed out on to his balcony in the Al Mansur Hotel, on the banks of the Tigris in the city centre, just in time to see four McDonnell Douglas F-4 Phantoms flying straight at him, engines screaming above the wailing air raid sirens and heavy anti-aircraft fire. Three of the jets veered one way, one the other, before dropping their bombs and returning home.[16]

Fourteen months after liquidating his opponents, just as Baghdad was hosting a conference on 'Our Architectural Heritage and the New Arab Architecture', Saddam led Iraq to war. His enmity towards Iran went back to his earliest childhood. In the absence of his father, who is thought to have disappeared, Saddam had been brought up by Khairalla Talfa, his maternal uncle and a former governor of Baghdad. Talfa was a nationalist army officer, author of a Baathist tract called *Three Whom God Should*

Not Have Created: Persians, Jews and Flies. In it Persians are described as 'animals God created in the shape of humans', Jews as a 'mixture of the dirt and leftovers of diverse peoples'. [17] Saddam's capacity for meting out violence went back just as far. As a boy he used to carry an iron bar as protection from bullies. For amusement he would heat it until it was red hot, then plunge it into the stomach or anus of a stray dog.

There had been plenty of sabre-rattling over the months preceding the war. In March diplomatic relations between Baghdad and the new revolutionary regime of Ayatollah Khomeini in Tehran were broken off. A month later, Saddam expelled Shia 'fifth columnists'. On 17 September he ripped up the 1975 Algiers Treaty, which gave both Iraq and Iran rights to the strategic Shatt al Arab waterway between the two countries. Advised by the shah's exiled generals that he would be victorious within three weeks, thanks to the disarray of the Khomeini regime in Tehran, Saddam decided to precipitate what turned out to be the twentieth century's longest conventional war. By its end, more than a million had died, half of them Iraqis, and the economies of two of the world's richest oil nations lay in ruins. For Baghdad itself, the Iranian strike was the opening salvo of a conflict that for Iraqis ultimately defined – and annihilated – an entire decade. [18] No family in the city was left untouched.

To the existing lies of Saddam's regime were quickly added the daily deceits – and grinding propaganda – of war. While Tehran stated 140 aircraft had attacked 15 targets, and only two planes were shot down in the opening assault, Baghdad claimed it had shot down 67 planes. [19] This was one man's war, as explicitly acknowledged in the state-sanctioned nickname of Kadisiyat Saddam, a reference to the Battle of Kadisiya in 635, when a smaller Arab army had crushed the Persians and forced them to convert to Islam.

During the first two years, Baghdad experienced the war largely as a distant phenomenon. While it affected some aspects of everyday life – blackouts and deserted roads at night – supplies remained plentiful and prices stable. In the short term, Saddam had sufficient financial reserves to insulate the country from shortages and rationing. In preparation for a confrontation, the regime had raised imports: from $4.2 billion in 1978 to $20.5 billion in 1981. Allies were helpful too. From January 1981 two Mirage F1s arrived in Baghdad every month, prompted by President Mitterrand's disgust with the Israeli attack on the French-supplied Tammuz nuclear reactor. [20]

Saddam was in ebullient form, determined that Baghdad should play a bigger role on the world stage. It had done so spectacularly on 17 December 1979, when Iranian rebels seized the Iranian Embassy in London in an operation masterminded by Iraqi intelligence.[21] Saddam also gave sanctuary to Israel's enemies, allowing the Palestinian terrorist and gun-for-hire Abu Nidal to base himself in Baghdad, where he planned, amongst other attacks, the failed assassination attempt on Shlomo Argov, the Israeli ambassador to London. At Salman Pak, south-east of Baghdad near ancient Ctesiphon, the Iraqi leader opened his first nerve gas plant with the assistance of what American senator Jesse Helms called 'Saddam's Foreign Legion' of West German and other companies.[22]

Those in khaki were well looked after. Bereaved families received a free car, a free plot of land and an interest-free loan to build a house, further fuelling the construction boom. Haj Mohammed Zuwat, a sixty-year-old market stallholder with a gleaming gold tooth, spoke for many, if not most, Baghdadis when he told a reporter, 'We hear about the war with Iran, but we don't really have to live with it here.'[23]

In fact, Baghdad was booming. Flush with oil revenues, Saddam raised public spending from $21 billion in 1980 to $29.5 billion in 1982. Cranes began to outnumber minarets on the city's skyline as a massive programme of construction got under way, transforming the ancient medieval city into an oasis of modernity. Six large areas in the central business and residential districts of Baghdad, including Karkh, Haifa Street and Kadhimiya – such was the city's sprawl that the one-time suburb was now part of the city proper – were earmarked for redevelopment. 'Overnight Baghdad became a giant construction site.'[24] By 1982, forty-five shopping centres had opened across the city. The frenzied building – a new airport, twelve bridges, new hotels and hospitals, parks, redevelopment zones, monuments, conference centres, roads and superhighways, hundreds of miles of new sewer and water lines – were an integral part of Saddam's attempt to host the 1982 Non-Aligned Movement Conference in Baghdad. The centrepiece of the city's new look was the $80 million, twenty-one-storey Sheraton on the east bank of the Tigris – unimaginatively named, like so many other things in Iraq (including bicycles, fridges and magazines), after Ishtar, ancient Mesopotamian goddess of fertility.

Just as the 1950s redevelopment of Baghdad had drawn in some of the world's most famous architects, so the international firms returned in their droves to help Saddam spend his oil money. The Architects Collaborative, Walter Gropius's old company, drew up a master plan for Khulafa Street, with new buildings, two squares, a civic centre, a huge extension to the Khulafa Mosque and rehabilitation of the old quarters (which were wildly romantic or shamefully dilapidated, depending on one's view). Arup Associates of Britain and Ricardo Bofill of Spain were charged with modernizing the lively Bab al Sheikh area; Arthur Erikson Associates of Canada offered a new vision for Abu Nuwas Street, running along the Tigris in East Baghdad; while Venturi and Rauch designed shops and offices, and masterminded a competition for a new Baghdad State Mosque.

Amid this often disconcerting transformation of old neighbourhoods, whole districts and the city's skyline, some things at least remained reassuringly familiar. The red double-decker buses so beloved by Baghdadis – their popularity was celebrated in the 1968 film *The Conductor* about a fat conductor and the daily travails of Baghdadis on an overcrowded bus – continued to ply their way along the city's roads new and old, just as they had since they were first imported from Britain in 1954.

Some architects raved about the transformation of the city, praising projects that reflected 'a clear sense of history and regionalism rooted in the history, climate and geographical location' of Baghdad, and boldly detecting a 'potential source of a new global architectural movement'. Tokyo's *Architecture* magazine devoted an entire issue to the 'New Baghdad' of 1979–83.[25]

Yet the new aesthetic was not to everyone's taste. Where 1960s Baghdad had been 'anarchic, schizoid, fragmented, but lively and human', Saddam's post-modern reinvention of the city was 'an exercise in alienation', as new tower blocks of boxlike accommodation – such as those along Haifa Street – punched into the skyline with only the weakest nod to Baghdad's heritage, not least its venerable tradition of projecting *mashrabiya* windows, intricately decorated with latticework screens.[26]

Regime propaganda underpinned much of the new architectural statement, deadening the effect and dulling the senses. Yet there were exceptions. In 1983 Saddam unveiled the extraordinary $250 million Shahid Monument in East Baghdad, south of Kassem's Thawra suburb, by then renamed Saddam City. Designed by the Iraqi artist Ismail Fattah al Turk to honour Iraq's martyrs, the Shahid was a circular platform

almost 650 feet in diameter, carrying a 130-foot-high split dome of piercing aquamarine floating over an underground museum on an artificial
lake. Built by Mitsubishi to the exacting specifications of Ove Arup and
Partners, of Sydney Opera House fame, the monument still dominates
wide sections of eastern Baghdad. It is an arresting sight. In the same
year Saddam also opened the Tomb of the Unknown Soldier on 14 July
Street, in the heart of the regime's heavily guarded inner sanctum in
Karadat Maryam. Intended by the sculptor Khalid al Rahal to represent
the traditional *diraa* shield falling from the grasp of a dying Iraqi soldier, it resembles instead a flying saucer halted in mid-flight. As the Iraqi
exile and intellectual Kanan Makiya wrote (under the pen name of
Samir al Khalil to protect his family), this was 'quintessential kitsch on
a grand scale'.[27] Beneath the artificial mound on which the monument
sits was a subterranean museum that told the story of Saddam's life as
a latter-day Prophet Mohammed.

Saddam was becoming ubiquitous in Baghdad and beyond. In the
parched lands of Iraq, the cult of Saddam found fertile soil. A nationally
disseminated family tree linked him – absurdly – to Ali, the fourth
caliph, and therefore to the Prophet Mohammed. The obvious lie was
all the more terrifying for being so brazen. Thirty-foot Saddam cut-outs
adorned city centres the length and breadth of the country. Radio listen-
ers heard Saddam's name mentioned thirty to fifty times an hour. There
were Saddam watches, presents for dutiful soldiers, Saddam notebooks,
Saddam pens and Saddam T-shirts.*

Saddam liked dressing up and posed in all manner of styles. He did
formal, smart-casual, peasant, tribal and Western chic. He was pictured
in the trenches in military uniform; in the fields with peasants, scythe in
hand, tilling the soil; in full parade uniform as he reviewed his troops;
in tailored Pierre Cardin suits as he met international leaders; in full
Kurdish costume as he talked reconciliation with the Kurds; in white
Arab robes as he embraced his Arab brethren.[28] A rueful Iraqi joke of

---

* Saddam's honorifics increased throughout the 1980s. He was President of the Republic,
Chairman of the Council of Ministers, Commander-in-Chief of the Armed Forces, Chairman of the Revolutionary Command Council, General Secretary of the Regional Command
of the Arab Baath Socialist Party, Chairman of the Supreme Planning Council, Chairman of
the Committee on Agreements, Chairman of the Supreme Agricultural Council, Chairman
of the Supreme Council for the Compulsory Eradication of Illiteracy, Leader-President,
Leader-Struggler, Standard Bearer, Arab Leader, Knight of the Arab Nation, Hero of
National Liberation, Father Leader and Daring and Aggressive Knight.

the time had it that the population of the country was 26 million, consisting of 13 million Iraqis and 13 million pictures of Saddam.

As the great Abbasid caliphs luxuriated in praise from their poets, so Saddam revelled in the sycophantic drivel of party hacks and ambitious writers showing the same taste for rewards that had animated their medieval ancestors. At the outset of war with Iran one poet likened him to:

> The perfume of Iraq,
> Its dates, its estuary of the two rivers,
> Its coast and waters,
> Its sword, its shield,
> The eagle whose grandeur dazzles the heavens.
> Since there was an Iraq,
> You were its awaited and promised one.[29]

Mayada al Askari, granddaughter of the great Iraqi patriot Jafar Pasha al Askari, briefly imprisoned by Saddam's regime, recalled another poem from 1982:

> Oh Saddam, our victories;
> Oh Saddam, our beloved:
> You carry the nation's dawn
> Between your eyes.
> Oh Saddam, everything is good
> With you.
> Allah! Allah! We are happy
> Because Saddam lights our days.[30]

*

As the war wore on, economic conditions worsened, and there was scant consolation to be found either in Saddam's grandiose posturing or in his architectural grandiloquence. In late 1982, by which time the war had put paid to Saddam's hopes of staging the Non-Aligned Movement conference and succeeding Cuba's Fidel Castro as its leader, inflation was peaking at 50 per cent. A series of Iranian victories on the battlefield earlier that summer led to Shia riots in Baghdad, Kerbala, Basra, Hilla and Nasiriya.

On 8 July, Saddam survived an assassination attempt in Dujail, a Shia town and stronghold of the opposition Dawa Party thirty-five miles north-west of Baghdad. It prompted the inevitable, savage retribution, in which almost 800 men, women and children were detained. Many died during their torture. Of the 148 men sentenced to death, most were executed. Obeying the orders of a modern-day Tamerlane, helicopter pilots dropped napalm, and bulldozers moved in to raze homes, farms and swathes of agricultural land containing date palms and fruit orchards. From this moment, Saddam abandoned all pretence of a walkabout, Harun-style of government.[31]

By 1983 Baghdad and Iraq were in an acute economic crisis. Iraqi oil revenues had crashed from $26.1 billion in 1980 to $10.4 billion a year later, sliding further to $8.4 billion in 1983. Imports meanwhile nose-dived from $20.5 billion in 1981 to $11.7 billion two years later. Foreign reserves, $35 billion before the war, had dwindled to $3 billion by the end of 1983. Construction and development projects ground to a halt. The oil-rich nation of Iraq became humiliatingly dependent on hand-outs from its Gulf neighbours. Saddam appealed to patriotic Iraqis to donate gold, jewellery and cash to the noble cause, a campaign that raised $400 million.[32] (It was hardly surprising that generous gifts did not always find their way to the right places. A well-heeled Baghdadi woman, who had reluctantly given up her extravagant gold and sapphire collection, subsequently spotted it on the notoriously avaricious, jewel-obsessed Sajida, Saddam's first wife.)[33]

Where favoured visitors to Saddam's office in 1981 moved through remarkably opulent ante-rooms and buffets groaning with foreign delicacies such as smoked salmon and Beluga caviar, by 1983, when war widows formed a steady procession to meet the Father Leader, a certain shabbiness had set in. Such were the Iraqi losses and the strain on the Baghdad exchequer that Saudi Arabia and Kuwait stepped in to make the traditional Islamic *diya*, payments made as compensation to the heirs of victims.

The once bountiful Fertile Crescent was no match for the human demands of the industrialized war machine, and agricultural production plummeted. In the mid 1970s Iraq had produced an average of 1.8 million tons of wheat annually. By 1982 the figure had dropped to 965,000 tons; two years later it was 300,000. The economist Abbas Alnasrawi has estimated that between 1980 and 1985 Iraq spent $94 billion on its war with Iran and lost $55.5 billion in oil revenues. The total cost to both countries during the same period was $416 billion. To put that figure into perspective, total oil revenues for both countries in the twentieth century up to the mid 1980s were $364 billion.[34]

Although Baghdad was never the battle front during the Iraq–Iran War, the conflict made itself felt in the capital in a number of ways. From a military perspective, Baghdad bizarrely remained the operational headquarters of the conflict for Saddam, who was completely unable and unwilling to delegate command to his senior military leadership. Saddam, who had never served in uniform, despite having promoted himself to the rank of general in 1976, insisted on total command from his bunker beneath the presidential palace in Baghdad. To the immense chagrin and frustration of his generals, every order down to platoon-level engagements had to be referred back to Baghdad for approval. To Baghdad also came the tide of reports from the tireless Baath Party political commissars, informing on the officers and men of the Iraqi Army. Baghdadis watching television were unable to escape the regular parade of grotesque pictures of dead Iranian soldiers, many of them mutilated, and the relentless shots of khaki-clad ministers and senior officials going about their business, after Saddam ordered the Baath Party leadership to ditch their suits for olive green fatigues in recognition of the growing toll of the war effort.

Funerals of soldiers killed on the front became a tragically regular feature of life in Baghdad. Wailing women provided the heart-rending accompaniment to the funeral processions: large, flapping black flags emblazoned with soldiers' names and the place of their death, together with a verse from the Koran ('Martyrs never die') and Saddam's war propaganda ('Martyrs are more generous than all of us'); coffins wrapped in the Iraqi flag carried through the streets on the shoulders of family and friends. In the early days of the war, before the coffers ran dry, families of the 'martyrs' received 5,000 Iraqi dinars (then worth around $15,500) in compensation, in addition to land and a car. A Baghdad wit duly adapted a children's song into a satirical war anthem:

> Now my father will return from the front
> Nailed to his coffin.
> My mother will marry another man,
> But I will ride a new Toyota.[35]

Whatever the military situation on the ground, Baghdad Radio continued its bombastic broadcasts day and night. On 28 February 1984 an announcer read out a cable sent earlier that day by Major-General Mahir Abdul Rashid, commander of the Basra-based Third Army Corps, to Saddam Hussein: 'Great Sir, we gladly inform you of the annihilation of thousands of harmful magian insects [pejorative reference to the Iranians] that carried out an abortive offensive late last night. We . . . will turn what is left of these harmful insects into food for birds of the wilderness and the fishes of the marshes.'[36]

From 1985 Baghdad experienced first-hand the terror of the conflict after Saddam opened the typically ill-conceived War of the Cities, which resulted in the launch of a series of surface-to-surface missile attacks, mostly Soviet-made Scud-Bs, against the Iraqi capital. On 12 September 1986, 21 were killed and 81 injured by an Iranian missile attack aimed at the main headquarters of Saddam's secret police, which missed by miles. It was, said Ayatollah Khomeini, 'a slap in the face' for Saddam Hussein in what was by now a highly personalized conflict between two leaders not known for valuing the lives of their countrymen.[37] As Henry Kissinger famously put it, 'A pity they both can't lose.'[38] On 26 November thousands of Baghdadis, led by Baath Party officials, marched through the city carrying coffins wrapped in the Iraqi flag after the regime reported fifty-three people killed by a missile strike.[39] A year later, on 13 October, television cameras played across the harrowing picture of injured teachers tearing at the rubble of a school hit by a missile, trying to rescue screaming children, while fathers wept as the blood-spattered corpses of twenty-nine children – all of them under ten – were removed. It was the sixteenth Scud missile to hit Baghdad that year.[40] A month later, as the Arab Summit opened in Amman, there were scores of casualties when two Iranian missiles hit a densely populated district of Baghdad.[41] Under this unpredictable but devastating barrage from the skies, it was little surprise that there were 'rifts in Iraqi morale'.[42]

By the later 1980s it was rare to find someone in Baghdad who had not been affected by the war. Most had a brother, a father, a cousin or an uncle fighting on the front. 'I remember we went to many funerals in the city at that time,' says Mohammed Ali, a Baghdadi restaurateur. 'Whole neighbourhoods would be crying "*Allahu akbar! Allahu akbar!*" and the women were wailing because these young martyrs had died before they were even married. It was a terrible time.'[43] After almost a decade of intense conflict, the war-wounded were a pathetically ubiquitous sight in the streets of Baghdad: 'Young men with burned faces, amputated legs, amputated arms. Desperate people with empty souls and expressionless eyes.'[44]

Something had to give. Both sides had fought themselves to a standstill – and economic ruin. The end, when it came, was quintessential Saddam. At midnight, on 8 August 1988, the Iraqi News Agency issued the 'Communiqué of Communiqués', calling on Iraqis to celebrate 'this great victory' over Iran. The announcement triggered a frenzy of gunfire and fireworks that lasted till dawn. Thousands of men, women and children surged on to the streets and piled on to car roofs and bonnets, driving through Baghdad beating drums, singing, waving flags and palms beneath banners celebrating 'The Hero of Peace, President Saddam Hussein' and 'Masses of Baghdad Congratulate the Hero of Victory'. There was so much celebratory fire that many were injured, and incoming aircraft were asked to delay their arrival in Baghdad for fear they would be hit by stray bullets or anti-aircraft rounds.[45] In what would retrospectively prove to be an ironic telephone call, Saddam accepted congratulations from the Kuwaiti amir Sheikh Jaber al Ahmed al Sabah and celebrated the 'victory' in Grand Festivities Square in Zawra Park.

Here, exactly one year later, he opened the infamous Victory Arch (or Crossed Swords monument), riding through the pair of arches on a white stallion. Designed by the Iraqi sculptors Khalid al Rahal and later Mohammed Ghani, under Saddam's close supervision, this was a Baathist Arc de Triomphe, only taller; its purpose was to 'announce the good news of victory to all Iraqis', as the invitation to the opening ceremony explained. Each 24-ton sword, made from the melted-down machine guns and tanks of Iraqi 'martyrs', was held aloft by a 20-ton forearm, an enlarged cast of Saddam's arm commissioned from the Morris Singer foundry in Basingstoke. The swords, replicas of that once wielded by Saad ibn Abi Wakas, commander of Arab armies at the Battle of Kadisiya, crossed 130 feet above the ground; and far beneath them were giant nets containing 2,500 helmets of Iranian soldiers.[46]

Baghdad now had a new parade ground and a Saddam Gifts Museum, displaying the presents given to the Iraqi president by world leaders – Saudi sabres, shotguns, pistols, Cartier cigarette lighters and fountain pens, a Finnish walking cane, Cuban cigars and a golden hand grenade in a custom-made leather and velvet presentation case, a gift from

Colonel Gaddafi of Libya. The new public space cut a Baathist swathe through Baghdad. It was 'Nuremberg and Las Vegas rolled into one'.[47]

The war was over. With combat operations ended, both countries withdrew their forces to respective sides of the – unchanged – international border over the following weeks and UN peacekeepers stepped in to monitor the ceasefire. To the casualties, already unthinkable, Saddam added a further 50,000 after unleashing a vicious campaign against the Kurds on the Iraqi side of the border during the autumn of 1988.[48] Whatever they thought of the victory Saddam had given them, Baghdadis could at last hope for a better future. After a desperate decade, peace had returned to the city.

*

For Baghdad, the war against Iran was only one part of the violence seeping through every level of society. It was fought against the backdrop of a far more relentless internal campaign of terror that Saddam was waging against his own people. In the mountains of northern Iraq the Kurds faced continuing persecution, including the suffocating horrors of a gas attack at Halabja that killed up to 5,000 people in the autumn of 1988. In the marshes and holy cities of the south, the perennially downtrodden Shia were abused with no less ferocity. In 1983 Saddam ordered the arrest of 125 close relatives of Ayatollah Mohammed Bakir al Hakim, scion of one of Iraq's oldest clerical families and one of the founders of the revolutionary Supreme Council of the Islamic Resistance in Iraq, an organization dedicated to the regime's overthrow, in punishment for his refusal to stop broadcasting opposition to Saddam from Iran. At least eighteen of the ayatollah's family were subsequently executed.[49]

Baghdad remained the engine-room of a giant machine carefully calibrated to control, cow and kill. Here were the headquarters and multiple offices of Saddam's feared quartet of security organizations that enabled an entire country to devour itself: the Amin al Am secret police in eastern Baghdad; the external intelligence service, the Mukhabarat, in Mansur; the military intelligence service, the Istikhabarat, overlooking the Tigris in Karrada; and, most powerful of all, the Amin al Khas, the special security organization for high-ranking officials. These extensive networks were just four of the numerous security and intelligence agencies that dominated Saddam's Iraq.

Saddam's presidential palace compound was six square miles of west bank Baghdad, the south-eastern wedge of land opposite Abu Nuwas Street, girdled by the Tigris in a languid loop. Bristling with military and security services, this was the heavily restricted zone bounded to the north and west by Yafa Road, and to the south and east by the river. Here, in the inner perimeter, were Saddam's private office, private secretaries' offices and interrogation centre, guarded by a meticulously vetted special protection squad. Beyond this inner sanctum, close to where Mansur's Round City once stood, were the presidential palace, a clutch of ministerial buildings and the headquarters of the Amin al Khas.

The Baghdad compound was where the loose ends were tied up. It was a mire of informing, treachery, revenge and reprisal, of greed and ambition fostered one moment, fatally punished the next. Innocence was irrelevant here and escape impossible. Its system was orchestrated around Saddam's uniquely ruthless appetite for power and its preservation, combined with an utter disregard for the sanctity of human life. As the Canadian writer Paul Roberts observed:

> A few had to be sacrificed for the good of many, and this was best achieved through fear. Just as no one ever returned from hell, from the demons with pitchforks and the vats of boiling sulphur, so no one ever returned from the covert human abattoirs, from the hooks, wires and grotesque parodies of internal medicine with which the Mukhabarat purged their compatriots of sin. Through such a perpetual Inquisition they maintained an orderly society.[50]

Saddam's torturers in Baghdad lacked neither imagination nor zeal for the task at hand. Professionally trained in tried-and-tested techniques by East German and Soviet intelligence and secret service advisers, they inflicted pain on their fellow Iraqis through myriad, mind-fogging methods, many of them recorded in a collection of videos kept by the 'Saddam Special Treatment Department'.

In one, a man is filmed tied to a chair screwed to the floor, huge crocodile clips attached to his nipples and genitals. His body twitches and shakes as the electric current is delivered, his eyes pop, saliva foams from his mouth. The camera zooms in on his contorted face. He screams and screams. Some have their arms and legs amputated with an electric saw or an axe; their mouths prised apart until their jaws break; their skin branded with iron skewers; their noses broken with a heavy hammer; their fingernails and toenails pulled out with pliers; others are secured to a bench with their hands tied behind their back, and then hauled up and down until their shoulders snap. A wiry man is tied naked to a gas ring, which is then turned on and burns through his skin.

One man stands by a wall with his head sandwiched between two wooden wedges, to which his ears are nailed. When he can no longer stand, he slumps to the floor and rips his ears off. Teeth are drilled. The corpses of murdered victims are thrown into cells to decompose in the heat of a Baghdad summer. Acid is sprayed on to bodies; snarling fighting dogs – Rottweilers and Dobermanns – are thrust into cells to attack men already weak from torture. Needles are pushed through tongues and under fingernails; feet and hands are immersed in boiling oil; insecticide is sprayed into eyes; arms are tied to an electric heater. Women are raped before husbands; glass bottles are shoved into men's anuses; a menstruating woman is hung upside down by her feet; wires are plunged into flesh. A blindfolded man stumbles around an empty room as loudspeakers blare a continuous, high-pitched cacophony to prevent sleep. One video shows Iraqis bound and kept for weeks in an airless room in which the temperature soars to 50°C. Parents are forced to watch their frantic children running naked around a cell containing a beehive, desperately trying to escape the squadron of stinging insects. A chainsaw slices through a man's genitals. One man has his arms broken with iron bars, another has his head crushed between the steel plates of a vice. His skull suddenly collapses with a jolt, and his brain squeezes out like toothpaste.[51] In all the terrible history of death and violence in Baghdad, there had been nothing as perverted as this.

*

If Baghdadis had hoped the 1990s would bring some respite after the follies and tragedies of the Iraq–Iran War in the 1980s, they were to be cruelly disabused. At an Emergency Arab Summit Conference hosted in Baghdad on 30 May 1990, Saddam accused Kuwait of 'economic warfare' against Iraq, claiming it had flooded the market with cheap oil. The Iraqi economy, crippled by the eight-year war with Iran, was in crisis. The conflict had cost Iraq an estimated $453 billion, during which time total oil revenues had been $104 billion. Inflation was rampant, foreign debt in a country that had been debt-free since the 1950s was soaring, unemployment was high, and rising, and generous state subsidies were no longer sustainable.[52] Saddam, whose views on economic recovery owed little either to John Maynard Keynes or to Friedrich Hayek, decided on direct action.

On 2 August 1990, less than a year after opening the Victory Arch commemorating the supposed defeat of Iran, he invaded the tiny amirate of Kuwait immediately to the south, across a border long regarded as contentious by many Iraqis, who believed Kuwait should always have been part of Iraq. Extraordinarily rich in oil, militarily weak and reluctant to pardon Iraq's massive war debt, Kuwait was a tempting target for Saddam, who was already in a war of words with its amir, Sheikh Jaber al Ahmed al Sabah, whom he accused of driving the oil price down through over-production. On 6 August, by which time Iraqi forces were in complete control of Kuwait (Sheikh Jaber and his government fled to Saudi Arabia within hours of the invasion), the UN Security Council passed Resolution 661, implementing economic sanctions against Iraq, a punitive measure that set the tone for an entire decade.

For a short while Baghdad enjoyed the unexpected benefits of defeating Kuwait. The city was suddenly deluged with foreign goods looted from Kuwaiti shops, many with their price tags still on. There was Norwegian salmon, chicken-liver pâté, state-of-the-art video-cameras, expensive perfumes, brand-new washing machines. Saddam's wife Sajida had numerous truckloads of marble ripped out of Kuwaiti palaces and mansions and brought to Baghdad. For Uday Hussein, Saddam's psychopathic eldest son, the victory brought a huge windfall in the shape of vast profits from stolen Kuwaiti cars. Thousands of Baghdadis hoping to snag a Cadillac ($4,000), Chevy ($5,000) or BMW ($8,000) flocked to the huge car sales organized by Saddam's son-in-law General Hussain Kamel, holder of four ministerial portfolios. By early September, Uday was reported to have made $125 million from these car sales.

With money and alcohol flowing more freely than ever among his inner circle, Uday's Baghdad parties, already infamously louche, became completely depraved. At one party, Uday left a bedroom door open so his guests could watch him tying women up and raping them, beating them with his favourite accessory, a black electric cable. Latif Yahia, forced against his will to serve as Uday's double, had a front-row seat at these parties. 'Naked girls roll screeching with bodyguards on the floor. At one point Uday has a girl jump onto a table on which various lamb dishes are laid out for a warm buffet. The girl rolls about in the pilau rice, smearing curry and all kinds of sauces over her breasts, and demands that we lick them off. Some of the men do.'[53]

If the war against Kuwait brought Saddam's family extreme financial and sexual gratification in the short term, for Baghdad and Iraq as a whole it was nothing less than a calamity. Having failed to comply with a UN ultimatum to withdraw its forces from Kuwait by 15 January, Saddam instead precipitated another ruinous war. Led by the US, with support from a broad coalition of thirty-four nations from the UK, France and Canada to Egypt, Syria, Kuwait and Saudi Arabia, the Allied response, which began with an extensive aerial bombardment campaign on 17 January 1991, was ferocious.

Baghdad was bombed nightly, its sky shot with flashes of red, white and yellow – a surreally beautiful, terrifying fireworks display. 'The first wave of attacks has never left my mind,' recalls Saad, a businessman friend. 'I was watching television at 1.30 in the morning when suddenly there was heavy bombing on the Karkh side. It came and went in waves with the F-117 Stealth bombers and lasted till 5.30. It was terrible. Many families huddled together on mattresses, mothers were trying to quieten down their hysterical, crying children. Baghdad became a city of ghosts, especially at night.'[54]

Jumhuriya Bridge was smashed into three pieces. Adhamiya Bridge, Martyr's Bridge and 14 July Bridge were all hit. In the darkness, families sheltered in cellars and air-raid shelters, shunning the ritual propaganda of Baghdad Radio for Radio Monte Carlo, the BBC and the Voice of America, as sirens wailed, wild dogs whimpered in terror, rockets, bombs and Cruise missiles fell, and the city shook all around them. Doors burst open in the explosions; windows shattered into flying shards of glass. Birds in cages died from the shockwaves. The Iraqi artist Nuha al Radi, who kept a compelling diary throughout the bombing of Baghdad, reported wild birds dying by their thousands across the city. Those that survived turned crazy somersaults and flew upside down, confused by the terrible noise and convulsions.[55]

Baghdadis rediscovered old ways and made their own bread, laying out unleavened dough on improvised wire meshes and baking it on old kerosene stoves. Men and women clutched smoking candles made from bottles filled with kerosene and a wick, sealed with a mash of dates. Many of those with friends and families outside Baghdad loaded their freezers on to the back of pick-up trucks and headed for the countryside, eating the food as it defrosted along the way. Electricity and water were cut, telephone lines went down, petrol was rationed. Families who stayed put had to contend with freezers piled with decomposing sheep, chickens, fish, legs of lamb and hunks of beef floating in stagnant water.

Baghdadis took to hauling water from the Tigris and washing clothes in the river. By day there were few cars and buses on the streets. Children took advantage of the relative quiet to play and career about on bikes. Now and then government trucks drove through neighbourhoods, throwing out sacks of bread to desperate crowds. Black columns of smoke drifted across the skyline as the regime burnt tyres in an effort to disorientate enemy pilots. Those living in the eastern district of Jadriya said there was no longer daylight: from the first hours of the bombing of Baghdad, the sky above the burning Dora refinery was permanently black.

The costs of Gulf War One, as it became known, were incalculable. Most of the country's electric-power stations were destroyed, knocking out 92 per cent of installed capacity. Oil refineries were bombed, eliminating 80 per cent of production capacity. Then there were the petrochemical factories, telecommunications centres and 135 telephone networks, more than 100 bridges, untold miles of roads, motorways and railways, trains and rolling stock, the state's radio and television broadcasting stations, cement plants, flour mills and factories producing everything from aluminium and textiles to electric cables and medical supplies – all obliterated from the air.[56] Economic assets carefully built up during five decades were destroyed in the two successive conflicts. Per capita GDP plummeted. In 1980, on the eve of war with Iran, it stood at $1,674. By 1990 it had slumped to $926. A year later it was $546.[57]

By the time American President George H. W. Bush announced the liberation of Kuwait and declared a ceasefire on 28 February, only four days after the ground offensive was launched, much of Iraq lay in ruins, although Allied forces did not march on Baghdad. Visiting Iraq from 10 to 17 March to assess the country's humanitarian needs, the UN's under-secretary-general, Martti Ahtisaari, the former president of Finland, was stunned by the scale of the destruction:

> nothing we had seen or read had quite prepared us for the particular form
> of devastation which has now befallen the country. The recent conflict has
> wrought near-apocalyptic results upon what had been, until January

1991, a rather highly urbanized and mechanized society. Now, most of modern life support has been destroyed or rendered tenuous. Iraq has, for some time to come, been relegated to a pre-industrial age, but with all the disabilities of post-industrial dependency on an intensive use of energy and technology.[58]

Or, in American Secretary of State James Baker's more concise version, issued as a pre-war threat, Iraq had been bombed 'back into the Stone Age'.[59]

*

Although the uprisings in March 1991 against Saddam were a largely southern Shia and northern Kurd phenomenon – every major city in the south and north bar Mosul briefly fell into rebel hands – Baghdad was once again in the thick of the action and at the centre of a national crisis. As the regime mobilized to suppress the rebellion with overwhelming force, many of those who bravely rose against the regime were rounded up, tortured and executed. In Kerbala, cats and dogs fed on corpses in the streets, family relatives too frightened to retrieve them for fear of further killings by a regime at bay. Many of the captured rebels were sent to Redwaniya, a large secret detention centre around nine miles west of central Baghdad next to Saddam International Airport. Here, according to eyewitness reports, Saddam Kamel, the 'butcher of Baghdad', supervised mass executions, personally shooting Shia and Kurd prisoners from his armchair in a courtyard for hours at a time. The prison stank of vomit, urine, faeces and decomposing flesh; the corpses of executed prisoners were thrown back into cells and removed only when the stench became intolerable for the guards. It was reported that Kamel received 20,000 dinars per man killed from Ali Hassan al Majid. At around the same time Saddam personally executed thirty prisoners, shooting them at point-blank range one by one in the grounds of his destroyed 'Project 2000' palace, a stone's throw from the Republican Palace, before declaring, 'I feel better now.'[60] The number of those killed during the uprising was unclear, estimated by one organization at 25,000–100,000. Both sides committed numerous atrocities.[61] Suppression of the uprising had one objective above all others: Saddam's survival as Iraqi ruler. By that measure, it was a complete success.

Recovery from the annihilating Gulf War campaign and its brutal aftermath would have been difficult enough in the best of times. Under the tightly enforced UN sanctions, it was impossible. America, the UK and France maintained the pressure on Saddam, enforcing two No-Fly Zones in the north and south to protect the Kurds and Shia respectively. Bombings continued throughout the 1990s and lasted until the invasion of 2003.

As the decade progressed, so Baghdadis started hearing stories of children dying of malnutrition. Saddam blamed the UN embargo; the UN blamed Saddam. Either way, the regime did not have to trim its sails when it came to looking after its own. While old scythe-wielding women in black *abayas* cut bulrushes on the banks of the Tigris as their ancestors had done for centuries, the lavish disco boats – accompanied with roaring jetskis – continued to ply the river, with fireworks, dancing girls, sumptuous banquets and prodigiously stocked bars. The severity of the sanctions regime led to one of the less publicized tragedies of modern Baghdad, which altered the city's appearance for good. The palm trees that had been such a distinctive feature of Baghdad and its riverfront for centuries started to disappear in droves as desperate families cut them down for fuel. This in turn led to worsening sandstorms, as more land turned to dirt, dust and desert.

Outside the tiny inner circle of the senior command and their cronies, shortages became the norm throughout Iraq: of food, medicine, any kind of equipment, spare parts. Already under political and psychological siege from Saddam's regime, Baghdadis now had to contend with a full economic blockade. Iraq was unique within the developing world in having received huge income in a very short time, only to have ended up with 'heavy foreign debt, heavy internal debt, a destroyed infrastructure, a shrinking and isolated economy, an impoverished and starved population, and staggering inequality in the distribution of income'.[62] As inflation soared, street-sellers, often children, sat by slabs of ragged cash, often measured by ruler. In 1990, $1 was worth 6 dinars. By 1995, when the official rate was 600 dinars, a dollar could be exchanged on the black market for around 3,000. A year later a doctor's salary was worth twenty-four eggs a month.

In the midst of this suddenly enforced poverty, Saddam's palace-building continued apace. Four new palaces suddenly sprang up along the Tigris, hidden from public view behind a 20-foot-high white concrete wall. One resembled a Spanish hacienda, another a shrunken air traffic control tower, the third an exercise in 1970s sci-fi. A 1999 US State Department study estimated that Saddam had spent at least $2 billion building almost fifty palaces from the time of Gulf War One.[63] For the writer Kanan Makiya, it was yet more pastiche masquerading as the revival of Mesopotamian and Islamic traditions. The 'totalizing sovereignty' of the dictator's kitsch had snuffed out art altogether: 'it is hard to imagine how anyone could so successfully combine the worst in everything'.[64]

Isolated from the world because of the actions of one man and his regime, the City of Peace withered and drew in on itself during the 1990s.

> What was once a rich and vibrant city, full of ambition, hope, discotheques and grandiose construction projects, was now an ugly, battered Third World slum, with not a single redeeming thing of beauty to be found anywhere throughout all its many miserable square miles . . . Here the outer circumstances pale in comparison with the inner carnage and horror. Not just the city has suffered from neglect and physical abuse; the minds of its inhabitants have been tampered with in an infinitely crueller, probably irreparable manner. For over twenty years, what has been happening to Iraq amounts to a psychological holocaust.[65]

Paul Roberts, the writer of that portrait of Baghdad, briefly interviewed Saddam on the eve of Gulf War One. When the dictator looked into his eyes, 'the shock hit like a column of iced mercury pumped up the spine'.[66]

Living in Saddam's Iraq induced a form of nationwide schizophrenia. An army psychologist spoke for many Iraqis when he acknowledged, 'It was as if I was living two personalities. I would do my best as an officer with my duties and then I would come home and speak against the regime. All Iraqis have two or more characters. It was the only way to survive under pressure for such a long time.'[67]

A chance remark, the sudden appearance of a car parked outside the house, a knock on the door, a telephone call, the summons from an unknown official, even an innocent glance – anything could change – and destroy – lives for ever. This was how Saddam's regime permeated Baghdad – through the osmosis of fear. No one was safe, and everyone knew it. The wrong look could be your last. The one-time prisoner Mayada al Askari recalled the horrifying story of fourteen-year-old twin brothers who were playing football in the streets when a car carrying security officials drove past. The boys were picked up for staring, taken away, tortured and executed. Only after extreme pleading and string-pulling were their distraught parents allowed to see the bodies. Their chests were covered with burns from an electric iron. They had been dissected from neck to stomach, and their eyeballs had been gouged out of their sockets. The parents were told they were lucky: many people simply disappeared and were never heard from again.[68]

Yet even Baghdadis shuddered when rumours circulated in February 1996 of the killing of Hussain Kamel, who had led Iraq's weapons-development programme, and his brother Saddam Kamel, Saddam's son-in-laws. They had been persuaded to return to Baghdad after having defected to Amman the year before. The message was clear: we can, and we will, destroy anyone.

Suffering under the twin evils of Saddam and the sanctions regime was endemic. At the Ministry of Health, propaganda portraits showed Saddam cradling a sick child, while young boys and girls in Baghdad perished in their tens of thousands. The Al Wiwa maternity hospital, once famous across the Middle East as a pioneer of 1970s in vitro fertilization, was reduced to a stinking unit in which two babies shared every incubator and little more than oxygen was available to treat the sick. Tuberculosis, typhoid, malaria and cholera, hallmarks of another era, returned to stalk the reeking wards of Baghdad's hospitals. Women died in childbirth of minor infections; doctors were forced to reuse surgical gloves and unsterilized needles.

In the poorest parts of town, such as Saddam City, haggard children as young as eleven became a regular sight on the streets, working for twelve hours as delivery boys or street vendors in sewage-flooded roads to bring back less than a dollar a day. Breakfasts were no more than leftover rice and beans, dinners a scrap of bread and oil. Under the terms of the controversial – and highly corrupt – UN Oil for Food Programme, by which Iraq was allowed to sell $2 billion of oil every six months to pay for food and medicine, the food basket distributed nationwide included flour, rice, sugar, tea, chickpeas, beans, salt, cooking oil and infant formula for children under two. There was no meat, fish, poultry, fruit or vegetables.[69]

The rations were not enough to live on. Some mothers were so malnourished they could not produce breast milk.[70] Infant mortality, according to UNICEF statistics, which relied largely on Iraqi government figures, doubled from 61 per 1,000 in 1991 to 117 per 1,000 in 1997. The average number of children under five killed by respiratory infections, malnutrition and diarrhoeal illnesses increased from 500 a month in 1991 to 8,000 in 1996. The UN estimate of one-third of Iraqi children suffering from malnutrition put the oil-rich country on a par with sub-Saharan Africa.[71] UNICEF estimated around 500,000 children under five had died unnecessarily as a result of the embargo, a figure that became an international rallying cry for campaigners against the sanctions.[72]

Schools and universities had no books, paper or pencils. Students were forced to take notes on the backs of receipts, bills, any scrap of paper. Some university students spent alternate years working and studying because their parents could not afford the bills.

Middle-class Baghdadis slid into begging. Iraqis with PhDs took to driving taxis, while uneducated smugglers, or 'embargo cats', grew rich through illegal trade and roared through Baghdad in top-of-the-range Mercedes and BMWs. On Mutanabbi Street, the traditional home of literary Baghdad, the booksellers hawked beautiful antiquarian volumes in Arabic and English, sold by their owners to buy medicines for their children. Most of Baghdad's cinemas were forced to close because the films and film-processing chemicals they required were prohibited under the UN embargo. Bitter resentment towards the outside world was the norm.

Foreign visitors arriving at Saddam International Airport in the 1990s were met with the legend WELCOME TO IRAQ: CRADLE OF CIVILIZATION beneath a vast mural setting out the great sweep of Iraqi history, as construed by the regime. It began with Nebuchadnezzar surveying his victorious troops marching through Babylon, raising swords in salute while they hauled along their Jewish prisoners in chains. On it went, through Caliph Mansur, surveying another military parade and more prisoners, and culminating with Saddam, pictured alongside the obligatory humiliated prisoners wearing either scruffy army uniforms or the black robes of the ayatollahs.

While those inmates of Baghdad Asylum who could muster the energy were singing to foreign visitors, 'We love Saddam Hussein. It is an honour to sing his name', fifteen of their weaker colleagues were dying every month. The meagre rations of soup, lentils, rice and tea provided only a third of their nutritional needs. Tuberculosis, diarrhoea and amoebic dysentery were the unit's most lethal problems. In 1996 a quarter of the 1,340 inmates had been taken there by their families because they had no food with which to feed them. In the absence of medication and other supplies, the asylum's most common treatment was electric-shock therapy.[73]

Survival was the order of the day. If beating Saddam's killing machine required great care and a measure of good luck, overcoming acute poverty, malnutrition and the illnesses they brought, especially for the young, demanded the greatest resilience. Families pawned silver, china, jewellery, anything worth something, to feed themselves. Years later the largely American and British shoppers who arrived on the coat-tails of the 2003 invasion would find in the elegant boutiques of the Al Rashid Hotel, among the Saddam-themed tat, expensive goods disposed of by once-wealthy Baghdadis reduced to dire straits: Dupont and Dunhill cigarette lighters, Cartier watches, silver-plated Christofle salvers, Mont Blanc pens, exquisitely engraved antique silver cigarette cases from Isfahan, Breitling watches given by Saddam to his airforce pilots during the Iraq–Iran War.

Thieves thrived. In the early 1990s, petrol, beer, cigarettes and chandeliers were the gangs' top choices. In a city where rumour was an essential way of life – a consequence of the regime's empty but all-encompassing propaganda system – stories swept through Baghdad about the latest outrageous theft. In one tale, a taxi driver returned home from the front with a coffin strapped on to the roof of his car; looking for the dead soldier's parents, he stopped to ask directions at a house and came out to discover the car and coffin had gone (cars parked in front of their owners' houses overnight were often discovered the following morning propped up on four bricks, their wheels removed). At times dignity disappeared altogether. Sacred occasions were sometimes just another opportunity for gangs to steal. Food brought to funerals as a donation to the bereaved family was often pilfered. As one woman who attended a funeral in 1995 recalled, by the time the sheep had been butchered, half of the meat had already walked, together with sacks of flour and sugar.[74]

One way to keep the prowling thieves at bay was to have a dog. Burglar alarms were less favoured, since there were no spare parts available. Displaying a characteristic combination of invention and aggression, Baghdadis started breeding a particularly ferocious 'wolf-dog', part

German shepherd and part Bedouin sheepdog, to deter all but the most reckless thieves.

*

One of the most popular shows in Baghdad in 2002 was *My Love Is the Moon*, a surrealist time-travel romp produced by Haidar Monather, a starry actor-director of the Iraqi stage. A young man called Faraj visits a Baghdad museum and is catapulted back to the Ottoman era on the eve of the British invasion in 1917. He falls in love with the beautiful young Kamar, only to discover she is earmarked for the sultan. For a while it looks desperate. But all is not lost, and after several scrapes the amorous Faraj manages to fast-forward with Kamar to modern Baghdad.

The play represented an exuberant and more or less affordable (2,000 dinars, or around $1 for a ticket) flight of escapism for Baghdadis weary after eleven years of sanctions. The National Theatre, with its marble lobby, built in the 1970s, still held on to a fading grandeur at a time when other public entertainment in Baghdad was scarce.

The venerable Baghdad Philharmonic, one of the oldest classical orchestras in the Arab world, hung on precariously, its musicians making do with frayed violin strings and cracked oboe reeds, their salaries cut from $300 a month to $3. One of the orchestra's scores in 2002 was 'To the UN', an angry piece of clashing cymbals and beating drums, a dramatic counterpoint to the more mournful 'Heartbeat of Baghdad'. UN sanctions hit everyone. The orchestra's conductor, Amin Izzat, lost his wife when their rickety gas stove, starved of proper maintenance and spare parts, exploded.

The themes of *My Love Is the Moon*, which included anti-imperialist swipes and allusions to caged animals caught in a circus of the absurd, were not difficult to distinguish. As one of the characters exclaims, 'First the Turks, then the British, now the Americans!'[75]

*

From the moment of the 9/11 attacks against New York's Twin Towers in 2001, the moustachioed face of Saddam Hussein was clearly in the crosshairs of President George W. Bush, son of the president who in 1991 had invaded Iraq – but who had refrained from moving on Baghdad to enforce 'regime change'. For many, this was a case of unfinished business, combined with the lure and lucre of oil. Supporters of war argued the world could no longer tolerate Saddam's weapons of mass destruction. Prime Minister Tony Blair's government declared Baghdad could threaten Britain within 'forty-five minutes'. It was just one of many egregiously misleading statements that helped to bring about the conflict.

As pressure mounted on Baghdad, Iraqis went to the polls on 15 October 2002, to vote for Saddam Hussein in a loyalty referendum called to extend his presidential term for another seven years. The official result was 100 per cent, a slight improvement from the 99.96 per cent Saddam won in 1995 on a voter turnout of 99 per cent.[76]

On 25 January 2003 three black double-decker buses bearing the words '500,000 dead Iraqi children "worth it" – TRUTH JUSTICE PEACE' left London for Baghdad. According to Stefan Simanowitz, co-founder of the Human Shield Action to Iraq, an anti-war campaign to prevent the American-led coalition from bombing certain targets, activists received a 'tumultuous welcome' when they arrived in Baghdad three weeks later, on 16 February. Yet, when idealism confronted Baathism, there could only be one winner. Many of the multinational shields, who came from the US, UK, Belgium, Germany, South Africa, New Zealand, Germany and Australia, were not 'comfortable' working closely with the regime. 'Others felt that they would rather be deployed in schools, hospitals and orphanages' and quickly left Iraq. There were two weeks of 'heated discussion' before the shields were given an ultimatum to 'start shielding or start leaving'.[77] The shields' host, Dr Abdul Razak al Hashimi, Saddam's adviser and head of the Organization of Friendship, Peace and Solidarity, deported the more independent-minded. Of the 500 shields who went to Iraq – 'pierced faces and dreadlocks were in abundance' – eighty moved to protect water-treatment facilities, power stations, food silos and other civilian infrastructure sites.[78]

Shields aside, the government continued its preparations, digging giant trenches near the Dora oil refinery and filling them with oil, ready to set alight and create a thick smokescreen to confuse American pilots. The Baath Party leadership across the city supervised more trench-digging and sandbagging. In their homes Baghdadis stockpiled emergency supplies of food and bottled water, dug wells in their gardens, fixed duct tape across their windows, bought 250-dinar particle masks to protect them in the event of the oil trenches being set alight. The once weekly *Humat al Watan – Guardians of the Nation* – television programme, an official Ministry of Defence production, started broadcasting nightly, railing against Western governments. Foreign correspondents scrambled for rooms at the Al Rashid Hotel, trailing flak jackets, helmets, satellite phones, chemical-biological warfare suits, boxes piled with MREs – meals ready to eat, as also used by the US Army. The queues at petrol stations were getting longer by the day. On 6 March the regime's *Iraq Daily* sent a warning message to Colin Powell and Donald Rumsfeld, recalling the British invasion almost a century earlier: 'We have prepared for you a nice and comfortable grave next to your inferior [*sic*] Stanley Maude.'[79]

In its long and troubled history, Baghdad had been besieged and placed under sanctions; it had been attacked, flooded, burnt and bombed. So for Baghdadis used to eking out a pitiful living under the regime of Saddam, a state of siege was, to a large extent, the natural order. The city once more braced itself for onslaught as the drumbeat of war sounded more urgently and sandstorms battered the city. The Americans called it 'Shock and Awe', a 1996 military doctrine from the National Defense University intended to bring about rapid victory through the use of power so overwhelming and spectacular that the enemy's will to fight is completely destroyed.[80]

*

The bombing of Baghdad began at 5.33 a.m., on 20 March, the day after the last 500 prisoners from the Iraq–Iran War had been exchanged. By this time Salam Pax was on his way to becoming the most famous blogger in the world with 'Where is Raed?', a brave, brash and seditious web diary from Baghdad. Had the security services discovered his identity at any time, he would have been 'pasta sauce'.[81] Two days after the first bombs fell on Baghdad, he wrote, 'The whole city looked as if it were on fire. The only thing I could think of was, "Why does this have to happen to Baghdad?" As one of the buildings I really love went up in a huge explosion I was close to tears.'[82] Salam Pax, the pseudonym it later emerged of a gay, twenty-nine-year-old architect called Salam Abdul Munem, was heralded as the Anne Frank of the Iraq War, writing brilliantly observed reportage with fierce conviction, lacerating humour and unsentimental clarity. 'Let me tell you one thing first,' he wrote in May. 'War sucks big time. Don't let yourself ever be talked into having one waged in the name of your freedom. Somehow, when the bombs start dropping or you hear the sound of machine-guns at the end of your street, you don't think about your "imminent liberation" anymore.'[83]

In addition to the bombs, Coalition aircraft dropped leaflets on Baghdad, warning Iraqi armed forces, 'We can see everything. Don't use nuclear, biological or chemical weapons.' Others followed. 'While your families struggle to stay alive, he lives in riches' showed Saddam sitting on a throne juxtaposed with an image of a woman holding a crying baby. 'Attention all Special Republican Guards! The Coalition forces are coming to rid Iraq from Saddam and his regime. You should not have to suffer their fate.'[84]

As war got under way, black humour was supplied by Mohammed Saeed al Sahaf, the black-bereted Iraqi information minister, whose colourful and counter-intuitive bombast quickly earned him the nicknames of Comical Ali and Baghdad Bob. When US forces seized control of Saddam International Airport after heavy fighting on 4 April – it was soon restyled Baghdad International Airport – Sahaf predicted a Dien Bien Phu-style slaughter of the 'villains', 'mercenaries' and 'animals'. While artillery rumbled on the outskirts of Baghdad, thousands rushed to leave on the highway heading west. Power was cut across the city.

Three days later Sahaf stood in front of the world's television cameras on the eastern bank of the Tigris and denied US forces had entered Baghdad. 'Their infidels are committing suicide by the hundreds on the gates of Baghdad,' he said with a theatrical flourish. 'We will encourage them to commit suicide more quickly.' He went on: 'Be assured, Baghdad is very secure, very safe. Baghdad is great.' As he spoke, US Abrams tanks were visible behind him on the other side of the river. By this time the most senior spokesman in Baghdad had won an international following – President Bush was a fan – and a website appeared devoted to his more outlandish pronouncements: 'There are no American infidels in Baghdad. Never!'; 'My feelings – as usual – we will slaughter them all'; 'Our initial assessment is that they will all die.' One of his last comments to a foreign reporter, quickly celebrated on T-shirts and mugs in the US, was 'I now inform you that you are too far from reality.'[85]

On 9 April, after a chaotically short-lived defence of the city, Baghdad fell. In Firdus Square in eastern Baghdad, Iraqis and American soldiers from 1 MEF, the Marines Expeditionary Force, joined forces to pull down a statue of the hated dictator. Photographs of it falling became iconic images. Saddam's rule was over. 'Big Moustache has had his day.'

Wild celebrations began throughout Baghdad as the news spread. 'Come, see, this is freedom!' came a cry as Baghdadis ripped down and smashed portraits of Saddam, beat them with shoes, stamped on them and tore them up, cursing him as a criminal, traitor and infidel.[86] Crowds clapped and cheered American soldiers and foreign correspondents in the same streets where Iraqi Army uniforms and boots had been discarded pell-mell as Saddam's dispirited armed forces evaporated.

From total control to lawlessness was a swift transition. Iraqis – and the world – watched in fascinated horror as looting broke out across Baghdad. Crowds descended on government buildings and ripped out air-conditioning units, computers, ceiling fans, curtains, refrigerators, hat-stands, desks and chairs, piling them into the back of pick-up trucks, precariously loading them on to car roofs or hand-pushed trolleys. Some hijacked police cars and motorbikes and raced off, hooting in delight. The Iraqi Olympics Committee headquarters, part of the despised Uday Hussein's empire, was ransacked and torched. His thoroughbred horses were immediately stolen from nearby stables. On Palestine Street, one of the regime's favourite venues for staging shows of support for Saddam, crowds pillaged freely from a trade ministry warehouse. 'This is our peace dividend,' a Baghdadi explained.[87] Many were appalled. 'To see your city destroyed before your own eyes is not a pain that can be described and put to words,' Salam Pax blogged on 10 April. 'It turns you sour (or is that bitter?). It makes something snap in you and you lose whatever hope you had. Undone by your own hands.'[88]

Yet, compared to what followed, the theft of government property, however reprehensible, was barely a footnote in the fall of Baghdad.

*

On a clear-skied morning in Baghdad I had an appointment to visit Dr Donny George, director of the Iraq Museum, which was still closed to the public. Over in the Salihiya district, on an 11-acre wedge of land at the intersection of Kahira and Nasir streets, a far greater disaster had taken place. On 8 April 2003, staff at the museum fled as a fire-fight broke out in front of the building. Saddam's forces entered the compound, and snipers were targeting American units from the museum galleries. An American tank round smashed into the museum façade. By the time the first workers returned to work on 12 April, some of the world's most priceless treasures, relics of the earliest civilizations, had been looted. Initial reports suggested 170,000 artefacts had been stolen, including the museum's finest pieces: the slender 5,000-year-old sacred Uruk Vase, a masterpiece of Sumerian art thought to be the world's oldest carved stone ritual vessel; the Bassetki Statue, an Akkadian figure of a man sculpted in copper in around 2300 BC; the two copper Ninhursag Bulls that had once adorned the temple built by the King of Ur in 2475 BC; the Treasure of Nimrud, 613 pieces of gold jewellery and precious stones from the eighth and ninth centuries BC; the Golden Harp of Ur from around 2500 BC, shattered into pieces and denuded of its gold; the Uruk Mask, perhaps the oldest naturalistic sculpture of a human face, from 3100 BC. Of the museum's collection of 15,000 cylinder seals, over 5,000 had been plundered. Priceless artefacts were hacked off walls, knocked off their bases, seized from smashed cabinets and displays. One of the most devastating blows was the vandalism and partial destruction of the museum's archaeological archives. The losses were unthinkable. Museum officials asked the Americans for urgent help in protecting the museum, but it took until 16 April for US tanks to arrive.[89]

Although US Defense Secretary Donald Rumsfeld brushed off the looting in Baghdad with the observation that 'freedom's untidy' and 'stuff happens', the world was horrified.[90] Piotr Michalowski, Professor of Near East Studies at Michigan University, offered some context. 'The pillaging of the Baghdad Museum is a tragedy that has no parallel in world history; it is as if the Uffizi, the Louvre, or all the museums of Washington DC had been wiped out in one fell swoop.'[91] Eleanor Robson of the British School of Archaeology in Iraq, another Gertrude Bell legacy, shared the sense of outrage. 'You'd have to go back centuries, to the Mongol invasion of Baghdad in 1258, to find looting on this scale.'[92]

Over the following weeks and months, many of the treasures were returned, 'rediscovered' or rescued by American and Iraqi authorities. Some were seized from international markets in Jordan, Lebanon, Syria, Kuwait, Saudi Arabia and the US. The final losses were much fewer than had first been feared. Up to 15,000 pieces had been stolen, but a year later 5,000 had been returned with a further 5,000 expected, as meticulously recorded by Colonel Matthew Bogdanos, the US Marine tasked with investigating the looting of the museum.[93] Nevertheless, the damage and outstanding losses were irreparable.

George was a portly, sad-eyed Christian, a distinguished archaeologist and scholar who had joined the museum in 1976. A year after the tragedy, he was still aghast that it could ever have happened. 'This is one of the greatest catastrophes in the history of Baghdad,' he said. 'But it's not just a disaster for Baghdad. Every piece we have lost represents a loss for humanity. It's a crime against the heritage of mankind. The Iraq Museum is the only place in the world where you can trace the beginnings of civilization and human culture – from art and agriculture to language and technology – on one site. There is nothing like it. What happened here beggars belief.' He was apoplectic about the damage done to Babylon. 'It's mankind's greatest heritage site. You don't just start digging it up to make more room for your tanks.'[94]

We padded together disconsolately through locked and shuttered galleries and sealed storehouses, shafts of sunlight stealing through the darkness, illuminating motes of dust thrown up by our procession. Treasures of classical antiquity, together with some of the greatest artefacts ever culled from the Muslim world, when Baghdad was the seat of the Abbasid caliphate, had been stolen in the latest dismal chapter of the city's history. A magnificent pair of Assyrian statues glowed gold amidst the gloom, winged bulls from the palace of Sargon in Khorsabad from the ninth century BC, standing tall like bearded sentinels, aloof from the chaos outside. Seeing these historical jewels that still stood proudly in the neglected galleries suddenly animated him. 'Just look at these,' he said, bobbing about in front of an arch-shaped panel of glazed bricks in faded green and brown, rich with floral and geometric decorations and pictures of animals. 'They're the oldest decorated bricks known to man, from Fort Shalmaneser in Nimrud – ninth century BC. Just imagine what they have survived to be here today.' There were gorgeously ornate statues of deities, stone *mihrabs* (the internal niche in a mosque indicating the direction towards Mecca in which the faithful should pray), friezes and tablets and statues hidden in darkened corridors, surrounded by piles of masonry and plaster, the odd wheelbarrow, broken windows, half-finished scaffolding. The cradle of civilization had been shattered.

The cultural losses were a catastrophe for Baghdad, a city that proudly considered itself the rightful guardian of the world's oldest civilizations. Yet even these savage thefts paled next to the extraordinary loss of life during the next several years, when Baghdad became a slaughter-house, the most dangerous city in the world. What happened to George in the aftermath of the 2003 invasion encapsulated the post-war tragedy of sectarian strife that tore Baghdad – and Iraq – apart. One of the more prominent members of Iraq's Assyrian Church of the East, which can trace its origins to the See of Babylon, said to have been founded by the Apostle Saint Thomas, he had dropped his family name of Youkhanna for professional purposes. He said he normally worshipped at St George's Church in Baghdad, where he was married, but it had been badly damaged in a recent terrorist attack and was now too dangerous to attend. 'Churches are being bombed in Baghdad and Mosul, Christian shops selling alcohol and music are being attacked and firebombed and we're receiving leaflets warning us to stop "corrupting Islamic society". That is what being a Christian in Iraq has come to.' Extremists were now threatening to kill him. In 2006, having received an envelope containing a Kalashnikov bullet and a letter accusing his younger son of disrespecting Islam, he fled Iraq.

*

On 1 May, when American war fatalities stood at 138, President Bush declared 'Mission Accomplished' in Iraq. By the end of the year the figure was 486. US forces completed their withdrawal at the end of 2011, and by 2012, when the last American death was confirmed, the final tally was 4,486.[95]

For much of the period in between, Baghdad was a surrealist dystopia divided between the six square miles of the Green Zone, formerly the heart of Saddam's regime, and the Red Zone, or everything that lay beyond it. From April 2003 the Green Zone was a heavily fortified enclave of Little America in which officials and contractors in Paul Bremer's Coalition Provisional Authority (CPA) had 'team huddles' and sat in front of computer screens prettifying PowerPoint presentations about 'metrics', 'deliverables' and the 'drumbeat' of progress.* Many of those who worked inside this bubble were contractually forbidden from leaving it in the course of their duties. They inhabited a cocoon of continually evolving acronyms, dodging IDFs as they shuttled between the multiple offices of IRMO, PCO, ORHA, ICC, GRD, LMCC and MNF-I before downing pens for a bacon cheeseburger, Baskin Robbins ice cream and a Gatorade at the DFAC and perhaps knocking back a few discreet beers and whiskies later in the BCC. Once in a while there would be a Rhino run down Route Irish – the most dangerous stretch

* Paul Bremer, a US diplomat and former businessman, was appointed administrator of the CPA in 2003, serving as the de facto head of the Iraqi state from 11 May that year to 28 June 2004, when power was transferred to the Iraqi Interim Government.

of asphalt in the world – to BIAP, on which passengers prayed hard to avoid VBIEDs, IEDs, RPGs and SAF.*

It was an improbable stage with an unlikely cast: a multicultural mix of neocons and ideologues, army officers in a permanent hurry, soldiers in grey T-shirts and black gym shorts with M4 rifles slung across their shoulders, close-cropped helicopter pilots in sweat-marked flight suits, smartly suited political advisers in button-down Oxfords and wrap-around shades, tattooed, goatee-bearded security contractors in Tactical 511 combats, impassioned gender advisers, rule of law and security-sector reform experts, tribal analysts, fast-talking IT systems managers, Filipino laundry staff, tractor drivers from Texas, catering staff from Bangladesh, rehatted South African mercenaries, American engineers, Chinese restaurateurs and masseuses, the occasional blue-bereted UN official from Britain or Australia, procurement and logistics contractors, would-be, latter-day Lawrences, war-profiteers, opportunists and poseurs, romantics, dreamers and schemers. 'We're going to sweep through the entire region, taking out every dictator one by one,' an American contractor said to me once. 'They're going to learn what democracy and freedom mean.'

Occasionally, you would see the odd Iraqi – perhaps a VIP, translator, political adviser or gardener. But this was a world, by and large, in which Iraqis were not welcome. Numerous signs around the CP checkpoints, bristling with barbed wire, 17-foot blast walls, sand-filled HESCO barriers and twitchy, heavily armed soldiers and security contractors, told drivers: DO NOT ENTER OR YOU WILL BE SHOT. Iraqis were not allowed to enter the Green Zone – later the International Zone, or 'Eye Zee' – unless they worked for the CPA or had lived there previously. I remember one dinner with a senior Iraqi politician at the Al Rashid Hotel, Saddam's bug-ridden trap for foreign visitors overlooking Zawra Park on the fringes of the Green Zone. The evening was ruined after a soldier slammed him against a wall for an aggressive body

* Indirect Fire; Iraq Reconstruction Management Office; Project and Contracting Office; Office for Reconstruction and Humanitarian Assistance; Iraqi Convention Centre; Gulf Region Division [of the US Army Corps of Engineers]; Logistics Movement Control Centre; Multi-National Forces – Iraq; Dining Facility; Baghdad Country Club; Baghdad International Airport; Vehicle-Borne Improvised Explosive Devices; Improvised Explosive Devices; Rocket-Propelled Grenades; Small Arms Fire.

search, completely unprovoked. 'They treat us like common criminals in our own country,' he said, shaking with anger. 'And this is liberation.'

For a time it was fashionable to post a quotation from T. E. Lawrence on office walls and desks – 'Do not try to do too much with your own hands. Better the Arabs do it tolerably than that you do it perfectly. It is their war, and you are to help them, not to win it for them – while doing precisely the opposite of what the quotation exhorted.[96] Almost as popular was the poster in which a smiling American soldier holds up a cup of tea above the legend HOW ABOUT A NICE CUP OF SHUT THE FUCK UP.

Bremer's otherworldly CPA evoked the dark unreality of Joseph Heller's *Catch-22*. Senior appointments tended to be politically driven. Knowledge of Arabic or experience of the Middle East mattered less than loyalty to the US Republican Party. As a result, Bremer's inner circle of advisers had no prior experience of Arab affairs or any knowledge of Arabic. A twenty-four-year-old official with no background in finance was given the job of resurrecting Baghdad's stock market. A reservist officer tasked with devising new traffic regulations for the capital simply downloaded those of the American state of Maryland from the internet. The private-sector development portfolio went to an investment banker and major Republican Party donor, a former Harvard classmate of the president, who vowed to privatize all of Iraq's state-owned enterprises within thirty days. 'I don't give a shit about international law,' he told a colleague. 'I made a commitment to the president that I'd privatize Iraq's businesses.'[97]

Bremer's political vision did not appear to be adequately guided or informed by local realities. He brushed off Grand Ayatollah Ali al Sistani's *fatwa* that Iraq's new constitution had to be written by elected representatives, treating the spiritual leader of the majority Shia, a man of unparalleled religious authority in Iraq, as though he were 'just another old man in a black turban'. A swathe of West Baghdad around Baghdad International Airport became the palace-filled American military base of Camp Victory, which included camps Liberty, Striker and Slayer, as well as a Pizza Hut, Burger King, Taco Bell, Subway, Cinnabon and Green Beans café. When asked why American helicopters were flying so low and terrifying young children at night, Brigadier-General Mark Kimmitt, a US military spokesman, advised Iraqis to tell their children that the ear-shattering noise of low-flying helicopters was 'the sound of freedom'.[98]

In the garden of Saddam's former Republican Palace, studded with palm trees and shaded by gazebos, young men sporting baggy trunks, wraparound Oakleys, tattoos, rippling six-packs and bulging biceps tanned themselves by the pool. Some sipped iced teas or chilled beer in the blinding light and stultifying heat, stealing admiring looks at the very few women brave enough to don a bikini in this almost exclusively male, testosterone-charged world. Hip-hop thudded from a boom box near by. Every few minutes Black Hawk helicopters thundered overhead on their way to or from 'Washington', the Green Zone landing area adjacent to the palace. In the evenings a crowd moved to the Chinese Restaurant for dinners of 'General Chicken' or spicy noodles and cold beers, while a regular flow of all-male traffic headed self-consciously upstairs for massages.

What happened inside the Green Zone had very little to do with what was happening outside. When heavy gunfire erupted on a steamy night in May 2004, CPA staffers drinking by the pool thought insurgents were storming the Green Zone and fled in panic to the palace's reinforced basement for safety. The noise was celebratory gunfire. The Iraqi football team had just beaten Saudi Arabia 3–1 in a critical game, thereby securing a place in the Olympics.

There was a honeymoon for several months in 2003, during which time an ever growing number of political parties scrambled to establish offices in Baghdad: the Patriotic Union of Kurdistan at the National Engineering Consultants' building, the Kurdish Democratic Party at the old Mukhabarat building in Mansur, the Iraqi National Congress in a former army conscription centre, Islamic Dawa at the children's public library. For this brief period many Iraqis were still pleased to see American forces in Baghdad. Then, from the late summer of 2003, security began to deteriorate dramatically.

On 19 August 2003 the UN's Canal Hotel headquarters in Baghdad was attacked in a deadly truck bombing that killed twenty-two, including Sergio Vieira de Mello, the charismatic Brazilian head of the UN mission. Al Qaeda in Iraq claimed responsibility for the attack, under its leader Abu Musab al Zarqawi, a Jordanian militant who styled himself the Amir of Al Qaeda in the Country of Two Rivers. The Iraq franchise of the global terror organization founded by Osama bin Laden in the late 1980s quickly established a deadly network of fighters in the aftermath of the 2003 invasion, complete with an apparently endless supply of suicide bombers. Violence in Baghdad and across Iraq then intensified after the Abu Ghraib torture scandal of 2004, in which American military police and other government agencies were revealed to have been abusing Iraqi prisoners in what had been one of Saddam's most notorious prisons, 20 miles west of Baghdad.

There were photographs of naked Iraqi men piled into a pyramid in front of grinning soldiers, guards terrorizing a prisoner with an attack dog, a hooded Iraqi man forced to masturbate in front of his guard and numerous other instances of prisoner abuse. American soldiers had urinated on detainees, poured phosphoric acid on them, ridden them like animals, sodomized them with batons or phosphoric lights, dragged them across the floor by tying ropes to their legs or penises, force-fed them with pork and alcohol, made them retrieve food from prison toilets and, in one case, beaten a prisoner to death. One of the most infamous pictures, of a hooded Iraqi standing on a box wearing nothing but a ragged blanket with electric wires attached to his hands, became global news and drew international opprobrium.[99]

Baghdad became a cauldron of killing. The stomach-hollowing sound of a suicide car-bomber destroying a Green Zone checkpoint became a regular feature of living in Baghdad, as did attacks on Iraqi politicians, crowded markets, Iraqis queuing to join the police, or enter a government ministry, or a foreign embassy, or the offices of a humanitarian agency. Sometimes an explosion at dawn was so powerful it shook you out of bed and on to the floor. At the time the steady flow of young men ready to blow themselves up for the *jihadi* cause seemed unending. Columns of thick black smoke drifting across the skyline from the latest explosion were a common view. Sometimes you wondered how anyone could even contemplate, let alone perpetrate, any act of violence in such mind-bending, paralysing heat. At other times the sheer brutality of the climate seemed the only explanation for levels of slaughter that were otherwise unfathomable. 'The heat in Baghdad hits you like concrete,' an Iraqi friend said to me once. 'Imagine what it does to your head.'

Shia death squads and Sunni insurgents began to reshape the city according to religious affiliation. In 2003 the majority of the city was mixed Sunni–Shia, with a number of Shia majority neighbourhoods (including Sadr City, renamed from Saddam City, Kadhimiya and Shula in the north) and Sunni majority areas (such as Adhamiya and Hurriya in the north, Washash, Karkh and Mansur in the centre, and Saeediya in the south). By 2005, when the Ministry of the Interior was under the control of the Islamic Supreme Council of Iraq's Badr Brigade, corpses were discovered daily, dumped in streets and rubbish tips across the capital. Overwhelmingly Sunni, their bodies carried the familiar signs of torture: cigarette burns on the skin, electric-drill holes in arms, legs and skulls, gouged-out eyes. Some had been garrotted; many had been shot in the back of the head. The year 2006 saw Iraq in open civil war and Baghdad mired in sectarian cleansing. Once again the Tigris became the dumping ground for the mutilated corpses of men, women and children, just as it had been during the vicious civil war between the brothers Amin and Mamun in the earliest days of the Abbasids.

Much of Baghdad was terrorized by Shia death squads operating with a nod and a wink from the interior minister Bayan Jabr.[100] A secret detention centre was discovered in which 169 emaciated prisoners, almost entirely Sunni, were being tortured. In 2006, following the bombing of the sacred Shia shrine at Samarra, the Mahdi Army of Muktada al Sadr, a firebrand from a distinguished clerical family, joined the fray, and Baghdad grew ever more polarized. Previously Sunni majority areas such as Saeediya, Hurriya and Washash became Shia majority areas. The previously mixed districts of Hay Aden, Sahab and Hay Sumer, north of Sadr City, became Shia dominated.

The once invulnerable Saddam Hussein was captured and subsequently executed on 30 December 2006, a date that was deliberately provocative for Iraq's Sunni, who were preparing to celebrate the holy festival of Eid al Adha. 'I spoke to Saddam during his last moments and prompted him to say his last prayers before he was hanged,' recalls Mowaffak al Rubaie, the then National Security Advisor, who presided over the execution. 'I pulled the lever and nothing happened. I apologized and he had to say his prayers again. Then I pulled it for the second time, the trapdoor opened and it was all over.'[101] Some hoped it would mark a turning point for peace. 'Your generous and pure land has got rid – and for ever – of the filth of the dictator and a black page of Iraq's history has been turned and the tyrant has died,' said Prime Minister Nouri al Maliki. Yet the execution did little to abate the violence, which continued to rip through Baghdad and Iraq. Violent civilian deaths in the city hovered between 300 and 1,200 a month in 2007 – across Iraq as a whole the monthly death-toll was 700–2,700.[102]

At the height of the inferno in 2006, shortly before he was driven out of Baghdad by extremists, Dr Donny George of the Iraq Museum managed to salvage some historical perspective – and even optimism – from the bloodletting. 'There are stages such as these, and then there are stages of calm. Each can last 100 years, but it passes,' he said. 'A famous Sumerian writer described the scene here in 2000 BC, saying that people are looting and killing and nobody knows who the king is. So you see, nothing is new.'[103]*

By 2008, when the mind-numbingly brutal sectarian war in Baghdad had finally subsided, partly as a result of the American 'surge' in early 2007, partly as a result of the Sunni Awakening militias abandoning attacks on the Coalition and targeting insurgents instead, the map of Baghdad had been redrawn. Adhamiya was the only large Sunni district left east of the river. Baghdad's Sunni population had been cantonized in a strip of western districts: Kindi, Khadra, Yarmuk, Ghazaliya and Amiriya, with a southern fringe in Dora and Muradiya. After concerted bursts of sectarian cleansing, Baghdad had become a segregated, and Shia-dominated, capital.[104] It remains one of the most dangerous cities in the world, with levels of violence difficult to comprehend.

For Baghdad's Christian population the recent years have been a shattering experience of hatred and intolerance, frequently murderous. Shootings, assassinations, bombings of churches and homes, attacks on stores selling alcohol, many of them owned by Christians – the campaign of violence against this ancient community has been extraordinarily fierce and unrelenting. An estimated 300,000 of the city's 400,000 Christians had fled the capital by 2010, and many of them had left Iraq altogether.[105] On Sunday, 31 October 2010, gunmen wearing suicide vests killed two armed guards outside the Iraq Stock Exchange in Karrada before crossing the street to Our Lady of Salvation, a Syrian Catholic church. After vaulting the security wall, they entered the church, started shooting wildly at the Madonna and crucifix, and took more than a hundred hostages from the terrified congregation, calling them 'dogs' and 'infidels'. By the end of the night, after Iraqi commandos had raided the building and a suicide bomber had detonated his vest, fifty-eight people, including two priests, were dead and seventy-eight wounded. Whole families had been exterminated. The Al Qaeda-linked

---

* Having left Iraq after repeated threats against his family, Dr Donny George was appointed a visiting professor at Stony Brook University in the US in 2006. He died of a heart attack in 2011 at the age of 60.

Islamic State of Iraq, which called the church 'the dirty den of idolatry', claimed responsibility for the attack, the worst suffered by Christians in Baghdad since 2003. Christians everywhere were 'legitimate targets', the group said. 'Those who say we are safe, that we can live peacefully in Iraq, they are liars,' said Reverend Douglas Yusef al Bazy, a colleague of the murdered priests. 'But we will stay in this country because still there are Christian people here and we still have a mission here.'[106]

At the time of writing in 2013, Canon Andrew White, the Anglican 'Vicar of Baghdad', ministers to a congregation of 4,000. Only the priests are Anglicans. The worshippers come from every Christian denomination in Iraq – Chaldean, Assyrian, Orthodox, Armenian Catholic and others – and generally speak Aramaic and Syriac, the most ancient of Christian languages. Canon White estimates that the Christian community of Iraq, which had once reached 1.5 million, has plummeted to around 100,000, of whom many have sought sanctuary in the Kurdish areas. 'Our Christians that remained have been tortured, killed and kidnapped. Many have fled Iraq to save their lives. I have personally had over 400 of my people killed since 2003. Most who could afford to leave have done so. Despite the tragedy that has beset our people, they remain full of joy because they say that when you have lost everything your faith is all you have left. That is so strong and keeps them going.'[107]

If the Christians were increasingly beleaguered in Baghdad, the Jewish community was virtually extinct. A community that predated Baghdad, that had peaked at around 150,000 nationwide in 1948, that shortly before then had represented almost 40 per cent of the city's population in around 1917, had crashed to just seven or eight – generally too small even to muster a *minyan*, the quorum of ten Jews required for any public religious service. For centuries they had been the motor of Baghdad's booming trade, excelling in business and banking, together with music and the arts. While the Jews prospered, Baghdad had thrived. Yet, as the twentieth century progressed, the city's genius for self-destruction reasserted itself. The political climate, already harsh, grew hotter still. Peaceful coexistence came to be a quaint anachronism. After the Farhud pogrom of 1941, the second half of the century dealt the Jews of Baghdad the most painful death blow. First there was a campaign of persecution that led to the mass emigration to Israel from 1951 to 1952. Even after that trauma, there was no respite, the virulent anti-Semitism of the Baath Party climaxing in the public hangings of 1969 and successive waves of departures in the 1970s. The horrors of Saddam Hussein's regime included still more harassment, intimidation, torture and arbitrary executions of Jews, so that at the dawn of the twenty-first century Baghdad's once mighty Jewish community was too small either to read the Torah in public or to recite a proper Kaddish for the dead – both of which were, besides, foolish to the point of fatal.[108]

The geographical marginalization of the Sunni population reflected the new political realities of Iraq after Saddam. Excluded from political power since the days of Mansur, Iraq's Shia were for the first time firmly in the driving seat. Their political dominance was underlined in the national elections of 2005 and 2010, which saw the Sunni minority relegated to an unaccustomed, highly unwelcome – and, in some cases, completely unacceptable – position on the sidelines.

After the misery of the Iraq–Iran War in the 1980s, the cataclysm of Gulf War One and the suppressed uprising that followed, after a decade of the harshest sanctions ever imposed by the UN, and after almost twenty-four years of misrule by Saddam, Iraqis longed for something better. Promised freedom, they slid instead into a chaos so violent that many openly admitted things had been better under Saddam.

Statistics reveal just a sliver of the tragedy that befell Baghdad. From the beginning of the war in April 2003 to the withdrawal of US forces at the end of 2011, there were 10,189 incidents in which at least one Iraqi civilian was killed in Baghdad province, with a total death-toll of 56,771. During the same period there were a staggering 322 suicide attacks in Baghdad, including 67 that killed 20 or more. Across Iraq the total number of civilians who met violent deaths exceeded 114,000, while the total number of violent deaths including combatants has been estimated at 162,000.[109] A more recent study, published in 2013, reached the much higher figure of approximately 500,000 Iraqi deaths from war-related causes between 2003 and 2011.[110] There was little sign of the carnage ending as this book went to press. 2013 was the deadliest year since 2008, with an estimated 8,955 killed in raging violence, a monthly average of 746, or 25 a day.[111]

'I came back with an idealistic and idealized vision of what life could and should be,' says Samir Sumaidaie, who returned to Baghdad from exile and opposition in 2003 and took up a string of senior political positions, the culmination of which was his appointment as ambassador to Washington in 2006. 'I was soon disabused of that idealism and in the last several years I have become much more pessimistic and uncertain about the future.'[112]

The city that had once exerted an irresistible gravitational pull, drawing in the greatest minds from across the world, was now driving out its own people: Jews, Christians, Sunni, Shia, anyone repelled by the tidal waves of violence breaking across Baghdad and the rest of the country. Iraqis scattered across the globe in disarray, from Jordan, Syria and Egypt to the US, the UK and Australia. In 2007, the UN warned that as many as five million Iraqi refugees had been displaced by the war.

*

The history of Baghdad, since its foundation by the caliph Mansur in 762, has been relentlessly tempestuous. The story of the City of Peace, once the noble apex of world civilization, has been written in blood. Baghdadis have been tremendously talented in creating beauty and culture and, tragically, just as skilled in destroying them. Yet one of the world's most violent cities is also one of its most resilient. Baghdad has seen foreign invaders come and go during the past 1,300 years, from eighth-century Byzantines to twenty-first-century Americans. It has survived the furious onslaught of Hulagu's Mongols in 1258 and Tamerlane's Tatars in 1401, when the Tigris ran red with blood and black with ink from the literary treasures of the ransacked House of Wisdom. It has shrugged off the indignity of falling under the rule of minor Turkmen chiefs, endured the Ottoman conquest of Sultan Suleyman the Magnificent in 1534, the Iranian incursion of Shah Abbas in 1623 and four centuries of haughty Ottoman pashas. 'The old Turkey-cock's city of Haroun al Rothschild' saw off the British invasion of 1917 and emerged from two world wars bloodied but unbowed. Beset by Baathist tyranny, Saddam's dictatorship, a shattering war against Iran and the pulverizing Gulf War One, Baghdad still managed to haul itself through a savage regime of UN sanctions, only to be met with the full fury of the Iraq War in 2003. Instead of bringing the longed-for peace and calm after decades of unimaginable suffering, the conflict ignited Baghdad's oldest demons, and sectarian strife exploded across the city and the nation. Once again the City of Peace was at war, and blood ran on the streets.

Yet, despite all this devastation, Baghdadis do not give up on their city. With a prodigious history of intellectual, cultural and Islamic pre-eminence, it stands for dignity, pride and, above all, endurance. 'It is a city unlike any one of its peers,' says Manaf, a retired diplomat steeped in the history of Baghdad. 'You have to wonder whether the good caliph Mansur, if he had had the slightest foresight of the city's bloody future, would have built his circular seat of power here. The cycle that sees Baghdad lurching between mayhem and prosperity has been long and gory, but of course we must have hope. May the City of Peace live up to its name before we ourselves depart to eternal peace.'

Anmerkungen

Appendix

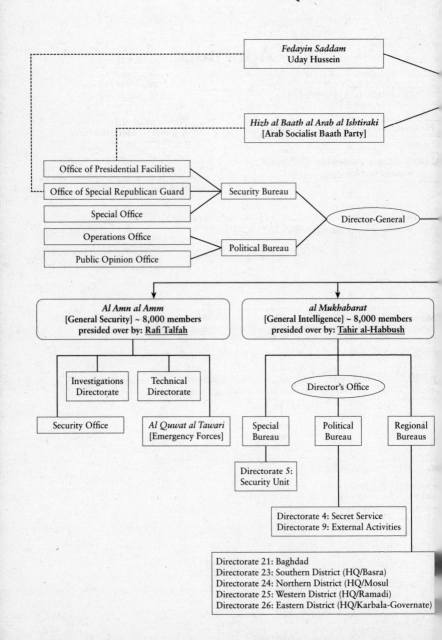

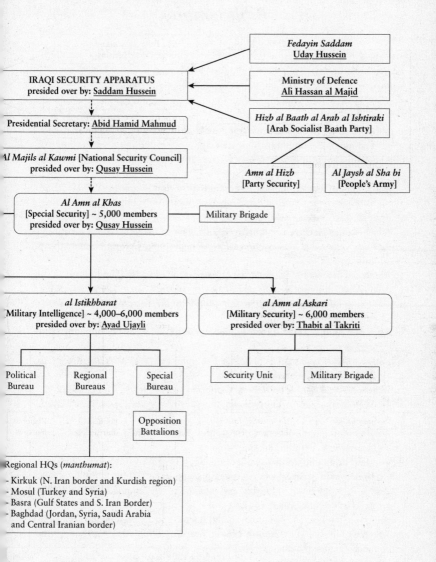

Bibliography

Abbott, Nabia, *Two Queens of Baghdad: Mother and Wife of Harun al Rashid* (London, 1986; reprint of 1946 original).

Abdullah, Thabit, *A Short History of Iraq: From 636 to the Present* (London, 2003).

Aboul-Enein, Youssef H., *Iraq in Turmoil: Historical Perspectives of Dr Ali al Wardi, from the Ottoman Empire to King Feisal* (Annapolis, Maryland, 2012).

Aburish, Said, *Saddam Hussein: The Politics of Revenge* (New York, 2000).

Adler, Marcus Nathan, *The Itinerary of Benjamin of Tudela* (Oxford, 1907).

Ágoston, Gábor, and Masters, Bruce, *Encyclopedia of the Ottoman Empire* (New York, 2009).

Ahsan, Muhammad Manazir, *Social Life under the Abbasids* (London, 1979).

Allaf, Abdul Kareem al, *Baghdad al Qadeemah min Sanat 1869 hatta Sanat 1917 (Old Baghdad from the Year 1869 until the Year 1917)* (Beirut, 1999; reprint of 1960 original).

Ali, Sayed Amir, *A Short History of the Saracens* (London, 1955; reprint of 1899 original).

— *The Spirit of Islam: A History of the Evolution and Ideals of Islam with a Life of the Prophet* (London, 1922).

Allawi, Ali A., *The Crisis of Islamic Civilization* (New Haven, Conn., 2009).

— *The Occupation of Iraq: Winning the War, Losing the Peace* (New Haven, Conn., 2007).

Alnasrawi, Abbas, 'Economic Consequences of the Iraq–Iran War', *Third World Quarterly*, 8, 3 (July 1986), pp. 869–95.

— 'Iraq: Economic Consequences of the 1991 Gulf War and Future Outlook', *Third World Quarterly*, 13, 2 (1992), pp. 335–52.

Amitai-Preiss, Reuven, *Mongols and Mamluks: The Mamluk–Ilkhanid War 1260–1281* (Cambridge, 1995).

Anderson, Jon Lee, *The Fall of Baghdad* (London, 2005; reprint of 2004 original).

Antonius, George, *The Arab Awakening: The Story of the Arab National Movement* (London, 1938).

The Arabian Nights: Tales of 1,001 Nights, translated by Malcolm Lyons, 3 vols. (London, 2008).

Arabshah, Ibn, *Timur the Great Amir* (London, 1936; reprint of 1935 original).

Arberry, A. J., *Arabic Poetry* (Cambridge, 1965).

Armstrong, Karen, *A History of God. From Abraham to the Present: The 4,000-Year Quest for God* (London, 1999; reprint of 1993 original).

Arnett, Peter, *Live from the Battlefield: From Vietnam to Baghdad* (London, 1994).

Ashtiany, Julia, et al. (eds.), *Cambridge History of Arabic Literature, vol. II: Abbasid Belles-Lettres* (Cambridge, 1990).

Athir, Ibn al, *The Chronicle of Ibn al Athir for the Crusading Period from Al Kamil fi al Tarikh (The Complete History)*, translated by D. S. Richards (Aldershot, 2006–8).
  — Part I: *The Years 491–541 / 1097–1146 – The Coming of the Franks and the Muslim Response*
  — Part II: *The Years 541–589 / 1146–1193 – The Age of Nur al Din and Saladin*
  — Part III: *The Years 589–629 / 1193–1231 – The Ayyubids after Saladin and the Mongol Menace.*

Atiyah, Ghassan, *Iraq, 1908–1921: A Socio-Political Study* (Beirut, 1973).

Atwood, Christopher P., *Encyclopedia of Mongolia and the Mongol Empire* (New York, 2004).

Audisio, Gabriel, *Harun al Rashid: Caliph of Baghdad* (New York, 1931).

Axworthy, Michael, *The Sword of Persia: Nader Shah, from Tribal Warrior to Conquering Tyrant* (London, 2009).

Azzawi, Abbas al, *Tarikh al Iraq bayn al Ihtilayn (History of Iraq between Two Occupations)*, 8 vols. (Baghdad, 1935–56).

Baig, Sulaiman Faiq, *The History of Baghdad*, translated by Mousa Kadhim Nawras (Baghdad, 1962).

Barbaro, Josafa, and Contarini, Ambrosio, *Travels to Tana and Persia* (London, 1873).

Barker, A. J. *The Neglected War: Mesopotamia 1914–1918* (London, 1967).

Barthold, W., *Turkestan down to the Mongol Invasion* (Oxford, 1928).

Batatu, Hanna, *The Egyptian, Syrian and Iraqi Revolutions: Some Observations on Their Underlying Causes and Social Character* (Georgetown, 1983).

— *The Old Social Classes and the Revolutionary Movements of Iraq: A Study of Iraq's Old Landed and Commercial Classes and of Its Communists, Baathists and Free Officers* (Princeton, N. J., 1978).

Battuta, Ibn, *The Travels of Ibn Battutah*, vols. I–IV, translated by H. A. R. Gibb (Cambridge, 1971).

Bayat, Fadhil, *Baghdad: min Khilal Wathaik al Arsheef al Othmani (Baghdad in the Light of Ottoman Archive Documents)* (Istanbul, 2008).

Beckford, William, *Vathek* (Oxford, 2008; reprint of 1786 original).

Bell, Gertrude, *Amurath to Amurath* (London, 1911).

— *The Desert and the Sown* (New York, 2001; reprint of 1907 original).

— *Diaries* and *Letters*, available on Newcastle University's Gertrude Bell Archive: http://www.gerty.ncl.ac.uk.

— *Review of the Civil Administration of Mesopotamia* (London, 1920).

Benjamin, Marina, *Last Days in Babylon: The Story of the Jews of Baghdad* (London, 2007).

Bennison, Amira, *The Great Caliphs: The Golden Age of the Abbasid Empire* (London, 2009).

Ben-Porat, Mordechai, *To Baghdad and Back: The Miraculous 2,000-Year Homecoming of the Iraqi Jews* (Jerusalem, 1998).

Bevan, Edwyn Robert, *The Land of The Two Rivers* (London, 1917).

Black, Edwin, *Banking on Baghdad: Inside Iraq's 7,000-Year History of War, Profit and Conflict* (Hoboken, N. J., 2004).

Blankinship, Khalid Yahya, 'The Tribal Factor in the Abbasid Revolution: The Betrayal of the Imam Ibrahim B. Muhammad', *Journal of the American Oriental Society*, 108, 4 (October–December 1988), pp. 589–603.

Bleaney, C. H., and Roper, G. J., *Iraq: A Bibliographical Guide* (Leiden, 2004).

Bogdanos, Matthew, 'The Casualties of War: The Truth about the Iraqi Museum', *American Journal of Archaeology*, 109, 3 (July 2005), pp. 477–526.

Boyle, John Andrew, 'The Death of the Last Abbasid Caliph', *Journal of Semitic Studies*, 6, 2 (1961), pp 145–61.

— (ed.), *The Cambridge History of Iran, vol. V: The Saljuq and Mongol Periods* (Cambridge, 1968).

Bracciolini, Poggio, *The Travels of Nicolò de' Conti, in the East in the Early Part of the Fifteenth Century* (London, 1857).

Bremer, Paul, *My Year in Iraq: The Struggle to Build a Future of Hope* (New York, 2006).

Bretschneider, Emil, *Medieval Researches from Eastern Asiatic Sources* (London, 1888).

Browne, Edward G., *Arabian Medicine* (Cambridge, 1921).

— *A Literary History of Persia*, 4 vols. (Cambridge, 1902–24).

Buckingham, James Silk, *Travels in Mesopotamia, including a Journey from Aleppo to Bagdad, by the Route of Beer, Orfah, Diarbekr, Mardin, & Mousul; with Researches on the Ruins of Nineveh, Babylon, and Other Ancient Cities*, 2 vols. (London, 1827).

Burgoyne, Elizabeth, *Gertrude Bell: From Her Personal Papers*, vol. II: 1914–1926, (London, 1961).

Butlin, Robin, 'Changing Visions: The RGS in the 19th Century', in Royal Geographical Society, *To the Ends of the Earth* (London, 2005).

Byron, Robert, *The Road to Oxiana* (London, 2004; reprint of 1937 original).

Callwell, Charles, *The Life of Sir Stanley Maude* (London, 1920).

The Cambridge History of Iran (Cambridge, 1968–91).

Candler, Edmund, *The Long Road to Baghdad*, 2 vols. (London, 1919).

Caractacus, *Revolution in Iraq: An Essay in Comparative Public Opinion* (London, 1959).

Çelebi, Evliya, *Seyahatnamesi (Book of Travels)*, 10 vols. (Istanbul, 1999–2007).

Çetinsaya, Gökhan, *Ottoman Administration of Iraq 1890–1908* (Abingdon, 2006).

Ceylan, Ebubekir, 'Carrot or Stick?: Ottoman Tribal Policy in Baghdad 1831–1876', *International Journal of Contemporary Iraqi Studies*, 3, 2 (November 2009), pp. 169–86.

— *The Ottoman Origins of Modern Iraq: Political Reform, Modernization and Development in the Nineteenth-Century Middle East* (London, 2011).

Chalabi, Tamara, *Late for Tea at the Deer Palace: The Lost Dreams of My Iraqi Family* (London, 2010).

Chambers, James, *The Devil's Horsemen: The Mongol Invasion of Europe* (London, 2001).

Chandrasekaran, Rajiv, *Imperial Life in the Emerald City: Inside Baghdad's Green Zone* (London, 2007).

Chesney, Francis Rawdon, *The Expedition for the Survey of the Rivers Euphrates and Tigris, Carried on by Order of the British Government, in the Years 1835, 1836 and 1837*, 4 vols. (London, 1850).

Christie, Agatha, *They Came to Baghdad* (London, 2003; reprint of 1951 original).

Chubin, Shahram, and Tripp, Charles, *Iran and Iraq at War* (London, 1988).

Clarke, George S., *The Baghdad Railway*, Memorandum prepared by the Direction of the Prime Minister, 26 January 1905 (London, 1905).

Clot, André, *Harun al Rashid and the World of the Thousand and One Nights*, translated from the French by John Howe (London, 2005).

— *Suleiman the Magnificent*, translated from the French by Matthew J. Reisz (London, 2005).

Cohen, Morris, 'Superstition among the Jews in Baghdad', extracted in *The Scribe: Journal of Babylonian Jewry*, 46 (January 1991), pp. 3–5.

Coke, Richard, *Baghdad: The City of Peace* (London, 1927).

Cooperson, Michael, 'Baghdad in Rhetoric and Narrative', *Muqarnas*, 13 (1996), pp. 99–113.

Cordesman, Anthony, and Wagner, Abraham R., *Lessons of Modern War, vol. II: The Iran–Iraq War* (Boulder, Colo., 1990).

Coughlin, Con, *Saddam: King of Terror* (New York, 2002).

— *Saddam: The Secret Life* (London, 2007).

Creswell, K. A. C., *Early Muslim Architecture*, 2 vols. (Oxford, 1932, 1940).

Damluji, Sadiq, *Midhat Pasha* (Baghdad, 1953).

Daniel, Elton L., 'Arabs, Persians, and the Advent of the Abbasids Reconsidered', *Journal of the American Oriental Society*, 117, 3 (July–September 1997), pp 542–8.

Dankoff, Robert, and Kim, Sooyong (eds. and trans.) *An Ottoman Traveller: Selections from the Book of Travels of Evliya Çelebi* (London, 2010).

Dann, Uriel, *Iraq under Qassem: A Political History 1958–1963* (New York, 1969).

Darke, Hubert (trans.), *The Book of Government or Rules for Kings: The Siyasat-nama or Siyar al Muluk of Nizam al Mulk* (London, 1960).

Darwish, Adel, and Alexander, Gregory, *Unholy Babylon: The Secret History of Saddam's War* (New York, 1991).

Dawisha, Adeed, *Iraq: A Political History from Independence to Occupation* (Princeton, N. J., 2009).

De Gaury, Gerald, *Three Kings in Baghdad: The Tragedy of Iraq's Monarchy* (London, 2008; reprint of 1961 original).

DeNovo, John A., *American Interests and Policies in the Middle East 1900–1939*, (Minneapolis, Minn., 1963).

Din, Rashid al, *The Successors of Genghis Khan*, translated by John Andrew Boyle (New York, 1971).

— *Jami al Tawarikh (Compendium of Histories)*, French translation by Etienne Quatremère, *Histoire des Mongols de la Perse* (Paris, 1836).

Ditmars, Hadani, *Dancing in the No-Fly Zone: A Woman's Journey through Iraq* (Northampton, Mass., 2006).

Dodge, Toby, 'The British Mandate in Iraq, 1914–1932' (http://www.gale.cengage.com/pdf/whitepapers/gdc/TheBritishMandate.pdf).

— *Inventing Iraq: The Failure of Nation Building and a History Denied (London, 2003)*.

D'Ohsson, Constantin, *Histoire des Mongols* (Amsterdam, 1834–5).

Drury, William Edward, *Camp Follower: A Padre's Recollections of Nile, Somme and Tigris during the First World War* (Dublin, 1968).

Dupuy, R. Ernest, and Dupuy, Trevo N. *The Collins Encyclopedia of Military History* (London, 1993).

Duri, A. A., 'Baghdad', in *Encylopaedia of Islam* (second edition), vol. I (London, 1971), p. 903.

Earle, E. M., *Turkey, the Great Powers, and the Baghdad Railway: A Study in Imperialism* (New York, 1923).

Effendi, Evliya, *Narrative of Travels in Europe, Asia and Africa in the Seventeenth Century*, translated by Joseph von Hammer-Purgstall, 2 vols. (London, 1834–50).

Egan, Eleanor Franklin, *The War in the Cradle of the World* (London, 1918).

Ellis, Tristram J., *On a Raft and through the Desert* (London, 1881).

Ellis, William S., 'The New Face of Baghdad', *National Geographic*, 167, 1 (January 1985).

Emberling, Geoff, and Hanson, Katharyn (eds.), 'Catastrophe! The Looting and Destruction of Iraq's Past', Oriental Institute Museum of the University of Chicago paper (Spring 2008).

Emin, Joseph, *Life and Adventures of Joseph Emin* (Calcutta, 1918).

Erskine, Beatrice, *King Faisal of Iraq: An Authorized and Authentic Study* (London, 1933).

Farmer, H. G., *A History of Arabian Music to the XIIIth Century* (London, 1929).

Faroqhi, Suraiya, *Approaching Ottoman History: An Introduction to the Sources* (Cambridge, 1999).

Farouk-Sluglett, Marion, and Sluglett, Peter, 'Review of *The Old Social Classes and the Revolutionary Movements of Iraq: A Study of Iraq's Old Landed and Commercial Classes and of Its Communists, Baathists and Free Officers*', *Arab Studies Quarterly*, 3 (1981), pp. 98–106.

Fathi, Saul Silas, *Full Circle: Escape from Baghdad and the Return* (Philadelphia, 2005).

Fattah, Hala, *The Politics of Regional Trade in Iraq, Arabia and the Gulf 1745–1900* (Albany, 1997).

Fawzi, Farouk Omar, *Abbasid Caliphate*, in Arabic, 2 vols. (Amman, 2003).

Ferguson, Niall, *Colossus: The Price of America's Empire* (New York, 2004).

Fernea, Robert A., and Louis, William Roger (eds.), *The Iraqi Revolution of 1958: The Old Social Classes Revisited* (London 1991).

Finkel, Caroline, *Osman's Dream: The Story of the Ottoman Empire 1300–1923* (London, 2005).

Foster, Benjamin R., and Polinger Foster, Karen, *Civilizations of Ancient Iraq* (Princeton, N. J., 2009).

Fraser, J. Baillie, *Travels in Koordistan, Mesopotamia, etc.*, 2 vols. (London, 1840).

Fromkin, David, *A Peace to End All Peace: The Fall of the Ottoman Empire and the Creation of the Modern Middle East* (London, 1989).

Gabriel, Albert, 'Les Étapes d'une campagne dans les deux Irak d'après un manuscrit turc du XVIe siècle', *Syria*, 9, (1928), pp. 328–49.

Gallman, Waldemar, *Iraq under General Nuri: My Recollections of Nuri al Said 1954–1958* (Baltimore, Maryland, 1964).

Ghanimah, Yusuf Rizk-Allah, *Nuzhat al Mushtak fi Tarikh Yahud al Iraq* (*A Nostalgic Trip into the History of the Jews of Iraq*), translated from the Arabic by Reading A. Dallal (Oxford, 1998).

Gibbon, Edward, *Decline and Fall of the Roman Empire* (London, 1937; reprint of 1776 original).

Glassé, Cyril, *The New Encyclopedia of Islam* (London, 2002; reprint of 1989 original).

Grant, Christina Phelps, *The Syrian Desert: Caravans, Travel and Exploration* (London, 1937).

Grousset, René, The *Empire of the Steppes* (New Brunswick, N. J., 1970; translation of 1938 original).

Groves, A. N., *Journal of a Residence in Bagdad during the Years 1830 and 1831* (London, 1832).

Gruendler, Beatrice, *Medieval Arabic Praise Poetry* (London, 2003).

Haim, Sylvia, 'Aspects of Jewish Life in Baghdad under the Monarchy', *Middle Eastern Studies*, 12, 2 (1976), pp 188–208.

Hakluyt, Richard, *Hakluyt's Collection of the Early Voyages, Travels, and Discoveries of the English Nation* (London, 1810; also 1903–5 edition).

Haldane, Aylmer, *The Insurrection in Mesopotamia 1920* (London, 1922).

Hammer-Purgstall, Joseph von, *Histoire de l'Empire ottoman*, translated from the German by J. J. Hellert (Paris, 1835–43).

Hammond, Josephine, *Battle in Iraq: Letters and Diaries of the First World War* (London, 2009).

Hamza, Khidhir, *Saddam's Bombmaker: The Terrifying Inside Story of the Iraqi Nuclear and Biological Weapons Agenda* (New York, 2000).

Hanne, Eric J., *Putting the Caliph in His Place: Power, Authority, and the Late Abbasid Caliphate* (Madison, N.J., 2007).

Hanway, Jonas, *An Historical Account of the British Trade over the Caspian Sea: with a Journal of Travels from London through Russia into Persia; and back again through Russia, Germany and Holland. To which are Added, the Revolutions of Persia during the Present Century, with the Particular History of the Great Usurper Nadir Kouli*, 4 vols. (London, 1753).

Harper, R. F., *Assyrian and Babylonian Literature* (New York, 1901).

Harris, John, *Navigantium atque Itinerantium Biblioteca; or, A Compleat Collection of Voyages and Travels*, 2 vols. (London, 1705).

Hasan, M. S., 'Growth and Structure of Iraq's Population 1867–1947', *Bulletin of the Oxford University Institute of Economics and Statistics*, 20, 4 (1958) pp. 339–52.

Hasluck, F. W., *Christianity and Islam under the Sultans*, ed. Margaret Hasluck, 2 vols. (Oxford, 1929).

Hathaway, Jane, and Barbir, Karl, *The Arab Lands under Ottoman Rule 1516–1800* (Harlow, 2008).

Hawting, G. R., *The First Dynasty of Islam: The Umayyad Caliphate AD 661–750* (London, 1986).

Haydar, Jamal, *Baghdad: Malamih Madina fi Dhakirat al Sitinat (Baghdad: Memories of a City in the 1960s)* (Casablanca, 2002).

Herodotus, *The Histories* (London, 2003).

Herrin, Judith, *Byzantium: The Surprising Life of a Medieval Empire* (London, 2007).

Heude, Lieutenant William, *A Voyage up the Persian Gulf, and a Journey Overland from India to England, in 1817* (London, 1819).

Hillenbrand, Carole, *The Crusades: Islamic Perspectives* (Edinburgh, 1999).

Hiro, Dilip, *The Longest War: The Iran–Iraq Military Conflict* (London, 1991; reprint of 1989 original).

Hitti, Philip, *History of the Arabs* (London, 1937).

Holt, Peter M., *Egypt and the Fertile Crescent 1516–1922* (London, 1966).

Horne, Charles F. (ed.), *Source Records of the Great War*, Vol. V (National Alumni, USA, 1923).

Hourani, Albert, *A History of the Arab Peoples* (London, 2005).

—, Khoury, Philip S., and Wilson, Mary C. (eds.), *The Modern Middle East: A Reader* (Berkeley and Los Angeles, Calif., 1993).

— and Stern, S. M. (eds.), *The Islamic City* (Oxford, 1970).

Howell, Georgina, *Daughter of the Desert: The Remarkable Life of Gertrude Bell* (London, 2006).

Howorth, Henry H., *History of the Mongols, from the Ninth to the Nineteenth Century*, 4 vols. in 5 (London, 1876–1927).

Huart, Clément, *Histoire de Bagdad dans les temps modernes* (Paris, 1901).

Hume-Griffith, M. E., *Behind the Veil in Persia and Turkish Arabia* (London, 1909).

Hurewitz, Jacob Coleman, *Diplomacy in the Near and Middle East: A Documentary Record 1535–1914*, 2 vols. (Princeton, N.J., 1956).

Hussain, Ishtiaq, *The Tanzimat: Secular Reforms in the Ottoman Empire* (http://faith-matters.org/images/stories/fm-publications/the-tanzimat-final-web.pdf).

Imber, Colin, *The Ottoman Empire 1300–1650: The Structure of Power* (New York, 2002).

— 'The Persecution of the Ottoman Shi'ites according to the Mühimme Defterleri 1565–1585', *Islam*, 56, 2 (1979) pp. 245–73.

Ionides, Michael George, *The Regime of the Rivers Euphrates and Tigris* (London, 1937).

Iraq Administration Reports 1914–1932 (Slough, 1992).

Irwin, Robert, *The Arabian Nights: A Companion* (London, 2004).

— *The Middle East in the Middle Ages: The Early Mamluk Sultanate 1250–1382* (London, 1986).

Isfahani, Abu al Faraj al, *Kitab al Aghani*, 25 vols. (Beirut, 2000).

Ives, Edward, *A Voyage from England to India, in the Year 1754 . . . Also a Journey from Persia to England by an Unusual Route* (London, 1773).

Jabra, Jabra Ibrahim, *Hunters in a Narrow Street* (London, 1960).

Jamali, Mohammed Fadhel, '*Iraq under General Nuri*: A Review of Waldemar Gallman's Book', *Middle East Forum*, 11, 7 (1964), pp. 13–24.

Jastrow, Morris, *The War and the Bagdad Railway: The Story of Asia Minor and Its Relation to the Present Conflict* (Philadelphia, 1918).

Jawad, Mustafa, *Baghdad al Qadeema wal Haditha* (*Baghdad: Ancient and Modern*) (Baghdad, 1969).

— and Susa, Ahmad, *Dalil Kharita Baghdad al Mufassal* (*A Detailed Guide to Baghdad's Map*) (Baghdad, 1958).

Jayyusi, Salma (ed.), *The City in the Islamic World* (Leiden, 2008).

Johnston, Norman, 'The Urban World of the Matraki Manuscript', *Journal of Near Eastern Studies*, 30, 3 (July 1971) pp. 159–76.

Jones, James Felix, 'Memoir on the Province of Baghdad', in *Memoirs by Commander J. F. Jones* (1998 edition; reprint of Bombay, 1857, original).

Jones Brgdges, Harford, *An Account of the Transactions of His Majesty's Mission to the Court of Persia, in the Years 1807–11, to which is Appended a Brief History of the Wahauby*, 2 vols. (London, 1834).

Juvaini, 'Ala-ad-Din 'Ata-Malik, *The History of the World-Conqueror*, translated from the text of Mirza Muhammad Qazvini by John Andrew Boyle, 2 vols. (Manchester, 1958).

Karsh, Efraim, and Rautsi, Inari, *Saddam Hussein: A Political Biography* (London, 1991).

Kathir, Ibn, *Al Bidaya wal Nihaya (The Beginning and the End)*, vol. XIII: *The Events of the Year 656 AH (1258 AD)* (Al Mostafa e-library: www.al-mostafa. com).

Kedourie, Elie, *England and the Middle East: The Destruction of the Ottoman Empire 1914–1921* (London, 1987; reprint of 1956 original).

Kennedy, Hugh, *The Armies of the Caliphs: Military and Society in the Early Islamic State* (London, 2001).

— *The Early Abbasid Caliphate: A Political History* (London, 1981).

— *When Baghdad Ruled the Muslim World: The Rise and Fall of Islam's Greatest Dynasty* (Cambridge, Mass., 2005; US edition of *The Court of the Caliphs*, London, 2005).

Kennedy, Philip, *Abu Nuwas: A Genius of Poetry* (Oxford, 2005).

Keppel, George, *Personal Narrative of a Journey from India to England*, 2 vols. (London, 1827).

Kerküklü, Rasul al, *Dawhat al Wuzara (The Lofty Tree of Ministers)*, translated from Turkish by Musa Kadhim Nawras (Beirut, [n.d.]).

Khadduri, Majid, *Republican Iraq: A Study of Iraqi Politics since the Revolution of 1958* (London, 1969).

Khaldun, Ibn, *An Arab Philosophy of History: Selections from the Prolegomena of Ibn Khaldun of Tunis*, translated by Charles Issawi (Princeton, N.J., 1987; reprint of 1950 original).

— *The Mukaddimah: An Introduction to History*, translated from the Arabic by Franz Rosenthal; abridged and edited by N. J. Dawood (London, 1978).

— *Tarikh ibn Khaldun* (Beirut, 2011).

Khalil, Samir al, *The Monument: Art, Vulgarity and Responsibility in Iraq* (London, 1991; pseudonym of Kanan Makiya).

Khalili, Jim al, *Pathfinders: The Golden Age of Arabic Science* (London, 2010).

Khallikan, Ibn, *Ibn Khallikan's Biographical Dictionary*, translated by Baron MacGuckin de Slane, 4 vols. (Beirut, 1970; reprint of 1842–71 original).

Khoury, Dina, 'Merchants and Trade in Early Modern Iraq', *New Perspectives on Turkey*, 5–6 (Fall 1991), pp. 70–82.

Kilpatrick, Hilary, *Making the Great Book of Songs: Compilation and the Author's Craft in Abu al Faraj al-Isfahani's 'Kitab al Aghani'* (London, 2002).

Kimball, Lorenzo Kent, *The Changing Pattern of Political Power in Iraq 1958 to 1972* (New York, 1972).

The Koran, trans. N. J. Dawood (London, 2000).

Kudret, Cevdet, *Fuzuli* (Istanbul, 2003).

Langley, Kathleen M., *The Industrialization of Iraq* (Cambridge, Mass., 1962; reprint of 1961 original).

Lassner, Jacob, *The Topography of Baghdad in the Early Middle Ages* (Detroit, 1970).

Lawrence, T. E., 'A Report on Mesopotamia', *Sunday Times*, 22 August 1920. Also available at the World War Document Archive at: http://wwi.lib.byu.edu/index.php/A_Report_on_Mesopotamia_by_T.E._Lawrence.

— *Seven Pillars of Wisdom* (London, 1935).

— 'Twenty-Seven Articles', *Arab Bulletin*, 20 August 1917.

Lees, William Nassau, *Jami: A Biographical Sketch* (Calcutta, 1859).

Le Strange, Guy, *Baghdad during the Abbasid Caliphate* (Oxford, 1900).

— 'A Greek Embassy to Baghdad in 917 AD', *Journal of the Royal Asiatic Society* (January 1897), pp. 33–45.

— *Lands of the Eastern Caliphate: Mesopotamia and Central Asia from the Moslem Conquest to the Time of Timur* (Cambridge, 1905).

— 'The Story of the Death of the Last Abbasid Caliph', *Journal of the Royal Asiatic Society* (April 1900), pp. 293–300.

Lewis, Bernard, *The Assassins: A Radical Sect in Islam* (London, 2010; reprint of 1967 original).

— 'The Ottoman Archives as a Source for the History of the Arab Lands', *Journal of the Royal Asiatic Society*, 3/4 (October 1951), pp. 139–55.

— *Race and Slavery in the Middle East: An Historical Enquiry* (Oxford 1992; reprint of 1990 original).

Long, P. W., *Other Ranks of Kut* (London, 1938).

Longrigg, Stephen Hemsley, *Four Centuries of Modern Iraq* (Oxford, 1925).

— *Iraq 1900–1950: A Political, Social and Economic History* (Oxford, 1953).

Low, Charles Rathbone, *History of the Indian Navy 1613–1863*, 2 vols. (London, 1877).

Lyons, Jonathan, *The House of Wisdom: How the Arabs Transformed Western Civilization* (London 2010; reprint of 2009 original).

Maalouf, Amin, *The Crusades through Arab Eyes* (London, 2006; reprint of 1984 original).

MacCulloch, Diarmaid, *A History of Christianity: The First Three Thousand Years* (New York, 2010; reprint of 2009 original).

McMeekin, Sean, *The Berlin–Baghdad Express: The Ottoman Empire and Germany's Bid for World Power 1898–1918* (London, 2010).

Main, Ernest, *In and Around Baghdad* (Baghdad, [n.d. but 1920s]).

Makiya, Kanan, *Republic of Fear: The Politics of Modern Iraq* (London, 1998; reprint of 1989 original).

Makkiya, Muhammad, *Baghdad* (London, 2005).

Makrizi, Al, *Book of Contention and Strife Concerning the Relations between the Banu Umayya and the Banu Hashim*, translated by Clifford Edmund Bosworth (Manchester, 1983).

Man, John, *Kublai Khan, The Mongol King Who Remade China* (London, 2006).

Mantran, Robert, 'Bagdad à l'époque ottoman', *Arabica*, 9, 3 (1962), pp. 311–24.

— *Histoire de l'Empire ottoman* (Paris, 1989).

Marcus, Abraham, *The Middle East on the Eve of Modernity: Aleppo in the Eighteenth Century* (New York, 1989).

Marozzi, Justin, *The Man Who Invented History: Travels with Herodotus* (London, 2008).

— *Tamerlane: Sword of Islam, Conqueror of the World* (London, 2004).

Marr, Phebe, *The Modern History of Iraq* (Boulder, Colo., 2012; reprint of 1985 original).

Marzolph, Ulrich, and Leeuwen, Richard van (eds.), *The Arabian Nights Encyclopedia*, 2 vols. (Santa Barbara, Calif., 2004).

Masudi, *The Meadows of Gold: The Abbasids*, translated and edited by Paul Lunde and Caroline Stone (London, 1989).

Matraki, Nasuh al, *Beyan-ı Menazil-i Sefer-ul Irakeyn (Description of the Stages of Sultan Suleyman's Campaign in the Two Iraqs)*, MMS 6964, University Library, Istanbul.

Maxwell, Donald, *A Dweller in Mesopotamia, being the Adventures of an Artist in the Garden of Eden* (London, 1921).

Maxwell, Gavin, *A Reed Shaken by the Wind* (London, 1957).

Meyer, Karl, and Brysac, Shareen, *Kingmakers: The Invention of the Modern Middle East* (New York, 2008).

Milstein, Rachel, *Miniature Painting in Ottoman Baghdad* (Costa Mesa, Calif., 1990).

Milton-Edwards, Beverley, and Hinchcliffe, Peter, *Jordan: A Hashemite Legacy* (Oxford, 2009; reprint of 2001 original).

Milwright, Marcus, *An Introduction to Islamic Archaeology* (Edinburgh, 2010).

Mishra, Jita, *The NPT and the Developing Countries* (New Delhi, 2008).

Moberly, Brigadier-General F. J., *History of the Great War Based on Official Documents by Direction of the Historical Section of the Committee of Imperial Defence. The Campaign in Mesopotamia 1914–1918*, 4 vols. (London, 1923–7).

Morgan, David, *Medieval Persia 1040–1797* (London, 1988).

— *The Mongols* (Oxford, 1986).

Mottahedeh, Roy, 'The Abbasid Caliphate in Iran', in *The Cambridge History of Iran, vol. IV: The Period from the Arab Invasion to the Saljuqs* (Cambridge, 1975), pp. 57–89.

Muir, William, *The Caliphate: Its Rise, Decline and Fall* (London, 1891).

Mukaddasi, *The Best Divisions for Knowledge of the Regions*, a translation of *Ahsan al Takasim fi Ma'rifat al Akalim* by Basil Anthony Collins (Reading, 1994).

Munro, John M. and Love, Martin, 'The Nairn Way', *Saudi Aramco World*, July–August 1981 (http://www.saudiaramcoworld.com/issue/198104/the.nairn.way.htm).

Murphey, Rhoads, *Ottoman Warfare 1500–1700* (London, 1999).

— 'Suleyman's Eastern Policy', in Halil Inalcik and Cemal Kafadar (eds.), *Suleyman the Second and His Time* (Istanbul, 1993), pp. 229–48.

Murray, Hugh, *Historical Account of Discoveries and Travels in Asia, from the Earliest Ages to the Present Time*, 3 vols. (Edinburgh, 1820).

Musil, Alois, *The Middle Euphrates: A Topographical Itinerary* (New York, 1927).

Nakash, Yitzhak, *The Shi'is of Iraq* (Princeton, N.J., 1994).

New Cambridge History of Islam, 6 vols. (Cambridge, 2010).

Nicholson, Reynold Alleyne, *A Literary History of the Arabs* (London, 1914; reprint of 1907 original).

Nicolle, David, *The Mongol Warlords: Genghis Khan, Kublai Khan, Hülegü, Tamerlane* (Poole, 1990).

Niebuhr, Carsten, *Voyage en Arabie et en autres pays circonvoisins* (Amsterdam, 1776–80).

Nieuwenhuis, Tom, *Politics and Society in Early Modern Iraq: Mamluk Pashas, Tribal Shaykhs and Local Rule Between 1802 and 1831* (The Hague, 1981).

Nissen, Hans, and Heine, Peter, *From Mesopotamia to Iraq: A Concise History* (Chicago, 2009).

Nunn, Wilfred, *Tigris Gunboats: A Narrative of the Royal Navy's Co-operation with the Military Forces in Mesopotamia from the Beginning of the War to the Capture of Baghdad 1914–1917* (London, 1932).

O'Leary, De Lacy, *Arabic Thought and Its Place in History* (London, 1922).

— *How Greek Science Passed to the Arabs* (London, 1948).

Oman, C. W. C., *The Art of War in the Middle Ages AD 378–1515* (Ithaca, N.Y., 1953; reprint of 1885 original).

Omari, Sua'ad Hadi al, *Baghdad fi al Qarn al Tasi Ashar Kama Wasafaha al Rahhala al Ajanib (Baghdad as Described by the Foreign Visitors)* (Beirut, 2002; reprint of 1954 original).

Ough, John, 'The Nairn Transport Company: Damascus to Baghdad' (http://ough-zone.blogspot.com/2009/08/nairn-transport-company-damascus-to.html).

Owen, Roger, *The Middle East in the World Economy 1800–1914* (London, 1981).

Parry, Ken (ed.), *The Blackwell Companion to Eastern Christianity* (Oxford, 2010; reprint of 2007 original).

Pax, Salam, *The Baghdad Blog* (London, 2003).

Pellat, Charles, *The Life and Works of Jahiz* (London, 1969).

Peters, Rudolph, *Jihad in Classical and Modern Islam* (Princeton, N.J., 2005).

Polo, Marco, *The Travels of Marco Polo* (New York, 1993).

Poole, Robert, 'Looting Iraq', *Smithsonian* magazine (February 2008).

Post, Jerrold, 'Saddam Hussein of Iraq: A Political Psychology Profile', *International Society of Political Psychology*, 12, 2 (June 1991), pp. 279–89.

Prawdin, Michael, *The Mongol Empire: Its Rise and Legacy* (London, 2005; reprint of 1937 original).

Prévite-Orton, C. W., *Shorter Cambridge Medieval History*, 2 vols. (Cambridge, 1952).

Purchas, Samuel, *Purchas His Pilgrimes* (London, 1905 [1625]).

Quataert, Donald, *The Ottoman Empire 1700–1922* (Cambridge, 2000).

Rachewiltz, Igor de, *The Secret History of the Mongols* (Leiden, 2004).

Radi, Nuha al, *Baghdad Diaries 1991–2002* (London, 2003; reprint of 1998 original).

Rauwolff, Leonhard, *A Collection of Curious Travels and Voyages. In Two Tomes. The First Containing Dr L. Rauwolff's Itinerary into the Eastern Countries, as Syria, Palestine, &c* (London, 1693).

Rawlinson, Henry, *Notes on the Early History of Babylonia* (London, 1854).

Rayess, Fuad, 'On a Bus to Baghdad', *Saudi Aramco World*, September–October 1966 (http://www.saudiaramcoworld.com/issue/196605/on.a.bus.to.baghdad.htm).

Raymond, André, *Arab Cities in the Ottoman Period* (Aldershot, 2002).

— *The Great Arab Cities in the Sixteenth to Eighteenth Centuries* (New York, 1984).

Reïs, Sīdi Ali, *The Travels and Adventures of the Turkish Admiral Sīdi Ali Reïs in India, Afghanistan, Central Asia, and Persia, during the Years 1553–1556* (London, 1899).

Rejwan, Nissim, and Beinin, Joel, *The Last Jews in Baghdad: Remembering a Lost Homeland* (Austin, Texas, 2004).

Rich, Claudius, *Narrative of a Residence in Koordistan, and on the Site of Ancient Nineveh; with a Journal of a Voyage down the Tigris to Bagdad and an Account of a Visit to Shirauz and Persepolis* (London, 1836).

Richard, Jean, *Le Comté de Tripoli sous la dynastie toulousaine (1102–1187)* (Paris, 1945).

Ricks, Thomas E., *Fiasco: The American Military Adventure in Iraq* (London, 2006).

Roberts, Paul, *The Demonic Comedy: The Baghdad of Saddam Hussein* (Edinburgh, 1999; reprint of 1997 original).

Robertson, William, *Soldiers and Statesmen 1914–1918*, vol. II (London, 1926).

Robinson, Chase, *Islamic Historiography: Themes in Islamic History* (Cambridge, 2003).

Robinson, Francis, *The Mughal Emperors and the Islamic Dynasties of India, Iran and Central Asia* (London, 2007).

Roemer, H. R., 'Timur in Iran', in *The Cambridge History of Iran, vol. VI: The Timurid and Safavid Periods* (Cambridge, 1986).

Rogan, Eugene, *The Arabs: A History* (London, 2009).

Rogers J. M., and Ward, R. M., *Suleyman the Magnificent* (London, 1988).

Roosevelt, Kermit, *War in the Garden of Eden* (New York, 1919).

Rouayheb, Khaled El, 'Opening the Gate of Verification: The Forgotten Arab–Islamic Florescence of the Seventeenth Century', *International Journal of Middle East Studies*, 38 (2006), pp. 263–81.

Rouleau, Eric, 'America's Unyielding Policy Toward Iraq', *Foreign Affairs*, 74, 1 (January/February 1995), pp. 59–72.

Runciman, Steven, *A History of the Crusades*, 3 vols. (London, 1951–4).

Sada, Georges, with Nelson, Jim Black, *Saddam's Secrets: How an Iraqi General Defied and Survived Saddam Hussein* (Brentwood, Tenn., 2006).

Sandes, EWC, *In Kut and Captivity with the Sixth Indian Division* (London, 1919).

Sarre, Friedrich von, and Herzfeld, Ernst, *Archäologische Reise im Euphrat- und Tigris-Gebiet* (Berlin, 1911).

Sasson, Jean, *Mayada: Daughter of Iraq. One Woman's Survival in Saddam Hussein's Torture Jail* (London, 2003).

Sassoon, David Solomon, *A History of the Jews in Baghdad* ([n.p.], 2006; reprint of 1949 original).

Saunders, John Joseph, *The History of the Mongol Conquests* (London, 1971).

— *Muslims and Mongols* (Christchurch, New Zealand, 1977).

Savory, Roger, *Studies on the History of Safavid Iran* (London, 1987).

—, and Karamustafa, Ahmet, 'Esmail I Safawi', in *Encyclopædia Iranica*, http://www.iranicaonline.org/articles/esmail-i-safawi.

Sawdayee, Max, *All Waiting to Be Hanged* (e-book, http://maxsawdayee.com/Sawdayee/Home.html).

Serjeant, Robert Bertram, *Islamic Textiles* (Beirut, 1972).

Shaban, M. A., *The Abbasid Revolution* (Cambridge, 1979).

Shaikhli, Mohammed Rauf Taha al, *Marahil al Hayat fi Baghdad Khilal al Fatra al Mudhlimah (Stages of Life in Baghdad during the Dark Period)* (Basra, 1972; reprint of 1956 original).

Shamash, Violette, *Memories of Eden: A Journey through Jewish Baghdad* (London, 2008).

Sherley, Anthony, *Sir Anthony Sherley and His Persian Adventure* (London, 1933).

Sicker, Martin, *The Islamic World in Ascendancy: From the Arab Conquests to the Siege of Vienna* (Westport, Conn., 2000).

Simon, Reeva Spector, 'The Education of an Iraqi Ottoman Army Officer', in Rashid Khalidi et. pl. (eds.), *The Origins of Arab Nationalism* (New York, 1991).

— *Iraq Between the Two World Wars: The Militarist Origins of Tyranny* (New York, 2004).

Siry, Joseph, 'Wright's Baghdad Opera House and Gammage Auditorium: In Search of Regional Modernity', *Art Bulletin*, 87, 2 (June 2005), pp. 265–311.

Sluglett, Peter, *Britain in Iraq 1914–1932* (London, 1976).

— and Farouk-Sluglett, Marion, *Iraq since 1958: From Revolution to Dictatorship* (London, 2001; reprint of 1987 original).

Spuler, Bertold, *History of the Mongols Based on Eastern and Western Accounts of the Thirteenth and Fourteenth Centuries* (London, 1972).

— *The Muslim World, vol. I: The Age of the Caliphs* (Leiden, 1960).

Stafford, Robert, *Scientist of Empire: Sir Roderick Murchison, Scientific Exploration and Victorian Imperialism* (Cambridge, 1989).

Stark, Freya, *Baghdad Sketches* (London, 1938).

— *Dust in the Lion's Paw: Autobiography 1939–1946* (London, 1961).

— *Riding to the Tigris* (London, 1959).

Steavenson, Wendell, *The Weight of a Mustard Seed* (London, 2009).

Strika, V., and Khalil, J., *The Islamic Architecture of Baghdad* (Naples, 1987).

Styan, David, *France and Iraq: Oil, Arms and French Policy Making in the Middle East* (London, 2006).

Suleyman, Hikmat S., *The Story of Oil in Iraq* (London, 1957).

Tabari, *The History of Al Tabari*, 40 vols. (Albany, 1984–2007).

Taeschner, Franz, 'The Itinerary of the First Persian Campaign of Sultan Suleyman 1534–1536, according to Nasuh al Matraki', *Imago Mundi*, 13 (1956), pp. 53–5.

Tanukhi, *Kitab Nishwar al Muhadara wa Akhbar al Mudhakara (Table Talk of a Mesopotamian Judge)*, e-book, http://www.al-mostafa.com, privately translated by Manaf al Damluji.

Tavernier, Jean-Baptiste, *The Six Voyages of John Baptista Tavernier, Baron of Aubonne, through Turky, into Persia and the East-Indies, for the Space of Forty Years. Giving an Account of the Present State of Those Countries, viz. of the Religion, Government, Customs, and Commerce of Every Country; and the Figures, Weight, and Value of the Money Currant all over Asia. To which is Added, a New Description of the Seraglio* (London, 1677).

Teixeira, Pedro, *The Travels of Pedro Teixeira; with His 'Kings of Harmuz' and Extracts from His 'Kings of Persia'*, translated and annotated by W. F. Sinclair (London, 1902; reprint of 1711 original).

Theophanes, *The Chronicle of Theophanes*, translated by Harry Turtledove (Philadelphia, 1982).

Thévenot, Jean de, *The Travels of Monsieur de Thévenot into the Levant*, translated by A. Lovell (London, 1687).

The Thousand Nights and One Night, translated by Powys Mathers, 4 vols. (London, 2005; London, 1996; reprints of 1949 original).

Tikriti, Abd al Rahman al, *Al Amthal al Baghdadiyya al Muqarana (Comparative Proverbs of Baghdad)*, 4 vols. (Baghdad, 1969).

Townshend, Charles, *When God Made Hell: The British Invasion of Mesopotamia and the Creation of Iraq 1914–1921* (London, 2010).

The Travels of Ibn Jubayr, being the Chronicle of a Mediaeval Spanish Moor Concerning His Journey to the Egypt of Saladin, the Holy Cities of Arabia, Baghdad the City of the Caliphs, the Latin Kingdom of Jerusalem, and the Norman Kingdom of Sicily, translated and edited by Ronald J. C. Broadhurst (London, 1952).

Tripp, Charles, *A History of Iraq* (Cambridge, 2010; reprint of 2000 original).

Ullman, Harlan, and Wade, James, 'Shock and Awe: Achieving Rapid Dominance', National Defense University paper (October 1996).

Valle, Pietro della, *The Pilgrim: The Travels of Pietro della Valle*, translated by George Bull (London, 1990).

Visser, Reidar, 'Centralism and Unitary State Logic in Iraq from Midhat Pasha to Jawad al-Maliki: A Continuous Trend?' (http://www.historiae.org/maliki.asp).

Voltaire, *Letters on England* (London, 1980).

Wardi, Dr Ali al, *Lamahat Ijtimaeeyah min Tarikh al Iraq al Hadith* (*Social Aspects of Modern Iraqi History*), privately translated by Manaf al Damluji (Baghdad, 1969).

— *Understanding Iraq: Society, Culture and Personality*, translated by Fuad Baali (Lewiston, N.Y., 2008).

Warraq, Ibn Sayyar al, *Annals of the Caliphs' Kitchens: Ibn Sayyar al Warraq's Tenth-Century Baghdadi Cookbook*, translated by Nawal Nasrallah (Leiden, 2007).

Warren, John, and Fethi, Ihsan, *Traditional Houses in Baghdad* (Horsham, 1982).

Webb, Frederick Charles, *Up the Tigris to Baghdad* (London, 1870).

Wellesley, Arthur Valerian, 'The Household Cavalry in Iraq and Syria 1941', private campaign diary.

Wellsted, James Raymond, *Travels to the City of the Caliphs*, 2 vols. (London, 1840).

Werr, Lamia al Gailani, 'Iraq: Destruction to Landmarks in the Cities', in *Culture in Development* (1 December 2010), available at: http://www.cultureindevelopment.nl/News/Dossier_Heritage_Iraq/632/Iraq:_destruction_to_landmarks_in_the_cities.

White, Andrew, *The Vicar of Baghdad: Fighting for Peace in the Middle East* (Oxford, 2009).

Wiet, Gaston, *Baghdad: Metropolis of the Abbasid Caliphate* (Norman, Okla., 1971).

Willcocks, William, *The Restoration of the Ancient Irrigation Works on the Tigris* (Cairo, 1903).

Wilson, Arnold Talbot, *Mesopotamia 1917–1920: A Clash of Loyalties* (London, 1931).

Winstone, H. V. F., *Gertrude Bell* (London, 2004; reprint of 1978 original).

Woods, John E., *The Aqquyunlu: Clan, Confederation, Empire* (Salt Lake City, 1999).

Yahia, Latif, *The Devil's Double: The True Story of the Man Forced to be the Double of Saddam Hussein's Eldest Son* (London, 2003).

Yapp, M. E., 'The Establishment of the East India Company Residency at Baghdad', *Bulletin of the School of Oriental and African Studies*, 30 (1967), pp. 323–36.

Yazdi, Sharaf al Din Ali, *The History of Timur-Bec, Known by the Name of Tamerlain the Great, Emperor of the Moguls and Tartars*, translated into English by John Darby, 2 vols. (London, 1723).

Yehuda, Zvi, 'Iraqi Jewry and Cultural Change in the Educational Activity of the Alliance Israélite Universelle', in Harvey Goldberg (ed.), *Sephardi and Middle Eastern Jewries: History and Culture in the Modern Era* (Bloomington, Ind., 1996).

Yergin, Daniel, *The Prize: The Epic Quest for Oil, Money and Power* (New York, 2008; reprint of 1991 original).

Yule, Henry, *Cathay and the Way Thither* (London, 1913–16).

Zahawie, Wissam al, 'The Cultural Scene in Baghdad and Its Socio-Political Backdrop on the Eve of the Revolution of 1958: A Memoir', unpublished paper.

Notes

Full bibliographical information for each note can be found in the Bibliography.

PREFACE

1. Philip Hitti, *History of the Arabs*, p. 283.
2. Cyril Glassé, *The New Encyclopedia of Islam*, pp. 11–12.
3. Hugh Kennedy, *When Baghdad Ruled the Muslim World*, p. 8.
4. Theophanes, *The Chronicle of Theophanes*, p. 114.
5. Tabari, *The History of Al Tabari, vol. XXVII: The Abbasid Revolution*, pp. 154–7. Quoted in Albert Hourani, *A History of the Arab Peoples*, p. 32.
6. See Roy Mottahedeh, 'The Abbasid Caliphate in Iran', in *The Cambridge History of Iran, vol. IV: The Period from the Arab Invasion to the Saljuqs*, p. 57.
7. Al Makrizi, *Book of Contention and Strife Concerning the Relations between the Banu Umayya and the Banu Hashim*, p. 92.

1 THE CALIPH AND HIS CAPITAL: MANSUR AND THE FOUNDATION OF BAGHDAD (750–75)

1. Mukaddasi, *The Best Divisions for Knowledge of the Regions*, p. 108.
2. R. F. Harper, *Assyrian and Babylonian Literature*, pp. 12–13.
3. Richard Coke, *Baghdad: The City of Peace*, p. 22.
4. Quoted in Gaston Wiet, *Baghdad: Metropolis of the Abbasid Caliphate*, pp. 10–11.
5. Mukaddasi, pp. 108–9.
6. Guy Le Strange, *Baghdad during the Abbasid Caliphate*, pp. 10–11.
7. *The Koran*, trans. N. J. Dawood, Sura 10:25–6, p. 149.
8. Tabari, *The History of Al Tabari, vol. I: The Reign of Abu Jafar al Mansur 754–775*, p. 144.
9. Coke, p. 24.
10. Diarmaid MacCulloch, *A History of Christianity: The First Three Thousand Years*, p. 3.

11. Chase Robinson, *Islamic Historiography: Themes in Islamic History*, p. 36.
12. Masudi, *The Meadows of Gold*, p. 33.
13. Ibid.
14. See Hugh Kennedy, *When Baghdad Ruled the Muslim World*, p. 135.
15. See Jonathan Lyons, *The House of Wisdom: How the Arabs Transformed Western Civilization*, p. 55.
16. Tabari, vol. I, p. 145.
17. See 'The Topography of Baghdad according to the Khatib al Baghdadi', in Jacob Lassner, *The Topography of Baghdad in the Early Middle Ages*, p. 46.
18. Le Strange, *Baghdad during the Abbasid Caliphate*, p. 23.
19. See ibid., p. 20.
20. Tabari, vol. I, p. 179.
21. Ibid., pp. 180–81.
22. Ibid., p. 181.
23. Quoted in Le Strange, *Baghdad during the Abbasid Caliphate*, p. 31.
24. Ibid., p. 36.
25. Ibid., p. 27.
26. Ibn Battuta, *The Travels of Ibn Battutah*, vol. II, p. 328.
27. Lassner, p. 49.
28. Tabari, vol. I, p. 180.
29. Ibid., pp. 183–4.
30. Quoted in El Ali, 'The Foundation of Baghdad', in Albert Hourani and S. M. Stern (eds.), *The Islamic City*, p. 94.
31. Lassner, p. 56.
32. Tabari, vol. I, p. 181.
33. Charles Pellat, *The Life and Works of Jahiz*, p. 259.
34. Le Strange, *Baghdad during the Abbasid Caliphate*, p. 78.
35. Ibid., pp. 64–5.
36. Tabari, vol. I, p. 215.
37. MacCulloch, p. 264.
38. Lassner, p. 55.

2 HARUN AL RASHID AND *A THOUSAND AND ONE NIGHTS* IN BAGHDAD (775–809)

1. 'IRAQ: Intellectuals Hail Reopening of Baghdad's Mutanabbi Street', *Los Angeles Times*, 26 December 2008 (http://latimesblogs.latimes.com/babylon beyond/2008/12/the-windows-on.html).
2. Violette Shamash, *Memories of Eden: A Journey through Jewish Baghdad*, p. 144.
3. Ibn Khallikan, *Ibn Khallikan's Biographical Dictionary*, vol. I, p. 205.

4. Masudi, *The Meadows of Gold*, p. 51.

5. Ibid., p. 53.

6. Ibid., p. 65.

7. Quoted in Hugh Kennedy, *When Baghdad Ruled the Muslim World*, p. 66.

8. Tabari, *The History of Al Tabari, vol. XXX: The Abbasid Caliphate in Equilibrium: The Caliphates of Musa al Hadi and Harun al Rashid AD 785–809/AH 169–193*, p. 256.

9. André Clot, *Harun al Rashid and the World of the Thousand and One Nights*, p. 218.

10. See *The Thousand Nights and One Nights*, trans. Powys Mathers, vol. I, p. 224.

11. For a brief summary of the Darb Zubayda, see Marcus Milwright, *An Introduction to Islamic Archaeology*, pp. 162–4.

12. For accounts of Arib, see Abu al Faraj al Isfahani, *Kitab al Aghani* (*The Songs*), vol. XXII, pp. 348–59. See also Ibn Kathir, *Al Bidaya wal Nihaya* (*The Beginning and the End*), vol. XIV, p. 630 (2003 edition).

13. Quoted in Hugh Kennedy, *When Baghdad Ruled the Muslim World*, pp. 177–8.

14. See ibid., pp. 174–5.

15. *The Arabian Nights: Tales of 1,001 Nights*, trans. Malcolm Lyons, vol. III, p. 190.

16. Ibid., pp. 190–1.

17. Ibid., vol. I, p. 123.

18. Ibid., vol. II, p. xi.

19. Letter from Gertrude Bell to her father, 3 January 1921.

20. For 'The Porter and the Three Ladies', see *The Arabian Nights: Tales of 1,001 Nights*, trans. Malcolm Lyons, vol. I, pp. 50–66.

21. Ibid., vol. II, p. 187.

22. Ibid., pp. 177–81.

23. Ibid., p. 204.

24. Tabari, vol. XXX, pp. 310–11.

25. Quoted in Hugh Kennedy, *When Baghdad Ruled the Muslim World*, pp. 71–2.

26. Tabari, vol. XXX, p. 215.

27. Masudi, p. 116.

28. Ibid., p. 123.

29. Ibid., p. 124.

30. *The Thousand Nights and One Night*, translated by Powys Mathers, vol. IV, p. 510.

31. Quoted in Clot, *Harun al Rashid and the World of the Thousand and One Nights*, p. 87.

32. Tabari, vol. XXX, p. 298.

3 'THE FOUNTAINHEAD OF SCHOLARS', CENTRE OF THE WORLD (809–92)

1. Quoted in Sayed Ameer Ali, *The Spirit of Islam*, pp. 368–9.
2. Hugh Kennedy, *When Baghdad Ruled the Muslim World*, p. 132.
3. Karen Armstrong, *A History of God*, p. 203.
4. Richard Coke, *Baghdad: The City of Peace*, pp. 48–9.
5. Amira Bennison, *The Great Caliphs*, p. 166.
6. Mukaddasi, *The Best Divisions for Knowledge of the Regions*, p. 104.
7. Quoted in Jonathan Lyons, *The House of Wisdom: How the Arabs Transformed Western Civilization*, p. 62.
8. Tabari, *The History of Al Tabari, vol. XXX: The Abbasid Caliphate in Equilibrium: The Caliphates of Musa al Hadi and Harun al Rashid AD 785–809/AH 169–193*, p. 182.
9. Tabari, *The History of Al Tabari, vol. XXXI: The War between Brothers: The Caliphate of Muhammad al Amin AD 809–813/AH 193–198*, pp. 145–6.
10. Ibid., p. 147.
11. Masudi, *The Meadows of Gold*, p. 169.
12. Jim al Khalili, *Pathfinders: The Golden Age of Arabic Science*, p. 78. For a discussion of the House of Wisdom, see pp. 67–78.
13. Ibid., p. 81.
14. Quoted in Gaston Wiet, *Baghdad: Metropolis of the Abbasid Caliphate*, p. 67.
15. Hugh Kennedy, *When Baghdad Ruled the Muslim World*, p. 117.
16. For a highly entertaining discussion of Abu Nuwas' poetic life, see 'Dangling Locks and Babel Eyes: A Profile of Abu Nuwas', in Philip Kennedy, *Abu Nuwas: A Genius of Poetry*, pp. 1–19.
17. Ibid., p. 11. The following Abu Nuwas verses are taken from this volume.
18. Masudi, pp. 43–5.
19. Ibn Khallikan, *Ibn Khallikan's Biographical Dictionary*, vol. I, p. 208.
20. Quoted in André Clot, *Harun al Rashid and the World of the Thousand and One Nights*, pp. 132–3.
21. Masudi, p. 99.
22. A. J. Arberry, *Arabic Poetry*, pp. 42–4.
23. Tabari, quoted in Hugh Kennedy, *When Baghdad Ruled the Muslim World*, p. 120.
24. Ibid.
25. Quoted in Wiet, p. 76.
26. Hugh Kennedy, *When Baghdad Ruled the Muslim World*, pp. 124–5.
27. See Jahiz's portrait of a singing slave-girl in Charles Pellat, *The Life and Works of Jahiz*, pp. 265–7.
28. Masudi, pp. 91–3.

29. Al Isfahani, *Kitab al Aghani*, quoted in Hugh Kennedy, *When Baghdad Ruled the Muslim World*, p. 180.
30. Wiet, pp. 76–7.
31. See Julia Ashtiany et al. (eds.), *Cambridge History of Arabic Literature, vol. II: Abbasid Belles-Lettres*, p. 81.
32. Pellat, p. 218.
33. Masudi, p. 249.
34. Quoted in Lyons, p. 73.
35. For a brief summary of Khwarizmi's achievements see ibid., pp. 70–74.
36. For a detailed description of the experiment, see Ibn Khallikan, vol. III, pp. 315–17.
37. Al Khalili, p. 89.
38. Ibid., p. 74.
39. Ibid., p. 75.
40. See Hugh Kennedy, *When Baghdad Ruled the Muslim World*, p. 255.
41. Al Khalili, p. 148.
42. Quoted in ibid., p. 149.
43. Ibid., p. 134.
44. Quoted in Bennison, p. 90.
45. Hugh Kennedy, *When Baghdad Ruled the Muslim World*, p. 214.
46. Tabari, *The History of Al Tabari, vol. XXXV: The Crisis of the Abbasid Caliphate: The Caliphates of al Musta'in and al Mu'tazz AD 862–869/AH 248–255*, pp. 49–50.
47. Ibid., p. 61.
48. Tabari, quoted in Hugh Kennedy, *When Baghdad Ruled the Muslim World*, p. 285.

4 THE LATER ABBASIDS: FAREWELL TO
THE MEADOWS OF GOLD (892–1258)

1. Quoted in Jacob Lassner, *The Topography of Baghdad in the Early Middle Ages*, pp. 88–9.
2. Amira Bennison, *The Great Caliphs*, p. 42.
3. Hugh Kennedy, *When Baghdad Ruled the Muslim World*, p. 295.
4. Masudi, *The Meadows of Gold*, p. 24.
5. Hugh Kennedy, *When Baghdad Ruled the Muslim World*, p. 251.
6. Masudi, p. 96.
7. Tanukhi, *Kitab Nishwar al Muhadara wa Akhbar al Mudhakara (Table Talk of a Mesopotamian Judge)* privately translated by Manaf al Damluji.
8. Charles Pellat, *The Life and Works of Jahiz*, p. 150.
9. Masudi, p. 352.

10. Ibn Akil, *Kitab al Funun*, quoted in *Al Ahram Weekly*, 'Baghdad Supplement', 17–23 April 2003.
11. Jacob Lassner, *The Topography of Baghdad in the Early Middle Ages*, p. 53.
12. Guy Le Strange, *Baghdad during the Abbasid Caliphate*, p. 233.
13. Richard Coke, *Baghdad: City of Peace*, p. 109.
14. Ibn Miskawayh, *The Experiences of the Nations*, translated by David Margoliouth (1921), cited in ibid., p. 112.
15. Le Strange, *Baghdad during the Abbasid Caliphate*, p. 319.
16. Mukaddasi, *The Best Divisions for Knowledge of the Regions*, p. 109.
17. See Lassner, pp. 108–9.
18. Ibn Sayyar al Warraq, *Annals of the Caliphs' Kitchens: Ibn Sayyar al Warraq's Tenth-Century Baghdadi Cookbook*, pp. 474–5.
19. Ibid., p. 482.
20. Ibid., p. 35.
21. Ibid., p. 517.
22. Ibid., p. 308.
23. Ibid., p. 309.
24. Ibid., p. 250.
25. Ibid., p. 251.
26. Masudi, pp. 191–2.
27. Warraq, p. 125.
28. Ibid., p. 31.
29. Ibid., p. 113.
30. Masudi, p. 95.
31. Quoted in Gaston Wiet, *Baghdad: Metropolis of the Abbasid Caliphate*, pp. 78–9.
32. Warraq, p. 502.
33. Ibid., p. 503.
34. Ibid., p. 506.
35. Ibid., pp. 508–17.
36. Ibid., p. 518.
37. Masudi, pp. 405–7.
38. For a brief summary of events around 1055, see Eric J. Hanne, *Putting the Caliph in His Place: Power, Authority, and the Late Abbasid Caliphate*, pp. 90–91.
39. Bennison, p. 44.
40. Hanne, p. 143.
41. *Encyclopaedia of Islam* (second edition), vol. I, pp. 69–70.
42. Amin Maalouf, *The Crusades through Arab Eyes*, p. xiii.
43. Ibn al Athir, *The Chronicle of Ibn al Athir for the Crusading Period from Al Kamil fi al Tarikh, Part I: The Years 491–541/1097–1146 – The Coming of the Franks and the Muslim Response*, p. 22.

44. Maalouf, p. xvi.

45. Manaf al Damluji, 'The Urban Masses of Baghdad', unpublished paper.

46. Le Strange, *Baghdad during the Abbasid Caliphate*, p. 329.

47. See Judith Herrin, *Byzantium: The Surprising Life of a Medieval Empire*, pp. 144–5.

48. For Benjamin's description of Baghdad, see Marcus Nathan Adler, *The Itinerary of Benjamin of Tudela*, pp. 35–42.

49. Ibn Khallikan records how Ibn Hanbal was 'beaten and imprisoned' for his refusal to declare that the Koran was created. See *Ibn Khallikan's Biographical Dictionary*, vol. I, p. 44.

50. Coke, p. 105.

51. Ibn al Athir, *Al Kamil fi al Tarikh*, vol. II, p. 257.

52. Ibid., p. 258.

53. For an account of his visit to Baghdad, see *The Travels of Ibn Jubayr*, trans. and ed. Ronald J. C. Broadhurst, pp. 226–32.

54. 'Iraqi Campus Is Under Gang's Sway', *New York Times*, 19 October 2009.

55. Le Strange, *Baghdad during the Abbasid Caliphate*, p. 335.

56. Coke, p. 123.

57. Masudi, p. 239.

5 'THIS PILGRIMAGE OF DESTRUCTION': THE MONGOL AND TATAR STORM (1258–1401)

1. Rashid al Din, *The Successors of Genghis Khan*, pp. 222–3.

2. Ibid., p. 223.

3. Henry Howorth, *History of the Mongols, vol. III: The Mongols of Persia*, p. 123.

4. William Muir, *The Caliphate: Its Rise, Decline and Fall*, p. 584.

5. John Joseph Saunders, *The History of the Mongol Conquests*, p. 110.

6. See Professor Farouk Omar Fawzi, *Abbasid Caliphate, vol. II: The Abbasid Caliphate – Decline and Fall*, pp. 248–60.

7. For a discussion of the strength of Hulagu's army, see Reuven Amitai-Preiss, *Mongols and Mamluks: The Mamluk–Ilkhanid War 1260–1281*, p. 15.

8. See David Morgan, *The Mongols*, pp. 145–66.

9. Rashid al Din, *Jami al Tawarikh (Compendium of Histories)*, pp. 238–9.

10. See Bertold Spuler, *History of the Mongols: Based on Eastern and Western Accounts of the Thirteenth and Fourteenth Centuries*, p. 115.

11. Ibid., p. 116.

12. Din, *Jami al Tawarikh*, p. 297.

13. See Ibn Kathir, *Al Bidaya wal Nihaya (The Beginning and the End)*, vol. XIII: *The Events of the Year 656 AH (1258 AD)*, pp. 235–7.

14. For a discussion of the casualties, see Morgan, p. 133. Such correspondence fuels a commonly held view amongst Arab historians that there was a secret

pact between Hulagu and some of the European monarchs to attack Baghdad, strengthening the Crusaders' push from the west. Such a policy, according to this argument, was encouraged by Hulagu's Christian wife, who was duly rewarded with the construction of a magnificent church in the heart of the caliphal complex of palaces and mosques.

15. Spuler, *History of the Mongols* pp. 120–21.

16. Kathir, p. 235.

17. Quoted in Saunders, pp. 111–12.

18. Din, *Jami al Tawarikh*, p. 301.

19. Howorth, p. 126.

20. Quoted in Justin Marozzi, *Tamerlane: Sword of Islam, Conqueror of the World*, p. 13.

21. Kathir, pp. 236–7.

22. Edward G. Browne, *A Literary History of Persia, vol. II: From Firdawsi to Sadi*, p. 29.

23. Marco Polo, *The Travels of Marco Polo*, pp. 551–2.

24. For the full text of the poem, see: http://www.hwlongfellow.org/poems_poem.php?pid=2052.

25. For an excellent discussion of Mustasim's demise, see Guy Le Strange, 'The Story of the Death of the Last Abbasid Caliph', *Journal of the Royal Asiatic Society* (April 1900), pp. 293–300, and John Andrew Boyle, 'The Death of the Last Abbasid Caliph: A Contemporary Muslim Account', *Journal of Semitic Studies*, 6, 2 (1961), pp. 145–61.

26. Howorth, p. 130.

27. Richard Coke, *Baghdad: City of Peace*, p. 152.

28. Stephen Hemsley Longrigg, *Four Centuries of Modern Iraq*, p. 12.

29. See Din, *Jami al Tawarikh*, pp. 307–9; Howorth, p. 130.

30. Ibid., pp. 287–8.

31. The opening lines, 'There is no god but God, and Mohammed is his Prophet', are the creed of all Muslims. Al Makrizi, *Kelavun*, vol. II, pp. 185–6. Cited in Coke, p. 159.

32. Edward Browne, *A Literary History of Persia, vol. III: A History of Persian Literature under Tatar Dominion*, quoted in Coke, p. 161.

33. Ibn Battuta, *The Travels of Ibn Battutah*, vol. II, pp. 322–5.

34. Ibid., pp. 329–30.

35. Ibid., p. 329.

36. Ibid., p. 332.

37. Ibid.

38. Ibid., pp. 340–41.

39. Sharaf al Din Ali Yazdi, *The History of Timur-Bec, Known by the Name of Tamerlain the Great, Emperor of the Moguls and Tartars*, vol. II, p. 213.

40. Ibn Arabshah, *Timur the Great Amir*, p. 158. For a graphic account of the city's sacking by Tamerlane's forces, see pp. 157–9.

41. Ibid., p. 165.
42. Yazdi, vol. II, p. 214.
43. Ibid., pp. 222–4.
44. Ibid., vol. I, pp. 433–4.
45. H. R. Roemer, 'Timur in Iran', in *The Cambridge History of Iran, vol. VI: The Timurid and Safavid Periods*, p. 65.
46. Yazdi, vol. II, p. 214.
47. Ibid.
48. Arabshah, p. 167.
49. Ibid., p. 168. According to the panegyrist Yazdi, each soldier was ordered to bring Tamerlane one head.
50. Yazdi, vol. II, p. 216.
51. Ibid.
52. Arabshah, p. 168.
53. Yazdi., p. 217.
54. Arabshah said he was told by the *kadi* Tajuddin Ahmad Namani, the Hanafite governor of Baghdad, that Tamerlane's army built about 120 towers of skulls (Arabshah., p. 168).
55. Ibid., p. 168.

6 BLACK SHEEP, WHITE SHEEP (1401–1534)

1. See Hugh Kennedy, *When Baghdad Ruled the Muslim World*, p. 296.
2. Ibn Arabshah, *Timur the Great Amir*, p. 169.
3. See R. Quiring-Zacher, 'Aq Qoyunlu', in *Encyclopædia Iranica* (http://www.iranicaonline.org/articles/aq-qoyunlu-confederation).
4. Cited in Richard Coke, *Baghdad: City of Peace*, p. 178
5. Ibid., p. 179.
6. Ibid.
7. Edward G. Browne, *A Literary History of Persia, vol. III: A History of Persian Literature under Tatar Dominion 1265–1502*, p. 285.
8. Ibid., p. 285.
9. Coke, p. 183.
10. Quoted in André Clot, *Suleiman the Magnificent*, p. 92.
11. See Poggio Bracciolini, *Travels of Nicolò de' Conti, in the East in the Early Part of the Fifteenth Century*, p. 5.
12. 'The Travels of the Magnificent M. Ambrosio Contarini', in Josafa Barbaro and Ambrosio Contarini, *Travels to Tana and Persia*, pp. 132–3.
13. William Nassau Lees, *Jami: A Biographical Sketch*, pp. 14–15.
14. Stephen Hemsley Longrigg, *Four Centuries of Modern Iraq*, p. 16.
15. 'The Travels of a Merchant in Persia', in Barbaro and Contarini, p. 191.
16. For details of Ismail's campaigns, see Roger Savory, *Studies on the History of Safavid Iran*, pp. 71–80.

17. See Roger Savory and Ahmet Karamustafa, 'Esmail I Safawi', in *Encyclopædia Iranica* (http://www.iranicaonline.org/articles/esmail-i-safawi).

18. Abbas al Azzawi, *Tarikh al Iraq bayn al Ihtilayn* (*History of Iraq between Two Occupations*), vol. III, pp. 336–43.

19. A. A. Duri, 'Baghdad', in *Encylopaedia of Islam* (second edition), vol. I, p. 903.

20. 'The Travels in Persia by Caterino Zeno', in Barbaro and Contarini, p. 65.

21. Ibid.

22. Clot, *Suleiman the Magnificent*, p. 30.

23. Giovanni Maria Angiolello, 'A Short Narrative of the Life and Acts of the King Ussun Cassano', in Barbaro and Contarini, p. 111.

24. See Caroline Finkel, *Osman's Dream: The Story of the Ottoman Empire 1300–1923*, p. 126.

25. See Rhoads Murphey, 'Suleyman's Eastern Policy', in Halil Inalcik and Cemal Kafadar (eds.), *Suleyman the Second and His Time*, p. 244.

7 OF TURKS AND TRAVELLERS (1534–1639)

1. Cited in Sīdi Ali Reïs, *The Travels and Adventures of the Turkish Admiral Sīdi Ali Reïs in India, Afghanistan, Central Asia, and Persia, during the Years 1553–1556*, p. 82.

2. Leonhard Rauwolff, *A Collection of Curious Travels and Voyages. In Two Tomes. The First Containing Dr L. Rauwolff's Itinerary into the Eastern Countries, as Syria, Palestine, &c.*, p. 179.

3. Ibid., p. 180.

4. Ibid., pp. 181–2.

5. Ibid.

6. Ibid., pp. 183–4.

7. Ibid., p. 187.

8. Ibid., pp. 190–91.

9. For Federici's journey, see Richard Hakluyt, *Hakluyt's Collection of the Early Voyages, Travels, and Discoveries of the English Nation* (1903–5), vol. V, pp. 365ff. For Balbi, see Samuel Purchas, *Purchas His Pilgrimes* (1905), vol. X, p. 145.

10. Richard Coke, *Baghdad: City of Peace*, p. 194.

11. William Shakespeare, *Macbeth*, Act I, Scene 3:

> FIRST WITCH: A sailor's wife had chestnuts in her lap,
> And munch'd, and munch'd, and munch'd: –
> 'Give me,' quoth I:
> 'Aroint thee, witch!' the rump-fed ronyon cries.
> Her husband's to Aleppo gone, master o' the Tiger:
> But in a sieve I'll thither sail,
> And, like a rat without a tail,
> I'll do, I'll do, and I'll do.

12. For the early years of British commercial representation in Baghdad, see M. E. Yapp, 'The Establishment of the East India Company Residency at Baghdad', *Bulletin of the School of Oriental and African Studies*, 30 (1967), pp. 323–36.

13. 'The Voyage of M. Iohn Eldred to Trypolis in Syria by Sea, and from thence by Land and River to Babylon and Balsara. 1583', Richard Hakluyt, *Hakluyt's Collection of the Early Voyages, Travels, and Discoveries of the English Nation* (1810), vol. II, p. 404.

14. Ibid., p. 372.

15. Ibid., p. 406.

16. Cevdet Kudret, *Fuzuli*, p. 189.

17. For an excellent introduction to art in Baghdad at this time, see Rachel Milstein, *Miniature Painting in Ottoman Baghdad*.

18. Ibid., p. 4.

19. See Colin Imber, 'The Persecution of the Ottoman Shi'ites according to the Mühimme Defterleri 1565–1585', *Islam*, 56 (1979).

20. Anthony Sherley, *Sir Anthony Sherley and His Persian Adventure*, p. 193.

21. Ibid., p. 192.

22. John Cartwright, 'Observations of Master John Cartwright', in Purchas, vol. VIII, p. 520.

23. Pedro Teixeira, *The Travels of Pedro Teixeira*, p. 62.

24. Ibid., p. 66.

25. Pietro della Valle, *The Pilgrim: The Travels of Pietro della Valle*, pp. 101–2.

26. Ibid., pp. 102–3.

27. Ibid., p. 105.

28. Ibid., p. 117.

29. Stephen Hemsley Longrigg, *Four Centuries of Modern Iraq*, p. 52.

30. Robert Mantran, 'Bagdad à l'époque ottoman', *Arabica* (1962), pp. 313–14.

31. Jean de Thévenot, *The Travels of Monsieur de Thévenot into the Levant*, 'Part II, pp. 62–3.

32. Ibid., Part I, pp. 287ff.

33. For an account of the siege, see the contemporary account of Ziyaeddin Ibrahim Nuri, *Fethname-i Bagdad*, summarized in Rhoads Murphey, *Ottoman Warfare 1500–1700*, pp. 115–22.

34. Thévenot, Part I, p. 288. The translation has been reworked into more modern English.

35. Ibid., p. 289.

36. Ibid.

37. Ibid.

38. Ibid., p. 290.

39. Ibid.

40. Ibid., pp. 290–91.

8 PLAGUES, PASHAS AND MAMLUKS (1639–1831)

1. Quoted in Bernard Lewis, *Race and Slavery in the Middle East*, p. 65.
2. Clément Huart, *Histoire de Bagdad dans les temps modernes*, p. 85.
3. For his description of Baghdad, see Jean-Baptiste Tavernier, *The Six Voyages of John Baptista Tavernier*, Book II, Chapter 7, pp. 85–6.
4. See Hugh Murray, *Historical Account of Discoveries and Travels in Asia*, vol. I, pp. 384–400.
5. For his description of Baghdad, see Jean de Thévenot, *The Travels of Monsieur de Thévenot into the Levant*, Part II, pp. 62–3.
6. Dr Ali al Wardi, *Lamahat Ijtimaeeyah min Tarikh al Iraq al Hadith (Social Aspects of Modern Iraqi History)*, vol. I, p. 150.
7. For a discussion of homosexuality in Mamluk Baghdad, see ibid., pp. 152–3.
8. Cited in Youssef H. Aboul-Enein, *Iraq in Turmoil: Historical Perspectives of Dr Ali al Wardi, from the Ottoman Empire to King Feisal*, p. 17.
9. Wardi, *Lamahat Ijtimaeeyah min Tarikh al Iraq al Hadith,* vol. I, p. 97.
10. See Hala Fattah, *The Politics of Regional Trade in Iraq, Arabia and the Gulf 1745–1900*, pp. 35–74.
11. Cited in ibid., p. 216.
12. 'It is reckoned a disgrace for a gentleman or soldier to mount a gelding or mare,' wrote the English traveller Dr Edward Ives. See *A Voyage from England to India, in the Year 1754 . . . Also a Journey from Persia to England by an Unusual Route*, p. 273n.
13. William Heude, *A Voyage up the Persian Gulf, and a Journey Overland from India to England, in 1817*, pp. 145–6.
14. Ibid., p. 146.
15. For a stirring study of Nadir Shah, see Michael Axworthy, *The Sword of Persia*.
16. Joseph Emin, *Life and Adventures of Joseph Emin*, p. 5.
17. Wardi, *Lamahat Ijtimaeeyah min Tarikh al Iraq al Hadith,* vol. I, pp. 112–13.
18. Emin, p. 7.
19. Joseph von Hammer-Purgstall, *Histoire de l'Empire Ottoman*, p. 521.
20. The figure of 100,000 is mentioned in Aboul-Enein, p. 21. See also Rasul al Kerküklü, *Dawhat al Wuzara (The Lofty Tree of Ministers)*, pp. 30–31.
21. Jonas Hanway, *An Historical Account of the British Trade over the Caspian Sea . . . To which are Added the Revolutions of Persia during the Present Century, with the Particular History of the Great Usurper Nadir Kouli*, vol. II, p. 91.
22. Heude, p. 148.
23. Ives, p. 282.
24. Stephen Hemsley Longrigg, *Four Centuries of Modern Iraq*, p. 169.

25. Ives, p. 284.

26. Heude, p. 149.

27. Ives, pp. 278–9.

28. See Tom Nieuwenhuis, *Politics and Society in Early Modern Iraq: Mamluk Pashas, Tribal Shaykhs and Local Rule Between 1802 and 1831*, p. 23.

29. Kerküklü, p. 159.

30. Carsten Niebuhr, *Voyage en Arabie et en d'autres pays circonvoisins*, p. 239.

31. Ives, p. 273.

32. Ibid., p. 281.

33. See report by Dr Lamia al Gailani Werr of the British Institute for the Study of Iraq, 'Iraq: Destruction to Landmarks in the Cities' (http://www.cultureindevelopment.nl/News/Dossier_Heritage_Iraq/632/Iraq:_destruction_to_landmarks_in_the_cities).

34. André Raymond, *Arab Cities in the Ottoman Period.*, p. 36, pp. 114–15.

35. Niebuhr, p. 250.

36. Ibid., p. 264.

37. Ibid., p. 240.

38. Ives, pp. 286–7.

39. Nieuwenhuis, p. 23.

40. Peter M. Holt, *Egypt and the Fertile Crescent 1516–1922*, p. 148.

41. Harford Jones Brydges, *An Account of the Transactions of His Majesty's Mission to the Court of Persia, in the Years 1807–11, to which is Appended a Brief History of the Wahauby*, vol. II, p. 190.

42. Longrigg, *Four Centuries of Modern Iraq*, p. 234.

43. Heude, pp. 169–70.

44. For his description of Baghdad, see James Silk Buckingham, *Travels in Mesopotamia*, vol. II, pp. 176–216.

45. Voltaire, *Letters on England*, pp. 53–4.

46. Jacob Coleman Hurewitz, *Diplomacy in the Near and Middle East*, vol. I, p. 90.

47. George Keppel, *Personal Narrative of a Journey from India to England*, vol. I, pp. 221–2.

48. Caroline Finkel, *Osman's Dream: The Story of the Ottoman Empire 1300–1923*, p. 435.

49. Longrigg, *Four Centuries of Modern Iraq*, p. 265.

50. Ibid., pp. 265–6. See in addition the vivid eyewitness accounts of A. N. Groves, *Journal of a Residence in Bagdad during the Years 1830 and 1831*, and James Raymond Wellsted, *Travels to the City of the Caliphs*, vol. I, pp. 280–91.

51. Wellsted, vol. I, pp. 282–3.

52. Ibid., p. 285.

53. Ibid., pp. 289–90.

54. Ibid., p. 290.

55. Hanna Batatu has the population of Baghdad at 80,000 at this time, of which he estimates 53,000 lost their lives in the plague, flood, siege and famine of 1831. See Albert Hourani, Philip S. Khoury and Mary C. Wilson (eds.), *The Modern Middle East: A Reader*, p. 505; see also *The Scribe*, 36 (September 1989), p. 4 (http://www.dangoor.com/TheScribe36.pdf), which estimates 100,000 lost their lives out of a population of 150,000; Groves estimates losses at more than two-thirds of an unquantified population, p. 236.

9 EMPIRES COLLIDE (1831–1917)

1. The English translation of the text of the 1914 Ottoman *jihad* is given in Rudolph Peters, *Jihad in Classical and Modern Islam*, pp. 56–7.
2. Ibn Battuta, *The Travels of Ibn Battutah*, vol. II, p. 334.
3. 'Baghdad's "Great Wall of Adhamiya"', *New York Times*, 20 April 2007.(http://thelede.blogs.nytimes.com/2007/04/20/baghdads-great-wall-of-adhamiya).
4. Dr Ali al Wardi, *Lamahat Ijtimaeeyah min Tarikh al Iraq al Hadith* (*Social Aspects of Modern Iraqi History*), vol. II, p. 82.
5. For a survey of these reforms, see the 2011 paper by Ishtiaq Hussain, *The Tanzimat: Secular Reforms in the Ottoman Empire*, pp. 5–11 (http://faith-matters.org/images/stories/fm-publications/the-tanzimat-final-web.pdf).
6. J. Baillie Fraser, *Travels in Koordistan, Mesopotamia, etc.*, vol. I, p. 211.
7. Stephen Hemsley Longrigg, *Four Centuries of Modern Iraq*, pp. 281–2.
8. Robin Butlin, 'Changing Visions: The RGS in the 19th Century', in Royal Geographical Society, *To the Ends of the Earth*, p. 17.
9. Robert Stafford, *Scientist of Empire: Sir Roderick Murchison, Scientific Exploration and Victorian Imperialism*, p. 95.
10. Abdul Kareem al Allaf, *Baghdad al Qadeemah min Sanat 1869 hatta Sanat 1917* (*Old Baghdad from the Year 1869 until the Year 1917*), pp. 10–18; see also Longrigg, *Four Centuries of Modern Iraq*, p. 294.
11. BOA.DH.ID 52/8. See Fadhil Bayat, *Baghdad: min Khilal Wathaik al Arsheef al Othmani* (*Baghdad in the Light of Ottoman Archive Documents*), p. 71.
12. M. E. Hume-Griffith, *Behind the Veil in Persia and Turkish Arabia*, p. viii.
13. Charles Rathbone Low, *History of the Indian Navy*, vol. II, p. 409.
14. See James Felix Jones, 'Memoir on the Province of Baghdad', in *Memoirs by Commander J. F. Jones* (1998 edition), p. 309.
15. For colourful descriptions of journeys on this service in 1947 and 1966 respectively, see John Ough, 'The Nairn Transport Company: Damascus to Baghdad'(http://ough-zone.blogspot.com/2009/08/nairn-transport-company-damascus-to.html) and Fuad Rayess, 'On a Bus to Baghdad', *Saudi Aramco World*, September–October 1966 (http://www.saudiaramcoworld.com/issue/196605/on.a.bus.to.baghdad.htm). See also John M. Munro and Martin

Love, 'The Nairn Way', *Saudi Aramco World*, July–August 1981 (http://www.saudiaramcoworld.com/issue/198104/the.nairn.way.htm).

16. Quoted in Richard Coke, *Baghdad: City of Peace*, pp. 272–3.

17. For an entertaining study of this ruinously expensive *Drang nach Osten*, see Sean McMeekin, *The Berlin–Baghdad Express*, p. 34.

18. Ibid., p. 239.

19. George S. Clarke, *The Baghdad Railway*.

20. Morris Jastrow, *The War and the Bagdad Railway*, p. 120.

21. See McMeekin, pp. 123–52.

22. BOA.A.MKT.MHM.2/4–84. Bayat, p. 50.

23. *Wardi, Lamahat Ijtimaeeyah min Tarikh al Iraq al Hadith*, vol. II, pp. 113–16.

24. Abbas al Azzawi, *Tarikh al Iraq bayn al Ihtilayn (History of Iraq between Two Occupations)*, vol. VII, pp. 98–9.

25. Ibid., p. 156.

26. BOA.A.MKT.MHM.702/78. Bayat, p. 54.

27. For an assessment of his pashalik, see Sulaiman Faiq Baig, *The History of Baghdad*, pp. 166–7.

28. Sua'ad Hadi al Omari, *Baghdad fi al Qarn al Tasi Ashar Kama Wasafaha al Rahhala al Ajanib (Baghdad as Described by the Foreign Visitors)*, p. 105.

29. Wardi, *Lamahat Ijtimaeeyah min Tarikh al Iraq al Hadith*, vol. II, pp. 211–14; Azzawi, pp. 121–5.

30. Wardi, *Lamahat Ijtimaeeyah min Tarikh al Iraq al Hadith*, vol. II, pp. 219–21.

31. Ibid., p. 239.

32. Allaf, pp. 21–3.

33. Longrigg, *Four Centuries of Modern Iraq*, p. 316.

34. See Mohammed Rauf Taha al Shaikhli, *Marahil al Hayat fi Baghdad Khilal al Fatra al Mudhlimah (Stages of Life in Baghdad during the Dark Period)*.

35. Coke, p. 274.

36. Sadiq Damluji, *Midhat Pasha*, p. 36.

37. Wardi, *Lamahat Ijtimaeeyah min Tarikh al Iraq al Hadith*, vol. II, pp. 248–51.

38. Marina Benjamin, *Last Days in Babylon*, p. 17.

39. Damluji, pp. 45–6.

40. Wardi, *Lamahat Ijtimaeeyah min Tarikh al Iraq al Hadith*, vol. II, pp. 260–62.

41. Ibid., pp. 263–4.

42. Yusuf Rizk-Allah Ghanimah, *Nuzhat al Mushtak fi Tarikh Yahud al Iraq (A Nostalgic Trip into the History of the Jews of Iraq)*, p. 137.

43. David Solomon Sassoon, *A History of the Jews in Baghdad*, p. 165.

44. Jones, p. 339.

45. Benjamin, pp. 36–7.

46. Zvi Yehuda, 'Iraqi Jewry and Cultural Change in the Educational Activity of the Alliance Israélite Universelle', in Harvey Goldberg (ed.), *Sephardi and Middle Eastern Jewries*, p. 137.

47. Quoted in ibid., p. 142.

48. Morris Cohen, 'Superstition among the Jews in Baghdad', extracted in *The Scribe*, 46 (January 1991), pp. 3–5 (http://www.dangoor.com/TheScribe46.pdf).

49. The figures come from the annual *Salnameh*, the annual Ottoman administrative and statistical survey published in each vilayet. See Shaikhli.

50. Sylvia Haim, 'Aspects of Jewish Life in Baghdad under the Monarchy', *Middle Eastern Studies*, 12, 2 (1976), p. 1.

51. See *Arab Bulletin*, 66 (21 October 1917).

52. See Mitchell Bard, 'The Jews of Iraq', *Jewish Virtual Library* (http://www.jewishvirtuallibrary.org/jsource/anti-semitism/iraqijews.html).

53. Quoted in Benjamin, p. 18.

54. For a full account of this incident, see the selection of contemporary reports extracted in *The Scribe*, 36 (September 1989), pp. 4–7 (http://www.dangoor.com/TheScribe36.pdf).

55. Benjamin, p. 27.

56. FO 371/1002/4234, Constantinople, 31 January 1910. Quoted in Ghassan Atiyah, *Iraq, 1908–1921*, p. 43.

57. Reeva S. Simon, 'The Education of an Iraqi Ottoman Army Officer', in Rashid Khalidi et al. (eds.), *The Origins of Arab Nationalism*, p. 155.

58. Gertrude Bell, *Letters*, 18 March 1911. See the Gertrude Bell Archive of Newcastle University Library, which contains an online collection of Bell's voluminous correspondence (http://www.gerty.ncl.ac.uk).

59. Manaf al Damluji, 'Sarah's Saga: The Story of a Popular Armenian-Iraqi Lady', unpublished paper. See also Wardi, *Lamahat Ijtimaeeyah min Tarikh al Iraq al Hadith*, vol. III, pp. 181–4.

60. McMeekin, p. 123.

61. E. M. Earle, *Turkey, the Great Powers, and the Baghdad Railway*, pp. 14–15.

62. See Hikmat S. Suleyman, *The Story of Oil in Iraq*, p. 29.

63. See Daniel Yergin, *The Prize: The Epic Quest for Oil, Money and Power*, p. 157.

64. Charles Townshend, *When God Made Hell: The British Invasion of Mesopotamia and the Creation of Iraq 1914–1921*, p. xxiv.

65. Brigadier-General F. J. Moberly, *The Campaign in Mesopotamia 1914–1918*, vol. I, p. 134.

66. See Atiyah, p. 134.

67. Tamara Chalabi, *Late for Tea at the Deer Palace: The Lost Dreams of My Iraqi Family*, p. 29.

68. Alois Musil, *The Middle Euphrates*, pp. 128–9.

69. Atiyah, p. 149.

70. Edmund Candler, *The Long Road to Baghdad*, vol. I, p. 3.

71. Chalabi, p. 32.

72. Quoted in Townshend, p. 232.

73. P. W. Long, *Other Ranks of Kut*, p. 25.

74. Ibid., pp. 26–7.

75. E. W. C. Sandes, *In Kut and Captivity with the Sixth Indian Division*, p. 284.

76. Long., p. 288.

77. Ernest Walker memoir, quoted in Townshend, p. 313.

78. Long., p. 34.

79. Josephine Hammond, *Battle in Iraq*, p. 162.

80. In the words of the subsequent parliamentary report 'it is certain that this desert journey rests upon those responsible for it as a crime of the kind we call historic, so long and terrible was the torture it meant for thousands of helpless men . . . to send the men out on such a journey and in such conditions was to condemn half of them to certain death.' See Moberly, vol. II, p. 464.

81. Atiyah, p. 150.

82. William Robertson, *Soldiers and Statesmen 1914–1918*, vol. II, pp. 75–6.

83. Eleanor Franklin Egan, *The War in the Cradle of the World*, p. 252.

84. Coke, p. 292.

85. Candler, vol. II, pp. 98–9.

86. A. J. Barker, *The Neglected War: Mesopotamia 1914–1918*, p. 367.

10 A VERY BRITISH MONARCHY: THREE KINGS IN BAGHDAD (1917–1958)

1. Cited in Arnold Talbot Wilson, *Mesopotamia 1917–1920: A Clash of Loyalties*, p. 338.

2. Brigadier-General F. J. Moberly, *The Campaign in Mesopotamia 1914–1918*, vol. III, p. 248.

3. Edmund Candler, *The Long Road to Baghdad*, pp. 97, 104

4. Moberly, vol. III, p. 249.

5. Eleanor Egan, *The War in the Cradle of the World*, p. 248.

6. Moberly, p. 255.

7. Edmund Candler, 16 March 1917, *Manchester Guardian*, reproduced in Charles F. Horne (ed.), *Source Records of the Great War*, vol. V.

8. Egan, pp. 253–4.

9. Quoted in Charles Townshend, *When God Made Hell: The British Invasion of Mesopotamia and the Creation of Iraq 1914–1921*, p. 267.

10. *The War Illustrated*, 24 March 1917, p. 131.

11. See Stephen Hemsley Longrigg, *Iraq 1900–1950*, p. 93. 'It made no great impression.'

12. Hansard, HC Debate, 21 March 1917, vol. 91, cols. 1,902–4.

13. *Iraq Administration Reports*, vol. I (1914–1918), pp. 520–21.

14. Georgina Howell, *Daughter of the Desert: The Remarkable Life of Gertrude Bell*, p. 60.

15. Karl Meyer and Shareen Brysac, *Kingmakers: The Invention of the Modern Middle East*, p. 158.
16. Gertrude Bell, *Letters*, 5 December 1918.
17. Ibid., 10 March 1917.
18. Ibid., 20 April 1917.
19. Charles Callwell, *The Life of Sir Stanley Maude*, p. 286.
20. Ibid., p. 311.
21. Hansard, HC Debates, 4 March 1918, vol. 103, cols. 1,747–53.
22. Bell, *Letters*, 22 November 1917.
23. Author visit, 25 April 2009. In August 2013, the Commonwealth War Graves Commission said it was working closely with the British Embassy in Baghdad and Commonwealth partners to 'develop a wider maintenance capacity via potential working partners'. Progress in recent years has included the erection of 500 new headstones at Baghdad North Gate War Cemetery.
24. Bell, *Letters*, 14 June 1920.
25. See Beverley Milton-Edwards and Peter Hinchcliffe, *Jordan: A Hashemite Legacy*, p. 17.
26. Longrigg, *Iraq 1900–1950*, p. 115.
27. See Elie Kedourie, *England and the Middle East: The Destruction of the Ottoman Empire 1914–1921*, p. 177.
28. Wilson, p. 336.
29. Gertrude Bell, *Review of the Civil Administration of Mesopotamia* p. 128.
30. George Antonius, *The Arab Awakening*, p. 313.
31. Ghassan Atiyah, *Iraq, 1908–1921*, p. 311.
32. Wilson, p. 257.
33. Bell, *Letters*, 14 June 1920.
34. Aylmer Haldane, *The Insurrection in Mesopotamia 1920*, p. 64.
35. Charles Tripp, *A History of Iraq*, p. 42.
36. Quoted in Kedourie, p. 195.
37. *Iraq Administration Reports*, vol. VI (1920–24), pp. 423–30.
38. Gerald de Gaury, *Three Kings in Baghdad*, p. 29.
39. Privately translated by Manaf al Damluji, 31 Jan. 2013.
40. For a first-hand account of the coronation, see Bell, *Letters*, 28 August 1921.
41. *Iraq Administration Reports*, vol. V (1920), pp. 155–6.
42. Tamara Chalabi, *Late for Tea at the Deer Palace*, p. 110.
43. Bell, *Letters*, 27 August 1922.
44. Longrigg, *Iraq 1900–1950*, p. 175.
45. Bell, *Letters*, 27 August 1922.
46. Ibid., 6 April 1926.
47. Quoted in H. V. F. Winstone, *Gertrude Bell*, p. 412.
48. See, for instance, Chalabi, pp. 142–4, 166–7. See also the Iraqi Makam classical music blog (http://iraqimaqam.blogspot.com).

49. Donald Maxwell, *A Dweller in Mesopotamia, being the Adventures of an Official Artist in the Garden of Eden*, pp. 91–2.
50. Ibid., pp. 71.
51. Robert Byron, *The Road to Oxiana*, p. 42.
52. Freya Stark, *Baghdad Sketches*, p. 30.
53. Ibid., pp. 40–41.
54. Ibid., pp. 70–71.
55. Ibid., p. 55.
56. Richard Coke, *Baghdad: The City of Peace*, pp. 316–17.
57. Author interview, 13 December 2011.
58. T. E. Lawrence, *Seven Pillars of Wisdom*, pp. 542, 519.
59. Bell, *Letters*, 24 February 1921.
60. Tripp, p. 69.
61. De Gaury, p. 60.
62. Ali al Wardi, *Understanding Iraq*, p. 66.
63. Hanna Batatu, *The Old Social Classes and the Revolutionary Movements of Iraq*, p. 78.
64. Beatrice Erskine, *King Faisal of Iraq*, pp. 229–30.
65. For a concise summary of the British Mandate period, see the paper by Dr Toby Dodge, 'The British Mandate in Iraq, 1914–1932' (http://www.gale.cengage.com/pdf/whitepapers/gdc/TheBritishMandate.pdf).
66. Batatu, *The Old Social Classes and the Revolutionary Movements of Iraq* p. 25.
67. Longrigg, *Iraq 1900–1950*, p. 235.
68. Kanan Makiya, *Republic of Fear: The Politics of Modern Iraq*, p. 170.
69. Chalabi, p. 183.
70. For details of the grand mufti's influence and activities in Iraq, see Reeva Spector Simon, *Iraq Between the Two World Wars: The Militarist Origins of Tyranny*, pp. 129–31.
71. Longrigg, *Iraq 1900–1950*, p. 276.
72. Marina Benjamin, *Last Days in Babylon*, p. 136.
73. Author interview, 12 July 2012. This account is also based on 'The Household Cavalry in Iraq and Syria 1941', the Duke of Wellington's private campaign diary.
74. Sarah Ehrlich, 'Farhud Memories: Baghdad's 1941 Slaughter of the Jews', BBC report (http://www.bbc.co.uk/news/world-middle-east–13610702).
75. Freya Stark, *Dust in the Lion's Paw*, p. 114.
76. Benjamin, pp. 140–41.
77. Ehrlich.
78. Benjamin, pp. 178–81.
79. Author interview, 18 June 2012.
80. Batatu, *The Old Social Classes and the Revolutionary Movements of Iraq* pp. 555–7.

81. See Joseph Siry, 'Wright's Baghdad Opera House and Gammage Auditorium: In Search of Regional Modernity', *Art Bulletin*, 87, 2 (June 2005), pp. 265–311.

82. See Wissam al Zahawie, 'The Cultural Scene in Baghdad and Its Socio-Political Backdrop on the Eve of the Revolution of 1958: A Memoir', unpublished paper.

83. Albert Hourani, *A History of the Arab Peoples*, p. 387.

84. Ibid.

85. See Mohammed Fadhel Jamali, '*Iraq under General Nuri*: A Review of Waldemar Gallman's Book', *Middle East Forum*, 11, 7 (1964), pp. 13–24.

86. See de Gaury, pp. 179–81.

87. For an account of the 14 July coup, see ibid., pp. 192–200.

88. Chalabi, p. 263.

89. See Batatu, *The Old Social Classes and the Revolutionary Movements of Iraq*, p. 802.

90. Quoted in ibid., p. 801.

91. 'The Pasha', *TIME Magazine*, 17 June 1957.

92. 'Iraq: After the Bloodbath', *TIME Magazine*, 4 August 1958.

93. Waldemar Gallman, *Iraq under General Nuri*, p. 230.

11 COUPS, COMMUNISTS AND THE BAATHISTS: THE MOTHER OF ALL BLOODSHED (1958–)

1. Quoted in Hanna Batatu, *The Old Social Classes and the Revolutionary Movements of Iraq*, p. 836.

2. See Waldemar Gallman, *Iraq under General Nuri*, pp. 207–8.

3. Adel Darwish and Gregory Alexander, *Unholy Babylon*, p. 21.

4. Quoted in de Gaury, p. 206.

5. Telegram from Ambassador Jernegan, 11 October 1959 (http://www.icdc.com/~paulwolf/iraq/Qasim%20relates%20attempt%20details%20Oct%2011%201959.htm).

6. Batatu, *The Old Social Classes and the Revolutionary Movements of Iraq*, p. 816.

7. Kanan Makiya, *Republic of Fear*, pp. 61, 105.

8. Uriel Dann, *Iraq under Qassem*, p. 368.

9. Batatu, *The Old Social Classes and the Revolutionary Movements of Iraq*, p. 977.

10. Ibid., p. 978.

11. Kassem's body was discovered in 2005. See 'Iraqis Recall Golden Age', *ICR* (Institute for War and Peace Reporting), 75, 21 February 2005 (http://iwpr.net/report-news/iraqis-recall-golden-age).

12. Max Sawdayee, *All Waiting to Be Hanged*, Part III, e-book, no page number.

13. Ibid.

14. A series of chilling films of the putsch can be seen on YouTube, beginning with: http://www.youtube.com/watch?v=JYmUzK1LVow&feature=relmfu.

15. For more details of the purge, see Con Coughlin, *Saddam: The Secret Life*, pp. 155–62; Efraim Karsh and Inari Rautsi, *Saddam Hussein: A Political Biography*, pp. 113–17; *Panorama: The Mind of Saddam*, 11 February 1991.

16. Author interview, 18 January 2012. See also 'Oil Sites in Iran and Iraq Bombed as Baghdad Troops Cross Border', *New York Times*, 24 September 1980.

17. Makiya, p. 17. The tract was published by Dar al Hurriya (Freedom House), the state publishing house, in 1981.

18. Anthony Cordesman and Abraham Wagner, in *Lessons of Modern War, vol. II: The Iran–Iraq War*, estimate that Iraq lost between 140,000 and 350,000 with 400,000 to 700,000 wounded and 70,000 captured. Iran is estimated to have lost between 450,000 and 730,000 with 600,000 to 1,200,000 wounded and 45,000 captured.

19. 'Oil Sites in Iran and Iraq Bombed as Baghdad Troops Cross Border', *New York Times*, 24 September 1980.

20. David Styan, *France and Iraq: Oil, Arms and French Policy Making in the Middle East*, p. 135.

21. See Coughlin, *Saddam: The Secret Life* p. 187.

22. Ibid., p. 190.

23. 'The War is Hailed in Iraq: Little Impact in the Capital in Spite of Air Raids – Baghdad Appears Nonchalant', *New York Times*, 30 September 1980.

24. Samir al Khalil [Kanan Makiya], *The Monument: Art, Vulgarity and Responsibility in Iraq*, p. 20.

25. See 'Baghdad: Breaking Tides in Process', *Architecture*, 58 (Tokyo, May 1985).

26. Khalil, p. 25.

27. Ibid., p. 74.

28. Ibid., p. 115.

29. 'The Megalomaniac Pitted against the Zealot', *Guardian*, 24 September 1980.

30. Jean Sasson, *Mayada: Daughter of Iraq*, p. 104.

31. Dujail returned to haunt Saddam in 2006. See 'Judging Dujail', Human Rights Watch report, 20 November 2006, p. 2 (http://www.hrw.org/reports/2006/11/19/judging-dujail-0).

32. Peter Sluglett and Marion Farouk-Sluglett, *Iraq since 1958*, p. 265.

33. Sasson, p. 121.

34. See Abbas Alnasrawi, 'Economic Consequences of the Iraq–Iran War', *Third World Quarterly*, 8, 3 (July 1986), pp. 874–6.

35. Sasson, p. 134.

36. Dilip Hiro, *The Longest War*, p. 108.

37. 'Iran Missile Hits Baghdad Homes', *Guardian*, 13 September 1986.

38. Niall Ferguson, *Colossus: The Price of America's Empire*, p. 118.

39. 'Deadly Consequences of Weapons Sales as Iran Fires Missiles into Bagh-dad', *Guardian*, 27 Nov. 1986.

40. 'Iraq Vows to Take Revenge as School Hit by Missile', *Guardian*, 14 October 1987.

41. 'Missile Hits Baghdad as Arab Leaders Open Summit', *Guardian*, 9 November 1987.

42. See Shahram Chubin and Charles Tripp, *Iran and Iraq at War*, p. 61.

43. Author interview, 18 March 2012.

44. Latif Yahia, *The Devil's Double*, p. 3.

45. 'Baghdad Celebrates with Gunfire and Fireworks', *Guardian*, 10 August 1988.

46. Khalil, p. 2. In February 2007, less than two months after Saddam Hussein's execution, the Iraqi government began demolishing the Victory Arch. Wide-spread protests forced it to reconsider and subsequently abandon the demolition, and in 2011 the controversial monument was restored.

47. Ibid., p. 51.

48. 'Hussein Charged with Genocide in 50,000 Deaths', *New York Times*, 5 April 2006. (http://www.nytimes.com/2006/04/05/world/middleeast/05iraq. html?_r=o).

49. For a brief biography of Grand Ayatollah Mohammed Bakir al Hakim, see the SCIRI website (http://www.sciri.btinternet.co.uk/English/About_Us/ Sayed/sayed.html) and the more recent website of the renamed Islamic Supreme Council of Iraq (http://isci-iraq.com/home/isci/biographies/49-a-biography-of-isci-co-founder-and-its-prominent-leader-late-ayatollah-sayyed-Mohammed-baqir-al-hakim). The Shia cleric was assassinated in a car bombing in front of the Imam Ali shrine in Najaf immediately after Friday prayers on 29 August 2003.

50. Paul Roberts, *The Demonic Comedy: The Baghdad of Saddam Hus-sein*, p. 20.

51. Yahia, pp. 67–75.

52. See Abbas Alnasrawi, 'Iraq: Economic Consequences of the 1991 Gulf War and Future Outlook', *Third World Quarterly*, 13, 2 (1992), pp. 336–42.

53. Yahia, p. 241.

54. Author interview, 17 March 2012.

55. Nuha al Radi, *Baghdad Diaries 1991–2002*, p. 27.

56. See Eric Rouleau, 'America's Unyielding Policy Toward Iraq', *Foreign Affairs*, 74, 1 (January–February 1995), pp. 59–72.

57. Alnasrawi, 'Iraq: Economic Consequences of the 1991 Gulf War and Future Outlook', pp. 347–8.

58. 'Report to the Secretary-General on Humanitarian Needs in Kuwait and Iraq in the Immediate Post-Crisis Environment by a Mission to the Area Led by Mr Martti Ahtisaari, Under-Secretary-General for Administration and Management', 20 March 1991, p. 5.

59. Jita Mishra, *The NPT and the Developing Countries*, p. 156.

60. Yahia, pp. 276–9. The palace was part of several command and control bunkers built during the Iraq–Iran War.

61. For an account of the rebellion, see 'Endless Torment: The 1991 Uprising in Iraq and Its Aftermath', Human Rights Watch report, 1 June 1992 (http://www.hrw.org/reports/1992/Iraq926.htm).

62. Alnasrawi, 'Iraq: Economic Consequences of the 1991 Gulf War and Future Outlook', p. 347.

63. 'Saddam Hussein's Palaces', Daily Telegraph, 16 July 2009 (http://www.telegraph.co.uk/news/worldnews/middleeast/iraq/5824615/Saddam-Husseins-palaces.html).

64. Khalil, pp. 77, 74.

65. Roberts, p. 214.

66. Ibid., p. 102.

67. Wendell Steavenson, The Weight of a Mustard Seed, p. 144.

68. Sasson, p. 107.

69. See Office of the Iraq Programme Oil-for-Food (http://www.un.org/depts/oip/food-facts.html).

70. Hadani Ditmars, Dancing in the No-Fly Zone, p. 11.

71. 'Iraqis' Suffering Widens as UN Sanctions Drag On', New York Times, 14 December 1997.

72. 'UN Says Sanctions Have Killed Some 500,000 Iraqi Children', Reuters report, 21 July 2000 (http://www.commondreams.org/headlines/072100-03.htm).

73. See 'The Wake of War', Guardian, 18 May 1996.

74. Radi, p. 78.

75. 'Artists Make Best of It in Oppressive Iraq', San Francisco Chronicle, 13 March 2002 (http://www.sfgate.com/cgi-bin/article.cgi?f=/c/a/2002/03/13/MN152757.DTL&ao=all).

76. 'Threats and Responses: Support for Hussein – A Show of Loyalty (Just Say Yes) In Iraq Vote for the One and Only', New York Times, 16 October 2002 (http://www.nytimes.com/2002/10/16/world/threats-responses-support-for-hussein-show-loyalty-just-say-yes-iraq-vote-for.html?pagewanted=all&src=pm); 'Saddam "Wins 100% of vote"', BBC News, 16 October 2002 (http://news.bbc.co.uk/1/hi/2331951.stm).

77. Stefan Simanowitz, 'The Human Shield Movement', Z Magazine online, 16, 11 (November 2003) (http://web.archive.org/web/20041107095821/http://zmagsite.zmag.org/Nov2003/simanowitz1103.html).

78. Jon Lee Anderson, The Fall of Baghdad, p. 73.

79. Ibid., p. 92.

80. See the paper by Harlan Ullman and James Wade, 'Shock and Awe: Achieving Rapid Dominance' (http://www.dodccrp.org/files/Ullman_Shock.pdf).

81. 'A Baghdad Blogger', New Yorker, 31 March 2003 (http://www.newyorker.com/archive/2003/03/31/030331ta_talk_zalewski).

82. Salam Pax, The Baghdad Blog, p. 130.

83. Ibid., p. 162.
84. For a selection of these leaflets, see http://salampax.wordpress.com/2009/03/24/blog-flashback-us-war-propaganda.
85. See http://www.welovetheiraqiinformationminister.com/.
86. 'Toppling Saddam's Statue is the Final Triumph for These Oppressed People', *Daily Mirror*, 10 April 2003 (http://www.thefreelibrary.com/GULF+WAR+2%3A+ANTON+ANTONOWICZ+WATCHES+THE+FALL+OF+BAGHDAD%3A+Toppling...-a099844046).
87. 'Looting Breaks Out as Baghdad Falls', *Sydney Morning Herald*, 10 April 2003 (http://www.smh.com.au/articles/2003/04/10/1049567757398.html).
88. Salam Pax, p. 148.
89. See the Oriental Institute Museum of the University of Chicago paper by Geoff Emberling and Katharyn Hanson (eds.), 'Catastrophe! The Looting and Destruction of Iraq's Past' (Spring 2008) (http://oi.uchicago.edu/pdf/oimp28.pdf).
90. 'Rumsfeld on Looting in Iraq: "Stuff happens"', CNN, 12 April 2003 (http://edition.cnn.com/2003/US/04/11/sprj.irq.pentagon/).
91. 'The Ransacking of the Baghdad Museum Is a Disgrace', History News Network, 14 April 2003 (http://hnn.us/articles/1386.html).
92. 'Experts' Pleas to Pentagon Didn't Save Museum', *New York Times*, 16 April 2003 (http://www.nytimes.com/2003/04/16/world/a-nation-at-war-the-looting-experts-pleas-to-pentagon-didn-t-save-museum.html?pagewanted=all&src=pm).
93. Colonel Matthew Bogdanos, a US reservist officer, led the US investigation into the looting of the Iraq Museum. See his paper 'The Casualties of War: The Truth about the Iraqi Museum', *American Journal of Archaeology*, 109, 3 (July 2005). See also Robert M. Poole, 'Looting Iraq', *Smithsonian* magazine (February 2008) (http://www.smithsonianmag.com/arts-culture/monument-sidebar.html#ixzz1u59x087U).
94. Author interview, 14 December 2004.
95. See Iraq Coalition Casualty Count (http://icasualties.org/); also http://www.globalsecurity.org/military/ops/iraq_casualties.htm.
96. T. E. Lawrence, 'Twenty-Seven Articles', *Arab Bulletin*, 20 August 1917.
97. For a withering portrait of Bremer's Coalition Provisional Authority, see Rajiv Chandrasekaran, *Imperial Life in the Emerald City*, pp. 216, 140.
98. Ibid., pp. 183, 141.
99. See 'Annals of National Security: Torture at Abu Ghraib', *New Yorker*, 10 May 2004 (http://www.newyorker.com/archive/2004/05/10/040510fa_fact?currentPage=all); also see 'New Details of Prison Abuse Emerge', *Washington Post*, 21 May 2004 (http://www.washingtonpost.com/wp-dyn/articlesA43783-2004May20.htm).
100. See 'The Minister of Civil War: Bayan Jabr, Paul Bremer and the Rise of the Iraqi Death Squads', *Harper's Magazine*, August 2006.
101. Author interview, 26 June 2013.

102. See 'Iraqi Deaths from Violence 2003–2011', Iraq Body Count (http://www.iraqbodycount.org/analysis/numbers/2011).

103. 'The Ghost in the Baghdad Museum', *New York Times*, 2 April 2006 (http://www.nytimes.com/2006/04/02/arts/design/02cohe.html?pagewanted=all).

104. http://thegroundtruth.blogspot.co.uk/2009/11/columbia-university-charts-sectarian.html.

105. 'In Grief and Defiance, Baghdad's Christians Return to Scene of Attack', *New York Times*, 7 November 2010 (http://www.nytimes.com/2010/11/08/world/middleeast/08baghdad.html).

106. 'After Baghdad Church Attack, Christians Shocked but Say "We Still Have a Mission Here"', *Christian Science Monitor*, 1 November 2010 (http://www.csmonitor.com/World/Middle-East/2010/1101/After-Baghdad-church-attack-Christians-shocked-but-say-we-still-have-a-mission-here).

107. Author interview, 15 December 2013.

108. Author interview with Cordia Ezekiel, the daughter of Max Sawdayee, 24 February 2012. See also 'Baghdad Jews have become a Fearful Few', *New York Times*, 1 June 2008 (http://www.nytimes.com/2008/06/01/world/middleeast/01babylon.html?pagewanted=all).

109. See 'Iraqi Deaths from Violence 2003–2011', Iraq Body Count (http://www.iraqbodycount.org/analysis/numbers/2011/).

110. See the report by Amy Hagopian and team, 'Mortality in Iraq Associated with the 2003–2011 War and Occupation: Findings from a National Cluster Sample Survey by the University Collaborative Iraq Mortality Study' (15 October 2013) (http://www.plosmedicineorg/article/info%3Adol%2F10.1371%2 Fjournal.pmed.1001533).

111. See 'Iraq 2013: A Year of Carnage' (http://Irag2013.rt.com).

112. Author interview, 17 March 2012.

Index

ALLEN LANE
an imprint of
PENGUIN BOOKS

Recently Published

Dominic Lieven, *Towards the Flame: Empire, War and the End of Tsarist Russia*

Noel Malcolm, *Agents of Empire: Knights, Corsairs, Jesuits and Spies in the Sixteenth-Century Mediterranean World*

James Rebanks, *The Shepherd's Life: A Tale of the Lake District*

David Brooks, *The Road to Character*

Joseph Stiglitz, *The Great Divide*

Ken Robinson and Lou Aronica, *Creative Schools: Revolutionizing Education from the Ground Up*

Clotaire Rapaille and Andrés Roemer, *Move UP: Why Some Cultures Advances While Others Don't*

Jonathan Keates, *William III and Mary II: Partners in Revolution*

David Womersley, *James II: The Last Catholic King*

Richard Barber, *Henry II: A Prince Among Princes*

Jane Ridley, *Victoria: Queen, Matriarch, Empress*

John Gray, *The Soul of the Marionette: A Short Enquiry into Human Freedom*

Emily Wilson, *Seneca: A Life*

Michael Barber, *How to Run a Government: So That Citizens Benefit and Taxpayers Don't Go Crazy*

Dana Thomas, *Gods and Kings: The Rise and Fall of Alexander McQueen and John Galliano*

Steven Weinberg, *To Explain the World: The Discovery of Modern Science*

Jennifer Jacquet, *Is Shame Necessary?: New Uses for an Old Tool*

Eugene Rogan, *The Fall of the Ottomans: The Great War in the Middle East, 1914-1920*

Norman Doidge, *The Brain's Way of Healing: Stories of Remarkable Recoveries and Discoveries*

John Hooper, *The Italians*

Sven Beckert, *Empire of Cotton: A New History of Global Capitalism*

Mark Kishlansky, *Charles I: An Abbreviated Life*

Philip Ziegler, *George VI: The Dutiful King*

David Cannadine, *George V: The Unexpected King*

Stephen Alford, *Edward VI: The Last Boy King*

John Guy, *Henry VIII: The Quest for Fame*

Robert Tombs, *The English and their History: The First Thirteen Centuries*

Neil MacGregor, *Germany: The Memories of a Nation*

Uwe Tellkamp, *The Tower: A Novel*

Roberto Calasso, *Ardor*

Slavoj Žižek, *Trouble in Paradise: Communism After the End of History*

Francis Pryor, *Home: A Time Traveller's Tales from Britain's Prehistory*

R. F. Foster, *Vivid Faces: The Revolutionary Generation in Ireland, 1890-1923*

Andrew Roberts, *Napoleon the Great*

Shami Chakrabarti, *On Liberty*

Bessel van der Kolk, *The Body Keeps the Score: Mind, Brain and Body in the Transformation of Trauma*

Brendan Simms, *The Longest Afternoon: The 400 Men Who Decided the Battle of Waterloo*

Naomi Klein, *This Changes Everything: Capitalism vs the Climate*